Lecture Notes in Computer Science 5169

Commenced Publication in 1973
Founding and Former Series Editors:
Gerhard Goos, Juris Hartmanis, and Jan van Leeuwen

Joseph Fong   Reggie Kwan   Fu Lee Wang (Eds.)

Hybrid Learning and Education

First International Conference, ICHL 2008
Hong Kong, China, August 13-15, 2008
Proceedings

 Springer

Volume Editors

Joseph Fong
Department of Computer Science
City University of Hong Kong
Kowloon Tong
Hong Kong, China
E-mail: csjfong@cityu.edu.hk

Reggie Kwan
Caritas Francis Hsu College
Hong Kong, China
E-mail: rkwan@cfhc.caritas.edu.hk

Fu Lee Wang
Department of Computer Science
City University of Hong Kong
Kowloon Tong
Hong Kong, China
E-mail: flwang@cityu.edu.hk

CR Subject Classification (1998): F.1.2, I.2.6, K.3-4, I.6, D.2.2, J.1

LNCS Sublibrary: SL 1 – Theoretical Computer Science and General Issues

ISSN   0302-9743

Springer is a part of Springer Science+Business Media

springer.com

© Springer-Verlag Berlin Heidelberg 2008

Typesetting: Camera-ready by author, data conversion by Scientific Publishing Services, Chennai, India
Printed on acid-free paper   SPIN: 12446520   06/3180   5 4 3 2 1 0

Preface

The First International Conference on Hybrid Learning was organized by City University of Hong Kong, Caritas Francis Hsu College and Caritas Bianchi College of Careers in August 2008. ICHL2008 was an innovative and consolidate experience for Hong Kong tertiary higher education. The conference aims to unify the traditional classroom face-to-face learning and Internet eLearning into one teaching and learning method—hybrid learning—for both teachers and students. Its audience are educators and eLearning practitioners. The conference obtained sponsorship from six local universities in Hong Kong: Hong Kong Baptist University, The Hong Kong Polytechnic University, The Hong Kong University of Science and Technology, University of Hong Kong, The Chinese University of Hong Kong, and Lingnan University. It was also sponsored by Pei Hua Education Foundation Limited, and K.C. Wong Education Foundation Limited.

Hybrid learning originated from North America in 2000 and is an ongoing trend. It is not merely a simple combination of direct teaching and eLearning, but comprises different learning strategies and important elements for teaching and learning. It focuses on student center learning and provides an environment for knowledge learning. Students are given more opportunities to be active learners and practice practical skills such as communication, collaboration, critical thinking, creativity, self-management, self-study, problem solving, analysis and numeracy.

It was our pleasure to have three keynote talks for the conference, namely, "You Can't Do That in a Classroom! Realizing the Potential of Distributed Learning for On-Campus Students" by Cath Ellis, "A Proposal for a Lifecycle Process for Hybrid Learning Programs" by Won Kim, and "Just-in-Time Knowledge for Effective Hybrid Learning" by Michel Desmarais.

We are thankful for the effort of all the conference Organizing Committee members for organizing the conference, and also all the conference Program Committee members for reviewing the papers. Special thanks must go to Frances Yao for the support of City University of Hong Kong in holding the conference. The conference attracted about 142 submissions, and only 38 papers were accepted for the conference proceedings in the series *Lecture Notes in Computer Science* published by Springer.

On behalf of the conference Steering Committee members—Reggie Kwan from Caritas Francis Hsu College, Philips Fu Lee Wang from City University of Hong Kong, Victor Lee from The Chinese University of Hong Kong, and Joseph Fong from City University of Hong Kong—we trust you will enjoy the papers in this volume.

August 2008

Joseph Fong
Reggie Kwan

Organization

Organizing Committee

Honorary Chairs	Keith Chan (The Hong Kong Polytechnic University)
	Lionel M. Ni
	(The Hong Kong University of Science and Technology)
	Victor S. K. Lee (The Chinese University of Hong Kong)
	Daning Sun (Lingnan University)
	Enoch Young (The University of Hong Kong)
Conference Chairs	Joseph Fong (City University of Hong Kong)
	Reggie C. Kwan (Caritas Francis Hsu College)
Program Chair	Philips Fu Lee Wang (City University of Hong Kong)
Organization Chairs	F. T. Chan (The University of Hong Kong)
	William Cheung (Hong Kong Baptist University)
Local Arrangements Chairs	John Lee (The Hong Kong Polytechnic University)
	W. L. Yeung (Lingnan University)
	Siu Cheung Kong (The Hong Kong Institute of Education)
	Oliver Au (City University of Hong Kong)
Registration Chair	Titus Lo (Caritas Francis Hsu College)
Financial Chair	Kat Leung (Caritas Bianchi College of Careers)
Publication Chair	Tak-Lam Wong (The Chinese University of Hong Kong)
Publicity Chair	Victor C. S. Lee (City University of Hong Kong)
Academic Liaison Chair	T. C. Pong
	(The Hong Kong University of Science and Technology)
Sponsorship Chair	Will W. K. Ma (Hong Kong Shue Yan University)
Activities Chair	Jonathan Diu (The Chinese University of Hong Kong)

Steering Committee

Chair	Joseph Fong (City University of Hong Kong)
	Reggie C. Kwan (Caritas Francis Hsu College)
Members	Victor S. K. Lee (The Chinese University of Hong Kong)
	Philips Fu Lee Wang (City University of Hong Kong)

International Program Committee

Oliver Au	City University of Hong Kong, Hong Kong
Philip Alberts	Brunel University, UK
Keith Barker	University of Connecticut, USA
Vic Callaghan	University of Essex, UK
F. T. Chan	The University of Hong Kong, Hong Kong

Keith Chan	The Hong Kong Polytechnic University, Hong Kong
William Cheung	Hong Kong Baptist University, Hong Kong
Giuliana Dettori	Istituto per le Tecnologie Didattiche, Italy
Michael Gardner	University of Essex, UK
Le Gruenwald	University of Oklahoma, USA
Joseph Fong	City University of Hong Kong, Hong Kong
Reggie C. Kwan	Caritas Francis Hsu College, Hong Kong
Wolfgang Halang	Fern Universität in Hagen, Germany
K. P. Hewagamage	University of Colombo, Sri Lanka
Raquel Hijón-Neira	Universidad Rey Juan Carlos, Spain
Wen-Chi Hou	Southern Illinois University, USA
Siu Cheung Kong	The Hong Kong Institute of Education, Hong Kong
John Lee	The Hong Kong Polytechnic University, Hong Kong
Victor C. S. Lee	City University of Hong Kong, Hong Kong
Kat Sze Ming Leung	Caritas Bianchi College of Careers, Hong Kong
Qing Li	Hong Kong Web Society, Hong Kong
Will W. K. Ma	Hong Kong Shue Yan University, Hong Kong
Sabine Moebs	Dublin City University, Ireland
Dennis McLeod	University of Southern California, USA
Sham Navathe	Georgia Institute of Technology, USA
Diana Perez-Marin	Universidad Autonoma de Madrid, Spain
Liping Shen	Shanghai Jiao Tong University, China
Stefanie Sieber	Otto-Friedrich-Universität Bamberg, Germany
Wei Sun	Beihang University, China
Stefan Trausan-Matu	Politehnica University of Bucharest, Romania
Philips Fu Lee Wang	City University of Hong Kong, Hong Kong
Tak Lam Wong	The Chinese University of Hong Kong, Hong Kong
Lei Xu	Tsinghua University, China
W. L. Yeung	Lingnan University, Hong Kong
Liming Zhang	University of Macao, Macao
Wanlei Zhou	Deakin University, Australia

Organizers

City University of Hong Kong
Caritas Francis Hsu College
Caritas Bianchi College of Careers

Sponsors

ACM, Hong Kong Chapter
Hong Kong Baptist University
Hong Kong Computer Society
Hong Kong Pei Hua Education Foundation
K. C. Wong Education Foundation
Lingnan University
The Chinese University of Hong Kong, School of Continuing and Professional Studies

The Hong Kong Polytechnic University
The Hong Kong University of Science and Technology
The University of Hong Kong, School of Professional and Continuing Education

In Co-operation with

IEEE, Computer Society, Hong Kong Chapter

Table of Contents

Trends

Pervasive Learning

Mobile and Ubiquitous Learning

Technologies

Contextual Attitude and Cultural Effects

'You Can't Do That in a Classroom!': How Distributed Learning Can Assist in the Widespread Adoption of Hybrid Learning Strategies

Cath Ellis

School of Music Humanities and Media,
University of Huddersfield, Huddersfield, HD1 3DH United Kingdom
c.a.ellis@hud.ac.uk

Abstract. Achieving the widespread adoption of Hybrid Learning in Higher Education is desirable but difficult and to accomplish this requires significant institutional change. This paper suggests that this kind of change can be achieved by the strategic harnessing of Distributed Learning opportunities. It takes as its main point of focus the lecture which, despite significant advances in communication and information technology still prevails as a dominant teaching and learning strategy in Higher Education. It suggests that using screencasting to deliver lectures in a Distributed Learning context can trigger the kind of widespread change required.

Keywords: Distributed Learning, Hybrid Learning, Lecturing, Screencasting.

1 Introduction

In a rapidly changing world, Higher Education is also having to adapt. In this context, there is little doubt that hybrid learning strategies are highly desirable in terms of maximising student engagement and learning achievement. This is particularly since the advent of widening participation and open access whereby students join the academy with a widely divergent range of qualifications, abilities, expectations, preferences and aspirations. While blended learning strategies have been used for a considerable length of time in distance learning provision, this kind of hybridity is only just starting to have a significant impact on the lives and experiences of main-campus, full-time, students. Indeed, there is overwhelming evidence in the literature to show that hybrid learning strategies can bring important rewards for academic staff, students and institutions alike in terms of both increased quality and efficiency. Yet, despite these obvious benefits *and* the weight of scholarly evidence supporting them, the reality is that the Higher Education industry as a whole is still some distance from achieving widespread or even substantial adoption of hybrid learning strategies, particularly for the provision of courses to full-time, main-campus students. In order to accomplish this, the industry needs to undergo significant change the likes of which Barr and Tag refer to as a paradigmatic shift [1].

J. Fong, R. Kwan, and F.L. Wang (Eds.): ICHL 2008, LNCS 5169, pp. 1–16, 2008.

In this paper I propose an approach which may prove more effective in achieving this kind of change, than strategies already attempted. I argue that making strategic use of distributed learning opportunities, such as the opening of new remote campuses and the adaptation of courses for flexible delivery, can be an effective means of bringing about change across an institution. In short, strategically targeting those moments when academics realise that teaching distributed student cohorts cannot be 'done in a classroom' can be an effective catalyst for bringing about useful change. To argue this I will focus specifically on lecturing as one of the mainstays of traditional teaching and learning practice. In terms of its influence and impact on student learning, the lecture's ubiquity is matched only by its obduracy. Evidence abounds that as a teaching and learning strategy, lecturing has little to commend it, yet it still makes up the bulk of the student learning 'diet'. I will argue that harnessing distributed learning opportunities strategically can be an effective mechanism by which to 'wean' academics off lecturing and can consequently encourage them to adopt more interactive, student-centred hybrid learning in their teaching practice. Using these opportunities systematically can be an effective catalyst for bringing about widespread change.

2 Understanding VLE Use as a Series of 'Step Changes'

The achievement of this particular paradigm shift requires quite specific changes in the way that Virtual learning Environments (VLE) and other kinds of teaching technologies are used in Higher Education. Making this change in the provision of teaching and learning to full-time, on-campus students is, I argue, most usefully understood as a series of step changes: first to the adoption of VLEs as repositories of resources; secondly the use of VLEs as interactive learning environments to augment or supplement the use of traditional face-to-face learning environments; and thirdly the use of VLEs as interactive learning environments which replace some use of traditional face-to-face learning environments (Hybrid learning).[1] It is useful to take these one at a time.

First, the use of VLEs as repositories for learning resources has a relatively long history, starting with the use of university intranets which were then organised into home grown VLEs. This eventually shifted onto the widespread adoption of proprietary VLEs in the mid to late 1990s. Some two decades later, this use of VLEs has become very widespread, with most institutions in the developed world holding a proprietary or open source VLE license, and having a recommendation or even requirement that all modules have a dedicated site on it [2-4]. This is, if nothing else, testament to the fact that this step change has been relatively easy to achieve. This type of use of the VLE is indeed a good first step, and undoubtedly provides many useful benefits to staff and students alike such as having convenient and flexible ways of distributing and accessing learning resources. However, studies have found that for the most part, this remains the extent of VLE use, with, in many instances, it being used for little more than the module handbook being made available [2-5]. While some academics and even some institutions may believe that this constitutes genuine

---

[1] Gilly Salmon has also usefully described this transition as a stepped process in her excellent article 'Flying not Flapping: A Strategic Framework for e-Learning and Pedagogical Innovation in Higher Education Institutions' [2].

achievement in the adoption of e-learning, as John Cowan points out, this 'is a mis-
nomer' and it is really better understood as 'e-reading' [5]. He goes on to criticise this
strategy, arguing that it simply defrays the costs of printing from the institution (who
can do it cheaply and efficiently *en mass*) to the students (for whom it costs more in
money and time even though they can least afford it, especially as they have, in many
cases, already paid for it in their course fees), [see 5]. Worst of all, while this step
change has been easy to achieve, in the end nothing really changes, which is perhaps
why it has been so easy to achieve! All that's really happening is that information is
being sent from teacher to student, teaching strategies continue as they have done for
centuries and the VLE becomes little more than a glorified and rather expensive virtual filing cabinet.

In comparison, the second step change, to the use of the VLEs as an interactive
learning environment to augment traditional, face-to-face classes, is relatively difficult to achieve. This step achieves many of the important objectives of hybrid
learning and as such there is much to commend it. In particular it brings benefits by
making access to the learning more flexible and by suiting a wide range of learning
styles and student preferences. There is also a considerable body of scholarship that
shows how this approach to teaching and learning is more suited to student-centred,
and often constructivist, approaches than traditional face-to-face strategies [see for
instance 6]. While this change is an important second step, it is ultimately not an
ideal outcome in itself. In this situation, face-to-face teaching still prevails and
thereby remains routinely hierarchised over VLEs. As such, VLEs are only ever
used as supporting or as supplemental to classroom-based activities such as lectures
or seminars (often in the forms of preparation activities, follow-up activities, and/or
non-compulsory extension or enrichment activities). The biggest problem this strategy presents is an increased workload for both staff and students. In the end, staff
have more work to do constructing, maintaining and moderating online activities in
addition to their classroom hours. Similarly, students are asked and sometimes expected to do more things on top of their classroom activities. While these extra
activities may bring benefits to student learning (which can be significant), they
have the very real tendency to eat into the inexorably finite time and energy of staff
and students alike. As such, they often tend to 'fizzle out' after a while, becoming
especially vulnerable towards the end of term when assessment and marking loads
impinge significantly on participants' lives. Because it is seen as supplemental,
students tend to drop their involvement or interaction in favour of investing their
energy in compulsory activities and assessable coursework components, and staff
simply run out of time and energy to effectively maintain it. At worst, academics
become disenchanted and tend to blame the technology or (even worse) the students
for the strategy's failure. They use it as an excuse to return to old, established and
'safe' teaching and learning strategies and consequently become even more reluctant to adopt hybrid strategies in the future. It also runs the risk of being perceived
by students as 'gimmicky' and a waste of their time and effort, and thereby they
become disinclined to become involved again in the future preferring to concentrate, instead, on the 'real' face-to-face learning environment. As such, this strategy
runs the risk of doing more harm than good. While these blended learning strategies
achieve significant change, it is ultimately not enough and traditional face-to-face
learning strategies continue to prevail.

The third step change, to the use of the VLE as an interactive learning environment that replaces aspects of traditional face-to-face strategies, is harder again to achieve but is an ideal and final step. There are many reasons why this change is so difficult to achieve and it is impossible to cover them all adequately here, however, it is worth briefly considering those which are most significant. These include the large number of substantial institutional barriers in place whereby everything from teaching work-loads (in terms of hours and student load), to timetabling, student evaluations, valida-tion documents, position descriptions, job titles, part-time hourly pay rates and even institutional architecture is designed on the assumption that the main activity of the teaching academic will be in the delivery of face-to-face lectures, seminars and tutori-als. Stepping outside of this system to undertake a different pattern of teaching and learning immediately presents academics with a long series of administrative hurdles to jump which of course involves extra work in comparison to their colleagues. As such, making such a change immediately puts these academics out of step with the activities of the majority of their colleagues and it can also often be something that is poorly understood, and consequently not well supported, by line managers. This alone can be disincentive enough and thereby provide enough encouragement to keep marching into the lecture hall week after week [see 7]. Even if the individual, the department, the school and even the institution as a whole are keen to make this step change, there are significant obstacles put in the way by Quality Assurance agencies which, in some instances, require such things as more rigorous and detailed (and in some cases external) validation for modules and courses which use a significant pro-portion of e-learning strategies in their delivery [8, 9]. As Oliver points out: "In cater-ing for the diversity, most exercises in quality assurance steer towards the activities with the highest levels of technology use and dependence; for example, distance edu-cation and online learning [10]." On top of these barriers, for the average 'grassroots' academic there is little real impetus for change, no matter how much the executive management of schools and institutions want it to happen. Indeed, this step change is something, I would argue, that executive management *are* increasingly wanting to achieve. From my personal experience as an *ad hoc* academic developer in a British Higher Education institution, I'm increasingly being approached by colleagues with academic management responsibilities to help them find ways of having academic staff do less lecturing and make better use of e-learning. This, of course, appears to contradict, if not fly in the face of the institutional barriers described above, whether they be perceived or real, that academics face. This appears to leave things in a strange state of stale mate. Gilly Salmon agrees, arguing that: "despite the fact that e-learning (and its role as a change agent) figures highly, and sometimes even wistfully, in the aspirations of many policy-makers and senior managers, there is considerable evidence that most HEIs are still struggling to engage a significant percentage of students and staff in e-learning [11]." Regardless, it is a change that is worth striving for as it accomplishes an ideal hybrid situation where VLEs and face-to-face envi-ronments are regarded as equal and as supporting and feeding into each other.

For academic staff, then, this strategy becomes a matter of moving away from a situation where all of the learning activities need to be able to be accomplished in a classroom, to matching the right tool (whether it be in a face-to-face or virtual envi-ronment) to the (learning) job. As such, curriculum development becomes being about finding the right mix of tools and learning environments to suit the learning objectives.

The outcome for students means improved flexibility of, accessibility to and even, in an ideal situation, choice of learning environments. In a well-designed hybrid situation, for staff and students alike, the workload can remain more or less the same. Indeed, the construction of reusable learning objects can see a significant reduction in delivery workload after the initial investment in development time. So while academic staff do the same amount of work, they are doing different types of work and, in many instances, more interesting, varied and rewarding work. Similarly, students are expected to do the same amount of learning work but this work is often significantly different (and in many instances more 'active' learning work) than that which would have been expected of them in a traditional face-to-face learning situation. As such, hybrid learning environments are easier to maintain than those which use VLEs to supplement face-to-face learning environments. This is because students are confident that their work in these environments is important and, in some instances, compulsory and assessable, and therefore they remain encouraged to contribute. Similarly, staff have enough time, energy and reason to maintain and moderate them. In this hybrid situation, genuine change occurs because teachers find the best teaching tool for the specific learning outcome and students see, consequently, better benefits to their learning.

The million dollar question still remains: how do we achieve this final step change to the widespread adoption of hybrid learning? As described above, the change is difficult to make which is, of course, why it is yet to happen. As Salmon points out 'research is currently not providing answers to this problem and more models are needed' to demonstrate the transferability and scalability of e-learning' [11]. This paper proposes that one potential answer to that question may lie in the area of distributed learning.

3   Distributed Learning

The terms 'hybrid learning' and 'distributed learning' are sometimes seen as being interchangeable. Indeed in its 'purest' sense, distributed learning can be understood as the delivery of teaching and learning which is distributed over as much of the students' life (in terms of time and environment) as possible, thereby constituting a hybridised combination of virtual and face-to-face learning environments. In practice, distributed learning tends to acquire a more 'work-a-day' definition *viz* the delivery of teaching and learning to distinct cohorts of students who are separated from each other in time and/or place. This could include any or all combinations of student cohorts spread around multiple and/or remote campuses, those that are undertaking their study part-time and those studying full-time, those that are studying on-campus (internally), those studying at a distance (externally), those that are studying within industry, those that can attend day-time classes only and those who can attend only in the evening and so on. With this more practical definition we are immediately presented with a single, inescapable fact: that it is difficult, if not impossible to gather students in all cohorts on a single module together regularly for a class that is synchronous in terms of both time and place. For these students, learning activities simply cannot be done in the rigidly synchronous learning environment which is a classroom. For academic staff there are really only two options. The first option is duplication of effort, either personally repeating the class or employing someone else to repeat it at a different time and/or location. This duplication of effort is necessarily costly and if any travelling time and expense is also incurred it can make this solution both unappealing and prohibitively expensive. The second option is to find some other means of delivering the teaching, which increasingly sees staff turning to technology to effectively join the cohorts together.

This simple obstacle – that the teaching can't be done in a classroom – triggers a series of interesting, useful and often unexpected results. In the first instance, the simple act of having to rethink teaching in this way requires a certain degree of reflection which is often enough to bring about significant change [see 12]. Many academics can find this experience quite liberating, as suddenly the restrictions that the rigidly synchronous nature of face-to-face teaching in classrooms imposes (in terms of both time and place) become apparent. From this, new possibilities emerge that were previously unviable. For instance, seeing the impositions of timetabling disappear and realising that lectures do not need to be 50 minutes long can be quite a liberating experience. Because new things are being attempted, the very act of piloting these new strategies means that unexpected things are more likely to happen, something that John Cowan cheekily refers to as 'unintended learning outcomes' [5]. One of the most profound 'unintended outcomes' is that these experiences start to have an impact on the main campus as academics recognise that these benefits can also be made available for full-time, main-campus students. Sometimes referred to as the 'Petri dish' approach, the impact that distributed learning initiatives designed for delivery to remote and often small campuses can have on the teaching and learning practice across the whole institution is becoming increasingly well documented [see 13, 14, 15]. For the purposes of this paper, I will focus on the practice of lecturing, and use it as an example of how the approach of distributed learning can be used to bring about wider institutional change.

4 Lecturing

Lecturing clearly has a place in hybrid learning alongside other forms of classroom-based and virtual learning strategies. Yet because its ubiquity, prevalence and, arguably, obduracy stands in such marked contrast to its efficacy it is an obvious candidate to target as a point of change. For there is little doubt that as a teaching and learning strategy, lecturing is of dubious quality. Diana Laurillard's dismissal of it in her highly influential *Rethinking University Teaching* is perhaps best exemplified by the fact that she affords it a little over two pages in the 240 page monograph, and only then begrudgingly. She introduces the segment on lectures by insisting it is 'under consideration here only to provide a baseline for comparison, as the traditionally favoured university teaching method' [16]. She goes on to say that 'if we forget the eight hundred years of university tradition that legitimises them, and imagine starting afresh with the problem of how best to enable a large percentage of the population to understand difficult and complex ideas, I doubt that lectures will immediately spring to mind as the obvious solution [16]. Similarly, Graham Gibbs's 'Twenty Terrible Reasons for Lecturing' (where the title says it all) provides a trenchant but accessible critique of lecturing as a teaching and learning strategy. In his conclusion he asserts: "I do believe there is far more lecturing going on than can reasonably be justified by the evidence concerning the efficiency of lectures, especially bearing in mind the nature of the educational goals we claim to be striving for. [...] I believe both institutions and validating bodies ought to be asking serious questions about courses which appear to be based primarily on lecturing as the dominant teaching method [17]." Given the weight of this kind of scholarly evidence, even books which purport to condone lecturing as a valuable teaching and learning strategy are now obliged to place considerable emphasis on how ineffectual they are.[2] Even one of the most comprehensive and widely cited studies on lecturing to date, Bligh's *What's the Use of Lectures?* has a certain hesitancy evident in the title. In this work, Bligh sets out the four main reasons which are usually offered to justify lecturing: 1 – that they assist students in the acquisition of information, 2 – that they promote thought, 3 – that they change student attitudes and 4 – that they enhance behavioural skills. Of these four, Bligh's findings demonstrate that it is only in the first of these objectives that the lecture can be effective and even then only *as effective* as other methods in transmitting information [18]. Brown and Race acknowledge Bligh's research, and concur that as a means of giving students the information they need, lecturing is not a particularly efficient method simply because the amount of information now available is huge and it is impossible to get everything done in the timescale lecturing allows [7]. Surveying such literature does leave you wondering, alongside Gibbs, why on earth there's so much of it going on [17].

If it ever *did* have a useful teaching and learning function, arguably lecturing is obsolete in a widening participation, information rich world. It is useful to consider these issues in turn. First, is the issue of open access and widening participation. In her trenchant criticism of the lecture as a teaching strategy, Diana Laurillard points out that lecturing can only ever work as an effective teaching methodology if lecturers know very well the 'capabilities of the students, and on the students having very similar capabilities and prior knowledge' [16]. She goes on to suggest that in a world where 'students were selected through standardised entrance examinations' [16] for admission to university, this was something about which a lecturers *could* be fairly certain. They could be confident that students would share and understand their idiolect, cultural references, social aspirations and, until relatively recently, their gender. Lecturers could also be confident that their prior knowledge and training in things such as essay writing was almost uniform, that their learning needs and that their potential employer expectations were fairly similar. Laurillard suggests that 'open access and module courses make it most unlikely that a class of students will be sufficiently similar in background and capabilities to make lectures workable as a principal teaching method' [16]. Students in Higher Education today come from an ever growing array of backgrounds with vastly differing prior qualifications and an equally vast array of learning needs. Of course hybrid learning acknowledges how ridiculous it is to assume that all of these needs can be met in a learning environment of lecturing alone.

---

[2] See for instance Brown and Race *Lecturing: A Practical Guide.* The authors make the rather astonishing circular claim that one of the principle justifications for lecturing is that 'despite all concerns that are expressed about the method, lecturing is likely to remain a central part of the higher education scene for the foreseeable future' [7] and so are worth doing if done well. They then go on to explain that to be done well, lectures need to involve something *other than* 'lecturing'.

Secondly, is the issue of living in an information rich world. Arguably in a time where information was stored only in books which were, like the libraries that held them, expensive and scarce, lecturing was a cheap and effective means of providing students with useful textual material. Lecturing was, in effect, a kind of cheap and efficient transcription tool. As Brown and Race point out the early history of lecturing in European universities involved Masters reciting memorised tracts of text, which the students then transcribed [7]. The lecturer's skill was in reciting the information faithfully, clearly and slowly enough to allow students to write it down! In this context, the lecturer was one of the most if not *the* most important sources of knowledge available to students. But in an e-world where the students' information cup is full to overflowing, the lecturer cannot and really should not be the main source of information. Clearly what students need is help and support in gathering, managing, filtering, evaluating and using the information available to them, not more of it. As Knight and Wood point out, while there is now more information to learn than ever before, "the increasingly easy accessibility of facts on the Internet is making long-term memorization of details less and less important. Students [...] will be required to apply conceptual knowledge to problem solving rather than simply to know many facts [19]." If all the lecture can and does do well is provide students with information, then we are doing them a disservice and under-preparing them for their future careers in our continuing use of them.

With these criticisms and the sheer weight of scholarly evidence, it is remarkable that there is still so much lecturing going on. Again, there are many reasons for this and here I only have to cover the important ones. Firstly, most academics were taught by lectures and feel obliged and expected to do it themselves. For many, a key aspect of joining the academy is performing that role and some scholars have argued that the lecture is, in this sense, inherited behaviour [20]. Others have argued that there is a general lack of reflection on teaching strategies in the academy which, as Bligh points out, would appear to be strangely at odds with the dedication to the 'disinterested search of truth by research' and the emphasis placed on 'discouraging expression of opinion not based upon careful study of publicly verifiable facts' which is at the heart of scholarly practice [18]. Others have suggested that academics are reluctant to give lecturing up simply because we like it – that the lecture provides a kind of self-indulgent, ego-boosting platform that is rarely matched in other settings [7, 19] . As suggested earlier, the very architecture of institutions is explicitly designed to encourage and reward lecturing [7, 19, 21, 22].

Even the two newest buildings that are nearing completion at my own institution have a considerable amount of space dedicated to lecture theatres, complete with a central rostrum and tiered seating, which are virtually impossible to use for anything other than lecturing. Many academics are also reluctant to give up lecturing because they perceive it to be their responsibility to 'cover the content'. Knight and Wood refer to this as the 'content problem' and argue that it doesn't really need to be solved because the 'ability to solve problems and in-depth understanding of underlying concepts will probably be of more use to them in the long run than any particular piece of factual information [19]. Astonishingly, some studies suggest that with lectures being seen as an easy solution to growing class sizes, we're actually doing more of it now than ever [7].

Another pressure which encourages the use of lectures is student expectation. As the research of Sander et al shows, for students entering Higher Education, the most frequently expected teaching and learning methods are formal lectures even though this ranked very highly in terms of the teaching and learning methods that students did *not* want [23]. This would seem to suggest that many students are embarking on a University education *despite* the fact that they will experience lectures not *because* of it. This begs the question, how many students are choosing not to embark on it at all precisely *because* of the lecturing? As Knight and Wood have pointed out, confounding this expectation can have a negative effect on student evaluations: 'because students at present are used to having most large courses taught in the lecture format, the unfamiliar demands of an active-engagement course may take them out of their comfort zone, resulting in lower student ratings for the instructor' [19]. It is possible that some students may prefer the lecture experience precisely *because* it is a passive learning experience that does not require much effort on their part. Knight and Wood report how students complained about a more interactive teaching and learning format because academics 'were not teaching them very much, but rather making them learn the material on their own' which, while quite gratifying for the teachers, serves to emphasise how entrenched and normative the passive lecture experiences has become for students [19]. To put it simply, attending lectures becomes a learning habit for students that becomes hard to break and is therefore easy to articulate as an expectation. This expectation can be difficult for academics to refuse to meet. It is hardly surprising then that lecturing has proved so difficult to shift and indeed why there is so much literature encouraging better lecturing practice.[3]

In my experience of working with teams of academics, both in Australia and the United Kingdom, on distributed learning development, similar patterns of change emerge time and time again. As outlined above lecturing is difficult if not impossible to achieve efficiently when there are two or more cohorts of students distributed by time and/or space. Even if duplication is cost effective, the ridiculous and tedious nature of repeating teaching soon becomes apparent and alternatives that make use of technology become more attractive. This breakthrough is, I argue, strategically useful from an academic development point of view, and it is precisely this that needs to be exploited if the aims of a more widespread adoption of hybrid learning are to be achieved. It is strategically useful precisely because by using technology to replace lecturing, academics are reassured that they are doing what they feel is expected of them – the lecturing is 'covered'. This immediately overcomes many, if not all, of the barriers described above that are currently maintaining and encouraging the continued use of lecturing as a teaching and learning method. In this process, academics find

---

[3] What is striking about this literature is that the strategies they offer to academics to improve their lectures is often not well suited to the classroom. Many of them are actually things which would be more easily, more efficiently and more effectively accomplished online. For instance, Brown and Race suggest getting students to work 'independently in groups all around the room, with the lecturer taking a position at a 'help desk' in the middle to answer questions, check and chase progress and occasionally address the whole group while briefing for tasks, taking in responses and coordinating plenary discussion' [7]. I for one find the prospect of this quite daunting in a strictly synchronous setting, but find this kind of learning activity is not just achievable in an online asynchronous environment, but actually easier to manage there.

that it is easier to accomplish things that are actually difficult or impossible to achieve in a classroom setting – literally doing things that cannot be done in a classroom.[4] They also find that the learning objects they create are so effective that they are worth deploying to the main cohort as well and thereby bring unexpected learning outcomes to the student body as a whole. With the confidence that the lecturing is 'covered', academics also feel more able to devote more time to managing follow-up activities, such as moderating discussion either inside a classroom or online. Again, this corresponds to Bligh's research on lecturing which suggests that 'discussion is more important than lecturing'. He declaims that: 'lecturing should always be pursued as a means to some other end. [...] Otherwise lectures become useless – necessarily useless' [18]. Exploiting this pattern to achieve impetus for change is, therefore, potentially an important strategic step for universities to take to achieve the goal of widespread adoption of hybrid learning. To illustrate, I offer a vignette which serves as a useful example of the kinds of methods that have be employed to replace lecturing in a distributed learning context and which can be used strategically to develop hybrid learning situations for full-time, on-campus students as well: Screencast lectures.

5   Screencast Lectures

Screencast lectures are not especially new or even innovative. Arguably the sets of 'advisory notes' that were distributed to distance learning students in their course packs were effectively a print-based version of the same thing. In my experience, students have been recording lectures on audio tape for as long as portable recording devices have been readily and cheaply available. Likewise, some academics and institutions have systematically audio- and/or video-taped lectures, for both on and off-campus student use for some time. More recently, various technologies which enable the accessing of lecture material in audio and video format online have become more widely available. These strategies are sometimes known as Web-based Lecturing Technology (WBLT), lecture streaming and podcasting [see 24, 25, 26]. These systems offer various combinations of the audio of a lecture, a video headshot of the lecturer and/or the presentation that accompanies it (such as PowerPoint slides). These can also be made available for downloading to devices, such as MP3 players for mobile access. Screencasting specifically refers to a combination of the audio recording of a lecture played synchronously with the PowerPoint presentation using SCORM software such as Camtasia Studio which can then be embedded within a VLE and/or downloaded onto a portable device.[5]

In a distributed learning scenario, these kinds of strategies are usually initially adopted to increase efficiency primarily by reducing the need for duplication of effort. Equally, they have been adopted to improve quality primarily by providing an equivalent learning experience to all students across distributed cohorts, thus ensuring that

---

[4] Again, this corresponds in interesting ways to much of the literature available which is designed to improve lecturing.

[5] The specific benefits and problems associated with mobile as opposed to streamed or embedded screencasts is in itself an interesting and complex issue which is outside the scope of the present paper. Also, it is evident that recent advances in software have successfully overcome many of the difficulties encountered with earlier attempts at synchronisation (see [26]).

all students have the same access to the academic expertise, regardless of where it is located, thus reinforcing the research/teaching nexus. As I shall discuss in more detail below, research shows that staff are often reluctant to adopt and in some instances even actively resist this technology being made available to students on the main campus. Conversely, research also shows that students report positive feedback on their use of screencasts finding them both convenient to use and beneficial to their learning sometimes in ways that are unanticipated [26]. For instance, Natalie Simpson's research found students hinting that their ability to maintain concentration and to react and reflect upon questions addressed to them by the lecturer were not hindered by the one-way nature of the experience and were perhaps even enhanced in comparison to the live lecture experience [27]. Overall, for students using some form of screencast lecture, the benefits are clear.

The research shows that these benefits fall into four main categories. First they can be easily, flexibly and multiply accessed on demand 24 hours a day, seven days a week. Because they are always available, they can be used by students, for reflection on their learning achievement through the module and for revision purposes as they prepare for assessment. Secondly, they can be used selectively in that students can select a specific section to listen to without having to go through the whole recording, and they can pause and replay the recording. This enables students to target specific aspects of the lecture to check and clarify their understanding. This has shown to be particularly attractive to and useful for students whose main language is other than the language of instruction [see 27]. Students can break the lecture into smaller chunks that suit their level of concentration rather than struggling to maintain it over the full 50 minutes. This corresponds with the extensive research which shows how student vigilance and arousal declines over the course of a one-hour lecture [see 18]. Lecturers can actually exploit this by breaking the lecture into smaller 15-20 minute chunks themselves and interspersing these with private and/or group reflection activities. Thirdly, at a time when many students are chronically time-poor, by not requiring them to travel to campus, and by beginning when the lecturer starts speaking and ending when they stop, it can save a considerable amount of student time.[6] Fourthly, students are able to compile more detailed and more meaningful notes. Here it is useful to consider Brown and Race's distinction between note *taking* and note *making*. They argue that 'most lecturers would actually *like* students to be [making notes] in lectures – not just copying things down, but *processing* what's being show and said, and turning it into their own notes' [7, emphasis theirs]. They suggest that many students resort to 'note taking' in a live lecture in an attempt to 'capture' it 'so that there's more chance of being able to get to grips with the content later' [7] . Knowing that the lecture is available for multiple viewings, students are less likely to feel this obligation and more likely to concentrate on making notes which record their own responses to and syntheses of the presented material. Together, these provide a significant benefit to students, whether they have access to the live lecture event or not,

---

[6] As Lammers and Murphy have shown, the amount of time in a formal face-to-face lecture where no one is actively involved in learning (because the lecturer is occupied with such things as setting up technology, distributing hand outs etc) can average as much as 15 per cent of the actual scheduled class time [30].

which is reflected in the accumulated body of evaluation evidence on student perceptions of screencast lectures [13, 24-29][7]

As suggested earlier, this kind of technology has attracted its fair share of criticism. Much of it is, however, unfounded. Phillips et al refer to the work of Donnan, Kiley and McCormack who told how the use of WBLT was met with resistance by academic staff at an Australian university because it was perceived to be technologically rather than pedagogically led innovation [Donnan, Kiley and McCormack, cited in 24]. These concerns are effectively discredited by the very real pedagogical advantages that are demonstrated widely in the literature, as described above, and this resistance can be seen as symptomatic of a pervasive, albeit unsupportable, investment in live lecturing amongst academic staff in general. As suggested earlier, there is also considerable evidence in the literature about academic anxiety relating to falling attendance at live lectures even though there is little evidence to suggest that this actually occurs [24, 26] This, again, confirms the amount of residual investment by academics that lecturing is, in itself, a good thing and to be preserved at all costs. Even if falling attendance did eventuate, this can be read positively as students 'voting with their feet' and choosing to adopt the learning strategies and environments that suit them best and benefit their learning most. Rather than feeling anxious about falling attendance, academics could instead be encouraged to read it as their providing a better and more valuable learning experience for their students through screencasting. Choosing not to make screencast lectures available simply as a means of forcing students to continue attending live lectures, even if they learn less from this arrangement, is illogical in the extreme! Of a similar nature is concern of what Wilson and Weiser refer to as 'massive instructor obsolescence', that having 'tapes' of lectures available on demand will result in a reduction in the need for academic staff [13]. However, just as with live lectures, screencast lectures require updating to keep abreast of developments in the field in order to maintain the research/teaching nexus. The availability of digital audio recording and editing software which can run on standard staff desktop computers makes such updating relatively easy and cheap to accomplish. More importantly, perhaps, the replacement of lectures with screencasts releases academic staff time to undertake more student-centred activities which guide students in the management of information and support them in the development of conceptual knowledge. Arguably, in this scenario academic staff are needed more than ever before!

Concerns are also often raised about a perceived lack of 'immediacy' and 'interactivity' with screencast lectures. Of course, many students do not find live lectures particularly interactive to start with [see 30]. As we have seen in the research of Simpson (outlined earlier), questions directed to students for reflection in a live-lecture are still just as effective in a screencast lecture (Simpson). It is entirely possible that some students find such reflection activities even more effective in a screencast setting given that they have more control over the amount of time they devote to their reflection and may feel reluctant to contribute a response in a lecture hall in any case. Further, some research has

---

[7] Interestingly, as Smith points out, these benefits 'correlate positively with students' attitudes to distance learning' which is a useful reminder that face-to-face classes have limitations and should never be regarded as the ideal learning environment against which others are measured [29].

shown students reporting a greater sense of intimacy and engagement with the lecturer in a screencast lecture than a live one. As Simpson puts it: 'the sound captured on video was devoid of environmental noise, while the view framed by the cameras created the impression of sitting quite close to the speaker' [27]. Simpson supports this with evidence from a student reporting that while she's easily distracted by such things as people walking in late and by her friends sitting around her in a typical classroom setting, in contrast her engagement with the screencast, where she is alone at home, affords her greater degrees of focus and concentration. Of course there are fewer opportunities for peer-learning activities such as 'buzz groups' and the lecturer is not immediately available to answer questions. Arguably these can be more than adequately compensated by the academic being freed to commit more time to follow up activities that achieve the same ends. Anecdotal evidence from my own students, who are studying at a campus remote from the main campus and have lecture material screencast by academics from the main campus, suggests that they feel they know these academics well even if they have met them only once or twice. There is little evidence then to suggest that screencasts result in less 'interactivity' and 'immediacy' for the students and, perhaps counter intuitively, some evidence to suggest that they are actually enhanced through screencasting.

Of more serious concern is the criticism from Donnan, Kiley and McCormack (reported by [24]) that screencast lectures are simply another way of reinforcing lecturing as a transmission model of teaching and encourage passive behaviour. This is difficult to dispute because while they are infinitely preferable to a lecture in terms of their accessibility, controllability and repeatability, they are still lectures nonetheless. Of course, the strategies that the literature on good lecturing technique advocates can and should be deployed with screencasts, just as they would be in a live lecture situation.

Even Laurillard, who is so scathingly dismissive of the lecture as a teaching strategy, is positively enthusiastic about screencasting (which she refers to as audiovision).[8] She argues that by using the 'auditory channel in combination with something for the visual channel to focus on [...] it creates an additional representation [...] of the descriptions being given in sound' [16]. Arguably, however, this should also be true in most modern live lectures since the advent of PowerPoint and other kinds of presentation software which are now truly pervasive both within and outside academia.[9] Where once visual aids were rare in a lecture, now the opposite is true, and lectures without a PowerPoint presentation are almost unheard of. So, the linking of audio (a lecturer speaking) and visual (a PowerPoint presentation) are now quite common in a live lecture.

There is a growing body of evidence that people everywhere are indeed sick of being subjected to 'death by PowerPoint' [31]. Of course students are not immune to this, and arguably, because they are subjected to more PowerPoint than most, 'death' rates for them are probably highest of all. I would agree with scholars, such as Mahin, who argue that PowerPoint itself is not at fault, but rather bad and over use of it, and

---

[8] Her concerns about audiovision being difficult to browse or index (and therefore being less 'controllable' than print) are for the most part rendered obsolete with the advent of modern digital recording and screencasting software, than can be broken into chapters [16].

[9] According to Linda Mahin, one estimate by Microsoft is that an astonishing 1.25 million PowerPoint presentations take place every hour [32]!

probably over reliance on it, is really the problem. In the light of this, perhaps 'death by dotpoint' is a more accurate term. Mahin concurs, saying that providing 'visual information such as photographs, charts, or diagrams [...] which enrich the message, not become the message' is the most effective way of using presentation software [32]. Further, those screencasts that more accurately mimic a television documentary, again something about which Laurillard is enthusiastic, are better still. She argues that televisual techniques, such as montage, can allow an academic who wants to convey a 'complex theoretical idea' to offer a way of 'supplanting the process the student must follow in order to understand the meaning' [16]. Supplanting, she suggests, "allows perception of the world through television to imitate our perception of the real world. As television offers a 'vicarious perception' of the world, it acts as a solution to the logistical problem of enabling large numbers of students to experience that aspect of the world directly [16]." Of course, the production of good quality televisual lectures, with high production values, is beyond the budgetary capacity of most teaching departments. However, the production of high quality, screencasts with synchronous audio and images, which mimic televisual strategies and thereby offer 'vicarious perception' are, arguably, of equal value and significantly cheaper while also offering the high degree of accessibility and controllability that live lectures lack.

Having said all this, screencasts still undeniably subscribe to a fundamentally instructional teaching and learning paradigm. Yet, as I have suggested above, they are strategically important and useful if harnessed as a means of triggering the step change required to achieve the widespread adoption of hybrid learning. As we have seen, academics are remarkably wedded to lectures as a teaching and learning method, despite the overwhelming and long standing accumulation of evidence that proves they are of dubious quality in terms of benefiting student learning. Without any real impetus or imperative *to* give them up, it is unlikely that academics will do so *en masse* any time soon. It is here that distributed learning is significant.

6 Conclusion: Why Distributed Learning Is Strategically Important

As Universities seek to attract a broader range of students and accommodate the ever-growing demand for greater flexibility of access to learning environments, distributed learning is becoming increasingly important as an efficient and effective teaching and learning strategy. Many Universities around the world have already established, or are in the process of establishing, multiple remote campuses which, in some instances, are based overseas.[10] Many Universities are also seeking to boost student numbers by attracting more distance or external students, part-time students and mature-age students who also stand to benefit from increased access to distributed learning envi-

---

[10] My own institution, the University of Huddersfield in West Yorkshire, has recently opened two new campuses in Oldham (Greater Manchester) and Barnsley (South Yorkshire). My previous institution, the University of Wollongong, has established four remote campuses and access-centres in the South Coast and Southern Highlands of New South Wales. In both of these campus networks, distributed learning is being used to some extent to deliver teaching and learning to students based there. The University of Wollongong has also established a campus in Dubai.

ronments. Many Universities are also establishing more formal partnerships to provide training and qualifications to industry which is usually reluctant to indulge in more than the bare minimum of work release. All Universities are ultimately in competition with each other to provide learning options and environments which will attract more students to them. Distributed learning can and should play an important part in enhancing all of these enterprises.

It is important, however, that the benefits to the institution are not seen to end there. As a growing body of scholarship is arguing, the very real benefits of hybrid learning environments should also be made available to full-time, main-campus students as well. As we have seen, the adoption of these strategies is simply not happening and there remain so many barriers in place. The experience of distributed learning development shows, however, that embarking on strategies to solve the problem of not being able to gather all students into a classroom can and should be strategically harnessed to trigger this change. As I have argued, in the particular case of the lecture this strategy has particular efficacy.

By reassuring academics that the work of 'lecturing' is covered by strategies such as screencasting, they can effectively be used to 'wean' academics off it. In doing so, academics are more likely to feel able and ready to dedicate contact time to undertaking a greater range of student-centred, interactive activities such as discussion, group work, role play and so on. If institutions are genuine in their commitment to achieving a more widespread adoption of hybrid learning, they would do well to invest in appropriate academic development that facilitates, encourages and empowers academics to redeploy distributed learning strategies to full-time, main-campus students as well. By harnessing the potential of distributed learning and making strategic use of those instances where teaching 'can't be done in a classroom', institutions can come a step closer to achieving the ideal objective of the widespread adoption of hybrid learning.

References

1. Barr, R.B., Tagg, J.: From Teaching to Learning. In: DeZure, D. (ed.) Learning from Change. Kogan Page, London (1995)
2. Browne, T., Jenkins, M., Walker, R.: A longitudinal perspective regarding the use of VLEs by higher education institutions in the United Kingdom. Interactive Learning Environments 14, 177–192 (2006)
3. Bell, M., Bush, D., Nicholson, P., O'Brien, D., Tran, T.: A survey of online education and services in Australia (2002)
4. Garrot, T., Psillaki, M., Rochhia, S.: Describing E-learning Development in European Higher Education Institutions Using a Balanced Scorecard. RUSC 5 (2008)
5. Cowan, J.: Introduction. In: O'Donoghue, J. (ed.) Technology Supported Learning and Teaching, pp. 1–13. Information Science Publishing, London (2006)
6. Neo, M.: Web-enhanced learning: engaging students in constructivist learning. Campus-Wide Information Systems 22, 4–14 (2005)
7. Brown, S., Race, P.: Lecturing, a practical guide. Kogan Page, London (2002)
8. QAA: Code of Practice for the Assurance of Academic Quality and Standards in Higher Education. Section 2: Collaborative Provision and Flexible and Distributed Learning (Including e-Learning) (2004)
9. IHEP: Quality On the Line Benchmarks For Success in Internet-Based Distance Education (2000)

10. Oliver, R.: Quality assurance and e-learning: blue skies and pragmatism. ALT-J. 13, 173–187 (2005)
11. Salmon, G.: Flying not flapping: a strategic framework for e-learning and pedagogical innovation in higher education institutions. ALT-J. 13, 201–218 (2005)
12. Hammersley-Fletcher, L., Orsmond, P.: Reflecting on reflective practices within peer observation. Studies in Higher Education 30, 213–224 (2005)
13. Wilson, R.L., Weiser, M.: Adoption of Asynchronous Learning Tools by Traditional Full-Time Students: A Pilot Study. Information Technology and Management 2, 363–375 (2001)
14. Collins, R.: Small campus, collegial development, a community and learning: Some reflections on developing reflective practice amongst part time casual tutors. In: 14th Annual Teaching Learning Forum. Murdoch University, Perth (2005)
15. Curtis, S., Lefoe, G., Merten, M., Milne, C., Albury, R.: Passing through the pain barrier: making a flexibly delivered degree. HERDSA, Melbourne (1999)
16. Laurillard, D.: Rethinking University Teaching. RoutledgeFalmer, London (2002)
17. Gibbs, G.: Twenty terrible reasons for lecturing. SCED, Birmingham (1981)
18. Bligh, D.: What's the Use of Lectures? intellect, Exeter (1998)
19. Knight, J.K., Wood, W.B.: Teaching More by Lecturing Less. Cell Biology Education 4, 298–310 (2005)
20. Cockburn, B., Ross, A.: Why Lecture? School of Education. University of Lancaster, Lancaster (1978)
21. Jamieson, P.: Designing more effective on-campus teaching and learning spaces: a role for academic developers. International Journal for Academic Development 8, 119–133 (2003)
22. Biggs, J.: Teaching for quality learning at university. Society for Research into Higher Education and Open University Press, Buckingham (1999)
23. Sander, P., Stevenson, K., King, M., Coates, D.: University Students' Expectations of Teaching. Studies in Higher Education 25, 309–323 (2000)
24. Phillips, R., Gosper, M., McNeill, M., Woo, K., Preston, G., Green, D.: Staff and student perspectives on web based lecture technologies: Insights into the great divide, Ascilite, Singapore (2007)
25. Gosper, M., McNeill, M., Woo, K., Phillips, R., Preston, G., Green, D.: Web-based Lecture Recording Technologies: Do Students Learn From Them? Educause Australasia, Melbourne, Australia (2007)
26. McNeill, M., Woo, K., Gosper, M., Phillips, R., Preston, G., Green, D.: Using web-based lecture technologies – advice from students. HERDSA, Adelaide, Australia (2007)
27. Simpson, N.: Asynchronous access to conventional course delivery: a pilot project. British Journal of Educational Technology 37, 527–537 (2006)
28. Soong, S.K.A., Chan, L.K., Cheers, C.: Impact of video recorded lectures among students, Ascilite (2006)
29. Smith, C.: Lecturing by Streamed Video: Blood, Sweat, Tears and Success. In: O'Donoghue, J. (ed.) Technology Supported Learning and Teaching, pp. 309–322. Information Science Publishing, London (2006)
30. Lammers, W.J., Murphy, J.J.: A Profile of Teaching Techniques Used in the University Classroom: A Descriptive Profile of a US Public University. Active Learning in Higher Education 3, 54–67 (2002)
31. Taylor, D.: Death by PowerPoint. Developmental Medicine & Child Neurology 49, 395 (2007)
32. Mahin, L.: PowerPoint Pedagogy. Business Communication Quarterly, 219–222 (2004)

A Proposal for a Lifecycle Process for Hybrid Learning Programs

Won Kim

Sungkyunkwan University
Suwon, S. Korea
wonkim@skku.edu

Abstract. A hybrid learning program is a mixture of traditional in-class learning components and e-learning components. A learning program may be a single course or an entire curriculum. A learning program and courseware must be designed to help learners learn. As such, a hybrid learning program is a rather complex artifact. Commercial software is in general a very complex artifact that has a clearly defined lifecycle for planning, development, deployment, maintenance & upgrade, and termination. Although learning programs and courseware are not nearly as complex as commercial software, adapting the lifecycle process for the creation and managing of commercial software to hybrid learning programs and courseware should make it possible for the learning program managers and courseware developers to take a holistic and disciplined approach to the creation and management of hybrid learning programs and courseware. This paper proposes a lifecycle process for hybrid learning programs and e-learning courseware.

Keywords: hybrid learning, blended learning, lifecycle process, software development process, courseware development.

1 Introduction

[1] provides rigorous definitions of hybrid learning and hybrid learning programs, and shed light on the many possible types of hybrid learning. Further, it outlines a methodology for creating and managing hybrid learning programs. One common aspect of every type of hybrid learning is that it is a mixture of traditional instructor-led in-class learning and e-learning which does not require the instructor and students to be concurrently present in the physical classroom. E-learning programs are in general more complex to create and manage than the traditional in-class learning programs, since e-learning programs must take into account not only the capabilities and limitations of various technologies that can be used in creating and delivering the learning contents, but also the fact that in general instructors do not lead the learning in real-time. Since hybrid learning programs combine e-learning and traditional in-class learning, creating and managing hybrid learning programs is inherently more complex than either the traditional in-class learning programs or e-learning programs alone. If the learning program is not just for a single course, but for a curriculum, it obviously becomes even more complex.

J. Fong, R. Kwan, and F.L. Wang (Eds.): ICHL 2008, LNCS 5169, pp. 17–30, 2008.
© Springer-Verlag Berlin Heidelberg 2008

There is considerable similarity between the process of creating and managing e-learning or hybrid learning programs and that of commercial software. Intuitively, they are both complex and therefore require upfront planning. After planning, they are developed. After development, they are deployed and assessed based on feedback from the customers (users and learners). They are then maintained and upgraded. Once their usefulness or value dissipates, they are retired. To be sure, there are some important differences between creating and managing learning programs and commercial software. In general, learning programs are not nearly as complex as software, with respect to the logic and logic branches. For learning programs, "learnability" is the most important objective, while it is in general not nearly as important for commercial software. Despite such differences, adopting the lifecycle process for creating and managing commercial software should help in creating and managing both e-learning and hybrid learning programs. It will allow the managers and developers of the learning programs to take a holistic and disciplined approach to creating and managing the learning programs, including the setting of the objectives, assessing the achievement of the objectives, learning program (and courseware) development (schedule, budget and resources), quality of the learning program (and courseware), usability of the courseware, learnability of the program, learning asset management, etc.

In this paper, I will propose a lifecycle process for creating and managing hybrid learning programs. The process is a sequence of steps. I will discuss considerations in each step in some detail. A major subset of the process is obviously applicable to creating and managing e-learning program and courseware, a subset of a hybrid learning program and courseware.

2 Lifecycle Process

The lifecycle of commercial software consists of three primary phases: planning, development and deployment, and maintenance and upgrade. The development phase in turn consists of the upstream phase and the downstream phase [2]. The upstream phase includes three key steps: requirements specification, design specification, and test planning. The downstream phase also includes three key steps: implementation, testing, and release. The design specification includes both basic (or architecture) design, and detailed design. Often the basic design step belongs to the upstream phase, and the detailed design step is pushed to the downstream phase. Further, detailed design, implementation, and testing are often done concurrently.

During the planning and development phases, documents are produced and they are reviewed by the stakeholders (i.e., people who need to know their contents). There are two types of document: one is for internal use, and another is for release to the customers. The internal-use documents include a plan document, a requirements specification, a basic design specification, a detailed design specification, a test plan, source code with block comments. The "for-customers" documents include executable code, release notes, user manuals and references. During the maintenance and upgrade phase, most of these documents undergo changes. Further, during this phase, a defect database is maintained to keep track of defects reported and resolved.

Table 1. First-level Comparison of the Lifecycle Process for Commercial Software and Hybrid Learning Programs

	Commercial Software	Hybrid Learning Programs
Planning	Product planning (plan document) & review	Program planning (plan document) & review
Upstream development	Requirements gathering & analysis (requirements spec) & review	Requirements gathering & analysis (requirements spec) & review
	Basic design (basic design spec) & review	
		Basic design (basic design spec) & review
	Test planning (test plan) & review	
		Test planning (test plan) & review
Downstream development	Detailed design (detailed design spec) & review	Detailed design & implementation (courseware, courseware notes) & review
	Implementation (source code, source code block comments) & code review	
	Testing: unit testing, integration testing, system testing, acceptance testing (test suite, test script) & test suite review, test results review	Testing: unit testing, integration testing, courseware testing & test results review
	Release (executable code, release notes, user manuals & references) & review	Release (courseware, program guide, learners guide to e-courseware)
Deployment & assessment	Deployment & customer training	Deployment & customer training
	Customer support & assessment	Customer support & assessment
Maintenance & upgrade	Maintenance & maintenance release	Maintenance & maintenance release
	Upgrade & upgrade release	Upgrade & upgrade release
Retirement	Retire the product	Retire the program

Table 1 provides the highest-level outline of the lifecycle processes for commercial software and hybrid learning programs. At this level, the two processes seem almost the same, although the details are considerably different, as I will show in the remainder of this paper. Each process consists of several phases, and each phase in turn consists of one or more steps. In Table 1, the items in parentheses after each step are the deliverables (output) of the step. Each of the deliverables needs to go through a review process by the stakeholders.

Note that in Table 1, the basic design is placed in the upstream development phase, while the detailed design is in the downstream phase. Most commercial software development is done under very compressed schedule, and implementation and detailed design are done concurrently, along with unit testing and integration testing. The implementation and detailed design of e-learning courseware can also proceed concurrently.

There are 7 steps before the release step. These are planning, requirements analysis, basic design, test planning, implementation, detailed design, and testing. I note that these 7 steps in general need to be iterated at least a few times, to allow for changes and improvements to "earlier" steps as shortcomings in them are discovered while the "later" steps expand and flesh out the deliverables of the "earlier" steps. For example, during implementation, inadequacy in basic design may be discovered, forcing changes to the basic design, and possibly the test plan as well. During implementation, problems with the development schedule may be discovered, requiring changes in the product development plan or the requirements specification, which in turn may force changes in the basic design.

Further, all of the deliverables of the development steps before the deployment step need to be synchronized shortly before or shortly after the release step. In other words, all of the documents (the plan document, requirements specification, basic design specification, detailed design specification, test plan, user manuals and references) and product assets (source code and source code block comments, test suite, test script) produced must be made consistent among themselves. For example, all the features included in the requirements specification should be reflected in the design specification, source code, user manuals and references; while those features not in the design specification, source code, user manuals and references should not be in the requirements specification.

3 Lifecycle Process for Hybrid Learning Programs

Despite the similarity at the highest level between the lifecycle processes for commercial software and hybrid learning programs, the details of most of the steps the lifecycle processes are very different. In this section, I will describe in some detail each step of the lifecycle process for the creation and managing of hybrid learning programs. Although documents and/or program assets are generated in each step of the process, and they are to be reviewed before proceeding to the subsequent step, for expository convenience, I will discuss them in a separate subsection at the end of each phase.

3.1 Program and Courseware Planning Phase

The learning program manager, or someone he designates, leads the planning efforts. The leader forms a planning task force to plan a learning program, with some people assigned on a full-time basis and others on a part-time basis as needed. Whom he should bring into the task force depends on the nature of the learning program, the structure and business model of the organization that is to create and manage the learning program. In general, a program planner, some courseware designers and developers, some instructors, a technical support leader, a quality assurance leader, and a program assessor should be included.

The planning phase for hybrid learning programs needs to define the program, set objectives and strategy; stipulate the schedule, resources, budget, and finance; and program assessment. I will explain these below.

1. The definition of the program includes a description of what the target learners will learn (including a list of the major subjects that program will cover), duration of the program, purpose of the program (i.e., certification, academic credit, self-satisfaction), and the profile of the target learners. The profile of the learners includes the knowledge prerequisites for taking the program.
2. The objective of the program may be a combination of increased learning effectiveness for the learners; and any combination of revenue generation, cost savings, space (classroom) savings, reduced congestion on or near the campus, relief in parking space, etc. for the organizations that create and/or manage the program [1]. The strategy is the strategic means of achieving the objectives.
3. The schedule includes the dates for all key milestones in the planning, development, deployment, and assessing the learning program; and securing the resources and budget.
4. The resources include people, computers and equipment, software tools, etc. that will be available for creating, delivering, managing and supporting the courseware; administering, managing and assessing the learning program; and marketing and selling the programs. People resources include program planners, courseware designers and developers, instructors, tutors, teaching assistants, program administrators, system administrators, program assessors, marketing and sales people, etc.
5. The budget is to pay for all the resources, and other expenses.
6. Finance includes the means of providing the budget, and also revenue projection for the learning program.
7. The assessment is to assess how well the program's objectives will have been met, and should specify the means to be used.

Documentation and review
Before the planning phase concludes, a plan document needs to be written, which will serve as a guide for the development phase. The document should be reviewed by all members of the planning task force, and the key people who will be involved in the upstream development phase.

3.2 Upstream Development Phase

This phase includes 3 steps: requirements gathering & analysis, basic design, and test planning. The requirements gathering & analysis step defines, based on the plan document generated in the planning phase, "what to" develop, and what the constraints are. The basic design step defines "how to" develop, largely, the e-learning courseware, and, to some extent, the overall hybrid learning program. The test planning step specifies how the e-learning courseware, and the overall hybrid learning program, will be tested before deployment.

The learning program manager, or someone he designates, leads the requirements gathering & analysis and basic design efforts. The leader forms a requirements analysis and basic design task force, with some people assigned on a full-time basis and others on a part-time basis as needed. Whom he should bring into the task force depends on the nature of the learning program, the structure and business model of the organization that is to create and manage the learning program. In general, a learning program planner, some courseware designers and developers, some instructors, a technical support leader, a quality assurance leader, and a learning program assessor should be included.

The quality assurance leader, or someone the learning program manager designates, forms a test plan task force, with some people assigned on a full-time basis and others on a part-time basis as needed. In general, a learning program planner, some courseware designers and developers, some instructors, a technical support leader, and a learning program assessor should be included.

In the remainder of this section, I will discuss each of the 3 steps in some detail.

Requirements gathering & analysis step
This is the most important step, as it serves as the basis for all subsequent steps, especially the basic design and test planning steps. This step needs to bring out, and document, all the requirements associated with the contents of the courseware; and the development, deployment, and management of the learning program and the courseware. The first set of the requirements to analyze, above all else, is the plan document created in the learning program planning phase, particularly the definition, objectives and strategy of the program; resources, and schedule. The requirements fall into at least 8 categories. These include the learning program architecture, learning program contents, learnability, e-learning usability, e-learning look & feel, e-learning management system architecture quality attributes, e-learning tools and environment, and learning program assessment.

Learning program architecture
As a hybrid learning program is a mixture of traditional in-class learning and e-learning, the "contents" will be some sequences of the two types of learning, that is, the use of in-class learning for some topics, and the use of e-learning for other topics. This sequence, or the learning program architecture, needs to be specified.

Learning program contents
All major topics the learning program is to cover, along with the scope of coverage for each topic, the level of difficulty for each, and the duration for each major component of the program should be specified, guided by the definition of the program in the plan document.

Exercises and exams in general need to be included in a learning program and courseware. Exercises help the learner to absorb the concepts effectively, and exams give the learners an opportunity to focus on learning and to put various concepts together into a coherent bigger picture. There are various types of questions for the exercises and exams, including true-false questions, multiple choice questions, filling in blanks, subjective questions, individual projects, and team projects. Appropriate types of questions should be selected that will cover the full range of topics covered in courseware or learning program.

Learning program contents can often be augmented by such learning aids as the table of contents, summarization, (in the case of e-learning courseware) links to related Web pages, etc. A guideline for including such learning aids may be set forth as well.

Further, new learning program contents may be created by reusing parts of existing learning programs. Reusable parts of existing learning programs should be specified for each topic of the new learning program. Some of the contents may be reusable with no changes at all. Some of the contents may be reusable with some changes, while others may only be usable as base references.

Learnability

The biggest problem with many of the e-learning programs has been the result of the courseware developers' focusing on wrapping the contents with technology, and losing focus on helping learners learn [3]. There are at least 4 types of techniques that can be used to help learners learn. Some or all of these may specified as requirements for the courseware developers.

1. The courseware content developers must invest the time necessary to properly organize the contents, present concepts progressively from small and simple to large and complex, illustrate concepts with examples, summarize concepts with figures and tables, etc. – all the standard techniques people use (or should use) in technical writing and preparing lectures and seminars, etc.
2. Various learning-enhancement techniques, not based on the use of technologies, may be applied, including the use of interactivity to engage the learners [4], themes (relevant to the topics of learning) [5], problem-solving challenges found in online games [6], etc.
3. Technologies may be used to engage the learners and/or to convey concepts better. Relevant technologies include audio (voice, music, sound) [7], motion graphics, animation [8], 3-d images [9], podcasts [10], video [11], simulations [12], etc..
4. Additional relevant results from learning theory may be applied.

E-learning usability

The "usability" here refers only to the usability for the learners, not for the courseware developers or designers or the learning program support staff. The usability of a hybrid learning program refers only to the e-learning component. The e-learning component includes not only the courseware, but also the learning management system, if the learners are to use one. An e-learning Web site combines the courseware with a learning management system.

The "ease of use" of the learning management system is about how easy it is for the learners to operate it [13]. It includes a "non-technical" aspect such as clear and intuitive operating instructions for non-technical learners, mechanisms for accident prevention (e.g., unintended deletion of the answers to an exam), etc. A technical aspect includes facilities to register for a program, take exams and submit answers, check grades, navigate the contents forward and backward, keyword-based search for topics, scroll a Web page, post a note or annotation to courseware, communicate with the instructor or classmates, etc.

The usability of e-learning courseware has two aspects. One is accessibility, and another is "extensional" quality. Accessibility becomes problematic if the learner cannot access the courseware in his learning environment. There may be many reasons, including software and software version mismatch, the use of a firewall, capacity of memory and hard disk drive on a computer, Internet access speed, etc. [3] Extensional quality includes avoidance of undefined terms and acronyms, typographical errors, inconsistent presentation style and look & feel.

E-learning look & feel
The "look & feel" of a hybrid learning program refers to the e-learning component, that is, both the e-learning management system and the e-learning courseware. The look & feel, along with the usability, should also be a key criterion for selecting a learning management system.

The look & feel of e-learning courseware is concerned with the style, including the layout, background design; font style, font size; colors for the letters and drawings, background colors; the use of upper case and lower case letters; the positioning of visual aids and their captions; types and design of icons; etc. The courseware content developers must invest the time necessary to follow widely accepted industry practices, where innovation and differentiation are not needed, use them consistently throughout the courseware, and introduce some deviations, where innovation and differentiation will help. It would be best to provide a style template for courseware developers to use.

E-learning management system architecture quality attributes
The requirements specification for commercial software has a long list of architecture quality attributes. They include performance, scalability, reliability, modifiability, extensibility, portability, testability, security, availability, etc. All of these are applicable to the e-learning management system, including e-learning Web sites. However, only those whose consequences are visible to the learners need to be included in the requirements specification. The following architecture quality attributes, and the goals for each, should be included:

– Performance refers to the response time.
– Scalability refers to performance as the number of learners increases who concurrently access the courseware, and as the volume of course contents or the number of Web pages increases.
– Reliability refers to the ability of the learning management system to recover from system crashes to provide integrity of stored data. For example, the learners' registration data, exam answers, grades, etc. should never be lost or corrupted.
– Portability refers to the porting of the learning management system to different hardware and software operating environment, including different multimedia formats & media players, different plug in technology, etc.
– Security refers to the safeguarding of the learners' private data from unauthorized access or unintended deletions or changes.
– Availability refers to the e-learning courseware and the learning management system being available all the time or at least most of the time.

Other architecture quality attributes, such as modifiability and testability, are meaningful only to the developers of learning management system itself, and are not relevant to the requirements specification.

I further note that such architecture quality attributes as performance, scalability, reliability and availability are met by the facilities of the database systems used by the learning management systems, and, as such, they depend on a proper selection and administration of the database systems (often by the data centers that host the e-learning management system).

E-learning tools & environment
The tools & environment refers to the e-learning component of hybrid learning programs. The requirements for the following 3 types of tools and environment should be specified:

- for designing and developing e-learning courseware.
- for managing e-learning courseware and the learning program.
- for the learners to access the e-learning courseware and learning management system.

Learning program assessment
The assessment of a hybrid learning program is to quantitatively establish the extent to which the objectives of the program have been met. Key requirements related to assessment need to be specified, including a methodology to use, the scheduling of assessment, resources and budget.

- The methodology may test a focus group that did not take the learning program, and compare the results against those of tests given to the learners who took the learning program; or compare the results of tests given to the learners before they took the learning program and after. The choice of a methodology depends to a large extent on the nature of the learning program.
- The scheduling of the assessment includes when the assessment is done, and how many times it is done.
- The resources for the assessment include people resources to design and develop the assessment, the equipment and tools needed to conduct the assessment, and the facilities needed for the assessment.
- The budget for the assessment is the cost of paying for all the resources and other related expenses.

Basic design step
I note that for developing an e-learning Web site, rather than just e-learning course contents, the basic design needs to specify all key aspects of designing a Web site. It is beyond the scope of this paper. For developing e-learning course contents, the basic design necessary is fairly limited, as shown below. Only some of the elements specified or defined in the requirements gathering & analysis step need to be elaborated into guides for the courseware developers.

Learning program architecture
N/A

Learning program contents
Key subtopics of each of the major topics in the learning program architecture specified in the requirements specification should be listed and described. Guidelines for

the number and types exercises and exams should be provided for each subtopic. Further, if parts of an existing learning program contents are to be reused with changes, brief descriptions of the extent of the changes need to be provided.

Learnability
The use of technologies should be specified for each topic.

E-learning usability
N/A

E-learning look & feel
If a style template is not available, create one for use by the e-learning courseware developers.

E-learning management system architecture quality attributes
N/A

E-learning tools & environment
N/A

Learning program assessment
A basic outline of the assessment should be specified, including the types of questions to ask or tests to be given.

Test planning step
Here "test" refers to the quality assurance of the learning program and the e-learning course contents, not the examinations that the learners will take. Test planning includes people resources and budget, testing schedule, and testing tools and environment, similar to the assessment planning and the overall program planning.

Test planning also includes checking the quality of the learning program and the learning contents. The quality check is to be done by the courseware developers and quality assurance people, and cover the following aspects of the courseware and learning management system:

- Intensional quality: includes inadequate materials, superfluous materials, inadequate visual aids, superfluous visual aids, etc.
- Learnability of e-learning courseware: includes consistent use of a theme; proper use of game-like challenges, multimedia data, simulations; adequate exercises, exams; etc.
- Errors: includes typos, conceptual errors, incorrect answers to exercises and exam questions, etc.
- Content flow: the smoothness of transition between separate component of the courseware, and the extent of overlap among the components (A little overlap is good and even desirable sometimes, but much overlap is not).
- Extensional quality: includes undefined terms, undefined acronyms, etc.
- Usability of e-learning courseware: includes consideration of the learner's environment, intuitive operating instructions, error prevention, etc.
- Look & feel: includes the layout, font style, font size, colors, icons, etc.
- Style: includes overall consistency of presentation style and look & feel.

Commercial software vendors often make a beta release of their software to a limited number of customers ahead of a general release. This is to receive feedback on the quality and features of the software. A hybrid learning program and/or e-learning courseware may similarly be beta-tested before general release. The actual learners are often better judges of the quality, learnability and usability of learning programs and e-learning courseware than the courseware developers and the quality assurance staff. If beta testing is to be included, it should be included in the overall program development and release schedule, and the beta-testing learner group should be identified and specified in the test plan document.

Documentation and review
Before the upstream development phase concludes, a requirements specification, a basic design specification, and a test plan need to be written, which serve as guides for the downstream development phase. The documents should be reviewed by all members of the task force, and the key people who will be involved in the downstream development phase.

3.3 Downstream Development Phase

The downstream development phase basically includes the implementation step and testing step. As with commercial software, implementation and testing should proceed concurrently.

Detailed design & implementation step
In the case of e-learning courseware development, there is little distinction between detailed design and implementation, while the distinction is clear in the case of e-learning Web site development or e-learning management system. However, considerations of the development of an e-learning Web site or e-learning management system is beyond the scope of this paper.

The learning program manager needs to plan the courseware development efforts, and subsequently work with the courseware development leaders to ensure that the development efforts proceed on schedule.

Testing step
The testing of commercial software is best done by dividing the testing work between the developers and the quality assurance staff [2]. The developers test the software roughly in 3 granules: unit testing (of single functions), integration testing (of modules, or subsystem, of multiple functions), and full system testing. Further, they inspect their own code, and review other developers' code periodically. The quality assurance staff performs performance and stress testing on the full system, and the release staff performs acceptance testing of the full system.

The same testing discipline may be applied to the testing of e-learning courseware (and e-learning management system).

The testing granules for e-learning courseware would include a unit (a subsection), a module (a section), and full courseware. The e-learning courseware developers should perform quality assurance at each granule as the development efforts proceed. The quality assurance staff should put on the learners' "hat" and test the full courseware and full learning program.

The testing must cover every quality aspect of the courseware outlined in the test planning step.

Release step
After the e-learning courseware and the full learning program have been tested, either the learning program "release" staff, or the learning program manager, should approve the release of the program and e-learning courseware.

When commercial software is released, often the release staff write "release notes" that explain how to get around some serious defects that have not been fixed. If circumstances require the release of e-learning courseware or learning program with some defects that have not been fixed, the release staff, or their equivalent, should write release notes.

If the release is a beta release, the beta testing learners should be managed, and the results should be incorporated in the general release. In effect, a beta release may be viewed as a "real" release, and the learning program and courseware may be considered to have entered into the maintenance & upgrade phase for the "general" release.

Documentation and review
The deliverables of the downstream development phase include the full e-learning courseware and full learning program, a guide to the learning program (as an overview to the learners), release notes, and learners guide for operating the courseware or learning management system.

3.4 Deployment and Assessment Phase

Once the learning program and e-learning courseware have been released, feedback from the learners flows in through various channels, including comments on the e-learning Web site, emails, instructors, tutors, learning support staff, etc. The feedback includes compliments, justifiable misunderstanding on the part of the learners, suggestions for improving the learning program and courseware contents, complaints about usability and look & feel, etc. Some of the compliments from satisfied learners can be used as testimonials in promoting the learning program. Some of the feedback or trends seen in the feedback can serve as a part of the requirements for subsequent changes or upgrades to the learning program and courseware.

The feedback should be segmented and saved in separate databases, including a "feedback database," a "compliments database," a "defect database," and "requirements database." Such databases are valuable learning program assets.

3.5 Maintenance and Upgrade Phase

It is best to plan the maintenance and upgrade of a learning program and courseware. The plan includes the people resources and budget, and the management of a defect database and a requirements database. The resources are the people who will make the changes to the learning program and courseware, record learner feedback to the defect database and requirements database. The budget is to pay for the people, tools and equipment, and related expenses. The management of a defect database and a requirements database includes the selection of a database system and application for recording and managing defect reports and change requirements from the learners.

3.6 Termination Phase

Commercial software is terminated when it becomes better to terminate it than to continue support the customer base that uses it. Similarly, a learning program and courseware need to be terminated if it makes no business sense to further support the learner base that uses them. The termination decision can have financial and legal consequences, and the organizations that provides the program and courseware must weigh them carefully and plan to address such consequences before taking the termination action.

4 Concluding Remarks

I proposed a lifecycle process for planning, developing, and managing hybrid learning programs and courseware. The process was adapted from one developed for commercial software. Because the learning programs and courseware are in general far less complex than commercial software, the process is simpler. However, because of the nature of the learning programs and courseware, each of the steps within the lifecycle process involves very different issues to consider. The process may serve as a guide to help learning program managers and courseware developers take a holistic and disciplined approach to the creation and management of the learning programs and courseware.

Acknowledgments

This research was supported by the MKE (Ministry of Knowledge Economy), Korea, under the ITRC (Information Technology Research Center) support program supervised by the IITA (Institute of Information Technology Advancement) (IITA-2008-(C1090-0801-0046)).

References

1. Kim, W.: Towards a Definition and Methodology for Blended Learning. In: Proc. of the First International Workshop on Blended Learning, Edinburgh (August 2008)
2. Kim, W.: On Software Quality Assurance and Curbing Development Cost. Journal of Object Technology (July 2006)
3. Kim, W.: Directions for Web-Based Learning. In: Liu, W., Li, Q., Lau, R.W.H. (eds.) ICWL 2006. LNCS, vol. 4181, pp. 1–9. Springer, Heidelberg (2006)
4. Elsenheimer, J.: E-Learning 1.0 Terms of Engagement: Keeping Learners Online, http://www.learningcircuits.org/2003/feb2003/elearn.html
5. Vogel, D.: E-Learning 1.0 Themes Add Creative Spark to Online Classes, http://www.learningcircuits.org/2002/sep2002/elearn.html
6. Klaila, D.: Game-Based E-Learning Gets Real, http://www.learningcircuits.org/2001/jan2001/klaila.html
7. Millbower, L.: The Auditory Advantage, http://www.learningcircuits.org/NR/exeres/6AF8D013-30DC-4CBA-BA15-09DBFD9B0E68.htm
8. Toth, T.: Animation – Just Enough, Never Too Much, http://www.learningcircuits.org/2003/aug2003/toth.html

9. Kaplan-Leiserson, E.: Trend: 3D Training, http://www.learningcircuits.org/2005/nov2005/0511_trends.htm
10. Kaplan-Leiserson, E.: Trend: Podcasting in Academic and Corporate Learning, http://www.learningcircuits.org/2005/jun2005/0506_trends.htm
11. Mayberry, E.: New Territory: Adding Video to Online Learning Offerings, http://www.learningcircuits.org/2005/jul2005/mayberry.htm
12. Dobrovolny, J.: Effective – and Ineffective – Instructional Strategies, http://www.learningcircuits.org/2004/jan2004/dobrovolny.htm
13. Smulders, D.: E-Learning 1.0 Web Course Usability, http://www.learningcircuits.org/2001/aug2001/elearn.html

Just-in-Time Knowledge for Effective Hybrid Learning

Michel C. Desmarais

Computer and Software Engineering Department
Polytechnique Montréal
michel.desmarais@polymtl.ca

Abstract. The means for Hybrid learning take on many forms. In this paper, we look at learning facilitators that can be embedded within the user interface. We argue that these means of learning can be even more effective than formal training. We describe different features of the user interface that can provide just-in-time knowledge that fosters learning: immersing the student into a rich environment where he can readily have access to the information for the task at hand.

1 Introduction

The European Commission is devoting over 50M Euros annually in recent years to fund projects that are aimed at developing new means of learning, and new means of creating and managing digital content[1]. Few of the funded research, if any, aim to develop technologies intended for the classroom. Instead, the emphasis is on developing technologies to make the delivery of learning content more individualized, interactive, and embedded into our everyday environment.

2 Learning Occurs Naturally, but It Can Use Facilitators

Why would such means of learning have a great potential of being effective?

Looking at the learning phenomena in general, we know that most of what we learn occurs outside of a structured context such as a classroom. Any researcher in Artificial Intelligence can attest that most cognitive tasks that humans perform involve a phenomenal amount of knowledge that was acquired throughout life. Much of this knowledge has to do with problem solving skills and "common sense" inference, which is mostly acquired in a semistructured or non structured environment, through practice. This huge amount of knowledge is, needless to say, not found in textbooks.

Language is a good example of our ability to learn in an unstructured context. Learning a language starts with the imperative need to communicate, and with the environment in which that language is omnipresent. The combination of *need* plus *environment* is sufficient to incur the learning of a complex skill.

---

[1] http://cordis.europa.eu/fp7/ict/telearn-digicult/telearn_en.html (last consulted on 2008.05.12).

J. Fong, R. Kwan, and F.L. Wang (Eds.): ICHL 2008, LNCS 5169, pp. 31–39, 2008.

Now, this is not to say that we should do away with structured learning and that unstructured learning is the only and best way to learn a subject mater. The point is that when we get the co-occurrence of the *need to know* something, or the *need to perform* some task, and an environment that *provides the elements to learn and perform*, then learning will naturally occur. What makes unstructured learning so powerful, is that learners often have a constant need to know or to perform. It is up to us to provide them with the proper environment that can foster that learning. The constant availability of that environment and the prevalence of the need to know and perform can far outweigh the time and the attention the learner can devote to learning in a structured context, such as a classroom.

The question is, how can we best leverage over this type of learning in the context of hybrid learning? A key factor is the constant progression, in recent decades, of the computerization of our environment, and of our access to knowledge and information that has dramatically increased. That opens an opportunity to enrich our environment with the right features that can foster unstructured learning towards specific learning objectives, and complement the more traditional structured learning. Learning through our computerized environment is already well under way, and our purpose here is to reflect on the most the most exiting developments.

3 Environments That Support Learning

Let us take that idea of fostering autonomous learning and look at the kinds of means we deploy to enrich the learner's environment towards that goal. We focus on the transformation of standard user interfaces that were originally designed with the goal of providing functionality, **to interfaces that embed the goal of inducing the learning of complex task**.

We start with an example that we had the opportunity to work on, the THEO Electronic Performance Support System (EPSS).

3.1 The THEO Example

THEO is a system designed for the customer support centers at a large utility company with millions of clients. The original interface is displayed in Figure 1.

The tasks that the user can perform with THEO are quite diversified and sometimes non trivial, such as explaining how a fixed monthly payment is derived from year to year, or making a diagnostic of a sudden increase of electricity consumption in a household. As a consequence, the classroom training for a new employee required three weeks.

In order to reduce the training period, we integrated a number of additions to the original THEO interface that are meant to provide a kind of just-in-time training, often referred to as an Electronic Performance Support System (EPSS) [1]. These features are accessible from the original interface in Figure 1 and are not intended to replace it. Their intent is to allow learning through the user interface.

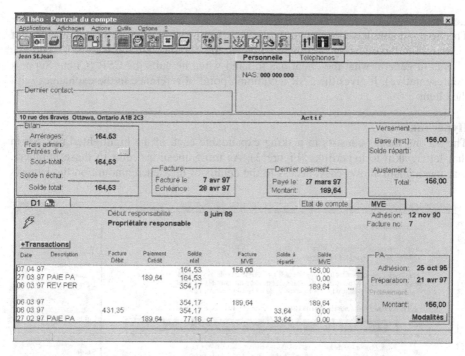

Fig. 1. Original THEO interface

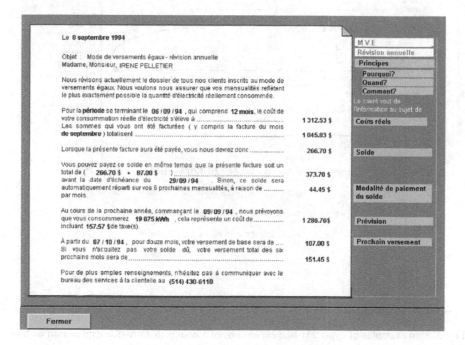

Fig. 2. Access to the letter sent to the client

Letter

The first and simplest mean of support consists in providing access to the most recent letter sent to the client by the company where the numbers are highlighted (Figure 2). This is in general what the client has in hand when he calls the CSR (Client Support Representative). It gives the CSR a common point of reference in the exchanges with the client.

Hyperlink

The second means consists in making expandable each of the highlighted number in that letter, akin to hyperlinks (Figure 3). As most questions refer to these numbers, that mechanism allows easy, access to the details of how each amount on the letter is

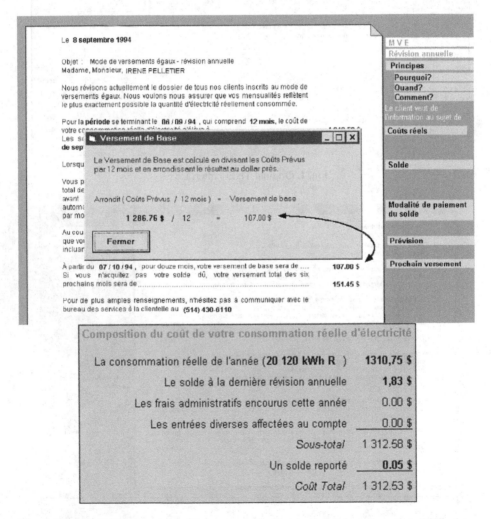

Fig. 3. Two examples of hypertext-like expansions of amounts that provide explanation on how they are derived

derived. The user clicks on a number and a window shows how this number is derived. The numbers in the explanation window can be further explored this way.

Diagnostic and documentation
Another feature of the interface is its ability to facilitate access to the relevant information by inferring the most likely causes of a CSR call. It allows direct access to the part of the system that is needed to answer the client's question. For example, Figure 4 shows the three most likely causes of a CSR call based on a statistical analysis of the client's profile. If the reason for the call is, say, the first item shown (a 26% increase of annual electricity consumption), the plausible causes are reminded to the CSR and can be discussed with the client. When applicable, all numbers shown are computed to reflect the actual impact in dollars for that particular client to make the information more relevant.

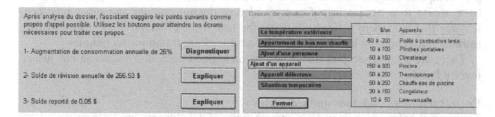

Fig. 4. Inference of the three most likely causes of a CSR call (left) and a corresponding explanation of cause 1 (right). Each tabbed text display in the explanation windows highlights, for that particular customer, the amount that corresponds to the different causes.

Evaluation Results
The impact of introducing the EPSS to the original THEO interface were investigated in an informal experiment (see [1] for details). The results of this experiment show that two out of three users with no training at all were able to perform the standard 15 out of 15 tasks relating to the topic chosen for the experiment (the equal payment plan that normally requires three weeks training). The other subject was able to perform 10 out of the 15 task. In comparison with the original interface without the EPSS, only one of the tasks was succeeded by a person without training. However, the trained CSR representatives were able to do almost all of them, as expected.

These results form a compelling argument for the effectiveness of the EPSS enhanced user interface. Considering that two out of three subjects were able to complete all of the 15 CSR tasks without training, it is quite reasonable to consider that the original three weeks training could be substantially reduced given the EPSS.

A qualitative questionnaire was also administered to investigate non performance related factors. Results from this questionnaire were very positive. All subjects, whether novices or experts, had positive comments on the EPSS. They all considered this tool to be useful, especially for novices. The number inspection technique was preferred over the hierarchical decomposition. It was unanimously considered "very useful" by all five of the subjects who filled out the questionnaire, whereas the hierarchical decomposition technique was considered by two subjects as "very useful" and by the three others as "rather useful".

The authors concluded from this investigation that an EPSS like THEO can substantially reduce the training period, and even improve the quality of the CSR service in general. The investigation clearly showed the power of rethinking the user interface to extend its purpose beyond the sole goal of providing the functionality, to the goal that encompasses the training and the learning of the most complex tasks to perform with the system.

3.2 Interactive Development Environment Examples

The power of embedding, within the user interface, means to help the user learn complex tasks has now been recognized within some communities. One of the most notable example is in the computer programming community where IDE (Interactive Development Environment) have evolved into highly sophisticated interfaces to support computer program development. These environments allow the programmer to have access to a large array of contextual tips, documentation, and other interface features that help them not only in doing the task more efficiently, but also to better learn the programming language and more advanced programming techniques.

There are many examples that could be mentioned here, and we name but just a few for brevity.

Project template skeletons and examples
The typical software project development types (GUI, library, etc.) are provided as template code that is complete with default structure and configuration, relieving the programmer from the initial effort of finding sample code to start from, and providing a useful example for the novice programmer.

Syntax
When typing, all syntactically incorrect lines are highlighted and, when possible, the correction is suggested.

Auto-completion
A powerful feature is the ability of the IDE to analyse the code and display a list of possible completions to the expressions as the user is typing them, such as the list of all methods that can be called upon a given object. Not only does this feature relieve the load on the user's memory, it also allows him to explore and learn the possibilities of the library.

Source code
All of Java's source code base is available by clicking over the corresponding function call in the user's program. Exploring the inner architecture of Java's source code helps the programmer understand the framework and learn advance programming tips and patterns.

The result of these features is twofold :

1. the user has fewer things to know, and thus fewer things to learn;
2. the learning occurs naturally as the user performs the tasks.

The case of *auto-completion* is a clear example of how this result can occur (Figure 5). It is taken from the NetBeans IDE[2]. The two popup windows of the NetBeans interface screendump show the auto-completion feature in action (refer to the two popup windows pointed to by the "completion and documentation" bubble text in Figure 5). The user is typing the name of the "System" class and the top window shows the applicable methods for that class, whereas the bottom window shows some details about the highlighted choice.

In this example, the cognitive load of remembering the name of the methods is reduced to a task of recognition and, in the case where the method is actually unknown, it provides immediate documentation to find and learn the method that should be used for the intended goal.

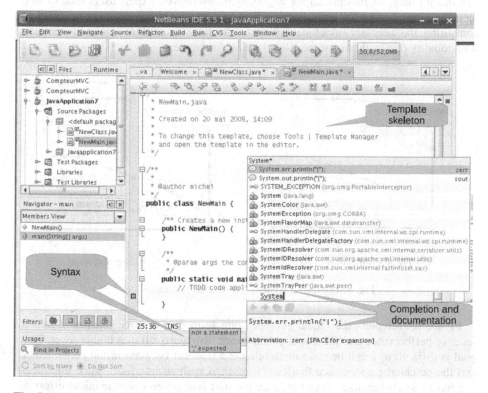

Fig. 5. Some features of the NetBeans IDE interface such as Auto-completion as when the user is typing the name of the class "System", syntax correction, and code template skeleton

All the other features mentioned above serve the same purposes of reducing the amount of learning, providing examples, highlighting errors at the very moment the user makes any and of providing highly precise and context sensitive documentation to learn to do a task.

---

[2] See http://www.netbeans.org/. The same could be said of most popular IDEs such as Microsoft's .NET, Borland's Turbo series, or IBM's Eclipse.

4 Interface Design, Learning, and Performance

The observations from the THEO and NetBeans interfaces bring us to a larger under-standing of the interactions between interface design, learning, and performance. These interactions are illustrated in Figure 6.

The learning curve of Figure 6(a) is typical of the evolution of performance. It fol-lows the well known Power law of practice [2]. As the user gets familiar with the tasks and the application, he develops strategies to perform better. The performance increases from an initially low level to an expert level and then levels off. However, this curve is not necessarily the best that can be achieved. Often, interface designers settle for a design that allows the user to perform at an acceptable level quickly, but that design may not be optimal for expert users. Moreover, expert users tend to stop their learning process too early because they lack the incentive to make the effort of consulting the necessary documentation, or the time to explore new and complex functionality that could him to new levels of performance.

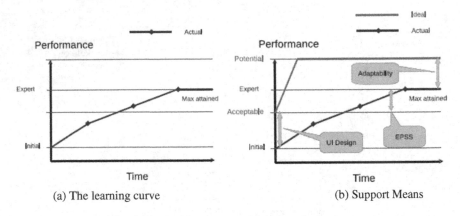

(a) The learning curve   (b) Support Means

Fig. 6. The learning curve and interface design issues

Figure 6(b) depicts the "Ideal" curve. Long term performance reaches a greater level of performance and the initial performance also starts off at a higher level. This goal is difficult to reach because there often is a tradeoff between initial performance and the potential performance that can be reached with an interface. Some interfaces can have a steep learning curve but, once the user has gotten over the initial effort of mastery, the performance can be much greater than with a simpler interface to start with. On the contrary, interfaces that are very easy to use for novice users often do not meet the needs of high performance for expert users.

Three means can be deployed to avoid this tradeoff between initial ease of use and the optimal performance for experts, and, thus, to transform the "actual" performance curve into the "ideal" one:

UI Design
The first one is the best known and consists in good User Interface (UI) design. Pro-ponents of the user-centred approach to developing interactive software know that a

good UI design can make a substantial difference in the user productivity. Studies have shown that a gain of 35% in productivity is what can be expected [3] by properly applying a user-centred approach to UI design. One of the key element of the design here is to support the diversity of users, namely experts as well as novices.

EPSS
The second means consists in using Electronic Performance Support Systems (EPSS). This is what is depicted in the THEO and NetBeans examples. As argued above, it enriches the user environment with embedded mechanisms to foster learning in a just-intime, context sensitive and on-demand fashion. The user can learn to gradually perform more complex tasks, more efficiently, in a naturally occurring manner that is akin to how most of our learning is acquired.

Adaptability
Finally, the third mean refers to the ability of an interface to adapt to its user. For the purpose of training and learning, one of the most important adaptation is the ability to adapt the interface help, documentation, and guidance to what the user knows and his level of skills for a given task. Another is the ability to infer what is the current user's goal. The auto-completion is such an adaptation feature. This feature is the most diffi-cult to implement and the advances in the field are slow, in spite of substantial re-search efforts in the field during the last two decades[3]. However, in the long term, it should yield significant returns.

5 Conclusion

Our daily environment is becoming more computerized than ever before. We argue that we need to think of the user interface of our computerized environment not only as a tool to perform tasks, but as a tool to help increase our skills and learn through that very interface. We have outlined different means of doing so and shown that they can prove very effective towards that goal.

At a time where the constructivist approach is paramount and where learning by doing is perceived as a key element for most programs in schools, the potential of reaping the benefits of enriching our computerized environments with learning facili-tators is great. The opportunity for teachers to leverage on such learner centered envi-ronments is something to consider.

References

1. Desmarais, M.C., et al.: Cost-justifying electronic performance support systems. Communi-cations of the ACM 40(7), 39–48 (1997)
2. Newell, A., Rosenbloom, P.S.: Mechanisms of skill acquisition and the law of practice. In: Anderson, J.R. (ed.) Cognitive Skills and their acquisition, pp. 1–55. Erlbaum Associates, Hillsdale N.J (1981)
3. Landauer, T.K.: The Trouble with Computers. MIT Press, Cambridge (1995)

---

[3] See, for example, the User Modeling and User Adaptive Interfaces Journal.

Critical Review of the Blended Learning Models Based on Maslow's and Vygotsky's Educational Theory

Esyin Chew[1], Norah Jones[1], and David Turner[2]

[1] Centre for Excellence in Learning and Teaching (CELT),
[2] Education Department at Faculty of Humanities and Social Science,
University of Glamorgan, United Kingdom, CF37 1DL.
{echew,njones2,dturner}@glam.ac.uk

Abstract. Blended learning involves the combination of two fields of concern: education and educational technology. To gain the scholarly recognition from educationists, it is necessary to revisit its models and educational theory underpinned. This paper respond to this issue by reviewing models related to blended learning based on two prominent educational theorists, Maslow's and Vygotsky's view. Four models were chosen due to their holistic ideas or vast citations related to blended learning: (1) E-Moderation Model emerging from Open University of UK; (2) Learning Ecology Model by Sun Microsoft System; (3) Blended Learning Continuum in University of Glamorgan; and (4) Inquiry-based Framework by Garrison and Vaughan. The discussion of each model concerning pedagogical impact to learning and teaching are made. Critical review of the models in accordance to Maslow or Vygotsky is argued. Such review is concluded with several key principles for the design and practice in blended learning.

Keywords: Hybrid Learning, Blended learning, Educational Theory, Educational Technology, Higher Education.

1 Introduction

"It is challenging to find a widely accepted definition of blended learning, and even more difficult to find a core set of literature on blended learning mythologies or framework." [18, p.137]

Of all instructional methods in the modern day, the term "blended learning" or "hybrid learning" is increasingly popular among UK higher educational institutions. Bonk and Graham [6] capture a vast amount of methods and applications of worldwide blended learning case studies in universities and commercial training and development units. Other researchers such as Littlejohn and Pegler [24], Allan [2], and Garrison and Vaughan [17] also provide comprehensive resources related to blended learning models in the context of higher education. The pervasiveness of blended learning has, however, increased the diversity and debates on its definitions and models. In higher education, there is neither standard nor simple framework to scaffold blended learning for all disciplines. The practices of blended learning are often

J. Fong, R. Kwan, and F.L. Wang (Eds.): ICHL 2008, LNCS 5169, pp. 40–53, 2008.

tailored by different needs and requirements of individual or organisation. There are too many ways and models of 'blends' depending on the blender and context. In a crude manner, blended learning involves the combination of two fields of concern: education and educational technology. To understand the richness of this term and its scholarly recognition from educationists, it is necessary to revisit its models and educational theory underpinned. This paper respond to this issue by reviewing models related to blended learning based on two educational theories.

2 Method and Overview of Chosen Educational Theory

This paper is neither empirical nor development project. It is an educational and critical review aimed to revisit current blended learning models from educationists' stand. First, the theories by Maslow and Vygotsky in educational context are explained. Four models were chosen due to their holistic ideas or vast citations related to blended learning: (1) E-Moderation Model emerging from Open University of UK [31, 32]; (2) Learning Ecology Model by Sun Microsoft System [42]; (3) Blended Learning Continuum in University of Glamorgan [21, 7]; and (4) Inquiry-based Framework by Garrison and Vaughan [17, 39]. The discussion of each model concerning pedagogical impact to learning and teaching are made. Critical review of the models in accordance to Maslow or Vygotsky is argued. Such review is concluded with several key principles for blended learning practitioners.

Two prominent educational theories, Maslow's theory and Vygotsky theory, were selected as grounding for the evaluation of blended learning models. Vygotsky considers socio-cultural factors in cognitive learning and education. For this reason, his idea is increasingly adopted as welcome guidance for classroom practice [23]. Vygotsky believes that learner's knowledge is developmentally constructed in a social or cultural interaction [11]. These interactions include those with educators, parents, classmates, family members and friends. They involve relationships with significant objects, such as books or toys, and culturally specific practices that learner engage in the school, at home, and in the community. This is called the Vygotsky's Cultural-Historical Theory [14], in particular to integrate historical and psychological processes into an untied theory of human consciousness [38]. In addition, this social and cultural construction of knowledge is mediated by words and language.

The Zone of Proximal Development (ZPD) is Vygotsky's terms for the range of tasks that are too difficult for learner to master alone but that can be mastered with guidance and assistance from educators or more-skilled peers [35]. Vygotsky views that learning could lead development if it occurs within the learner's ZPD. A simple but powerful principle lies behind ZPD: the quality of learner's thinking and performance is much better if he is aided with a more skilful and knowledgeable educator rather than he works independently [1]. For the skills and concepts that lie outside a learner's ZPD, even significant instructional efforts may fail to produce developmental gains. Vygotsky recognises that the kind of assistance needed to help learner develop new skills and concepts within their ZPD takes different forms for learner of different ages [14]. Vygotsky's view on the role of the educator is as a facilitator. The nature of this role is reflected in ZPD model. To facilitate the learning among learners, the educators utilise modelling and supporting techniques when they teach learners concept which are above their current skills and knowledge level in ZPD, motivating them to excel beyond their current level. The facilitating process from the educator is essential to encourage the learner to achieve higher level of ZPD. In summary, Vygotsky emphasises the social interactions, language and culture of their total learning environment, with the educators' and more-skilled peers' facilitation in learners' ZPD.

Abraham Maslow [26] is a famous contemporary theorist who put forward the hierarchy of needs. His model can be implied in educational context especially to understand the motivation of learning and teaching for learners [15, 22, 41] as well as educator [5, 10, 28, 29]. The educational implications of his ideas are summarised in the table below:

Table 1. Pedagogical Implication for Maslow's Hierarchy of Needs (Modified from [1])

Stage	Needs	Pedagogical Implication
Stage-1	Physiological well-being	Learners will lose attention and not be able to learn well if their physical conditions such as accessibility, hungry, insufficient sleep, illness and indistinct noises are not well attended. No physical obstacles that hinder the accessibility to the learning materials in this stage.
Stage-2	Safety	The learning environment must be safe and sound for all students from any background and at any age. For example the inclusive facilities for disabled learners or international students. Psychologically the learners feel safe to communicate with the peers and tutor in this stage.
Stage-3	Love and sense of belonging - Social	The individual learner needs to be cared and loved by the peers and educator. The educator shall create such learning community to provide the sense of belonging to the learners.
Stage-4	Self-esteem	The personal strength, qualities and uniqueness within the individual learner is developed and found in the learning process. Learners who are given tasks to play role in the learning environment can contribute to this perception.
Stage-5	Self-actualisation	The learner will develop the full potential as a human being to realise the purpose driven learning process and the cultural life.

3   Revisit Current Models

3.1   Salmon's e-Moderation and e-tivities

"The UK Open University (OU) was founded on the idea of blended learning long before the phrase came into common use." [34, p.387]

Gilly Salmon [30, 31] is perhaps one of the most popular researchers on blended learning or online education in the UK in the last decade. Her classic books on e-tivities and e-moderations have shifted the typical terms such as e-learning or online education to a new paradigm. A new term namely "e-moderator" was created to substitute online tutor or e-tutor. E-moderation model has widely adopted by the higher educational institutions across the world [33]. Salmon's e-moderation model was apparently built on Maslow's model for hierarchy of needs. To understand Salmons' model, it is necessary to revisit the profound concept developed by Maslow. In Maslow's context, McFadzean [25] defines the aim of education as to assist learners to achieve self-actualisation and thus fulfil their potential for personal growth. Through the social interaction, learners feel loved and sense of belonging to the learning group. Educators may contribute to the sense of belonging and self-esteem by ensuring the engagement of learners in the community which is socially and academically reinforced [27]. This idea is clearly presented in Salmon's model for e-moderation. In accordance with Maslow's model, her stage-like model consists of 5 phases as shown in Figure 1. At Stage 1, the warm induction, motivation and accessibility for all learners are the key agenda. E-moderators shall provide an interesting introduction to the use of the technological platform, and acknowledgement the feeling surrounding using technology and meeting new people through the online environment [30].

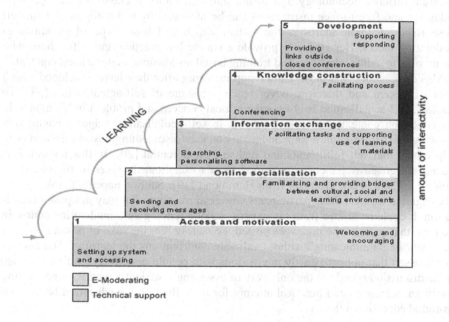

Fig. 1. E-moderation (Salmon, 2000, 2001)

Salmon [30] emphasise socialisation with peers and e-moderator are the essential activities in Stage 2. The learners are familiarising with each other and developing bridge between cultural and social barriers. Information will start to exchange in the following stages if the bridge are built. Rather than merely reading from the online materials, interactions with the materials and interactions with e-moderator and peers will be stimulated at individual own pace. In stage 3, the sense of belonging to this community may grow in parallel. By stage 4, learners start constructing the knowledge and facilitating each other. The personal strength and knowledge within the individual learner is developed and constructed along the way. Learners will take control for their own knowledge construction where as e-moderators merely facilitating the knowledge constructing and sustaining the groups' communication in a little noticeable manner. Ideally, the learners will successfully handling their own group dynamically as the learning proceeds. At the last stage, learners become responsible for their own learning and for their group. They also become critical and self-reflective. Ultimately, learners are confident in reflection, assessment and achieve self-actualisation in the whole e-moderation process.

Salmon [32] claims that this e-moderating model is a proven resource that provides a clear blueprint for education and e-learning. Hammond [19] also addresses the strength of e-moderating lies in its pragmatic and practical nature. One of the authors attended an e-moderating course in the year 2006. Based on such personal experience, these claims are rather valid. E-moderating is a simple but useful guide to scaffold the blended teaching and learning for the educator. In the past few years, there have been an increasing number of studies dealing with the blended issues such as (1) how to integrate different technology and media into conventional classroom and (2) how pedagogy and face-to-face instructions can be mediated by technologies. To support these issues, Salmon addresses the "what, which and how" type of questions e-moderating model. Her aim is to provide a simple but practical guide for those who are involve in online education and training based on Maslow's educational concept.

Maslow cautions that most learner stop maturing after they have developed a high level of esteem and therefore never reach the stage of self-actualisation [35]. To Maslow, self-actualisation is always the critical concern and problem in his model. In the education context, the learner who is in self-actualisation stage is cognitively knowing and exploring new knowledge, to connect to something beyond the ego or to help others find self-fulfilments and realise their potential [20]. In this respect, it is indeed the greatest challenge for e-moderator to facilitate learners to the last stage (stage 5). There is one criticism from Hammond [19]: Salmon appears to take generally negative view on those participants who read messages but may not post a contribution. It could be argued from my experience of attending an e-moderating course in the past, that some of the messages posted are merely "for the sake of posting" or "for the sake of communicating" without valuable contributions the learning. The authors would assert that not necessarily interactions with people or actively posting message in the discussion board are the only way of assessing a student. Overall, e-moderating is still an interesting and practical attempt for modelling online education based on a profound educational theory.

3.2 A Learning Ecology Model by Sun Microsoft System

According to Wenger and Ferguson [42], world-wide Sun Microsystem corporate adopted an ecology framework as a guide to their blended learning model. This model enables them to map the current possibilities as well as new possibilities of technology and learning design for IT training in global corporate. The major strength of this model is that it contains a broader and stable view of the totality and at the same time accommodates a constant changing set of components (refer to Figure 2). Wenger and Ferguson [42] suggest five important backgrounds to this learning ecology framework as (1) Quality of Learning experience; (2) Control over Learning Experience; (3) Formal versus informal learning; (4) Social nature of learning and (5) Cost effectiveness. These are essential values to construct the framework but the authors would like to argue that not all of them were embedded and applicable in the model, for instance, the measurement for the "quality" and the "cost effectiveness" of learning experience. This model presents a methods-rich framework for blended learning. They named the methods and opportunities as "learning elements" for learners to construct the knowledge and perform social interactions. Each learning element in Figure 2 demonstrates the learner-focus or educator-focus idea behind. With the above spiral type of learning modalities, the ecology framework is flexible enough to tailor the learners' and educators' needs.

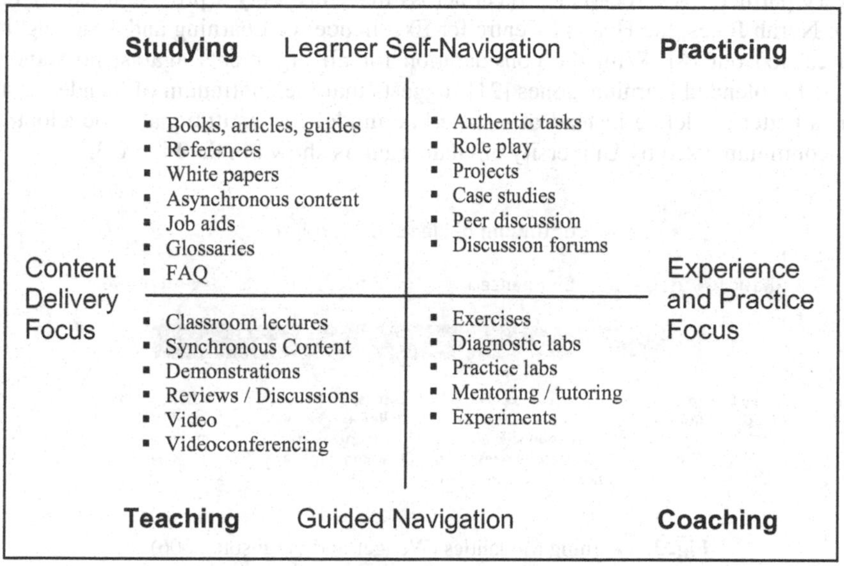

Studying Learner Self-Navigation	**Practicing**
• Books, articles, guides • References • White papers • Asynchronous content • Job aids • Glossaries • FAQ	• Authentic tasks • Role play • Projects • Case studies • Peer discussion • Discussion forums
• Classroom lectures • Synchronous Content • Demonstrations • Reviews / Discussions • Video • Videoconferencing	• Exercises • Diagnostic labs • Practice labs • Mentoring / tutoring • Experiments
Teaching Guided Navigation	**Coaching**

Content Delivery Focus — Experience and Practice Focus

Fig. 2. Learning Modalities (Wenger and Ferguson, 2006)

A research in Canada, Siemens [36] spectacularly indicates that learning is a dynamic, living and evolving state and learners always learn from evolving process more than static content. In this respect, it could be argue that learning modalities shown in Figure 2 provides less dynamic and evolving environment. There is no specific learning element which is undoubtedly distinguishable from the adjacent elements in another column. For instance, case studies can be learned by "studying" or "teaching" instead of "practicing" in certain circumstances; and exercises can be carried out in self-initiative manner without guided coaching. The line between studying and practicing, teaching and coaching is therefore ambiguous. There is no clear distinction between self-navigation versus guided navigation. The learning could be took place in an overlapping circumstances as described by Vygotsky in ZPD in which the learner constructs the knowledge (self-learning) in the aid of a senior facilitator (guided learning). On the other hand, the authors would argue that this model pays too little attention to the cognitive factors such as reflection and assessment along the learners' development. However, this Learning Ecology addresses the criticism raised by Stevens and Frazer [37] about the concept of "coaching" is the missing ingredient in blended learning strategy. Nevertheless, Vygotsky's ZPD is clearly revealed in "Coaching" element in Figure 2 as the Learning Ecology model emphasises coaching as one of the four elements.

3.3 Jones's Blended Learning Continuum

The University of Glamorgan (UoG) is one of a number of UK HEIs which has taken a whole institutional approach to the adoption of Blended Learning. It made a commitment in 2005 to the adoption of Blended Learning across the institution and its delivery partners. A three-year project across the University's provision led by Professor Norah Jones, the Head of Centre for Excellence for Learning and Teaching, has been carried out [8]. With the consideration for all arguments against no standard models for blended learning, Jones [21] suggests that the continuum of blended learning is a better guideline instead of a stage-like model for institutional wide adoption. Such continuum used by University of Glamorgan is shown in the Figure 3.

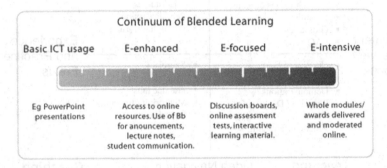

Fig. 3. Learning Modalities (Wenger and Ferguson, 2006)

Jones [21] identifies that PowerPoint presentations and basic web-facilitated learning resources through VLE are the indication for the category of "Basic ICT Usage" and "E-enhanced". The next point is "E-focused" where discussion boards, online assessment tests and interactive materials take place. More online facilities are used extensively and creatively here. E-intensive is the last category in the continuum, where whole teaching and learning is delivered online with face-to-face inductions. Similarly, this Jones's continuum tally with Garrison's and Vaughan's [17] view on the rejection for dualistic thinking of choosing between conventional face-to-face and online learning. A continuum provides more flexibility for practitioners to decide at which point the best option is, in order to suite the individual's epistemology and disciplines. At the same time, one may be able to conduct self evaluation and understand more options along the way. The available directions are well-defined for anyone who adopts this continuum. The "E-intensive" in this model, however, is not asserted as the best solution. It is a subject dependency and flexible model acting as a guideline to individual discipline and requirement via different mode of category. It provides an unambiguous method to the institution that is new to blended learning.

Jones's Continuum of Blended Learning is a simpler but more practical model than Learning Ecology Model (refer to section 3.2) in terms of practical adoption of the technology. It shows the progress and direction of blended learning for a higher educational institution where as this is not clearly expressed in other models. The Continuum of Blended Learning provides the educators an idea of what and how to embed blended learning in their teaching process. In this respect, this model provides an overall picture especially on the choices and indications that can be made in producing uncomplicated but effective blended learning experiences, from individual's module to the whole programme. Allen, Seaman and Garrett [3] conducted an extensive survey among the universities in the State. They provide a very similar indication to Jones's Continuum. Thus the authors attempt to relate both ideas as the Figure 4. To compare the Jones's continuum and Allen et al.'s classification, it could be summarised that "Basic ICT usage" is fall into the category of "Traditional"; "E-enhanced" is more likely to be the type of "Web Facilitated"; where as "E-focused" is labelled as "Blended/Hybrid" course; and "E-intensive" is apparently fall into the category of "Online" module. In practice, Allen et al.'s classification may be easier for one to identify the current stage from the exact percentage. It could be argued at that, however, this may again provoke disagreement from the educationalists as it is a typical stereotype. Cross [13] affirms that the classification by percentage is not useful blends as they are "oversimplified" (p.xviii). Jones's continuum on the other hand, provides more thinking space and flexible variation, which commonly required in the context of education. Overall, Allen et al.'s [3] idea does not stand comparison with Jones's continuum.

Proportion of Content Delivered Online	Type of Course	Typical Description	Jone's Continuum
0%	Traditional	Course with no online technology used — content is delivered in writing or orally.	Basic ICT usage
1 to 29%	Web Facilitated	Course which uses web-based technology to facilitate what is essentially a face-to-face course. Uses a course management system (CMS) or web pages to post the syllabus and assignments, for example.	E-enhanced
30 to 79%	Blended/Hybrid	Course that blends online and face-to-face delivery. Substantial proportion of the content is delivered online, typically uses online discussions, and typically has some face-to-face meetings.	E-focused
80+%	Online	A course where most or all of the content is delivered online. Typically have no face-to-face meetings.	E-intensive

Fig. 4. Indications for Blended Learning Continuum [3]

If there is one point of criticism for the continuum, it is that its emphasis on technology rather than pedagogy. Pedagogical considerations such as instructional activities and social interactions are not directly described in the continuum. Furthermore, it does not reveal the role of educators and learners as depicted in the Learning Modalities [42] and Salmon's models [30]. It is essential due to the focal point of education are people and followed by pedagogy, not technology. Hence, the authors assert that practitioners with pedagogical knowledge and practice, winged by technological tools, are the initial principles of blended learning model. The main challenge is perhaps to convince the academics that this continuum is not a new initiative but an attempt to improve professional development in a systematic manner. Ultimately it acts as an impetus for academics to move forward in view of the pedagogical issues and of their ICT competencies.

3.4 Garrison and Vaughan's Inquiry-Based Framework

In the context of blended learning, the authors perceive that Garrison and Vaughan are perhaps one of the most pioneer and prominent researchers, in terms of the understanding of the nature of both educational process and educational technology. Garrison and Vaughan [17] precisely assert that "reflection and discourse" (p.31) are the two inseparable elements at the heart of a meaningful educational experience. They promote blended learning design which recognise and maximise such educational experience through: (1) thoughtfully integrating online learning and face-to-face learning for better reflection and discourse; and (2) fundamentally revisiting and rethinking the learning and teaching to optimise students' engagement. Based on the immerse experience grounded in the field of education, Garrison et al. [16] developed the Framework for Community of Inquiry (CoI) as a guideline for online and face-to-face learning and teaching. As a result, Arbaugh [4] reports that Garrison et al.'s work [16] has shown considerable promise and becomes the most cited piece of research in the journal of *The Internet and Higher Education* to date. According to Garrison and Vaughan [17], CoI framework is rooted on Dewey's idea on constructivism. They understand Dewey in the sense that educational inquiry is neither to memorise nor seeking final answers but a practical process to investigate problems and issues. They believe the ideal educational process is the route for a collaborative constructivist who focuses on inquiry. The key of CoI is heavily relies in the process of inquiry. In such process, knowledge is shaped and constructed through social interaction and collaboration.

Figure 5 depicts the idea of educational experience from the process of inquiry. Cognitive presence consists of information exchange, connections of ideas and the creation and testing of the concepts. Teaching presence establishes the reasonably structure and process of the learning and teaching. It also provides the quality design and direction for educational experience. Garrison and Vaughan [17, p.15] thus argue that "education defined as a process of inquiry goes beyond accessing or even assimilating information. Inquiry joins process and outcomes (means-end) in a unified, iterative cycle. It links reflection and content by encouraging students to collaboratively explore and reasonably question the organization and meaning of subject matter." Social presence represents a group communication that facilitates the collaborative learning. A community of inquiry will be formed through its presence. The personal educational experience will be enhanced when all teaching, cognitive and social presences occur at the same time and facilitating each other. The categories and indicators for CoI are clearly presented in the Table 2 and from that table, one may think of many educational technologies that are able to facilitate these elements. Many blended learning researchers merely provide and analysis a list of technologies that can be adopted in learning and teaching. It could be asserted, however, that Vaughan and Garrison [39] have successfully shifted the focus of blended learning from "technology" to "learning", yet simultaneously trigger the exploration and interests on possible technologies or ways to enhance the educational experience. In addition to these issues, the framework of CoI is facilitated heavily by educational technologies and they can also be used in faculty level rather than at the individual level. Vaughan and Garrison [39] conclude from their findings that blended learning was successfully supporting a development community of inquiry in a faculty. Vaughan and Garrison [40] further highlight that a blended faculty community of inquiry provides the necessary structure to support and sustain the course redesign process. The blended faculty CoI will provide support and recognition for participants to revisit and reflect on their course design, pedagogy and the uses of educational technology. Presumably, blended learning in this sense may represent the integration of pedagogy and technology in a community-based inquiry development. This is a different dimension of view from Salmon [30] and Jones [21]. Both Salmon and Jones define the blended learning model in a structured and practical manner where as Garrison and Vaughan [17] illustrate blended learning in a more descriptive and wider way. According to a recent research, Arbaugh [4] reports on the empirical verification of the CoI framework and assert that this research needs to move beyond exploratory descriptive studies.

Fig. 5. Community of Inquiry Framework (Garrison and Vaughan, 2008)

Garrison's and Vaughan's model remarkably responds to Maslow's hierarchy needs and Vygotsky's Socio-Cultural theory. CoI create a socio-cultural educational environment for educators as well as learners. That setting inevitably leads to Maslow's perception from the stage of physiological well-being to self-esteem. Blended learning, in the eyes of Garrison and Vaughan [17] is not simply embedding educational technology into face-to-face instruction. Rather than suggesting "what and how" type of questions as Salmon [30, 31] did, they precisely introduce a holistic, reflective and self-sustainable Community of Inquiry Framework grounding on a strong educational theory. It acts as a conceptual tool that helps the academics and blended learning practitioners who wish to evaluate and position the value of blended learning. It also acts as a stimulation of positive and informed change through such reflections. If there is one point of criticism, it is that assessment - an important element of learning and teaching is not depicted in the framework.

Table 2. Community of Inquiry Categories & Indicators (Garrison and Vaughan, 2008)

Elements	*Categories*	*Indicators (examples only)*
Cognitive presence	▪ Trigger event ▪ Exploration ▪ Integration ▪ Resolution	▪ Having sense of puzzlement ▪ Exchanging information ▪ Connecting ideas ▪ Applying new ideas
Teaching presence	▪ Design and organizing ▪ Facilitation of discourse ▪ Direct instruction	▪ Setting curriculum and methods ▪ Sharing personal meaning ▪ Focusing discussion
Social Presence	▪ Open communication ▪ Group cohesion ▪ Affective/personal	▪ Enabling risk-free expression ▪ Encouraging collaboration ▪ Expressing emotions, camaraderie

4 Conclusion

In the context of blended learning, Croft [12] suggests that two challenges faced by educators and learners when technology-focus is in place: (1) we should have a distinct idea of the purpose(s) we wish to serve; (2) we must maintain the flexibility and imagination to adapt the tool to new uses as they arise. The blended learning models discussed above serve the later challenge but not the first challenge. In this sense, educational theory is always the foundation of educational purposes.

Again, all models are not argued as equally good. Some models are better than others and it is almost impossible in contrary, to design a perfect model as blended learning resides in the field of education or social science rather than in computer science. At this point, the authors would like to assert that, without strong educational philosophy priming the blend, all principles are rather instrumental, stereotypes and trivial [9]. Today, blended learning researchers seem to have an emphasis toward practices without a clear understanding of or underpinned educational theories. Technologist possibly seldom takes the time to develop educational technology that is informed by pedagogy and sound educational reasoning. If things go well, educators simply assume that it works; but ironically, they will blame as "the system is not right" or "this is useless and it is not what I want". It could be argues that the latter phenomenon is more likely to happen. Most often, this is caused by the disciplinary and epistemological differences for educationalists and technologists. The heart of blended learning lays on deep understanding for the trends of both educational theories and technology. Hence, the need to explore educational theory and its relationship with technology is essential.

Social interactions, language and culture of learners total learning environment, with the educators' and more-skilled peers' facilitation shall be regarded as one of the keys design principles of blended learning. Pedagogical implications based on Maslow's hierarchy of needs (stage 1-4 only) are recommended to be considered during the design and practice. Theories of education provide insight into important components of blended learning models, however it is a practical and empirical question whether blended learning can be structured yet having the same benefits with practitioners from different disciplines using the similar model and if so, how. This area is suggested for future research in blended learning. It is also suggested that blended learning researchers should investigate and develop principles or framework which recognising disciplinary differences and grounded on educational theory.

References

1. Alexander, P.A.: Psychology in Learning and Instruction. Pearson Prentice Hall, New Jersey (2006)
2. Allan, B.: Blended Learning Tools for Teaching and Training. Facet Publishing, London (2007)
3. Allen, I.E., Seaman, J., Garrett, R.: Blended. In: The Extent and Promise of Blended Education in the United States. Sloan-Consortium, Needham (2007)
4. Arbaugh, J.B.: An Empirical Verification of the Community of Inquiry Framework, Sloan Consortium. Journal of Asynchronous Learning Networks 11(1) (2007) (Retrieved January 20, 2008), http://www.sloan-c.org/publications/jaln/v11n1/v11n1_9arbaugh.asp
5. Blase, J., Blase, J.: Effective instructional leadership Teachers' perspectives on how principals promote teaching and learning in schools. Journal of Educational Administration 38(2), 130–141 (2000)
6. Bonk, C., Graham, C.R.: The Handbook of Blended Learning: Global Perspectives, Local Designs. Pfeiffer Publishing, San Francisco (2006)
7. Chew, E., Jones, N., Blackey, H.: Embedding Blended Learning Across a Higher Education Institution. In: Proceedings of the First Annual Blended Learning Conference: Blended Learning – Promoting Dialogue in Innovation and Practice, pp. 64–73. University of Hertfordshire Press, Hatfield (2006)
8. Chew, E., Jones, N., Law, A.: Education for Social Change: The Education of Entrepreneurship in Wales. In: FACE Annual Conference 2006, Swansea (2006)
9. Chew, E., Jones, N., Turner, D.: The Marriage of Rousseau and Blended Learning: An Investigation of 3 Higher Educational Institutions' Praxis. In: WISE Workshops 2007. LNCS, vol. 4832, pp. 641–652. Springer, Heidelberg (2008)
10. Conley, S.: Teacher role stress, higher order needs and work outcomes. Journal of Educational Administration 38(2), 179–201 (2000)
11. Cortazzi, M., Hall, B.: Vygotsky and learning. Education Libraries Journal 42(3), 17–21 (1999)
12. Croft, R.S.: What Is a Computer in the Classroom? A Deweyan Philosophy. Journal of Educational Technology Systems 22, 301 (1994)
13. Cross, J., Forewords, I.C.J., Bonk, C.R.: Handbook of blended learning: Global Perspectives, local designs. Pfeiffer Publishing, San Francisco (2006)
14. Deborah, J.L., Bodrova, E.: Lev Vygotsky: Playing to learn. Scholastic Early Childhood Today 15(4), 48 (2001)
15. Dickinson, M.: Giving undergraduates managerial experience. Education and Training 42(3), 159–169 (2000)

16. Garrison, D.R., Anderson, T., Archer, W.: in a Text-based Environment: Computer Conferencing in Higher Education. Elsevier: The Internet and Higher Education 2(2-3), 87–105 (2000)
17. Garrison, D., Vaughan, N.: Blended Learning in Higher Education: Framework, Principles and Guidelines. Jossey-Bass, San Francisco (2008)
18. Hanson, K.S., Clem, F.A.: To blend or Not to Blend. In: Bonk, C.J., Graham, C.R. (eds.) Handbook of blended learning: Global Perspectives, local designs, ch. 10. Pfeiffer Publishing, San Francisco (2006)
19. Hammond, M.: Book Reviews: G.Salmon E-moderating: The Key to Teaching and Learning Online (second ed.). Computers & Education 48, 329–333 (2007)
20. Huitt, W.: Maslow's hierarchy of needs. Educational Psychology Interactive. Valdosta State University, Valdosta, GA (2004); (Retrieved May 24, 2006), http://chiron.valdosta.edu/whuitt/col/regsys/maslow.html
21. Jones, N.: E-College Wales, A Case Study of Blended Learning. In: Bonk, C.J., Graham, C.R. (eds.) Handbook of blended learning: Global Perspectives, local designs, ch.13. Pfeiffer Publishing, San Francisco (2006)
22. Kabouridis, G., Link, D.: Quality Assessment of Continuing Education Short courses. Quality Assurance in Education 9(2), 103–109 (2001)
23. Lipman, M.: Natasha: Vygotskyian Dialogues. Teacher College Press, New York (1996)
24. Littlejohn, A., Pegler, C.: Preparing for Blended e-Learning: Understanding Blended and Online Learning (Connecting with E-learning), Routledge, London (2007)
25. Mcfadzean, E.: Supporting virtual learning groups. Part 1: a pedagogical Perspective Team Performance Management: An International Journal 7(3), 53–62 (2001)
26. Maslow, A.H.: A Theory of Human Motivation. Psychological Review 50, 370–396 (1943)
27. Nodding, N.: The Challenge to Care in Schools. Teachers College Press, New York (1992)
28. Rowley, J.: Motivation and Academic Staff in Higher Education. Quality Assurance in Education 4(3), 11–16 (1996)
29. Rowley, J.: Motivation of Staff in Library. Library Management 17(5), 31–35 (1996)
30. Salmon, G.: E-Moderating: The Key to Teaching and Learning Online. Kogan Page, London (2000)
31. Salmon, G.: E-tivities: The Key to Active Online Learning. Kogan Page, London (2002)
32. Salmon, G.: All Things in Moderation - Reviews (2004) (Retrieved December 20, 2007), http://www.atimod.com/e-tivities/reviews.shtml
33. Salmon, G.: All Things in Moderation - People (2004) (Retrieved January 19, 2008), http://www.atimod.com/e-moderating/people.shtml
34. Salmon, G., Lawless, N.: Management Education for the Twenty-First Century. In: Bonk, C.J., Graham, C.R. (eds.) Handbook of blended learning: Global Perspectives, local designs, ch.28. Pfeiffer Publishing, San Francisco (2006)
35. Santrock, J.W.: Educational Psychology. McGraw-Hill Higher Education, New York (2004)
36. Siemens, G.: Learning Ecology, Communities and Networks, extending the classroom, elearnspace (2003) (Retrieved June 10, 2006), http://www.elearnspace.org/Articles/learning_communities.htm
37. Stevens, G.H., Frazer, G.W.: Coaching: the Missing Ingredient in Blended Learning Strategy. Performance Improvement 44, 8–13 (2005)
38. Ussher, B., Gibbes, C.: Vygotsky, physical education and social interaction. Journal of Physical Education New Zealand 35(1), 76–87 (2002)

39. Vaughan, N.D., Garrison, D.R.: Creating Cognitive Presence in a Blended Faculty Development Community. Internet and Higher Education 8(1), 1–12 (2005)
40. Vaughan, N.D., Garrison, D.R.: How Blended Learning can Support a Faculty Development Community of Inquiry. Journal of Asynchronous Learning Networks 10(4), 139–152 (2006)
41. Watson, M.: Supporting pupils with Diabetes. Health Education 4, 148–153 (1998)
42. Wenger, M.S., Ferguson, C.: A Learning Ecology Model For Blended Learning from Sun Microsoftsystems. In: Bonk, C.J., Graham, C.R. (eds.) Handbook of blended learning: Global Perspectives, local designs, Pfeiffer Publishing, San Francisco (2006)

A Mixed Reality Teaching and Learning Environment

Victor Callaghan[1,*], Michael Gardner[1], Bernard Horan[2], John Scott[1], Liping Shen[3], and Minjuan Wang[4]

[1] University of Essex, UK
{vic,mgardner,jrscott}@essex.ac.uk
[2] Sun Microsystems Laboratories, UK
bernard.horan@sun.com
[3] Shanghai Jiao Tong University, China
lpshen@mail.sjtu.edu.cn
[4] San Diego State University, USA
mwang@mail.sdsu.edu

Abstract. This work in progress paper describes collaborative research, taking place on three continents, towards creating a 'mixed reality teaching & learning environment' (MiRTLE) that enables teachers and students participating in real-time mixed and online classes to interact with avatar representations of each other. The longer term hypothesis that will be investigated is that avatar representations of teachers and students will help create a sense of shared presence, engendering a sense of community and improving student engagement in online lessons. This paper explores the technology that will underpin such systems by presenting work on the use of a massively multi-user game server, based on Sun's Project Darkstar and Project Wonderland tools, to create a shared teaching environment, illustrating the process by describing the creation of a virtual classroom. We describe the Shanghai NEC eLearning system that will form the platform for the deployment of this work. As these systems will take on an increasingly global reach, we discuss how cross cultural issues will effect such systems. We conclude by outlining our future plans to test our hypothesis by deploying this technology on a live system with some 15,000 online users.

Keywords: Hybrid learning, online education, eLearning, mixed reality, learning technology, smart classrooms, cultural engagement.

1 Introduction

The world is witnessing radical changes as information technology alters how we communicate with each other and the machines that serve us. The arrival of the Internet and mobile phones has spearheaded these changes making possible the vision for "anyone, anytime, anyplace" communication, accelerating the pace of globalisation, as services become affordable international commodities.

Education is such a global service. Ron Perkinson, the Principal Education Specialist for the International Finance Corporation (part of the World Bank Group)estimated

---

* Alphabetical ordering.

J. Fong, R. Kwan, and F.L. Wang (Eds.): ICHL 2008, LNCS 5169, pp. 54–65, 2008.
© Springer-Verlag Berlin Heidelberg 2008

that the value of the global education market in 2005 was a little over US$2.5 trillion with the private higher education market being worth over $400 billion worldwide (about 17% of the overall education market). In 2005 the international student population worldwide was 115 million, growing at a rate of approximately 15% per annum, with about half of this increase being due to China [1]. Education is becoming increasingly important in modern knowledge-based economies [2] where learning is rapidly becoming a life long process.. The focus of this paper is to examine how emerging technology might address this challenge. To these ends we describe a state-of-the-art network education college in Shanghai that delivers real-time online education to almost 20,000 students. We discuss a parallel online phenomenon, the rise of massively multi-user game (MMUG) servers. We contend that network education and MMUG technology share a common computational framework and that the massive investment in games technology could be synergistically exploited to provide cost effective forms of educational service. This paper seeks to explore this hypothesis by investigating the use of MMUG technology in the form of Sun's Project Darkstar and Project Wonderland platforms, to create a shared teaching environment. We illustrate the process by describing the creation of a virtual classroom. In addition, the international dimension of such global education services poses significant culture-based challenges for developers, and providers—another issue we seek to explore.

1.1 Related Work

1.1.1 Online Learning Systems

The rapid evolution of information technology has led to new ways of learning and education. eLearning has been promoted by most education institutions and numerous corporations to facilitate better learning and teaching environments. Products such as WebCT (www.WebCT.com) and Blackboard (www.Blackboard.com) have been in use for the past few years. Many online colleges such as the UK Open University (www.open.ac.uk), the Hong Kong Open University (www.ouhk.edu.hk) and the Network Education College Shanghai Jiao Tong University (www.nec.sjtu.edu.cn), have developed and deployed their own eLearning platform and infrastructure to provide adaptive and efficient eLearning services. Today, eLearning becomes heavily learner-centred, emphasizing pervasive and personalized learning technologies [3]. As both the traditional classroom learning and web-based learning offer strengths and suffer from limitations, it is now a trend for eLearning systems to combine the strengths of the two into blended learning [4].

1.1.2 Online Games

The computer games industry is the primary user of virtual worlds which vary in complexity from a basic simulation such as a chess board, to a complex virtual environment the size of a country, continent, planet or universe.

The latest generations of computer games consoles have been designed for broadband internet connectivity, allowing traditional offline game genres (such as racing) to be updated so players can challenge opponents online from anywhere in the world. The success of online gaming has led to a new genre of online social communities (for example Second Life) where a user can log-in to the virtual world "seeing" and "interacting" with other users, without any of the mission-based objectives or tournaments found in traditional online computer games. Second Life (secondlife.com/) has expanded to the point where businesses have been established in the virtual environment, with real-world money being exchanged for products and services traded within the virtualised space. Traditional Universities are also beginning to offer services in online virtual worlds; for example, Harvard Law School, has set up a simulated court room in Second Life where students can practise their advocacy skills whereas Edinburgh University uses it to deliver an MSc course on elearning [5]. Currently (2008), over one hundred higher education institutions are listed on the Second Life site with many enthusiastically pursuing the vision for a globally networked virtual classroom environment (secondlifegrid.net/how/education_and_training). Another notable example is Sun Microsystems' MPK20; a virtual meeting environment for supporting Sun's business activities (research.sun.com/projects/mc/mpk20.html).

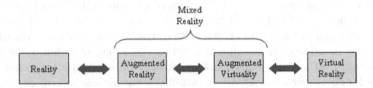

Fig. 1. Milgram's Reality-Virtuality Continuum

More advanced approaches are exploring the area connecting the real-world with a virtual environment. Collectively known as Mixed Reality, this term can be broken down further using the Reality-Virtuality Continuum [6] into: a) Augmented Reality, where the system consists of virtual components being added to a real-world environment [7]; and b) Augmented Virtuality, where real-world features are added to a virtual environment [8]. Such technological advances underpin our vision to bring innovative mixed-reality solutions to remote education environments.

1.1.3 Cultural Issues - Models in Designing Culturally Sensitive Instruction

Teaching is, by its very nature, a profoundly cultural act. Challenges associated with any cross-cultural interaction, such as the misunderstandings that arise from the assumptions we unknowingly make also influences teaching and learning [9]. As Pai & Adler have argued, culture and education are inextricably related; so much so, in fact, that, in a sense, they "define" each other. "The processes of teaching and learning are influenced by the core values, beliefs, and attitudes, as well as the predominant cognitive and communication styles and linguistic patterns, of a culture" [10].

With the increasing global outreach of online programs and courses, there is a great need to design and deliver online learning that can be engaging to a culturally diverse audience. Several models have been suggested that could assist those creating online instruction, each illuminating important considerations. Thomas, Mitchell, and Joseph [11] suggested adding a cultural dimension to the widely used ADDIE (Analyze, Design, Develop, Implement, and Evaluate) instructional design model. This cultural dimension would have three aspects: intention, interaction, and introspection. The intentional attribute of learning would encourage the designer to consider and make their cultural bias explicit. The interaction parameter would involve the collaboration of designer, subject matter expert, and end user throughout the model phases to facilitate the melding of culture into the end product. Finally, introspection on the part of designer ensures that he or she is considering his or her own thoughts, beliefs, attitudes, desires, and feelings toward the cultures represented in the instruction.

Edmundson [12] proposed the Cultural Adaptation Process model, which ideally helps to categorize course complexity and culturally adapt materials for particular learner groups based on the type of content, instructional methods, and media used. Henderson's [13] [14] "multiple cultures model" emphasizes the importance in sustainable learning outcomes of including elements from both the learner's own culture and those from the emerging global academic or training culture (from industry, government, or higher educational institutions).

Cultural factors are also a factor for the underlying technology. For instance, differing cultures and political groupings may react differently to the potentially invasive nature of the technology raising issues such as how privacy might be compromised by the sensing and monitoring aspects of these systems [15].

2 Sun's Project Darkstar and Project Wonderland

Sun's Project Darkstar is a computational infrastructure to support online gaming (www.projectdarkstar.com) [16]. Project Wonderland[1] is an open-source project offering a client server architecture and set of technologies to support the development of virtual and mixed reality environments. A noteworthy example of this is Sun's MPK20 application; a virtual building designed for online real-time meetings between geographically-distributed Sun employees.

In more detail, Project Wonderland is based on several technologies including Project Looking Glass to generate a scene, and jVoiceBridge[2] for adding spatially realistic immersive audio. The graphical content that creates the visible world as well as the screen buffers controlling the scene currently use Java3D. Additional objects/components to Wonderland (such as a camera device to record audio and video seen from a client), make use of other technologies such as the Java Media[3] Framework. Graphical content can be added to a Wonderland world by creating objects using a graphics package such as Blender or Maya. Project Wonderland provides a rich set of objects for creating environments, such as building structures (such as walls) and furniture (such as desks) as well as supporting shared software applications, such as word processors, web browsers and document presentation tools.

Thus, for example, a virtual whiteboard can be drawn on by one or several users, PDF documents and presentations can be viewed. A user is represented as an avatar augmented with the user's login name. A user can speak through their avatar to others users in the world via the voice-bridge and a microphone and speaker, or use a dedicated chat window for text-based messages. The scene generated by Wonderland can be viewed from first-person or several third-person perspectives.

---

[1] lg3d-wonderland.dev.java.net
[2] jvoicebridge.dev.java.net
[3] java.sun.com/products/java-media/jmf

Fig. 2. Sun's MPK20 Environment

3 The Shanghai e-Learning Platform

3.1 Overview

The Shanghai eLearning platform (Figure3) developed at the Online College of Shanghai Jiao Tong University delivers fully interactive lectures to PCs, laptops, PDAs, IPTV and mobile phones. The core of the platform includes a number of "smart classrooms" distributed around Shanghai, the Yangtze River delta, and even in remote western regions of China such as Tibet, Yan'an, Xing Jiang and Nin Xia.

The smart classrooms (Figure 4) are equipped with numerous smart devices/sensors and specially developed software. For example, the touch screen of the room displays presentations (such as PowerPoint), while also acting as a whiteboard for handwriting. The lecturer can write on materials projected on the screen using a laser E-Pen. To optimize the video quality, a pan-camera automatically follows the lecturer as he/she moves around in the classroom. RFID (Radio-frequency identification) tags are used to identify and track students. Another tracking camera is mounted in the front of the classroom and it captures students' attention status by recognizing the blink frequency of their eyes.

During the class session, lecturers can load their pre-prepared PowerPoint and Word documents and write on the whiteboard (even when they are away from the whiteboard). The students can also write individual notes to the lecturer's handwriting window. All these live lecture scenes can be recorded and archived for later access. Using this environment, the teacher can move freely, demonstrate his or her body language, and interact with learners as naturally and easily as in a traditional face-to-face classroom.

Currently, the Network Education College has about 17,000 Students; 99% of them are working professionals who attend the University part time. The large number of students in this College and its expansive course delivery systems make it a perfect place to test our mixed reality technology: MiRTLE.

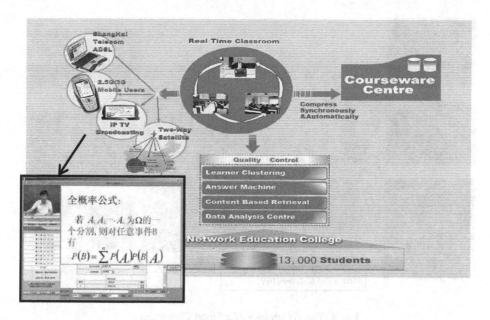

Fig. 3. The SJTU eLearning System Architecture (inset - Option 1 display)

3.2 The eLearning Platform in Use

Figure 3 illustrates the architecture of the SJTU eLearning system, which includes mobile phone broadcasting and a classroom management sub-system. Classrooms are connected to two servers (broadcasting and management) either through CERNET (China Education and Research Network) or cable network providers. Mobile phones can use the General Packet Radio Service (GPRS) network.

The teachers use the presentation station to teach in their usual ways. At the same time cameras and microphones capture the live scenes of the classroom. A recording system records all these media components: audio, video, handwriting, and any programs or documents shown on the computer. Students can view these live online, or they can download them for later viewing. If a student uses a mobile phone to connect to a class, the teacher periodically receives a screenshot of the student's mobile device so that the teacher can monitor the student's progress and the students can send SMS messages to the teacher. Students' messages are displayed on a screen that the teacher can view. Frequently asked questions are answered automatically by a computerized answer machine [17] and for more special cases teachers can provide oral explanations or reply via SMS text messages. In addition students can participate in polls and class activities initiated by the teacher. A computer analyses the poll results and immediately displays them to the teacher so that they may adjust or improve the lecture. To improved the efficiency of the system further, matching algorithms are employed to assemble student groups of similar attainment and ability [18].

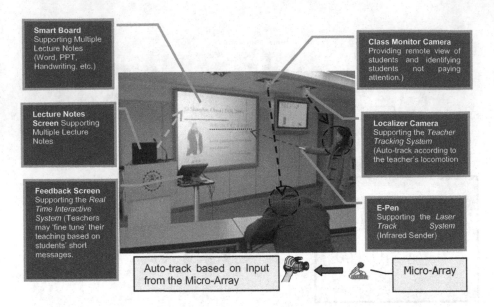

Fig. 4. The Technology of a Smart Classroom

When connecting to a live class, students have four options:

1) text, audio, and a small video of the real-time classroom,
2) video of the instructor only,
3) enlarged display of the course material shown at that time, and
4) a close-up display of the instructor's facial expressions and their body language.

We have found that 85% of the students prefer option (1): text, audio, and video (see Figure 3). Previous surveys with several samples of students in Shanghai NEC all reveal their preference to study alone, by listening to the archived recordings of live class sessions [19]. In theory, the text, audio, and video mode (option 1 above) can create a better context for learning as its closer to the feel of being in a real classroom with the teacher. Our current work on MiRTLE seeks to use mixed reality to reinforce this sense of a learning community further.

4 MiRTLE

The objective of the MiRTLE (Mixed Reality Teaching & Learning Environment) is to provide a mixed reality environment for a combination of local and remote students in a traditional instructive higher education setting. The environment will augment existing teaching practice with the ability to foster a sense of community amongst remote students, and between remote and co-located locations. The mixed reality environment links the physical and virtual worlds. 'Where students are distributed across geographically dispersed locations the hybrid learning environment allows an

Fig. 5. Lecturer view of remotely located students   **Fig. 6.** Student View of Lecture

increase in teaching productivity by enabling teachers to deliver only one lecture to all students rather than duplicate lectures which incur time and travel costs

Our longer term vision is to create an entire mixed-reality campus but in this paper we describe our first component in this process: a mixed-reality classroom. In the physical classroom the lecturer will be able to deliver the lecture in their normal way but they will have the addition of a large display screen mounted at the back of the room that shows avatars of the remote students who are logged into the virtual counterpart of the classroom (see figure 5). Thus the lecturer will be able to see and interact with a mix of students who are present in the real world or the virtual world whilst delivering the lecture. Audio communication between the lecturer and the remote students logged in to the virtual world is made possible via the voice bridge mentioned earlier. Two additional items of equipment located in the physical world are a camera placed on the rear wall of the room, and a microphone situated in the centre of the room—these combine to provide a live audio and video stream of the lecture to the virtual world.

From the remote students' perspective, they log into the MiRTLE virtual world and enter the classroom where the lecture is taking place (see figure 6). Here they see a live video of the lecture as well as any slides that are being presented, or an application that the lecturer is using. Spatial audio is employed to enhance their experience such that it is closer to the real world. They have the opportunity to ask questions just as they would in the physical world via audio communication. Additionally a messaging window is provided that allows written questions or discussion to take place.

A means by which a student can feedback their emotional state to the lecturer is also being investigated [20] [21] [22] together with the use of Sun's Small Programmable Object Technology[4] (SPOT) as a means of interfacing between physical and virtual worlds. The MiRTLE world has been developed using open source tools. Blender has been used to create the objects that populate the world. These objects are then exported to the X3D file format for use in the world. The platform employs a client-server architecture and to aid ease of use and to ensure that users receive the current version of the client Java Web Start Technology[5] has been employed. A short video showing an early Mirtle prototype is available on YouTube[6].

---

[4] www.sunspotworld.com
[5] java.sun.com/products/javawebstart
[6] http://www.youtube.com/watch?v=FYS6YzgPujc

5 Multicultural Aspects

With the increasing global outreach of online education, designing online learning that can be engaging to a global audience is critical to its success. Recent studies have found that students learn better when they are socially, cognitively, and emotively immersed in the learning process [23]. Social presence is about presenting oneself as a "real person" in a virtual learning environment. Cognitive presence is about sharing information and resources, and constructing new knowledge. Emotive presence is about learner's expression about their feelings of self, the community, the learning atmosphere, and the learning process. Learners' cultural attributes affects how they perceive an online learning setting and how they present themselves online, cognitively, socially, and emotively [24] [23] [24]. Therefore, it is essential that cross-cultural issues in online learning be more critically examined [10]. With the increasing global outreach of online programs and courses, there is a great need to design and deliver online learning that can be engaging to a culturally diverse audience.

For this paper, we are interested in learning how learners from different cultures present themselves online, either through learning interactions or avatars. Further, we will explore how culture affects student learning in educational online games. There is still a dearth of research in this area. In the new millennium, one of our main challenges is to learn to live with difference. [19] assert that "within the broader filed of education, online education may well have the greatest potential for enabling people to develop tolerance and learn to live with difference." Of course, the condition is that "this potential will only be realized if we as researchers and developers take issues related to culture more seriously." This assertion grounds a "call to action" and emphasizes the power that online learning environments can have to better prepare all of us for operating in a global environment.

6 Bringing It Together

In this paper we have described three areas of our research; *eLearning*, *mixed-reality* and *cultural diversity* in education. Whilst these areas are individually successful and productive, our plans are to bring these together. The way we have chosen to do this is to use the SJTU eLearning platform as the educational delivery platform. In particular, we are focusing on the SJTU smart-classroom which the MiRTLE simulation will be developed to model as closely as we can. Sun Microsystems are providing two Darkstar servers for the project, one of which will be located at the SJTU eLearning laboratory and will serve out MiRTLE. A server will offer a forward looking camera view of the smart-classroom (that is, from a student's position, towards the teacher), together with a number of simulated instances of the smart-classroom (each instance being a particular student's environment and view). The Darkstar server will be interfaced the existing smart classroom servers and processors, enabling Darkstar-based students to access the full range of educational media available in the smart-classroom. To access the system students will need to use the Internet (broadband or GPRS) to log into the Sun Darkstar server in Shanghai which will create an avatar representation of them (which they will have previously selected as part of customising their account). We are planning to use this customisation as one of the vehicles to explore the effects of cultural diversity by providing a rich set of operational modes which will reflect social preferences. For example, students will be able to create environments in which they are isolated or highly social avatars. Likewise the amount of personalised information available to other online students will be under their control, as will some of the options for interaction with lecturers and other students. Currently, we are still debating the ways we will integrate the three strands of our collaboration and this discussion is offered as by way of providing an insight to some of the issues that have arisen. Finally, although this is a long-term collaboration, in which the results will emerge over a period of years, we plan to deploy an initial experimental prototype during the summer of 2008 which we hope to report at ICHL08.

7 Conclusions and Further Work

In this paper we have described 'work in progress' aimed at augmenting online eLearning systems with mixed reality technology which we argue will counter the isolation of remote network-based learners, engendering a sense of community and social presence which Wang has shown can improve student engagement and the overall learning experience. At the heart of our vision is the hypothesis that a mixed reality version of the smart-classroom, with avatar representations of teachers and students, will help the social environment that Wang's work has shown can improving student engagement in online lessons.

Thus an important component of this work is the mixed reality environment and, to these ends, we have described how we are applying an online games server, based on the Sun's Project Darkstar and Project Wonderland tools, to create a shared virtual classroom which will be based at the Shanghai NEC. We have discussed that, not only does Wang's findings drive some of our objectives, but that the technology itself will form a vehicle to advance the cultural insights into the design of eLearning systems which are becoming increasing global in reach and nature. Looking further into the future, we recognise that other human qualities can play an important factor in learning performance and, as part of the social space, we are integrating some of our work on emotion monitoring and mediation, as part of this experimental framework. Thus, whilst we are aiming to use this work for shorter term deployment of mixed-reality technology on the Shanghai NEC system, we are also seeking to create a framework for much longer term research addressing more speculative and less understood aspects of remote education, such as the role of culture and emotion. We look forward to reporting on these as our research progresses.

Acknowledgements

We are grateful to Sun Microsystems for their financial support of the MiRTLE project. We are pleased to acknowledge the important role Kevin Roebuck of Sun Microsystems has played in enabling the MiRTLE project. We also wish to thank Professor Ruimin Shen, Dean Network Education College (NEC) and head of the E-Learning Lab Shanghai Jiao Tong University (SJTU), for giving us access to the SJTU E-Learning facilities and for his support throughout this work. We also wish to acknowledge Marc Davies whose work has contributed to the mixed reality review and

Chris Fowler whose insights on the psychology of education permeate the Mirtle model.

References

1. Perkinson, R.: International Higher Education. In: Plenary Address Going Global2 The UK's international education conference, Edinburgh, UK, December 6-8 (2006)
2. Clarke, G., Callaghan, V.: Ubiquitous Computing, Informatization, Urban Structures and Density. Built Environment Journal 33(2) (2007)
3. Thomas, S.: Pervasive Scale: A model of pervasive, ubiquitous, and ambient learning. IEEE Pervasive Computing 7(1), 85–88 (2008)
4. Kim, W.: Towards a Definition and Methodology for Blended Learning. In: International Workshop on Blended Learning 2007 (WBL 2007), August 15-17. University of Edinburgh, Scotland (2007)
5. Shepherd, J.: It's a world of possibilities. The Guardian (Tuesday May 8) (2007)
6. Milgram, P., Kishino, A.F.: Taxonomy of Mixed Reality Visual Displays. IEICE Transactions on Information and Systems E77-D(12), 1321–1329 (1994)
7. Hughes, C.E., Stapleton C.B., Hughes D.E., Smith E.M.: Mixed Reality in Education, Entertainment, and Training. IEEE Computer Graphics and Applications 25(6), 24–30 (2005)
8. Davies, M., Callaghan, V., Shen, L.: Modelling Pervasive Environments Using Bespoke & Commercial Game-Based Simulators. In: Li, K., et al. (eds.) LSMS 2007. LNCS (LNBI), vol. 4689, pp. 67–77. Springer, Heidelberg (2007)
9. Hall, E.: Beyond culture. Doubleday, New York (1976)
10. Rogers, P.C., Wang, M.J.: Cross-cultural issues in online learning. Encyclopedia of Distance and Online Learning (In press)
11. Thomas, M., Mitchell, M., Joseph, R.: The third dimension of ADDIE: A cultural embrace. TechTrends 46(2), 40–45 (2002)
12. Edmundson, A.: Globalized E-Learning Cultural Challenges. Information Resources Press, Arlington, VA (2007)
13. Henderson, L.: Instructional design of interactive multimedia: A cultural critique. Educational Technology Research & Development (ETR&D) 44(4), 85–104 (1996)
14. Henderson, L.: Theorizing a multiple cultures instructional design model for e-learning and e-teaching. In: Edmundson, A. (ed.) Globalizing e-learning cultural challenges, pp. 130–153. Information Science, Hershey (2007)
15. Callaghan, V., Clarke, G., Chin, J.: Some Socio-Technical Aspects Of Intelligent Buildings and Pervasive Computing Research. Intelligent Buildings International Journal 1(1) (2008)
16. Burns, B.: Darkstar: The Java Game Server. O'Reilly, Sebastopol (August 2007) ISBN 10: 0-596-51484-0 I ISBN 13:9780596514846
17. Shen, L.P., Shen, R.M.: Ontology-based intelligent learning content recommendation service. International Journal of Continuing Engineering Education and Life-Long Learning 15(3-6), 308–317 (2005)
18. Shen, R.M., Yang, F., Han, P.: A dynamic self-organizing e-Learner communities with improved multi-agent matchmaking algorithm. In: Australian Conference on Artificial Intelligence 2003, Perth, Australia. Springer, Berlin / Heidelberg (2003)
19. Wang, M.J.: Designing online courses that effectively engage learners from diverse cultural backgrounds. British Journal of Educational Technology 38(2), 294–311 (2007)

20. Shen, L., Leon, E., Callaghan, V., Shen, R.: Exploratory Research on an Affective eLearning Model. In: International Workshop on Blended Learning 2007 (WBL 2007). University of Edinburgh, Scotland (2007)
21. Kalkanis, X.: Towards end-user physiological profiling for video recommendation. In: The 4th IET International Conference on Intelligent Environments (IE 2008), University of Washington, Seattle, USA, July 21 - 22 (2008)
22. Shen, L., Callaghan, V.: Affective e-Learning in Residential and Pervasive Computing Environments. Journal of Information Systems Frontiers (special issue on Adoption and Use of Information & Communication Technologies (ICT) in the Residential/Household Context) 10(3) (october 2008)
23. Wang, M.J., Kang, J.: Cybergogy of engaged learning through information and communication technology: A framework for creating learner engagement. In: Hung, D., Khine, M. (eds.) Engaged learning with emerging technologies. Springer Publishing, New York (2006)
24. Wang, M.J.: Correlational analysis of student visibility and learning outcomes in an online setting. Journal of Asynchronous Learning Networks 8(4), 71–82 (2004) (Retrieved October 1, 2004), http://www.sloan-c.org/publications/jaln/v8n4/index.asp (also available in print)
25. Wang, C.-M., Reeves, T.C.: The Meaning of Culture in Online Education: Implications for teaching, learning, and design. In: Edmundson, A. (ed.) Globalizing e-learning cultural challenges, pp. 2–17. Information Science, Hershey (2007)

Towards a Design Theory of Blended Learning Curriculum

Ronghuai Huang[1], Ding Ma[1,2], and Haisen Zhang[1,3]

[1] Beijing Normal University, Beijing, 100875, China
huangrh@bnu.edu.cn
[2] Chinese People's Police Security University, Beijing, 100038, China
mading70@126.com
[3] University of International Business and Economics, Beijing, 100029, China
haisenzhang@uibe.edu.cn

Abstract. The purpose of this article is to develop a design theory of blended learning curriculum in ways of establishing a model for designing such a curriculum and a model for designing an activity in a blended learning curriculum as well as demonstrating how these models can be utilized in a curriculum design. It first attempts to define what the essence of blended learning is by drawing on definitions of previous studies. Then, it goes on to identify the characteristics and rationales of blended learning. Finally, it exemplifies the devised BLC activity model, which is supported by the BLC design model and the BLC process model.

Keywords: Blended Learning, Blended Learning Curriculum (BLC), BLC Design Model, BLC Activity Model, BLC Process Model.

1 Introduction

Blended learning is not a new concept [6, 13]. It originates from corporate training and development in the U.S.A. and is believed to have made its first appearance in the late 1990s [3]. Blended learning has become a buzzword and has grown increasingly in demand and popularity in both corporate and academic settings. It has been broadly researched across the globe in the educational circle over the past couples of years. However, the term of blended learning has been defined differently since its birth and its meaning has been changing with time [12]. Many define it as a combination of two pedagogical approaches [3, 5, 6, 16], in our view, with their focus merely on the superficial level while few have had it defined like Singh & Reed [14] do as "optimizing achievement of learning objectives by applying the [']right['] learning technologies to match the [']right[']personal learning style to transfer the [']right['] skills to the [']right['] person at the [']right['] time" (p. 2), which we believe goes beyond the superficial form and penetrates the essence of blended learning.

In blended learning design, "five key ingredients" are known to be involved in a blended learning process [2]. However, when we design a blended learning curriculum,

J. Fong, R. Kwan, and F.L. Wang (Eds.): ICHL 2008, LNCS 5169, pp. 66–78, 2008.
© Springer-Verlag Berlin Heidelberg 2008

we still have no clue to the way how such design can be produced. As blended learning has been practiced across various disciplines at various levels of educational institutions and in various part of the globe, little has been done in establishing a theoretical framework which is used to guide blended learning curriculum design and believed to be highly desirable to ensure effective blended learning. This paper attempts to make just such an endeavor, with the hope of laying a theoretical foundation for blended learning curriculum design.

2 Characteristics of Blended Learning

Blended learning takes many forms. In general, it has three characteristics. The first one is flexibility of providing learning resources. Blended learning is treated as an instructional strategy, which is developed in a networked environment. Such a strategy is usually supported by virtual learning environments (VLEs), which are a computer-based standardized learning system and are used to sustain content delivery of online learning as well as to promote online communication between an instructor and learners [7]. Studies [1, 8, 15] show that, with the medium of VLEs, the three most common uses in blended learning are providing course information, supplementing on-campus studies as well as accessing Internet resources. It can help diversify the provision of learning resources through BBS, E-mail, and other functions.

The second is support of learning diversity. As learners are diverse in terms of learning styles, learning proficiency, as well as learning ability, blended learning can come to the rescue by making it possible for individualized learning and self-regulated learning to happen. Teachers can use combined approaches to cater for the needs of the diverse student body and to create an opportunity to make everyone's learning an equally successful experience.

The third is enrichment of e-learning experience on campus. From the faculty's perspective, blended learning can enable them to improve their existing teaching practices. For example, we used to ask students to submit their weekly assignments by the paper, but now we ask them to submit their work by email and then we evaluate their performance by e-Portfolios. One more specific example, we used to teach students with the typically teacher-centered approach, but now individualized learning is no longer a rarely seen phenomenon. Learning systems also help teachers to reduce the burden of calculating the marks of the papers, for the systems can do the whole trick automatically. From the learners' perspective, learning has become rights of their own, which they can make own decisions on what they do each day and what they are going to achieve by certain deadlines for the same goal and how they are going to achieve them. Moreover, learning anytime and anywhere has become a reality. From the administrators' perspective, tons of paper work has been replaced by limited e-work. Educational administration brought about by blended learning has become as easy as mouse-clicking.

3   Rationales of Blended Learning

3.1   Theoretical Rationales of Blended Learning

Blended learning does not come out of nothing but has a solid theoretical foundation. In addition to the theoretical bases of constructivism and other learning theories, the first principles of instruction, which are advocated by Merrill [9], also give rise to blended learning. According to him, "[l]earning is promoted when learners are engaged in solving real-world problems[,] … when existing knowledge is activated as a foundation for new knowledge[,] … demonstrated to the learner[,] … applied by the learner[,] … [and] integrated into the learner's world" (pp. 44-45).

Briefly speaking, effective learning can happen when the learner is given the right task (problem-centered tasks) to accomplish by informing them of the right method (such as activation, demonstration, application, and integration) to use. As the goal of blended learning is to optimize learning outcomes and cost of program delivery, which is indicated by Singh & Reed [14], effective learning can be undoubtedly achieved because blended learning enables effective instruction to come into play as learners are not only presented with real-world problems to solve but also provided with how to solve the problems.

3.2   Educational Rationales of Blended Learning

Blended learning is intended to promote learning in the best manner possible. Before we find out the rationales for blended learning, let's first take a look at what learning is. Learning has two kinds [17]: One is regarded as "shallow learning," which is characterized with memorizing while the other, "deep learning," which is featured with "taking [new] knowledge, understanding it and checking that it fits in with one's existing knowledge, and incorporating it into one's present framework of knowledge" (p. XXII). The former simply involves "recall of information", which is a less effective way of learning. In contrast, the latter involves a process of "digestion" and is therefore referred to as problem-solving learning. Obviously, blended learning is encouraged for the promotion of "deep learning."

Furthermore, blended learning is embraced for promoting situated learning, which refers to learning in terms of activity and participation in a community of practice. As students observe their peers, reflect what they do, and practice apprenticeship, they develop habits, beliefs, identities, and skills that are shared by the community through interaction. Blended learning enables learners to learn in various ways possible, including problem-based and activity-based learning, such as those mentioned above.

4   Rationales of Blended Learning Design

There are three other fundamental reasons why blended learning design is created. First, large group teaching requires blended curriculum designs. For example, in China, as larger enrollments were allowed in colleges and universities by China's Ministry of Education, both class sizes and group sizes grew significantly. In order not to sacrifice instructional effectiveness and efficiency, as well as to ensure instructional quality, both higher education administrative staff and faculty had to face the challenging problem and to come up with something that was different from what they did in the past in terms of curriculum design.

Blended learning could be an effective means of enhancing learning by blending traditional classroom learning and online learning. Then, a blended curriculum design is desirable to respond to the situation, which may include designing tasks for dealing with difficult topics, creating extension activities for some learners of the entire learner population; providing additional feedback opportunities, helping students with practical work, encouraging dialog opportunities within small groups, and promoting interactivity in class [11].

Second, blended learning design is needed to engage learners outside of class. Traditionally, learner can only have access to direct teacher support during face-to-face class sessions. Because learners remain little contact with their instructors outside of class, they may find it hard to gain an easy access to faculty for support when they have problems with their academic work. This situation requires that a novel curriculum design be produced to support learners during periods of little faculty and learner contact. For example, Clarke, Lindsay, McKenna, & New [4] provided student support during the period of absence of learner faculty contact by creating sets of multiple choice questions to complement an introductory series of first-year undergraduate management lectures. All these blended course designs can effectively make learners' learning a pleasant experience when making them feel at "home" while away from "home." According to Sharpe [11], these curriculum designs may comprise the following: discussions which are used to guide study, between face-to-face sessions, discussion boards for sharing ideas about course topics of common interest, multiple choice questions to check progress in preparation for exams, and interactive tasks that students can deal with outside of class sessions.

Last, blended learning design is sought after for developing professional skills. Corporate adoption of blended learning design mainly derives from enhancing employees' professional skills and eventually their work efficiency. Likewise, institutions of higher learning are also following that path, namely, to develop professional skills of future professionals, which are needed in the current fiercely competitive job market.

Research [10] shows that the driving force of course redesigning stems from the requirements for use of IT as a competency in some disciplines while Sharpe, Benfield, & Francis (as cited in [12]) reveal that course redesigning is initiated by enhancing learners' skills which are required in the modern business world. Obviously, the latter case is also true in China. For a little while, most Chinese universities are making great efforts to distinguish themselves from their counterparts by gaining an edge over others. These endeavors are made not only by raising higher academic research standards for faculty but also by offering learner unique professional programs with cutting-edge curriculum designs through integrating technology into curriculum. Take a course of international trade practice in a Chinese university for instance. Originally, this course was designed for traditional face-to-face settings. Students were presented with some fundamental theories and practice. For giving students a better idea about how international trade was performed, and, more importantly, in order to enhance students' practical skills in international trade, the course was redesigned after an online platform for international trade practice and trade processes was brought forth in 2001. Students took the course in two separate locations: classroom and laboratory. The lab instruction engaged students in trade simulations covering wide range of issues, such as product promotion, quotation, offer, counter-offer, negotiation, signing contract, delivery, and so on, and so forth. Apparently, this new design is intended to familiarize learners with business knowledge and practical skills.

5 The Blended Learning Curriculum (BLC) Design

5.1 The BLC Models

Blended learning is now promoted in educational circles worldwide. It is ubiquitous in both corporate and academic settings. However, how to design such a curriculum still remains tricky because there are few models that can be applied to the guidance of such curriculum design.

The following model depicts the design procedures that can be followed when designing a blended learning curriculum (see Fig. 1). The ultimate goal of this model is for instructional implementation. The procedures are made up of three main components: (1) pre-analysis; (2) activity and resource design; and (3) instructional assessment.

Pre-analysis. In order to ascertain whether blended learning could be used, several observations and analyses need to be conducted. These analyses chiefly are composed of three factors: (1) analysis of learner characteristics, in terms of regular assessment of learners' prior knowledge, learning styles, learning preferences, etc.; (2) analysis of learning objects (knowledge taxonomy), in terms of defining what should be taught based on knowledge taxonomy; and (3) analysis of blended learning environments, in terms of finding out the environmental features. The purpose of this component is to identify learners' proficiency level and spell out learning tasks so as to lay a sound foundation for organization of learning activities. The result of this pre-analysis is represented by an analysis report, which is a brief summary of the starting point of instruction based on these analyses.

Design of Activities and Resources. This component consists of three subcomponents, that is, overall design of blended learning, unit (activity) design, as well as resources design and development. The overall design of blended learning predetermines the other two subcomponents in terms of the fact that it sets the tone for what can be done in the other two designs by laying out the general objectives and making appropriate arrangements for specific activities. The byproduct of this overall design is a detailed design report, which can be regarded as a roadmap for the other two designs. It is the basic document for blended learning and focuses teachers' instructional methods for organizing course events and activities and also the basic principles for curriculum assessment. The most important feature of the design that differs from the usual instructional design is that it focuses on which activities and resources fit in the learning context and which fit in the typical classroom instruction context.

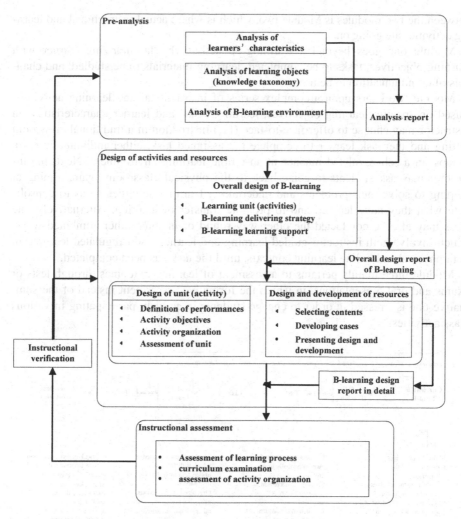

Fig. 1. The BLC design model

Instructional Assessment Design. The assessment design depends on the activity objectives, performance definition, and the general environment of blended learning. It mainly uses the assessment of the learning process (for example, using e-portfolios), the examination of curriculum knowledge (for example, online tests), and the organization of learning activities.

To clarify what is to be done in teaching a unit, which is, in essence, the overall design of blended learning encompassed in the middle component of the BLC design model, let's take a look at the BLC process model (See Fig. 2). This model is a detailed illustration of this subcomponent, which elaborates the processes where instructional activities are performed. The whole process can be broken down into three modules. Module one is curriculum lead-in and Module three is Review and Assessment. In between the two modules is Module two, which is where actual instructional and learning activities are going on.

Module one goes beyond a warming-up activity by familiarizing learner with learning objectives, tasks to be completed, learning materials to be studied, and channels of communication to be used.

Module two bears upon a complex series of instructional and learning activities. Based on specific learning objectives, learning tasks, and learner characteristics, an instructor may choose to offer face-to-face (f2f) instruction in a traditional classroom setting and then ask learner to complete the assigned task, either individually or in groups, in a self-regulated manner in an online learning environment. Next, the instructor may ask students to come back to the physical classroom again, aiming at helping to solve their problems and undertaking learning activities so as to consolidate what they have learned and to promote transfer of learning. Alternatively, the class may also be conducted the other way round or in some other combined ways, which involve both instructor-guided learning and learners' self-regulated learning in both physical and online learning contexts, until the task has been completed.

Module three mainly pertains to assessment of learning outcomes through tests or exams and oral presentations, in which the formative assessment instead of the summative one is stressed in order to engage students in actively participating in various class activities.

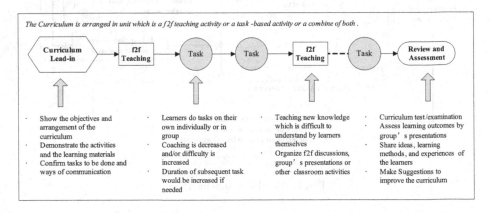

Fig. 2. The BLC process model

In order to better understand how the design of a unit (activity) works in the BLC design model, an activity-based blended learning model is set up for that purpose (See Fig. 3). Having been built upon the first principles of instruction and above-mentioned learning theories, this model demonstrates what methods we may use to design a problem-based and "learning-centered" blended learning activity. There are four main components in the whole procedure: (1) Lead-in; (2) Planning; (3) Acting; and (4) Reviewing.

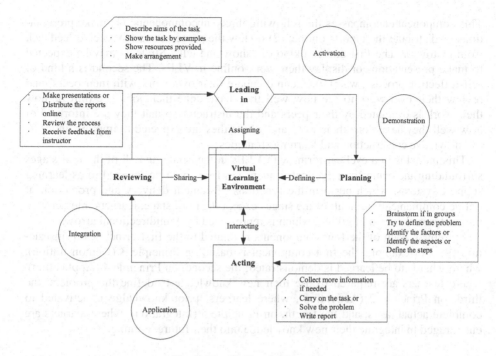

Fig. 3. The BLC activity model

Lead-in. It is the starting point of the activity. The main objective is to demonstrate the task to learners. In this component, there are four subcomponents, which are: (1) describe aims of the task; (2) show the task by examples; (3) show resources provided; and (4) make arrangements. The first one is intended for students to have an idea what they are expected to achieve after completion of the task. The second is meant to let students have a better understanding of the task. The third is set to provide students with resources that they can use to complete the task. The last is to make instructional arrangements, which are mainly referred to as the general planning for how this course will be carried on through the whole semester.

Planning. The objective of this component is to define the task by learners themselves through using their knowledge. There are three subcomponents, which are: (1) brainstorm if in groups; (2) define the problem; and (3) identify the factors or aspects or define the steps. If learners work in groups, they may be required to work out various issues related to the given problem and to define the steps that you can follow to deal with the problem.

Acting. The objective is to deal with an actual task or problem by completing task-related requirements. This component distinguishes itself from other components by interacting with VLEs. It has three subcomponents: (1) collect more information if needed; (2) carry on the task or solve the problem; and (3) write reports. Through interacting with VLEs, learners are able to acquire needed information and support from both their peers and their instructor.

Reviewing. The objective is to have newly constructed knowledge transferred to learners' future learning through sharing their work with their peers and the instructor.

This component encompasses the following three subcomponents: (1) make presentations or distribute the reports online; (2) review the process; and (3) receive feedback from instructor. The first one is a kind of "show and tell". Students may be expected to make presentations or display their work online in VLEs. The second is a kind of self-reflection process, where they can compare their own work with their peers' and review their own work to see how well they have done their job. The third is how their work is evaluated by their peers and the instructor so that they are informed of how well they have done their work and where they are expected to improve in terms of knowledge construction and learning strategies.

This model is in a cyclical form, with VLEs in the center and all of the four stages surrounding the center in a cyclical sequence. VLEs could be referred to as learning support systems, which perform the functions of content delivery and promotion of online communication. In all of the stages except the third stage, learners interact with the center in the form of giving, which is represented by a unidirectional arrow.

Moreover, each of the four components is related to the first principles of instruction [9]. For example, the first component is based on Principle 3 (Demonstration), where what is to be learned is demonstrated; the second, on Principle 4 (Application), where learners are required to use their new knowledge to define the problem; the third, on Principle 2 (Activation), where learners' prior knowledge is activated to complete actual tasks; and the fourth, on Principle 5 (Integration), where learners are encouraged to integrate their new knowledge into their future learning.

5.2 Case Study

To shed light on how the BLC activity model works, we could use as an example a hands-on design of the "Career Development Planning" activity in an introductory course titled "An Introduction to Educational Technology." This course has been offered to freshmen of the educational technology major in every first semester since 1985, which is intended to open the window for the learners to have a general idea about what educational technology is all about, to arouse their interest, and to enhance their motivation to probe more into this field so that they can improve their learning strategies and abilities in their future exploration of the field of educational technology throughout the rest of the academic years.

In the course of their study, the learners work as a group and, based on their group's interest, choose one of the five career orientations in the field of educational technology, namely, instructional design and curriculum development; information technology education; distance education; educational software development as well as educational media development. After the completion of this introductory course, they are expected to know what they might need to learn for a particular career in their four-year undergraduate studies of educational technology. At the end of the semester, the groups are required to bring their completed written reports to the classroom and to give an oral presentation. Over the past two decades, this course has been developed into one of the key courses in the field of educational technology in China and it has also been rewarded as an excellent course in the educational quality initiative launched by China's Ministry of Education. The curricular activity design presented here is chosen for the course instruction in the first semester of the 2006-2007 academic year. The design has been proven to be effective and it still provides

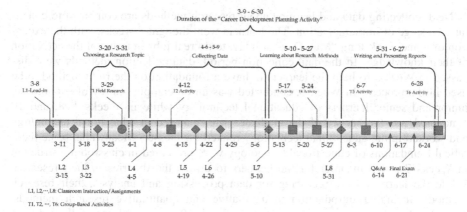

Fig. 4. A course schedule for the "An Introduction to Educational Technology" course

guidance for instructors to teach this course. A brief description of the course schedule goes as follows (Fig. 4):

In Fig. 4, the timeline indicates weeks of the whole semester. Bigger square symbols represent activities while smaller square symbols refer to face-to-face instructions, with the only circle symbol on the timeline signifying field research, which is a field study of the applications of educational technology at a Chinese distance learning company in Beijing. From this figure, we could see that the activity lasted almost throughout the whole semester, which was composed of 17 weeks from March 8 to June 28, 2007.

The activity design followed the four design stages of lead-in, planning, acting, and reviewing. The lead-in was instruction-intensive, which was intended for the learners to know about the goal of this course and basic information about future career paths and prospects in the field of educational technology. The activity as a group assignment was also made available to the learners so that they could know where they would be going right from the start. Supplementary learning resources and communication support channels were demonstrated so that they could be better informed of where to find support from.

Then, planning would be the next stage of the activity design. Planning, which was known as planning of the activity by the learners themselves, mainly involved choosing a research topic through the application of their prior knowledge and of what they learned in the classroom. In order for the learners to choose a topic appropriately, classroom instruction was brought into the classroom in Weeks 2 and 3, which covered an introduction to the brief history of educational technology development and the disciplinary system of educational technology. With a fundamental understanding of what educational technology was, the learners were made to have a field trip to a Chinese distance learning services business in Week 4, which was intended to give the learners an opportunity of experiencing what was covered in the lectures was actually referred to in the real world. In the meantime, this field research could also give rise to a better understanding of their career orientations and ultimately help them to have a better idea about their own research topics.

Next, collecting data and learning about research methods are combined to constitute the stage of implementation. The learners went thought 8 weeks, with the exception of a one-week-long "May Day" holiday, to do real jobs in terms of the activation of their knowledge. In the data collection period, data collection methods were discussed in Week 5 to help the learners to have a foundation on the right method to be used in the process. In Week 6, conducted was an on-campus survey of sophomore, junior and senior learners of educational technology while in Weeks 7, 8, and 10 conducted was the survey of the graduates who majored in educational technology and worked in the educational technology-related businesses. Meanwhile, basic theoretical foundations of educational technology were presented in classroom instruction in Weeks 7 and 8 in order for the learners to utilize the theories in their research. While the learners were preparing for data processing and analysis, their research methods, including introduction to qualitative and quantitative research methods, were developed in classroom instruction in Week 10. This week was followed by a one-week research method seminar in Week 11 and a one-week group presentation on research methods that the learners could adopt in their research in Week 12.

Starting from Week 13, the learners came to the stage of presenting their "products", which was the last stage of the activity design. This stage was manifested by integrating what they learned throughout the semester into the problem-solving reports of their group's career development planning. Report writing was taught in a lecture form in Week 13 and learners started to discuss the outline of their reports and research methods with which the available data could be presented in Week 14. In Week 15, a Q&A session was held to help solve the learners' problems in the process of report writing. Finally, the learners made oral presentations on their findings coupled with the instructor's comments and their peer's critical review of each individual group's completed project. Then, each group gave a response to how their reports needed to be improved.

To summarize, this curriculum design starts with a curriculum lead-in, which is mainly intended to familiarize learners with the goal of this course and tasks to be completed. Then, it moves on to a blended approach which is aimed at helping learners to achieve effective learning in the best way possible. Finally, the design winds up with revision and assessment. For the BLC activity design, the four stages of activity lead-in, planning, acting, and reviewing are inseparable from the backbones of the first principles of instruction as advocated by Merrill [9].

6   Conclusions

The BLC Design Model is developed on the basis of the first principles of instruction and constructivism as well as a renewed view of behaviorism. It is intended to provide instructors with a conceptual framework and practical design guidance before blended learning is implemented. When BLC is designed, the following two aspects in activity design may deserve full attention:

The first is concerned about the sequential features of activity design. In curriculum lead-in, instructors should make it clear about learning objectives and overall instructional arrangements. Also, learning activities and resources should be demonstrated with examples so that learners could have the right target to shoot. Moreover, tasks should be clearly identified and modes of interaction should be put in place right from the start. In classroom instruction, the emphasis should be laid on the learning content that is hard to comprehend for an individual learner's self-regulated learning. Face-to-face discussions and group-based presentations could be effective inside-of-class activities. In non-instructional activities, instructors' guidance should be gradually decreased while the difficulty level of given tasks could be increased little by little. In the process of evaluation, course exams could be a form of evaluation. However, having learners' share their learning experiences through presentations and critical reviews might be also a good form of evaluation.

The second involves how a BLC activity can be better designed to help learners perform an activity effectively. In general, the following four steps are crucial: activity lead-in, in which the goal of an activity is presented, a specific task to be completed is exemplified, and the supplementary learning resources that are accessible to learners are demonstrated; planning, in which possible ways to accomplish the task are brainstormed, the research problem is defined, and concrete steps to resolve the problem are identified; implementation of the plan, in which the task is completed by collecting required data and working on the task collaboratively, as well as reviewing and sharing, in which research findings are presented and shared among fellow learners and the instructor with critical comments from the both.

Blended learning is transforming education in every corner of the world. Its unique characteristics go beyond those of any of its counterparts. With the changing of educators' traditional concepts and deepening of their theoretical explorations in blended learning curriculum design and practical applications of the theoretical findings, it will benefit not merely the learners in one region but all the learners on the entire globe.

References

1. Bricheno, P., Higgison, C., Weedon, E.: The Impact of Networked Learning on Education Institutions. UHI Millenium Institute & Bradford University—INLEI, Bradford (2004), http://www.sfeuprojects.org.uk/inlei/
2. Carman, J.M.: Blended Learning Design: Five Key Ingredients (2005), http://www.agilantlearning.com/pdf/Blended%20Learning%20Design.pdf
3. Clark, D.R.: Blended Learning (2007), http://www.nwlink.com/~Donclark/hrd/elearning/blended.html
4. Clarke, S., Lindsay, K., McKenna, C., New, S.: INQUIRE: a case study in evaluating the potential of online MCQ tests in a discursive subject. ALT-J, Research in Learning Technology 12(3), 249–260 (2004)
5. Garrison, D.R., Kanuka, H.: Blended learning: Uncovering Its Transformative Potential in Higher Education. Internet and Higher Education 7, 95–105 (2004)
6. He, K.K.: The New Developments in the Theory of Educational Technology from the Perspective of Blended Learning (I). E-Education Research 2004(3), 1–6 (2004)
7. Huang, R.H., Zhou, Y.L., Wang, Y.: Blended Learning: Theory into Practice. Higher Education Press, Beijing (2006)

8. JISC: Study of Environments to Support E-learning in UK Further and Higher Education: A Supporting Study for the Joint Information Systems Committee. Joint Information Systems Committee (JISC): Bristol (2005),
   http://www.jisc.ac.uk/uploaded_documents/
   e-learning_survey_2005.pdf
9. Merrill, M.D.: First Principles of Instruction. ETR & D 50(3), 43–59 (2002)
10. Molesworth, M.: Collaboration, Reflection and Selective Neglect: Campus-Based Marketing Students' Experiences of Using a Virtual Learning Environment. Innovations in Education and Teaching International 41(1), 79–92 (2004)
11. Sharpe, R. (n.d.).: Why blend? Rationales for blended e-learning in undergraduate education. The Higher Education Academy,
   http://www.heacademy.ac.uk/assets/York/documents/ourwork/
   research/literature_reviews/blended_elearning_why_blend.pdf
12. Sharpe, R., Benfield, G., Roberts, G., Francis, R.: The Undergraduate Experience of Blended E-Learning: A Review of UK Literature and Practice. The Higher Education Academy (2006), http://www.heacademy.ac.uk/assets/York/documents/ourwork/
   research/literature_reviews/blended_elearningfull_review.pdf
13. Shaw, S., Igneri, N.: Effectively implementing a blended learning approach: maximizing advantages and eliminating disadvantages (2006),
   http://adlcommunity.net/file.php/11/Documents/
   Eedo_Knowledgeware_whitepaper_Blended_Learning_AMA.pdf
14. Singh, H., Reed, C.: A White Paper: Achieving Success with Blended Learning. Centra Software (2001),
   http://www.centra.com/download/whitepapers/
   blendedlearning.pdf
15. Ward, G.: Flexible delivery: A report on an evaluation of the use of the virtual learning environment in higher education across Scotland. The Quality Assurance Agency for Higher Education (2006),
   http://www.enhancementthemes.ac.uk/documents/
   flexibleDelivery/Flexible_delivery_QAA_128.pdf
16. Whitelock, D., Jelfs, A.: Editorial. Journal of Educational Media 28(2–3), 99–100 (2003)
17. Wood, E.J.: Review: Problem-based learning. Acta Biochimica Polonica Quarterly 51(2), XXI–XXVI (2004), http://www.actabp.pl/pdf/2_2004/XXI.pdf

Transnational Education Programs: Student Reflections on a Fully-Online Versus a Hybrid Model

Iwona Miliszewska

Victoria University, School of Computer Science and Mathematics, P.O. Box 14428,
Melbourne Vic 8001, Australia
Iwona.Miliszewska@vu.edu.au

Abstract. With rapid expansion of the transnational education market, more and more universities join the ranks of transnational education providers, or expand their transnational education offerings. Many of those providers regard online provision of their programs as an economic alternative to face-to-face teaching. Do the transnational students support this view? This paper discusses student responses to the fully-online provision of education programs in several important transnational markets: Hong Kong, Malaysia, Singapore, and Vietnam. The paper reports on a study of the perceptions of transnational students in those locales of the importance of the hybrid learning environment with an emphasis on face-to-face interaction in their courses, and discusses the importance of cultural sensitivities on those perceptions. The paper concludes by considering the future of the hybrid education model in the transnational context.

Keywords: Face-to-face interaction, online learning, transnational education.

1 Introduction

In recent years a particular stream of distance education called 'transnational education' has become widespread [1,2,3]. While there may be many definitions of transnational education, the one used in this paper describes that type of education, often referred to as offshore education, *in which the learners are located in a country different from the one where the awarding institution is based* [4].

It is estimated that the demand for transnational higher education in Asian countries (excluding China) will reach nearly 500,000 students by 2020 [5]. This presents both a challenge and an opportunity for those universities, and in particular Australian universities, who are key transnational providers in the region. The Australian Department of Education, Science and Training estimates that, already *approximately one in every four international students in the Australian education and training system is enrolled offshore* [6] (p. 7).

Competition for students in the transnational education arena is intense. For Australia, one of the main providers of transnational education in South East Asia [1,3], satisfying the needs of highest demand disciplines in the region – computing and business – is of vital importance. With the growing number of transnational education offerings, students will be able to choose more widely and will increasingly demand

J. Fong, R. Kwan, and F.L. Wang (Eds.): ICHL 2008, LNCS 5169, pp. 79–90, 2008.

high quality programs. According to [7], this power of consumer choice will drive universities to acknowledge and respond to student needs; it will also force universities to increasingly consider the effectiveness of their educational offerings in terms of their value to students. As [8] concluded:

If universities are to attain a 'goodness of fit' between the needs of their offshore students and the resources of the university, student expectations about quality need to be taken into consideration. [8] (p. 236)

One aspect of this *goodness of fit* that needs to be considered is the delivery mechanism of transnational programs. While advances in technology, and the Internet in particular, have created new ways of delivering education, and fully-online provision of transnational programs has been viewed by many providers as an economic alternative to face-to-face teaching [9], others believe that fully-online learning cannot be regarded as a suitable alternative in transnational settings [10]. The tension between traditional classroom learning and e-learning underpins this discussion. The high cost of the delivery of transnational programs has tended to skew the discussion in terms of the benefits of fully-online learning, but most of this debate has proceeded without the input of the students themselves. What is the transnational students' view on the matter? What kind of delivery mechanism do they want and/or prefer? The views of South Asian students are of vital importance to Australian providers, as this region is the main and fastest growing market for Australian transnational education. This paper discusses the issue of fully-online provision of transnational programs, and reports on the results of a study that sought the views of such programs from current transnational students in Hong Kong, Malaysia, Singapore and Vietnam.

2 Online Delivery: Constraints and Concerns

Fully-online provision of transnational programs raises many concerns regarding the learning experience, particularly about the extent of feedback and guidance that can be provided to students [11]. [12] agrees that fully-online provision of offshore programs is generally perceived to be less effective than options including a face-to-face component and emphasises the strong recognition of the value of (Australian) academics meeting and interacting with the offshore students population; such regular teaching input by these academics significantly enriches the transnational program [12,13].

Another aspect of transnational education that online delivery might find difficult to support is localisation of teaching. As [14] pointed out, the curriculum of a transnational program is usually standardised across several campuses, which may be located in different countries. While the curriculum is sometimes tailored to local conditions, the modifications are usually minimal; they may only involve assignment questions for example. In such circumstances, teachers, through face-to-face interaction, can play an important role contextualising and interpreting the content of study materials: *the relationship between students and face-to-face teachers is crucial in making foreign materials relevant to students* [14] (p. 33).

Technology, too, may be yet another constraining factor. Although some advanced technologies, such as streaming media technologies, are very capable of supporting voice and video and afford the possibility to emulate face-to-face interaction, they are out of reach for many transnational learners. For example, videoconferencing for learning over the Internet requires more bandwidth that is usually available to a regular Internet subscriber [16]. It should also be noted that even universal access to computers by offshore students, for example in China, is not a safe assumption and for many Chinese learners their offline education could be supplemented, but not replaced, by ever-advancing online technologies [17]. In China, the limited equipment and infrastructure for transnational online education in many institutions is only one factor that reduces its viability; one other important factor is *the strict legislation of central government regarding online education services provided by foreign countries* [18] (p. 203).

The availability of technology is not the only prohibitive factor; there are also aspects of curriculum and teaching that are difficult to emulate through technology. For instance, *demonstration of theoretical knowledge in Internet classes is below that of traditional classes* [19] (p. 16). Having measured online students' ability to apply programming theory, [19] concluded that the Internet did not lend itself to the deployment of subjects that involved problem solving and higher analytical reasoning, such as advanced computing subjects – the online students in their study performed significantly worse than their counterparts in a traditional classroom. They identified several factors that determined poorer performance of online learners in their study including: inadequate instructional methods, technology differences, and differences in group interaction. With respect to instructional methods, they pointed out that *instruction in the online environment is still in its infancy and faculty, as instructors and course designers, have not yet developed the most effective methods for delivering some type of content in this context* [19] (p. 17). They went on to say that application of theory in particular, might be effectively illustrated in the classroom through the choice of suitable examples or through answers to students' questions; technology could not easily emulate this kind of interaction. Moreover, *simple repetition can be effective in a classroom, but it is difficult to implement online* [19] (p. 17). The authors also suggested that group interaction in a classroom setting could be an important contributor to the learning process. However, this kind of interaction is difficult to emulate in the online environment even through thoughtful use of online forums, chat sessions, and email; *the cohesiveness and satisfaction of class discovery is not duplicated online* [19] (p. 17).

3 Importance of Face-to-Face Communication

Related to the importance of direct group interaction is the community aspect of face-to-face contact [20]. [20] found that dialogue not only allows students to assess their learning, but also to develop a sense of community with other students; this sense of community can alleviate the problem of isolation often reported by distance students. [21] agree and state that *students need dialogue with their teachers and with other students in order to consolidate and check on their own learning* (p. 278). Moreover, they list the inability to offer dialogue in the way that conventional face-to-face education does as one of three most significant weaknesses of distance education; the inflexibility of content and study method, and the isolation and individualisation of the student are cited as the remaining two weaknesses.

[22] reported on a two-year study by Thomson Learning. Launched in 1999, the study compared the results of three sets of adult learners: the first – the *blended* group – were taught to use Microsoft Excel with a mix of online and face-to-face instruction; the second group took an online course; the third group – the control group – received no training. The study report concluded that the blended group performed tasks 30% more accurately than the online-only group. The blended group and online group both performed better than the control group with no training in accuracy, by 159% and 99% respectively. In addition, the blended group performed tasks 41% faster than the online group.

A recent meta-study aimed at identifying factors that affect the effectiveness of distance education has led to some important data-driven conclusions including the importance of face-to-face communication, live human instructors, and the right mixture of human involvement and technology [23]; the study suggested that programs combining face-to-face component and technology mediated distance component resulted in the most positive outcomes.

4 The Hybrid Model

Given the importance of face-to-face interaction, successful distance learning programs are increasingly moving towards a new model known as *hybrid* or *blended* learning. The hybrid model adds a human touch to distance learning by using facilitators or mentors and promoting various types of interactions between students, instructors, and resource centers [16,23,24,25]; its goal is to *enhance student learning by offering students a combination of face-to-face instruction and distance learning* [26]. The hybrid model combines various instructional strategies (teacher-facilitated, self-study, practicum, lab), delivery modes (online, face-to-face, print-based), paces (self-paced, group-paced), times (synchronous, asynchronous) and learning objects (print material, video, lab kits, animation, audio, simulation, case study). The various combinations of face-to-face instruction and distance learning are flexible in that they can involve the different components to different degrees: it need not be for example 50% face-to-face and 50% online. Table 1 depicts some of the possible combinations:

Some of the successful distance education programs which blend the traditional distance learning model with face-to-face teaching sessions include the programs at Purdue University West Lafayette, Indiana University, and Penn State University[16]. [24] supports the hybrid approach maintaining that media alone cannot offer students guidance and personal engagement.

Table 1. Hybrid model – possible combinations of face-to-face instruction and distance learning (derived from [26])

Instructional strategy	Lab	Teacher-facilitated	Practicum	Self-study
Delivery mode	Online	Face-to-face	Face-to-face	Online
Pace	Self-paced	Group-paced	Group-paced	Self-paced
Time	Asynchronous	Synchronous	Synchronous	Asynchronous
Learning object	Simulation	Video	Video	Audio

[15] pointed out the importance of face-to-face interaction in transnational programs, as well as the decreasing interest in such programs if they are provided fully online. Recent Australian statistics confirm the declining interest in fully online transnational programs in South East Asia: in 2004 the number of distance online students declined by 15% on semester two, 2003, while there was a 1% growth in on-campus students [27]. Having examined various modes of transnational program delivery in Australia and elsewhere, [15] suggested that the future of transnational programs belongs to programs that include face-to-face interaction facilitated largely by an offshore partner of the educational provider; he used the term *joint delivery* to describe such programs, whereas they would now be referred to as *hybrid* programs.

Evidence internationally shows that fully on-line delivery is proving unpopular except in small niche programmes, due to the lack of face-to-face contact, an unwillingness on the part of students to pay high fees and significant start-up costs. Branch campuses are faced with problems of scale and expose the provider to considerable financial risk through capital investment offshore. Perhaps the best approach, both in terms of mode of delivery and financial risk, is seen to be "joint delivery" with local, established partners, using on-line delivery in some form (for enrolment and general information for example). [15]

5 Perspective of Transnational Students

To evaluate transnational students' attitude towards fully-online provision of the programs, a study was conducted among students in eight transnational computing programs offered in Hong Kong, Malaysia, Singapore and Vietnam by Australian universities. The study was conducted in 2007; four-hundred- and-sixty-nine students participated. Table 2 presents a breakdown of student numbers across providing universities, locales and programs; it also includes information about the mode of study (part-time, full-time) and the mode of teaching (both Australian and local staff, or local staff only).

Table 2. Number of students participating in the study

	Hong Kong	Malaysia	Singapore	Vietnam
University1	Program1 (131) p/t, both	Program2 (44) f/t, both		
University2		Program3 (69) f/t, local	Program4 (46) p/t, local	Program5 (33) f/t, local
University3	Program6 (44) p/t, both	Program7 (32) f/t, local		
University4			Program8 (70) p/t, both	

The choice of locales, and students in computing programs was deliberate for two reasons. First, Hong Kong and Singapore are important markets for Australian transnational programs, and are also well-developed territories where English is commonly spoken [28,29,27]; hence, students participating in the study were unlikely to oppose online education because of lack of suitable technological infrastructure or limited linguistic skills. Malaysia and Vietnam were chosen to check if limited technological infrastructure and language proficiency would have a bearing on student perceptions. Second, the intention was to seek the views of students who were technology savvy; hence, they were least likely to oppose online education because of techno-phobia alone.

The programs operating in part-time mode involve students who have previous approved tertiary qualifications. Students are normally in full-time employment, and usually study six subjects per year – two subjects per term. The full-time programs typically involve students who are high school leavers.

In the programs where teaching is shared by Australian and local academics, lecturers from Australia are responsible for the design of curriculum, detailed teaching plans, continuous and final assessment, as well as face-to-face delivery of twenty five percent of the programs; local lecturers teach the remaining part of the programs. The programs rely on the Internet for communication, e.g. subject Web sites, bulletin boards, and email. Students meet with lecturers and fellow students through face-to-face sessions, and benefit from Web based support between sessions. Programs taught exclusively by local staff still follow the curriculum detailed by the *host* university from Australia and access online resources provided by the *host* university; however, Australian lecturers do not participate in face-to-face teaching.

Data was collected through a survey and group interviews with students. The survey was administered to approximately six hundred students in the selected programs; four-hundred-and-sixty-nine completed surveys were returned. One-hundred-and-eighty-four students participated in group interviews.

5.1 Survey Responses

Responses from the survey revealed that the majority of students opposed fully-online provision of transnational programs and stressed the importance of face-to-face communication with both lecturers and fellow students. The support for possible fully-online provision of the programs ranged from a marginal 7%-14% in programs 6, 7 and 8, through a moderate one-third of participants in programs 3 and 4, and a *high* of 39% and in programs 1 and 5, and the highest rate of 56% in program 2. Students repeatedly stated the importance of face-to-face communication as the most important reason for preferring the current, hybrid, program model that is one that combined face-to-face teaching with Internet-based resources and learning objects. Respondents did, however, acknowledge the usefulness of the Internet as a means for provision of course material and communication with instructors and fellow students. A summary of survey results is presented in Table 3.

The results of the survey revealed that student perceptions were not necessarily determined by the locale. For example, two programs from Hong Kong, 1 and 6, both involved part-time students and were both taught by Australian and local staff, yet the support for online provision varied greatly between the programs: 7% as opposed to 39%. It should be noted, that a study of three transnational computing programs in Hong Kong conducted in 2004 revealed a more uniform lack of support for fully-online delivery: it varied from 0%, through 9%, and 13 % [30].

Table 3. Percentage of students in favour of online delivery of transnational computing education programs

	Hong Kong	Malaysia	Singapore	Vietnam
University1	Program1 (39%) p/t, both	Program2 (56%) f/t, both		
University2		Program3 (35%) f/t, local	Program4 (28%) p/t, local	Program5 (39%) f/t, local
University3	Program6 (7%) p/t, both	Program7 (7%) f/t, local		
University4			Program8 (14%) p/t, both	

The survey also revealed that the quality and availability of the technological infrastructure did not seem to determine student perceptions. For example, students in two programs in Malaysia, 2 and 3, as well as students from Vietnam (program 5), were more in favour of fully-online delivery than their counterparts in the more technologically advanced Singapore. Likewise, the mode of study, part-time or full-time, or the mode of teaching (both Australian and local staff, or local staff only) did not correlate with student perceptions.

The only pattern that could be observed in relation to student preferences was the association with the Australian university offering a given transnational program. It appears that the support for fully online provision was greatest among students of programs offered by University1 (39% and 56%); the support was somewhat lower among students of University2 (35%, 28%, and 39%); and, at 7%, it was lowest in both programs (6 and 7) offered by University3.

Face-to-face communication was preferred as, according to the respondents, it offered instant feedback, afforded easier communication with fellow students and instructors, was better suited to the resolution of study problems, and gave better motivation to study. A summary of student comments is presented in Table 4.

The students who were in favour of fully-online provision, qualified their assent with a variety of conditions including:

But web site must have full support (24x7) and be helpful for the user (S1).

I guess an online course would be great as long as support is highly considered (S2).

If video function is available but in Malaysia internet speed is still far too slow for that (S2).

If the program organised a good interactive or interesting multi-media material and online response (S6).

But if the tutors and lecturers were available anytime to contact via mails, discussion boards it shouldn't be a problem (S7).

Table 4. Student attitudes towards fully online provision of transnational computing education programs

	% of students in favour of online delivery	Student comments
Program1	39	Although it's tempting, I think face-to-face contact with the lecturer is invaluable. Nothing beats face-to-face contact. I want to communicate with instructors. I like face to face learning. Distance learning is not always applicable learning - need interaction not just material. Motivation decreases (with online study). I think it (online learning) will not work for Hong Kong culture.
Program2	56	I would prefer to have classroom based courses. Distance learning would not be effective in degree courses; there are a lot of subjects which are better taught and explained in class. Save time, save money, save resources (petrol, paper) to protect environment. Full use of technology. (Fully-online) effective and convenient.
Program3	13	It's a way of future learning. (Online learning is) easy and reliable. I wouldn't feel and experience student-lecturer relationship and it's easier if it's only semi-online. I still prefer the traditional (hybrid) way.
Program4	28	Self-study will be flexible for working adults. Face-to-face classroom discussions are important in learning.
Program5	39	Beside the lecture or materials, communication with instructors or other students is very important. If the program is offered online only, there will be no discussions in class, after class and in a coffee shop. I don't want to sit in front of a computer all the time. It will reduce all of my communication skills. (Online learning would be) difficult for Vietnamese students.
Program6	7	Some material and course topics really need instructors. Traditional teaching methods are more effective. Direct communication with lecturers makes me pay attention to what I study. Online learning is not for me. I enrolled in an online course and withdrew after one semester. I can't learn and the schedule is too hard to follow.
Program7	7	"Actual" learning is much better: we can interact with lecturers and other students. This program needs an instructor to be beside the student to guide them. Our country connection speed is lousy.
Program8	14	Face to face communication is still the best way in learning. Fully online means less interaction and learning. Classroom interaction is important.

(To ensure anonymity, participating students have been identified only by their program identifier; that is, S1 refers to a student in Program1, S2 identifies a student in Program2, and so on).

5.2 Group Interviews' Responses

The group interviews addressed this issue again to explore further the reasons behind the students' views. Students again responded in favour of the hybrid model of the programs. They regarded face-to-face communication as: more conducive to the learning process; affording better opportunity to share knowledge and ask for help; and, *easier* and more interactive:

Face-to-face communication is more effective (S1).

Face-to-face is interesting, fully online is boring (S1).

(Fully-online learning is) not recognised in this (Hong Kong) society (S1).

Without a lecturer's explanations it would be difficult to understand some material (S2).

It (online learning) would be tough for someone who learns programming language for the first time (S2).

Face-to face interaction often yields better results (S3).

It's easier to understand the subject if we meet the lecturer directly (S3).

There are some things that you can't do online (S3).

We need to meet with lecturers in face-to-face conversation (S4).

For some courses, direct communication with lecturers is necessary (S5).

It is difficult to self-learn (S6).

I'm lazy and there would be no one to ask if I had a problem (S6).

Having group discussions in person is more effective (S7).

I believe face-to-face contact with lecturers and students is very important. Education is as much about the physical relationships made as it is about the knowledge gained (S8).

Having classes forces me to allocate enough time to the program and subject (S8).

However, students welcomed the Internet as a means for providing course material and enabling communication with lecturers outside classes.

Students should be given a choice whether to attend lectures or go online. Students who cannot leave home can still access lectures (S3).

Internet is good for obtaining study material and emailing the lecturers (S6).

6 Discussion

The results of the study appear to confirm the views of [9,10,13] who opined that, although many universities view online learning as an economic alternative to face-to-face teaching, fully-online learning could not be regarded as a suitable alternative in transnational settings. [13] argued that *fully-online global delivery has failed to capture the imagination of students and teachers in the same way as it has excited senior administrators* (p. 2). They looked at the existing transnational programs in South East Asia and concluded that distance education programs with no local support had not been popular; and, they found that Australian institutions offering transnational programs in the region have learned to appreciate the importance of local presence. Students, especially in South East Asia, respect teachers and want and expect to be taught by teachers; those transnational providers that intend to *rely more heavily on online teaching and learning run the risk of eroding students' perception of quality* [13] (p. 10).

[31] attributed the low acceptance of online education in Asia, as compared to the West, to cultural differences. Since online learning is representative of highly developed technologies and Western values in education that emphasise individual development, self-management, active learning, and mutual communications, it may not appeal to students from non-Western cultures. [32] reported on the low number of applicants to the Korea National Open University, and students' lack of confidence in the quality of education from a distance. In addition, [33] indicated that although 67 public universities in China have implemented online courses, most courses were *simply an extension of conventional classroom teaching* (p. 26) with the majority of teachers not ready to change their traditional way of instruction. All of this evidence seems to indicate that hybrid learning rather than online learning is the preferred choice of Asian students. Further research is needed into the possibility of an *Asian* preferred learning style, or even to collect evidence of a learning style shared by students in a particular locale. If support eventuates, cultural considerations would need to be factored into future research and to the design, marketing, and delivery of transnational education programs.

In the meantime, the Australian government officially acknowledged the importance of face-to-face interaction in transnational teaching and incorporated a requirement for face-to-face interaction in the recently developed definition of *Australian Transnational Education* [6]. In contrast to the general definition of transnational education, this definition includes two additional requirements: one, that the transnational program be delivered and/or assessed by an accredited Australian provider; and two, that the delivery should include a face-to-face component. It further stresses that transnational education should include *a physical presence of instructors offshore, either directly by the Australian provider, or indirectly through a formal agreement with a local institution* [6] (p. 6).

7 Conclusions

Australian universities have had over two decades of experience in the provision of transnational higher education programs, particularly in South East Asia, and lessons learnt from this experience should guide decisions concerning the delivery models of those programs. The implementation and utilisation of current and emerging technologies offers many potential advantages including ready access to a vast store of the latest information, and facilitation of communication between students, and students and instructors. However, the advantages to be gained from introducing new technologies will depend on the ability and willingness of the students to use them. Therefore, an assessment of educational needs should be conducted, and potential consequences in the classroom considered, prior to the deployment of those technologies.

This paper discussed the issue of fully-online provision of transnational programs, and reported on a recent study of the perceptions of transnational computing students in Hong Kong, Malaysia, Singapore and Vietnam on fully-online provision of such programs. The study found that the majority of students opposed an online-based delivery model and, instead, preferred a hybrid delivery format; they emphasised the importance of face-to-face interaction, and regarded the Internet as a useful, but only supplementary, means of support.

It appears that despite earlier predictions that globally offered fully-online programs would dominate the transnational education market, the hybrid model – Web-supported face-to-face delivery – is likely to emerge as the principal model of transnational tertiary education programs. Further research is needed to determine the composition of the hybrid model for each transnational destination; the blueprint for each program would include the proportion of face-to-face and online delivery, as well as selection of the most suitable types of learning objects.

References

1. IDP Education Australia: Transnational education providers, partners and policy: Challenges for Australian institutions offshore. In: Davis, D., Olsen, A., Böhm, A. (eds.), IDP, Canberra (2000)
2. McBurnie, G., Pollock, A.: Opportunity and risk in transnational education – issue in planning for international campus development: An Australian perspective. Higher Education in Europe 25(3), 333–343 (2000)
3. van der Vende, M.C.: Globalisation and access to higher education. Journal of Studies in International Education 7(2), 193–206 (2003)
4. UNESCO & Council of Europe: Code of good practice in the provision of transnational education. UNESCO-CEPES, Bucharest (2001), http://www.cepes.ro/hed/recogn/groups/transnat/code.htm
5. GATE (Global Alliance for Transnational Education): Demand for transnational education in the Asia Pacific. Global Alliance for Transnational Education, Washington (2000)
6. DEST (Department of Education, Science and Training): A national quality strategy for Australian transnational education and training: A discussion paper (2005), http://aei.dest.gov.au/AEI/GovernmentActivities/QAAustralian EducationAndTrainingSystem/QualStrat_pdf.pdf
7. Moore, M.G., Kearsley, G.: Distance education: a systems view, 2nd edn. Wadsworth, Toronto (2005)
8. Chapman, A., Pyvis, D.: Quality, identity and practice in offshore university programmes: Issues in the internationalization of Australian higher education. Teaching in Higher Education 11(2), 233–245 (2006)
9. Davis, D., Meares, D.: Transnational education: Australia online – critical factors for success. IDP Education Australia, Sydney (2001)
10. Emil, B.: Distance learning, access, and opportunity: Equality and e-quality. Metropolitan Universities 12(1), 19 (2001)
11. Knipe, D.: The quality of teaching and learning via videoconferencing. British Journal of Educational Technology 33(3), 301–311 (2002)
12. Debowski, S.: Lost in internationalised space: The challenge of sustaining academics teaching offshore. In: 17th IDP Australian International Education Conference, Securing the future for international education, Melbourne (2003), http://www.idp.com/ 17aiecpapers/
13. Ziguras, C., Rizvi, F.: Future directions in international online education. In: Davis, D., Meares, D. (eds.) Transnational Education: Australia Online, pp. 151–164. IDP Education Australia, Sydney (2001)

14. Ziguras, C.: New frontiers, new technologies, new pedagogies. Educational technology and the internationalisation of higher education in South East Asia. Monash Centre for Research in International Education, Melbourne (2000)

15. Ziguras, C.: Education beyond our shores: Defining the way forward. In: Workshop report (2002), http://www.minedu.govt.nz/web/downloadable/dl7382_v1/workshop-report-final.doc

16. Hentea, M., Shea, M.J., Pennington, L.: A perspective on fulfilling the expectations of distance education. In: CITC4 2003, pp. 160–167. ACM Press, New York (2003)

17. Singh, M., Han, J.: Globalizing flexible work in universities: Socio-technical dilemmas in internationalizing education. International Review of Research in Open and Distance Learning 6(1) (2005), http://www.irrodl.org/content/v6.1/singh_han.html

18. Huang, F.: Transnational higher education: A perspective from China. Higher Education Research and Development 22(2), 193–203 (2003)

19. Marold, K., Haga, W.: Measuring online students' ability to apply programming theory: Are Web courses really working? Journal of International Technology and Information Management 13(1), 13–20 (2004)

20. Chen, L.: Distance delivery systems in terms of pedagogical considerations: A revolution. Educational Technology 37(4), 34–37 (1997)

21. Kirkup, G., Jones, A.: New technologies for open learning: The superhighway to the learning society? In: Raggatt, P., Edwards, R., Small, N. (eds.) Adult learners, education and training 2: The learning society – challenges and trends, pp. 272–291. Routledge, London (1996)

22. Kiser, K.: Is blended best? E-Learning 3(6), 10 (2002)

23. Zhao, Y., Lei, J., Yan, B., Lai, C., Tan, H.S.: What makes the difference? A practical analysis of research on the effectiveness of distance education. Teachers College Record 107(8), 1836–1884 (2005)

24. Riffee, W.R.: Putting a face on distance education programs. Syllabus, pp. 10–13 (February 2005), http://www.campus-technology.com/article.asp?id=7233

25. Woodworth, P., Applin, A.G.: A hybrid structure for introductory computers and information technology course. Journal of Computing Sciences in Colleges 22(3), 136–144 (2007)

26. Norquest College: Distance learning: Hybrid learning (2007), http://www.norquest.ca/distance/hybridlearning.htm

27. IDP Education Australia: International students in Australian universities. Report, semester 2, 2004. IDP, Canberra (2004), http://www.idp.com/research/fastfacts/Semester%20Two%202004 %20-%20Key%20Outcomes_Web.pdf

28. Garrett, R., Verbik, L.: Transnational higher education, part 1: the major markets – Hong Kong and Singapore. The Observatory (November 14, 2003a)

29. Garrett, R., Verbik, L.: Transnational higher education, part 1: shifting markets and emerging trends. The Observatory (December 15, 2003b)

30. Miliszewska, I.: Is it fully 'on' or partly 'off'? The case of fully-online provision of transnational education. Journal of Information Technology Education 6, 499–514 (2007)

31. Wang, H.: Teaching Asian students online: what matters and why? PAACE Journal of Lifelong Learning 15, 69–84 (2006)

32. Park, D., Kim, S.: Challenges facing the open university: The case of the Korea National Open University. Open Education Research 10(6), 28–33 (2004)

33. Zhu, Z.T., Gu, X.P., Wang, Q.Y.: A panorama of online education in China. Educational Technology, 23–27 (2003)

Building an Assessment Learning System on the Web

Reggie Kwan[1], Kenneth Wong[2], Chi-wing Yu[3], Philip Tsang[4], and Kat Leung[1]

[1] Caritas Francis Hsu College and Caritas Bianchi College of Careers
rkwan@cihe.edu.hk
[2] Hong Kong Institute of Higher Education
[3] Po Leung Kuk Tang Yuk Tien College
[4] The Open University of Hong Kong

Abstract. This paper presents the design and a preliminary assessment of an online assessment system for learning purposes. The prototype aims to enhance learning by helping teachers teach Key Stage 3 (KS3) Mathematics in Hong Kong The system was built on the concept domain model and the Rasch model to provide an adapting feature to students, such as, navigation support, optimal study path and direct guidance. This is based on the Response Theory (IRT) model to determine students' estimated ability level.. When an individual student enters the system, different problems depending on student's estimated ability level will be assigned to students. Once the system senses an individual student's responses are converging to a particular competence level, the system immediately calculates the student's estimated ability level, identifies his strengths and weaknesses, etc. An immediate score, solution of items, feedback recommended study path and direct guidance can be give instantaneously.

1 Introduction

Web-based learning is growing rapidly worldwide; more and more schools in Hong Kong are integrating learning materials on the Web as part of the standard pedagogy. Most believe that web-based education has the potential not only to provide savings in time and money, but, more importantly, it's flexibility and convenience may also revolutionize the way to live and play. Assessment for learning can be one of the ways of improving learning by gauging students' competency, e-assessment should be an integral part of any e-learning system [1]. As a matter of fact, the Curriculum Development Council published a report entitled *"Learning to learn: The Way Forward in Curriculum Development"* in 2001 to urge schools to put more emphasis on assessment for learning [2]. It is a process in which teachers seek to identify and diagnose student learning problems, and provide quality feedback for students on how to improve their work.

Most students, however, treat assessment as difficult or even a necessary evil. Fortunately, there are techniques that can turn assessment into something effective and efficient but not threatening. Unfortunately, much of the current assessment methods in Hong Kong schools are still the conventional paper-and-pencil test (PAPT), they are bounded by *time* and *place*. It is no easy task to design an online assessment system that focuses on "Assessment for Learning", not to mention the migration process [3].

J. Fong, R. Kwan, and F.L. Wang (Eds.): ICHL 2008, LNCS 5169, pp. 91–102, 2008.
© Springer-Verlag Berlin Heidelberg 2008

Mathematics is a challenging subject for students at all levels. Although, textbook publishers and software vendors have developed a lot of digital materials in learning of mathematics, not many of them put an emphasis on assessment for learning and using concept model to build the online learning kits. Most online assessment systems do not provide immediate feedback and recommend study path to make use of the assessed result to help students learn. Our prototype of the online assessment system, on the other hand, aims to enhance learning by helping teachers teach Mathematics from Secondary 1 to 3 (Key Stage 3) in Hong Kong. The system is built on the concept domain model and the Rasch model [4], [5], and [6]. The two integrated models are used for providing adapting features to students, such as, navigation support, optimal study path and direct guidance.

2 Rasch Model and Computer Adaptive Test

The Rasch model is a fairly simple Item Response Theory (IRT) model. IRT can overcome some of the problems and assumptions associated with Classical Test Theory (CTT) and to provide information for decision-making that is not available through CTT. The Rasch model is based on objective measurement [5]. It is based on the probability that an examinee with a given ability level will correctly answer a question representing a given difficulty [7]. Rasch models are also used for analysing data from assessments to measure things such as abilities, attitudes, and personality traits. The Rasch model can be used as an interval scale of scores for both the difficulty of items and the ability of the examinee tested. Interval scores are constant differences along the scale, add & subtract possible; e.g., ratings on students' ability, the difference between 3 and 2 is equal to the difference between 2 and 1, but still a student with 4 is not twice as good/bad as that of 2. These scores are reported in units called logits. Since Logits unit can do addition, subtraction, multiple, and division, it makes useful for educational gains, displays of strengths and weaknesses, and comparisons of different groups.

Rasch model presents a simple relationship between the examinee and the difficulty of items. The mathematical formula of the Rasch Model is given bellow:

$$Log \left(\frac{P_i}{1 - P_i} \right) = \theta_j - b_i \tag{1}$$

Where

P_i : probability for an examinee responding correctly.

θ_j : ability parameter of an examinee.

b_i : difficulty parameter of an item.

Figure 1 is the Rasch Model Test Characteristic Curve [8]. It shows the relationship between the probability $P(i=1)$ and ($\theta_j - b_i$) the difference between the examinee's ability level θ_j and the item difficulty b_i.

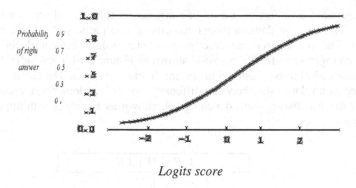

Logits score

Fig. 1. The Rasch Model Test Characteristic Curve [8]

If an examinee's ability level exactly equals to the difficulty level b_i of the item, he/she will have a 50% chance of passing an item. Similarly, if the examinee's ability level is greater than the difficulty level of the item, he/she will have over a 50% chance of responding correctly to this item. Conversely, if the examinee's ability level is less than the difficulty level of the item, he/she will have less than a 50% chance of responding correctly to this item. The best design for the selection algorithm of items is that the difficulty level of an administrated item is close to the current ability level. The examinee ability level parameter and item difficulty parameter can be estimated iteratively through application of a process such as Conditional Maximum Likelihood estimation.

In analyzing Rasch data, there are two chi-square fit statistics should be concerned - Outfit and infit statistics [9]. Outfit statistics are more sensitive to extreme scores and infit statistics are more sensitive to unexpected patterns. Use of this two fit statistics information, the Rasch model helps the user identify any items that are not fitting the model, and any examinee whose scores do not appear to be consistent with the model.

Computer Adaptive Test (CAT) works like a good oral exam. Examinees receive the question in accordance with their ability. After the response is given, the result is calculated immediately. If an answer is correct, the next question generated will give a higher difficult item. If the answer is incorrect, the procedure will be reversed. The examinee's ability level can be estimated during the testing process [10]. Since the item selected next for obtaining ability estimates is based upon one's previous item performance, an algorithm must be chosen for sequencing the set of test items administered to the examinees. Therefore, using Rasch model to design such algorithm is very suitable.

3 Concept Domain Model

However, CAT may be optimal for determining an individual's overall ability level, it doesn't assure content balance and doesn't guarantee that one could obtain subtest scores. To overcome this concern, the algorithm should develop a set of construction rules to select the best questions. To optimize the online assessment system, the

research team decided to construct a set of construction rules based on a concept domain model. The concept domain model consists of two parts: skillful tree and curriculum tree. The skillful tree can descript as a relationship between different skill
interconnected together to form a network, shown as Figure 2 with appendix A shows
the Mathematics Skill to be mastered in solving linear equations. The curriculum tree
can described as a relationship between different knowledge elements interconnected
together to form a network (with dependency), shown as Figure 3 with appendix B
shows an example .

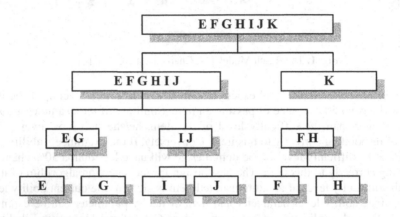

Fig. 2. A Skillful Tree

4 Building an Item Bank

To implement a CAT, an item bank containing all items is necessary. "An item bank
is a large collection of test items organized and catalogued to take into account the
content of each test item and also its measurement characteristics." [6]. Actually, the
item bank is a database of items. The size of the item bank should be big enough to
cover the wide range of test content. The great advantage of an item bank is its flexibility. Tests can be long or short, easy or difficult depending on the aim of the test.
Normally, the questions in CAT are drawn from an item bank. All individual items
are carefully calibrated and ranked in difficulty. However, there are several disadvantages of building an item bank. No item bank is perfect. The items in an item bank
must be continually re-calibrated. Therefore, all item bank has to continually maintain
its standard. Such ongoing work requires a lot of resources.

It is expensive and time-consuming to establish an item bank especially on this
CAT. Initially, there are about 100 existing items from the past few year tests which
are suitable to the assessment system. However, those items are not calibrated and
with difficulty levels. To assign difficulty levels of the items, research team members
will first guess intelligently. As they have expertise in Computer Science, Education
and Mathematics, they know what topic areas are harder than others for those at any
stage of development and know which item is suitable for the assessment system. In
addition, inspection of individual items gives indications of their relative difficulty.

Initially, items are stratified into 10 different difficulty levels and related topic areas. Each research member gives his/her scale first, then an average will be derived accordingly. Consequently, a fairly stratifying of items by expert-perceived difficulty can often be accomplished.

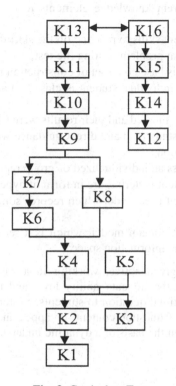

Fig. 3. Curriculum Tree

Nevertheless, this is only a preliminary state of estimated items' difficulty levels, all initial items must be examined and re-calibrated by a pilot conventional test. The pilot test will be administered later this year with students in this very course. The results of the test will be used to verify the item whether it is functioning as specified and to ascertain the item's precise difficulty. Then the item can be made part of the item bank.

5 System Design and Architecture

There are tools that can do adaptive testing, and tools that can do tutoring, and tools that can do analysis of results from students doing on-line tests; but there is no single tool that incorporates all three of these functions. One of our goals is to develop an online assessment system incorporates all three of these functions.

5.1 System Features

The distinctive features of our online assessment system are:

- students have choice to select Knowledge mode or Skilful mode to learn;
- students can select different knowledge elements to learning on the Knowledge mode;
- students can select different skills to practice on the skilful mode;
- students are given different problems during the test;
- selection of test question is based on a set of construction rules and Rasch model;
- the level of ability of the individual student is classified according to the their performance;
- students are automatically marked and their results were summarised in a report;
- feedback, recommended study path and direct guidance would be given to studnets when he complete a question.
- Teachers are able to access an individualized or group report of the students.
- all test questions and content materials are in form of hypermedia;
- the system have an explicit user-model which records some features of the individual student; and
- the system has a concept domain model, which is a set of relationships between knowledge elements in the information space;

System should be strongly adaptive, working in a well-structured information space; gathering data about the students' ability level and using this information to dynamically generate an optimal question to students. System should also be capable of altering the sequencing of question content, or appearance of the direct guidance and, an optimal study path on the basis of a dynamic understanding of the characteristics of the individual user.

5.2 Selection Algorithm

An algorithm to choose the next best items is based on a set of construction rules and the Rasch model. To estimate examinee's ability, the algorithm is based on Rasch model. We use the algorithm described by [11] to estimate an examinee's ability. The next item generated will give an appropriate difficulty with the examinee's ability. This iterative process is part of the Rasch Model. Similarly, to estimate an appropriate content of next item, the algorithm uses a set of construction rules. We employs the concept domain model. If the user selects the Knowledge mode, the construction rules will focus on the content balance on different knowledge elements. If the user selects the Skilful mode, the construction rules will focus on the content balance on different skill type. The steps are shown on figure 4.

As examinees answer each question, the computer scores the question and uses that information together with the responses of the previous questions to determine which question is presented next. If an examinee gets a correct answer with a given item, the system will generate an item from the pool with slightly more difficult than the current one. Then the best next item will be selected with some constraints from this item pool based on a set of construction rules. If the examinee gets the item wrong, the process is similar, however the next item received will be easier. When the

Stopping condition is obtained, the testing session ends. The stopping conditions are crucial factors for our system, they are when:
1. no more relevant questions are left in the item bank; or
2. a pre-determined time-limit was reached; or the examinee decided to quit the test.

The current estimated ability level was the final ability level of the examinee. Then examinees will be given an immediate feedback, study guides if any and score on their performance and examinees' performance can be tracked by using the computer to store performance data.

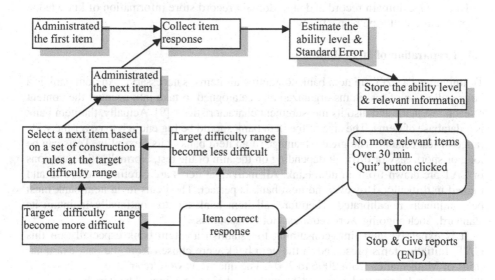

Fig. 4. The Algorithm of the online assessment system

5.3 Design of the Database

The system contains several main records: the item record, the item frequency record, the student record, the student response record, student test record, student ability record, knowledge domain record, and skill domain record. Details are elaborated as follows.

Item records stores all relevant item information, e.g. the item ID (*Qid*), content topic (*Qtype*), skill type(*Stype_A, Stype_B,...*) , date of upload (*Qdate*), question statements (*Stem, Alt_A, ..., Alt_D*), keys (*Key_A, ..., Key_D*) and difficulty level (*Rindex*).

The item frequency record contains the item ID (*Qid*), the number of right (*R_freq*) and wrong (*W_freq*) responses by students, total operation time (*Total_time*) by the students).

The student record stores all relevant student's information. The record consists of student ID (*SID*), first name (*F_Name*), last name (*L_Name*), class (*Class*).

The student response record stores student's information examine one item, e.g. student ID (*SID*), test indicator (*Tid*), item ID (*Qid*), student response on item(*R_time*), login date and time (*Date_test*).

The student test record stores student's information during the test,

e.g. student ID (*SID*), test indicator (*Tid*), executive time on item (*Ex_Time*), and executive time for the whole test (*Finish_Time*).

The student ability record stores student's ability information during the test, e.g. estimated ability level (*Ability_L*), standard error (*SE*), knowledge_domain(*K_1, K_2,K_3, ...*), skill_domain(*S_1, S_2, ...*)

Knowledge domain record and skill domain record store information of knowledge elements and skill type respectively.

5.4 Preparation of Item Bank

To implement a CAT, an item bank containing all items is necessary. "An item bank is a large collection of test items organized and catalogued to take into account the content of each test items and also its measurement characteristics." [9]. Actually, the item bank is a database of items. The size of the item bank should be big enough to cover the wide range of test content. The great advantage of an item bank is its flexibility. Tests can be long or short, easy or difficult depending on the aim of the test. Normally, the questions in CAT are drawn from an item bank. All individual items are carefully calibrated and ranked in difficulty. However, no item bank is perfect. The items in an item bank must be continually re-calibrated. Therefore, all item bank has to continually maintain its standard. Such ongoing work requires a lot of resources.

It is expensive and time-consuming to establish an item bank especially on this CAT. Initially, items presented in the item bank were chosen from the past examinations of Mathematics from 2006 to 2007. The questions were restricted to only one of the modules. It consisted of over 100 multiple-choice questions. The item bank was of smaller size compared with a real CAT for this pilot test. All items were categorised into different sub-sections based on the Concept Domain Model. All items were pre-calibrated by a software program called WINSTEP. WINSTEP gave a ranking of the difficulty level of all items. It was the only information used in this system. We employed the difficulty scale unit called logits [5].

5.5 System Architecture

The online assessment system architecture (Figure 5) consists of a Web Interface, a Main system, Database, Rasch Model and Concept Domain Model. The Web interface provides a communication channel between the system and examinees. It operates in conjunction with examinees and the online assessment system.

The main system is the core module in the system, which provides the main tasks in the system: database connection, authentication, estimating the ability level and standard error, selecting the next item, determining the end of the test, giving feedback and generate summary reports. The Database contains item bank which all the pre-calibrated items of information, and examinee response record which contains all the relevant examinees information. The Concept Domain Model contains a set of relationships between different knowledge domains and different skill type domain.

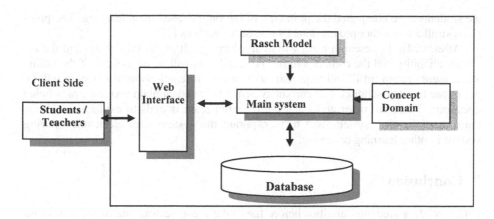

Fig. 5. Architecture of the online assessment system

5.6 Choice of Web Tools and Working Platform for Building the System

Although the Web framework has some limitations especially in its interface, it gives the system great benefit. The main advantage of the Web is that a user can access the system from anywhere on the Internet without any special interface programs. Two identical online assessment systems were developed, one on Linux and the other one on Window XP. The one using Linux provides a stable and economy working platform for students while the other one using Window XP was chosen for its popularity and the fact that XP is the most used operating systems in Hong Kong schools. In Linux system, an Apache server was used together with PHP and JavaScript to build the front pages and CGI, and uses mySQL as a database for handling information. In Window's platform, the system uses the Window 2003 server as a web server, PHP and JavaScript to build the front pages and CGI, and uses SQL server as a database for handling information.

6 Deployment and Further Development

Several schools are being selected to attend two pilot tests for the online assessment system. A single-group pretest-posttest evaluation design will be used to evaluate the effectiveness of the system. This design compares the same group of participants before and after the programme. The purpose of the single group pretest-posttest design is to determine if students improved after receiving such assessment system.

The research team will request the students to do both tests. Two tests are in traditional PAPT format that is multiple-choice questions; all items are selected from the item bank. Each participant has to answer all questions within the test period. They will not be allowed to leave the test until test session ends. Each participant will give feedback by filling in a questionnaire at the end. The result of the test will be analysed, items will be verified and the difficulty level of each item will be re-calibrated. Then, all re-calibrated items will be used as a part the regular item bank. A pretest pilot test will be deployed in December 2007. The protest pilot test will be scheduled on April 2008 after the students have completed the prototype of the online assessment learning. The process is similar to another project done by one of the authors [12].

Afterwards, the research team will analyse the result of the pilot tests, and the internal reliability and the content validity [13] and [14] will be measured. If the online assessment system fulfills all requirements from the research team, the system will be put in use to other schools. The current system only handles plain text multiple-choice questions. There are other areas that the research team intends to explore, such as a multi-media testing system, and to incorporate the system with electronic tutoring system in other learning programs.

7 Conclusion

Differentiating students' abilities before they take a course was one of the concerns. An online assessment system has been built and focused on "Assessment for Learning". The system can be an effective method of assessment in which the computer selects and presents test items to examinees according to the estimated examinees' ability levels. Using the Rasch Model, the system can estimate students' ability effectively and the estimated ability was a useful indicator for instructors' reference. We learned that building such a system is an on-going process that requires a systematic and meticulous approach. The effectiveness of such a system remains to be seen and will be a great interest of the research team.

References

1. Kwan, R., Chan, J., Lui, A.: Reaching an ITopia in Distance Learning—A Case Study. AACE Journal 12(2), 171–817 (2004)
2. CDC: Learning to learn: The Way Forward in Curriculum Development. The Curriculum Development Council, Hong Kong SAR (June 2001)
3. Kwan, R., Wong, T.M.: Migrating to the On-line Environment: the experience of OUHK's School of Science & Technology. In: International Conference on Learning and Teaching On-line, Guangzhou, China (2001)
4. Linacre, J.M.: Computer-Adaptive Testing: A Methodology Whose Time Has Come, Memo#69 Iom Research Memoranda, Institute for Objective Measurement, Inc. (2000), http://rasch.org/memo69.pdf
5. Keeves, J.P., Alagumalai, S.: New Approaches to Measurement. In: Masters, G.N., Keeves, J.P. (eds.) Advances in Measurement in Educational Research and Assessment, Pergamon, pp. 23–48. Pergamon, Oxford (1999)
6. Umar, J.: Item Banking. In: Keeves, J.P. (ed.) Educational Research, Methodology, and Measurement. Pergamon Publishing, Oxford (1997)
7. Wright, B.D., Stone, M.K.: Best Test Design. MESA Press, Chicago (1979)
8. Wright, B.D.: Reliability and Separation. Rasch Measurement Transactions 9(4), 472 (1996)
9. Linacre, J.M., Wright, B.D.: Chi-Square Fit Statistics. Rasch Measurement Transactions 8(2), 350 (1994)
10. Rudner, L.M.: An On-line, Interactive, Computer Adaptive Testing Mini-Tutorial, ERIC Clearinghouse on Assessment and Evaluation (1998)

11. Linacre, J.M.: Individualized Testing in the Classroom. In: Masters, G.N., Keeves, J.P. (eds.) Advances in Measurement in Educational Research and Assessment, pp. 186–194. Pergamon, New York (1999)
12. Wong, K.: Web-based Tool for a Computerised Adaptive Test System. Master Thesis. University of Victoria Wellington, New Zealand (2000)
13. Wong, K.R., Kwan, R., Chan, J.: A Preliminary Evaluation of a Computerized Adaptive Test System on the Web. In: Kwan, R., et al. (eds.) Web-based Learning: Men & Machines, pp. 123–134. World Scientific Publishing, New Jersey (2002)
14. Wong, K., Kwan, R.: Building a Web-based Computerized Adaptive Testing System. In: International Conference on Information and Communication Technologies in Education, Badajoz, Spain, vol. I, pp. 62–66 (2002)

Appendix A. Mathematics Skill to be mastered in solving linear equations

Code	Skill
A	Appropriate use of letters to represent numbers
B	Understand the language of Algebra
C	Formulation of Linear Equations in one unknown
D	Formulation of Linear Equations in 2 unknowns
E	Simplify +− on one side
F	Simplify ÷× on one side
G	Moving +− terms
H	Moving ÷× terms
I	Grouping
J	Removal of brackets
K	Simplification
L	Changing of subject of equation
M	Technique of substitution
N	Multiplication of Equations by a factor
O	Technique of Elimination

Appendix B. Example of Content Model

Code	Concepts
K1	Use Symbols or letters to represent numbers
K2	Understand the language of algebra including translating word phases into algebraic expressions or write descriptive statement for algebraic expressions
K3	Understand the concepts of equations
K4	Formulation of Linear Equations in one unknown
K5	Formulation of Linear Equations in two unknowns
K6	Solve simple equations involving one step in the solutions and check answers (involving whole numbers only)
K7	Solve problems by simple equations (involving only one step in the solution)
K8	Solve equations involving almost two steps in the solutions
K9	Solve problems by simple equations (involving at most two steps in the solutions)
K10	Solve linear equations in one unknown
K11	Solve literal linear equations
K12	Plot and explore the graphs of linear equations in 2 unknowns
K13	Solve simultaneous equations by algebraic method
K14	Solve simultaneous equations by graphical method
K15	Awareness of the approximate nature of the graphical method
K16	Explore simultaneous equations that are inconsistent or that have no unique solution

A Qualitative Analysis on Collaborative Learning Experience of Student Journalists Using Wiki

Will Wai Kit Ma[1] and Allan Hoi Kau Yuen[2]

[1] Department of Journalism & Communication, Hong Kong Shue Yan Univeristy,
Braemar Hill, North Point, Hong Kong SAR, China
wkma@hksyu.edu
[2] Faculty of Education, The University of Hong Kong, Pokfulam, Hong Kong SAR, China
hkyuen@hkucc.hku.hk

Abstract. Education in journalism emphasizes internships, apprenticeships, and other opportunities to learn journalism by doing journalism; however, most computer-mediated communication tools do not have such a provision. The fully open structure of Wiki matches the principles of learning journalism while, from a technical point of view, Wiki provides a very easy way for users to report, write and edit. In a case study, a group of undergraduate journalism students were exposed to a student-written Wiki to jointly compose news reporting. Analysis of student journalists' responses to the open-ended questions revealed revision as the core processing capability of Wiki. The motivational factors to revision include accuracy (fact checking), story enrichment, and personal interest toward the news topic. In addition, learners are also affected by the social interactions among the community users within Wiki. The qualitative data shows students both value the process and face challenges in managing the complexity of shared editing.

Keywords: Wikis, Journalistic Writing Processes, Revision, Social Interaction.

1 Introduction

Since its introduction in 2004, Wikipedia.org has grown rapidly into one of the largest reference Web sites on the Internet. It is more popular than all other reference sites, including Britannica.com. It is also ahead of all English language news and media sites, excluding only YouTube. Basically, Wikipedia, utilizing the Wiki technology, provides only a platform out of scratch. Wiki is defined and described as *"a type of website that allows users to add, remove, or otherwise edit and change all content very quickly and easily"*[1]. In turn, could we apply the Wiki technology to support teaching and learning of news writing?

In education, Wikis have been applied simply as an efficient means for knowledge sharing between teachers and students such as sharing notes, co-working projects, sharing list, notes, and recipes [2, 3]. Empirical studies suggest that Wikis could support collaborative knowledge creation and sharing in an academic environment [4] and support teaching and learning [5, 6]. In order to maximize the effective use of a

J. Fong, R. Kwan, and F.L. Wang (Eds.): ICHL 2008, LNCS 5169, pp. 103–114, 2008.

web-based knowledge management system using Wikis, Raman [7] concluded that management should consider a better "fit" between the system and the applied context after a case investigation of the implementation of an emergency preparedness at an American university consortium.

On the other hand, the media industry is one of the first disciplines to grasp the full potential of Wikis. Former reporter has implemented Wikis since 2004 for a social networking web site to allow its users to submit, choose and rank content on news stories (www.digg.com) [8]. Wikis have also helped collected a multi-layered body of knowledge and linked together disparate bits of information in one place, in an example of advertising application [9]. It is argued that news reporting would be an appropriate application and promising area of implementing Wikis to manage the relevant knowledge [10], for example, Wikinews (http://www.wikinews.org) and USC Online Journalism Wikis (http://www.ojr.org/ojr/wiki/). Wikis have been found employed in a number of mainstream media news sites, for example, Los Angeles Times and its Wikitorial – invite visitors to rewrite the newspaper's editorials using Wikis.

In particular, journalists practice writing as their single or most important professional activity. Prior literature [11] suggest generic steps in news writing where revising is one of those key steps. Previous study [12] on text production processes including text production (drafting a document), feedback (reader commentary) and revision (revising the text) from a socio-cognitive approach where peer interactions in the social context affect the text production processes in the discourse community of engineering. Prior study suggests an effective model in writing that includes two sections: section one encourages reflection on all aspects of the message leading revision while section two informs error-analysis and further revision [13].

Apart from revision capability that helps the process of writing, Wiki also helps create a community of Wiki users to interact with each other within its environment. Empirical studies found that providing feedback constitutes an integral part of the learning process in writing [14]. Another study investigated [15] the social interaction of peer revision of a group of Spanish-speaking college students enrolled in a second language writing course. They revealed an extremely complex interactive process that highlighted the importance of activating and cognitive processes enhanced through social interaction in the writing classroom. Other study explored group interaction patterns to include power relations and social goals, even among first grade children [16].

As a result, it is important to explore how this emergent technology Wiki interacts with the pedagogical needs of teaching and learning of news writing. The paper is organized as follows: after a brief review of related literature, we describe a case study utilizing a student-written Wiki and the method to collect reflections of users on their learning experience. Focused on the revising processes, the paper analyzes the open-ended responses in order to identify the factors or categories. The last section concludes with a discussion of the implications to instructional design in the implementation of Wiki as a learning medium to news writing.

2   Wikis and Journalistic Process

News writing does not only include the reporting process (e.g., interviewing eyewit-nesses and experts, checking facts, writing an original representation of the subject), but also include the editorial review processes (e.g., reporter researches and writes a story, editor ensures that it meets her requirements) in accordance to the objective to produce a consistent product that is informed by the news agency's standards and journalism principles [11].The essence of Wiki is its fully open and inherently democ-ratic structure that closely matches with the journalistic processes.

The essence of Wiki and its relevance to learning journalistic writing can be sum-marized by these statements:

(1) *A wiki allows all users to edit any page or to create new pages within the wiki web site while using only a standardized Web browser.* The core activity of learning journalism is news writing. Wiki becomes a learning platform for learners to freely publish content with the minimal barrier. Editorial review is a necessary and impor-tant step in the journalistic processes. However, it only allows scheduled update for static web page and for repository database. On the contrary, anyone can edit any page at any time. Therefore, student journalists may easily change their roles from a reporter (contributor) to an editor of their own news writing, or review over other reporters' work. Education in journalism emphasizes reporting, writing, and editing as a whole [17], while Wiki helps integrate the learning of these instrumental skills at a one-stop centralized platform.

(2) *A wiki allows all users to make hyperlinks between wiki pages by easy and sim-ple markups for cross-referencing related topics in order to create context for news stories.* For example, in using one of the Wiki derivatives, MediaWiki (http://www.mediawiki.org/), users can simply type the text, say "John" in double parentheses, [[John]] to create a hyperlink to the wiki page "John", if no such page exists, MediaWiki will create such a page in edit form and invite users to add content. For a static webpage, it is difficult to do effectively, and it is hard to change or update, while broken links due to change is also a typical problem. For a repository database, it depends on query and serving engine, where only search is possible in most cases. Nonetheless, Wiki allow anyone to edit and to create cross-links and create topic page for searchers. The essence of journalism is a discipline of verification while Wiki's capability of facilitating these following site links and cross-referencing provide so much an easy method for verification. Users can browse a wiki site in a free-form structure. They can easily search relevant news writing by topic or by keywords. The ease to create and to browse cross-referencing for information, material, or back-ground to provide context within Wiki is the best way to help learners to understand the process of journalism.

Therefore, utilizing Wikis, student journalists can produce news in a similar man-ner as they work and think every day. They perfect their performance in the repetition of doing, until these elements of journalism become second nature. This is what will breed clarity of purpose, confidence of execution, and public respect [18]. This is the way Wiki which helps the learning of journalistic writing.

3 Method

The selection of sample is no easy as Wiki is still not popular in local higher educational settings. There may be individual applications in certain department or course; however, it may not be comparable to the scale of usage, or relevant to the context under investigation. In view of this, this study designs to select the sample which will provide appropriate data to address the research aims. Therefore, this study chooses a case study method to explore the collaborative news writing process using learning medium Wiki. A student-written Wiki (named, HKNews at http://hknews.hksyu.edu) has been setup for the Department of Journalism & Communication at a private local university in Hong Kong. HKNews Wiki is open to the public; however, its primary aim is to support teaching and learning by allowing 548 student reporters in the department to contribute original news reporting. Up till April 15, 2007, there were 10,622 Wiki pages (including discussion and user pages), and among them, there are 4203 news reporting articles, and a total of 54,049 edits (5.09 edits per article), with a total of 2,474,818 view counts in the whole site. There are 1,497 registered users, of which 3 (or 0.20%) are System Operators (Sysops). At the beginning of the second semester, 23 students enrolled in the course, *Application of Information Technology for Communication*, at the Department of Journalism & Communication. They were the subjects in this study.

There was a seminar on February 6, 2007. Before that, a Wiki page was setup about introducing the speaker and the talk. Throughout the week, all the students in the department were encouraged to edit the Wiki page and to add content to it. They might also create links and additional Wiki pages to provide extra information for any content in the article. The 23 students joined this collaborative news writing task for one week.

In order to understanding the processes of collaborative news writing and the individual learners' perceptions on using Wikis, they were asked to complete an open-ended survey expressed in details in the writing processes and their reflection on their experiences in the Wiki environment. For the analysis of qualitative data from the open-ended questions, we copied the responses into a word processor, sorted and grouped them, and labeled the major themes and categories that emerged.

4 Results

4.1 Goals of Using Wiki for the Writing Task

Congruent goals are important to direct learners' effort in collaborative work. It is found that all of the subjects share the common goal that Wikis provide an open platform for people to collaborate together to create and to share updated knowledge. Typical comments included:

> • *The goal of wiki is providing a platform for people editing openly and freely. The contributions of different people enrich the information...*
> • *To provide and share accurate information on every aspects of everyday life.*

• *Everyone can write and re-write the information without time and place limit, to attain the mutual sharing in knowledge.*

Half of the respondents agreed that goals were achieved while using Wiki. They try and they find that they can really write and edit together to complete the writing task. Typical comments included:

• *Everyone can be writer and editor......Therefore, the aim collaborative creation and sharing can be achieved.*
• *Everyone can correct other contents freely. The updating is non- stop.*
• *We edit and elaborate more and more information inside the Wiki. We do not only edit Cheung's (the speaker) information but also provide more information based on what she said. Everyone provides his/her own information to expand the Wiki page.*

However, one-fourth of the student journalists have reservation to the attainment of the goals. Goals were achieved only to a certain extent. They point out that, although Wikis are capable to provide such a collaborative platform, it is also highly dependent on the motives of the community users who really use the platform. Moreover, they also care much about the quality of the final writing work, especially the accuracy. Typical comments included:

• *However, some information is wrong and there is not every Wiki user or computer user enjoys being an editing for the Wiki, but a reader.*
• *The success of WIKI depends heavily on the users.*

The remaining one-fourth of the student journalists is more skeptical to the quality of the final writing. The final written work has errors, incomplete and is not organized. They think that the goals are not achieved. Typical comments included:

• *Our work cannot form a complete piece of writing. Some parts of the writing are missing.*
• *It is hard to ensure things written on Wiki are accurate.*
• *The information is provided but is not very organized at all.*

4.2 Satisfaction over Using Wiki for the Writing Task

Nearly half of the respondents are satisfied with the use of Wiki for this collaborative writing task. One quarter of the respondents are satisfied with some reservations. They are content with the use of Wiki, for example, "*I can compare how good or bad writing skills so that I can improve it (my own writing)*," "*I can (easily) see other people's effort in writing the task*," "*after you get familiar with the system, it is easy to obtain information, edit a page and link each page*," "*it is easy to add, edit, remove a page by just few clicks*," "*As I am a junior user, it quite satisfies me. The process is not hard to handle.*"

The remaining one quarter of the respondents are not satisfied with the use of the Wiki environment. The dissatisfaction results reveal a lot of the details in the writing process and the worries. For example, someone does not like working with others ("*I enjoy working from zero but not following others' suit*"); someone does not satisfied with the final quality overall ("*the quality of it (the final writing piece) is not stable*");

or the accuracy of the final work ("*someone adds fake information easily. It affects the accuracy*"); someone thinks that it is not the appropriate task to work together ("*group work is more suitable for some difficult topics*"); someone has difficulties in the technical aspect ("*We need to memorize several format how to make a title and create a new sub-heading. This may cause problems*"; "*the page may crash when more than one user are editing the same page. It is quite annoying*"; "*The "knowledge" write in the article may not be true. Sometimes, I needed to search for more information to ensure the "knowledge". Moreover, some people only created a new page, but when I click into the link, the page is blank. That's make the Wiki writing not professional.*")

4.3 Revision

Revision is the key processing capability of Wiki. However, all the users are able to join the writing task does not mean that they really participate. The quality of the final piece depends a lot on the contribution of some of the early users, then the revisions of the then coming users to add new information, to fill the missing gap, to revise inaccurate information, and to format the presentation. Revisions become a major step in the collaborative writing process. However, who really take part in the revision? When do they think there is a need to revise the writing piece? What do they choose to revise? These all affect the final quality of the written work. The best way to understand all of these is to ask the student journalists how they think while utilizing Wiki to complete the writing task.

Key Motivators to Revising Wiki page: Accuracy, Enrichment and Interesting

What determine them to decide to revise his or her Wiki page? Half of the respondents point out that accuracy is the key motive. It seems quite a clear consensus that student journalists cannot bear any inaccurate information on the Wiki. Typical comments included:

- *When there is a mistake or out-dated information, I will revise it.*
- *If I find the mistakes from the Wiki page, I will do my revision for it.*
- *Whether there is wrong information.*

Moreover, more than one-fourth would consider enrichment by adding new information or further details to the writing as the key motive to revise a Wiki page. Typical comments included:

- *When I find new details about the topic, I will revise my page.*
- *Discover new ideas or receive comments.*

It is also interesting to find that two of them will work on the article if they find it interesting. This is important. In a Wiki project, everyone writes. However, it is not necessary everyone writes on the same article. Rather, everyone finds the topic that he or she is most interested in and they would contribute to their best. At last, every article is to their best as each article is contributed or edited by the most interested and capable ones. We also find other reasons. Someone does it because it is required as a course task while another one revise an article when there are few readers.

On the other hand, what if it is not his or her written Wiki page? What determine them to decide to revise others' Wiki page? This may not be the same factors. To edit others' Wiki page requires additional courage to do so. One will have reservation if he or she cares about how other community users view his or her editing behavior.

Accuracy is still the key motive to revise a Wiki page though this is other's contributing work. Half of the respondents list it as the major motive. However, there are also other factors suggested, including completeness (e.g., *"whether there are missing information"*); enrichment (e.g., *"I have new ideas,"* "I want to add the same views with more explanation," and "I want to add more information on it."); better one's own knowledge (e.g., "I will (force myself to) check other materials from other websites first before I revise others work"); interesting article (e.g., "mainly from curiosity," "when I want to see their opinion (to see other's feedback to my revision).").

Social Interaction in the Writing Process

Social interaction appears in several key steps in the writing process.

In the planning stage, ideas generation and reading Wiki articles become major activities of the writing process. Instead of writing alone, everyone writes on the Wiki site. Any individual would then be a part of the community and be affected by the presence of other users and other written work in the Wiki site. For example,

- *Reading sources is the most significant process of preparing.*
- *First read all text other students have written before writing my own text to avoid repetition which spends me most of the time.*

In the drafting stage, an individual has a lot of concerns. Firstly, s/he knows that there are a lot of other users in the Wiki community. S/he needs to read a lot to take care of others' idea to avoid writing too similarly. Secondly, if s/he needs to build on a previous work, s/he needs to think hard to understand the idea flow before s/he can write further. It is sometimes not easy to understand others, if not one's own writing. Thirdly, there is an anxiety that his or her writing will be revised by others. S/he needs to check on and on to see if there are any changes and if s/he needs to response to those changes. Therefore, the analysis reveals that the presence of other Wiki community users does have impact on the individual learner. It is good to provide a lot of referencing articles for one to generate new ideas; however, it also creates anxiety over too much information. Individual learners typically work independently but are not used to interact with others. This perception will affect much of the effectiveness of peer review in the writing process. Moreover, the unique process capability of Wiki to facilitate editing, on the other hand, post extra burden to individual learners. Typical comments include:

- *The content of articles is too many and too scattered*
- *The greatest problem is that there is already too much information in wiki. I cannot repeat the thing that have already considered. So I must find more information or give up writing.*
- *The greatest problem in using Wiki to write is sometimes I would have problem in understanding other people's writing and don't know how to continue the passage.*

• *It is difficult to start writing because of many suggestions and argue for what we are going to focus. It is hard to find a focus.*
• *The article is easily changed by other users and their work will take the place of mine. The feeling of being replaced is not good.*
• *The greatest problem is the others can change your article content easily. And you can not prevent they add any fake information in the pages.*

After completed the draft, some may stop writing any more while others go on with the revising stage to improve one's writing. Analysis of the reflection reveals that learners do not just totally depend on the system to complete the writing task. They may meet and discuss face-to-face, before, after, or whenever they meet problems in the writing process. Their discussion does not only about the writing details, but also any other problems they meet, especially, technical know-how on presenting their written work on Wiki. Nevertheless, about one-third of the respondents depends totally on the Wiki and do not do any face-to-face discussion. It is important to learn from this analysis that learners find way to solve problem, for example, face-to-face discussion, in addition to the Wiki environment can provide. Typical comments include:

• *I discuss with others before and after I write.*
• *I have discussed with my classmate before I write. After that, if my writing is modified by someone, I will also discuss with them. Through the discussion, we may understand more about the talk.*
• *I discuss the content just because I'm not sure how to write my article or ask others if I have any confusion about the Wiki code I want to use.*
• *Yes, when I cannot sure of the information I find or I cannot find the information.*
• *Yes, I discuss with others before you write, it can make my text contain more ideas, and the accuracy will rise after the discussion.*

Social interaction also affects the revision behavior. In the analysis on the factors to motivate learners to revise his or her Wiki page, one suggests that the browsing hit rate will be one factor (*"I will revise the page when the number of reader is low."*).

On the other hand, in the analysis of the revision work, some will totally leave the hand to the peers. More than half report that they revise their own Wiki page; the remaining half report that they leave the review and revise job to their peers. This is a conflict in thinking. Individual learners leave the burden to peers to revise their own work; however, individual learners have reservation, or are not accustomed to edit others' work. These conflicting perceptions affect the writing process and finally the quality of their written work. Someone must take the initiative and take the role to edit Wiki page should the collaborative process effective. In fact, some learners do have this division of labor to arrange the role of writer and the role of editor in completing the writing task. Typical comments include:

• *I will ask others to help me revise an article...Because the wrong information can be correct by others.*

- *Only by all people's effort can make an article better and better.*
- *I ask others to revise my work because they are in objective position to look at it and add or delete the information which is relevance...Base on the collaboration view, everyone should not only have the responsibility to write but also edit and revise the others work for abundance the whole Wiki page.*
- *Ask groupmates to do. Because we have a common consensus that two groupmates are responsible for writing Wiki and others are searching information.*

The respondents also indicate they have different style in dealing with others in completing the written work. Some are very critical (n=7), some are easy come easy go (n=6), while others are more objective and are only based on facts/content (n=5). Some also mention that they want to be critical but have difficulties in directly voicing out their opinion. Typical comments include:

- *I think I am very critical to others' work and this style forces me to seek for a better outcome of the task.*
- *"Easy come easy go" style. Since the Wiki suggests that people do their own work on the platform and everyone has his/ her style. If I am very critical to others' work, other groupmates cannot express their style (views freely) on the project.*
- *My style is based on fact. If they write something wrong, I will ask them to revise. But if they express their own views, I will respect them and let them go.*

In the revising stage, social interaction also has effects on the revision behavior. Individual learners need to go back and review their work before they would actually revise and improve their work. If they never go back, there is no chance to revise one's article. However, what motivates them to go back and read again their own work? The analysis reveal that half of the respondents do regularly review their own work for mistakes, new ideas and enrichment because of their own style, habit or personal goal of self-improvement. However, in addition to individual characteristics, a lot of them also mention the effects from other community users in the Wiki site. They are expecting comments, revision from other Wiki users, and reviewing the changes. They also care about whether their Wiki page is popular by checking the click rate. Typical comments include:

- *Every time when I go back to review my work, I always think that it is inadequate, no matter contents, information or even page editing, it is not enough. If I am a reader, I want more than that.*
- *Yes, I would like to know (if there is) any amendment of my revision, if there is amendment, I would see how different with my writing and learn from it*
- *I look for the click rate of the pages to determine their popularity.*

Wiki as a Learning Medium to Writing: How Learners Really Use the Wiki and Does the Unique Processing Capability of Wiki Really help?

It is found that half of the respondents do not write directly on Wiki. They write on a Word Processor and then copy and paste their draft to Wiki. Less than half write directly on Wiki. Two other respondents do not indicate clearly the way they do. However, after they post their draft on Wiki, all further revision will be done through Wiki. Wiki records all editing log, with time, date and login ID of the editor. Therefore, although we may miss the preliminary planning and drafting process in the history log, we do record all the revision behavior in Wiki and the learners are interacting with Wiki during the revision process.

5   Discussion, Limitations and Future Research

5.1   Learning News Writing Could Be a Continuous Iterative Revision Process

Individual learner's mental model is affected by the task, the learner and the medium in the learning process [19]. The task in this study is to complete news reporting for the speaker and the talk taken place in the campus. The medium can be in a broad sense to include the technology platform Wiki and each other learners in the Wiki community. Analyzed from the self-reflection of participants using the Wiki, individual learners are being affected in their formation of mental models in the different stages of the writing processes through the use of Wiki. This is not just the individual learner alone learning through his or her own cognition. The present of other users, the written work of them, and the act of revision of others' written work on Wiki all influence each individual learner, as reflected from their self-reflection of the writing process.

While revision is a key to writing as found in prior research, the results of this study consistently reveal that individual learners improve their writing in accuracy, enrichment, new ideas, and presentation through a continuous revision process.

5.2   Student Journalists Benefit from Social Interaction in the Process of Learning News Writing

What motivates learners to revise their work? The results find that individual learners do care about the presence of other users, supported by prior studies on social comparison [20]. They care about whether their work has been viewed and/or has been revised. No matter it really takes place or not, this expectation becomes a motive for individual learners to regular review their written work, and in a higher chance to revise their own work for accuracy and enrichment of content or idea.

Wiki provides a platform for all learners to write and post their written work. It keeps a complete record of any further revisions, including the time, date, editor login ID, and the complete changes. Individual learners can revert any of the previous version as s/he likes. S/he can compare and check any changes in content of the written work. This unique processing capability, on the one hand, facilitates writing processes of individual learners; on the other hand, this also improves the interactions between community users of Wiki, to read others' work, to edit others' work, to read any changes made from other users, and to learn from a different perspective to the same issue.

The result of this study supports the wider social perspective on online learning which reveals that students experience isolation, loneliness, and feelings of alienation and low sense of community [21-23]. The findings show that we cannot disregard the concerns and anxiety of individual learners. These factors would finally affect the motives in using Wiki. For example, the history log of all the prior revisions are complete and useful, however, it is also too much for any individual learners to review once again all the changes every time. Individual learners put great emphasis on accuracy in the written work; however, as it is so easy to edit each others' work, it poses great pressure for each individual learner to validate all the time the truth of for any additional information. There seems lots of information in the Wiki community. To avoid duplication of idea would also put on extra mental burden to individual learners.

5.3 Limitations and Future Research

This is a preliminary study on a specific context, utilizing Wiki for a group of student journalists to collaborate and complete a writing task. The results may only apply with limitations. Future research should expand the study to other disciplines in order to understand better on the impact of Wiki. The results and analysis are based on the self-reflection of respondents who participate in completing the writing task, although this is the appropriate way to capture all the details in understanding the writing process, future research should consider data from various sources, for example, the usage behavior captured by the Wiki. Furthermore, the project groups' design of the present study assumes all group members as contributors and knowledge creators. It would be interesting to see how learning takes place if there are readers (knowledge users) who do not involve in the knowledge creation process, for example, students from other courses. It will also be interesting to see how learning takes place if groups are encouraged to review other groups' work, in addition to his or her group.

6 Conclusion

This preliminary study reflects from the learning experience of a group of student journalists that Wiki provides a unique learning environment to facilitate writing and to enhance learning during the writing process. It provides both a platform for any individual learners to work alone, with the help of the complete editing record; and a platform for all the community users in the Wiki environment to interact with each other and to learn from each other through the revision of each others' written work where the revision behavior is well recorded and transparent to any one of the individual to benefit from it. The qualitative data shows students both value the process and face challenges in managing the complexity of shared editing. Further study in the area, for example, comparing the various use of the Wiki to complete different tasks in different contexts will surely be a promising area to enhance learning and writing.

References

1. Wikipedia: Wiki, vol. 2006 (2006), http://Wikipedia.org
2. Bulik, B.S., Kerwin, A.M.: Media Morph: PBWiki. Advertising Age 77, 35 (2006)
3. Guzdial, M., Rick, J., Kehoe, C.: Beyond Adoption to Invention: Teacher-Created Collaborative Activities in Higher Education. The Journal of the Learning Sciences 10, 265–279 (2001)
4. Raman, M., Ryan, T., Olfman, L.: Designing Knowledge Management Systems for Teaching and Learning with Wiki Technology. Journal of Information Systems Education 16, 311–320 (2005)
5. Ma, W.W.K., Yuen, A.H.K.: Learning News Writing Using Emergent Collaborative Writing Technology Wiki. In: Fong, J., Wang, F.L. (eds.) Blended Learning, pp. 296–307. Pearson, London (2007)
6. Ma, W.W.K., Chan, Y.: Student Journalist Acceptance on Collaborative Writing Wikis. In: Khosrow-Pour, M. (ed.) IRMA 2008 and published in the Proceedings of Information Resources Management Association International Conference. IGI Publishing, Vancouver (2007)
7. Raman, M.: Knowledge Management for Emergency Preparedness: An Action Research Study, p. 300. The Claremont Graduate University (2005)
8. Bulik, B.S.: Media Morph: Digg.com. Advertising Age 77, 19 (2006)
9. Oser, K., Kerwin, A.M.: Media Morph: Wiki. Advertising Age 76, 38 (2005)
10. Dorroh, J.: Wiki: Don't Lost That Number. American Journalism Review 27, 50–51 (2005)
11. Ward, M.: Journalism Online. Focal Press, Oxford (2002)
12. Pogner, K.-H.: Writing and Interacting in the Discourse Community of Engineering. Journal of Pragmatics 35, 855–867 (2003)
13. Roundy, N., Thralls, C.: Modeling the Communication Context: A Procedure for Revision and Evaluation in Business Writing. Journal of Business Communication 20, 27–46 (1983)
14. Jacobs, G., Opdenacker, L., Van Waes, L.: A Multilanguage Online Writing Center for Professional Communication: Development and Testing. Business Communication Quarterly 68, 8–22 (2005)
15. Villamil, O.S., Guerrero, M.C.M.d.: Peer Revision in the L2 Classroom: Social-cognitive Activities, Mediating Strategies, and Aspects of Social Behavior. Journal of Second Language Writing 5, 51–75 (1996)
16. Lomangino, A.G., Nicholson, J., Sulzby, E.: The Influence of Power Relations and Social Goals on Children's Collaborative Interactions While Composing on Computer. Early Childhood Research Quarterly 14, 197–228 (1999)
17. Deuze, M.: Global Journalism Education: A Conceptual Approach. Journalism Studies 7, 19–34 (2006)
18. Kovach, B., Rosenstiel, T.: The Elements of Journalism: What Newspeople Should Know and the Public Should Expect. Three Rivers Press, New York (2007)
19. Kozma, R.B.: Learning with Media. Review of Educational Research 61, 179–221 (1991)
20. Festinger, L.: Informal Social Communication. Psychological Review 57, 271-282 (1950)
21. Mansour, B.E., Mupinga, D.M.: Students' positive and negative experiences in hybrid and online classes. College Student Journal 41, 242–248 (2007)
22. Allan, J., Lawless, N.: Stress caused by on-line collaboration in e-learning: A developing model. Education + Training 45, 564–572 (2003)
23. Conrad, D.L.: Building and maintaining community in cohort-based online learning. Journal of Distance Education 20, 1–20 (2005)

Improving Web-Based Learning by Means of Narrative

Giuliana Dettori

Institute for Educational Technology –National Research Council, Italy
dettori@itd.cnr.it

Abstract. Web-based learning mostly relies on written, asynchronous interaction, which grants learners time for reflection and freedom in the organization of their activity. Written communication, however, is considered an impoverished means by many people, because it lacks non-verbal cues, with consequent negative influence on the quality of the learning process, as concerns both its cognitive and motivational/emotional aspects. Hence, the research on web-based learning is increasingly giving attention to ways to overcome this problem. Based on the analysis of three different examples drawn from the literature, this paper argues that introducing a targeted narrative activity in the design of web-based learning can represent a valuable way to contextualize the learning activity and enhance social presence, in that narrative is a multifaceted form of communication which results natural in all cultures and is suitable for any learning subject.

Keywords: Social presence, narrative, web-based learning.

1 Introduction

It is increasingly recognized in the literature that successful online teaching and learning involve dialogue, that is, the discussion and sharing of ideas among all the subjects involved [1]. Online discourse, however, taking place mostly in written, asynchronous way, is often criticized as an impoverished form of communication, since it lacks non-verbal cues, such as face expression and tone of voice [2], with consequent limited reach and negative influence on the quality of the learning process, in both its cognitive and motivational/emotional aspects. The situation is made worst by the fact that often online participation is affected by some level of anonymity, either because participants use a nickname or simply because they have scarce or none opportunities to meet in person.

Therefore, possible ways to overcome this problem have increasingly been an object of investigation. A number of research studies carried out in the past years have spotted lack of context, of ownership and of social presence as sources of uneasiness in online learning situations, with consequent negative effects on the learning outcomes. A number of approaches to improve online learning in this respect were also proposed, as mentioned in the next section.

In this paper, we argue that including some narrative task in the design of online activities could help learners develop social presence, contextualize their work and

J. Fong, R. Kwan, and F.L. Wang (Eds.): ICHL 2008, LNCS 5169, pp. 115–124, 2008.

gain a sense of ownership of the learning environment, therefore overcoming the limitations of written asynchronous interaction and improving learning effectiveness. To this end, we discuss three examples, drawn from the literature, of different narrative activities that appear suitable for online learning environments, highlighting that narrative can be used in different ways, but with similar benefits, to enhance learning through the development of social presence.

2   Towards Rich Online Learning Experiences

Among the many research studies aiming to improve online learning by overcoming the current limitations of virtual settings, three orientations emerge, that is, attention to context, to feeling of ownership over the learning space and to social presence.

The importance of setting a suitable learning context is highlighted, for instance, by Afonso [3], who points out that virtual educational settings often pay scarce attention to the construction of an appropriate learning context, that is, "everything individuals find as relevant to perform a certain task and make sense of it" (p. 153). Without a relevant context, learning appears much less meaningful. Communities - such as groups of learners working together in virtual settings - help to create contexts for an effective management of learning if they promote interaction, collaboration and a sense of belonging.

Feeling of ownership and inclusion in the learning space are emphasized by Christiansen [4], who attributes the uneasiness of many participants in online learning activities to the "lack of dwelling" which is consequent on the lack of a physical reference point for the learning activities. She observes that the source of problems is not virtuality *per se*, nor written communication (in that letters have always been an effective medium of communication and academic reflection), but the fact that learners need to know that their experience has a place and counts as a contribution in the learning space, where they can feel included, guided and able to transform. This can hardly be achieved if the lack of a physical space is not compensated by suitable features in the organization of the online environments and learning activities.

Social presence, that is, *"the degree to which a person is perceived as a* real person *in mediated communication"* [5, p. 9] is widely discussed in the literature. This concept, which has its roots in previous studies concerning face-to-face communities [6], [7], received much attention after becoming part, with cognitive presence and teaching presence, of the three characterizing dimensions of the Community of inquiry Framework proposed by Garrison, Anderson and Archer [2]. These three kinds of presence correspond to the three kinds of interaction that usually take place in learning activities, that is, with teacher, with content and with the other learners. These authors define it as *"the ability of learners to project themselves socially and emotionally as 'real' people into a community of learners"* [p. 94] and point out that being present entails interacting and relating with people, expressing one's feelings and reacting, being recognized, perceived, accepted, changing or trying to change the others.

It appears from the above definitions that these three orientations are not in contradiction with each other, but only express in different ways the need to set up online learning spaces where the learners may experience inclusion, control and affection, and are encouraged to put themselves deeply into play. In other words, all of them proceed in similar ways to add a dimension of reality to virtual environments, overcoming the lack of social and non-verbal cues by means of suitable, and consistent, activities. We can, therefore, make reference to any of these ways to address the problem with the peace of mind that we are not disregarding the possibilities suggested by other approaches.

Social presence is recognized as very important for the realization of cognitive aims and the development of critical thinking skills [8], [9]. It is rooted in social interaction but does not reduce to it [10], [11]. Since learning in online environments arises from a purposeful integration of cognitive, social and teaching presence, social interaction should be strictly intertwined with learners' cognitive engagement. As Garrison and Cleveland-Innes point out [10], it is not the quantity of interaction that matters, but the quality of discourse. Social interaction and presence may create the conditions for sharing and challenging ideas but does not directly create cognitive presence, which makes learning happen. It appears therefore important to find ways to foster social presence not *per sè* but in relation with the cognitive task at hand.

The realization of social presence is not automatic nor easy, but needs to be stimulated and supported by means of appealing, engaging, and rewarding group interactions. Several authors in the literature (e.g. [6], [11]) offer a number of suggestions to support its creation, addressed either to course designers - such as posting welcome messages, including participants' profile, structuring collaborative activities - and to course participants (tutors and learners) - such as improving expressiveness by means of emoticons, replying promptly, asking thought-provoking questions, keeping focused). Aragon [6] also mentions that tutors and learners should share personal stories and experiences as a way to achieve credibility and to improve active participation.

We go further, suggesting that a purposeful use of narrative - in the form of stories and narrations - should be included in the design of online learning activities, so as to make use of it systematically and in relation with the learning tasks, rather than leaving its presence depend on voluntary and sporadic actions of individual participants, with outcomes that are possibly unrelated with each other and with the learning task. As we will argue in the next sections, narrative can be a valuable tool in supporting the creation of social presence, and deserves to be exploited more widely than it is at present.

3   Learning Potential of Narrative

Narrative has been increasingly used in education in the past decade, since it is recognized as a natural expressive form for people of any age and culture [12], as well as a privileged way to help develop cognitive abilities and organize knowledge [13]. It leads people to engage in symbolic activities to construct and make sense of themselves and work out a coherent meaning for their experiences [14].

The roots of this rich cognitive potential can be recognized in the definition that Bruner [14, p. 43] gives of narrative as "...*a unique sequence of events, mental states, happenings. ... But these constituents do not have a life or meaning of their own. Their meaning is given by their place in the overall configuration of the sequence as a whole*" . This definition spots the presence of logical relationships among narrative elements as a key point provoking active thinking and supporting meaning construction. This concerns both invented narratives (stories) and true ones (history and narrations of experience) [15].

The literature highlights that narrative's positive influence on learning concerns not only cognition, but also motivation and emotions. As Bruner [14] points out, *"narrative in all its forms is a dialectic between what was expected and what came to pass"* (p.15), as well as *"an invitation to problem finding, not a lesson in problem solving"* (p. 20). For this reason, the use of narrative in learning can be challenging and stimulate curiosity and fantasy, which are major components of intrinsic motivation. The support to emotions raises from the fact that narrative is based on an interplay between characters and causation [16], which leads the user to highlight aspects of personality, emotional state and social standing, as well as the motives and intentions which underlie actions.

Narrative can help the creation of social presence of the participants in online learning activities in a variety of ways, for several reasons:

- Narrative always has a narrator, hence it is told from an explicitly declared perspective, which can help people get aware of the existence of many agents and different points of view.

- Narrative concerns actions and events, which are something concrete and apt to raise mental images in its readers/listeners; this helps overcome the abstractness of virtual environments and constitute solid ground for discussion and reflection; as Wenger [17, pg. 203] points out, *"stories ... can be appropriated easily because they allow us to enter the events, the characters and their plights by calling upon our imagination"*.

- Sharing stories is traditionally a social activity, hence narrative is particularly suitable to create a social atmosphere; this is important from the point of view of learning, in that *"the cultural contexts that favour mental development are principally and inevitably interpersonal"* [18, p. 68].

- Narrative can be useful in the creation of learning contexts engaging learners from the emotional/motivational point of view and connecting this aspect with content knowledge [19].

4 Supporting Social Presence by Means of Narrative

4.1 Sharing Personal Experiences

Arnold et al. [20] report the case of a group of students involved in a distance education degree program, who autonomously organized a discussion space, independently of their study provider, where they used to share personal stories concerning their learning strategies, issues, feelings and attitudes. Stories shared in this space were often prompted by participants' questions on how to organize online learning or how to carry out some task, and were reported in narrative form. The authors do not specify the study subject of this group of students, nor the structure and social organization of the courses they were enrolled in. We may suppose, however, that the social aspects of the course they were taking were not well supported, since the students felt the need to create an external social space to exchange information and opinions and to reflect together on the online learning experience.

As the authors point out, personal stories narrated in this example represent a potential learning resource for all participant. With this mean, learning actions become visible and provoke reaction and reflection. Thanks to these personal narrations, the strategies suggested to tackle tasks or to cope with the novelty of online learning are perceived quite differently than analogous suggestions possibly provided by official booklets, whose authors remain invisible. This kind of stories let the participants' context emerge, both at individual and community level.

This case exemplifies well the need of online students to develop a social dimension. This is pointed out by the fact that the community was started by the students themselves, independently of the study provider, and by their need to get support avoiding the anonymity of user manuals and online helps. We can view the social activity carried out in this environment as a kind of technical support concerning online learning, realized by means of stories. This narrative form of communication appears to play a central role in the existence and meaning of such a community: giving each other support in plain technical way would probably be perceived as a plain time-consuming service, and therefore, on the long run, as a burden to drop. Sharing personal narrations, on the contrary, appears enriching for the authors as much as for the readers, in that narrating is a powerful way to make sense of one's own experience, as pointed out in the literature (see Section 3). A narrative activity of this kind within an online community is a way to disclose one's own presence in a rich and meaningful way, as well as a useful support to reflection on one's own learning process.

Moreover, narrating personal experiences, helps the students acquire awareness of one's own strategies and achievements, prompted by the questions of peers, and therefore supports self-awareness and self-efficacy; it also stimulates reflection and meta-reflection, through comparison of the perspectives of different narrators. Since all these are important components of self-regulated learning [21], making oneself socially visible by means of this reciprocal narrative activity appears not only as a good way to acquire knowledge, but also as an occasion to consolidate learning competence.

4.2 A Narrative Simulation Game

In a master on juridical translation to several languages, run for the past 5 years by the Faculty of Foreign languages of the University of Genoa [22], a socio-professional simulation game is proposed at the beginning of the course. This master, which is addressed to graduate students with at least an average knowledge of the language of their interest, aims to build competence in the translation of juridical documents. It is run completely online, lasts 25 weeks and includes both individual and collaborative activities. At the beginning of the course, participants are split in groups of 4 to 6 people, with heterogeneous background and different language levels.

The simulation game proposed consists in asking the groups to get organized as real "translation agencies". Based on this assumption, all the master activities are seen as steps of a context in which the agencies take part to win a big translation job offered by the European Community. This gives a slightly playful flavour to the various tasks proposed during the master, and motivates the students to tackle them in professional way, committing to obtain the best scores and hence win the context. The first of the assigned tasks is a self-presentation that each "translation agency" is asked to build, so as to look professional and appealing. The invitation to behave like a real translation agency is then carried on throughout the master, with the aim to encourage the students to take advantage as much as possible from the collaboration with the group mates.

Lupi and colleagues [22] analysed the interactions inside the course from different points of view, and compared the outcomes of an edition of the master in which the simulation game was widely exploited with another edition where it was not. They remarked that the interactions were much more numerous and alive in the first case, and the participants obtained better results in the final exam.

The apparently childish task to prepare a professional presentation for a hypothetical translation agency is actually the occasion to learn expressive forms which may be useful at professional level, and at the same time has several positive side-effects on the overall learning. It helps group members to get acquainted with each other, which is essential to establish and exploit social presence; it helps set up negotiation dynamics inside the groups, which is crucial in the subsequent joint translation work [23]; and it boosts a creative attitude towards the course work, which is important non only because creativity appears to support social presence [24], but also because the law systems of different countries are not completely congruent and hence translating juridical documents is not simply a matter of learning technical words, but also, and especially, to find the best possible correspondent of the juridical concepts in the documents assigned for translation. Hence, we clearly see in this case a strict intertwinement of social interaction and cognitive activity.

This simulation is actually a narrative activity, in that the students are invited to take part in a role playing game, where the roles played are imaginary but realistically connected with the (possible) future profession of the participants, and the actions they are asked to perform in such roles leads them to show their presence in group work and at the same time to immerse themselves in the cognitive task assigned. The stories that come out from this role playing are the daily activities of groups of professional translators who put into play their own abilities and personality to emerge over their competitors. The effect on social presence is therefore evident, and so is also the boost granted to motivation and learning.

The positive influence on social presence and learning of asking the students to act as if they were in a given role is underlined by Garrison and Cleveland-Innes [10], who point out that it leads the students to bypass their own social identity as students and work with the course material from a different (and hopefully wider) perspective.

4.3 Narrating by Means of Metaphors

Delfino & Manca [25] and Delfino [26] describe two studies on the use of metaphors in the online component of a blended course in educational technologies, addressed to trainee teachers.

In the first study, the use of metaphors spontaneously arose during the course, without being encouraged by the tutors. They were equally used by students with any background, and emerged more frequently in relation with meaningful or critical events. They were used by course participants as a means to express in a vivid way their view of the learning environment and to disclose their identity, emotions, feelings, without the need to talk of themselves directly, in first person.

In the second study, on the other hand, the use of metaphors was explicitly stimulated, by asking the students to tackle the course as a sea journey and by giving the discussion conferences in the familiarization area the name of different types of boat (e.g., fishing boat, caravel, cruise liner etc.). The study reports that participants mostly accepted without problem the request to use the metaphor of navigation, expressed a good amount of creativity in its use, and even extended it beyond the end of the familiarization phase where it had been proposed.

Summarising the outcomes of the two studies, Delfino [25] concludes that figurative language proved to be beneficial to support the participants' social interaction, in particular by facilitating the expression of emotions associated with the learning experience. It resulted to be a creative way to give concreteness to the virtual space where the course was taking place. It allowed the students to alleviate their anxiety for the new way to take a course by expressing their emotions in disguised but effective form, that is, by describing themselves and their actions by means of images of animals, vehicles, fictional characters, etc. (e.g. "In this brand-new activity, I feel like a little turtle going slowly, slowly ..."). Hence, the use of metaphors resulted as a non intrusive and very expressive way to develop social presence and at the same time reflect on the learning experience carried out.

Certainly figurative language can not always be viewed as narrative, when it consists of static images depicting a situation rather than narrating actions, mental states and events. It appears proper, however, to consider it a narrative form in this example, since the use made by the students was actually to share with the course mates actions and feelings that it would have been difficult, for subjective or objective reasons, to communicate in other form. Moreover, in the second case metaphors followed the students throughout the course, creating a sort of continuing story of the various boats while finding their way through the difficult sea of the unusual learning environment.

The association with vivid and concrete images allowed by figurative language appears, therefore, as a powerful way to make oneself present in a shared virtual space. Moreover, the choice of unreal characters and features to describe one's actions and feelings allows, better than plain language, the modulation of emphasis (for instance, the turtle in the above example is defined as "small", and this adjective, modifying the image, points out something important concerning its authors, who likely, with plain language, would not have defined herself as "small" to convey her sense of humility with respect to the task at hand). This image-based emphasis appears to compensate for the lack of non-verbal cues in written language, and hence, despite its making reference to imagined things and events, it helps to cope with the virtuality of online environments.

5 Concluding Remarks

The three examples selected represent different ways to use a narrative activity in web-based learning to support the development of social presence, and by this means favour understanding and learning. They obviously do not cover all possibilities in this respect; they, however, can well give an idea of the range of possibilities offered by narrative for this purpose.

In the self-organized community of students, real stories are narrated; the students talk from their own position and disclose themselves to their peers, giving concreteness, by this means, to their own person and at the same time to the competence they share. Social presence is created by providing each other support, with a positive influence on both the cognitive and emotional aspects of learning.

In the simulation game, the narrative is between real and unreal, in that the students are invited to play a role which is not their true one at the moment, but is one they could be playing for real in the near future, thanks to the competence they are acquiring in the course. Hence, narrative appears here as a way of conceptually situating learners in their possible future working contexts, helping them to establish a mental connection with the professional community in which the competence they are acquiring makes most sense. Playing their role in the simulation appears as a way for the learners to intertwine and make explicit their social and cognitive presences.

In the courses where metaphors were used, the narrative is completely unreal. Nevertheless, the narrative framework set up by figurative language resonates with learners' perception of the course as a journey into an unknown world, and allows them to express their feelings and thoughts in an imaginative and not embarrassing way. Social presence is induced by the rich possibilities to express oneself, and reinforced by the narrativity of metaphors, which, in turn, boosts cognitive presence by stimulating reflection.

Despite their differences, all the described ways to establish social presence by means of a narrative activity appear to have been effective, and to have induced a positive influence on learning. This is independent of the content knowledge addressed in the respective learning activities. This is not surprising, since, as pointed out in Section 3, narrative is not simply an activity, but rather a form of thought which is innate in human beings, as well as a natural form of communication.

None of these different ways to use narrative appears to be preferable to the others, but rather they have different aims and effects; hence, the choice for one or the other can only be determined by the features and requirements of the context of use, as well as the inclination of the course designers, teachers/tutors and participants.

In all cases, the use of other kinds of discourse - such as descriptions or argumentations - does not appear as much suitable to induce the same effect, since none of them entail like narrative the presence of narrating voices, which socially recalls the presence of narrators.

In the three examples, the generated narrations appear to be connected to learning in a subtle way, that is, not only to the content knowledge which is object of study, but especially to the learning process and competence growth. In this respect, in all three cases the narrative activity, besides helping to develop social presence, constitutes a useful starting point for meta-reflection. This suggests a consideration regarding the educational power of web-base learning, that is, making good use of it entails to put effort on aspects, like social presence, which are usually taken for granted in face-to-face learning, but this extra effort required is in the end rewarded by students' achievement of a better awareness of their learning.

In conclusion, this study underlines, in the wake of other recent studies, that communication within web-based learning environments is not necessarily impoverished with respect to face-to-face one. Learners can avoid feelings of isolation and anonymity in several ways; the implementation of a narrative activity can very well serve this purpose.

References

1. Forret, M., Khoo, E., Cowie, B.: New Wine or New Bottles: What's new about online teaching. In: Figueiredo, A.D., Afonso, A.P. (eds.) Managing Learning in Virtual Setting: the role of context, pp. 253–273. Information Science Publishing, Hershey (2006)
2. Garrison, D.R., Anderson, T., Archer, W.: Critical inquiry in a text-based environment: computer conferencing in higher education. The Internet and Higher Education 2(2-3), 87–105 (2000)
3. Afonso, A.P.: Communities as Context Providers for Web-Based learning. In: Figueiredo, A.D., Afonso, A.P. (eds.) Managing Learning in Virtual Setting: the role of context, pp. 135–163. Information Science Publishing, Hershey (2006)
4. Christiansen, E.: Space as a learning context: The role of Dwelling in the Development of Academic Reflection. In: Figueiredo, A.D., Afonso, A.P. (eds.) Managing Learning in Virtual Setting: the role of context, pp. 84–97. Information Science Publishing, Hershey (2006)
5. Gunawardena, G.N., Zittle, F.J.: Social presence as a predictor of satisfaction within a Computer-mediated conferencing environment. The American Journal of Distance Education 11(3), 8–26 (1997)
6. Aragon, S.R.: Creating Social presence in Online Environments. New Directions for Adult and Continuing education 100, 57–68 (2003)
7. Garrison, D.R., Arbaugh, J.B.: Researching the community of inquiry framework: Review, issues and future directions. The Internet and Higher Education 10, 157–172 (2007)
8. Rourke, L., Anderson, T., Garrison, D.R., Archer, W.: Methodological Issues in the Content Analysis of Computer Conference Transcripts. International Journal of Artificial Intelligence in Education 12, 8–22 (2001)
9. Rovai, A.P.: Facilitating online discussion effectively. The Internet and Higher Education 10, 77–88 (2007)
10. Garrison, D.R., Cleveland-Innes, M.: Facilitating Cognitive presence in Online learning: Interaction is not enough. The American Journal of Distance education 19(3), 133–148 (2005)
11. Goertzen, Ph., Kristjánsson, C.: Interpersonal Dimensions of Community in graduate online learning: Exploring social presence through the lens of Systemic Functional Linguistics. The Internet and Higher education 10, 212–230 (2007)
12. Bruner, J.: Acts of meaning. Massachusetts. Harvard University Press, Cambridge (1990)
13. Shank, R.C.: Tell Me a Story - Narrative and Intelligence, 3rd printing. Northwestern University Press, Evanston (2000)
14. Bruner, J.: Making Stories. Harvard University Press, Cambridge (2003)
15. Ricoeur, P.: Hermeneutics and the Human Sciences. Thompson, J.B.(ed), 17th edn. Cambridge University Press, Cambridge (2005)
16. Aylett, R.: And they both lived happily ever after? In: Dettori, G., Giannetti, T., Paiva, A., Vaz, A. (eds.) Technology-Mediated Narrative Environments for Learning, pp. 5–25. Sense Publishers, Rotterdam-Taipei (2006)
17. Wenger, E.: Communities of Practices. Learning meaning and identity. Cambridge University Press, Cambridge (1998)

18. Bruner, J.: The culture of Education. Harvard University Press, Cambridge, MA (1996)
19. Dettori, G., Morselli, F.: Accessing Knowledge through Narrative Context. In: IFIP Int. Conf. WCC 2008. ED-L2L (in print, 2008)
20. Arnold, P., Smith, J.D., Trayner, B.: Narrative: designing for context in virtual settings. In: Figueiredo, A.D., Afonso, A.P. (eds.) Managing Learning in Virtual Setting: the role of context, pp. 197–218. Information Science Publishing, Hershey (2006)
21. Shunk, Zimmermann: Self-regulated learning. From teaching to Self-reflective practice. The Guildford Press, New York (1998)
22. Lupi, V., Pozzi, F., Torsani, S.: La dimension sociale dans un Master post-universitaire a distance: outils, animations et analyse des interaction (Social dimension in a post-graduate, online master: tools, animations and interaction analysis). In: Lamy, Mangenot, Nissen (eds.) Actes du colloque Echanger pour apprendre en ligne (EPAL), Grenoble, june 7-9 (2007) (in French) http://w3.u-grenoble3.fr/epal/actes.html
23. Torsani, S.: Didattica delle lingue in rete e ambienti virtuali di apprendimento (Online language teaching and virtual learning environments). Doctoral Dissertation in Language, Culture and ICT, University of Genoa, Italy (in Italian) (2008)
24. Manca, S.: Presenza sociale e apprendimento in rete: stato dell'arte e prospettive di ricerca (Social presence and online learning: state of the art and research perspectives). In: Proceedings of Didamatica 2004, pp. 369–378 (2004) (in Italian)
25. Delfino, M., Manca, S.: The expression of social presence through the use of figurative language in a web-based learning environment. Computers in Human Behavior 23(5), 2190–2211 (2007)
26. Delfino, M.: How to create places with words: The role of spatial metaphors in web-based learning environments. Doctoral Dissertation in Languages, Culture and ICT, University of Genoa, Italy (2008)

Analyzing Peer Interactions in Computer-Supported Collaborative Learning: Model, Method and Tool*

Yanyan Li and Ronghuai Huang

Knowledge Science & Engineering Institute, School of Education Technology,
Beijing Normal University, 100875, Beijing, China
liyy1114@gmail.com

Abstract. One of the most important facets in CSCL research is the interaction between individual and collaborative learning activities. This paper proposes a holistic and complementary analysis model of the collaborative interactions base on three dimensions – process pattern, social relationship and topic space. By making use of content analysis, social network analysis and text mining technologies, asynchronous discussion transcripts are semi-automatically processed to address the questions concerned with peer interactions in collaborative learning: what are they talking about, who are talking to whom, and how do they talking with others. An integrated tool with comprehensive functionalities is designed and implemented to support collaborative interaction analysis with intelligence and visualization features. With the assistance of the tool, a case study is conducted to analyze the discussion records of a class composed of 18 graduate students who enrolled in a course along with online discussion in knowledge forum platform.

Keywords: CSCL, Interaction Analysis, Text Mining, Content Analysis Tool, Social Network Analysis.

1 Introduction

Currently, there is a growing adoption of computer-based facilities in educational practice to foster online collaboration. This practice is commonly described as the field of Computer Supported Collaborative Learning (CSCL). In CSCL environments, online asynchronous discussion takes a central place, which allows learners to share information, exchange ideas, address problems and discuss on specific themes. All exchanges of information between students are stored in the discussion transcripts. These transcripts can be used by teachers and students for reflection purposes or they can serve as data for research [9]. This asynchronous interaction, confined in the transcripts of the discussion, is thus the object of a large body of recent educational research.

So far, several approaches have been put forth to analyze interactions in the computer-supported collaborative learning (CSCL). The typical methods include analysis

---

* The research work was supported by the National Science Foundation of China (NSFC: 60705023).

J. Fong, R. Kwan, and F.L. Wang (Eds.): ICHL 2008, LNCS 5169, pp. 125–136, 2008.

of computer-generated quantitative log files, social network analysis, discourse analysis and content analysis [4]. Quantitative log files generated and stored in the CSCL environments serve as an easily accessible source for analyzing collaborative process, but Nurmela et al. point out that researchers should not heavily depend on the information recorded in log files, but to combine this with an analysis of its content, especially the content of collaborative dialog or discourse [11]. Social network analysis (SNA) is usually used to study the way people participated and interacted with each other, especially investigates the relationship between participants rather than the discussion content. Discourse analysis is a broad and complex interdisciplinary field involving linguistics, anthropology, and sociology, which focuses on studying the naturally-occurring speech or conversation in context. But the indetermination of context causes the difficulty for understanding language use. Content analysis is defined as "a research methodology that builds on procedures to make valid inferences from text" [2]. Wever et al. [16] give an overview of different content analysis schemes that reflect the diversity in the theoretical base, the amount of information about validity and reliability, and the choice for the unit of analysis. Compared with other methods, content analysis is widely used to analyze and assess the collaborative interaction. The traditional content analysis mainly depends on the manual coding, which is time-consuming and tedious for the researchers. So it is indispensable to make use of tools to facilitate coding process for the interaction discourse analysis.

The aim of this kind of research is to provide a more complete picture of peer interaction in CSCL based on interaction analysis. We believe that these understandings will contribute to the development of better pedagogical frameworks and software that more effectively support learning and tutoring by design. Therefore, by incorporating content analysis, text mining, and social network analysis, this paper proposes a multidimensional analysis model to study peer interactions, expecting to provide an integrated foundation for in-depth investigation of collaborative learning in CSCL. The three methods are used to triangulate and contextualize our findings and to stay close or connected to the first-hand experiences of the participants themselves. Furthermore, this paper describes the design and implementation of an intelligent content analysis tool by adopting the quantitative statistics for participation and interaction analysis, and text analysis in addition to the semi-automatic coding support.

2 A Multidimensional Analysis Model to Study Collaborative Interaction

Discussion boards are one of the most commonly used facilities to support collaborative learning. Asynchronous text-based discussions present several advantages as compared to synchronous discussions: students get more opportunities to interact with each other and students have more time to reflect, think, and search for extra information before contributing to the discussion [17]. The facts that all communication elements are made explicit in the written contributions to the discussions. By browsing the discussion transcripts, teachers and researchers are mostly interested in the following three questions.

- How do the students talking with others?
- What are the students talking about?
- Who are talking to whom?

When the teachers find out the answers to the questions, it is helpful for them to further understand the students' collaborative process, discover the possible existing problems with regard to the collaborative interaction, and accordingly take the necessary intervention strategies to facilitate collaborative learning.

Inspired by the three questions, we propose a multidimensional research model for studying peer interaction in CSCL, as shown in figure 1. The model comprises three dimensions: Process Pattern, Topic Space, and Social Network. Process Pattern reflects the interaction patterns among students involved in the collaborative learning, which emphasizes probing the diverse speech intentions and changing trend. Topic space reflects the knowledge or concepts that students used in collaborative learning process, which focuses on recognizing the discussion topics emerged in the participants' interaction. Social relationship reflects the dynamic mechanism influencing knowledge flow. It is to find out the relationship between the participants in collaborative learning, and the diverse roles the participants play to fulfill a specified task.

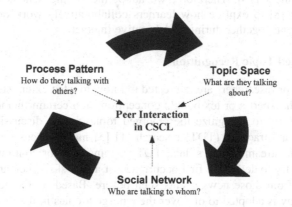

Fig. 1. A Multidimensional research model for studying collaborative interaction

3 Methods

3.1 Content Analysis

Content analysis is often adopted to unlock the information captured in transcripts of asynchronous discussion groups with the aim to reveal information that is not situated at the surface of the transcripts. To find out how do the students talking (interacting) with others, we adopt content analysis to investigate the possible process patterns within the collaboration interaction. That is, annotate the speech intention of discourse records and then make a quantitative analysis to discover the distribution of speech intentions and changing trend.

Although this research technique is often used, standards are not yet established [16]. The applied coding schemes reflect a wide variety of approaches and differ in their level of detail and the type of analysis categories used. Further differences are related to diversity in their theoretical base, the amount of information about validity and reliability, and the choice for the unit of analysis. So far, many researchers have proposed diverse coding schemes for content analysis. Henri proposes a coding scheme consists of five dimensions: participative, social, interactive, cognitive and metacognitive [5]. Newman et al. argue that there is a clear link between critical thinking, social interaction and deep learning, and accordingly developed a coding scheme composed of 10 categories [10]. Based on the combination of Vygotsky's theory and theories sof cognitive and constructive learning, Zhu divides the social interaction into vertical interaction and horizontal interaction [18]. The coding scheme developed by Veerman and Veldhuis-Diermanse [14] identifies two categories of messages: task-related and non-task-related messages. Task-related messages are further subdivided into three categories: new ideas, explanation, and evaluation. [2] presents the coding scheme for measuring cognitive, social, and teaching presence.

Nevertheless, Rourke and Anderson [12] suggest that instead of developing new coding schemes, researchers should use schemes that have been developed and used in previous research. Applying existing instruments fosters replicability and the validity of the instrument [13]. Therefore, we adopt the coding scheme developed by Chen-Chung Liu [8] to explore how learners collaboratively work on the task and formulate arguments together during collaborative interaction.

3.2 Theme-Based Topic Recognition

Usually teachers or researchers are interested to know to what extent students' discussion overlap with expert's or textbook's conception on a certain themes in a discussion. So, it is useful to recognize the emerged topics in the discussion transcripts. Topic detection and tracking (TDT) research [1] [3] mainly focus on detecting and tracking events in streaming news data. TDT systems monitor continuously updated news stories and try to detect the first occurrence of a new story; i.e., an event significantly different from those news events seen before. Based on the approaches, text mining technology is adopted to discover the emerged topics in the discourse records of students. The key idea is that teachers initially present the themes that are expected to be talked by the students, and then the postings in a discussion thread are combined into a document. Afterwards, parse the documents and compute the semantic similarity with the theme vector proposed by the teachers. If the document is similar to an existing theme, the postings in the documents will be labeled with such theme; otherwise, it will be labeled as a new theme with related keywords description.

Assuming that the postings in a discussion thread represent the same topic, we combine them into a summary document and then process it. Each document is represented as a weighted term vector $d = (d_1, d_2, \ldots)$ with the standard TFIDF function.

$$d_i = TF(w_i, d) \cdot \log(\frac{|E|}{DF(w_i)}) \tag{1}$$

Where the term frequency $TF(w_i, d)$ is the number of times word w_i occurs in document d, $|E|$ denotes the total number of documents in the training set and the $DF(w_i)$ is the number of postings containing the word w_i at least one time.

We consider the text in title field and body field of postings separately but discriminatively. Usually, title is the outline of body contents, so words in title filed are more descriptive and discriminative in contrast to the words in body field. Thus, words in title field are assigned larger weights to reinforce their stronger impact. For TF(w_i, d), one time appearance in title field equals to t times appearances in body field. The cosine method is adopted to compute the similarity between the document vector and the theme vector defined by the teachers, and thus the documents belong to the certain concept with the maximum similarity value.

3.3 Augmented Social Network Analysis

Social Network Analysis (SNA) is an established method to derive person-person relations in the form of sociograms from "traces" of communication in a networked community [15]. It is widely used to study the way people participated and interacted with each other in discussion boards [6], which provides information about the activities of such a community and the way they learn collaboratively. The discussion transcripts can be treated as relational data and stored away in a case-by-case matrix to analyze interaction patterns. A few of indicators are computed in SNA, such as betweenness, centrality, clique, cohesion, to indicate the activities of such a community and the way they learn collaboratively. But this method is simply based on the information flow between learners but ignore the content of postings, so the constructed social network is very large and complex. To better reflect the peer collaboration in CSCL, we focus on the theme-centered social network of the peers who are engaged in the same theme.

After determining the theme of each threaded-notes with above-mentioned method, the following formula are used to compute several criteria for evaluating a student's performance in the collaborative interaction, including participation, authority, novelty, coverage, and activity.

Participation

$$P_i = \beta \cdot \sqrt{\frac{I_i}{\sum_{f=1..l} I_f}} + (1-\beta) \cdot \sqrt{\frac{R_i}{\sum_{f=1..l} R_f}}, \beta \in [0,1] \qquad (2)$$

Where Ii denotes the number of postings initiated by the ith person, Ri denotes the number of postings replying to others posted by the ith person, l denotes the total number of students involved in the theme discussion.

Authority

$$A_i = \frac{\sum_{t=1..I_i} \left(\frac{I_t^c}{max(I^c)} + \frac{I_t^r}{max(I^r)} \right)}{2I_i} \qquad (3)$$

Where I_t^c denotes the times of clicking by others for the tth posting initiated by the ith person, I_t^r denotes the times of replying by others for the tth posting initiated by the ith person. Ii denotes the total number of postings delivered by the ith person. max(Ic) and max(Ir) denotes the maximum clicking-times and replying-times for a posting.

Novelty

$$N_i = \frac{M_f}{M} \qquad (4)$$

Where M_f represents the number of theme-related keywords mentioned for the first time by ith student, M represents the total number of keywords mentioned by the ith student.

Coverage

$$C_i = \frac{I_i^k}{I_i} \qquad (5)$$

Where I_i^k denotes the number of postings pasted by the ith student that belong to the kth theme, I_i denotes the total number of postings pasted by the ith student.

Activity

$$AC_i = \frac{N_i}{\Delta t_p} \times \frac{1}{(t - t_d) + \tau} \qquad (6)$$

Where N_i represents the number of postings posted by the ith person during the period Δt_p, t is the current date and t_d is the date the ith person posted the latest posting in the forum. τ is the adjust parameter to avoid the denominator is zero, and it is initially assigned 1.

4   Implementing a Tool to Support Collaborative Interaction Analysis

We have developed a tool VINCA (Visual Intelligent Content Analyzer) with C# language to support interaction analysis. It is implemented by using C/S architecture and can be installed stand-alone or support the online downloading of the forum text from CSCL platform to conduct analysis. The tool provides a plug-in interface allowing for flexible addition of more modules. Figure 2 shows the framework to design the content analysis tool. It mainly comprises three modules: data preparation, text analysis, as well as visualization & Export. The preparation module allows the users to import data in the format of HTML files, XML files, database, or text from different CSCL platforms, and then transforms the data into a standard relational database format automatically. The text analysis module is to analyze the raw transcripts or the coded transcripts with the support of keyword extraction, concordance viewing, and text similarity computation. The visualization & Export module provides visualization (e.g. graphs, curves, tables) of analysis results or export the multiple analysis results in the format of .csv files for further quantitative and code co-location explorations. More information can refer to [7].

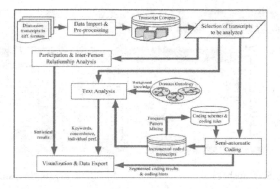

Fig. 2. Framework for designing the content analysis tool

Figure 3 - figure 6 are the snapshots of the tool interface. Figure 3 shows the semi-automatic coding interface. As the figure shows, the coding hint is marked with red color and its corresponding recommended candidate codes are listed in the right part of the interface with the support percentage and confidence percentage. During the coding process, VINCA will scan each segment to locate the coding hints, highlight the hints, and then recommend the candidate codes with two computerized indicators: support and confidence percentage. The support indicator represents the hints appearance frequency in the transcripts corpus, while the confidence indicator means the reliability of the recommended codes. Users can accept the recommended codes or refuse it by selecting other code. The coding process and coding errors will be recorded. Thereafter, VINCA will make use of the hints, mistakes and missing lists of discourse segments and the coding effectiveness statistics to improve on the coding rules. Figure 4 illustrates the visualization of the coding results, including the coding distribution and coding changing trends. Figure 5 shows the interface to set the analysis parameter and show the extracted keywords, frequency, speakers, etc. The users can also click any keyword to view its concordance in the lower part of the interface. Furthermore, after importing the domain ontology constructed by the teachers or the researchers, VINCA support the evaluation of individual's performance by computing the topic relevance, novelty, and extension. One outstanding feature of VINCA is its coding rule learning mechanism by discovering the frequent pattern from the database of increased coding

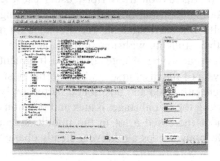

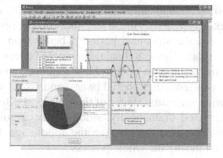

Fig. 3. Snapshot1   **Fig. 4.** Snapshot2

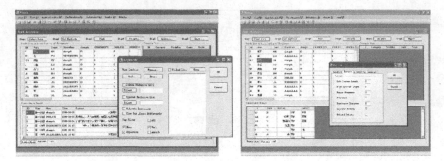

Fig. 5. Snapshot3   **Fig. 6.** Snapshot4

expertise. As figure 6 illustrates, the users can set the configuration for the pattern discovery and then check the resulting pattern in the lower part of the interface. Users can then select all or some patterns to add into the coding rules database.

5   A Case Study

We conduct an experiment to investigate the peer interaction in CSCL. A class of 18 graduate students majoring in Education Technology" enrolled in the course "Key Technologies in E-Learning and Application". During the semester from Sep. 2007 to Jan. 2008, the students took the course with a hybrid learning of two-lesson face-to-face learning each week as well as collaborative learning in Knowledge Forum (KF: http://kf.cite.hku.hk) anytime. Except the learning in the classroom, the graduate students were required to fulfill the assigned activities through online discussion. We chose a set of discourse data recorded in the KF platform as data source, and then use the coding component, text analysis, and data export component of VINCA to help analyzing the sampled data, for the purpose of unveiling the students' peer interaction in terms of process pattern, topic space and social network.

- **Process Pattern**

With the assistance of VINCA, two coders took the meaning unit as the basic analysis unit and performed the coding with the coding schema. The coding scheme is tabulated in table 1. After finishing the coding of discussion transcripts, users use the coding visualization module to view the coding distribution and coding changing trends. Figure 7 illustrates the coding results for each student. As the histogram shows, the student 8 performs better than other students with maximum notes. Furthermore, figure 8 displays the change trend of each type of notes during a fragment of the discussion period. Time sequence analysis of the discourses indicated that positions often outnumbered issues, and issues were proposed and positioned increasingly during the initial stages of the activity. Following the initial stage, issues and positions decreased dramatically. Additionally, argument increased a lot in the middle stage, but decreased sharply after the middle age. Response keeps a relatively steady change trend during the whole process.

Table 1. Coding scheme

Type	Meaning
Issue	What needs to be done and problems to solved, and related to the concepts and skills being learned by students.
Position	Methodologies for resolving an issue, and are answers from peers in response to issues that have been raised.
Argument	Opinions that support or object to a position
Group development	Questions raised to coordinate members to work together
Response	A suggested answer to a group development question
Acceptance of response	The acceptance or agreement of a response
Objection to response	Student objection or disagreement to responses
Conflict	Contradiction occurs among students
Support request	A request for resources and help from other group members

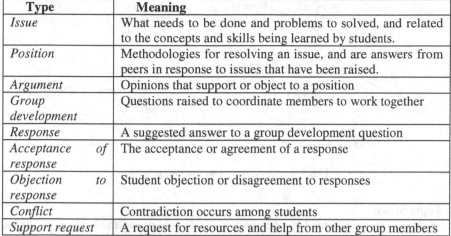

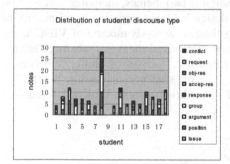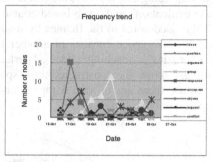

Fig. 7. Visualization of coding statistics   **Fig. 8.** Changing trend of each type of notes

Additionally, students were divided into five groups and were assigned an activity of "Design of vertical search engine". Each group was asked to collaboratively determine the topic of the search and task allocation through online discussion in knowledge Forum. Afterwards, their discourse records were analyzed via using VINCA to further investigate the interaction pattern among members. Herein we select two groups (group A and group B) for illustrative purpose. Figure 9 shows the interaction pattern graphs for the two groups, respectively. As the figure indicates, two groups has quite different interaction pattern. Regarding group A, a2 plays a central role within the group by organizing the group collaboration and receiving many responses from other members. This kind of interaction can be defined as centralized knowledge exchange. By contrast, there is no central member within group B. All of the members in group B interact with each other by expressing opinions or giving answers to other's question. So, this kind of interaction is more likely to be called distributive knowledge exchange.

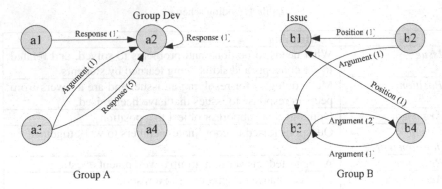

Fig. 9. Peer interaction within two groups

- **Topic Space**

A learning activity assigned by the teacher is "discussing on the web-based course analyzing", and all the students were required to exchange their ideas via the KF platform. Regarding this activity, the teacher assigned two themes, including "web-based course evaluation" and "web-based course design". After computing the similarity of each threaded-notes to the themes by using the text analysis module of VINCA, the resulting topic space consists of another new discovered themes, including "learner characteristics", "teaching effect", "perfect course", "person of ability". Figure 10 intuitively shows the constructed topic space for the students' discussion. As the figure shows, there are in total 6 topics, and t4, t5 involve more students' discussion compared to other topics.

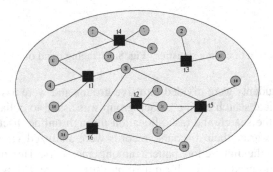

Fig. 10. Topic space

- **Social Network**

Different from the traditional social network analysis, we herein focus on the analysis of the social relationship between students who are involved in the discussion on the same theme. Figure 11 shows the social network on the theme "perfect course". From the figure, we can see that 5 students participated in the discussion with active interaction among them. The wider the edge between the students is, the more interactions between them occur. S16 plays a central role in the discussion by drawing attentions from other students and especially S18 responses to S16 a lot. To further illustrate the learner characteristics in the collaborative learning, we compute the several indicators for the selected two students: S8 and S16. As figure 12 shows, S8 has higher level of participation and activity compared to S16, but his other characteristics such as authority, novelty, and coverage are relatively lower than S16. It implies that though S8 are very active engaged in the collaborative learning, his speeches do not draw a lot of attention from others, whilst S16 attains others' more responses with relatively small speeches.

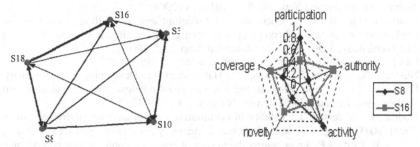

Fig. 11. Theme-centered social network   **Fig. 12.** Learner characteristics

6 Conclusions

By incorporating content analysis, social network analysis, and data mining technologies, this paper puts forward a three-dimensional model to help researchers understand what happened behind online peer interactions in CSCL. This paper also designs and implements an intelligent content analysis tool VINCA to support analyzing peer discussion transcripts. An experimental study is conducted to explore the discussion topics, process pattern and social network with respect to the students' online interaction, while illustrating the viability and usefulness of VINCA during the analyzing process.

References

1. Allan, J., Wade, C., Bolivar, A.: Retrieval and novelty detection at the sentence level. In: 26th annual ACM SIGIR Conference, Toronto, Canada (July 2003)
2. Anderson, T., Rourke, L., Garrison, D.R., Archer, W.: Assessing teaching presence in a computer conference context. Journal of Asynchronous Learning Networks (2001) (Retrieved: August 15, 2004),
   http://www.sloan-c.org/publications/jaln/v5n2/pdf/
   v5n2_anderson.pdf
3. Brants, T., Chen, F., Farahat, A.: A system for new event detection. In: 26th annual ACM SIGIR Conference, Toronto, Canada (July 2003)
4. Hakkinen, P., Jarvela, S., Makitalo, K.: Sharing perspective in virtual interaction: Review of methods of analysis. In: Wasson, B., Ludvigsen, S., Hoppe, U. (eds.) Designing for Change in Networked Learning Environments, proceedings of the International Conference on Computer-support for Collaborative Learning 2003, pp. 395–404. Kluwer, Dordrecht (2003)

5. Henri, F.: Computer conferencing and content analysis. In: Kaye, A.R. (ed.) Collaborative learning through computer conferencing. The Najadan Papers, pp. 117–136 (1992)
6. Laat, M.D., Lally, V.: Investing group structures in CSCL: some new approaches. Information Systems Frontiers 7(1), 13–25 (2005)
7. Li, Y., Wang, J., Liao, J., Zhao, D., Huang, R.: Assessing Collaborative Process in CSCL with an Intelligent Content Analysis Toolkit. In: IEEE International Conference on Advanced Learning Technologies (IEEE ICALT), Japan, pp. 257–261 (2007)
8. Liu, C.C., Tsai, C.C.: An analysis of peer interaction patterns as discoursed by on-line small group problem-solving activity. Computers & Education (2006)
9. Meyer, K.: Evaluating online discussions: four different frames of analysis. Journal of Asynchronous Learning Networks 8(2), 101–114 (2004)
10. Newman, D.R., Webb, B., Cochrane, C.: A content analysis method to measure critical thinking in face-to face and computer supported group learning. Interpersonal Computing and Technology, 3, 56–77 (1995) (Retrieved August 15, 2004),
http://www.qub.ac.uk/mgt/papers/methods/contpap.html
11. Nurmela, K., Palonen, T., Lehtine, E., Hakkarinen, K.: Developing tools for analyzing CSCL process. In: Proceedings of the International Conference on Computer-support for Collaborative Learning 2003, Bergen, Norway, pp. 333–342 (2003)
12. Rourke, L., Anderson, T.: Validity in quantitative content analysis (Retrieved August 1, 2004) (2003), http://communitiesofinquiry.com/sub/papers.html
13. Stacey, E., Gerbic, P.: Investigating the impact of computer conferencing: content analysis as a manageable research tool. In: Crisp, G., Thiele, D., Scholten, I., Barker, S., Baron, J. (eds.) Interact, integrate, impact: Proceedings of the 20th annual conference of the australasian society for computers in learning in tertiary education, Adelaide, December 7–10 (2003) (Retrieved September 1, 2004)
http://www.ascilite.org.au/conferences/adelaide03/docs/pdf/495.pdf
14. Veerman, Veldhuis-Diermanse, E.: Collaborative learning through computer-mediated communication in academic education. In: Euro CSCL 2001, pp. 625–632. McLuhan institute, University of Maastricht, Maastricht (2001)
15. Wassermann, S., Faust, K.: Social Network Analysis: Methods and Application. Cambridge University Press, Cambridge (1994)
16. Wever, B.D., Schellens, T., Valcke, M., Keer, H.V.: Content analysis schemes to analyze transcripts of online asynchronous discussion groups: a review. Computers & Education 46(1), 6–28 (2006)
17. Wever, B.D., Schellens, T., Valcke, M.: Samenwerkend leren via informatie- en communicatietechnologie [Collaborative learning through ICT]. In: D'haese, I., Valcke, M. (eds.) Digitaal leren. ICT Toepassingen in hethoger onderwijs [Digital Learning. ICT applications in higher education]. Lannoo Campus, Tielt (2004)
18. Zhu, E.: Meaning negotiation, knowledge construction, and mentoring in a distance learning course. In: Proceedings of selected research and development presentations at the 1996 national convention of the association for educational communications and technology. Indeanapolis: Available from ERIC documents: ED 397 849 (1996)

eSurvey: A Survey Record Based eLearning System for Research Degree Study

Joseph Fong and Herbert Shiu

Department of Computer Science, City University of Hong Kong, Hong Kong
csjfong@cityu.edu.hk

Abstract. In research studies, a student starts with writing a research proposal, followed up by intensive literature and industrial survey in his/her own research area. The student must perform his/her own research with validation under supervisor's guidance. The student's own research work must be differentiated from others work in order to demonstrate the unique originality and significance of the students' contribution. The information explosion on the Internet makes the survey analysis much more difficult. This paper suggests a solution by recording both the students' own research work and others work into a meta data, and compare them for further analysis as part of student's dissertation. The record based eLearning system can track the progress of student's research studies in, problem statement, proposed solution, analysis, findings, publication and feedback, in an eLearning system.

Keywords: research study, research proposal, research method, eLearning.

1 Introduction

In research study, a feasibility study is very crucial to the success of the student' work. It determines the direction of the student's research. As a result, the title and the scope of the research study should be wide open in order to provide room for the student to contribute his/her own part of body of knowledge. Otherwise, years of work may be in vain due to no significant result. Very often, a critical analysis is required to evaluate the significance of the findings in the research. In this case, a comparison table on the uniqueness of the students' own work is needed to differentiate it from the others work in the same area.

The process of producing a research proposal is very useful. First of all, the student must define the aims and objectives of the research project, along with the research parameters such as performance analysis, design methodology and derived rules for business operations etc. The student must assess the feasibility of the research parameters to construct a research plan. Basically, a research method must consist of problem statement, survey, experiment empirical case study, validation by prototype or mathematical induction etc. The deliverables of the research can be a law in science, a new model in design and simulation, a set of stepwise procedure in methodology, improved techniques in engineering, and a validated business rule etc. The

J. Fong, R. Kwan, and F.L. Wang (Eds.): ICHL 2008, LNCS 5169, pp. 137–146, 2008.
© Springer-Verlag Berlin Heidelberg 2008

research result must be validated by use of prototype, mathematical induction, survey, and/or experiment. The research resources requirement must be prepared with respect to man power, computer hardware and software, and testing data. A schedule states the time table of the research project.

To begin with, a research student must write up a research proposal in a formal document which consists of the following structure:

1. Title of the research project – the main theme and focus of the Research.
2. Introduction to proposal – the scope of the research
3. Background to research – the motivation of the research
4. Aims and objectives – the intended accomplishment of the research
5. Intellectual challenge – the academic merit of the research
6. Ethical basis of project – the originality issue of the research outcome
7. Research method – the process of performing the research
8. Deliverables produced – the outcome and the result of the research
9. Resources needed–required manpower & computer resources of the research
10. References – the referred articles and industrial work of the research

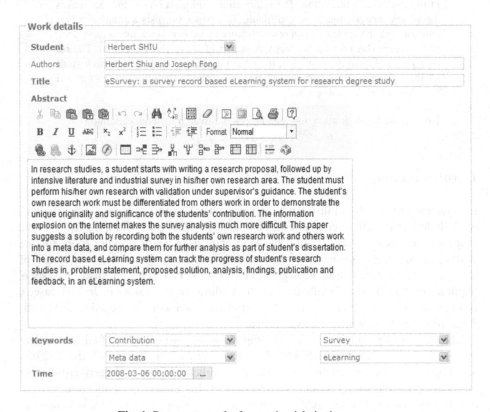

Fig. 1. Data capture of referenced article in the survey

2 Data Capture the Research Proposal Survey

To capture users input, we allow users enter his/her article's title, authors' name, time of publication, abstract and keywords as shown in Figure 1.

Figure 2 allows supervisors to enter comment on the student and the others work.

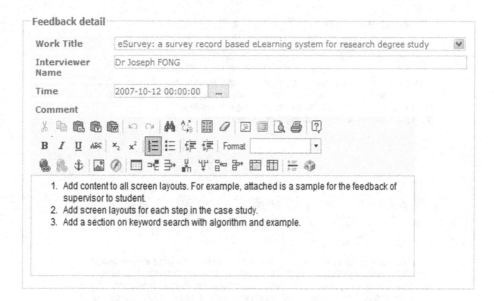

Fig. 2. Supervisor and examiners comment on the student and others work

Figure 3 shows the regular interview record between the student and his/her supervisor. The student reports his/her work after previous interview, and the problem encountered. The supervisor recommends follow up actions for students.

In order to record the student's survey, we need to develop a meta data to store the student's own work and his/her referred articles and their abstracts into the computer records. We can then browse them according to the authors name, time stamps, subject areas, and keywords. The students' supervisors can also provide feedback to the student's work, and which can be stored into the meta data for records. In fact, for each meeting with the research, it will be beneficial for both parties to record the minutes of the interview. For example, the accomplishment of the student's record from the previous interview to the current interview, what kind of the problems that the student is facing, and what are the supervisors recommendation for the student to continue the research work. In order to implement the eSurvey system, we can develop a meta data with its Entity Relationship Model as shown in Figure 4.

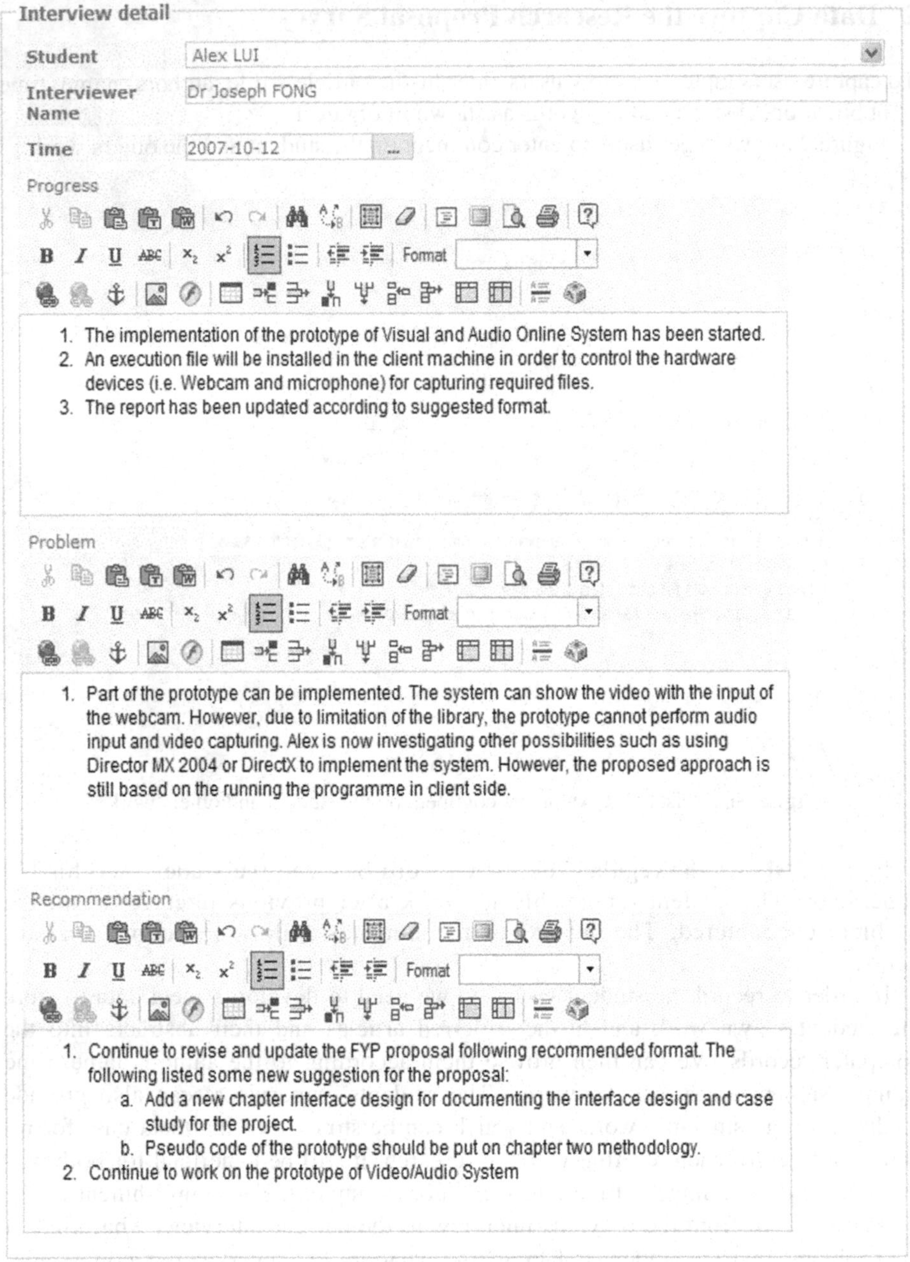

Interview detail

Student	Alex LUI
Interviewer Name	Dr Joseph FONG
Time	2007-10-12

Progress

1. The implementation of the prototype of Visual and Audio Online System has been started.
2. An execution file will be installed in the client machine in order to control the hardware devices (i.e. Webcam and microphone) for capturing required files.
3. The report has been updated according to suggested format.

Problem

1. Part of the prototype can be implemented. The system can show the video with the input of the webcam. However, due to limitation of the library, the prototype cannot perform audio input and video capturing. Alex is now investigating other possibilities such as using Director MX 2004 or DirectX to implement the system. However, the proposed approach is still based on the running the programme in client side.

Recommendation

1. Continue to revise and update the FYP proposal following recommended format. The following listed some new suggestion for the proposal:
   a. Add a new chapter interface design for documenting the interface design and case study for the project.
   b. Pseudo code of the prototype should be put on chapter two methodology.
2. Continue to work on the prototype of Video/Audio System

Fig. 3. Interview record between student and supervisor

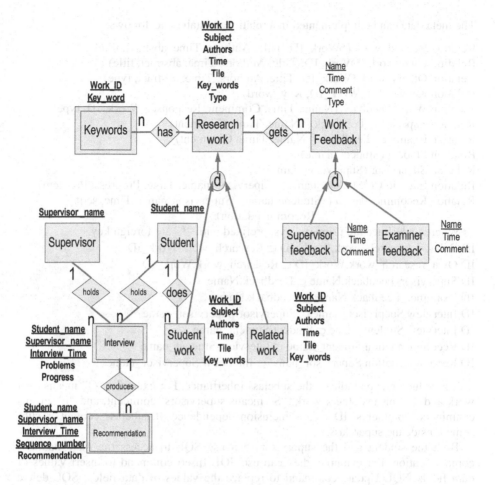

Fig. 4. The Entity Relationship Diagram of the research survey data

In this meta data with entities in parenthesis, the student (student) does many research work (Student work). The student (student) has many-to-many interviews with his/her supervisor (supervisor). In each interview, the supervisor gives many recommendation (recommendation). The student has done much survey (research work), which includes both his/.her own work (student work) and others' work (related work). In each work (research work), there are many keywords (keywords). In each survey article (research work), the student obtains many feedback (work feedback), which consists of supervisors comment (supervisor feedback), and examiners comment (examiner feedback). In each feedback, the supervisors may give many recommendations (Recommendation) for follow up actions for the students to act, ordered by a Sequence number.

The meta data can be implemented in a relational database as follows:

Relation Related_work (*Work_ID, Title, Authors, Time, abstract, title)
Relation Own_work (*Work_ID, Title, Authors, Time, abstract, title)
Relation Others_work (Work_ID, Title, Authors, Time, abstract, type)
Relation Keywords (*Work_ID, Key_word)
Relation Work_Feedback (Name, Time, Comment, Response, *Work_ID, type)
Relation Supervisor_Feedback (*Name, Time, Comment)
Relation Examiner_Feedback (*Name, Time, Comment)
Relation Student (Student_name)
Relation Supervisor (Supervisor_name)
Relation Interview (*Student_name, *Supervisor_name, Time, Progress, Problem)
Relation Recommendation (*Student_name, *Supervisor_name, Time, seq#,
                         Recommendation)
    Where underlined are primary keys, prefixed with "*" are foreign key.
ID Related_research_work.Work_ID ⊆ Research_work.Work_ID
ID Own_research_work.Work_ID ⊆ Research_work.Work_ID
ID Supervisor_Feedback.Name ⊆ Feedback.Name
ID Examiner_Feedback.Name ⊆ Feedback.Name
ID Interview.Sueprvisor_name ⊆ Supervisor.Supervisor_name
ID Interview.Student_name ⊆ Student.Student_name
ID Recommendation.Student_name ⊆ Interview.Student_name
ID Recommendation.Supervisor_name ⊆ Interview.Supervisor_name

    The value of Type indicate the subclass inheritance. For example, "O" means own work and "T" means others work. "S" means supervisors' comment, and "E" means examiners' comments. ID means inclusion dependence of subclass content is subsumed inside the superclass.

    Both the student and the supervisors can use SQL to access the meta data for communication. For example, they can use SQL Insert command to insert values of data fields, SQL Update command to replace the values of data fields, SQL delete command to delete tuples, and SQL select command to browse the inserted tuples as follows:

    For example, we can insert the student's publication record into meta data by using insert statement:

Insert into others_work (work_id, title, authors, time, abstract, type) values
(1,
'Bin Feng',
'A methodology for XQuery processing in distributed native XML data bases",
'01-October-2007',
'As XML becomes more and more important, it is used not only for data exchange but also for the XML data storage. ....',
'own'
);

    We can update the time stamp of the surveyed article in update statement:
Update Time Set Time = "14-January-2008" Where work_id = 1;

We can delete a surveyed reference in a delete statement:
Delete others_work where work_id = 1;
We can browse the abstract of a surveyed reference in a select statement:
Select * from Others_work where work_id = 1;
We can record an interview between student and supervisor in an insert statement:
Insert into Interview (Student_name, Supervisor_name, Time, Progress, Problem) values
('Herbert Shiu',
'Joseph Fong',
'16-1-2008',
'Research Proposal on distributed heterogeneous XML database. Finished
the initial feasibility study on survey in this area. Start to design a methodology on designing an XML database',
'Can two phase commit be done in an XML database?. What is the XML database management system to be used in the research project?'
);

3 Application of eSurvey with Cases Study

We can apply eSurvey as a cross reference between research contribution and the examiners and supervisors' comment to them. It can also be used as a communication record between student and supervisors, and between student's dissertation and examiners feedback as follows:

I Cross References on the Subject

In a research topic, many outstanding issues may come up in the research. Each one of them may involve others' work against student's own contribution. We need to analyze their differences, and evaluation the significance of the student's contribution on each subject as a result.

II Minutes on Research Progress Meeting

In general, student will meet with his/her supervisors on the progress of the research project. In each interview, the student must show their incremental work and seek for the feedback and approval of the supervisors. Very often, supervisors will analyze student's research work, identify the problem in the unresolved issues, and recommend actions to resolve them. It is important for student to record his/her supervisors' comment in a minutes, and which can be reviewed in the next interview meeting.

III Record the Issues between Student's Dissertation And Examiners' Unresolved Concern

After reviewing student's dissertation, both the internal and the external examiners usually come up with many questions for the student's written and/or oral examination. It is important for the student to answer each question correctly in good detail. A record tracking system is helpful for student to revise his/her dissertation to satisfy the examiners' demand.

4 Searching Features

Searching is an important feature of the application for locating the works and hence their progresses, comments and feedbacks. Based on the proposed entity-relationship behind the application, the Keywords table plays an important role in locating the Research Works and hence the corresponding interviews and feedbacks.

Another significantly useful searching feature is to search the Research Works based on their contents. For instance, the proposed database schema only maintains the abstracts. A possible enhancement is to maintain the contents of the entire research work documents by uploading the works to the application in their native file formats, such as Microsoft Word document, Portable Document Format (PDF), Latex and so on. Once a research work file is uploaded to the application, it is stored centrally at the server and its contents are extracted by an appropriate module to be maintained by the back-end relational database. As a result, it is possible to perform textual search in the research work contents other than the abstracts.

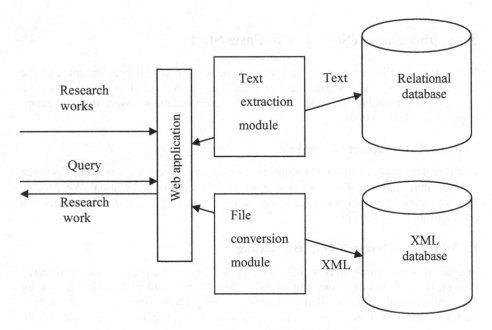

Fig. 5. Data flow of research works stored in relational/XML databases for search

Another possible enhancement of the application is to make use of an XML database to maintain the related works, such as Tamino [7], that can convert popular document formats into XML format and subsequently maintained by the XML database. As such, it enables the user to search the XML database with the more feature rich X-Query language that involves single or multiple research works, compared with the pattern or sub-string searching by relational databases.

Figure 5 shows the data flow for key word text search among research articles which are stored into relational database and/or XML database. The related works in the form of articles can be scanned and stored into a PDF file. The text of the PDF file can be extracted and stored into either relational database or XML database in memo data type, and then retrieved by using SQL for relational database, or XQuery for XML database.

While relational database can store research work contents in pure textual format and sub-string or pattern searches are possible, native XML database mostly stores XML documents with indexing on entire textual data. As such, the performance of keyword and text searches is more efficient. Besides, the flexibility and capability of the native query language for XML database, X-Query, provides user more possible ways to query and manipulate the research work contents.

For example, Figure 6 demonstrates the keyword search box for searching works by keyword. By clicking the drop-down list box, the list of existing keywords will be shown for selection. Click the Search button to start searching.

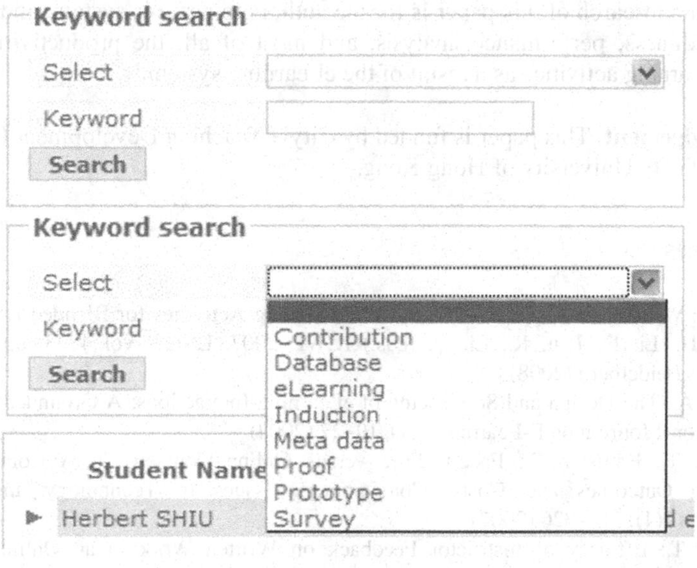

Fig. 6. Screen layouts for keyword search

Besides, it is possible to enter a keyword to the keyword field for searching as shown in Figure 7.

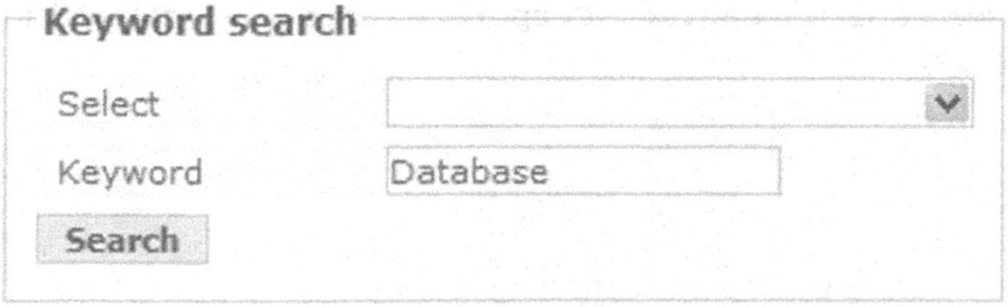

Fig. 7. Screen layouts of data entry for keyword search

5 Conclusion

This paper helps a research student keep track of his/her research studies work in an eLearning system. The student can log the research literature and industrial survey into a database, store his/her own published and/or un-published working papers into system, and put the interview minutes between the students and the supervisors into tables, and insert the supervisors' comments and recommendations into records. Then, the students can cross reference his/her own work against others work in an online report. The significance of the system is a powerful search agent for students research effort. In case of implementing this eLearning system by use of XML document, the student can search for the keywords and/or key phrases of the whole article, not limited to an abstract of the referenced paper. In this case, the practical application of the system is enormous to the student because it can save much time in his/her research studies.

The future research of this paper is for the authors to use this system, and report its users friendliness, performance analysis, and most of all, the productivities of the student's learning activities as a result of the eLearning system.

Acknowledgement. This paper is funded by CityU Teaching Development Grant 6000152 of City University of Hong Kong.

References

1. Fong, J.: Web-Based Logging of Classroom Teaching Activities for Blended Learning. In: Leung, H., Li, F., Lau, R., Li, Q. (eds.) ICWL 2007. LNCS, vol. 4823, pp. 597–605. Springer, Heidelberg (2008)
2. Hirumi, A.: The Design and Sequencing of eLearning Interactions: A Grounded Approach. International Journal on E-Learning 1(1), 19–27 (2002)
3. Herman, T., Banister, S.: Face-to-Face versus Online Coursework: A Comparison of Learning Outcomes and Costs. Contemporary Issues in Technology and Teacher Education 7(4), 318–326 (2007)
4. Wolsey, T.: Efficacy of Instructor Feedback on Written Work in an Online Program. International Journal on E-Learning 7(2), 311–329 (2008)
5. Chesapeake, V.A.: AACE. Taran, C, Best Practices for Creating Quality Rapid eLearning. In: Pearson, E., Bohman, P. (eds.) Proceedings of World Conference on Educational Multimedia, Hypermedia and Telecommunications 2006, Chesapeake, VA: AACE, pp. 2089–2094 (2006)
6. Tamino – The XML database, http://www.softwareag.com/Corporate/products/wm/tamino/default.asp

5i: A Design Framework for Hybrid Learning

Anthony Tik Tsuen Wong

Caritas Francis Hsu College
1D Oxford Road, Kowloon, Hong Kong
awong@cfhc.caritas.edu.hk

Abstract. Existing challenge in offering education is the use of information technology in delivering contents and providing an interesting platform to enhance students' learning. Hybrid learning is becoming one of the important applications by integrating electronic learning and traditional learning platforms together. Teachers and course designers are interested in how to design a hybrid course in a more effective way. The author proposes a 5i design framework for designing course using hybrid learning approach. The 5i includes initiative, interaction, independent, incentive and improvement. The supporting arguments of the 5i framework are from the most recent and critical literatures in hybrid learning with most updated examples in teaching approaches. The author conducted a qualitative study in collecting feedback about the proposed 5i framework from students who are studying in different programmes and at different years of studies. The purpose of this paper is to suggest a design framework for teachers and course designers to design their hybrid course in a more effective manner.

Keywords: initiative, interaction, independent, incentive, improvement, hybrid learning and course design framework.

1 Introduction

Learning is the acquisition and development of memories and behaviors, including skills, knowledge, understanding, values, and wisdom. It is the product of experience and the goal of education. The contemporary challenge in education is the use of information technology to enhance students' learning interests (Naqvi, 2006). Online learning (or e-learning) uses information and communication technology to build up a computer-based or web-based system platform for learning. It can be used as an independent tool for changing the behavior and experiences of learners. It can also be used as a supplementary tool to traditional classroom learning, which is called hybrid learning. Hybrid learning is to combine face-to-face classroom learning and learning by computer-based system (Brunner, 2007) and is becoming one of the most popular learning modes. This paper proposes a 5i design framework to facilitate course designers and teachers to design more performing hybrid related courses. The aim is to provide a framework with the most essential elements for hybrid course design. Comments from students on hybrid course design and the 5i framework were collected through a qualitative research approach.

J. Fong, R. Kwan, and F.L. Wang (Eds.): ICHL 2008, LNCS 5169, pp. 147–156, 2008.
© Springer-Verlag Berlin Heidelberg 2008

2 Background

Hybrid learning is necessary because face-to-face learning and online learning each have their shortcomings. The deficiencies of face-to-face learning include the need for teachers and students to meet at the same time. This mode of learning has lower flexibility and leads to inconsistent learning progress of students (Mansour and Mupinga, 2007). Online learning also carries the defect that students might be lost in their cyberspace (Mansour and Mupinga, 2007). Hybrid course design provides flexibility for institutions to engage in face-to-face classroom and online learning by providing students with relevant meaningful content while maintaining student-teacher relationship (Teeley, 2007). The strength of a hybrid course is to increase student performance and retention, giving them more time flexibility, the availability of multiple modes of learning, deeper sense of community and greater interaction (Brunner, 2007).

There are three strategies for online course: provides contents in multiple formats, allows for individual locus of control, and encourages active and collaboration interaction (Zapalska and Brozik, 2007). Zapalska and Brozik suggested that online environment can provide online projects, online work in groups, small group discussion in synchronous sessions, and virtual field trips and videos. However, most teachers got frustrated in designing online course because they feel their role is being eroded. Teachers' role has been changed to facilitator of learning rather than knowledge transferring in hybrid learning (Brunner, 2007). It leads to an argument between andragogical and pedagogical approaches in hybrid learning. Andragogy approach is a process of engaging adult learners in the structure of the learning experience that requires more self-directed learning style. It is commonly utilized in online learning. Pedagogy is a process of being a teacher to provide teaching and learning strategies of instruction. Pedagogy is used in traditional classroom learning. However, Muirhead (2007) suggested that a mixture of two approaches is more appropriate.

Lee, Tseng, Liu and Liu (2007) found that digital content is important to learners' satisfaction towards online learning. However, pedagogy approach is still considered vital in a classroom setting. They claimed that the role of teacher should play a less important role with weaker influences in online learning. This is quite different to the traditional classroom learning in which teachers are liked performers on stage and has more influences to the students' learning motivation and attitudes. With less interaction and influence of teachers in online mode, teachers find difficulties in designing an effective hybrid course to strike off a balance of their roles between andragogical and pedagogical approaches. The literatures reflect that each mode of learning has their own advantages and deficiencies. A blend learning approach by using both modes of learning together could take the advantages over others and diminish the effect of the deficiencies. However, there are few studies in proposing the factors in designing a course by using a hybrid learning approach. It leads to an important issue to uncover the essential elements required in designing a hybrid course, especially the relevant core activities required in face-to-face and online modes, and their mutual relationship.

3 5i Design Framework

The following discussion is about a proposed 5i design framework for a hybrid course. The 5i are initiative, interaction, independent, incentive and improvement.

3.1 Initiative

Students might be easily initiated to attend traditional classroom training. However, motivating them to attend online sessions is always a problem. A hybrid course should contain elements to initiate students to actively participate in online learning (Bates and Watson, 2008) and classroom training. Verbal communication is often used in traditional classroom training (Bates and Watson, 2008) because it is more convenience to instruct students to read notes and have discussion in class. However, the lack of monitoring and direct instruction in online environment has popularly resulted in communication problem and inactive participation of students.

In hybrid learning, students may take half of their time in classes and half of their time online. It implies that both students and teachers under the traditional teaching mode may need special training on how to communicate online (Bates and Watson, 2008). Teacher's role is being changed. The concept of teaching is moving to 'learning' because the responsibility of learning will depend on the initiative of students (Bates and Watson, 2008). Traditional way in learning by reading notes, conducting project and doing homework are no longer sufficient (Bates and Watson, 2008). Online learning allows students to seek the most up-to-dated knowledge and discover the underlying theories in order to enhance their initiative. In order to increase students' initiative to use hybrid mode of studies, direct instructions and guided discoveries should be incorporated (Clark, 2000 cited in Bates and Watson, 2008). Direct instructions are essential in face-to-face lecturing so students can understand the fundamental knowledge by the explanations of teachers. Guided discoveries are to let students learn on their own by observing the theory, asking questions and discussion, which can play a better role in online mode. More interactive activities in online learning could even help to improve students' initiative. Bates and Watson (2008) suggested the use of games, puzzles and flash exercises but not tests because of the problems of cheating and identity. Those activities could initiate students' capabilities in self-discovery and self-directing (Teeley, 2007) both in the traditional and online modes of learning.

3.2 Interaction

There are two ideas in interaction here. One is the interactivity of activities in online learning. Second is the interaction of activities between traditional classroom mode and online mode. One critical feature of online learning is to provide group interaction opportunities (Lee, Tseng, Liu and Liu, 2007) among students, and between students and teachers. High level of group interactivities including learning communities and peer review is required (Bates and Watson, 2008). This heavily depends on the creativity of teachers and course designers and the availability of the relevant technology. The emergence of new technology, such as the introduction of Web 2.0 provides new platforms for more creative applications for interactions. The importance of interactivities in hybrid learning is to cater for different learning style of students (Negas, Wilcox and Emerson, 2007). Teachers do not have the time to care for each student's learning progress in classroom mode because of large class size, however, online learning provides teacher better interaction with individual student's enquiries. It puts problems back to the teachers requiring them to have new mindset for teaching. Teachers should transit from being standing on stage to a facilitator role in learning. They should have more interactions and sharing of knowledge with students through socialized activities online apart from just the delivery of knowledge (Brunner, 2007).

Second area of interactions is to integrate activities in classroom mode and online mode. Most researchers and teachers emphasize interactivities in each mode of learning only. Few of them suggest interactivities between the two modes of learning in order to have effective hybrid course design and learning. Some hybrid courses have applied one side of interactions such as requiring students to attend a class and work on assignments or projects online. However, teachers should discuss the work done by students. Currently most teachers provide their comments in online environment. Teachers could discuss students' work that done online in class. Teachers can also discuss in classrooms about the online communication among students. These activities will further enhance the other 'i' that would be discussed later.

3.3 Independent

Students should work and think independently in both modes of learning. Online mode of learning emphasizes social interactions by group discussions. One disadvantage is that students still encounter difficulties in doing homework, assignments and arranging their workload outside classroom environment (Lee, Tseng, Liu and Liu, 2007). In hybrid learning, teachers play an important role in online environment for students' pace of learning (Negas, Wilcox and Emerson, 2007). Teachers should design a hybrid course with training in students' self-regulation and control of learning (Negas, Wilcox and Emerson, 2007). It is definitely critical now because students spend too much time on the Internet in surfing irrelevant information for studies. They will be lost in the virtual environment. Their online peers easily affect their thinking. A hybrid course should be designed to allow for independent study and working (Teeley, 2007). Pre-set case studies and projects might lead to similar answers that students might depends on each others' ideas, so students could be requested to apply the knowledge learnt in classroom to design their own scenario of cases and projects. Details of the requirements are briefed in the classroom mode. Students need to search information on the Internet and think and work independently to design their own case. Their peers will act as inputs to discuss the requirements but not the final answers.

3.4 Incentive

Students should be motivated to learn in the two learning modes. Incentive approach is then required. As mentioned above, proper design of interactivity between online learning and classroom will affect learners' intention to use online system (Lee, Tseng, Liu and Liu, 2007). Current practices in compulsory participation or summative assessment to stimulate discussion might not be appropriate for motivating students (Muirhead, 2007). Students will be motivated to attend both modes of learning if activities are cross-referenced between them. Students also will be motivated if the activities or functions they are familiar are used in the hybrid course. For examples, students may prefer to have games in classroom instead of intensive direct lecturing (Bates and Watson, 2008). Web blogs, as one of the most common online activities, are used in online mode for students to post and express their views. They can be used to enhance students' motivation to join the online activities (Bates and Watson, 2008). Students will also be motivated by allowing them to build up their own community (Brunner, 2007). This could be achieved by allowing students to freely raise any topic for discussion rather than discuss the topics defined by teachers.

3.5 Improvement

A hybrid course must be designed such that students know there are improving in learning. Traditional way of assessing students' learning progress provides marked and graded works to students who, then can check whether they have improvement in attending the course (Teeley, 2007). This could be achieved by using integrating technology in providing statistical results to students about their learning progress. However, intangible improvement should be catered. Some students might be reluctant to give comments and voice out opinions in classroom environment (Teeley, 2007). Online environment gives less pressure to them and encourage them to actively express their views. These students will feel improvements in initiation and independence activities. Their comments could be further discussed in classrooms for motivating them to continuingly express their ideas (Teeley, 2007). Peer review is another approach for improvements. Some students may feel more comfortable in listening comments and feedbacks from peers (Teeley, 2007). Teachers can allow students to mark other students' assignments and allow them to discuss other students' work in class. Students will have more positive attitude towards the mistakes and would be more likely to make corrections.

4 Methodology

The study uses qualitative methodology in collecting opinions from a group of students enrolling in a general education course - "Information Technology and Modern Life".

Qualitative approach focuses on measuring people's experiences on an event processed and structured inside a social environment (Skinner, Tagg and Holloway, 2000). Researchers using qualitative research would like to investigate the issues in complex, messy and a situation that involves different stakeholders. Qualitative research helps practitioners and researchers have a deeper understanding and rich insights (Cassell et. al., 2006) of an unstructured problem circumstance. Qualitative approach, as an interpretative paradigm, is appropriate in understanding the social setting and theories of a hybrid course design.

Focus group was employed in collecting information from students. Focus group has the original idea as being a focused interview by emphasizing a specific theme or topic for each group. The members of the focus groups, the students, have certain level of understanding and experience about the research topic (Bryman, 2004). Using focus group is appropriate because it is a popular method for researchers to examine the way the participants in conjunction with one another (Bryman, 2004).

There were two rounds of forming focus groups for collecting information. The participants are students studying a general education course. The students are from different programmes and years of study. The reason in selecting those students is to avoid any possible bias in one profession such as business administration, computing studies, etc. The students were to form groups with three to four members voluntarily. In the first round of focus groups, twenty-four students participated and totally seven groups were formed. The researcher designed a set of questions for them to discuss. The second round of focus group discussion took place a week after. Twenty-eight students participated and nine groups were formed. Again, the researcher designed questions for discussion. In the second round of focus groups, the researcher has briefed the students about the proposed 5i design framework before the discussion.

The focus group discussions were conducted in a computer laboratory in which each student has a personal computer with Internet access. The students were allowed to search information from the Internet for discussion. The researcher did not take part in this discussion. The durations allowed for the first round and second round focus group discussion were 45 minutes and 50 minutes respectively.

5 Results

Content analysis was used to explore the information collected from participants. A summary of the major comments in the first and second rounds of focus group discussion is listed below:

Table 1. Major comments from first and second round of focus groups

First round of focus groups	Second round of focus groups
Activities in online learning mode:	Activities in online learning mode:
1. Online discussion 2. Upload assignments 3. Check marks 4. Video in classroom instructions. 5. Material for download 6. Sample questions and answers	1. Online discussions 2. Gaming 3. Tests 4. Sample papers 5. Search information on the Internet
Activities in classroom mode:	Activities in classroom mode:
1. Discussions 2. Tests 3. Presentations 4. Lecturing	1. Discussions 2. Tests 3. Presentations 4. Field studies 5. Debates

Major comments from students on the proposed 5i design framework are listed in the following table.

Table 2. Major comments from students on the proposed 5i framework

5i design framework	Comments from students
Initiative:	1. Attendance 2. Reward 3. Assignment available in classroom only 4. Rich and variety of information for download
Interaction:	1. Game 2. Use MSN for communication 3. Discussion forum 4. Apply knowledge to the case the youth is familiar 5. News cutting and discussion by students
Independent:	1. Individual work 2. Using web blogs to express opinions
Incentive:	1. Bonus for attendance 2. Student with higher bonus can have priority to join special functions 3. Scholarship
Improvement:	1. Collective results on marks 2. Peer reviews 3. Samples of good works from other students and give comments

6 Discussion

When the 5i design framework was described to students, a significant difference in students' feedbacks was found in favoring the framework. From the activities identified by students in the two rounds of focus groups study, it was found that the success of hybrid learning could be achieved by designing a hybrid course with focus on the 5 "i" of the proposed framework.

Although the students are having all of their classes in traditional classroom instruction mode and the college's WebTL system does not provide sophisticated function in allowing them to communicate with teachers and other students very frequently, it was observed that the activities suggested by students show that they understand the two types of teaching and learning approach: andragogy and pedagogy, which Muirhead (2007) suggested that a mixture those two is more appropriate in hybrid learning. The activities suggested in the two rounds of focus groups even though were very similar, but lecturing is considered as most significant activity in the first round of focus group but is considered as less significant in the second round. The debate activity was not mentioned in any one focus group in the first round of discussion but was mentioned in the second round of study. It is quite important that as students understand the importance of the 5 "i" elements in designing a hybrid course, they could mention what activities should be used. Debate is definitely an andragogical approach that requires students' self-motivation and self-directed attitude in searching relevant and arguable information. It also shows that students should need to come back to classroom mode to present their ideas. Learning is an active process that students construct their personal understanding and meaning of the subject matter (Seyhan and Morgil, 2007). Construction approach enhances students' learning by integrating the 5i elements in a hybrid course. This shows that after students learnt that hybrid course should be designed with the five elements, they would expect more variety of peer activity that they did not think of before.

By comparing the activities proposed from the two rounds of focus groups, the ones from the first one are quite passive. This is not surprising because the current students are using the college's WebTL system that is mainly for downloading materials. Few teachers allow uploading of works from students and even fewer teachers use discussion groups. The activities they identified and proposed were one-way communication, such as "materials for download", "upload assignments", "video", "check marks" and "sample questions and answers". After the students were introduced the 5i design framework, they started suggesting different activities. Two typical activities are "Gaming" and "Search information on the Internet". This echoes the ideas from Bates and Watson (2008) and the proposed "initiative" and "interaction" of the 5i framework. The activity "search information on the Internet" reflects students' ability of self-talk and self-interaction. It is also the "independent" of the 5i framework.

The comments from students concerning the 5i are quite different. For initiative, the comments are quite passive and operational. Students' comments about initiative in attending classroom and online mode by teachers include taking attendance and reward. For incentive, students suggested that they would be motivated if they have bonus marks or scholarship. These two findings could be explained by the fact that the students in the college were usually with less satisfactory results in public examinations (HKCEE and HKALE). Their initiative and motivation are quite insufficient. However, this fact should lead to same argument for other 3i. However, some of the comments on "interaction", "independent" and "improvement" were not so passive. Students commented that using "MSN" can achieve interaction, using web blogs can achieve independence and using peers review can achieve improvement. Their comments support the above descriptions that by using the online activities the students will get familiar to and can enhance the effectiveness of online usage. This shows that incentive can be achieved indirectly but not being recognized by the students. The comments reflect that effectiveness of a hybrid course relies on how the teacher designs the hybrid course to facilitate students' participation and learning.

The qualitative study collected information from students concerning their ideas about hybrid learning environment. The views about the 5i design framework support the importance of the 5 "i" but cannot fully validate the 5i design framework. From the literature review, the 5 "i" framework sounds general idea but it is significant in considering an integration of activities between two modes of instruction in hybrid learning. Further evaluation of the proposed framework is recommended. The qualitative study gives positive results towards the framework and it is part of the author's research. The author is planning to design a course with hybrid approach and to apply the 5 "i" in designing the course content and activities. An empirical research will be followed in evaluating the results after the 5 "i" techniques are used. The author also recommends other researchers and practitioners to evaluate their hybrid course by focusing the 5 "i" and carry out similar evaluation by a quantitative study.

The proposed 5i design framework is constructed by critically identifying the work of other researchers and practitioners. Although the value of the framework depends on further application and evaluation, it could act as a foundation for designing hybrid course. When practitioners design a hybrid course, they know there are 5 "i" elements that are necessary in deploying different activities between traditional classroom mode and online mode of learning. The current limitations of the proposed 5i design framework include limited validation since feedbacks were collected from students studying in a general education course and further validation of the framework's value by an empirical study is necessary. The feedbacks from the current students were limited to their experiences in using hybrid course and the WebTL in the college. However, the advantage of examining the ideas of the current group of students is their variety of backgrounds, such as programme, level of study and the nature of a general education course. The comments were expected not to be bias to any one discipline. It is recommended to further elaborate and examine the 5i design framework by designing and applying a hybrid course and collect feedback from students after they have practical experience in both modes of learning.

The proposed 5i design framework provides focus to teachers in designing hybrid course activities. Technology is one of the current research issues in designing a hybrid course in order to provide more variety of functions to students, however, the overall approach in delivering the teaching and learning package in hybrid learning is equally important. The 5 "i" design framework provides useful and understandable guidelines to design a hybrid course structure and aims at encouraging students to achieve initiative, interaction, independent, incentive and improvement in hybrid learning environment and gain the most effective and efficient learning outcomes.

7 Conclusion

Online learning is a growing trend in education. Students are increasingly spending more time on the Internet. This has forced educators to move some of the learning process to online mode. Hybrid learning is a new trend of education approach by combining the advantages of classroom training and online learning. However, it is challenging to teachers in designing an effective hybrid course that can enhance students' learning. This paper studies the results from other researchers and proposes a 5i design framework for hybrid learning. The author conducted a qualitative study in collecting their comments about the proposed framework. The results are positive towards the framework. The author expects the 5i design framework can work as a foundation for course designers and teachers in designing their hybrid course.

References

1. Bates, C., Watson, M.: Re-learning teaching techniques to be effective in hybrid and online courses. Journal of American Academy of Business, Cambridge 13(1), 38 (2008)
2. Bird, L.: The 3 'C' design model for networked collaborative e-learning: a tool for novice designers. Innovation in Education and Teaching International 44(2), 153 (2007)

3. Brunner, D.L.: Using "Hybrid" effectively on Christian higher education. Christian Scholar's Review 36(2), 115 (2007)
4. Bryman, A.: Social Research Methods. Oxford University Press, Oxford (2004)
5. Cassell, C., Symon, G., Buehring, A., Johnson, P.: The role and status of qualitative methods in management research: an empirical account. Management Decision 44(2) (2006)
6. Lee, Y.K., Tseng, S.P., Liu, F.J., Liu, S.C.: Antecedents of learner satisfaction toward e-learning. Journal of American Academy of Business, Cambridge 11(2), 161 (2007)
7. Mansour, B.E., Mupinga, D.M.: Students' positive and negative experiences in hybrid and online classes. College Student Journal 41(1), 242 (2007)
8. Muirhead, R.J.: E-learning: is this teaching at students or teaching with students? Nursing Forum 42(4), 178 (2007)
9. Negas, S., Wilcox, M.V., Emerson, M.: Synchronous hybrid e-learning: teaching complex information systems classes online, vol. 3(3) (2007)
10. Naqvi, S.: Impact of WebCT on learning: an Oman experience. International Journal of Education and Development using Information and Communication Technology 2(4), 18–27 (2006)
11. Seyhan, H.G., Morgil, I.: The effect of 5E learning model on teaching of acid-base topic in chemistry education. Journal of Science Education 8(2) (2007)
12. Skinner, D., Tagg, C., Holloway, J.: Managers and research: the pros and cons of qualitative approaches. Management Learning 31(2) (2000)
13. Teeley, K.H.: Designing hybrid web-based courses for accelerated nursing students. Educational Innovations, vol. 46(9) (2007)
14. Zapalska, A., Brozik, D.: Learning styles and online education. Campus-Wide Information Systems 24(1), 6–16 (2007)

When Hybrid Learning Meets Blended Teaching: Online Computer-Mediated Communication (CMC) Discourse and Classroom Face-to-Face (FTF) Discourse Analysis

Zhichang Xu

English Department, The Hong Kong Institute of Education, Hong Kong SAR, China
zhichang@ied.edu.hk

Abstract. This paper reports on a research project about the emerging hybrid or blended learning and teaching environments. These new environments result from the introduction of new technologies (e.g. 'Blackboard' learning and teaching systems) into the educational setting. The new technologies, rendered as innovative tools in the education sector, have helped integrate the classroom and online learning environments into a variety of "productive spaces" referred to by researchers as "the third space" [1]. This research project has explored the major issues arising in this "third space" in a higher education institute in Hong Kong. These issues include 1) the relationship between the traditional knowledge transmission and the current technology-enhanced knowledge generation in education; 2) the changing relationship between the teachers and the students in the new learning and teaching environments; 3) the discourse nature of interactions through differing modes, e.g. face-to-face (FTF), and interactive electronic media. In addition, this project has also addressed, through a case study of two courses offered in the blended mode, the issues concerning the context and content of the two courses, and the opinions of the participants of these two courses towards the new learning and teaching mode.

Keywords: Hybrid learning, blended teaching, computer-mediated communication, classroom discourse analysis.

1 Introduction

Hybrid learning and blended teaching, the emerging modes as a result of the introduction of new technologies into education, have become increasingly popular worldwide. These emerging modes, consisting essentially of a face-to-face (FTF) component and a computer-medicated communication (CMC) component, reflect the hybrid and blended nature of our current schools, universities and workforce, and "the natural process of how people really learn" [2]. Smith & Kurthen [3] have summarized that "combined e-learning FTF courses go by a number of terms, including 'hybrid', 'blended', and 'web-enhanced' learning". They have also proposed a practical taxonomy of four distinct categories including *web-enhanced*, *blended*, *hybrid learning* and *fully online*.

J. Fong, R. Kwan, and F.L. Wang (Eds.): ICHL 2008, LNCS 5169, pp. 157–167, 2008.
© Springer-Verlag Berlin Heidelberg 2008

"Web-enhanced courses incorporate a minimal number of web-based elements, such as the syllabus and course announcements, into an otherwise traditional FTF course. In blended courses, the instructor adds, beyond an online syllabus and a few online documents, some significant online learning activities. For example, a blended course might have online quizzes or have a few online discussions, which account for a certain limited percentage of the course grade. But an important point is that these online activities do not replace any of the regular FTF class meetings and account for only a limited percentage of course activities – less than 45%. If the online activities replace 45% to 80% of FTF class meetings, then the course is hybrid. Class with 80% or more e-learning are considered fully online" [3].

By these definitions, the two courses that are investigated in the research project belong to the "blended" category. However, taking the actual online time of the participants' learning into consideration, the participants can also be regarded as engaging in "hybrid" learning. While this paper acknowledges the distinction between "hybrid" and "blended" learning and teaching, it makes use of the terms interchangeably as both of them share the meaning of combining FTF and CMC components.

The two 'blended' courses involved in this project are "Vocabulary Studies" and "Language and Societal Modernization". They were taught and delivered through a "blended" mode of teaching, i.e. 80% FTF and 20% CMC by means of synchronous 'Blackboard' discussion forums. "Vocabulary Studies" is one of the core courses offered to participants of Bachelor of Education (BEd) and Bachelor of Arts in English Studies and Education (BAESE) programs. There are approximately 180 students studying in this course in the 2006-2007 semester with 36 participants, as a tutorial group, having participated in "blended" mode of learning as research subjects for this project. "Language and Societal Modernization" is a General Education (GE) course offered to students of all BEd programs. For the purpose of this research project, a relatively small number of 12 participants were selected. These participants took the course in a tutorial group.

The purpose of this research project is three-fold interwoven with the three stages of the project. Firstly, although the modes of classroom FTF teaching supplemented by online CMC delivery have been gaining popularity, what has been happening in online CMC discussion forums still remains a "mystery" to some teachers. The first stage of the project is to describe and analyze the online interactions among teacher-student, student-student, and teacher-student-(re)sources and to tease out certain discourse patterns. The purpose of this stage is to illustrate the interactive dynamics of the online discussions, e.g. topic initiation and development, exploitation of varying (re)sources of input, the changing roles of the teachers and the students. Secondly, the conventional classroom FTF learning and teaching have been revisited through a discourse analysis (DA) approach in the second stage. A number of DA theories, e.g. classroom discourse hierarchy and classroom IRF/E (Initiation-Response-Feedback/Evaluation) patterning [4] have been applied in the analysis of the classroom discourse data of the two courses. The purpose of this stage is to explore how technology-enhanced classroom learning and teaching discourse (including the use of interactive and communicative media) has evolved from the traditional classroom discourse. Thirdly, the issues that arise in the "blended" mode of learning and teaching are addressed and discussed in the third stage. The purpose of this stage is to explore the characteristics, potentials, implications and the educational significance of the "blended" mode of learning and teaching.

2 Literature Review

Since the project involves the analysis of online CMC discourse and classroom FTF discourse analysis, the literature or the theoretical and analytical framework underpinning the conceptualization of the project covers a "blend" of three areas including discourse analysis (DA), online education, and classroom-based learning and teaching.

Discourse analysis is "the study of the relationship between language and the contexts in which it is used" [4]. As the project mainly looks into language and content-based learning and teaching through different educational media, DA theories permeate across the three stages of the project. As far as the classroom FTF discourse and the online CMC discourse are concerned, the data for the project has been analyzed based on the theories of the "hierarchy of classroom interaction" [5], and the "social conventions of classroom interaction" [6]. The "written" texts in the CMC context are of a very unique type, which not only contains features of "hypertext" [7] but also features of both written and spoken discourse. This type of written texts can be located on a continuum of spoken-written discourse proposed by Leech, Dechar & Hoogenraad [8], where "conversation", "e-mail message", "lecture", "newspaper", and "a serious printed book" are placed between typical speech and typical writing.

Online education is a broad term encompassing any kind of learning that is done online. People have widely accepted that technology transforms knowledge, and that new technologies make "new things" possible "in a new way" [9]. Recent publications on online education, e.g., Warschauer & Kern [10], Kwan & Fong [11], and Juwah [12], have focused on e-learning pedagogy, and the features of interaction and interactivity in the new online learning and teaching environments. While this project takes "online education" as part of its research paradigm, its focus is on the synchronic online "Blackboard" discussion as a supplementary tool for the FTF classroom teaching. In this regard, this project draws on, as its theoretical and analytical framework, the research and publications by Davis & Brewer [13] on the "context and contact in electronic discourse" and by Laurillard [14] on her classification of five different media types for learning and teaching, i.e., "narrative", "interactive", "adaptive", "communicative", and "productive" media. In addition, this project also draws on the literature on the combination, hybrid or blend of online CMC and classroom FTF interactions, including Topper [15], Skill & Young [16], Larson & Keiper [17], Ellis & Calvo [18], Pearson [19], Jones, Garralda, Li & Lock [20], Ng, Yeung & Hon [21], Xie, DeBacker, & Ferguson [22], Condie & Livingston [23], Reisetter, Lapointe, & Korcuska [24], and Smith & Kurthen [3].

On the classroom-based research front, according to van Lier [25], "most current views of language education are based on the assumption that social interaction plays a central role in learning processes, as a quick glance at the dominant terminology shows. Communication, negotiation of meaning, co-construction, cooperative learning, responsive teaching, and many other terms like them testify to a fundamental shift from conditioning, association, and other laboratory-based notions of learning to human learning as it is situated in the everyday social world of the learner".

The traditional classroom environments have undertaken considerable transformations due to the development in teaching and learning theories and the introduction of new technologies. Nunan [26] has investigated "collaborative" classroom teaching and learning. Ellis [27] has explored the relationship between classroom-based teaching and tasks, and illuminated areas of "task-based" course design and methodology. As far as classroom technologies are concerned, Craig & Amernic [28] have presented a wide-ranging analysis of the use of PowerPoint technology in higher education. Lowerison, Sclater, Schmid and Abrami [29] have investigated the student perceived effectiveness of computer technology use in post-secondary classrooms. Hill [30] has compared the similarities and differences in traditional learning and technology-enhanced classroom, including online flexible learning environments. The purpose of looking at classroom-based learning and teaching is to find out the extent to which the introduction of multimedia in the traditional classroom changes the narrative nature of the classroom discourse.

3 Methodology

This research project involves multiple methods adopting both qualitative and quantitative research approaches. It is based on 1) online CMC discourse data analysis, 2) classroom FTF discourse data analysis, and 3) a questionnaire survey. The questionnaire survey is mainly concerned with the opinions of the participants on the blended mode of learning and teaching of the two courses.

This project consists of three stages of investigation: 1) describing and analyzing the interactions in online 'Blackboard' discussion forum CMC data, 2) describing and analyzing discourse features of the classroom FTF learning and teaching, 3) investigating the characteristics, potentials, implications and the educational significance of the blended mode learning and teaching.

The research questions for this project include: 1) what are the emerging discourse patterns in online CMC discourse? 2) to what extent are contemporary classroom learning and teaching different from the traditional classroom IRF/E (Initiation, Response, Feedback/Evaluation) discourse patterns? and 3) to what extent does the blended mode affect quality learning and teaching as far as the changing roles of the teachers and the students, and the dynamic interactions among the teachers, students and the course content are concerned?

4 Analytical Framework

The analytical framework for the research project is primarily based on the "blend" of the three areas of literature as discussed in the literature review section of the paper. It is particularly developed from differing stages for computer-mediated discourse analysis proposed by Job-Sluder & Barab [31].

There are three guiding principles for establishing the current analytical framework for the "blended" learning and teaching discourse analysis. These include 1) the analysis draws on insights from traditional or conventional discourse analysis, including spoken discourse, written discourse, and classroom discourse, and it is grounded in empirical, textual observations of online CMC and classroom FTF interactions for learning and teaching purposes; 2) the analysis accounts for certain unique features of the technology-enhanced classroom FTF discourse and the online CMC discourse in relation to hypermedia or hypertext, (a)synchronicity, netiquette and the use of Netlish/Weblish (as in chatgroup, BBS, Instant Messaging, MSN or Blackboard discussion forums and in Weblogs or blogs); and 3) the analysis characterizes language use that is above or beyond the level of sentence or utterance in both online CMC and classroom FTF discourse, with a focus on the emerging patterns of language use, interaction, and participation.

The analytical framework consists of *context* analysis and *content* analysis. Content analysis includes *structural* analysis, *semantic* analysis, *interaction* analysis, and *participation* analysis. The major components for each of these analyses are illustrated as follows:

1) *Context* analysis
• course information (course titles, objectives, major content, modes of teaching or delivery)
• participant demographics (age, gender, educational background)
• medium variables (language, the degree of technology-enhancement, temporality, synchronicity, and classroom or online discourse conventions, i.e. the netiquette)
• social context (identities and power relationships of participants)
2) *Content* analysis
• *structural* analysis, including classroom FTF and online CMC discourse hierarchy, i.e. lesson-transaction-exchange-turn-move-act versus forum-thread-exchange-posting-move-act; teacher-talk/posting versus student talk/posting; text versus hypertext
• *semantic* analysis, including discourse move and act identification and categorization, functions of the utterances/postings, i.e. recreational (affective and cohesive) or educational (interactive), and topic development
• *interaction* analysis, including interaction as a means of knowledge construction (sharing, negotiating, and applying newly constructed knowledge), teacher-student-content interactions
• *participation* analysis, including the contribution and engagement of the teachers and the students, the changing roles of the teachers and the students.

5 Results

In terms of the *context* analysis, this project has involved two courses offered in the "blended" mode of learning and teaching. They are "Vocabulary Studies" and "Language and Societal Modernization". The former course provides grounding in concepts, theory and research underlying effective approaches to vocabulary teaching and learning. The major topics covered include morphology, word formation and semantics, vocabulary knowledge, frequency and size, and vocabulary learning strategies. The latter course explores the relationship between societal modernization and language in Asia. It takes into account multiple perspectives on how language is tied to time, place and socio-historical and socio-cultural context. The major topics covered include the invention of writing and printing, the spread of languages through colonization and migration, the people's language, standard language and exoglossic language, language planning, language change and variation, electronic-mediated discourse, and the digital revolution and its effect on societal communication. Both courses are taught and delivered in the form of a combination of lectures, FTF tutorials, and online Blackboard discussion forums with the medium of instruction being English. The ratio for the FTF and CMC tutorial components is 8:2, i.e., eight FTF tutorials and two online synchronous "Blackboard" discussion forums.

In terms of the content analysis, two lectures on "Vocabulary Studies" and two lectures on "Language and Societal Modernization" were recorded and transcribed; two "Blackboard" discussion forums for each of the two courses were downloaded (with the consent of the course participants) for data analysis purpose. Due to the limited space for this paper and the selective nature of discourse analysis, the data of one lecture and one "Blackboard" discussion forum are selected and analyzed in terms of discourse hierarchy, and discourse "act" identification and categorization.

As far as "discourse hierarchy" and discourse "act" are concerned, the lecture consists of transactions, exchanges, turns, moves and acts. Transactions are topic based. There are eight transactions in the lecture including the introduction of the lecture topics, a narrative "word" story, the Old English period, the Middle English period, the Early Modern English period, the Modern English period, language change, and language variation. There are 30 exchanges. An exchange is "the smallest interactive unit consisting, minimally, of two turns" [32]. The teacher has 34 turns, while the students have 30 turns. A turn is "everything the current speaker says before the next speaker takes over" [32]. The teacher has four more turns than the students, because on four occasions, the teacher was "interacting" with the teaching materials, like the sound recording of Shakespeare's Sonnet XVIII. There are also a number of moves to "initiate", "repair", "respond", "re-open", and to "follow-up" in the lecture. A move is "what the speaker does in a turn in order to start, carry on and finish an exchange, i.e. the way he or she interacts" [32]. For the purpose of finding empirical evidence for the classroom FTF discourse analysis, "acts" have been carefully identified and categorized. An "act" signals "what the speaker intends, what he or she wants to communicate". "It is the smallest interactive unit" [32]. Stenstrom [32] has categorized 28 "primary acts" in spoken discourse. These include "accept", "acknowledge", "agree", "alert", "answer", "apology", "call-off", "check", "closer", "confirm", "disagree", "evaluate", "greeting", "inform", "invite", "object", "offer", "opine", "query", "question", "react", "reject", "reply", "request", "smoother", "statement", "suggest", and "thanks". In the 50-minute lecture, a total number of 666 acts have been identified and classified. The teacher performs a total of 644 acts while the students 22. The distribution of the different types of the teacher's acts in the sequence of frequency is as follows (with the number of acts in brackets): statement (189), inform (144), filler (113), opine (62), suggest (59), question (15), invite (14), request (13), offer (12), thanks (6), evaluate (6), check (5), acknowledge (2), agree (1), apology (1), confirm (1), and greeting (1). Note that in Stenstrom's [32] terms, a filler is a secondary act. However, it is listed here as a primary act because of its high frequency of occurrence in the classroom FTF discourse. In contrast, distribution of the students' acts is as follows: accept (11), answer (7), react (2), greeting (1), and query (1).

In contrast with the classroom FTF discourse, the online CMC Blackboard discussion forum has explicit variations. The forum displays a discourse hierarchy of a forum, threads, exchanges, postings, moves, and acts. There are 16 threads, with each thread centering around a loosely defined topic. A considerable number of threads are initiated by the students. The number of exchanges is difficult to determine, because in online discussion forum, multiple participants upload postings, with no explicit pattern of two participants interacting to each other on a traditional turn-by-turn basis. Instead, the number of postings is apparent. There are 127 postings (also named "messages") in the 120-minute synchronous discussion forum. The teacher has 24 postings whereas the students, as a whole, have 103 postings, with each of the students having between 1 to 10 postings among the 36 students. There are also identifiable moves and acts. For the comparison purpose, the primary "acts" in the forum have been identified and classified. There are 999 acts in the forum. The teacher has 277 acts, whereas the students have 722 acts. The distribution of the different types of the teacher's acts in the sequence of frequency is as follows (with the number of acts in brackets): statement (55), inform (54), evaluate (43), thanks (32), opine (17), agree (12), request (11), suggest (9), greeting (7), answer (5), alert (5), closer (4), question (4), offer (3), react (3), reply (3), confirm (3), call-off (2), check (2), accept (1), invite (1) and apology (1). In contrast, distribution of the students' acts is as follows: inform (150), statement (135), opine (80), question (70), greeting (51), agree (43), evaluate (39), alert (34), suggest (23), react (19), thanks (17), answer (13), reply (13), invite (8), object (8), apology (7), check (6), query (4), acknowledge (4), offer (3), closer (2), confirm (2), request (1) and call-off (1). Notice that in Stenstrom's [32] terms, a reply act "responds to a statement", while an answer act "responds to a question or request".

In addition to the classroom FTF discourse and online CMC discourse analysis, a questionnaire survey has also been conducted among the 36 participants in the "blended" mode of "Vocabulary Studies" learning at the end of the course. The questionnaire results are as follows. 83.3% of the participants agree or strongly agree that "it is good to have a combination of FTF and online tutorials"; 97.2% of the participants agree or strongly agree that "FTF tutorials form an integral part of the module learning"; 94.5% of the participants agree or strongly agree that "online tutorials give us a sense of freedom, leisure and autonomy in terms of our involvement and participation in the discussion forums"; and 80.6% of the participants agree or strongly agree that "the current ratio of FTF and Online tutorials (8:2) is appropriate".

6 Discussion

The research project centers around quality learning and teaching through investigating classroom FTF discourse, online CMC discourse and the mixed mode of "blended" learning and teaching. "Good learning is a process of socially based, active co-construction of contextualized knowledge and webs of relations among its nodes" [33]. With the advent of the new era of technology-enhanced or network-enhanced education, traditional notions and practices on learning and teaching have been changing. Interaction and discussion play a crucial role in the learning and teaching processes. Ellis & Calvo argue that "learning through discussions is a key aspect of the student learning experience in higher education" [18]. Smith & Kurthen suggest that "interaction, between instructor-student and between students, is at the heart of education, whether FTF, fully online, or blended-hybrid" [3]. The research data analysis shows that the "blended" mode of learning and teaching can enhance discussion and interaction between the teacher and the students, among students themselves, and between the teacher, students and the course content materials. The classroom FTF and online CMC data analysis also shows the following changes and shifts in terms of the notions and practices on the "blended" mode of learning and teaching.

1) There is a shift from knowledge transmission to knowledge construction in the "blended" mode of learning and teaching. The classroom FTF discourse data shows that the teacher plays a dominant role in terms of disseminating knowledge or leading the classroom discourse. Among the total discourse "acts" in a typical lecture, the acts of "statement", "inform", "opine" and "suggest" come almost exclusively from the teacher, while the students only perform the discourse "acts" of "accept" and "answer". In the online CMC discourse, the students play a leading role as far as the "act" variety and distribution are concerned. The "inform" and "statement" and "opine" acts by the students outnumber those by the teacher significantly. In addition, the total acts by the students in an online discussion forum far exceed those by the teacher. All these data indicate that the "blended" mode of learning and teaching facilitates the shift from knowledge transmission to knowledge construction. The "blended" mode helps create rich zones of development "in which all participants learn by jointly participating in activities in which they share material, socio-cultural, linguistic, and cognitive resources" [1]. In addition, these "hybrid" zones also provide a model for "understanding how meaningful collaboration can be created and sustained and how difference and diversity can serve as resources for learning" [1].

2) The traditional IRF/E (Initiation, Response, Feedback/Evaluation) pattern of classroom discourse pattern has been challenged in the "blended" learning and teaching contexts. New patterns are emerging due to the introduction of new technologies in education and the emerging "blended" learning and teaching practices. The classroom FTF discourse data shows a significant deviation from the traditional IRF/E pattern in that with the introduction of new teaching technologies, such as PowerPoint and multimedia presentation equipment in the classroom and Blackboard discussion platform in online delivery of the courses, complex and dynamic patterns of discourse are emerging. In addition to the interaction between the teacher and the students, there is also a new dimension of interacting with the course content materials in the form of varying media, text or hypertext.

3) The traditional roles of the teachers and students have shifted and become increasingly dynamic. The CMC component in the "blended" mode of learning and teaching has a "democratization effect" [3]. According to Gutiérrez, Baquedano-López, Alvarez, & Chiu [1], learning in the "blended" context requires participants to constantly "negotiate their roles and understandings as they co-participate in various problem-solving activities". It is also essential for the teachers to make new adjustments as far as their roles are concerned in the "blended" context. "Instructors often feel a 'star' quality as they lecture to their students. The online environment divests instructors of their teaching persona, charisma, and years of FTF teaching skills" [3]. The classroom FTF and online CMC discourse data shows that the teacher takes on new roles as an expert learner, a participant, a course designer, an organizer, a

facilitator, a manager, a monitor, an assessor, a team-leader, and also a researcher. In the meantime, the students also perform new roles in addition to being learners, participants, and respondents. They have increasingly become information providers, topic contributors, strategic communicators, meaning makers and negotiators, monitors and team-builders.

4) New dimensions have been added in the consideration of such issues as participation and interaction in both classroom FTF discourse and online CMC discourse. In the "blended" learning and teaching contexts, "students' participation is based on authentic competence, rather than on traditional school criteria such as age, language background, education, or ability" [1]. The interaction in the "blended" context has increasingly included the interaction among the students themselves and a learning community largely due to the changing roles of the students. In addition, interaction in the "blended" context also involves the interaction with course content materials in the form of multimedia text and hypertext. Even the traditional interaction between the teachers and the students is also increasingly mediated through written discourse. "Students of online classes have to decipher written instructions, announcements, examples, or assignments to understand what is expected of them and what is of importance" [3].

5) It can be suggested that teachers and educators should be "synchronous" with the students' positive attitudes towards "blended" learning and teaching. The questionnaire survey data on the combination of classroom FTF and online CMC shows that the students favor both modes of learning and teaching. The majority of the 36 participants consider the combination of FTF and online tutorials to be a good mode. A great majority of the participants agree or strongly agree that online tutorials give them a sense of freedom, leisure and autonomy in terms of their involvement and participation in the discussion forums. In addition, around 80% of the participants think that the 8:2 ratio of FTF and CMC tutorials is appropriate. This shows that the students generally have a positive attitude towards "blended" learning and teaching. This also indicates that the teachers should keep pace, i.e. be "synchronous" with the students' positive attitudes and expectations, and consider ways to include or expand the CMC components in their existing teaching practices.

7 Conclusion

This paper has reported the major objectives, procedures and findings of a research project on the classroom FTF and online CMC discourse analysis in the context of a Hong Kong higher education institute. It argues that the combination of classroom FTF and online CMC helps create a dynamic space for learning and teaching. In this dynamic environment, the notions on education shift from knowledge transmission to knowledge construction. The traditional classroom discourse patterns also shift and become dynamic. In line with these changes and shifts, the teachers and the students also take on new roles in the "blended" learning and teaching environments. New dimensions have been added to the interpretation of participation and interaction in the new educational settings. It is suggested that the teachers should keep "synchronicity" with the students in terms of their positive and embracing attitudes towards the "blended" learning and teaching.

According to Skill and Young [16] "the likely future will be neither solely online learning nor solely instructor-led classroom learning". They propose that "for many of us who have been working with various learning models, it appears that hybrid or blended models most frequently emerge as the most effective learning strategy. This likelihood suggests that the creation of new learning environments should embrace both virtual and real spaces. Understanding how best to integrate these two modes of learning is and will continue to be a significant challenge for educators" [16].

Acknowledgment. This paper is based on an Internal Research Grant (IRG) funded research project (RG27/2006-2007) of the Hong Kong Institute of Education. The author wishes to acknowledge the support, assistance and valuable feedback from Professor Andy Kirkpatrick, Professor Phil Benson, Dr. Lixun Wang, Miss Jieying Zhou and the two anonymous reviewers from the ICHL 2008 Program Committee.

References

1. Gutiérrez, K.D., Baquedano-López, P., Alvarez, H.H., Chiu, M.M.: Building a Culture of Collaboration Through Hybrid Language Practices. Theory Into Practice 38(2), 87–93 (1999)
2. Masie, E.: The Blended Learning Imperative. In: Bonk, C.J., Graham, C.R. (eds.) The Handbook Of Blended Learning: Global Perspectives, Local Designs, ch. 2 (pp. 22–26), p. 26. John Wiley & Sons, Inc, San Francisco (2006)
3. Smith, G.G., Kurthen, H.: Front-Stage and Back-Stage in Hybrid E-Learning Face-to-Face Courses. International Jl. on E-Learning 6(3), 455–474 (2007)
4. McCarthy, M.: Discourse Analysis for Language Teachers, pp. 5–7, 14–17. Cambridge University Press, Cambridge (2002)
5. Coulthard, M.: An introduction to discourse analysis, pp. 99–100. Longman Group Limited, London (1977)
6. Walsh, S.: Analyzing Classroom Discourse: a Variable Approach. In: Hughes, R. (ed.) Spoken English, TESOL and Applied Linguistics: Challenges for Theory and Practice, pp. 216–242. Palgrave MacMillan, Basingstoke (2006)
7. Orsinger, R.R.: The future of managing information: Hyper-text & Hyper-media. 9th Annual Advanced Evidence and Discovery Course (1996) (Retrieved January 08, 2007)
8. Leech, G., Deuchar, M., Hoogenraad, R.: English Grammar for Today: A New Introduction, 2nd edn., p. 151. Palgrave MacMillan, London (2006)
9. Noss, R., Pachler, N.: The challenge of new technologies: doing old things in a new way, or doing new things? In: Mortimore, P. (ed.) Understanding Pedagogy and its Impact on Learning, p. 195. Paul Chapman Publishing Ltd, London (1999)
10. Warschauer, M., Kern, R.: Network-based Language Teaching: Concepts and Practice. Cambridge University Press, Cambridge (2000)
11. Kwan, R., Fong, J.: Web-based Learning: Technology and Pedagogy. World Scientific, Hong Kong (2005)
12. Juwah, C.: Interactions in Online Education: Implications for theory and practice. Routledge, London and New York (2006)
13. Davis, B.H., Brewer, J.P.: Electronic Discourse: Linguistic Individuals in Virtual Space. State University of New York Press, New York (1997)
14. Laurillard, D.: Rethinking University Teaching: A Conversational Framework for the Effective Use of Learning Technologies, 2nd edn., pp. 81–174. RoutledgeFalmer, London and New York (2002)

15. Topper, A.: Comparing Face-to-Face and Electronic Discourse: Issues and Questions Raised in a Research Study, Chicago, IL (1997)
16. Skill, T.D., Young, B.A.: Embracing the Hybrid Model: Working at the Intersections of Virtual and Physical Learning Spaces. New Directions For Teaching And Learning 92, 23–32 (2002)
17. Larson, B., Keiper, T.A.: Classroom Discussion and Threaded Electronic Discussion: Learning in Two Arenas. Contemporary Issues in Technology and Teacher Education 2(1), 45–62 (2002)
18. Ellis, R.A., Calvo, R.A.: Learning Through Discussions in Blended Environments. Educational Media International 41(3), 263–274 (2004)
19. Pearson, J.: Investigating ICT using problem-based learning in face-to-face and online learning environments. Computers & Education 47, 56–73 (2006)
20. Jones, R.H., Garralda, A., Li, D.C.S., Lock, G.: Interactional dynamics in on-line and face-to-face peer-tutoring sessions for second language writers. Journal of Second Language Writing 15, 1–23 (2006)
21. Ng, C., Yeung, A.S., Hon, R.Y.H.: Does online language learning diminish interaction between student and teacher? Educational Media International 43(3), 219–232 (2006)
22. Xie, K., DeBacker, T.K., Ferguson, C.: Extending the traditional classroom through online discussion: The role of student motivation. J. Educational Computing Research 34(1), 67–89 (2006)
23. Condie, R., Livingston, K.: Blending online learning with traditional approaches: changing practices. British Journal of Educational Technology 38(2), 337–348 (2007)
24. Reisetter, M., Lapointe, L., Korcuska, J.: The Impact of Altered Realties: Implications of Online Delivery for Learners' Interactions, Expectations, and Learning Skills. International Jl. on E-Learning 6(1), 55–80 (2007)
25. van Lier, L.: Constraints and resources in classroom talk: Issues of equality and symmetry. In: Candlin, C.N., Mercer, N. (eds.) English language teaching in its social context: a reader, pp. 90–107. Routledge, London and New York (2001)
26. Nunan, D.: Collaborative language learning and teaching. Cambridge University Press, New York (1992)
27. Ellis, R.: Task-based Language Learning and Teaching. Oxford University Press, Oxford (2003)
28. Craig, R.J., Amernic, J.H.: PowerPoint Presentation Technology and the Dynamics of Teaching. Innovative Higher Education 31, 147–160 (2006)
29. Lowerison, G., Sclater, J., Schmid, R.F., Abrami, P.C.: Student perceived effectiveness of computer technology use in post-secondary classroom. Computers & Education 47, 465–489 (2006)
30. Hill, J.R.: Flexible Learning Environments: Leveraging the Affordances of Flexible Delivery and Flexible Learning. Innovative Higher Education 31, 187–197 (2006)
31. Job-Sluder, K., Barab, S.A.: Shared We and Shared They Indicators of Group Identity in Online Teacher Professional Development. In: Barab, S.A., Kling, R., Gray, J.H. (eds.) Designing virtual communities in the service of learning, pp. 377–403. Cambridge University Press, Cambridge (2004)
32. Stenstrom, A.-B.: An introduction to spoken interaction, pp. 38–46. Longman, London, New York (1994)
33. Okan, Z.: Edutainment: is learning at risk? British Journal of Educational Technology 34(3), 255–264 (2003)

Learning Environment for Digital Natives – Web 2.0 Meets Globalization

Crusher Wong, Lilian Vrijmoed, and Eva Wong

City University of Hong Kong, Hong Kong SAR, China
{crusher.wong,bhlilian,eva.wong}@cityu.edu.hk

Abstract. Web 2.0 services and communities constitute the daily lives of digital natives with online utilities such as Wikipedia and Facebook. Attempts to apply Web 2.0 at the University of Illinois at Urbana-Champaign demonstrated that the transformation to writing exercises could improve students' learning experiences. Inspired by their success, blogging technology was adopted to pilot a writing-across-the-curriculum project via the learning management system at City University of Hong Kong. Instead of promoting peer assessment, one-on-one tutoring interactions were induced by providing feedback to written assignments. Taking the advantage of the "flat world", tutors were hired from the United States, Canada, Australia, New Zealand and Spain to experiment with outsourcing and offshoring some of the English enhancement schemes. For the university wide project deployment in the fall of 2008, a globalized network of online language tutors needs to be built up with support from universities in countries with English as the native language.

Keywords: e-Learning, Web 2.0, Globalization, Blog, Writing Across the Curriculum, Language Learning, Online Tutoring.

1 Introduction

The impact of digital technology on the new generation can be likened to television and its effects on post WWII baby boomers, but the influence is far greater in this digital age. With video games engaging networks of players via Wi-Fi connection on the Internet, cyber worlds are as real as the physical world to digital natives [1]. How can a traditional lecture compete with a virtual gaming experience in terms of attracting young minds? Obviously, educators have to speak the students' language in order to communicate and transfer skills, knowledge and value to the generation of digital natives.

Nonetheless, the notion of "speaking the students' language" should be limited to the adoption of communication methods instead of the actual language. The official medium of instruction at City University of Hong Kong (CityU) is English hence course instructors are obligated to conduct classes and assess students in English. However, most of the faculty staff is not trained to assess students' English competency so only the knowledge in subject matter is gauged. Although students are required to study academic English courses through out the three years of their university

J. Fong, R. Kwan, and F.L. Wang (Eds.): ICHL 2008, LNCS 5169, pp. 168–177, 2008.

life, they usually treat the courses as a constraint and never have any genuine interest in studying English. One of the reasons is those courses are mostly designed for all students and lack the connection to the students' subject disciplines. As a result, improving students' English proficiency in the context of subject discipline has becomes a new direction in CityU's language enhancement scheme.

2 Writing across the Curriculum Online

A pilot project entitled Language Companion Course (LCC) started in February 2007 (Winter Semester) to provide a small group of students with English support in their subject assignments at CityU. With a dedicated online essay marking interface provided by Prof David Wible [2] at Tamkang University in Taiwan, tutors gave specific feedback to guide students in refining their written assignments. Improvements were observed by comparing errors frequencies between different versions of the same essay and different assignments from the same student. The system assisted project evaluation and served as an archive but it lacked the integration with our central e-learning platform for institution-wide deployment.

2.1 The Web 2.0 Learning Environment

Web 2.0 applications have been around for years [3] but cyber citizens may not have realized the significance until the term entered common usage. In essence, it describes the trend from passive to proactive involvement on the web such as collaborating in editing Wikipedia articles or mobilizing people by building a group on Facebook. The power of co-creation generated by all these Web 2.0 tools energizes new opportunities in education [4], from schools to society, facilitating lifelong learning for everyone.

In the summer of 2007, Web 2.0 applications registered strongly in the mind of the CityU delegates after engaging with presenters from Washington State University, Dartmouth College and the University of Illinois at Urbana-Champaign in an e-learning conference in Boston. Blogs and wikis were the most common instruments in their studies. To enhance individual student writing proficiency, private blogs [5] were selected rather than wikis where team work was emphasized. Journal LX from Learning Objects for blogging (Fig. 1) was an add-on feature on CityU's Blackboard system, thus it was the obvious choice for the task.

The second pilot involved three courses from different disciplines - Microbiology, Services Operation Management and Electronic Publishing, with around 150 students. To control resources, each course could elect up to three 500-word essay assignments to join the scheme. In line with requests from the language tutors, special grouping was supplied to maintain tutor to student ratios at 1 to 15 or below.

Entering the winter term of the 2007/08 academic year, the pilot broadened to involve over 600 students registered in ten courses from various faculties and schools. 48 language tutors were deployed, 29 of them stationed in overseas countries.

2.2 Workflow and Timeline

The key to gaining acceptance by students was the relevance to the subjects they were studying. Instead of a separate English assignment, students merely needed to

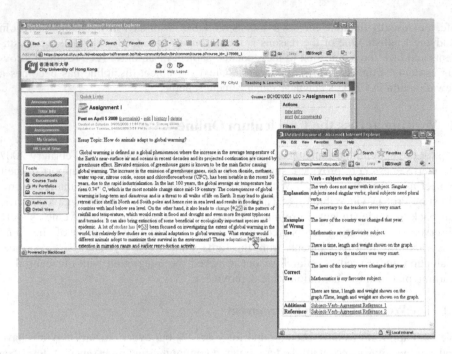

Fig. 1. Student view of a specific feedback on a blog

increase their effort in an existing one. On the other hand, the management did not want to increase the burden on course instructors so usually no alternation would be applied to the assignment in all respect - length, topic, format, due date, etc.

For each assignment attached to the LCC scheme, a blog were opened in advance for students to post the drafts. Tutors would locate the problematic areas and indicate the types of errors using a standard comment bank (Fig. 2) developed at CityU. Structural issues and overall comments were also available but were given as free format notes. Besides the locally produced essay writing resources, links to public websites such as Just the Word (http://193.133.140.102/JustTheWord/) for collocation query were supplied. Then, students could rewrite their essays accordingly as second drafts for one more round of formative feedback. All the editing histories were available for the students and tutors to track the chances and gauge the improvement on students' writing skills. Two chances of getting feedback were the manageable limit at that point.

Time was an important factor in carrying out the feedback exercise. The iteration of feedback and revision guided students to a converging path of writing refinement. Nevertheless, asking a student to prepare an assignment one month in advance might not be practical. To maximize the benefit of learning from the feedback, a model timeline (Fig. 3) was formulated.

T1 was the assignment deadline set by the course instructor. Around 10 days prior to T1, a blog was opened (boxed area in Fig. 3) to let students post their draft work. If a student posted an entry before T3, feedback would be ready by T3 + α. Hence,

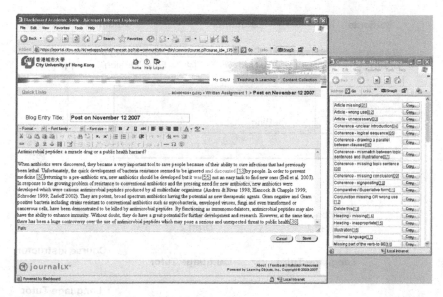

Fig. 2. Insertion of specific feedbacks by a language tutor using the WYSIWYG editor of the blog tool and the custom made comment bank interface

α (usually 72 hours) represented the time limit for the language tutor to provide feedback. The student then had β, 24 hours in most cases, to improve their writing according to the feedback. The tutor would start giving feedback on the second draft at T2 and finish the work by T2 + α. After another round of refinement, the student submitted the final version to the course instructor and the language tutor separately.

Initial observation showed only around 15% of the students posted their first drafts before T3. After the students were accustomed to the LCC logistic, over 80% of them took the full advantage of two times feedback in most courses. However, the law students had total confidence with their English writing skills and less then 10% participated in the feedback exercise.

The essence of this project was to help students improve their written English. Hence, the feedback activities were voluntary and those with confidence in their English could skip the drafting. To help students gauge their writing proficiency, the final submissions were graded by the same online language tutors. Course instructors counted the English grades as 5 to 20 percent against the whole assignment to retain the subject-driven idea of writing across the curriculum.

3 Logistic and Technical Support

The logistic and technical support team consisted of staff members from the Academic Regulations and Records Office, the Computing Services Centre, the Education Development Office, the Enterprise Solutions Office and the Office of the Dean of Student Learning. They collaborated in tasks including user interface development, account management, user training, and enquiry service.

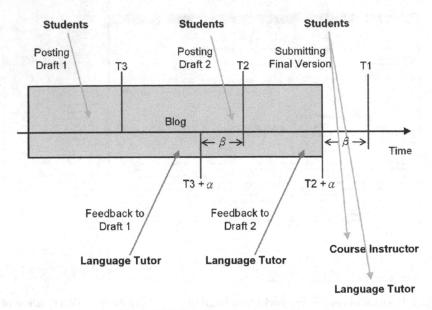

Fig. 3. LCC Timeline of an assignment

3.1 User Interface and Account Management

To reduce the effort of customization, the blog feature in Blackboard course sites together with the in-house developed comment bank interface served as the apparatus for students and tutors to interact. Each course site was populated manually with a group of students, the assigned language tutor, the course instructor and the evaluation team members. Besides the Blackboard course sites, blog and wiki sites were launched to encourage sharing of new ideas and practice by the pilot team members. Over thirty special user accounts were created for the overseas tutors and coordinators to work on our Blackboard system and SharePoint wiki site since they were not regular CityU members.

3.2 User Training

In person workshops were arranged for the CityU English Language Centre (ELC) colleagues acting as online tutors. With their background knowledge in Bb, the blog feature was relatively easy to follow. Overseas tutors mostly trained themselves by watching the online workshop video clips with the Blackboard training account provided. All of them managed to give feedbacks on blog to students with support from the technical team. Hence, online training modes should be a sufficient means for overseas tutors to comprehend the technical procedures. However, involvement in the LCC project required more than technical know-how and English teaching skills; the responsibility of each member, the delay when collaborating with people in different time zones, managing the tight feedback timeframes, and the different subject disciplines and level of students were much more difficult for the online tutors to grasp effectively.

The submission and editing procedures of the blog entry for the LCC scheme were demonstrated to students during the class visits. The enquiries statistics showed that most students could handle the blog feature very well. With more courses joining the project, the class visit exercise could be supplemented or even substituted by online tutorials.

The instructor user guide had been updated numerous times according to requests by language coordinators and tutors. The ever expanding content, such as introduction of SafeAssign as an optional device for plagiarism detection, made it an unattractive reading. Since the ELC had developed another document entitled Guidelines for LCC tutors, there was a possibility to completely separate the logistics from the technical steps. On the contrary, the student user guide remained as simple as it could be and no complaints were received. It was not clear, however, whether students had simply relied on trial and error or consulted the document.

3.3 Enquiry Service

Over 300 phone calls and e-mail enquires had been answered within one of the four categories – the use of the application (50%), the application technical problems (5%), the connection problems (5%) and the user requests (40%).

The use of the application referred to tutors asking for the steps to create a blog or to set a deadline. These procedures had been incorporated in the workshop and the user guide but obviously some re-enforcement was needed. Such problem also led to students' quires when they could not see the assignment drop box.

The small number of application technical problem confirmed that the platform was relatively bugs free. However, diagnosing technical problem remotely was always time consuming. The connection problems were coursed by user behavior, client side bandwidth and CityU server restart schedules. Only fine tunings from both sides was able to fix the issues.

Most enquiries from students were not exactly technical, ranging from requesting permission for late submission to complaining about delay in receiving tutor feedback. After confirming that no genuine technical issues were involved, the support team contacted the related parties to sort out the arrangement.

4 Tutor Search in the "Flat World"

The advent of internet technology not only creates a new medium for communication and collaboration indigenous to the digital natives but also breaks the geographic boundaries of human resources. Hong Kong is amongst the most populated metropolis in the world with a heavy cost of living. Local English language training experts are in demand due to the vital linkages between Hong Kong and the rest of the world in business, academic, political and legal issues. The Web allows anyone with the right skill set to cultivate our students' English writing ability without being physical present in Hong Kong. In summary, the human resources of the flat world [6] guarantee a sufficient amount of capable language tutors to participate in the LCC project. "Flat world" refers to a level playing field in terms of academic competition, providing opportunities to everyone.

The colleagues in the ELC had assisted the introduction of the LCC scheme as language tutors from the beginning. Their contributions were highly appreciated but they had regular face-to-face teaching duties. Recruitment of a new population of English teaching experts dedicated to the LCC project was essential to any future development. In addition, interacting with tutors from around the world expand student language and culture awareness.

During the fall semester pilot, two overseas tutors were hired from Los Angeles and Chicago independently to probe the feasibility of outsourcing. Besides minor technical problems and time zone issues, our Web 2.0 writing-across-the-curriculum experiment had been autonomous with regard to location. This result further encouraged the CityU management to launch a large scale world-wide tutor search to the exploit the flat world resources powered by the latest information and communication technology.

In addition to the isolated overseas tutors from the US, New Zealand and Spain, connections were established with institutions in English speaking countries to cope with the expanding population of students for the winter semester 2007/08. Postgraduate and undergraduate students in Teaching English as a Second Language (TESL) or linguistics programs were recruited from the University of Sydney, the Brigham Young University in Utah and the University of British Columbia. Giving feedback and grading in the LCC project became part of their studies. This win-win situation enabled both the student tutors (TESL or linguistics students) and CityU's undergraduate students to improve their skills. The addition of the overseas student tutors giving the project new source of energy.

5 Student Participation

From another point of view, our approach was an early bird assignment scheme similar to the study by Unsworth and Kauter [7]. Students often claimed they were too busy to join voluntary schemes even if they believed the activity might help them to achieve a higher grade. Besides the time management competency of the students, the appreciation to language learning was essential to participation to the LCC scheme. Course instructors and language tutors played crucial role in motivating students.

5.1 Course Instructors' Role in Motivating the Students

The attitude of the course instructor had a major impact on the participation rate of the students. In addition to promoting the scheme and providing a well designed essay assignment, the project management team suggested that the grade on the final version given by the online tutor accounted for 10 to 30 percent of the whole assignment. However, some course instructors were reluctant to do this and thus some students perceived the scheme, in particular the final version submission, as voluntary instead of compulsory.

Some assignments could not be prepared for in advance. For example, an applied physics laboratory course was included in the pilot with the focus on writing discussion sections in the lab report. Naturally, one had to complete the experiment before starting the lab report write-up. To join the LCC scheme, postponing the lab report deadline date was unavoidable. Fortunately, the course instructor appreciated the importance of expressing experimental findings in written English and allowed more than two weeks, rather than the usual one week, for students to participate in the feedback process. Otherwise, there would have been insufficient time to iterate the draft-feedback loop process.

5.2 Workload Distribution on Language Tutors

When the grouping of one language tutor with around fifteen students made the workload looked evenly distributed, it was strongly coupled with the subject discipline. Even thought the tutors supported students on only the English writing, they had problem giving suggestions when they were not familiar with the subject matter. The law courses had most severe problem as the profession adopted a different writing style. Likewise, tutors without any science background were unable to comprehend the discussion of an applied physics lab report. To adept to these specific forms of writing, diligent tutors had put in extra efforts. Law students were always the students with the best English proficiency at CityU and most of them skipping the feedback and went straight to the final submission. That translated to low workloads for tutors in the law courses.

Some dedicated tutors, mostly the student tutors from overseas, communicated with the CityU students, building a more social relationship to stimulate their learning. Rather than following the LCC assignment timeline, they minimized the feedback response time in order to give more opportunities for feedback within the ten day period. Nevertheless, another population of tutors behaved exactly like typical students and gave the feedback in the last minute. Some even avoided providing any language support to the students besides the feedback to assignment. Unfortunately, the Web 2.0 environment in the LCC project was partly driven by monetary reward as opposed to the self-directed Wikipedia and the open source movement.

6 Future Development

Providing formative feedback to draft versions of the assignments via the blog interface is believed to be an excellent method of improving students' language skills. Nevertheless, our experience indicates coordinating the LCC scheme with course instructors, language tutors and students in ten courses demands the manpower of a dedicated office. One of the major difficulties in the workflow is scheduling the feedback and submission process. All online tutors must work according to the deadline of a particular assignment which may vary due to the progress of content delivery.

6.1 Creating a Self-directed Learning Environment

One of the proposed solutions is to decouple the grade of the LCC from the subject courses. By creating a credit-bearing LCC course, students can register to take the benefit of getting online tutor feedback in addition to earning extra credits. Students will be told to prepare their written assignments as early as possible in order to receive feedback from tutors before their assignment deadline. Even after the formal assignment deadline, students can keep improving their writing with the language tutors. The target is to avoid the inflexible nature of the LCC assignment timeline. Grading may rely on a final e-Portfolio highlighting all the learning experience and improvement from the student's point of view. Shifting the responsibility of learning back to the students is the only way to lead them to the path of lifelong learning.

6.2 Other Dimensions in Language Learning

English writing skill is the focus in the initiation of the LCC scheme. The expansion to reading, listening and speaking skills are all technically possible in our Blackboard system. The University of Sydney LCC coordinators will co-design reading materials with course instructors at CityU in the summer of 2008. Winba Voice Tools, providing audio recording and play back capability via internet browser, have always be a building block on CityU's Blackboard system to facilitate oral language learning. Subject expert in Management Sciences have asked for English support in oral presentation. The technology to video tape student's presentations and host them online has existed for years. It is a matter of time to source the flat world for experts on presentation skills.

7 Conclusion

In the LCC project, the power of social networking [8] observed in the globalized world was harnessed to enhance student learning. The blog tool facilitated an environment for collaboration in writing skills development with student posting subject assignments and tutor giving formative feedbacks. The detailed history of the blog presented the chronological progression in essay writing enabling evaluation by everyone in the project including the students themselves. Coupling with other online resources, the system promoted the culture of self-directed learning. Allowing more flexible feedback workflow should encourage more student initiated interactions.

The reward systems to both students and online tutors were extrinsic as scores and money were not originally involved in the practice of social networking. Partnership with institutions from countries with English as the native language has shed new light on the future recruitment model. Observation showed some overseas student tutors were more pro-active in communicating with CityU students due to their personal attributes – intention to support language learning and comprehension of Web technologies. As a result, the new target is to build an online community concerned about improving students' English proficiency more than the financial reward. Further sharing is on the way as over a thousand of students will participate in the fall semester of 2008/09.

References

1. Prensky, M.: Digital Natives, Digital Immigrants. On the Horizon 9(5) (October 2001) NCB University Press (2001)
2. Wible, D., Kuo, C., Tsao, N., Liu, A.: An Online Writing Platform for Language Learners. J. UCS. 7(3), 278–289 (2001)
3. O'Reilly, T.: What Is Web 2.0, http://www.oreilly.com

4. Franklin, T., van Harmelen, M.: Web 2.0 for Content for Learning and Teaching in Higher Education. JISC Report (2007)
5. Forrest, S.: Using Blog in Course Work Helps Improve Students' Writing. News Bureau, University of Illinois at Urbana-Champaign 25(20) (2006)
6. Friedman, T.L.: The World is Flat: A Brief History of the Twenty-First Century, Farrar, Straus and Giroux (2005)
7. Unsworth, K., Kauter, K.: Evaluating an Earlybird Scheme: Encouraging Early Assignment Writing and Revising. Higher Education Research & Development 27(1), 69–76 (2008)
8. Tapscott, D., Williams, A.D.: Wikinomics: How Mass Collaboration Changes Everything. Portfolio (2006)

The Pervasive Learning Platform of a Shanghai Online College – A Large-Scale Test-Bed for Hybrid Learning

Liping Shen and Ruimin Shen

Computer Science & Engineering Dept., Shanghai Jiao Tong University
{lpshen,rmshen}@sjtu.edu.cn

Abstract. The rapid evolution of Information and Communication Technologies has led to new ways of learning and education. In Shanghai, researchers and developers of an online college actively seek technological interventions to provide first-class e-learning services for about 17,000 enrolled students. They developed a cutting-edge pervasive learning platform that provide "always on" education. It aims to support "Learning Anytime, Anywhere", which is accomplished through extending the real classrooms and also supporting web-based self-paced learning. The platform is composed of three components: a) distributed Standard Natural Classrooms, the smart spaces to provide natural interaction for teachers and students; b) large-scale media streaming for multi-mode terminals delivering fully interactive lectures to PCs and mobile devices; c) dynamic and personalized web-based learning systems. Multi-modal interactions are supported that students learning on this platform change from passive learners to truly engaged learners who are behaviorally, intellectually, and emotionally involved in their learning activities.

Keywords: e-Learning, pervasive learning, hybrid learning, learning platform.

1 Introduction

The rapid evolution of Information and Communication Technologies (ICT) has led to new ways of learning and education. e-Learning systems have been promoted by most education institutions and numerous corporations to facilitate a better learning and teaching environment. Products such as Virtual-U [3], WebCT[17] and Blackboard [2] have been in use for the past few years. These systems have implemented a number of fundamental components such as synchronous and asynchronous teaching systems, course-content delivery tools, polling and quiz modules, virtual workspaces for sharing resources, whiteboards, grade reporting systems, and assignment submission components. Many online colleges such as the UK Open University[7], the Hong Kong Open University[8] and the Network Education College of Shanghai Jiao Tong University (SJTU)[6], have developed and deployed their own e-Learning platform and infrastructure to provide adaptive and efficient e-Learning services. Today, eLearning becomes heavily learner-centered, emphasizing pervasive and personalized learning technologies[13]. As both the traditional classroom learning and web-based

J. Fong, R. Kwan, and F.L. Wang (Eds.): ICHL 2008, LNCS 5169, pp. 178–189, 2008.

learning offer strengths and suffer from limitations, it is now a trend for e-Leanring systems to combine the strengths of the two into hybrid learning [5].

In china, more than half of the right age students are not admitted to higher education institutions every year. The data from the Ministry of Education press Sept 2007 showed that 77% of the right age youngsters (about 19 million) were not able to take higher education. From 2001, Chinese government began to authorize colleges and universities to establish online colleges to boost occupational and adult education and to ensure more access to higher education. Online colleges usually have large numbers of distributed students in one class, so it is not feasible for traditional classroom lecturing. Many online colleges use the hybrid mode of delivering lecture CDs and web-based asynchronous learning. But the main problems there are the lack of learning-inducing stress for learners and the resulting high non-completion-rate. The traditional instructor-led classroom learning is proven to be an effective and successful education method which is fresh, original, interactive and on-the-spot. We have conducted a survey among 5000 online college students which shows that only 280 students prefer to learn traditionally web-based courses while most students select real-time learning.

Researchers in the SJTU online college have been holding the vision that the most import thing is to provide live and interactive lectures to the distributed students. Great efforts have been made by the researchers and developers of the college to leverage existing and emerging ICT to augment the function of traditional classroom and then digitalize them, and finally deliver them to diverse devices. In addition to the synchronous live lecturing, asynchronous web-based learning is also provided, allowing students to study according to their needs and preferences. Learners appear to enjoy this flexible, student-centered approach. Within seven years (2001-2007), this College's enrollment has grown from 120 students to 17,000 students.

This paper presents a pervasive learning platform which is developed and used at the SJTU online college, where we are motivated to research on exploiting new and emerging ICT to provide effective learning services for students. This online college currently has about 17000 enrolled students which make the platform a large-scale test-bed for hybrid learning. We will start by outlining the pervasive learning platform (Section 2). Then we describe three main components of the platform in section 3~5 respectively. Finally conclusion is made in section 6.

2 The Shanghai Pervasive Learning Platform

The e-Learning system developed at the SJTU online college is kind of pervasive learning platform that provide "always on" education[13]. It aims to provide "Learning anytime, anywhere", which is accomplished through extending the real classrooms and also supporting web-based self-paced learning. It differs from the previous platforms by the feature of heavily learner-centered, and by using wireless computing and pervasive computing technologies.

Figure 1 gives the architecture of the platform. It is composed of three main parts: a) distributed Standard Natural Classrooms (SNC), the smart spaces to provide natural human-machine interaction and context-aware services for teachers and students; b) large-scale media streaming for multi-mode terminals delivering fully interactive

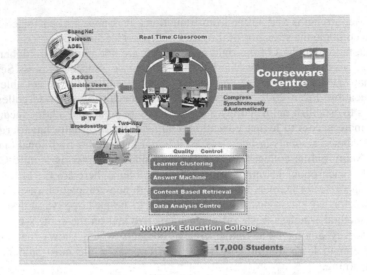

Fig. 1. The Shanghai Pervasive eLearning Platform

lectures to PCs, laptops, PDA, IPTV and mobile phones through heterogeneous networks; c) dynamic and personalized web-based learning providing multiple services for learning management and quality control, such as dynamic learning services, collaborative learning communities and personalized recommendations. The core of the platform is interconnected SNCs distributed around Shanghai, the Yangtze River delta, and even in remote western regions of China such as Tibet, Yan'an, Xing Jiang and Nin Xia. They are equipped with numerous smart devices/sensors and specially developed software. The live interactive lectures are digitalized and then delivered to PCs, laptops, PDA, IPTV and mobile phones through various networks such as Shanghai Telecom ADSL, GPRS, IPTV, two-way satellite and the Internet. A recording program records all the media components including audio, video, handwriting and files shown on the computer into coursewares. Students can tune into these recordings live online, or they can download them later for review. The web-based learning services consist of the content based retrieval search engine which enables the students to find their desired materials conveniently and quickly, the answer machine which responds to students' questions automatically, the data analyze center and self-organized learning community which analyze students learning patterns and provide personalized services, and other learning tools such as assignment system and examination system.

Chinese classrooms, whether on school grounds or online, have long suffered from a lack of interactivity. Researchers and developers of this platform actively seek technologic interventions that could greatly increase interactivity in large blended classroom. The platform support real-time multi-modal interactions such as audio, video, text, short message and pen-based etc. In conclusion, this platform has five distinctive characteristics: broadband, wireless, real-time, interactive and multimedia. These five factors integrate together and supplement each other, servicing the whole e-Learning framework.

3 The Standard Natural Classrooms – The Headwaters for Learning

Being the most popular way for off-campus education in China, many real-time e-Learning systems deliver live lectures through satellite in a way like Television University or using commercial video conference systems. Most of these systems are desktop based that the teacher must remain at the computer, using the keyboard and mouse to manage the lecture, which not only have deficiencies in interaction, scalability, mobility and maintenance but also loss the effectiveness of classroom education to a large extent. Many efforts have been made to bridge the gap between real-time remote classroom and traditional classroom activities such as the Smart Classroom project in Tsinghua University[12].

By applying pervasive technologies in real classrooms, we developed numerous distributed Standard Natural Classrooms both in Shanghai area and across the whole China. These SNCs are equipped with high-tech devices, tools and software infrastructure that all the SNCs are configured in a unified STANDARD way. In SNCs, teachers can move freely, use multiple NATURAL modalities to give the lecture and interact with remote students in the same way as the traditional classrooms. All these SNCs are distributed around Shanghai, the Yangtze River delta, and even in remote western regions of China such as Tibet, Yan'an, Xing Jiang and Nin Xia. They are interconnected either through the broadband IP network or through two-way satellites. During a lecture, students could select to attend the class in the primary SNC with lecturers, in the nearest remote SNC or even in their own home. Figure 2 is the classroom setup of a typical SNC in use at the online college. The smart board and lecture notes touch screen display presentations (e.g. PowerPoint), while also act as a whiteboard for handwriting. The instructor can write on materials on the touch screen with a pen or on the projected whiteboard with a laser E-pen. To optimize the video quality, a pan-camera could track the instructor when he/she moves around in the classroom, which actually is installed at the rear end of the SNC. Another monitor camera is mounted in the front of the classroom and it captures students' attention status by recognizing their face expressions. The feedback screen supports the real-time multimodal interaction and displays the questions and poll results based on which the teachers could fine tune their lecturing in a positively way. Other devices are provided and installed to collect the context information and to control the classroom equipment, for example RFID (Radio Frequency IDentifier) tags are used to identify and track students and context-aware light controller to switch on/off the light intelligently. Using this hi-tech environment, the teacher can move freely, demonstrate his body language, and interact with learners as naturally and easily as in a traditional face-to-face classroom.

The SNC involves a number of component technologies that make the interaction between the teacher and remote students as natural as that in a physical classroom. Due to space limitations, we only describe three of them and how these technologies function in the SNC.

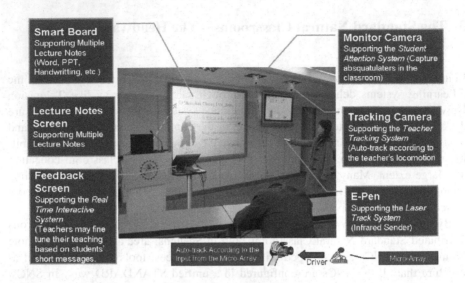

Fig. 2. The typical SNC setup

3.1 Multi-modal Natural Interaction

In this part, the phrase "interaction" refers to both human computer interaction and teacher student interaction. Technologies are leveraged to support multi-modal interactions in SNC, that at one side, students and teachers could communicate and interact as naturally as the face-to-face education, and at the other side, teachers could teach in a usual way through handwriting, audio command and laser pen, thus eliminating the limit of desk based interaction in traditional tele-education systems. As the data collected from this platform reported, interactions could much better engage students in the learning process and students changed from passive learners to truly engaged learners who are behaviorally, intellectually, and emotionally involved in their learning tasks[16].

The interaction modes involve video, audio, text and pen-based handwriting. During lecture, the live classroom scenes are transmitted to remote SNCs and displayed on wall-mounted large screens, at the meantime, the remote SNC video are also sent back to the lectures' SNC. For learners using PC at home and mobile devices on the way, the live teacher's video is delivered together with the audio and lecture notes. When a teacher talks with a specific student, this student's video will also be transmitted to all the other SNCs. The teacher could use voice-commands to perform some common tasks such as "next slide" or "go back to the last one". Meanwhile, students can send text messages to the instructor through cell phone Short Message Service or the text window of the SNC system. Students' messages will be displayed on the instructor's feedback screen, to inform the instructor their learning progress, questions, or any other feedback, that the instructor could respond in a positive way.

Teachers in real classrooms often write on chalkboards or whiteboards. Most current tele-educations, however, confine teachers to their computers by requiring them to use the mouse and keyboard. We address this problem by allowing the teachers to write on the touch screen with a touch pen. With the help of this pen, teachers could write on their prepared lecture notes in the same way as writing on a sheet. There are advantages of pen-based handwriting over the traditional chalk. The touch pen could write directly on the lecture notes, no need to re-write to the chalkboards which could improve the efficiency greatly. And the erasure job is easier and healthier with a digital eraser or just opening a new page. The remote students could see the same lecture notes and handwriting on the smart board as local students do. A remote student who has a PC or mobile devices could also write on this board freely—for instance, a student might write the solution to a question the teacher has just posed. This kind of pen-based interaction is very important for some science courses such as Math and Physics. When teachers leave the touch screen, for example, walking into the students or holding a model, they could even use a laser pointer to write on the projected smart board. A computer-vision-based module turns an ordinary laser pointer into an E-pen.

3.2 Movement Tracking and Intelligent Focusing

In a conventional classroom, students naturally follow the class's focus as it changes from time to time. For instance, when the teacher writing on the electronic whiteboard, the focusing should be the content of handwriting; when the teacher answering questions, the focusing might be his gesture and expression; when a teacher holds up a model, the model becomes the object of general interest. Yet in most current tele-education systems, remote students only see a fixed scene regardless of the changing context of the class, which hampers their understanding of the instruction. Although a human camera operator can select the proper view for live video, the high labor cost often makes this infeasible.

The intelligent focusing module we developed overcomes this problem. This module consists of a pan-camera and a decision module. By drawing clues from the classroom context, the intelligent focusing module automatically distinguishes among several activities during a typical class. Using this information, the decision module selects the most appropriate view and control the pan-camera to focus on the proper on-spot object. In SNC, instructors could move arbitrarily. Movement tracking module is implemented and used to focus on the moving instructor's video. The movement tracking module employs face detection technology and RFID localizer system.

3.3 Emotion Detection and Affective Learning

Researches have demonstrated that emotion is an important factor in learning and that the human brain is not just a purely cognitive information processing system, but also a system in which both affective functions and cognitive functions are inextricably integrated with one another[4]. Of course nobody denies the role of 'affect' or emotion in learning. Teachers know that it plays a crucial role in motivation, interest, and attention. But in most current e-Learning systems, there has been a bias towards the cognitive and relative neglect of the affective[9]. We conducted a primary study on affective learning model and built a prototype to detect emotions from physiological signals. The goal is to help improve students' learning experience by adapting existing e-Learning systems based on the learner's emotional state.

The physiological data for emotion detection were collected from three bio-sensors: a skin conductance (SC) sensor measuring electrodermal activity, a pho-toplethysmyograph measuring blood volume pressure (BVP), and a pre-amplified electroencephalograph sensor measuring EEG activity from the brain. We have achieved a best-case accuracy (86.5%) for four types of learning emotions[11]. And we have built two prototypes to make use of the sensed emotions. One is emotion-aware SNC. Expert teachers are able to recognize the emotional state of their students and respond in ways that positively impact on learning. But in the e-Learning case, there are large numbers of remote students in distributed classrooms and mobile users. We provided a solution for such problems via the incorporation of students' emo-tional information into the pervasive eLearning platform. Firstly we simply feedback the students emotions back to the lecturer in real-time, that the lecturer would adapt the lecture style, speed and content based on the students' emotional statistics. And then we are collecting data to investigate the computational model of emotion-aware group interaction dynamics so as to enhance the information flow within the group by smoothing the emotion flow. Another one is emotion-aware adaptive content delivery. Based on our previous work[10], we built a prototype to provide personalized service based on the learner's emotions.

4   Large Scale Media Streaming for Multi-terminals – Channels in All Directions for Learning

The aim of pervasive learning is to provide end users the ability to access education resources using any available network devices anytime anywhere. Our platform supports three types of multimedia access: tuning into live lecture broadcast, Lec-ture-on-demand (LOD), and downloading archived lectures. The challenges here are, at one side the adaptation of education content based on the current context such as the device computing capacity, screen size and network bandwidth; and at the other side to provide efficient reliable media transmission mechanism even for large scale concurrent user accessing. We now introduce two cases to manage these issues.

4.1   Hybrid Multicast Model for Media Streaming

Currently, the typical media streaming e-Learning systems are one-to-many (lectur-ing) or many-to-many (interaction and collaboration) interaction modes. So using multicasting for learning content transmission can dramatically improve the quality of service and network bandwidth efficiency. Multicast can be either performed in Inter-net Protocol (IP) layer or application layer. IP multicast has the advantage of effi-ciency, but the critical requirements of routers ,scalable inter-domain routing protocol and robust congestion control mechanism make it difficult to be implemented on heterogeneous inter-networks such as CERNET, telecom ADSL, dial-up network as well as mobile network. Application layer multicast is based on a high-level virtual network leveraging unicast to perform multicast by data replication. As there is no need for supporting from routers, flexible congestion control mechanism could be used to ensure the quality of data transmission. In recent years, application layer mul-ticast (ALM) has gained more and more attention among researchers. In the pervasive learning environment, users might be either in a remote classroom, at home or on the way learning with mobile devices. And users are distributed in a heterogeneous sparse-aggregation way. Therefore, we designed and implemented a hybrid multicast model that combine ALM and IP multicast. The network topology is tree-like architecture. Data is distributed in two ways: one is tunnel distribution which is based on UDP unicast at the application layer across different multicast domains; the other is IP multicast within a multicast domain.

As there is a lack of necessary QoS control mechanism in current IP network and the variety of end devices and network conditions, distribution of media data suffers due to limited bandwidth, delay and package loss rate, so there is an urgent need to provide QoS control mechanisms to ensure all these steams to be distributed according to their priorities to different devices. Our strategy is to periodically probe the network variables such as bandwidth, delay, package loss rate etc, and adapt the multicast routing algorithm based on measurement of these network metrics.

4.2 Content Adaption and Interaction Patterns for Mobile Learning

When tuning into the live class, students presently have four options: 1) presentation, audio, and a small video of the real-time classroom, 2) video (including audio) of the instructor only, 3) enlarged display of the presentation shown at that time, and 4) a close-up display of the instructor's facial expressions and their body language. Our recent survey shows that 85% of the students prefer option 1. In theory, the presentation, audio, and video mode can create a better context for learning. That is, the feeling of being in a real classroom with the instructor and many other students nearby. Catering to this need, three types of streams are provided for mobile users: a) an instructor's presentation screen from his desktop b) the instructor's facial expressions from a video camera, and c) the audio stream of an instructor's voices from a microphone. For mobile phones to retrieve these learning contents, they have to get access to the Internet by GPRS (General Packet Radio Service). Whereas the bandwidth of GPRS is quite limited, which are approximately 28.8kbps for downloading and 10kbps for uploading, to successfully deliver the learning contents to mobile phones, they are further compressed. Each of the three streams are reduced to as low as 8kbps, so that it can better adapt to the bandwidth of GPRS. Figure 3 shows the course display on the mobile phone Nokia 6600. Based on the GPRS network conditions and the students' preferences, the transmission and rendering pattern could be customized, for example, close the video or presentation function.

The mobile learning system not only delivers learning materials and live classrooms to mobile devices, but also encourages interactions in large blended classrooms. Once a student's mobile phone connects to a class, the instructor periodically receives a screenshot of the student's mobile device so that the instructor can monitor the student's progress. Meanwhile, students can send text messages to the instructor through cell phone Short Message Service. To address these messages, the instructor can give oral explanations or can reply through short text-messages. Students can also participate in polls and class activities which are often related to the various aspects of course conduct, content, pace, clarity, structure etc. The poll results are immediately sent back to the instructors so that they could adjust or improve the instruction accordingly. In addition, audio interaction could be initiated when necessary. This could

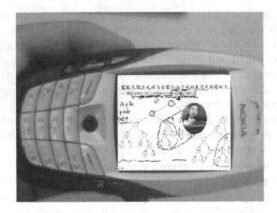

Fig. 3. Course display on the mobile phone Nokia 6600

help alleviate the problem of slow typing on a mobile phone. Language classes, especially, would benefit from an audio enhancement enabling listening and speaking practice under the teacher's guidance.

5 Dynamic and Personalized Web-Based Learning Services – The Quality Control of Learning

The web-based learning services is a platform students could conduct asynchronous self-paced learning anytime anywhere. It is comprised of the content based retrieval search engine which enables the students to find their desired materials conveniently and quickly, the answer machine which responds to students' questions automatically, the data analyze center and self-organized learning community which analyze students learning patterns and provide personalized services, and other learning tools such as assignment system and examination system. In this section, we introduce two existing distinctive services and one innovative web2.0-based service as the dynamic and personalized learning service examples.

5.1 Answer Machine, the Intelligent Q&A System

Because of the large number of the students in online teaching, a lot of teaching tasks have to be supported by the computer. Let's take Answer Machine[15], the Question and Answer system as an example. If there are 200 students online and each student asks only one question, then it will take a teacher several hours to answer all these questions. From our experience, many questions usually have the same or similar meanings. The solution to this problem is to share the answers among the students and let a computer recognize similar questions and answer them automatically. If the computer cannot find an answer, it transfers the question to a teacher. After the teacher answers the question, the answer is added to the Q&A database. Therefore, as the Q&A database accumulates questions and answers, the hit rate grows over time. Beyond these functions, the Answer Machine also provides other services, such as the Hot Spot of Lesson, the Hot Spot of each chapter which is likely to help students to find out what questions are frequently asked and what the correct answers are.

5.2 Data Analyze Center and Learning Community

In china, the size of E-Learning classes is much larger than normal classes. As against the traditional education, there are several challenges: we have many more students with dramatic differences that they have different backgrounds with the dynamic knowledge structure; given such diversity, how do we construct learner profiles and analyze students learning behaviors? How do we provide personalized services based on the learner profiles and learning behaviors? Furthermore, how do we send the feedbacks of learning states to teachers? In order to answer these questions, we developed a system ---the Data Analysis Centre, to monitor the whole process of teaching and learning, to analysis the student study behavior, and then to provide personalized learning services (Figure 4). As is well known, the learning behaviors are very complex. During the learning process, learners will browse online courses, query the course materials, submit questions, perform examinations, and so on. All of these behaviors represent the learning interest and intent of the learners. We collect all these activities in the log files for further analysis.

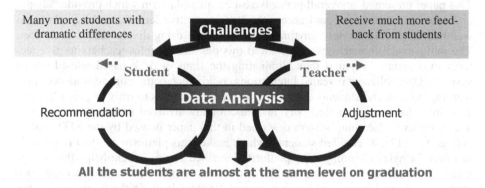

Fig. 4. Data analysis center

From traditional face-to-face lecturing to virtual network classroom learning, users have experienced the deficiencies of lonely learning. Thus collaborative learning is proposed to tackle this problem. Learners exist in learning communities and learn through communities. Every learner in learning community is either the consumer or the provider of knowledge. And the learning goals could be fulfilled though helping one another in the learning community. We implemented a prototype of self-organizing learning community[18] to cluster learners automatically and quickly, which also could help learners share their learning experiences and insights and exchange learning materials during the learning process.

5.3 Personalized Course Generation Based on Social Annotated Resources

The big ideas of 2.0 encourage participation, are inherently social and open. These principles are in line with modern educational theories such as constructivism and connectionism and thus make Web 2.0 applications very attractive for teachers and learners. Wikis, blogs, and social bookmarking are now commonly used in learning [1]. Web based courses have become popular ways to distribute learning content to learners but "one size fits all" solutions are no longer enough to satisfy the learner's educational needs. The lack of sharable and reusable learning resources put most personalized systems into the embarrassment of cooking a meal without rice. Authoring learning resources is a time consuming and difficult task. We proposed and implemented a mechanism of harnessing the power of the crowd (principle of web 2.0) to social annotate learning resources for the personalized course generation system[14]. With this method, the lectures and developers could use very few effort and time to make very tedious and complicated work easier and feasible. Students from both traditional classes and online learning could benefit from our personalized course generation system. We are currently using this system to collect data for the SJTU course of "Web Services and .NET Technologies".

6   Conclusion

This paper presented an overall pervasive e-Learning platform which provide "always on" education. Students could access the live interactive lectures and asynchronous web-based learning services anytime from anywhere using diverse network devices. The multi-modal interactions supported at this platform enables teachers to give lectures in a natural way and thus eliminating the limit of desk based tele-education systems. Data collected revealed interactions could much better engage students in the learning process and students changed from passive learners to truly engaged learners who are behaviorally, intellectually, and emotionally involved in their learning tasks. The pervasive e-Learning system described in this paper is used by the SJTU online college with 17,000 enrolled students, which makes this platform an ideal large-scale test-bed for hybrid learning. The platform described in this article helps the college yield higher profits than ordinary colleges that one administrator could manage 1000 students and one teacher could give a class of 1000 students. In the future, researches on leveraging emerging technologies to provide more efficient learning services on this pervasive learning platform will always be encouraged and conducted.

References

1. Alexander, B.: Web 2.0: A new wave of innovation for teaching and learning. EDU-CAUSE Review 41(2), 32–44 (2006)
2. Blackboard Company, http://www.blackboard.com
3. Groeneboer, C., Stockley, D., Calvert, T.: Virtual-U: A collaborative model for online learning environments. In: Proceedings of the Second International Conference on Computer Support for Collaborative Learning, Toronto, Ontario, pp. 122–130 (1997)

4. Isen, A.M.: Positive affect and decision making. In: Lewis, M., Haviland, J. (eds.) Handbook of emotions, p. 720. The Guilford Press, Guilford, New York (2000)
5. Kim, W.: Towards a Definition and Methodology for Blended Learning. In: International Workshop on Blended Learning 2007 (WBL 2007), pp. 15–17. University of Edinburgh, Scotland (2007)
6. Network Education College, Shanghai Jiao Tong University, http://www.nec.sjtu.edu.cn
7. UK Open University, http://www.open.ac.uk
8. Hong Kong Open University, http://www.ouhk.edu.hk
9. Picard, R.W., Papert, S., Bender, W., Blumberg, B., Breazeal, C., Cavallo, D., et al.: Affective learning — a manifesto. BT Technology Journal 22(4), 253–269 (2004)
10. Shen, L.P., Shen, R.M.: Ontology-based intelligent learning content recommendation service. International Journal of Continuing Engineering Education and Life-Long Learning 15(3-6), 308–317 (2005)
11. Shen, L.P., Callaghan, V., Shen, R.M.: Affective e-Learning in Residential and Pervasive Computing Environments. Journal of Information Systems Frontiers (special issue on Adoption and Use of Information & Communication Technologies in the Residential/Household Context) 10(3) (October 2008)
12. Shi, Y.C., Xie, W.K., Xu, G.Y., et al.: The Smart Classroom: Merging Technologies for Seamless Tele-Education. IEEE Pervasive Computing, 1536-1268/03, 47–55 (2003)
13. Thomas, S.: Pervasive Scale: A model of pervasive, ubiquitous, and ambient learning. IEEE Pervasive Computing 7(1), 85–88 (2008)
14. Ullrich, C.: Course generation based on HTN planning. In: Proceedings of 13th Annual Workshop of the SIG Adaptivity and User Modeling in Interactive Systems, pp. 74–79 (2005)
15. Shen, R.M., Li, X.J.: A web automatic answer system based on WWW. Computer Engineering 25(09), 49–51 (1999)
16. Wang, M.J., Shen, R.M., Novak, D., Pan, X.Y.: The Impact of Mobile Learning on Learning Behaviors and Performance: Report from a Large Blended Classroom. British Journal of Educational Technology 38(2), 294–311 (2007)
17. WebCT Company, http://www.webct.com
18. Yang, F., Han, P., Shen, R.M., Kraemer, B.J., Fan, X.W.: Cooperative Learning in Self-organizing E-Learner Communities Based on a Multi-Agents Mechanism. In: Gedeon, T.D., Fung, L.C.C. (eds.) AI 2003. LNCS (LNAI), vol. 2903, pp. 490–500. Springer, Heidelberg (2003)

Towards Blended Learning Environment Based on Pervasive Computing Technologies[*]

Yue Suo and Yuanchun Shi

Key Laboratory of Pervasive Computing, Ministry of Education
Department of Computer Science and Technology, Tsinghua University, Beijing 100084, China
suoy@mails.thu.edu.cn, shiyc@tsinghua.edu.cn

Abstract. Nowadays Internet-based multimedia learning has been entered into our daily life over various end user devices including mobile phone. Whereas, participating in the classroom and book reading are still major modalities of learning. Pervasive computing technologies will accelerate the progress and help to build a more convenient learning environment for learners. Smart Space technologies can augment real classroom to help teachers and students having class with the support of natural tangible UIs and context aware aids where teaching is still in a similar fashion with what happens in traditional classroom. Books can also be fabricated with bits for browsing multimedia learning materials. Bits from cyberspace and atoms from real world will be more and more blended into each other. And learning will be pervasive and blended which is beyond today's e-learning.

Keywords: Blended Learning, Pervasive Computing.

1 Introduction

Thanks to the booming development of the information technology in recent years, multimedia and internet has become common in our daily life. People are able to reach multimedia information via numerous various devices, including PC, Laptop, Smart Phone and PDA, as long as they connect to the internet. Learning has also been influenced by this trend: many e-learning [1] systems appear to enable the students to learn the knowledge shown in multimedia and attend the "class" at home with just a personal computer connected to the internet.

Whereas, traditional learning that students participate in the classroom and book reading are still major modalities of learning and has its unrivaled advantages. Researchers [2] [3] report that besides the aspect of the difference in knowledge transmitting methods, the traditional learning is more important for its cultural effect on the learners. Students learning at school or in the campus form tighter social relationship with each other. The teacher can interact with and convey enthusiasm to the students through face-to-face interaction, which is exactly what the e-learning lacks of.

---

[*] This work is supported by National High-Tech Research and Development Plan of China under Grant No. 2006AA01Z131 and National High-Tech Research and Development Plan of China under Grant No. 2008AA01Z132.

J. Fong, R. Kwan, and F.L. Wang (Eds.): ICHL 2008, LNCS 5169, pp. 190–201, 2008.

Therefore a new learning type called blended learning is born. Of the various definitions of blended learning, combining the e-learning and traditional learning is the key point. Blended learning tries to address the problems of traditional learning such as weak scalability and lack of fidelity while keeps the cultural effect as much as possible.

The emergence of Pervasive Computing [4] and Smart Space [5] provides new methods and accelerates the progress for the educators to build a more convenient blended learning environment. Several research projects in Smart Space [6] [7] [8] [9] [10] aiming at educational issues share the common idea that keeping the main learning place in the classroom while providing Smart Space technologies to enhance its functions and experiences: enabling remote students to join in the class, allowing the students to report feedback quietly to the teacher during the class, capturing the whole instruction for students to review after the class and so on. Blending Smart Space technologies with traditional learning and e-learning provides novel and better experience for both of the teacher and the students.

The Learning process encompasses four sub-processes: teaching, reading, discussing and reviewing. Besides teaching and reviewing explained in the above paragraph, Smart Space technologies also augment the reading and discussing process. Paper-based textbook could be fabricated with bits for browsing multimedia learning materials [11] in cyberspace using mobile devices by Pervasive Computing technology and makes the text-object to be the "internet of things" [12]; discussion in one real classroom could be enhanced to be in several connected classrooms. All these features lead to build a more convenient blended learning environment by combining bits from cyberspace and atoms from real world together, which is beyond both of the today's e-learning and the traditional learning environment.

The rest of the paper is organized as follows: We introduce traditional learning, the developing history of the learning and its latest steps blended learning in Section 2. Then in Section 3, we explore blended learning based on pervasive computing technologies and its achievement. Section 4 presents the prospect for future p-blended learning environment. And we make the final conclusion in the last Section.

2 Traditional Learning and Blended Learning

Blended Learning is the latest steps in the history of learning from traditional learning to more and more enhanced technology-based learning [2]. In this chapter, we will first articulate the advantage of traditional learning, introduce the evolution of learning, and then present several important aspects of blended learning.

2.1 Traditional Learning

Nowadays, traditional learning mode is still the major modalities of learning. Traditional learning has a classroom-based learning environment with an instructor such as teacher, professor or subject-matter expert. The instructor organizes the knowledge, adjusts the pace, changes the direction according to the context of students in the classroom, while the students immerse in a learning environment listening to the instruction. It has been proven to be an effective and pervasive mean of learning for years. Besides conveying the knowledge to the students, traditional learning has a cultural effect more importantly: people interact and learn from one another [2] and students have full opportunities to communicate with the instructor and other students, forming strong relationship with others [3].

Additionally, traditional learning still uses real-paper textbook for students. Compared to the e-learning material, although it has several disadvantages such as heavy-weighted, high-cost and hard to search by keyword, paper-based textbook gives the students better experience on much higher resolution, easy annotation, easy skimming and natural reading manner.

The biggest challenge of traditional learning is lack of scale [2]. Cultural benefits are great, whereas teaching thousands of students consumes larger classrooms (reducing effectiveness greatly) and lots of travel (very expensive). The second challenge of traditional learning is lack of equipments in the classroom that sometimes makes the instructor difficult to teacher certain topics effectively [3]. Moreover, because of the limitation of the classroom and the paper-based textbook, the teaching is of less fidelity than multimedia-based e-learning to a certain extent.

2.2 The Developing Trend of Learning

As given by [2], blended learning is the latest step in a long history of technology-based training/learning. From the traditional learning to today's blended learning, there are mainly six phases of learning types (Figure 1); in order is classroom-based learning, mainframe-based learning, distance learning by satellite-based live video, CD-ROM based learning, web-based virtual classroom learning and blended learning. Classroom-based learning is the traditional learning, which suffers lack of scale and lack of fidelity. As to solve the lack of scale problem, the next three types emerge. Mainframe-based learning forms the basis for the thinking about blending technologies with traditional learning. Satellite-based live video and CD-ROM based learning are two successful solutions for "lack of scale" problem in that era. Satellite-based live video was once very popular in the 1980s in China since the government is lack

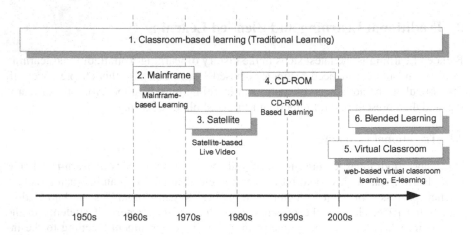

Fig. 1. The timeline of the developing trend of learning

of instructor and too many students. CD-ROM based learning uses CD-ROM to deliver multimedia learning material to the end user. However, as the rapid development of the high-speed internet and common to normal people, satellite-based live video and CD-ROM based learning are to be faded and replaced by the web-based virtual classroom learning which is cheaper, more effective and less cost of maintenance. Today the training organization and educational institution have a wide range of options for learning. Therefore the last type, blended learning, is born to try to integrate the former learning types in order to build a better learning environment.

2.3 Blended Learning

- Definitions

Graham [13] in his book discusses the three most commonly mentioned definitions of blended learning: combining instructional modalities, combining instructional methods and combining online and face-to-face instruction. The first two suffer the problem that the definitions are given so broadly that almost encompass all learning systems while the third definition is thought to be the more accurate one, which is the foundation of the Graham's definition: "Blended learning is the systems combine face-to-face instruction with computer-mediated instruction".

Won Kim in his keynotes paper [3] defines the blended learning more precisely that it is "a combination of two or more of all possible learning types" with two qualifiers that at least one type must be physical class-based type and one must be e-learning type.

From these definitions, the face-to-face instruction, physical class-based type and e-learning involvement are the key points of blended learning, which is also the foundation of our blended learning environment based on pervasive computing technologies as well.

- Significance of blended learning

Of those advantages that choosing blended learning for the instructor rather than other possible options, there are three important reasons that can not be neglected [13]: 1) Improved pedagogy. Blended learning provides new modes for the learners to learn, to collaborate and to discuss while keeps the cultural effect of traditional learning; 2) Improved access/flexibility. Aided by the growth of distance learning environment, blended learning enlarges the scope for the learners to access the knowledge and also provides more flexibility for the learners to choose the most convenient learning environment from physical classroom to virtual learning forum; 3) Improved cost effectiveness. Blended learning provides the opportunities for the education and corporate institutions to achieve cost saving while assures the didactical quality enhancement.

Face-to-face instruction in the physical class-based type keeps the cultural effect among the instructor and the students; computer-mediated instruction enhances the scalability and fidelity of the knowledge transmitting from the instructor to the students. As the rapid growth in computer-technology area, especially coming to the era of pervasive computing, blended learning environment is enhanced by pervasive computing technology and will become more convenient and effective for learners.

3 Blended Learning Based on Pervasive Computing Technologies

3.1 Smart Space

Smart Space embodies the key features of pervasive computing and is thought to be the test-bed for it. As Smart Space focuses in a limited-space such as classroom or meeting room, it is suitable for using Smart Space technologies to enhance blended learning environment.

As Smart Space develops, we propose three successive phases of Smart Space, each of which brings new opportunities to provide better experience for blended learning environment (Figure 2). The three phases are listed in logical order rather than temporal order, where new features added continuously from the left to the right to make Smart Space more powerful.

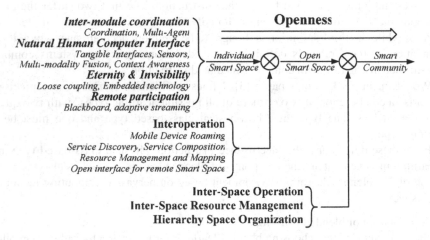

Fig. 2. Three successive phases of Smart Space

- Individual Smart Space

In first phase, the research focuses on building a smart human-computer interactive space. Communication and the coordination mechanism among the software modules is the basis for building the computer-mediated learning environment. Also, lots of tangible UIs [14], such as sensors and awareness modules, have been applied to achieve natural human computing interaction. Modules in Smart Space are loose-coupled in order to maintain system robust and embedded technologies are involved to remove the computing devices from people's sight. Remote participation enables the people outside Smart Space to communicate and collaborate with the people inside. Rebuilding the traditional classroom into the Smart-Space-based classroom provides enhanced experience for the instructor to give class to large number of students outside of the classroom at the same time while keeps the similar fashion as before with the help of natural tangible UIs.

- Open Smart Space

In the second phase, Smart Space becomes more open. The mobile and handheld devices roaming with users, which becomes more and more popular in pervasive computing environment, can discover the existence of smart space environment and spontaneously take use of the resources and the services in the space to perform tasks of the users in an enhanced fusion. Other Smart Spaces could connect in to build a virtual larger Smart Space. Classroom based on Open Smart Space enables the instructor and the students to bring their personal mobile devices to augment teaching and learning experience. Instructor could bring learning materials such as PPT or interesting video via his Smart Phone to show and share to the students. Students can also using their mobile devices to give real-time comments or questions to the teacher while not interrupt the teacher's talking. Other classrooms settled in different places or even in different countries with different languages could connect in and have class with local classroom together.

- Smart Community.

In the third phases, as [15] refers that it is almost impossible to establish an union pervasive computing environment all over the world in the near future, while great plenty of self-governed Smart Spaces exist by their own. Smart Community consisting of multiple Smart Spaces needs to address the inter-space operation and inter-space resource management mechanism issues. For blended learning, this would refer to the future collaborating learning environment involving many classrooms together, which combines with others automatically in terms of the shared schedules.

3.2 p-Blended Learning

Based on pervasive computing technologies and Smart Space, blended learning environment could be enhanced to provide better features than ever before. We call this type of blended learning as p-Blended learning. P-Blended learning emphasizes on combining face-to-face instruction in the classroom built as a Smart Space (regardless of whether it is a Individual Smart Space, Open Smart Space or Smart Community) with pervasive computing technologies enhanced instruction (such as synchronous distance learning by remote participation, asynchronous learning by the experience record of the past class, textbook fabricated with special tags for browsing multimedia learning materials).

Graham [13] introduces four dimensions of the interaction in face-to-face and distributed learning environment in order to explain the trend of fusion between these two archetypal learning environments: space, time, fidelity and humanness. Space reaches from live or physical to virtual reality; time ranges from live synchronous to asynchronous. Fidelity reflects the level of the interaction from high (all senses) and Medium (e.g. audio only) to Low (text only). And the humanness addresses the ratio of human interaction and machine interaction. Based on above dimensions, we extend the dimensions of the interactions to show the features of p-blended learning type in Figure 3.

P-blended learning fuses synchronous and asynchronous learning mode in the Time dimension. For the synchronous mode, the local students receive face-to-face instruction with high fidelity aided by multimedia learning material displayed by the

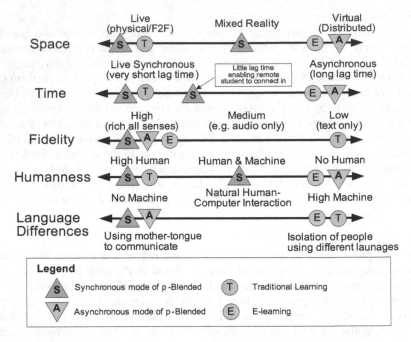

Fig. 3. Dimensions of p-blended learning

interactive blackboard in the classroom. The interaction of synchronous mode is the mix of high humanness interaction and human & machine interaction, in which the latter provides better experience thanks to natural human computer interaction provided by Smart Space. The remote students attend the class in real time by their personal computer, which is a little longer lag time. The remote students have to interact with the class by the help of the machine. For the asynchronous mode, the learning environment turns to be like web-based learning. Moreover, p-blended learning takes cultural differences and language barrier into account in the class. P-blended learning provides mechanisms for the students to solve these language differences problems by involving language transformation services.

3.3 Progress Achieved: Smart Classroom

P-blended learning combines the face-to-face and computer-mediated learning together based on pervasive computing technologies. Some achievements have been made in building such kind of learning environment: Smart Classroom [7] and Open Smart Classroom [9].

Smart Classroom aims at building a primitive prototype of futuristic p-blended classrooms, which integrates voice-recognition, computer-vision, experience record, natural human interfaces and other technologies to provide a tele-education experience similar to a real classroom experience. By applying pervasive computing technologies in a real classroom, the Smart Classroom combines the tele-education or web-based education mode with the traditional classroom activities and makes these

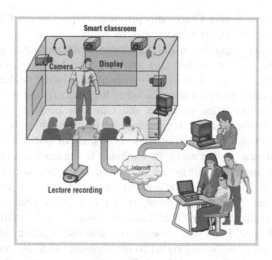

Fig. 4. The Smart Classroom system [7]

two separate educational practices seamlessly bound together. Figure 4 gives an overview of the Smart Classroom. As in a real classroom, the teacher can gives his class while moving freely and using conventional teaching methods to instruct both of the local and remote students. Beside this kind of synchronous learning, the whole process of the lecture which contains the live video of the whole class, all of the context and events occur in this lecture will be recorded as a hypermedia courseware, which is available for playback after class for the asynchronous learning mode.

Additionally, Smart Classroom provides multiple human computer interfaces and modalities to enhance the teacher's experience of teaching. We extend the user interface of a legacy desktop-based tele-education system into the real augmented classroom. The teacher uses SMART Board [16] similar to the blackboard in traditional learning classroom, while it can show multimedia learning materials and could be controller by the teacher's hand. Laser Pointer interface enables the teacher to make annotations on the blackboard and interact with remote students while roaming in the classroom. Speech-capable assistant enhances the effectiveness of the class by saving the teacher from sending some common command (such as "turn to next page of the slide") by hand.

Smart Classroom successfully embodies several convenient features of p-blended learning: it holds the benefit of the cultural effect in face-to-face instruction, even for remote students; it enhances the experiences of the teacher by involving a multimedia blackboard; it keeps the interactions in the traditional learning as much as possible, naturally to the experienced instructors; it provides both of the synchronous and asynchronous learning mode to meet the needs of different learners.

Smart Classroom has been proven to be effective and used in real campus for several years. As the technology develops from Individual Smart Space to Open Smart Space, we enhance the Smart Classroom to be more open and therefore develop the prototype of Open Smart Classroom [17].

Beside the features Smart Classroom provided, Open Smart Classroom emphasizes on enabling other Smart Classrooms to connect in and have class together. Language barrier may occur when the classroom from another country speaking of different languages joins in the learning environment. Language Grid [18][19] and Langrid Blackboard [20] as aid tools are involved to help the students with different mother-tongue to communicate with each other together. As the primary experiment, two Smart Classrooms settled in Japan and China respectively are combined together. We constrain the teaching language to be English which is understandable to both of the participations from the two classrooms. Participations are able to use aid tools to discuss with each other and give feedback to the teacher as the class goes on. It is an interesting attempt to form two communication channels at the same time: teacher is giving his class to the students as formal channel while the students are discussing with other in different languages as the informal channel. Another interesting experimental approach in Open Smart Classroom is supporting personal devices (e.g. Smart Phone, PDA and Laptop) to seamlessly connect into the classroom system and even has some access rights to interoperate with the system, such as the teacher is able to use his personal Smart Phone as a controller of the classroom to navigate the slideshow.

At last, organizing this kind of class is valuable experience. Japan and China has lots of difference, from complicated cultural difference to simple one-hour time difference. How the p-blended learning system leverage the issues caused by difference is still an interesting open question.

4   Future Prospect of p-Blended Learning

After introducing achieved progess, we are going to make a prospect for future p-Blended learning. Organizing the p-blended learning encompasses four separate steps: teaching, reading, discussion and reviewing, which will be explained in detail as follows.

4.1   Teaching

As Derntl in his research results [21] indicates that "faculty preferred a more traditional, discipline-based course design model for online course planning and shunned high-level instructional design, opting for lighter-weight, dialog-rich instructional design emphasizing real-time, faculty-student interaction." Therefore, p-blended learning environment should provide a teaching mode whose experience is more similar to the traditional one in the classroom for the instructors. Classroom-based teaching mode while enabling the remote students to join in and to interact with the class in real-time is a good approach.

Moreover, [22] and [24] point out different skills are required on the side of the instructor, both socially/didactically and technically. The instructors always lack time and technical expertise to use e-learning platforms or other "high technology" tools conveniently. Smart Space technologies, which tend to make computer invisible, proactively provide the service for the user and the natural human interface alleviating the instructor to learn and adapt to the new "classroom", enable the instructors to give the class in the similar fashion with what happens in the traditional learning but with enhanced experience.

As the Smart Space technologies improve, although it is easier and more natural for the teacher to give class to the people all over the world synchronously and asynchronously, the educators still need to think about how to design and develop new learning theories making full use of the new p-blended learning mode. Neither learning platforms nor learning theories in isolation can provide effective p-blended learning scenarios. Therefore co-considering educational concerns and p-blended learning platforms in order to take full advantage of pervasive-computing-enhanced educational practices is crucially important and needs further research.

4.2 Reading

Paper-based textbook is still the main reading material in learning process. It is interesting to realize that the emergence of e-book based on internet does not eliminate the traditional paper-based book. However, the total number of the paper-based book even continues to grow in a faster speed. Having several advantages such as saving space, full of fidelity by multimedia technology, fast searching, easy sharing and delivering, the e-book is still lack convenience of reading than traditional book in several aspects so far: low resolution, hard to make annotation, reading is restricted by the screen of computing devices and uncomfortable feeling caused by unnatural reading manner. Many people choose to print out the e-material to read instead of reading it directly. It is quite obvious that the e-book and textbook will co-exist for such a long time in the near future.

In p-blended learning environment providing an enhanced classroom-based fashion, local students are still suggested to use paper-based textbook as their main reading material and make notes on it while listening to the class, as well as the remote students, whose PC screens are used for displaying live-video and blackboard of the class and no room for displaying reading material. However, paper-based textbook is only able to show text-based knowledge lacking of vitality and animation, which should be enhanced in p-blended learning environment.

Therefore, the paper-based textbook "connected" with the cyberspace by embedding tags that can be identified by students' mobile devices such as PDA or Smart Phone is recommended. The tags could be a website link, 1-D/2-D barcode embedded with corresponding cyberspace's information or just predefined patterns. Mobile devices recognize these tags, fetch the related multimedia learning material from the internet and show it to the reader. Through this mechanism, paper-based textbook is enhanced to be more vivid and animated, and more importantly, connect with p-blended learning environment more tightly to improve the effectiveness of the students' reading.

4.3 Discussion

Class discussion is one of the pervasive instructional methods focusing on students interaction, aiming at having the students negotiate and co-construct an understanding of the learning topic. Traditional class discussion is more spontaneous but hard to ensure the participation and flexibility, while web-based discussion is more "Depth of reflection" [23] and flexibility but difficult to ensure spontaneity and weak to build human connection.

P-blended learning combines these two types of discussions together: traditional class discussion during the class and the web-based discussion after the class. Both of these discussions should take language barrier into account for supporting multi-language multi-space discussion in the new p-blended learning environment.

4.4 Reviewing

Traditional learning environment is hard for the students to review the whole class after the class. In p-blended learning environment, the whole class, not only the live-video of the class but also all the notes of the blackboard and all of the events occur will be captured by the learning environment in order to help the students to make further review and absent students to catch up with the learning progress. Also, with the help of current developing summary and index technologies of the class [25], the class record could become more and more effective for students to learn and understand.

5 Conclusion

This paper aims at introducing the idea of building more convenient blended learning environment based on pervasive computing technology. Blended learning environment absorbs the advantages of traditional learning and e-learning and it may even become so pervasive that eventually we just call it as "learning" itself [13]. Pervasive Computing and Smart Space technologies augment the blended learning environment in each of its aspects including teaching, reading, discussing and reviewing, assisting both of the teacher and students through the learning process and finally provide enhanced experience for the class which is beyond today's e-learning.

References

1. Electronic learning, http://en.wikipedia.org/wiki/Electronic_learning
2. Bersin, J.: How Did We Get Here? The History of Blended Learning. In: The Blended Learning Handbook: Best Practices, Proven Methodologies, and Lessons Learned. Pfeiffer Wiley, Chichester (2004)
3. Kim, W.: Towards a Definition and Methodology for Blended Learning. In: The Proceedings of Workshop on Blended Learning 2007, pp. 1–8 (2007)
4. Weiser, M.: The computer for the twenty-first century. Scientific American 265(3), 94–100 (1991)
5. Rosenthal, L., Stanford, V.: NIST Smart Space: Pervasive Computer Initiative. In: Proceedings of IEEE 9th International Workshop on Enabling Technologies: Infrastructure for Collaborative Enterprises (WETICE), pp. 6–11 (2000)
6. Abowd, G.: Classroom 2000: An Experiment with the instrumentation of a living educational environment. IBM Systems Journal 38(4), 508–530 (1999)
7. Shi, Y., Xie, W., Xu, G., et al.: The smart classroom: merging technologies for seamless tele-education. IEEE Pervasive Computing 2(2), 47–55 (2003)

8. Ratto, M., Shapiro, R.B., Truong, T.M., Griswold, W.G.: The ActiveClass project: Experiments in encouraging classroom participation. In: Proceedings of CSCL 2003, pp. 477–486 (2003)

9. Suo, Y., Miyata, N., Ishida, T., Shi, Y.: Open Smart Classroom: Extensible and Scalable Smart Space Using Web Service Technology. In: Leung, H., Li, F., Lau, R., Li, Q. (eds.) ICWL 2007. LNCS, vol. 4823, pp. 428–439. Springer, Heidelberg (2008)

10. Johanson, B., Fox, A., Winograd, T.: The Interactive Workspaces Project: Experiences with Ubiquitous Computing Rooms. IEEE Pervasive Computing 1(2), 67–74 (2002)

11. Shih, T.K., Chang, W.-C., Wang, T.-H., et al.: The hard SCORM LMS: reading SCORM courseware on hardcopy textbooks. In: The Proceeding of Fifth IEEE International Conference on Advanced Learning Technologies, pp. 812–816 (2005)

12. The internet of things, http://www.itu.int/internetofthings/

13. Graham, C.R.: Blended Learning system: definition, current trends and future directions. In: Bonk, C.J., Graham, C.R. (eds.) The Handbook of Blended Learning, San Francisco Pfeiffer (2006)

14. Tangible User Interface, http://en.wikipedia.org/wiki/Tangible_User_Interface

15. Kindberg, T., Fox, A.: System software for ubiquitous computing. IEEE Pervasive Computing 1(1), 70–81 (2002)

16. SMART – SMART Board interactive whiteboards, http://smarttech.com/products/smartboard/index.asp

17. Suo, Y., Miyata, N., Morikawa, H., et al.: Open Smart Classroom: Extensible and Scalable Learning System in Smart Space using Web Service Technology. Special Issue of IEEE Transactions on Knowledge and Data Engineering for e-learning, Major Revision (submitted)

18. Ishida, T.: Language Grid: An Infrastructure for Intercultural Collaboration. In: IEEE/IPSJ Symposium on Applications and the Internet (SAINT 2006), pp. 96–100 (2006)

19. Murakami, Y., Ishida, T., Nakaguchi, T.: Language Infrastructure for Language Service Composition. In: International Conference on Semantics, Knowledge and Grid (SKG 2006) (2006)

20. Language Grid – Langrid Blackboard, http://langrid.nict.go.jp/en/ blackboard.html

21. Derntl, M., Motschnig-Pitrik, R.: The Role of Structure, Patterns, and People in Blended Learning. The Internet and Higher Education 8(2), 111–130 (2005)

22. Motschnig-Pitrik, R., Mallich, K.: Effects of Person-Centered Attitudes on Professional and Social Competence in a Blended Learning Paradigm. Educational Technology & Society 7(4), 176–192 (2004)

23. Mikulecky, L.: Diversity, discussion, and participation: Comparing web-based and campus-based adolescent literature classes. Journal of Adolescent & Adult Literacy 42(2), 84–97 (1998)

24. Power, M.: A dual-mode university instructional design model for academic development. International Journal for Academic Development 13(1), 5–16 (2008)

25. Yu, Z., Ozeki, M., Fujii, Y., Nakamura, Y.: Towards Smart Meeting: Enabling Technologies and a Real-World Application. In: Proceedings of the 9th International Conference on Multimodal Interfaces (ICMI 2007), pp. 86–93 (2007)

Techniques for Enhancing Pervasive Learning in Standard Natural Classroom

Chenping Lu, Jiaji Zhou, Liping Shen, and Ruimin Shen

Computer Science Department, Shanghai Jiao Tong University, Dong Chuan Rd. 800,
200240, Shanghai, China
fullfree@sjtu.edu.cn, zhoujiaji@live.cn

Abstract. Standard Natural Classroom (SNC) is a real-time classroom based on smart space and design principles of e-learning, aiming at creating face-to-face, interactive and pervasive learning scene for students who are far from live classroom. We use various techniques in developing different kinds of components in SNC. Two components among them are specially described in this paper: E-pen and Emotion Understanding. E-pen focuses on helping teachers mark on the projection screen and several recognition algorithms are mentioned, while Emotion Understanding focuses on affective learning and is used to estimate students' emotion.

Keywords: SNC, E-pen, Emotion Understanding, e-Learning.

1 Introduction

Learning is a process of interaction, communication and thinking. In a world of information and knowledge today, people have the requirement to be educated whenever they want and wherever they are in order to keep up with the changing world. E-Learning is what we have created to fulfill such a requirement. In the classical e-learning environment, however, there exists a critical defect that teacher and students are lack of interaction. Standard Natural Classroom (SNC) is a concept proposed by our e-Learning Laboratory, which tries to create pervasive learning scene for students who are far from live classroom.

In this paper, we focus on two techniques, so called components, contained in SNC as instances of technical details: E-pen and Emotion Understanding. They help SNC to provide integrated and friendly teaching environment. E-pen system consists of a laser pen, a digital camera connected to the computer and software to process the video captured by the camera. E-pen enables teachers to "write" directly on the projection by the laser pen which solves the problem that electrical courseware is not as interactive as the blackboard. Emotion understanding system is made up of physiological sensors and algorithms to process data received from the sensors attached to students in SNC. It helps teachers to grip the emotional states of students so that teachers could deliver courses in the best way that students could accept. Cooperation among all components in SNC, however, is of great importance and an information fusion system is being developed.

J. Fong, R. Kwan, and F.L. Wang (Eds.): ICHL 2008, LNCS 5169, pp. 202–212, 2008.

2 Background

Our e-Learning system is kind of pervasive learning platform. It extends the real classrooms by using pervasive computing technologies. The system architecture of the platform is composed of three main parts: a) distributed Standard Natural Classrooms (SNC), providing human-machine interaction and context-aware services for teachers and students; b} media streaming for multi-mode terminals delivering interactive lectures; c) personalized web-based learning with dynamic learning services, collaborative learning communities, and personalized recommendations.

The core of our e-Learning system is SNC, which is equipped with numerous smart devices or sensors and specially developed software. We try to digitalize interactive lectures and deliver them to different kinds of terminals live online. Meanwhile, offline students may also attach vivid classrooms by different kinds of techniques in our e-Learning system. So well-designed SNC could help us provide lively and natural learning scene, which students certainly prefer.

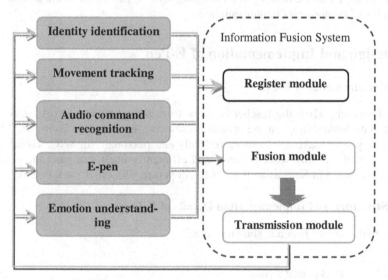

Fig. 1. Design of Standard Natural Classroom

As is shown in Fig.1, SNC has five components and an important information fusion system:

1. **Identity identification.** Identity is important information to context aware applications or other components in SNC, especially identities of teachers.
2. **Movement tracking.** In normal classroom, teacher often moves arbitrarily. It is helpful for students that one video flow always focuses on the teacher in order to accurately record what has happened on him.
3. **Audio commands recognition.** It is interesting to recognize teachers' frequent used commands, which may be used further to free hands. For

example, we try to use the recognized content from teacher's audio to tone up the content-based multimedia retrieval.

4. **E-pen.** When teacher is away from dais, he may control his courseware or simulate handwriting on the projection drawing by a simple laser-pen.

5. **Emotion understanding.** Emotion understanding component is to inform the teacher the emotional states of the students.

6. **Information fusion system.** This system is used to collect and fuse data, thus make all components communicate with each other easily. For the moment, we have a prototype system called *InfoIntegrator*. As is shown in Fig.1, a register module manages the elements; a fusion module receives and fuses information from elements; a transmission module transmits information to elements. Besides, a special self-defined communication protocol is used inside this system.

In this paper, we'll focus on techniques of SNC for enhancing pervasive learning. So the information fusion system will not be deep discussed. Due to the space limit, details of *E-pen* and *Emotion Understanding* will be discussed in the next sections as examples of components implementation.

3 Design and Implementation of E-Pen

3.1 Requirements of E-Pen

In a classroom, when the teacher is away from dais, he can control his courseware or simulate handwriting on the projection drawing by a simple laser-pen. Therefore, E-pen may help making lessons more freely and personally in SNC. To achieve this, E-pen should not only work properly and efficiently itself, but meet the needs of information fusion in SNC as well, so as to cooperate with other components.

3.2 Structure and Implementation Details of E-Pen

The actual scene of E-pen is shown in Fig.2.

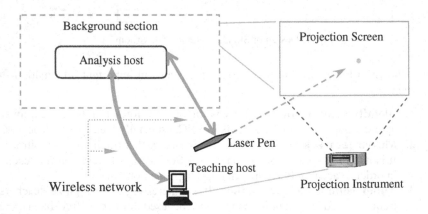

Fig. 2. Actual Scene of E-pen

3.2.1 Work Flow of E-Pen

1. Background Section in Actual Scene of E-pen
As shown in Fig.2, an indication tool, such as a laser-pen, is used to produce light points on the projection screen. A camera is used to sample the video information of the projection screen and transmit the video information to *the analysis host*, who runs *the light point recognition algorithm* to get the light point position. Before introduction to this algorithm, some specific words are explained as follows:

Light Point Position (LPP): The target position to find in this algorithm.

Suspicious Position (SP): Potential light point position which needs further estimation.

The images, or called frames, caught from camera arrive 1-by-1, each of which will be dealt with through the steps in Table-1.

The entire algorithm can be concluded as: scan-by-line, merge-across-line. In the implementation, we do some optimizations mentioned below, together with the Time Complexity analysis:

Table 1. Process of Light Point Recognition Algorithm on One Frame

Step	Action	Additional aspect
i	Get the current frame as: img_1	
ii	Compare old img with img_1, get all the possible light point coordinates as *SPs*.	*SPs* are estimated based on gray level.
iii	Pick out SPs aggregated together and record the average coordinates of them to represent LPPs.	Details are omitted here to avoid verbosity and will be given in other papers before long.
iv	Reject those LPPs with unreasonable coordinates.	Reject those with too more or too less SPs and those cover too large area.
v	Get new img by old img and img_1	img(i,j)=img(i,j)×a+img_1(i,j)×(1-a)

Step (ii), (iii) and (v) can be executed pixel-by-pixel. So each pixel in one frame would be considered only once. It is easy to have that the Time Complexity is $O(MN)$, if we neglect Step (v), where M, N represent the width and height of frame respectively, determined by the camera. Step (v) could be done independently after all other steps and does not influence the Time Complexity.

2. Other Sections in Actual Scene of E-pen
Besides background part, other parts are working as follows:

Light point positions are transmitted to the teaching host through network, point-by-point. When a point arrives, the teaching host does a coordinate-conversion between camera video and projection screen. Then it begins to display the track information of those points. Two steps are needs in display:

First, point track is formed by connecting points one-by-one, using simple lines or curves. At the same time, we offer another function for users: light point position represents mouse position of teaching host, and if light point disappears, a left-click event occurs in teaching host. Users may choose from those two functions. The Second step below works only if the former function is chosen.

Second, after getting numbers of points, we try to find track information in those points. If succeeded, we use those tracks, for instance, simple graphs or letters, to replace the track in the first step. This step could be partitioned as below:

1. Points partitioning. There are two ways to choose: Time-based partition and User-behavior-based partition.
2. Do track recognition for each partition based on the track-type users set in advance. Types of track include simple shapes, digits and letters. In E-pen, handwriting recognition differs from [3], [6] because of the actual scene we've set up. We modify traditional BP networks and feature sets but it is still in developing as we'll mention in experimental results below. Details of our method would be given before long if we get the chance.
3. Process track optimization if necessary. Use improved light point track form to display instead of printed form.

3.2.2 Communications between E-Pen and Other Components in SNC or Users

Accepted commands to receive from users or information transmission module: start E-pen; stop E-pen; change track-type.

Accepted information to be sent out from E-pen to information fusion module: E-pen started, E-pen stopped, track-type changed.

3.3 Experiments and Results

We've completely implemented the light point recognition algorithm and done some tests under different conditions. The results are shown in Table-2. Every test lasts for 2 minutes.

Table 2. Results of Light Point Recognition Algorithm Test

No.	Screen Size (Meters)	User Position (from Screen)	Result (fps)	Camera (fps)	Recall	Precision
1	2×2	2m	20	25	80%	100%
2	2×2	10m	20	25	80%	100%
3	1×0.8	2m	22	25	88%	100%
4	1×0.8	10m	22	25	88%	100%

We may conclude that the distance between the user and the screen doesn't influence the precision or the recall, but obviously, the further users stand from screen, the harder indication tools would be to use.

The smaller screen gets a higher recall in test. However, the precision is very good and we may summarize that the light point recognition algorithm is feasible. On the other hand, 20 or higher fps is enough for use, so noise-reduction has been added after light point recognition in order to reject the points that possibly results from the shake of hand and finally we get a frame-rate of 10 fps.

Track-recognition tests have been partly finished and we've got some results in Table-3, all of which are tested under Condition 1 of Table-2. It is inspired that shape recognition and digit recognition are practical to some extent.

Table 3. Results of Track-recognition Test

Test object	Classification object	Partition	Error rate
Simple shapes	ellipse, line, triangle, rectangle	User-behavior-based partition	6.5%
Digits	10 digits	User-behavior-based partition	5%
Letters	26 capitals or lower-cases	Time-based partition	In developing

4 Preliminary Results of Emotion Understanding Component

People tend to focus on the cognitive ingredient of learning process, while most of them neglect the affective factor. "...expert human tutors... devote at least as much time and attention to the achievement of affective and emotional goals in tutoring, as they do to the achievement of the sorts of cognitive and informational goal...", concluded in the early work of intelligent tutoring systems by Lepper M. R. and Chabay R. W.[12].

We have noticed the importance of affective factor of learning and launched a research project trying to develop a system to inspect the emotional states of learners during the learning process. The emotion understanding module will be integrated into SNC as the result of the project. In this paper we want to show some preliminary results of the project under progress.

4.1 Emotion Model

Several previous works in emotion detection and measuring are listed in Table-4.

Table 4. Related Works

Method	Related Works
EEG	Alicia Heraz et al, *Emomental Agent* [7]
Skin Conductivity	R. W. Picard et al., *Galvactivator* [15] ; Liping Shen et al., *XVast* [8]
Facial Image	Arman Savran et al. [9]
Pressure	C. J. Reynolds, *Pressure Mouse* [10]

These works show a strong implication that human emotion relates tightly with physiological signals. We believe that internal emotional state of a subject could be revealed by analyzing his or her physiological responses. Based on this hypothesis, we designed a system trying to find out the relationship by applying machine learning algorithms.

We model the emotional state of a person as a pair of sets:

$$S=\{P,E\} \tag{1}$$

P represents a set of *Physiological Signals*. **E** is a set of *Emotional States*. They are described in detail in the next two sections.

Emotional State Set (E)
The emotional state set defines emotion directly related to our research.

Russell's circumplex model of affect [11] is our reference model since we consider it simple and suited our purpose. Russell's model divides human emotion into two base states: *Valance* and *Arousal*. All emotions are represented as a dot in a 2D coordinate with x-axis representing *Valance* and y-axis representing *Arousal*. (Fig. 3)

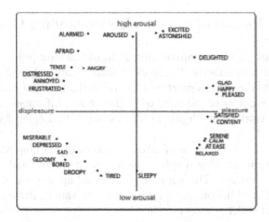

Fig. 3. Russell's Circumplex Model

Though simple, Russell's emotion set are too rich for us, we need to select some particular emotions out which relate most tightly to our concern. In the previous work by Liping Shen et al. [11], they confine the emotion set to: *interest, engagement, confusion, frustration, boredom and hopefulness*. We reduce it more, we only consider four of them since *engagement* is more often mixed with *interest* and also *boredom* is more often mixed with *frustration*. The emotional state set is shown in Table-5.

Table 5. Emotional State Set

Emotional State Set	Description
Interest	Curious about the new knowledge, attentive, eager to learn
Confusion	Faced with problems, trying to solve the problems
Frustration	Completely unable to understand the course material, reluctant to learn
Hopefulness	Difficulties solved, pleased with the new findings, willing to explore more.

Physiological Signal Set (P)

Human affection is subtle and complex, no exception in the process of learning. Multiple-aspects of physiological signals are needed. On account of this reason, we choose to sample multi-channel signals of learners including SC (skin conductivity), BVP (Blood Volume Pressure) and EEG (electroencephalography).

Some frequencies of brainwave show tight relation with the brain activity (Table-6) so that we separate them from the raw EEG data.

Table 6. Brainwaves

Wave Type	Frequency	When wave is dominant
Delta	0-4 Hz	Deep sleep
Theta	4-8 Hz	Creativity, dream sleep, drifting thoughts
Alpha	8-12 Hz	Relaxation, calmness, abstract thinking
Beta	+12 Hz	Relaxed focus. High alertness, mental activity.

By putting these signals together, the Physiological Signal Set is composed of:

$$P = \{(SC, BVP, EEG\_RAW, Alpha, Beta, High\ Beta, Theta, Delta)\} \qquad (2)$$

Table-7 describes the definition of each physiological signal in detail.

4.2 Experimentation

The experimentation is conducted by simulating a virtual distant education environment. The learner watches video records from a real classroom and each learning session takes 40 minutes which is just the same length as a real class in order to get emulational result. We conducted four separated learning sessions altogether with video records from an algorithm course, a mathematic course, a Chinese history course and an economic course respectively.

Table 7. Physiological Signal Set

Signal	Description	Unit
SC	Skin Conductivity	μS
BVP	Blood Volume Pressure	N/A
EEG Raw	Raw brain wave	μV
Delta	Delta wave 2-4 Hz	μV
Theta	Theta wave 4-8 Hz	μV
Alpha	Alpha wave 8-13 Hz	μV
Beta	Beta wave 15-20 Hz	μV
High Beta	High Beta wave 20-40 Hz	μV

ProComp5 Infiniti™ encoder [16], a multi-modality device, is used to collect real-time physiological data of the learner during the experimentation.

To record the emotional state during the learning process, we arrange an assistant to watch the learner from a distance who is responsible for estimating and noting down the emotional state of the learner by his judgment. However we notice that even

Fig. 4. Program Records Emotional States

a well trained psychologist may not be able to catch every emotion transition by watching the learner, we ask the learner to do some self-evaluation during the learning process. In order not to attract the learner from learning to recording of emotional state, we design a program to help the learner. (Fig. 4) The learner needs only to click on a colored button once he feels the transition of his emotion. The program records the emotional states and the timestamp when the transition of states occurs. After a session is completed the program will generate a report of the emotional states of the learner during the learning session.

We merge these two reports together to generate a summary of the emotional states and combine the emotional states to the data recorded by matching the timestamp when each piece of data is recorded. If the two reports conflict with each other, we trust the learner's self-evaluation.

4.3 Data Preprocessing

Raw data needs preprocess before they can be inputted into the algorithm.

Because EEG signal is so weak that prone to be interfered by tiny movements of the learner, we need first do some selection on the raw data by reviewing the recorded EEG waveform to delete obviously interfered data sections.

After removing noise data by naked eyes, we use algorithms to smooth the data.

4.4 Algorithms

We applied k-nearest neighbors (kNN)[13] and SVM to the preprocessed data, 80% of which are used as training data and the rest are used as testing data.

The maximum accuracy is reached when k is set between 2 and 4. Fig. 5(a) shows the results when k is set to 3.

We use libSVM [14] library and choose radial basis function as the kernel. Fig. 5(b) shows the results by applying SVM.

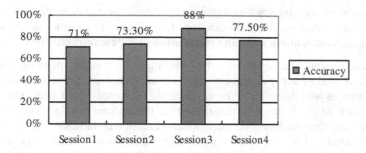

Fig. 5(a). kNN Results

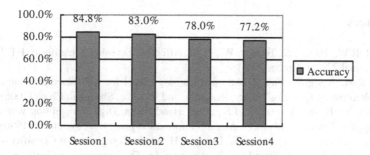

Fig. 5(b). SVM Results

4.5 Discussion of Results

Obviously the results strongly support our hypothesis that physiological responses of human body do reflect his or her emotional state.

This initial experimentation shows that SVM gives better result and is much more stable than kNN and is very prospective to be the algorithm we use for future research. The model we are currently using, however, is still rough and needs to be evolved. We expect higher accuracy so that we could apply the model to practice.

5 Conclusion and Future Work

We've introduced Standard Natural Classroom, a core member in our E-learning lab, which is constructed based on smart space and E-learning concept. Two technical components in SNC have been put forward: E-pen and Emotion Understanding. Our works on those two components results in some practical sub-system or integrated idea. Definite goals of them are also brought forward, which means further efforts on framework or experiment are in process.

The current E-pen component has already become practical except for part of the functions in track-recognition. Communications between E-pen software system and other components or users have also been completed. Our future work includes:

- Create a self-developed laser-pen instead of current ones, in order to facilitate the communication between users and teaching host and provide more functions.

- Continue implementing track-recognition and track-optimization algorithm. We are trying to specialize the methods mentioned in [4] and [5] so as to make them suitable for digit recognition and letter recognition in E-pen, respectively.

Our future work on emotion understanding component includes improving the model, as well as applying the emotion sensing to the actual classroom education or asynchronous self learning. We are planning to simply feed back the students emotions back to the lecturer in real-time, that the lecturer would adapt the lecture style, speed and content based on the students' emotional statistics. We also plans to provide personalized service based on the learner's emotions. This service will incorporate the learner's emotional states together with the learner's cognitive abilities, and his/her learning goals, to generate appropriate responses to the learner.

References

1. Picard, R.W., Papert, S., Bender, W., et al.: Affective Learning - manifesto. BT Technology Journal 22(4) (October 2004)
2. Shen, R.M., Yang, F., Han, P.: An open learning model for web-based learning architecture, Web-Based Learning Theory, Research, and Practice, Shanghai, China (2006)
3. Le Cun, Y., Boser, B., Denker, J.S., et al.: Handwritten Digit Recognition with a Back-Propagation Network. Advances in neural information processing systems 2 (1990)
4. Bottou, L., Cortes, C., Denker, J.S., Drucker, H., et al.: Comparison of Classifier Methods: A Case Study in Handwritten Digit Recognition. In: The International Conference on Pattern Recognition, Jerusalem, Israel, pp. 77–82 (October 1994)
5. Júnior, J.J.O., de C. Carvalho, J.M., Freitas, C.O.A., Sabourin, R.: Evaluating NN and HMM Classifiers for Handwritten Word Recognition. In: The XV Brazilian Symposium on Computer Graphics and Image Processing, pp. 210–217. IEEE, Los Alamitos (2002)
6. de Oliveira, J.J., de Carvalho Jr., J.M., de A Freitas, C.O., Sabourin, R.: Feature Sets Evaluation for Handwritten Word Recognition. Frontiers in Handwriting Recognition (2002)
7. Heraz, A., Razaki, R., Frasson, C.: Using machine learning to predict learner emotional state from brainwaves. In: Proceedings of ICALT, Japan (2007)
8. Shen, L.P., Leon, E., Callaghan, V., Shen, R.M.: Exploratory Research on an Affective E-Learning Model. In: Proceedings of Workshop on Blended Learning (2007)
9. Savran, A., et al.: Emotion Detection in the Loop from Brain Signals and Facial Images. In: Proceedings of eNTERFACE 2006, Dubrovnik (2006)
10. Reynolds, C.J.: The Sensing and Measurement of Frustration with Computers. Master thesis, Massachusetts Institute of Technology
11. Russell, J.A.: A Circumplex Model of Affect. Journal of Personality and Social Psychology 39(6), 1161–1178 (1980); American Psychological Association
12. Lepper, M.R., Chabay, R.W.: Socialising the intelligent tutor: bringing empathy to computer tutors. In: Mandl, H., Lesgold, A. (eds.) Learning issues for intelligent tutoring systems, pp. 242–257 (1988)
13. Dasarathy, B.V.: Nearest Neighbor (NN) Norms: NN Pattern Classification Techniques, (1991) ISBN 0-8186-8930-7
14. Chang, C.-C., Lin, C.-J.: http://www.csie.ntu.edu.tw/~cjlin/libsvm/
15. Picard, R.W., Scheirer, J.: The Galvactivator: a glove that senses and communicates skin conductivity. In: 9th ICHCI, New Orleans (August 2001)
16. Thought Technology Ltd. Canada, http://www.thoughttechnology.com

Explorative Learning of Wireless Network Security with Tele-Lab IT-Security

Dirk Cordel, Christoph Meinel, Stephan Repp, and Christian Willems

Hasso-Plattner-Insitut für Softwaresystemtechnik GmbH, Prof.-Dr.-Helmert-Straße 2-3, 14482 Potsdam, Germany
{dirk.cordel,meinel,stephan.repp,
christian.willems}@hpi.uni-potsdam.de

Abstract. Recently, IT-Security education and awareness creation have become important issues – especially for companies. Enterprises noticed that employees are often unknowingly responsible for security incidents. Due to the significant costs that may arise from such incidents, many companies nowadays spend a lot of money on awareness campaigns. Because today pupils are already able to use current computer technologies and the internet at a young age, the idea arose to start security education and awareness raising early in schools. This paper investigates the feasibility of a special security education program at the "Berufsbildenden Schule für Gewerbe und Technik" (a school providing vocational education) in Trier, Germany. Considering that security education needs to train students to deal with security problems in real environments, the Hasso-Plattner-Institut in Potsdam developed a special interactive web-based security training system. Besides theoretical knowledge, the so-called Tele-Lab system provides students with hands-on experiences by means of a virtual laboratory. This virtual lab is realized on the basis of virtual machines. Every user receives a dedicated virtualized computer to perform practical security exercises with real-life tools in a secure way. Using Tele-Lab, students of the "Berufsbildenden Schule für Gewerbe und Technik" were able to explore wireless network security issues autonomously. This paper subsequently describes the technical foundations of Tele-Lab, the students' hybrid learning process and the evaluation of the Tele-Lab training system.

Keywords: Explorative Learning, Computer Science Education, IT Security, Awareness Creation, Virtual Remote Laboratory.

1 Introduction

Apprenticeship in Germany is based on a dual concept, the so-called *Duale Ausbildung*. This kind of education combines practical and theoretical components. While the theoretical part takes place in classes at specialized schools, the apprentice gains practical experience in a company. The apprenticeship usually focuses on certain aspects of a subject area. In computer science, software development, system administration or networking are possible domains.

J. Fong, R. Kwan, and F.L. Wang (Eds.): ICHL 2008, LNCS 5169, pp. 213–224, 2008.
© Springer-Verlag Berlin Heidelberg 2008

Due to the close cooperation between public educational institutions and companies, this successful system is considered to be worldwide one of the most exemplary. Nevertheless, some weaknesses of the dual concept have been reported in the past. Among these are high costs for enterprises, the lack of ability to teach many school graduates and the inadequate equipment in many schools – also in those with a technical orientation.

The last fact especially forces teaching personnel to focus on theoretical education. But particularly in the interest field of IT-Security, hands-on experience is indispensable but hard to provide – even with suitable hardware and software equipment. Tele-Lab IT-Security can help to overcome this problem.

Tele-Lab[1] is a web-based training system for IT-Security which was developed at the Hasso-Plattner-Institut in Potsdam. The original objective of the system was to provide users not only with theoretical security knowledge but also practical experience in a realistic environment. Especially in the field of IT-Security it is important to gain practical experience to be able to secure computers, communications between computers or even whole networks. After the development of a first prototype of the Tele-Lab system and first user feedback, it turned out that the architecture is also appropriate to increase the awareness of users regarding security issues.

Companies often spend a lot of money on security training for their employees. The reason for this is the high number of failures of computer systems, security leaks or attacks on computer systems caused by human factors. Employees or computer users in general often do not comply with instructions, because they are not aware of the potential consequences. The idea of Tele-Lab is to give users the chance to perform realistic security exercises and experience the consequences themselves which tends to result in increased security awareness. In a company, for example, an executive manager can tell his employees to use strong passwords for authentication but strong passwords are hard to remember and inconvenient. In Tele-Lab the users are able to crack passwords and find out how easy it is to reveal passwords that do not satisfy general security guidelines. In consequence of such hands-on experience, it is expected that the users will be willing to choose stronger passwords in future. Awareness has become an important topic as nearly every person nowadays owns a computer and has an internet connection. Even for pupils at a young age it is normal to make use of current computer technologies. Thus, the idea arose to start awareness training in schools. A computer tool cannot explain better than a human teacher could, but it can present information in a clearer, maybe a better way than a teacher could. Currently, students tend to be more visual learners than in previous generations because their world is rich in visual stimuli [1–3].

This paper describes the application of Tele-Lab in a German school in a hybrid course. Besides providing knowledge and hands-on experience on a security topic relevant to the students, the special kind of explorative learning (described in chapter 4) intends to increase the motivation of learning and the extent of awareness regarding security issues. Furthermore the learning activities have been moved online and time traditionally spent in the classroom is reduced.

---

[1] See http://www.hpi-web.de/meinel/projects/tele-lab_it-security.html and http://www.tele-lab.org

2 Tele-Lab Architecture

When performing practical security exercises on a computer, special requirements arise. Users usually need privileged rights to execute special programs or must have access to certain computer resources like configuration files. If such rights are granted to users, it's very likely that, after a while, the computer system will be damaged due to faulty operation and has to be recovered. Furthermore, the privileged rights could be misused, e.g. to attack other computers in the network. Tele-Lab therefore uses virtual machines as a kind of virtual laboratory.

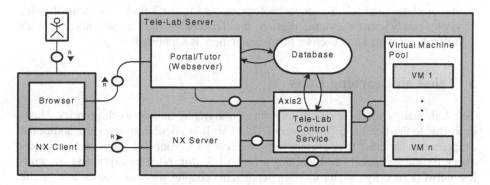

Fig. 1. Tele-Lab architecture (FMC notation)

They are integrated in the online training system to provide the users with hands-on security experience in a secure and efficient way. Figure 1 illustrates the architecture of Tele-Lab. The Tele-Lab Server consists of the following main components:

- **Portal/Tutor (Web server):** A web server provides the portal of the Tele-Lab training system and presents the different security chapters to the users. On this portal a user can log into the system and take part in the training course. The web server with its dynamic WebPages can also be seen as a tutor that offers users the learning material especially didactically.
- **Database/Repository:** A database is used to store several types of information. Besides general information about the users like name, credentials, group, etc. it contains individual information about the user's learning progress. Thus a user is able to continue his training at a later date without repeating already completed exercises. Furthermore, information about the virtual machines is stored in the database which is used to control their management. Finally, the structure of the learning units is stored here.
- **Virtual Machine Pool:** The virtual machine pool is a collection of prepared virtual machines that build the virtual laboratory for the users. Instead of using real computers, several virtual machines are operated on one powerful physical computer. Those virtual machines already contain all needed security applications for the exercises. This saves hardware resources, eases the management of the system and increases the overall security. Due to the isolated operation mode of a virtual machine it can be easily recovered in case of failure without affecting other running

virtual machines or the host computer. For this reason it is even possible to grant users privileged rights on the virtual machines. Currently VMware Server[2] is used in the Tele-Lab system as virtual machine monitor (VMM), i.e. as technology to build and operate the virtual machines.

– **Tele-Lab Control Server:** The control server is responsible for managing the state of the virtual machines and to guarantee an efficient interaction between the user and his dedicated virtual machine. For this reason the control server, for example, handles the assignment of users to virtual machines, the automatic recovering of failed virtual machines, etc.
– **NX Server[3]:** In order to provide the users a remote graphical interface to the virtual machines, the NX Server technology is used in the Tele-Lab system. Besides saving bandwidth for communication, this technology has the advantage that all traffic is encrypted and user session management is supported.

3 Tele-Lab Learning Units

Tele-Lab mainly offers learning units on cryptography and network security. However, due to the flexible architecture of Tele-Lab it is possible to integrate additional chapters e.g. for other user groups with different background or interests [4]. Subsequent, the general structure of learning units will be illustrated by explaining the wireless network security chapter more in detail. This chapter was also chosen to train the participants of the grade of school. Since nowadays wireless networks are very popular but often still not secured by encryption, the chapter seemed to be interesting for the students and also appropriate to increase their awareness.

Before starting the security training a user has to access the Tele-Lab portal (http://www.tele-lab.org) and log-in. For this purpose all scholars in the computer science course were registered to the system with a unique user account in advance. After login an overview of available security units/chapters is displayed. Besides a chapter on authentication and port scanning the "Wireless Network Security" unit is selectable for standard users at the moment. Further units on e.g. firewalls, intrusion detection, e-mail security, etc. are already integrated in Tele-Lab, but not yet open to the public.

Figure 2 shows the user interface of the Tele-Lab training environment: the tutoring system within the browser window and the virtual machine for exercising. In general every chapter is divided into three different parts, each marked with a symbolic icon in the tutor's chapter overview. In the Tele-Lab learning unit on e.g. "Wireless Network Security", those parts consist of the following kinds of information and challenges:

– **Introduction:** This part provides the users with relevant background knowledge on the respective topic. In the "Wireless Network Security" chapter the user gets familiarized with different WiFi technologies like Wireless LAN or Bluetooth.

---

[2] See http://www.vmware.com/products/server
[3] NX is a remote desktop access protocol that allows secure access to Windows RDP-, VNC- and X11-Servers (see http://www.nomachine.com)

Furthermore, the functionality of mechanisms and protocols is explained and related security weaknesses are described [5].

- **Tools:** In this section important hacker tools and security-relevant applications for Windows and Linux are presented. "Kismet" or the "Aircrack Suite" are examples for relevant tools that are described in the "Wireless Network Security" unit. Thus, the user learns to operate these tools to use them in the exercises later on.

- **Exercises:** Especially this section makes Tele-Lab a unique training system for IT-Security. Users can gain practical knowledge by performing exercises with real-world tools on their dedicated virtual machines. For each exercise which requires a realistic computer environment, the user can request a virtual machine by simply pressing the appropriate button displayed on the webpage. A remote desktop connection will be established to the user's virtual machine. The participant of the Tele-Lab training system needs nothing more than a standard browser with java support for being able to control the virtual machine's desktop via the NX-applet. In the "Wireless Network Security" chapter e.g. the user can crack the key of a WEP-encrypted WLAN communication on the virtual machine and directly see the weaknesses of WEP-encryption. It is expected that after such an experience and additional recommendations provided in the Tele-Lab system the participant will have the needed knowledge and awareness to operate a wireless network in a secure way.

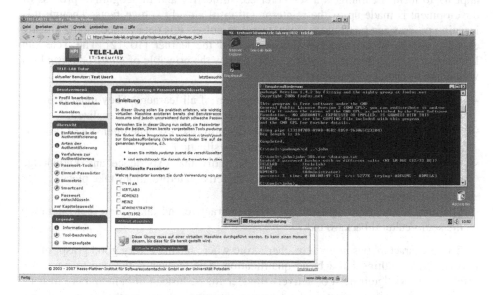

Fig. 2. Tele-Lab training environment (Tutor and Virtual Machine) [6]

4 Lecture Style

Traditional pedagogy distinguishes between different learning styles. These distinct learning styles are closely related and take into consideration different personality types. Many learning style models have been developed and used over the years.

Some of the most widely used pedagogy theories which take into consideration the different personality types mentioned have been proposed by Carl Jung, Myer Briggs, Kolb, and Howard Gardner [7]. The commonly used Visual / Auditory / Kinesthetic Learning Style Model classifies people into three main categories [8].

Visual Learners: these people learn through seeing. They prefer to think in terms of pictures, and learn best from visual aids such as: diagrams, videos and printed handouts. *Auditory Learners:* these people learn through listening. They like listening to lectures engaging in discussions and talking things through. For them, nuances of audio such as tone and speed have a profound effect on their level of understanding. *Kinesthetic Learners:* these people learn by touching or building physical models and are therefore also called Tactile Learners. Some of them may find it hard to sit still in lectures as they want to experience things physically, and can not just listen to the descriptions or read about them [9]. But an individual commonly possesses different learning styles.

Therefore, our educational concept is based on the assumption that acquiring knowledge takes place in an active and knowledge-enriching process which is initiated by the learner himself.

Teaching in the sense of knowledge transfer is not just a uni-directional process. Knowledge is gained in relation to the specific individual background and experiences of the student. People do not perceive the world as it exists (objective), but the way it appears to them. Learning is a self-referred, subjective and the cognitive process of development is made up of the reinterpretation of already known facts. Though this learning process can be triggered by external impulses, it is determined by the already existing and developed individual structures of the learner [10–12]. The Tele-Lab learning units described in the paper at hand obey the principle of *constructivism* [13] which can be characterized as follows:

- Learning happens through active participation of all learners. They must be motivated and interested in what they do and how the objective can be realized.
- The learners control and guide their own learning-process. The intensity of this self guidance may vary depending on the learning situation.
- Learning is practiced constructively. The individual experience and knowledge background is taken into consideration. Subjective interpretations take place.
- Learning takes place in a specific context.
- Learning is socially orientated by being interactive and taking into consideration the socio-cultural background.

These characteristics imply a teacher's role where having a very good grasp of the knowledge is nothing but a basic qualification. The teacher is the one to passively offer the knowledge instead of actively transferring it. Instead of being a pure instructor, the teacher will be creator of a learning environment and must also care of progress management besides promoting, moderating and attending to the self-controlled learning [14, 15, 12].

Koubek [16] describes two meta-levels when developing competences in the education of information scientists: the level of technology and the level of discourse analysis. The first level expresses the importance of providing knowledge on concrete areas of technology (i.e. IT Security) and should be the main focus. The discourse level defines the scope of activity concerning the above technologies. Moreover, [17]

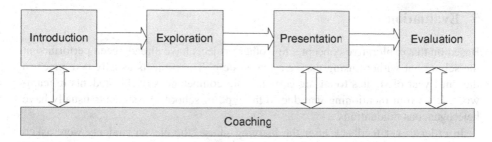

Fig. 3. Lecture style overview

gives ideas on a competence model for computer scientists. Brinda specifies that the learners' perspective should be transformed to the state of mind of a computer science expert during the education process. The student performs a role alternation and becomes an IT specialist. The objective is to enable him or her to learn completely autonomously after finishing the formal education. An example of such a learning style is described in [18].

Based on this theoretical foundation, the lesson concept is introduced as follows:

- **Introduction (20 min):** For motivation, the lecturer presents sensational headlines from newspaper articles on WLAN security problems, such as: "30% of all wireless LANs unprotected", "Secure enterprise WLAN needs complex infrastructure" etc. These headlines are used to trigger a general discussion on wireless security. The discourse should introduce the students to security problems at home or in enterprises. Students are assigned the task of developing a secure concept for a wireless network in the exploration phase. Finally, they are asked to prepare a presentation of their results.
- **Exploration (120 min):** Using the Tele-Lab system, the students explore autonomously the theoretical and practical matters of wireless security in groups of two. In addition to Tele-Lab, the learners are allowed to use other different information sources such as the tele-TASK[4] archive, the Internet in general or textbooks. The important aspects of the exploration phase are the independent work of the students and the self controlled learning guided by the Tele-Lab system. At the end of this phase the students have to work out their presentation.
- **Presentation (90 min):** All groups introduce their results to other students in a presentation of 10 minutes. Afterwards, they discuss the solutions to reflect and analyze their work. Open issues and questions will also be answered during the discourse.
- **Evaluation (90 min):** The students have a written exam on the theoretical background and the practical applications. They also give an evaluation of the Tele-Lab system and the constructive learning concept.
- **Coaching:** The function of the teacher in our concept is to act as a kind of coach – instead of being a lecturer. The teacher must introduce topics and objectives, and motivate the students. If problems arise, the coach gives help and hints for solutions.

---

[4] Tele-TASK is a state-of-the-art e-Lecturing toolkit; its archive provides publicly recorded lecture series on different topics (see http://www.tele-task.de)

5 Evaluation

Based on this explorative concept a few other projects have already been performed at the school but without using the Tele-Lab system. The projects usually take place in the third year of studies to ensure certain basic competences of the students in team-work. It's worth mentioning that due to the type of school, the students usually have heterogeneous graduations.

In order to get feedback after the learning phase, the eleven students were asked about their personal opinion on the Tele-Lab system. For this reason, they had to fill out a questionnaire comprising 21 questions. The questions covered various aspects concerning usability, interestingness, satisfaction and information content. In this paper only four questions were chosen for a more detailed discussion.

The first question was about the all-over satisfaction with the Tele-Lab system. Figure 4 shows the general contentment of the users with 18.2 percent "satisfied" and 81.8 percent "rather satisfied". None of the students said they were rather dissatisfied or even dissatisfied.

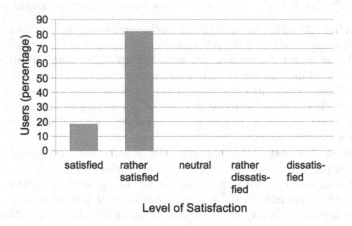

Fig. 4. Overall satisfaction with Tele-Lab

One part of the questionnaire covered the usability of the system. Among certain questions about the structure or navigation of the system there was one question about the first-time ease of use of Tele-Lab. Figure 5 illustrates that it wasn't difficult for the participants to use the system for the first time.

Figure 6 shows the result of the students' opinions regarding the usefulness of the practical exercises (one student didn't mark this field). Since this is a special feature of Tele-Lab which also distinguishes the system from traditional learning systems, this question was one of the most important ones for the Tele-Lab project team. For the majority of students (70%) the practical exercises were useful or rather useful. However, 20 percent of the users evaluated the exercises as rather useless.

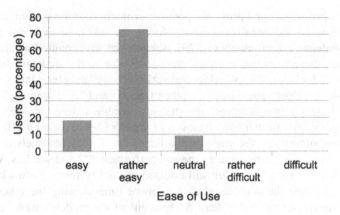

Fig. 5. First time ease of use

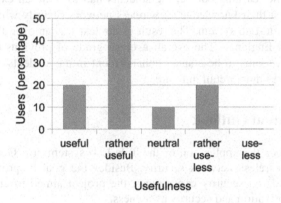

Fig. 6. Usefulness of practical exercises

Besides the presentation of the training system, the learning content has to attract the users. For this reason one question asked about the interestingness of the system. The result of the answers was positive as well (see figure 7).

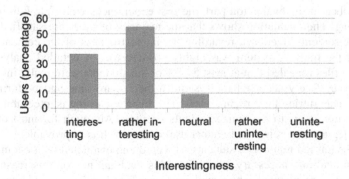

Fig. 7. Overall interestingness of Tele-Lab

In order to investigate and prove the positive evaluation of the system, the log files of the system were additionally analyzed. During the two hour exploration phase of the eleven students, a total number of 292 website hits was counted within the Tele-Lab. Although there were two other chapters accessible to the students, they focused on their task to deal with the "Wireless Network Security" chapter. Only 2.05 percent of website hits were performed in the "Authentication" and "Port scanning" chapter.

After the learning time in school, the students' accounts were not deactivated. It's worth mentioning that further investigations of the log files revealed a 110.27 percent increase of website hits by the students at a later time. 6 students freely accessed the Tele-Lab system again in their spare time and performed 322 website hits. With about 75 percent, most of the clicks were still counted in the "Wireless Network Security" chapter but this time the students also spent more time viewing the other chapters. Thus, the analysis shows that at least 54.5percent of the students were really interested in the Tele-Lab system and the students learn in a self-directed way.

At the end of the learning course, the students had to write an exam. This exam was intended to test their knowledge on wireless network security which they gained by means of the Tele-Lab system. The result of the test was an overall average grade of 2.0 (B Mark in England). The overall average grade of previous exams was approximately 2.3. It seems to be a small enhancement in the students' results but this has to be analyzed in more detail in future.

6 Conclusion and Outlook

This paper describes the application of the Tele-Lab system at a German school to train students in wireless network security. Besides the goal of providing students with practical hands-on security experiences, the project aimed to enhance the students' learning motivation and security awareness.

Our hybrid course-style with Tele-Lab can be used in different situations. In our blended learning approach, we used it to introduce a new subject in an autonomous and explorative way. It can also be used for distance learning, where a student (or a professional) can learn at home. Another interesting aspect is for collaborative learning. The Students worked in a group and collect information, which they share and discuss.

As described in the evaluation part, the first experiences with Tele-Lab in schools are promising. The evaluation shows that the majority of users are satisfied with the system. The students' feedback regarding the interestingness of the contents and the usability of the training system was highly positive too. A detailed analysis of the system's log files revealed that at least 54.5% of the students were really interested in Tele-Lab. They freely accessed the system in their spare-time and performed more website hits than during their regular class. This hybrid learning is to combine the two learning environments to maximize students learning. Although for most of the students the integrated exercises were rather useful, the result is improvable.

Due to the limited number of students who used and evaluated the system there are deeper investigations necessary to confirm this evaluation. For this reason further school projects are planned which will integrate Tele-Lab in their classes too. For the upcoming projects other existing chapters of Tele-Lab on network security or cryptography will be chosen for a security training course. Thus, it is also possible to determine which topics are most appropriate for security education in schools.

References

1. Owston, R.D.: The world wide web: A technology to enhance teaching and learning? Educational Researcher 26, 27–33 (1997)
2. Linckels, S., Repp, S., Karam, N., Meinel, C.: The virtual tele-TASK professor: semantic search in recorded lectures. In: Russell, I., Haller, S.M., Dougherty, J.D., Rodger, S.H. (eds.) Proceedings of the 38th SIGCSE Technical Symposium on Computer Science Education, SIGCSE 2007, Covington, Kentucky, USA, March 7-11, pp. 50–54. ACM, New York (2007)
3. Linckels, S., Dording, C., Meinel, C.: Better results in mathematics lessons with a virtual personal teacher. In: Nagorski, A., Brouilette, G., Rhodes, C. (eds.) Proceedings of the 34th Annual ACM SIGUCCS Conference on User Services 2006, Edmonton, Alberta, Canada, November 5-8, pp. 201–209. ACM, New York (2006)
4. Hu, J., Cordel, D., Meinel, C.: New media for teaching applied cryptography and network security. In: Nejdl, W., Tochtermann, K. (eds.) EC-TEL 2006. LNCS, vol. 4227, pp. 488–493. Springer, Heidelberg (2006)
5. Willems, C.: Tele-Lab IT-Security: An architecture for practical IT security education on the web. In: Proceedings of the 2nd International Workshop on eLearning and Virtual and Remote Laboratories (2008)
6. Willems, C.: Eine erweiterte Architektur für den Tele-Lab Server: Implementierung eines generischen Interfaces für Virtual Machine Monitors. Master's thesis, Universität Trier (2006)
7. Schroeder, C.: New students - new learning styles (accessed, October 2007), http://www.virtualschool.edu/mon/Academia/KierseyLearningStyles.html
8. Bogod, L.: Learning styles (accessed, December 2007), http://www.ldpride.net/learningstyles.MI.htm
9. Sharda, N.K.: Authoring educational multimedia content using learning styles and story telling principles. In: Friedland, G., Hürst, W., Knipping, L., Mühlhäuser, M. (eds.) Proceedings of the International Workshop on Educational Multimedia and Multimedia Education 2007, Augsburg, Bavaria, Germany, September 28, pp. 93–102. ACM, New York (2007)
10. Arnold, R., Schüssler, I.: Wandel der Lernkultur. Wissenschaftliche Buchgesellschaft, Darmstadt (1998)
11. Bonz, B.: Wandel der Lernkultur. Schneider Verlag GmbH, Hohengehren (2003)
12. Siebert, H.: Pädagogischer Konstruktivismus. Luchterhand, München (2003)
13. Schelten, A.: Pädagogischer Konstruktivismus. Franz Steiner Verlag, Stuttgart (2000)
14. Gudjons, H.: Krisen als Wandlung im Lehrerberuf. Pädagogik 11, 6–12 (2002)
15. Frey, K.H.: Selbstorganisiertes Lernen in (berufs-) biographischer Reflexion. Julius Klinkhardt Verlag, Bad Heilbrunn (1998)
16. Koubek, J.: Informatische Allgemeinbildung. In: Friedrich, S. (ed.) Unterrichtskonzepte für informatische Bildung, INFOS 2005, 11. GI-Fachtagung Informatik und Schule. an der TU Dresden, September 28-30. LNI, vol. 60, pp. 57–66. GI (2005)

17. Brinda, T., Schulte, C.: Beiträge der Objektorientierung zu einem Kompetenzmodell des informatischen Modellierens. In: Friedrich, S. (ed.) Unterrichtskonzepte für informatische Bildung, INFOS 2005, 11. GI-Fachtagung Informatik und Schule. an der TU Dresden, September 28-30. LNI, vol. 60, pp. 137–148. GI (2005)
18. Repp, S., Ziegler, R., Meinel, C.: Lernortkooperation in der IT-Ausbildung – Kompetenzentwicklung in Projekten. In: Schubert, S. (ed.) Didaktik der Informatik in Theorie und Praxis, INFOS 2007, 12. GI-Fachtagung Informatik und Schule, Siegen, September 28-30. LNI, vol. 112. GI (2007)

Mobile 2.0 Leads to a Transformation in mLearning

Shudong Wang[1] and Michael Higgins[2]

[1] Faculty of Law, Hiroshima Shudo University, 1-1-1 Oozukahigashi,
Asaminami-ku, 731-3164, Hiroshima City, Japan
[2] Faculty of Engineering, Yamaguchi University, Tokiwadai 2-16-1, 755-8611,
Ube City, Yamaguchi Prefecture, Japan
peterwsd@shudo-u.ac.jp, higginsm@yamaguchi-u.ac.jp

Abstract. This paper aims to delineate the impact of Mobile 2.0 on mobile learning (mLearning). Based on a thorough analysis on numerous Mobile 2.0 applications which can be used or are being used for learning purposes, the paper concludes that Mobile 2.0 brings a revolution to learning and will eventually lead to a transformation in the style of learning. The background for this conclusion includes introduction of the concept and technology of Mobile 2.0, its relationship to Web 2.0, empirical research, and actual use of Mobile 2.0 applications in education. The paper also offers a sneak peek at the future of Web 3.0 assisted learning. This Japan and China based research is also applied to other countries.

Keywords: mLearning, Mobile 2.0, learning transformation, Mobile 2.0 applications for learning, Web 3.0.

1 Introduction

1.1 Web 2.0 and Mobile 2.0: Potentiality for Learning

Web 2.0 on PCs has been proved to be significantly pragmatic in education [1]. Then to what degree has Mobile 2.0 been able to extend PC Web 2.0's educational applications to mobile devices? Mobile 2.0 is a term that has been used since the appearance of Web 2.0 in 2004. Mobile 2.0 constitutes the next generation of transferring data to mobile devices and it links Web 2.0 with the mobile platform to create something new: it creates a new set of services that has greatly increased mobility and is as easy to use as the Web. These services point the way forward for the mobile data industry [2]. Without exception, all Internet giants have stepped into the Mobile 2.0 market. Google, Yahoo!, and MSN can all be adapted to mobile devices that have Internet connection. Apple's iPhone has integrated the functions of the mobile phone, PDA, GPS, iPod and TV, and all of these functions can be activated just by finger touch. Yahoo! has mobile handset-oriented pages called Yahoo! Mobile. On Microsoft's mobile OS, Windows Mobile enables PC Office files to be viewable on mobile phones and PDAs. Mobile 2.0 is not device dependent: any mobile device which can be connected to the Internet can be considered to be a Mobile 2.0 carrier, including

J. Fong, R. Kwan, and F.L. Wang (Eds.): ICHL 2008, LNCS 5169, pp. 225–237, 2008.

Nintendo's DS Lite and other handheld game consoles. All functioning mobile phones, PDAs and iPods are within the realm of Mobile 2.0. Unlike Web 2.0, Mobile 2.0 is more concerned with user-led services and focuses more on the user-side than PC Web 2.0, as mobile handsets can be used almost anywhere.

Most multi-function applications developed in Java, Python, or open C/C++, run fairly well on mobile devices. This has given mobile phones qualities resembling small, handheld computers. It can also be argued that the built-in GPS, FM radio and both streaming and broadcast TV services on mobile phones make Mobile 2.0 more differential and even revolutionary than PC Web 2.0. Increasingly seamless integration of PC Internet and mobile networks has changed mobile devices into very powerful learning tools.

1.2   Research Purpose – Exploration of Mobile 2.0 for Learning

Web 2.0 for learning is widely practiced and has been well-researched. However, Mobile 2.0 for education has yet been to be fully explored. How can Mobile 2.0 be used for learning? What are the strengths and potential of Mobile 2.0 for learning? Are there any successful applications of Mobile 2.0 reported in education? Finally, Web 3.0 has also recently emerged. What kind of applications for learning can be predicted for Web 3.0? The above questions will be discussed in the following sections. Section 2 details the background of Mobile 2.0 for learning and delineates the actual use of Web 2.0 in education. Section 3 discusses the learning transformation that Mobile 2.0 is leading us to. The concept of Mobile 3.0 and how it can be used for education is predicted in Section 4. Section 5 provides a summary and conclusion of the previous sections.

2   Mobile 2.0 for Learning Purposes

2.1   Mobile 2.0 for Learning: An Infrastructure Background

In the last decade, mobile phone technology has witnessed incredible developments in technology: from analog to digital and from plain and simple mobile phones to the current 3G smartphones which can serve as a mini-computers, telephones, radios, televisions and cameras. This rise in technology has been so monumental that it is outpacing the devices that are currently on the market. In Japan, as of April of 2008, the number of contracts with mobile phone companies (mainly NTT DoCoMo, au-KDDI, Softbank and EMOBILE) was 102,724,500 [3], which is roughly 80% of Japan's population. China, the largest mobile phone market in the world, had 575 million mobile phone users as of April, 2008 [4]. When coupled with other formats of mobile devices, such a large figure has created an enormous number of potential learners who can learn anytime and anywhere. As impressive as the increasing numbers of mobile phone users are, equally surprising is the development in wireless telecommunication infrastructure and mobile device manufacturing technology. Mobile telecommunication in many countries have entered 3G, which is a generation allowing the transmission of 384 kbit/s for mobile systems and 2 Mbs for stationary systems. Japan, Europe and North America are already moving towards 4G networks (WiMax 4G networks show transfer speeds of 3Mbs and 4G Long Term Evolution —

LTE — networks are already achieving real-world transfer speeds of 180Mbs) [5]. These increasing speeds make mLearning less problematic and even more feasible. Infrared, Wi-Fi, WiMAX and Bluetooth technology enable data communication between mobile phones and other digital devices. In the case of Japan, all mobile phones have Internet connection capability.

2.2 Mobile 2.0 Applications for Learning

Some IT technologies are best suited for particular learning activities. For example, the SMS function on mobile phones is ideal for vocabulary learning as vocabulary items are naturally short and can be easily segmented to small, individual definitions and examples [6]. A similar situation exists with the nexus between Mobile 2.0 applications and learning. For example, text blogs are helpful for training writing ability and improving social identity. Wiki is useful for promoting collaborative topic discussion and writing. Podcasting can be used for a lot of educational purposes such as content dissemination. Thorne and Payne [7] cite some educational projects utilizing Wiki technologies for learning. For instance, L.Wiki (a particular Wiki to support Unicode encoding), supported by Pennsylvania State's foreign language resource center is used by a variety of groups and courses, including Chinese, German, Russian, Spanish, English composition, and also for English as a Second Language courses.

The primary uses of iPods include individual and collaborative student authoring, course project management, and multiparty running commentaries. In the case of Podcasting (combining iPods and broadcasting) for language listening, it is worth noting that Podcasting-assisted English learning programs started in April 2004 at Osaka Jogakuin College, Japan [8]. 15-gigabyte iPods were provided to 210 newly enrolled freshmen. These iPods came installed with audio materials designed to improve learners' listening abilities.

Real-time updating alerts of learning content via RSS and ATOM
In the PC Web 2.0 world, people need to sign into their accounts to generate Web 2.0 content such as blogs, SNS (Social Network Service) and share photos and videos. After that, content developers (users) must wait for others to view their messages or choose to subscribe to new ones through RSS feeds. Passive RSS has been an important web syndication protocol. More importantly, ATOM (Atom Publishing Protocol), which has been rapidly replacing RSS as the preferred syndication format, is already actually part of every major RSS reader and email client today. This move away from RSS towards ATOM is because RSS is a technically flawed implementation of a good idea and is, in fact, incompatible with itself to the frustration of many, and that, combined with numerous problems related to g11n feeds, has given rise to ATOM. However, depending on how one publishes the information, preferably automated and using a Content Management System such as Drupal or Joomla, it is mostly trivial to implement either one or both (which is most often done as many data consumers are not savvy enough to distinguish between the two).

The primary benefit to having a syndication feed is to increase exposure of something by submitting it to be regularly crawled by a feed search engine or community, such as Technocrati or Facebook as examples, to freely disseminate the information throughout the web to parties who are keeping abreast of trends particular to a broader interest. In the mLearning world, learning tips or new information for study (vocabulary items of the day, etc.) can be submitted to many sites that have been built for specific student populations (Moodle sites, etc.).

As a vehicle to keep students abreast of happenings, it is certainly acceptable. But trends do demonstrate that most people do not directly subscribe to such feeds in practice, and unless the originator of the feed is interested in a wider exposure to try to generate additional traffic to the original site created for the specific student population, its usefulness has more to do with the actualized relationship with the students and ironically, the better it is, the less likely they are to subscribe to the feed directly unless it is a forced subscription.

Even so, feeds are generally disregarded, as they need to be in constant motion to demand attention. Because of this, the learning situation would probably be better served by emailing updates to the students and having the same release available on the mLearning or e-learning website for syndication. The teacher would tend to get more attention out of the email than the feed and theoretically raise its urgency as opposed to a feed which is entirely passive and, unless it is part of a collection of topically relevant feeds that provide important information for the course and considered part of the requirements, it would likely be ignored by the majority of the students. Thus, we return to RSS/ATOM's actual value; pushing the feed to Google, or some other central source to broaden the mLearning/e-learning audience beyond a finite group and as a general promotional vehicle rather than an active resource.

The problem is that in order to perform all these functions (signing into their accounts to generate Web 2.0 content such as blogs, SNS, sharing photos and videos, etc.), users must be near a PC. This is not a restriction for Mobile 2.0 users, as they can send updated information to subscribers via mobile-based mail systems, which can be accessed in real-time. Mobile 2.0 can also spread information more effectively than Web 2.0 by utilizing existing mobile phone numbers.

Registered or un-registered Mobile 2.0 sites

The URLs that are built into mobile phone menus are known as *registered* sites. In Japan, these sites must sign contracts with mobile telecommunications companies and pay a fee in order for them to be incorporated into the phones. Further, the content of registered mobile sites is investigated thoroughly by mobile phone companies. For example, NTT DoCoMo, au KDDI, Ezweb, and Softbank Yahoo! Mobile have a large number of mobile sites registered with them. Users merely need to scroll through their menu lists to find their desired sites.

Most learning sites on mobile phones are registered sites, providing a surfeit of Mobile 2.0 services. Sites such as the one in Figure 1 offer online quizzes, message posting, Wikis, RSS feeds, photos and video sharing services (see Fig. 1, the front page of a registered Mobile 2.0 learning site.).

Some well-known examples of registered learning Mobile 2.0 sites in Japan include: English Forest <www.eigonomori.com/keitai.php>, from which mobile phone users can do listening exercises, download texts, and take online quizzes; and English People <http://eigojin.net> enables mobile phone users to learn English words though

Fig. 1. An example of registered Mobile 2.0 learning site

games and BREW (Binary Runtime Environment for Wireless) applications. Learners can download and run programs from the site for playing games, sending messages and sharing photos.

These registered learning mobile sites are mostly run by schools and other related companies for a profit. The obvious drawback of these sites is that users pay for the time they spend online and for the use of the learning site. For this reason, it may not be advisable for teachers to put time and money into building a registered site. In the case of Japan, it is also unlikely that an individual mobile site will be approved by the major mobile phone companies.

As a result of the drawbacks noted above, teachers may have to turn to *unregistered* mobile sites. These sites work much like a majority of sites on the Internet: they are made by users who have no affiliation to any specific site or company, and they are made for a user community with a specific purpose. Thus, teachers can take advantage of this option, as it is a much cheaper and more user-friendly option than registered sites. A further advantage of unregistered sites is that they are built to have exactly the same functions as the registered sites. In fact, the only added burden on the user of these sites is that he or she must manually input the URL of the site into his or her mobile phone. In fact, as more and more digital cameras built in mobile phones can "read" URLs and email address in QR (Quick Response) codes, the input of URLs has become easy.

Do-it-yourself: Free Mobile 2.0 sites for teaching purposes
A popular and free Mobile 2.0 site builder for teaching can be found at Winksite <http://winksite.com>. The site claims that it makes it easy to create mobile Websites and communities that can be viewed worldwide on any mobile phone. Winksite allows users to build their own blogs, chat forums, conduct polls and create journals on mobile phones.

It is truly user-friendly in that it does not require the user to download or install any software, and allows users to build and manage a mobile community over which they have total control [9].

Teachers can easily avail themselves of Winksite's functions. For example, teachers can make announcements to students, post homework assignments, give quizzes, and discuss tasks assigned in previous lessons. The use of mobile phones for these activities offers a multitude of educational opportunities for learners, as it promotes interactivity and gives them quick and easy access to discussion and timely feedback from teachers. Further, teachers can encourage learners to work collaboratively on writing assignments, read e-magazines, and conduct group work, all via their mobile phones by customizing services from this site.

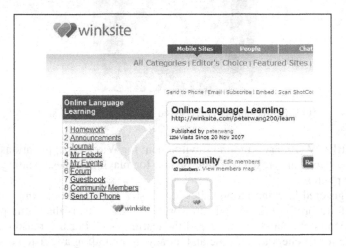

Fig. 2. A Do-it-yourself Mobile 2.0 site using Winksite

In Japan, there are several mobile page providers, such as HP Maker <http://hp.0zero.jp >, Forest Page <http://id.fm-p.jp>, and FHP <http://fhp.jp>, which all have similar services to Winksite.

Learning through mobile blogs, SNS, tags and games

Beginning with mixi <http://mixi.jp> in 2004, SNS in Japan has become extremely popular. As of May 15, 2006, Mixi had 4 million registered users and 130 million page views (PV) per day. Another popular blog site in Japan, Livedoor, had 8.6 million registered users by the end of April, 2006 [10]. Both sites can be accessed by mobile phones, with both having a large contingency of foreign community users. Japanese language learners using these mobile sites have access to everyday Japanese use at their fingertips. In addition to language communities, there are numerous other learning communities in many different fields. Community members raise questions, propose solutions and exchange ideas. Some regularly read and comment on the blogs on the sites. Mixi members can always find a community to meet his or her learning interests.

In the first half of 2004, SNS providers simply transferred their services from PCs to mobile phones without considering the special features of mobile phones. From the winter of 2004 to 2005, Japanese providers using SNS started to embed mobile phones with unique functions like GPS and mobile games. Coupled with these, Mobile Social Software (MoSoSo) can facilitate social encounters by allowing users to see others who are in the same geographic location as them. The implications for learning are clear: Mobile 2.0 users can easily find out who, in their community, is nearby and available to talk and/or learn simultaneously.

Mobile SNS integrated with online games is another new tendency in Mobile 2.0. One successful integration of SNS and online games in Japan can be found at Mobage-town < http://mbga.jp >, a free mobile site offering free online games and a wide variety of community functions such as blogs, email, chat, and message boards. The site has some English games on it that can be used by learners to gain a different perspective on English language learning. After all, teachers often employ games in their classrooms, so extending them to mobile phone usage is another facet of Mobile 2.0 that can greatly assist the learner.

One of the Mobile 2.0 features is "I am not a number, I am a tag." In Web 2.0, tags are essentially a classification system. Tags are different from keywords as keywords have to appear in the content, but tags can be created by the bloggers and page makers to reflect their thoughts about the content. Educators can use tags to associate specific learning references, class events and learning topics. Learners can make the best use of tags to look for desired blog entries, images, and other web publications for certain learning topics, as search engines can index tags to make relevant materials searchable in a uniform way. By using the above Mobile 2.0 community tools, mobile learners can be ubiquitously involved in content editing and sharing in mobile communities. Pedagogical research shows that mobile communication can significantly increase student extrinsic motivation without increasing the pressure on them [11].

Learning via animated media on Mobile 2.0 phones

Since Flash Lite 1.0 was released by Macromedia in 2004, it has been supported by most mobile phone companies. Flash Lite is very popular with mobile users who buy discount contracts with their providers, as they can usually view as many flash movies as they like for the same price each month. For learning, Flash Lite can be used for creating flash cards to review foreign language vocabulary and grammar: a very popular method of learning new words with many learners. Science teachers can use Flash Lite to create flow chart to indicate an experiment process and solving process of mathematical problems. Students who use smartphones can download Flash Lite software from the Internet and install it on their mobile phones. Learners can also choose to view flash movies by connecting to a Mobile 2.0 site. In Japan, <http://freedom-mobile.jp> is a good example of how flash can be used to provide rich format contexts on mobile phones.

Video possibly has more power than any other medium for learning. It has the power to engage, enlighten, and fascinate learners. With this in mind, YouTube is representative of Web 2.0 applications that are currently being widely used for various educational purposes. Teachers can post their lessons to the site for students to review. Science teachers can post recordings of experiment processes, language teachers can upload video clips, interviews, or selected clips from educational TV programs to YouTube for their class to view. In fact, learners can always find video clips which are perfectly, or at least partially, relevant to the topic being taught on

YouTube. Mobile YouTube has been available on many specifications of 3G mobile phones that support 3GP video format since 2006 in Japan. As the digital streaming video from mobile networks is still quite expensive for viewers, Mobile YouTube is not yet as popular in education as PC YouTube. The same reason applies to Second Life. Second Life is an online community, which has been in the headlines lately for creating a virtual community, whereby users pay for virtual goods and services. Some companies are providing game players with a virtual cell phone that works within the game and enables voice, SMS and basic mobile content services. But there are very few studies on, or practices that use Second Life on mobile phones found in education.

SMS integrated with instant messengers (IM)

SMS for learning has been gaining in popularity as of late. Levy and Kennedy [12] sent Italian words, idioms and example sentences to students ' mobile phones as SMS messages. The project proved successful for aiding in language learning and demonstrated that the use of SMS in learning is a pedagogically sound technique.

Instant messengers (IM) are also valuable tool for learners. Time and place-independent communication is one of the fundamental tenets of mobile assisted learning. Like SMS, has the potential to greatly enhance communication between learners and instructors. The integration of SMS and IM, which is advancing in the Mobile 2.0 world, serves as a connection between mobile phone users and PC users. Moreover, it connects mobile phone users even more closely to each other, giving them an advantage over conventional PC users. In China, people can send SMS messages to mobile phones using QQ, the most popular instant messenger with Chinese youth. Skype, Yahoo!, and MSN also allow users to send SMS to mobile phones by typing in the users' mobile phone number. Instant messengers like MSN and Yahoo! messenger are available on most mobile phones with, and mobile phone users can easily enter communities like mobile blogs from their phone's IM mode. Users can chat online with mobile phones partners or PC users. This allows potential learners to exchange information much more conveniently when they are on the move.

Li and Erben [13] report that learners are capable of increasing their intercultural awareness with prolonged use of instant messenger services. Li and Erben argue that these services can assist in boosting self-reflection capacities, critical thinking skills and create a greater sensitivity and respect for intercultural differences. In a time and age when these skills are so important for survival in an increasingly globalized world, teachers and learners cannot afford to overlook the benefits of acquiring these qualities.

Mobile search

In July 2006, Japan-based au-KDDI, in cooperation with Google, started a mobile search engine service that is available on their phone's menu bar. Then, the Japanese giant telecommunications company NTT DoCoMo, which was the first company in the world to create a mobile phone with Internet capability, embedded a whole host of Internet search engines onto its i-mode service: Google, R25, CROOZ! SeafTyy, and mobile Goo. Clients using these search engines can also obtain content from unregistered mobile sites and the original PC sites. Further, since the summer of 2006, Softbank has led the growing trend of Mobile 2.0 in Japan. Every Softbank mobile phone is now embedded with the following Yahoo! Products: search; calendar; mail; messenger; animated cartoons; comic books with their popularity ranked by readers; games, and news. As these services are quite new, many learners do not yet possess a concrete knowledge of them. Instructors can utilize these services in their classrooms by demonstrating how they work and by introducing potential peers with whom their learners can communicate.

Location Based Service (LBS) for context aware and adaptive learning

GPS navigation service allows people to find out a precise physical location with a high degree of accuracy. In Japan, by 2006 GPS functions had been built into 26% of mobile phones [10] and this ratio has been steadily increasing. As LBS on mobile devices provide services such as navigation, field services and "find my nearest", it obviously can be used for context aware or adaptive learning. Some ideas being explored are: Mobile Google Map service can be used for outdoor geography learning; learners can be sent "pinpoint" context aware learning materials; and on the learner side, using mobile LBS, they can always find their nearest community members. For example, a group of like-minded Japanese learners could use the mobile site <http://activo.jp>, an SNS site integrated with GPS.

Mobile 2.0 LMS/ CMS for learning

LMS (Learning Management System) or CMS (Course Management System) are complex software or platforms designed for planning and managing learning activities online or offline. Popular LMSs for educational use are Moodle, a free open source teaching and learning management platform, and Blackboard (WebCT), a widely used commercial LMS. In the era of Web 2.0, many of these LMSs have integrated Web 2.0 technologies.

It is natural to expect that the above types of LMS work on mobile handsets so that teachers can manage teaching and students can conduct learning remotely. Unfortunately, due to the fact that both the hardware and software on mobile handsets have inherent limitations in running a multi-functional LMS, it is difficult to transfer all types of LMS to mobile handsets. Hardware limitations include small screens, low bandwidths, low resolution of images, and the difficulty of typing on small handsets. Software limitations include the rejection of cookies and the problem that mobile handsets do not support as many applications as PCs. Moreover, mobile online learning security such as access control can only work reliably through integrating an operating system, which many current mobile phones do not have [14].

Poodle, a mini-LMS course-management system developed by Houser and Thornton, is designed to read quizzes in Moodle's own GIFT format, and randomly distribute questions and responses to learners of English, with each of these displayed in its own tiny webpage. The authors also built a Wiki and forum server, which enables students to collaboratively learn about American culture. Poodle was highly rated by learners, who cited its ability to be used anywhere and anytime as one of its main advantages of it [15]. With the exception of its online quiz function, Wikis and forums, other Moodle functions were not mentioned in Houser and Thornton's paper. Further, Researchers at Sapporo Gakuin University, Japan, have successfully converted PC Moodle to mobile phones, allowing feedback and quiz modules to be viewed on mobile phones, but not the other functions of Moodle.

Nevertheless, both Poodle and Moodle for Mobiles maintain their status as ground-breaking mobile LMS developments. With the increasing enhancement in mobile hardware and software, powerful and comprehensive LMSs are bound to emerge in the near future.

3 Mobile 2.0 – A Transformation of mLearning

The potential of Mobile 2.0 for learning was presented in the previous sections. In fact, not only has Mobile 2.0 changed learning for the better, but it has also funda-mentally altered the means of everything from conducting business to education. From shopping to making ticket reservations, and from finding accurate directions to learning, mobile devices have not only made our lives easier, but they also present us with opportunities we once may never have imagined. Throughout history, educa-tional technology has greatly increased the way in which we learn: technology like movies, which has brought the world into the classroom since 1920, was considered to be a progressive teaching approach in the 1920s and the 1930s. Moreover, radio was regarded as "the assistant teacher" in 1930s. The 1950s witnessed a teaching transformation when TV was first used in the classroom [16], and the 1990s wit-nessed the World Wide Web being introduced into educational settings. Nowadays, Mobile 2.0 has changed both the way we live our lives and the learning styles we use.

There has been a plethora of research that envisions e-learning as an educational paradigm shift from classroom learning to distance learning [17]. From 1996 onwards classroom teachers started to incorporate the Internet into their regular classroom teaching. In the past decade, mobile devices have presented educators and learners alike with new opportunities for learning. They bestow upon us innovative means with which to conduct research, gain access to course administration and manage-ment, provide learners with support and guidance, and offer us the up-to-the-minute knowledge we require to compete and succeed in today's increasingly wired world. Ally, Schafer, Cheung, McGreal, and Tin assert that mLearning is distinctive because it facilitates the manner in which learning is delivered to people at the right time and in the right place. In the near future, "mLearning will become a normal part of life-long education and self-directed learning" [18]. Accordingly, we believe the emer-gence of Mobile 2.0 will bring about a revolution in mLearning. Mobile 2.0 frees people's learning from a fixed place to any location while still maintaining a rich and interactive learning content. In Mobile 2.0 world, traditional SMS has been replaced with Mobile IM, MMS (Multimedia Messaging Service) has been replaced with mobile media sharing, WAP (Wireless Application Protocol) sites replaced with Mo-bile Web and Mobile search, Push-to Talk (PTT) with mobile VoIP, WAP Push with Mobile RSS reader, and LBS has been replaced with Mobile Google maps. Obviously Mobile 2.0 has made wired e-learning and wireless mLearning seamless. It makes the extension of in-house learning to outdoor learning much more of a reality.

Mobile 2.0 uniquely provides learners with a movable, sociable, community-based synchronous or asynchronous learning environment. Face-to-face learning is usually restricted to classrooms, and e-learning on wired networks is confined to PC desks. On the other hand, mLearning without Mobile 2.0 tends to be too individual, isolated and fragmented. Multi-featured Mobile 2.0 learning environments cannot be dupli-cated in any other contexts.

The limitations of mLearning [19] are likely to be overcome by the development of new technologies in the coming years. When mobile networks gain the capacity to reach broadband speeds, and when the inherent typing problems associated with mobile devices are eventually solved, the rich interaction and ease of content management that Mobile 2.0 promises will be fully functioning on mobile handsets. Mobile handsets will eventually integrate many more functions that the learner can use for learning. For example, the Apple iPhone is a mobile phone integrated with many of the functions of the iPOD, PDAs, digital cameras, GPS and TV. The iPod uses the Web as a back end and the PC as a local cache. In this sense, the Mobile 2.0 service is "driven by the Web and configured at the PC." With this concept in mind, we will begin to see a complete transformation into truly practical handsets that will also facilitate a transformation in learning.

4 Mobile 3.0 for Future Learning

Although very few people are as yet talking about Mobile 3.0, some indeed have started to research Web 3.0, which is a term that is sometimes referred to as the Semantic Web. In the coming Web 3.0 era, browsers will have the abilities to discover and organize massive amounts of disordered knowledge generated on Internet. The Web 3.0 world is a place where machines can read web pages much as human beings read them. Current keyword search on the Internet is not intuitive and does not reflect the underlying Intent of the query. Being semantic in nature, Web 3.0 will allow semantic sentence input and be able to linguistically interpret it, including any misspelling, then return with accurate results. When Web 3.0 is expanded to mobile devices, that is, Mobile 3.0, this kind of "artificially intelligent interpretation" will dramatically improve learning efficacy using Mobile search, as misspellings happen more often when users input words via built-in speech recognition software or touch pad into mobile devices while on the move than when using a fixed-base PC.

Another potentiality of Mobile 3.0 for learning is to realize 3D virtual classroom on mobile devices. Mobile Second Life is already being tested for business purposes on mobile phones. This would involve the Web transforming into a series of 3D spaces, taking the concept realized by Second Life further. This could open up new ways to connect and collaborate using 3D shared spaces in learning activities. As the virtual 3D world on PC starts to be widely used in education, we believe that mobile virtual 3D classrooms can be realized on mobile devices in the near future.

While some people feel that Mobile 2.0 carriers such as the Apple iPhone, Google Earth and GPS phones that integrate user-generated-content are in fact Mobile 3.0, most consider that these are but the first feeble steps in that direction. One thing that is certain, however, is that Mobile 3.0 for learning is a field that is wide open for exploration and exploitation.

5 Conclusion

This research focused on how to use Mobile 2.0 concepts and technology to benefit learning and teaching. The paper discussed how emailing, blogging, SNS, online games, mobile searching, and the integration of SMS and IM can be used on mobile devices, especially mobile phones, for learning. This community-based and user-led mobile educational style is undoubtedly leading to a transformation not only into mLearning itself, but also the whole e-learning world. This transformation is one that will positively affect the way in which we teach and learn. Arising from this discussion is the projected transformation from Mobile 2.0 to Mobile 3.0 that will eventually take place with a Semantic Web element possessing artificial intelligence being built-in to mobile devices. This can ultimately result in a virtual classroom that can be viewed on mobile phones and PDAs that will feature 3.5G and 4G technology expected to appear in 2009-2010 in Japan and some other countries.

Acknowledgment. We extend our heartfelt thanks to Professor Neil Heffernan for checking and proofreading the draft of this paper.

References

1. Franklin, T.: Web 2.0 for Content for Learning and Teaching in Higher Education (2008), http://www.jisc.ac.uk/media/documents/programmes/digitalrepo sitories/web2-content-learning-and-teaching.pdf
2. Appelquist, D.: What is mobile 2.0 (2006), http://www.torgo.com/blog/2006/09/what-is-mobile-20.html
3. Japan Telecommunication Carriers Association, http://www.tca.or.jp
4. Ministry of Information and Industry of the People's Republic of China. Monthly Statistical Report of China Telecommunication (2008), http://www.mii.gov.cn
5. Stokes, J.: Nokia 4G wireless tech hits 173Mbps in real-world test. Ars Technica, LLC (2007), http://arstechnica.com/news.ars/post/20071228-nokia-4g-wireless-tech-hits-173mbps-in-real-world-test.html
6. Levy, M., Stockwell, G.: CALL dimensions: Options and issues in computer assisted learning. Lawrence Erlbaum Associates, New Jersey (2006)
7. Thorne, S., Payne, J.: Evolutionary Trajectories, Internet-mediated Expression,and Education. CALICO Journal 22(3), 371–397 (2005)
8. McCarty, S.: Spoken Internet to Go: Popularization through Podcasting. The JALT CALL Journal 1(2), 67–74 (2006)
9. Winksite (2008), http://winksite.com
10. Mobile White Book, Impress R&D, Tokyo (2007)
11. Pei-Luen, P., Qin, G., Wu, L.: Using mobile communication technology in high school education: Motivation, pressure, and learning performance. Journal of Computers & Education 50(1), 1–22 (2006)
12. Levy, M., Kennedy, C.: Learning Italian via mobile SMS. In: Kukulska-Hulme, Traxler, J. (eds.) Mobile Learning: a handbook for educators and trainers, pp. 76–83. Taylor & Francis, London (2005)
13. Li, J., Erben, T.: Intercultural learning via instant messenger interaction. CALICO Journal 24(2), 231–291 (2007)
14. Weippl, E.: Security and Trust in Mobile Multimedia. In: Ibrahim, I.K. (ed.) Handbook of mobile multimedia, pp. 22–34. Idea Group Reference, New York (2005)
15. Houser, C., Thornton, P.: Poodle: A course-management system for mobile phones. In: Proceedings of the third IEEE workshop on wireless technologies in education (WMTE 2005), pp. 159–163 (2005)

16. Cuban, L.: Teachers and machines: The classroom use of technology since 1920. Teacher's College Press, New York (1986)
17. Ferguson, C., Keengwe, J.: Pedagogical paradigm shift: A shift from traditional to E-learning education. In: Richards, G. (ed.) Proceedings of World Conference on E-Learning in Corporate, Government, Healthcare, and Higher Education, Chesapeake, Virginia, pp. 2022–2024 (2007)
18. Ally, M., Schafer, S., Cheung, B., McGreal, R., Tin, T.: Use of mobile learning technology to train ESL adults. In: M-learning 2007 Conference Proceedings, Melbourne, Australia (2007)
19. Wang, S., Higgins, M.: Limitations of Mobile Phone Learning. In: International Workshop on Wireless and Mobile Technology in Education, pp. 179–181 (2005)

Integrating Incidental Vocabulary Learning Using PDAs into Academic Studies: Undergraduate Student Experiences

Yanjie Song and Robert Fox

Faculty of Education, The University of Hong Kong, Hong Kong, China
sonyj@hkusua.hku.hk, bobfox@hku.hk

Abstract. In higher education literature, no in-depth studies have been identified that investigate the value of integrating incidental vocabulary learning using mobile devices into undergraduate students' academic studies. This one-year multiple-case study investigated undergraduate students' dictionary and other uses of Personal Digital Assistants (PDAs) to enhance their incidental vocabulary learning in an English-medium (EM) university. The research findings show that the students made a variety of uses of PDAs to improve their vocabulary learning in the course of academic studies both in- and after class. The research results indicate that PDAs can be used in more flexible, novel and extended ways for English as a foreign language (EFL) vocabulary teaching and learning in both informal and informal learning environments in higher education.

Keywords: Dictionary use, EFL, incidental vocabulary learning, mobile technology, PDA use.

1 Introduction

English learning is important for university students in non-English speaking countries, especially those students from English-medium (EM) universities. Vocabulary learning is crucial for English learning because vocabulary constitutes the basic building blocks of English sentences [1]. Research into vocabulary learning for English as a foreign language (EFL) students has been prominent. Many research findings show that poor vocabulary frequently leads to incorrect inferences or misunderstanding of the content when reading English materials in their academic studies [1], [2] and [3]. The vocabulary learning strategy literature shows that the use of the dictionary has a positive effect on students' vocabulary learning in terms of their language course studies [1], [2] and [4]. However, in the digital age, few students bring along a thick dictionary to class or places of study. They may bring a handheld electronic dictionary, or a mobile device with downloaded dictionaries such as a mobile phone or a Personal Digital Assistance (PDA). Mobile devices have been increasingly developed, designed and used to 'ultimately support a lifetime of personal and social enrichment' that can support education [5]. How do EFL students make use of PDAs as a tool on

J. Fong, R. Kwan, and F.L. Wang (Eds.): ICHL 2008, LNCS 5169, pp. 238–249, 2008.

their own to help with their incidental learning of vocabulary in the course of pursing their degree in higher education? Research in this area remains limited. However, understanding EFL students' perceptions of PDA use for incidental vocabulary learning will help the EFL researchers and teachers understand students' needs and strategies in coping with vocabulary difficulties in their academic readings.

The following section of this paper reviews incidental vocabulary learning literature and identifies the research framework, followed by the research method adopted in a longitudinal multiple-case study. Research results are then presented, and implications relating to the results are discussed.

2 Literature on English Vocabulary Learning for EFL Students

2.1 Incidental Vocabulary Learning

Vocabulary learning activities generally fall into two types: *intentional* and *incidental* learning of vocabulary [1]. The former refers to activities that aim at vocabulary development predominantly. When vocabulary is learned predominantly through extensive reading, with the student guessing at the meaning of unknown words that do not have a predominant focus on vocabulary development, the activities are called incidental learning of vocabulary [6]. Incidental learning creates opportunities for inferring word meaning in context, enables vocabulary acquisition and reading at the same time, and is more individualized and student-based because the vocabulary being acquired is dependent on the student's own selection of reading materials [6]. However, studies have revealed that incidental learning of vocabulary may lead to such problems as incorrect inferences [3]. The problem of guesses may be due to the fact that unlike native speakers, EFL students often lack the word knowledge from context and do not use active reading strategies [6]. They need to be able to have constant access to word related resources such as dictionaries to help resolve problems in their academic study.

2.2 MALL in Terms of Incidental Vocabulary Learning

Some studies have attempted using computer-based dictionaries to improve EFL students' incidental English vocabulary learning in language courses [7]. Hill and Laufer's [7] research findings showed that the use of computer-based dictionaries could trigger more incidental vocabulary related learning activities for Chinese EFL university students [7]. In recent years, studies on mobile technology assisted vocabulary learning are on the rise [8] and [9]. These studies have experimented with improving students' vocabulary learning in the environment where students used mobile technologies for prescribed vocabulary learning tasks, or tested designed personalized learning systems to enhance student's vocabulary learning in a short term in language related courses. Dictionary use via mobile devices has often been considered simply a reference for students and is not assumed to induce other vocabulary learning activities [10] and [11]. The concerns regarding whether dictionary use of the PDA will be referential only for students' incidental vocabulary learning across their academic studies in higher education, and what other uses of the PDA can help students' incidental vocabulary learning activities are unknown. This empirical research was an attempt to fill this gap. It aimed at investigating students' free use of mobile devices - PDAs to foster their incidental vocabulary learning in terms of dictionary and other uses at an EM university in Hong Kong from the perspective of the students. The research questions are: (1) what dictionary use and other uses of the PDA did the students make to support their incidental learning of vocabulary in their academic studies? (2) how did dictionary use and other uses of PDA help the students with their incidental learning of vocabulary?

3   Research Methods

Qualitative research through a multiple case study approach was adopted for a period of one year from April 2006 to March 2007 to gain a deeper understanding of the processes and outcomes of the PDA use in incidental vocabulary learning by the students, and add confidence to the research findings [12].

3.1   Context

According to Hulstijin, Hollander, and Greidanus [13] intermediate and advanced EFL students enlarge their vocabulary to a great extent through incidental vocabulary learning. Students in EM universities in Hong Kong are considered advanced EFL learners as they passed certain English proficiency tests before being enrolled in these universities. These students often perceived a need to continue their study of English because most of the students' native language is Chinese. They need to read and understand lecture handouts, academic papers, and books with the help of a dictionary throughout the course of pursing a Bachelor's degree. Laufer and Hill [14] claimed that in EM universities in Hong Kong, no instruction is given on the usage of dictionaries in their English enhancement courses. This provided opportunities for this research study to examine students' optimal lookup conditions in their incidental vocabulary learning.

3.2   Student Profile

Three students were selected from first-year undergraduate students at a university on a voluntary basis. The criteria for student selection were: positive attitudes towards technology use, different disciplinary studies, gender, nationality/region. Finally, three students/cases were chosen for this research study. Their profiles are shown in Table 1. A consent letter containing terms and conditions in participating in this project was given to the students. In this project, each student was provided with one 1 G mini memory card and a PDA - a Dopod 818 Pro device for free use. Dopod 818 Pro is a wireless enabled device with both phone and PDA functionalities. In the university, free wireless access was available on campus and in university residential halls, where students could access the Internet using the device.

3.3   Data Collection and Analysis

Student electronic journals (e-journals), student artifacts as screenshots created using the PDA and face to face interviews (F-T-F interviews) were the main means of data

Table 1. Student profile

Student*	Age at the time of the study	Major	Year of study	Nationality at the time of the study
Ann	19	Journalism	1	Mainland Chinese
Andy	20	Engineering	1	Hong Kong permanent resident
Evan	20	Biotechnology	1	Hong Kong permanent resident

*Pseudonyms are used to protect the students' identities.

collection over a period of one year. Retrospective interviews were also made based on the questions raised from student e-journals and artifacts submitted. Categorizing and contextualizing strategies were adopted to analyze the data collected at different stages [15].

The data analysis underwent two stages. First, content analysis was used to categorize the data collected adopting Nvivo qualitative analysis software. Student data sources were initially coded on the broader themes: dictionary use, other uses, vocabulary learning, Coded themes of data were then recoded according to sub-themes. A constant comparative analysis was conducted on data to find sub-themes that initially emerged from student perceptions of the PDA use and their learning. A final list of sub-theme codes was placed in matrices by student names along with excerpts from F-T-F interviews, and e-journals. Afterwards, student artifacts and retrospective interviews were coded and put into the matrix by themes and sub-themes and student names in order to triangulate data. The triangulated sub-theme data were further analyzed for common themes that describe common practices and thinking among the three cases in using the PDA for their study. Another sub-theme: common uses and perceptions, from all three cases emerged. The sub-themes of other uses included other PDA functional uses. The sub-themes of learning included referential, data collection, situated, constructive, reflective, explorative and conversing uses. In the second phase of data analysis, a more descriptive method was adopted to contextualize PDA uses in each case to understand the 'true story' behind the uses for vocabulary learning in relation to the sub-themes.

4 Results

The following are results obtained from the analysis of the three cases. For the sake of clarity, the findings from the cases are presented individually. Then findings across the cases are also described. The research questions in relation to *what* dictionary and other uses of the PDA students made, *how* dictionary and other uses helped students' incidental vocabulary learning are answered.

4.1 Case 1: Ann

Ann, from Mainland China, lives in a university hall. Majoring in Journalism, she took as many opportunities as possible to improve her English as she considered her English was not good enough. She had used a handheld electronic dictionary to help with her studies. As soon as she participated in this research project, Ann gave up using the electronic dictionary, and downloaded the free Oxford English-Chinese Dictionary from 'Mdic' that consisted of a set of dictionaries. Ann also took advantage of Internet access using the PDA. The following are the main uses that Ann made in her incidental vocabulary learning.

Dictionary uses of the PDA: *what* and *how*
- Downloaded dictionary on the PDA provided more opportunities for her to refer to unknown words in context. Ann reported that the dictionary use increased her vocabulary retention by frequent exposure to unfamiliar words through repeated consultation, and helped solve problems in the reading materials such as the handouts and PowerPoint slides 'just-in-time' during lectures or self-study when a computer was not available.
- Downloaded dictionary on the PDA provided opportunities for her to understand unfamiliar words through discussion with classmates. Ann reported that she often discussed with classmates unfamiliar words encountered during their study.

Other uses of the PDA: *what* and *how*
- Online search using the PDA provided opportunities for her to gain deeper understanding of new words. Ann reported that she usually used the downloaded dictionary on her PDA to look up unfamiliar words. But if she still could not quite understand the word, she preferred to do an online search via Google 'define' using the PDA (See Figure 1), or browse Wikipedia using a computer if a computer was available.
- The Notes function on the PDA provided opportunities for her to take down useful English expressions in context and reflect on the meaning and use afterwards. Ann wrote down many expressions of English taken from lectures, talks or reading materials, and used them in her course work or project reports after reflection and reconstruction.
- Downloaded materials on PDA provided the opportunity for her to review English words and expressions whenever she wanted. In order to learn 'idiomatic' English, Ann downloaded passages and exercises from the book series 'New Concept English' to her PDA. She wanted to review and learn them by heart so that she could make free use of these expressions in her course work or project reports.

4.2 Case 2: Andy

- Andy is from the Department of Mechanical Engineering. Andy used to consult dictionaries using a computer. In many cases, when he encountered vocabulary problems, and a computer was not available, he could not solve his learning problems in time. As soon as he joined this project, Andy found the Mebook consisting of varied dictionaries from the Internet. He downloaded a Professional English-Chinese Dictionary in his disciplinary study to the PDA. Andy also used the device to get access to the Internet for his vocabulary learning. The following are the main uses of PDA by Andy.

Dictionary uses of the PDA: *what* **and** *how*

- Downloaded dictionary on the PDA provided the opportunities for him to solve the vocabulary problems during his revision of courses. Andy reported that he usually looked up engineering related new words and expression from hardcopy handouts distributed by the lecturers before, during and after lectures using the dictionary on the PDA. It was really helpful for his revision and reflection.

- Downloaded dictionary on the PDA provided opportunities for him to share the vocabulary knowledge with peers in context. Andy reported that when he worked in a group, they would from time to time encounter unfamiliar words and expressions. In such cases, he would consult the dictionary, and then share the knowledge with the group.

- Downloaded dictionary on the PDA provided opportunities for him to learn the pronunciation of unfamiliar words. Andy considered that his pronunciation of English was not proficient, so he downloaded the Professional English-Chinese Dictionary with a sound function. He could listen to the sound of the unfamiliar words. He said this helped him learn these words better (See Figure 2).

Other uses of the PDA: *what* **and** *how*

- The PDA provided opportunities for him to solve vocabulary problems by making phone calls to his classmates, or MSN chat with his friends. Andy reported that when he could not find the unknown academic words in the dictionary on the PDA, he would call his classmates for their help. He also used MSN to chat with his friends to solve vocabulary problems.

- Online dictionary accessed via the PDA provided opportunities for him to search academic terms online if those terms could not be found in the dictionary on his PDA. Andy preferred consulting the downloaded dictionary on the PDA. However, if there were some terms that could not be found in the PDA, he would connect the PDA to the Internet and look up 'Yahoo Online Dictionary'.

- Notes function on the PDA provided opportunities for him to take down unfamiliar words in context and re-read and look up meanings later. Andy would take down unfamiliar words using the Notes function on the PDA during lectures when he could not find these words in the downloaded dictionary on the PDA, and other means of communication were not convenient in the lecture rooms.

4.3 Case 3: Evan

Evan is from the Biotechnology Department. Though he is a local Hong Kong resident, he considered that his English was not proficient. Before joining this project, he always carried a paper dictionary. He used the downloaded English-Chinese dictionary Dr. eye on his PDA after he joined this project. He used dictionaries at home, university library, on campus, in transport, abroad during trips, etc. for vocabulary learning in his academic studies. The following are the main uses of PDA reported by Evan in his incidental vocabulary learning.

Dictionary uses of the PDA: *what* **and** *how*

- The downloaded dictionary on the PDA provided opportunities for him to consult academic vocabulary in context. Evan reported that the dictionary – Dr. eye played a key role during the situations when he encountered vocabulary problems in reading academic papers, handouts or books in biology. It was useful and convenient for his learning.

- The downloaded dictionary on the PDA provided opportunities for him to improve his understanding of lectures, and help him do his assignments on overseas trips. Evan reported that he used to guess new words and expressions during lectures if there was no dictionary available. With the PDA, he made fewer guesses as guessing sometimes caused serious misunderstandings.

- The downloaded dictionary on the PDA provided opportunities for him to learn the pronunciation of unfamiliar words. Dr. eye has a sound function. He reported that he frequently referred to this function. He felt that his pronunciation was considerably improved after the one-year trial, and practicing the pronunciation helped him remember words better.

- The downloaded dictionary provided opportunities for him to help construct and proofread his course work. Evan noted that when he was writing assignments, sometimes, he would forget how to spell a word, or express ideas. In such cases, he would use synonymous expressions with the help of the dictionary on his PDA. Evan also constantly reported that he used the dictionary on his PDA to do proofreading after he completed essay writing.

Other uses of the PDA: *what* and *how*

- The PDA provided opportunities for him to get access to the Internet and write emails to his lecturers to solve problems relating to academic terms. Evan mentioned one time when he had encountered an academic term 'chiaroscuro' that he could not understand even with the help of the online dictionary on his PDA. He then wrote an email to his teacher who responded immediately, explaining the term to him. He found this experience really enhanced his learning (See Figure 3).

- Camera function on the PDA provided opportunities for him to capture photos with academic terminology for later memorization and reflection. Evan used the camera function on the PDA to capture some pictures from books in the library or PowerPoint slides during lectures in relation to Bio-technology courses.

Fig. 1. Screenshot of 'Google define' online search

Fig. 2. Screenshot of word 'robustness' with pronunciation

Fig. 3. Screenshot of an email correspondence

4.4 Common Uses and Perceptions of the PDA from Cases 1, 2 and 3

It is noted that perceptions from all of the three students in some aspects are quite similar, if not identical. First, all of them reported that downloaded dictionaries on the PDA provided opportunities for them to get faster access to unknown words than using a computer. Secondly, all students felt more confident when they encountered problems during lectures or self academic studies and increased their self-efficacy. They could solve vocabulary problems in time during lectures, and better understood what lecturers conveyed by using different searching options such as dictionaries both on- and offline. They also reported that the PDA helped them improve their vocabulary learning efficiency as well as their academic studies in general. Moreover, all the students had kept on using the PDA to consult unfamiliar words in participating in the one-year project. However, Andy reported that he used the PDA as a dictionary less in the second half of the year as he knew most of the academic terms in his discipli-nary study. The other two students – Ann and Evan did not make such claims.

5 Discussions

Patten et al. [11] categorize the use of material such as dictionaries and e-books on mobile devices into a 'referential' function in terms of its mobile educational applica-tions in formal learning situations. They posit that referential applications generally do not go beyond information delivery. Based on this framework, Clough et al. [10] further developed an informal mobile learning framework derived from their survey of web forum users in terms of mobile learning activities. They classify the use of referential materials into individual and collaborative referential activities. These frameworks shed some light on analyzing incidental vocabulary learning activities using PDA of this study. However, in-depth analysis revealed that uses of referential materials via PDA rendered learning that is far more complex than these frameworks show. A diagram of the PDA uses derived from this study is presented in Figure 4.

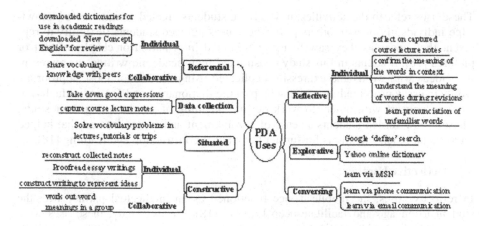

Fig. 4. Diagram of PDA uses for incidental vocabulary learning

5.1 Referential Uses

Referential applications provided student access to content at places where learning activities occur, taking advantage of the portability and mobility of mobile devices [11]. Such uses reported by the students include both individual and collaborative reference. Individual uses include the uses that the students made to refer to unknown words in revision of academic reading materials such as handouts, slides, articles or books. Collaborative uses were concerned with the use of PDA to look up unknown words, and share them with other students. This dictionary content access provided the students a chance to learn vocabulary 'just-in-time'.

5.2 Data Collection Uses

Data collection made use of the capability of the mobile device to record data and information about their environment [10] and [11]. Such uses described by the students using Notes on the PDA to take down good 'English expressions' or capture photographs of some images in academic books or lecture slides for later review and reflection. Such data collection was usually unfeasible or problematic without the use of the mobile device [11].

5.3 Situated Uses

Situated use refers to the mobile devices that offered the opportunities for spontaneous, personal, informal, and situated learning for a socially situated practice [16]. The PDA uses are shifting the focus from smart planning to smart situated actions [17]. In this study, such uses students made included: finding out the meaning of academic terminology during lectures or tutorials when the lectures or tutors raised questions, solving vocabulary problems when students used small chunks of time to do their academic assignments on buses, trains, planes and at hotels, etc.

5.4 Constructive Uses

These uses refer to the activities in which the students created or constructed knowledge individually or with others [10]. These uses allowed students flexibility to represent their ideas as they saw fit using collected information or chunks of text or pictures [18]. Students in this study constructed their academic writings to represent their ideas with words and expressions collected using the PDA, choose appropriate words in essay proofreading with the help of the dictionaries on PDA individually, or work in concert with others to work out the meaning of words during their study. These uses afforded students a sense of involvement and vested interest that helped them sustain their intentions for further knowledge construction and learning [18].

5.5 Reflective Uses

In reflective uses, the mobile device functioned as an intellectual partner with the student to engage and facilitate deep learning [18]. In this study, these uses were composed of individual and interactive reflective uses. In individual uses, students used dictionaries on PDA to compare and confirm the meanings of the academic terms when they revised their course materials. In addition, they reflected on their captured lecture notes or images using PDA in order to better understand the vocabulary in the pictures, which not only aided students' vocabulary retention [19], but also helped reflection when they were out of the learning environment. For interactive use, students used the downloaded dictionary with sound function so that they could consult the pronunciation of unfamiliar words for their own learning needs. Hill [20] found that Chinese learners appeared to benefit from hearing the pronunciation of unfamiliar words as a means of retention. In this case, the PDA functioned as an intellectual companion for them to interact with.

5.6 Explorative Uses

In explorative applications, students searched and interpreted the information that was related to their learning needs [18]. Students reported that whenever they wanted to get detailed explanations of certain words or academic terms, they would take the last resort by online searching via PDA or computer such as Google 'define' search, and the Yahoo online dictionary. Sometimes, they would use online or downloaded Wikipedia via a computer for the searching process. This process promoted meaning making by constantly forcing the students to interpret the information they were finding on website or downloaded resources in response to their intentional search, and determining how relevant it is to their intended purpose [18]. Rich information about the meaning of unknown words explored positively affects their learning [13].

5.7 Conversing Uses

Conversing use refers to the social interactions which led to learning mediated by the mobile device by taking advantage of the mobile device's unique characteristics of connectivity to the Internet and phone function [18]. In this study, students used the PDA to solve vocabulary problems by making phone calls, through emails or MSN chat. Evan reported that he understood what 'chiaroscuro' meant after he wrote to his teacher an email about it; and Andy mentioned how he and his classmates came to a common understanding of the word 'ductile' via MSN chat. In these applications, the PDA afforded 'conversation social interaction' for students to work together and socially reach a common understanding [18].

6 Conclusions

This research study examined undergraduate EFL students' use of dictionaries and other uses of the PDA to enhance their incidental vocabulary learning in pursuit of their undergraduate studies at an EMI university. In general, students' attitude towards the technology use was positive. Their experiences in using the tools on the PDA enhanced and extended the way they learned vocabulary. Students did not restrict themselves to make only a referential use of the PDA for their vocabulary learning, they also employed various tools on the PDA for data collection, situated, constructive, reflective, explorative, and conversing uses. In addition, students' uses of the PDA were not fixed but adaptable and dynamic in the learning processes.

These learning activities further drove students to make more creative PDA uses to improve their vocabulary learning in the course of their academic studies.

This three-case study is limited in its capacity for generalization, especially as the cases were chosen from highly motivated technology users. Nevertheless, the research indicates that the PDA can be used in more flexible, novel and extended ways for EFL vocabulary teaching and learning in higher education. It is not the technology itself that changes learning practices but students' use of the technology. The research results shed some light on how to improve incidental vocabulary learning practices using mobile technology in both formal and informal learning environments in higher education.

Acknowledgement. The research study was funded by a Small Project Fund and a Faculty Research fund at the Faculty of Education, the University of Hong Kong.

References

1. Nation, I.S.P.: Learning vocabulary in another language. Cambridge University Press, Cambridge (2001)
2. Gu, Y.: Fine brush and freehand: The vocabulary-learning art of two successful Chinese EFL learners. TESOL Quarterly 37(1), 73–104 (2003)
3. Huang, H.-T.: Vocabulary learning in an automated graded reading program. Language Learning & Technology 11(3), 64–82 (2007)
4. Laufer, B.: How much lexis is necessary for reading comprehension? In: Arnaud, L., Bejoint, H. (eds.) Vocabulary and Applied Linguistics, pp. 126–132. Macmillan, London (1992)
5. Roschelle, J., Sharples, M., Chan, T.W.: Introduction to the special issue on wireless and mobile technologies in education. Journal of computer assisted learning 21(3), 159–161 (2005)
6. Huckin, T., Coady, J.: Incidental vocabulary acquisition in a second language: A review. Studies in Second Language Acquisition 21(2), 181–193 (1999)
7. Hill, M., Laufer, B.: Type of task, time-on-task and electronic dictionaries in incidental vocabulary acquisition. International Review of Applied Linguistics in Language Teaching 41(2), 87–106 (2003)
8. Chen, C.-M., Chung, C.-J.: Personalized mobile English vocabulary learning system based on item response theory and learning memory cycle. Computers &.Education 50(1), 77–90 (2008)
9. Stockwell, G.: Vocabulary on the move: Investigating an intelligent mobile phone-based vocabulary tutor. Computer Assisted Language Learning 20(4), 365–383 (2007)
10. Clough, G., Jones, A.C., McAndrew, P., Scanlon, E.: Informal learning with PDAs and smartphones. Journal of Computer Assisted Learning (in press)
11. Patten, B., Arnedillo-Sanchez, I., Tangney, B.: Designing collaborative, constructionist and contextual applications for handheld devices. Computers & Education 46(3), 294–308 (2006)
12. Yin, R.K.: Applications of case study research, 2nd edn. Sage Publications, Thousand Oaks (2003)

13. Hulstijn, J.H., Hollander, M., Greidanus, T.: Incidental vocabulary learning by advanced foreign language students: The influence of marginal glosses, dictionary use, and reoccurrence of unknown words. Modern Language Journal 80(3), 327–339 (1996)
14. Laufer, B., Hill, M.: What lexical information do L2 learners select in a CALL dictionary and how does it affect word retention? Language Learning & Technology 3(2), 58–76 (2000)
15. Maxwell, J.A.: Qualitative research design: an interactive approach. Sage Publications, Thousand Oaks (1996)
16. Lantolf, J.P.: Sociocultural theory and second language learning. Oxford University Press, Oxford (2000)
17. Fischer, G., Konomi, S.: Innovative socio-technical environments in support of distributed intelligence and lifelong learning. Journal of Computer Assisted Learning 23(4), 338–350 (2007)
18. Jonassen, D.H., Hernandez-Serrano, J., Choi, I.: Integrating constructivism and learning technologies. In: Spector, J.M., Anderson, T.M. (eds.) Integrated and holistic perspectives on learning, instruction and technology: understanding complexity, pp. 103–128. Kluwer Academic Publishers, Dordrecht (2000)
19. Lai, C.-H., Yang, J.-C., Chen, F.-C., Ho, C.-W., Chan, T.-W.: Affordances of mobile technologies for experiential learning: the interplay of technology and pedagogical practices. Journal of Computer Assisted Learning 23(4), 326–377 (2007)
20. Hill, M.M.: What's in a word? Enhancing English vocabulary development by increasing learner awareness. In: Storey, P., Berry, V., Bunton, D., Hoare, P. (eds.) Issues in Language in Education, pp. 179–190. Hong Kong Institute of Education, Hong Kong (1996)

Hybrid Learning and Ubiquitous Learning

Ji-Ping Zhang

East China Normal University, Shanghai 200062, China
jpz@ecnu.edu.cn

Abstract. Ubiquitous learning (U-Learning) has an increasing trend as the coming forth of more new media and instructional ideas. U-Learning focuses on the combination of learning environment and substance space, emphasizing the learning can be happen as seeing, hearing, reading, or apperceiving whenever the learner wanted. Hybrid learning, sometimes called "blended learning", emphasizes to maximize student's learning within different learning environments (traditional and digital). It also means that learning requires students to meet for face to face classes while providing much of the learning content and interaction online via delivery software and instructional tools. This paper will discuss concept and characteristics of U-learning and H-learning, the different between the H- and U-learning, and their relationship.

Keywords: U-learning; Hybrid learning; Learning environments.

1 Introduction

With the development of digital information transfer, storage and communication methods having a significant effect, education has undergone major changes in recent years. This development has allowed for access to global communications and the number of resources available to students at all levels of schooling. After the initial impact and applications of computers in education, the introduction of e-learning and mobile learning epitomized the constant transformations that were occurring in education.

Now, the assimilation of ubiquitous computing in education marks another great step forward, with Ubiquitous learning (U-learning) emerging based on the concept of ubiquitous computing. It is reported to be both pervasive and persistent, allowing students to access education flexibly, calmly and seamlessly. U-learning has the potential to revolutionize education and removes many of the physical constraints of traditional learning. Sometimes, it can be viewed as the integration of M-learning and E-learning, allowing for personalization and customization to student's real needs. Simply, U-learning means "everywhere learning" (the internet or learning content follows people around). Core "knowledge pots" (work-related content, personal knowledge, internet) hold content and information. Various devices plug in and retrieve the information in the appropriate format (PDA, cell phone, laptop, or any other appliance). It fulfills e-learning's promise of "anytime, anywhere, and any context"[1].

J. Fong, R. Kwan, and F.L. Wang (Eds.): ICHL 2008, LNCS 5169, pp. 250–258, 2008.

H-learning provides the best opportunities for learning transition from classroom to e-learning. It involves classroom (or face-to-face) and online learning. This method is very effective for adding efficiency to classroom instruction and permitting increased discussion or information review outside of classrooms.

2 Concept of U-Learning

Mark Weiser coined the term 'Ubiquitous Computing' in the late 1980s. He introduced the idea of ubiquitous computing: a world in which computers and associated technologies become invisible, and thus indistinguishable from everyday life[2]. He also further indicated that Ubiquitous computing is the method of enhancing computer use by making many computers available throughout the physical environment, but making them effectively invisible to the user [3]. Based on the Weiser's view, UC refers to the process of seamlessly integrating computers into the physical world, in which the presence of computers is becoming less conspicuous and will eventually blend into our daily lives.

Of course, the computing and communication technologies required to achieve Weiser's vision did not exist around the late 1980s. But now, presented aspects of a ubiquitous (or pervasive) computing environment in which instances of Weiser's ubiquitous computing world could be explored, given the maturity of computing/communication technologies, such as wireless LANs, portable and wearable computers, and sophisticated embeddable sensors. Briefly described, a ubiquitous computing environment is a well-defined area, open or enclosed, that incorporates a collection of embedded systems (computers, sensors, user interfaces, and infrastructure of services).

From the system point of view, physical integration and spontaneous interoperation are two main characteristics of ubiquitous computing systems. Physical integration means that it involves some integration between computing nodes and the physical world. And spontaneous interoperation means the system must spontaneously interoperate in changing environments. A component interoperates spontaneously if it interacts with a set of communicating components that can change both identity and functionality over time as its circumstances change. From the user's point of view, in such an environment, anyone can make use of computers that are embedded everywhere in a public environment at any time. A user equipped with a mobile device can connect to any of them and access the network by using wireless communication technologies. Moreover, not only can a user access the network actively, but computers around the user can recognize the user's behavior and offer various services according to the user's situation, the mobile terminal's facility, the network bandwidth, and so on. User assistance via ubiquitous computing technologies is realized by providing users with proper decisions or decision alternatives.

That is, a ubiquitous computing technology-equipped system supplies users with timely information and relevant services by automatically sensing users' various context data and smartly generating proper results. So the characteristics of a pervasive computing environment can be mainly concluded as the following: User mobility, Resource and location discovery, Context awareness (user/time/location), Collaborative interaction, Ambient information, Calm technology, Event notification,

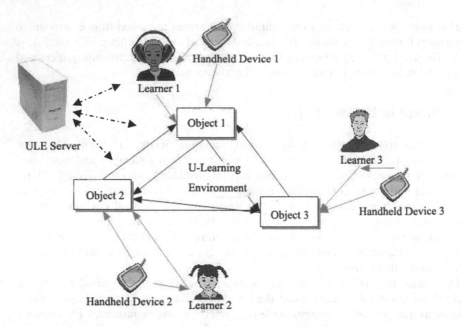

Fig. 1. Ubiquitous learning environment

Adaptive interfaces, Invisibility object augmentation, and Anytime/anywhere. An U-learning environment shows as Fig. 1.

Based on the characteristics of a pervasive computing environment, a number of higher education institutions have begun extensive research projects aimed at investigating with respect to what are a pervasive learning environments. These projects involve new learning spaces, class/instructor/student collaborative interactions, context-aware applications, event notification, enhanced collaboration and decision-making support for administrators and researchers, and more efficient facilities learning. Though not reaching a clear definition until now, it is a more general view that a ubiquitous learning environment is a situation or setting of pervasive (or omnipresent) education (or learning). Education is happening all around the student but the student may not even be conscious of the learning process. Source data is present in the embedded objects and students do not have to DO anything in order to learn. They just have to be there [4].

Essentially, U-learning is the extend and advance of E-learning, and also can be viewed as a combination of the advantages of E-learning and M-learning with the benefits of ubiquitous computing and the flexibility of mobile devices. Students have the freedom to learn within a learning environment which offers adaptability to their individual needs and learning styles, as well as the flexibility of pervasive and unobtrusive computer systems. According to Chen [5] and Curtis [6], the major characteristics of ubiquitous learning are the following:

Permanency: Learners never lose their work unless it is purposefully deleted. In addition, all the learning processes are recorded continuously everyday.

Accessibility: Learners have access to their documents, data, or videos from anywhere. That information is provided based on their requests. Therefore, the learning involved is self-directed.

Immediacy: Wherever learners are, they can get any information immediately. Thus, learners can solve problems quickly. Otherwise, the learner can record the questions and look for the answer later.

Interactivity: Learners can interact with experts, teachers, or peers in the form of synchronies or asynchronous communication. Hence, the experts are more reachable and the knowledge becomes more available.

Situating of instructional activities: The learning could be embedded in our daily life. The problems encountered as well as the knowledge required are all presented in their natural and authentic forms. This helps learners notice the features of problem situations that make particular actions relevant.

Adaptability: Learners can get the right information at the right place with the right way.

3   Concept of H-Learning

Hybrid learning, sometimes called "Blended learning," provides the best opportunities for learning transition from classroom to e-learning (now could be to U-learning). It refers to learning that require students to meet for face to face classes while providing much of the learning content and interaction online via content delivery software and learning tools. It provide students with an option of taking some learning materials fully online and some in class, or hybrid.

Currently, the term "hybrid learning" has evolved to encompass a much richer set of learning strategy "dimensions." A blended learning program may combine one or more of the following dimensions, although many of these have over-lapping attributes [7].

- Blending offline and online learning
- Blending self-paced and live, collaborative learning
- Blending structured and unstructured learning
- Blending custom content with off-the-shelf content
- Blending work and learning

The most common reason that an instructor, a learner, or a trainer might pick hybrid learning over other learning options is that hybrid learning combines the best of both worlds. Based on this, hybrid learning provides various benefits over using any single learning delivery type alone, such as pedagogical richness, learning effectiveness, access to knowledge, cost-effectiveness, ease of revision, etc. In fact, Hybrid learning brings a more natural way to learn and work. A blend is an integrated strategy that involves a planned combination of approaches, such as coaching by a supervisor; participation in an online class; reference to a manual and participation in seminars, workshops, and online communities, forums, chat etc. Table 1 presents some possibilities of what can constitute a blended learning approach.

Table 1. Possibilities of a blended learning approach [8]

Live face-to-face (formal)	Live face-to-face (informal)
• Instructor-led classroom • Workshops • Coaching/mentoring • On-the-job (OTJ) training	• Collegial connections • Work teams • Role modeling
Virtual collaboration/synchronous	Virtual collaboration/asynchronous
• Live e-learning classes • E-mentoring	• Email • Online bulletin boards • Listservs • Online communities
Self-paced learning	Performance support
• Web learning modules • Online resource links • Simulations • Scenarios • Video and audio CD/DVDs • Online self-assessments • Workbooks	• Help systems • Print job aids • Knowledge databases • Documentation • Performance/decision support tools

The up to the present day available research provides proof that hybrid learning can be equally or more effective and efficient compared with the model of entire e-learning and with the model of entirely traditional education. The students participating in programs of hybrid learning achieve the same or better learning results besides being more contented with the combining process [9] (Garrison & Kanuka, 2004). Rich, blended learning environments are giving learners greater control over their learning journeys and making learning more effective. The concept of hybrid learning is rooted in the idea that learning is not just a one-time event, but is a continuous process. Generally, the main characteristics of H-learning can be concluded as:

Mixed Mode: H-learning combines the socialization, group learning and hands-on opportunities of the classroom (face to face) with the learning possibilities of the online environment (also can call the U-learning environment).

Student Centered: Learning shifts from lecture to student-centered instruction. Faculty reconsider teaching strategies, becoming facilitators.

Communications Important: The key element underpinning a hybrid learning environment is the scope and nature of the communication channels provided to support learners.

Access flexibility: Blending is used to provide a balance between flexible learning options and knowledge access.

Cost-effectiveness: Hybrid learning provides an opportunity for reaching a large, globally dispersed audience in a short period of time with consistent, semi-personal content delivery.

4 Research Focus of the U- and H-Learning

Currently, the researches on U-learning are still at its early stage, especially the systematic theories and practice modes researches. But the academic circles have put great emphasis on U-learning and many countries have stepped into the practical applications. Theoretically, the researches on U-learning are carried in the following directions:

- Ubiquitous pedagogy
- Classroom-centered U-learning mode
- Specific curriculum-centered U-learning mode
- Faculty education for the implementation of U-learning
- Development standards of U-learning resources
- Development of U-learning instructional management system

Researches in the higher education have also been carried in many countries. Some representative projects are showed in Table 2.

Table 2. U-learning projects

University	Project	Network environment	Service content
UCSD	Active campus Active class	Mobile Device (G PS)	Navigation Service, Collaboration work in class
Honnover Univ. (Germany) ; VTT (Finland)	Ubi-campus	Mobile Devise IR	Navigation Service, Lecture note, Task Assignment
Thokoshima Univ. (Japan)	TAN- GO/JAPELES/ CLUE	Mobile Devise (RFID）	learning service,Information exchange between learners
MIT	Oxygen	Tangible Interface, AR, Image based Sensor, RFID	Intelligent Laboratory

The current research is at the transitional stage of from mobile learning to ubiquitous learning. Most of the research, not focusing on the frame-work of U-learning instructional mode, is just the application of ubiquitous technology through the link of ubiquitous computing and education.

Last five years, the research was emphasized in both academic and business literatures on hybrid learning. Hybrid learning is dominant in higher education, in corporate and in governmental training settings. It is seen in the linkages between instructors, learners, and classrooms located in different areas. Some researches in hybrid learning have been carried at places such as Microsoft, IBM, Thomson, the University of Pretoria, the University of Glamorgan, National University in California, and the Open University of Malaysia. According to our survey, the current researches are carried around the following questions:

- Does hybrid learning produce better learning outcomes than face-to-face instruction or e-learning alone?
- What models of hybrid learning are most effective?
- What channels of delivery are used to facilitate learning in hybrid mode?
- What are learner and instructor experience and perceptions of hybrid learning?
- What infrastructure and support is needed to support hybrid learning?
- What are the primary barriers associated with hybrid learning?

As online environments push into more extensive use in education, the forms and formats of hybrid learning will be extended as well. Hybrid learning has really come into its own and we are seeing a huge trend for integrating different forms of learning to provide real choice for learners. Some predicted trends in hybrid learning include mobile hybrid learning; greater visualization, individualization, and hands-on learning; self-determined hybrid learning; increased connectedness, community, and collaboration; linking work and learning; hybrid learning course designations; and the emergence of hybrid learning specialists (Bonk and Graham, 2005). Of course, there are still many challenges facing the hybrid learning, among of which, creating a formal faculty development program for teaching hybrid courses, allocating the necessary time for instructors to redesign traditional courses into hybrids and preparing students to learn effectively in hybrid courses are most challenging.

5   Relationship between U-Learning and H-Learning

It is clear that hybrid learning is a mixture of online and face-to-face learning using a variety of learning resources and communications options available to students and lecturers. In other words, hybrid learning mixes U-learning with traditional type (Classroom-based) of learning. The relationship between them shows in Fig. 2.

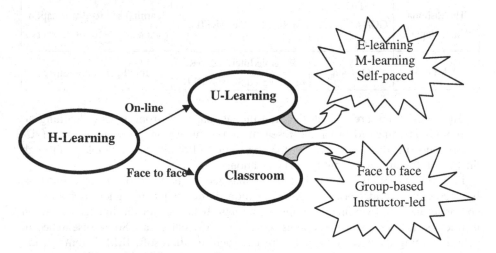

Fig. 2. Relationship between U-learning and H-learning

As illustrated in Fig.2, the traditional learning type is classroom-based and offers the learner face-to-face contact and support, in which the major learning modes are instructor-led and group-based. Ubiquitous learning, which can be delivered anywhere, anytime through mobile and handheld devices, provides the online program or resources for learners, in which the main leaning modes are self-paced and peer-to-peer. Of course, ubiquitous learning also has the affects that learners may feel isolated that sometimes may affect motivation and student retention. Hybrid learning offers some of the best of both worlds: face-to-face tutor support and contact with peers through the ability of online mobile communication. By practicing hybrid the conveniences of online courses and mobile learning are gained without the loss of face-to-face contact. So a learning environment is created that is richer than either a traditional face-to-face environment or a fully online environment. However, it is important to establish the equilibrium between face-to-face education and online mobile environments during the process of organizing hybrid learning environments.

When developing a hybrid learning experience we need to contemplate the whole spectrum with learning opportunities that are appropriate to the learner and the situation. It does involve very careful planning and preparation for it to be successful.

It is necessary for us to look beyond the traditional boundaries of classroom instruction by augmenting their current best practices with new advances in learning and collaboration technologies to maximize results. More importantly, we should seek to empower every learner to become an active participant in the learning and collaboration process. Anyway, not today also tomorrow, hybrid learning will be the best solution for learning.

References

1. George S.: Categories of E-learning, http://www.elearnspace.org/Articles/elearningcategories.htm
2. Weiser, M.: The Computer for the Twenty-First Century. J. Scientific American, 94–104 (September 1991)
3. Weiser, M.: Some Computer Science Problems in Ubiquitous Computing. J. Communications of the ACM (July 1993); (reprinted as "Ubiquitous Computing". Nikkei Electronics) (December 6) pp. 137–143 (1993)
4. Jones, V., Jo, J.H.: Ubiquitous learning environment: An adaptive teaching system using ubiquitous technology. In: Atkinson, R., Mc Beath, C., Jonas-Dwyer, D., Phillips, R. (eds.) Beyond the comfort zone: Proceedings of the 21st ASCILITE Conference, Perth, December 5-8, pp. 468–474 (2004)
5. Chen, Y.S., Kao, T.C., Sheu, J.P., Chiang, C.Y.: A Mobile Scaffolding-Aid-Based Bird - Watching Learning System. In: Proceedings of IEEE International Workshop on Wireless and Mobile Technologies in Education (WMTE 2002), pp. 15–22. IEEE Computer Society Press, New York (2002)
6. Curtis, M., Luchini, K., Bobrowsky, W., Quintana, C., Soloway, E.: Handheld Use in K-12: A Descriptive Account. In: Proceedings of IEEE International Workshop on Wireless and Mobile Technologies in Education (WMTE 2002), pp. 23–30. IEEE Computer Society Press, New York (2002)
7. Harvi, S., Chris, R.: A White Paper: Achieving Success with Blended Learning, http://www.centra.com/download/whitepapers/blendedlearning.pdf

8. Rossett, D., Frazee, H.: Strategies for Building Blended Learning (2003), http://www.Learning-circuits.org/2003/jul2003/rossett.htm
9. Garrison, D.R., Kanuka, H.: Blended learning: Uncovering its transformative potential in higher education. J. Internet and Higher Education. 7, 95–105 (2004)
10. Bonk, C.J., Graham, C.R.: Handbook of blended learning: Global Perspectives, local designs. In: Future directions of blended learning in higher education and workplace learning settings, ch.8.3. Pfeiffer (2005)

Experiences in Hybrid Learning with eduComponents

Mario Amelung and Dietmar Rösner

Otto-von-Guericke-Universität, FIN/IWS
P.O. Box 4120, 39016 Magdeburg, Germany
{amelung,roesner}@iws.cs.uni-magdeburg.de

Abstract. Since five years we practice hybrid learning in all our courses by combining classroom lectures and group exercises with Web-based e-learning. In this paper we reflect the experiences with our learning environment and discuss the changes in teaching and learning that resulted from the new approach as well as pedagogical concerns and policy issues.

1 Introduction

Before we introduced a hybrid learning environment—made up as a combination from classroom teaching and e-learning—for computer science courses at the University of Magdeburg, we were dissatisfied with some aspects of the traditional way of teaching, practicing and assessing. The traditional way of exercises in a classroom only manner may be sketched as follows:

- design or choose assignments for a weekly exercise sheet according to the state of the course,
- distribute a printed or online PDF version of the exercise sheet,
- students work through the exercise sheet at home,
- in classroom sessions
  - students present their solutions at the blackboard,
  - tutor and peers give (spontaneous) feedback,
  - peers take notes from the presentation and
  - the tutor may take notes about student's performance.

As a variation written submissions may be demanded for that are checked by tutors. But there is always a delay between submission and the reception of the corrected version with comments. For large groups of students manual correction is labor and time intensive.

However, we wished to offer students more detailed discussion on their solutions and problems, more timely feedback, as well as more opportunities to apply their knowledge and to exercise their skills. Especially for programming assignments, the traditional way of handing in programs on paper and discussing them on the blackboard was not very motivating for our students. This approach is only viable for very small programs, and practical problems (e.g., syntax errors) are hard to detect.

In addition, we also wished that teachers were liberated from avoidable (administrative) work and were provided a better overview of the performance and progress of the class.

J. Fong, R. Kwan, and F.L. Wang (Eds.): ICHL 2008, LNCS 5169, pp. 259–270, 2008.

Now, with the hybrid learning environment based on eduComponents (cf. below) the exercise courses for computer science and programming lectures follow a significantly changed process which may be summarized as follows:

- Design or choose tasks for weekly exercise sheet according to state of the course, additionally take automatic testability into account.
- Make online version of weekly exercise sheet accessible
- Students should work through exercise sheet and
- submit their solutions via an interactive Web interface (using ECAssignmentBox or ECAutoAssessmentBox, cf. below);
- They get immediate feedback and may re-submit improved versions.
- In preparation of the classroom session the tutor gets a complete overview over of the performance of the group as well as of each single student.
- During classroom session students present their solutions using laptop and beamer.
- Peers get online access to all alternative solutions.

In sum: in contrast to a traditional way of teaching which is primarily paper based, our hybrid learning environments makes extensive use of the benefits of electronic documents in combination with the Web.

We have reported about details of eduComponents and the aspects of computer-aided assessment (CAA) elsewhere (e.g., [1], [2], and [3]). In this paper we concentrate on the issues of hybrid learning, i.e., in our case the relation between face-to-face lectures and group exercises and the Web-based e-learning functionalities.

The paper is organized as follows: In section 2 we give an overview of eduComponents, our collection of modules for e-learning and computer-aided assessment. We then describe how eduComponents are employed in our hybrid learning environment. This is followed by a discussion of experiences and lessons learned in section 4. Finally, we summarize our experiences and illustrate some future options for further improving the learning opportunities for students.

2   eduComponents: Design, Implementation and Functionality

Instead of using a separate learning management system (LMS), which would have required additional training and administration, we have chosen a different approach for the hybrid learning environment: A component-based architecture using a general-purpose content management system (CMS) as the basis.

The use of a CMS as foundation for a hybrid learning environment is motivated by the observation that a large percentage of both traditional as well as e-learning is actually document management: Most activities in higher education involve the production, presentation, and review of written material. Thus, instead of re-implementing basic content management functionality, we base our environment on a general-purpose CMS, which provides a reliable implementation of basic document management functionality. In our case this is the open-source content management system *Plone*[1].

---

[1] http://plone.org/

The e-learning-specific functionality is implemented by extension modules for Plone. We have designed, implemented and deployed a number of Plone modules—collectively called eduComponents[2]—that provide specialized content types offering the following main functions (see also [2] and [4]):

- ECLecture: A portal for learning objects, course information and registration.
- ECQuiz: Electronic multiple-choice tests.
- ECAssignmentBox: Electronic submissions for assignments (e.g., essays) and support for the process of assessment and grading.
- ECAutoAssessmentBox: A version of ECAssignmentBox with automatic testing and assessment of assignments with immediate feedback.
- ECReviewBox: An add-on for ECAssignmentBox allowing teachers to create peer review assignments.

These components can be used separately or in combination and, since many basic functions are already provided by the CMS, they already implement much of the standard functionality required in an e-learning environment. If additional features are required, e.g., a discussion forum, bibliographies, a glossary, a Wiki, or domain-specific content types, they can be integrated by adding other Plone modules. The component-based architecture thus makes it easy to create tailor-made learning environments both for pure online learning as well as for hybrid learning scenarios. Also, all components use a uniform content representation. All objects in Plone are documents (or folders containing documents) and can be manipulated in the same way, regardless of whether the document is a multiple-choice test or an image. This ensures a consistent and easy-to-learn user interface. The rest of this section describes the individual components in more detail.

2.1 ECLecture

ECLecture is a Plone module for managing lectures, seminars and other courses. ECLecture objects group all course-related information—including course metadata (such as title, instructor, time, location, credits, etc.)—and resources. ECLecture objects can thus serve as a "portal" to all course-related materials like slides, exercises, tests, or reading lists. These materials are managed using the appropriate content types (e.g., ECAssignmentBox for assignments, ECQuiz for tests, or PloneBoard for discussion forums) and appear as resources to the course. Since an ECLecture object is a folder-like object, these resources can be stored inside of it, but they can also be stored somewhere else, even on another server. ECLecture also handles the online registration for courses and exercise groups.

2.2 ECQuiz

ECQuiz supports the creation and delivery of multiple-choice tests (see also [5]). Multiple-choice tests are especially useful as formative tests to quickly assess the performance of *all* students of a class without the need for extra grading work. ECQuiz also

---

[2] All eduComponents modules are freely available as open-source software licensed under the terms of the GNU Public License (cf. http://wdok.cs.uni-magdeburg.de/software/).

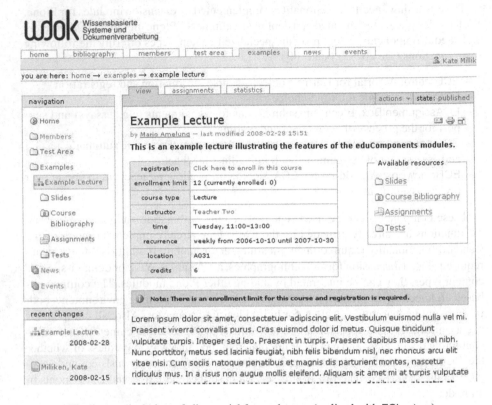

Fig. 1. A typical view of all material from a lecture (realized with ECLecture)

offers tutor-graded extended text questions, so that selected-response and constructed-response items can be mixed in a test to address different skills.

Another possible use of ECQuiz is for self tests with immediate feedback: In this case, students immediately get an overall score, an overview of wrong and right answers and possibly additional explanations, see figure 2. Since both the selection of questions from a pool of questions and the selection of possible answers can be randomized, the instructor may also allow that the test may be taken repeatedly.

2.3 ECAssignmentBox and ECAutoAssessmentBox

ECAssignmentBox supports creation, submission, and grading of essay-like assignments. The assessment of essay-like student submissions offered by ECAssignmentBox is semi-automated, meaning that the teacher does the assessing, but is aided by the tool during the entire process of grading students' work and giving feedback. ECAssignmentBox leverages the workflow capabilities of Plone to define a specialized workflow for student submissions. Modeling the grading process as a workflow structures it and makes it more transparent, but, as in typical content management workflows, it also enables the division of labor and online collaboration. For example, the detailed

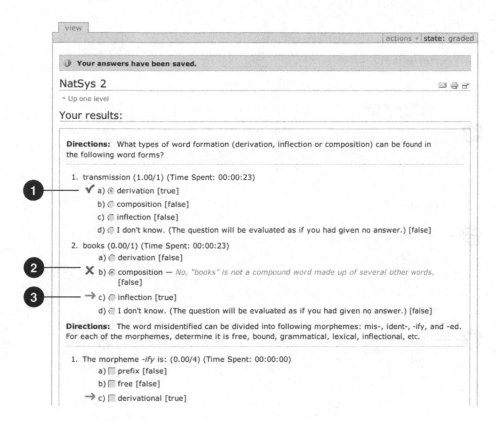

Fig. 2. Example of the ECQuiz instant feedback option for self-assessment tests. ❶ is a correct answer, ❷ is an incorrect answer with additional feedback provided by the test author, and the arrow ❸ indicates the correct answer that the candidate should have selected.

reviewing of submissions may be assigned to teaching assistants, while the decision about the eventual grades can be reserved to instructors.

ECAutoAssessmentBox is derived from ECAssignmentBox and was originally developed to allow students to submit their solutions for programming assignments via the Web at any time during the submission period and get immediate feedback (see figure 3). Automatic testing and assessment of assignments is handled by a Web-based service which manages a submission queue and several *backends*. Backends are also Web-based services, which encapsulate the testing functions for a specific type of assignments.

The exact testing strategy implemented by a backend depends on the application: For example, when testing programming assignments, the output of a student solution can be compared to that of a model solution for a set of test data, or the assignment can be tested for properties which must be fulfilled by correct programs. Currently implemented are backends for Haskell, Scheme, Erlang, Prolog, Python, and Java. However, with the appropriate backends, the system can also be used to test submissions in other formal notations or to analyze natural-language assignments (we have already experimented with style checking and keyword spotting [6]).

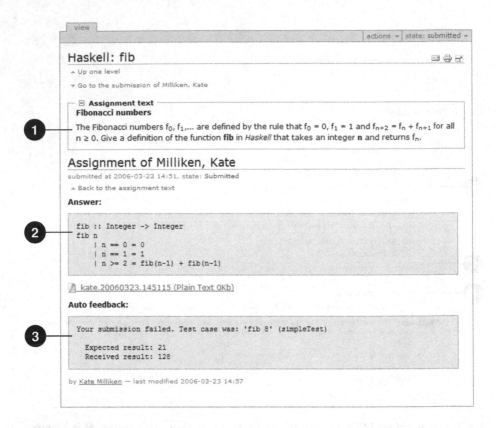

Fig. 3. The view a student gets after the automatic testing of a programming assignment with ECAutoAssessmentBox. ❶ is the assignment; ❷ is the student's submitted program, in this case an incorrect solution; ❸ is the automatic feedback, reporting an error, since the submitted solution does not yield the expected results.

Both ECAssignmentBox and ECAutoAssessmentBox objects represent single assignments. Online exercise sheets are simply created by placing the desired assignments in a special folder, which handles the presentation and provides statistics and analysis features for the student submissions for the contained assignments.

3   Employing eduComponents for Hybrid Learning

In Magdeburg, we are using the eduComponents modules (cf. section 2) as part of a hybrid learning strategy which consists of lectures, electronic exercise work and exercise groups as regular classroom sessions.

We are actively using eduComponents in **all** our lectures since several semesters. This includes advanced lectures in programming like "AI programming and knowledge representation" or "Functional programming: advanced topics" as well as lectures like "Natural language systems", "Document processing", or "Information extraction". In the latter student assignments deal with formal systems and formalisms beyond traditional programming, e.g., XSLT [3] in "Document processing" and regular expressions or UIMA annotators [4] in '"Information extraction".

The most recent and broad scale usage in programming was summer semester 2007 in a lecture called "Programming paradigms" with 2 hours lecture and 2 hours exercise per week. This course is obligatory for all CS bachelor students in their second semester. These students have already a background in Java programming from their introductory courses in the first semester and have thus been exposed to the imperative and the object oriented paradigm. Therefore "Programming paradigms" concentrates on complementing the students' perspective with functional programming (using Haskell, Scheme, and CommonLisp) and logic programming (using Prolog). It is essential that the students deepen their understanding by solving programming tasks in the different representatives of declarative languages. This can only be achieved when exercises and practice are very intensive. We therefore demand that students submit weekly programming assignment several hours prior to the weekly group meeting and get them checked and—hopefully— accepted by ECAutoAssessmentBox. This may involve a number of error corrections and re-submissions.

A group comprises approx. 15 to 20 students and is headed by an assistant as tutor. The tutor of the exercises—this is either an assistant or an advanced student—has prior access to all submissions. He can thus preview all submissions of his group members and look for recurring problems or alternative and outstanding solutions. This allows to better prepare the face-to-face group meetings. The tutor can now decide much better in advance how much time needs to be allocated for what tasks because he can judge the students' performance and their potential problems from the inspection of submitted solutions and solution attempts. During and after the group session all these documents are available online.

Students have to present their solutions as before, but during the classroom session, the assignments and the presented solutions are projected for all to see. This removes the need to copy solutions to and from the blackboard. The selected students have to comment on their solutions. If the solution and the presentation have been satisfactory, the submission gets moved to the corresponding workflow state (e.g., *accepted* or *graded*).

4   Experiences and Lessons Learned

We started to develop and exploit eduComponents as basis for our hybrid learning environment in winter semester 2003/2004. Since then we have been gathering experiences with this approach in all our lectures. During the last two semesters, automatic testing of programming assignments (using ECAutoAssessmentBox and backends for Haskell, Scheme, and Prolog) was actively used by a total of over 140 students. This resulted in almost 12.000 automatically tested submissions for about 200 assignments.

---

[3] http://www.w3.org/Style/XSL/

[4] http://incubator.apache.org/uima/

In the following we will discuss experiences with the hybrid learning arrangement:

– effects on students,
– effects on teachers,
– feedback from students,
– analysis of learning outcomes,
– stipulation of pedagogical experimentation.

4.1 Effects on Students

For programming assignments with automatic testing the demands for students' solutions are much more explicit and rigid with respect to correctness and quality. Students thus also have to ensure that their solution is working correctly. Consequently the intensity of work needed for the exercises has effectively increased.

On the other hand, students can gain access to a larger number of alternative solutions and to typical error cases. Students also reported that they feel much more motivated, since they get immediate feedback for their solutions. The motivation is also due to the fact that students know that their submissions are actually reviewed, while previously only a small number of solutions could be discussed. Maybe these advantages have compensated for the higher requirements.

Student behavior during classroom sessions has also changed: Many students no longer carry written notes to the classroom session, since they know that their submissions are available online. Some students were even tempted not to come at all to the group sessions if their submissions had passed the automatic tests. Our policy in this respect is that personal attendance and active participation in the discussion among peers is obligatory.

A very positive development is that many more students than before speak up in the groups and want to show and discuss their solution if it is different from other presented solutions.

4.2 Effects on Teachers

For teachers using automatic testing of programs, the most significant effect is that the effort for initially designing assignments has increased. This is an insight that other users of automated program testing systems have also reported (e.g., [7]). Automatic testing requires problems and tasks to be formulated much more formally and precisely. This is necessary to enable automatic testing and in order to avoid misunderstandings which could result in students trying to solve a different problem than the one the teacher had in mind and then getting puzzled about the reactions of the automatic testing system.

When they employ eduComponents, teachers are sometimes surprised by unexpected or unintended usage of the system by the students. The latter may demand for policy decisions.

Unexpected usage: ECAssignmentBox has been designed and implemented as lightweight solution. It was intended to support either direct typing of (short) answers or uploading of assignments (programs, texts) from a file; but it intentionally do not offer any sophisticated editor functionality. Nevertheless there were unanticipated usages of the system. Some students used it not only for the submission of their final solution, but also as a kind of "ubiquitous work place" to work on essay-like assignments: They started to work on an assignment from one computer, used the submission feature to store an intermediate version, and later continued to work on the same assignment from a different computer. This resulted in a large number of spurious superseded submissions.

Unintended usage: Other students abused ECAutoAssessmentBox as a Web-based interpreter to solve programming assignments. This was clearly unintended in our design. We therefore introduced a parameter for teachers to restrict the number of possible re-submissions for automatically tested programming assignments. We currently use a limit of three trials. Limiting the misuse of ECAutoAssessmentBox as a trial-and-error device by setting a limit on repeated submissions also enforces a secondary learning objective: We expect that our students are able to use the native programming environments and interpreters for the various programming languages and to leverage them instead of submitting untested sketches of a solution.

4.3 Feedback from Students

At the end of each semester we ask our students to complete a questionnaire on their experience with the learning environment. The questions cover three areas: The use of electronic submissions in general, their effect on the students' working habits, and the usability of eduComponents. The results—based on feedback from up to now more than 200 students—in all three areas are consistently very positive. Students especially value the reporting and statistics features, which help them to track their learning progress, again resulting in better motivation. Furthermore students find it helpful that their assignments are stored centrally, and can quickly be accessed for discussion in the course. Students also report that they work more diligently on their assignments because the teachers can now access and review all assignments.

A seemingly minor change in the organization and technical basis of exercises—i.e., introducing that all assignments and all solutions of students are electronic documents in a content management system—resulted in significant changes in the learning environment and changed learning processes much more fundamentally than expected in the beginning of the transition to the new system. When we started using CAA and other e-learning components we had the primary motivation to relief teachers and students from administrative burdens by automating certain processes and supporting others. Our experience is, however, that the change in the way how assignments are submitted has lead to many other changes in our courses because of the new possibilities offered by the system. But the new opportunities also pose new demands for both teachers and students.

Although the workload for students has increased there is a broad acceptance of the new system and students would welcome its use in other lectures as well. We interpret this as a positive reaction on the new opportunities and as an indication that students accept the higher intensity of their own engagement because they experience and appreciate an improved return on investment for their learning outcomes.

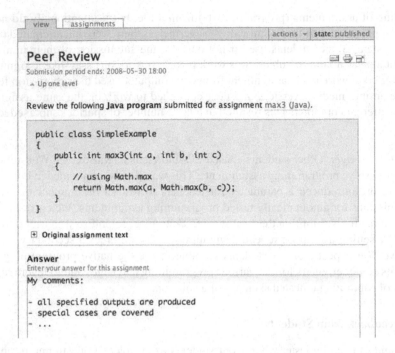

Fig. 4. Review of an assignment using ECReviewBox (student view; simple Java program for illustration purpose)

4.4 Analysis of Learning Outcomes

On the other hand an in depth analysis of recent examination results (lecture on "Programming paradigms" from Summer 2007 with first exam in September 2007 and repetition exam in February 2008; N = 55 students) and the recorded data from the respective exercise groups (e.g., final number of accepted solutions, number of presentations of solutions in the group) reveals that not all students make already the intended use of the offered opportunities for self study. In this analysis we distinguished "minimalist" students from "overperformers". We counted those students as minimalists that achieved just those numbers that were obligatory as prerequisite for access to the final exam (a two hour written exam with tasks similar to those from the exercises). Overperformers in contrast have submitted solutions to all or almost all assignments and additionally were much more active in the exercise groups. Whereas all overperformers from the exercise groups—except one, but he got a "very good" as score in the repetition of the exam—excelled their peers with very good or at least good results in the exam, many of the minimalists showed only poor performance or failed, some even twice (i.e., as well in the repetition exam), and no minimalist excelled positively.

4.5 Pedagogical Innovation

There is another effect of our hybrid learning environment: The availability of eduComponents and the relative ease of extending them with new functionality stipulate pedagogical experimentation. The recent development and first employment of the so called ECReviewBox is a point in case.

Computer science students need not only be able to write programs themselves, they must as well be able to understand and evaluate programs written by others. This is, by the way, an excellent example from CS education for the cognitive learning objective of "evaluation" in Bloom's taxonomy [8]. ECReviewBox is a new module of eduComponents that to a large extent automates a peer review process of student solutions to assignments (cf. fig. 4). We have employed this new functionality for several more complex programming assignments for the first time in summer 2007. First, students have been asked to supply their solutions to the programming task. In the subsequent week, all submitters were eligible for acting as anonymous reviewer and commenter on the anonymized submission of some randomly selected other student. Finally the reviews were made available as feedback to the original authors. Please note that such a type of assignment would hardly be possible in a traditional paper-based environment.

5 Summary and Prospect

Since we started with the hybrid learning environment based on combining classroom lectures and exercises with e-learning and especially computer-aided assessment our teaching has changed significantly.

This starts already when preparing a lecture. When the content is selected and the slides and/or notes are prepared we habitually devise both an accompanying multiple choice questionnaire as well as the assignments for the weekly exercise group. Of course we now do no longer have to create all of this from scratch because we can choose from the repository of former tests and assignments.

The following point illustrates, in our opinion, in a nearly prototypical way the interrelation of pedagogical concerns and policy issues. In summer 2007 we had—as we usually do up to now—demanded that at least 66 percent of the assignments were successfully solved (i.e., accepted by the automatic checking module prior to the exercise groups). We have at several occasions tried to convince our students with arguments that plagiarism is counterproductive and in the long run destructive for themselves. On the other hand we decisively did not regularly check students' submissions for suspected plagiarism (also technically possible within limits), because we did not want to start an "arms race" between plagiarism hiding and plagiarism detection. We now think about a change in policy for future semesters. We will experiment with a combination of relaxing the demands on the one hand (i.e., we will only demand that solutions to a minimum number of assignments have been seriously *attempted*, but they need not necessarily be fully correct and automatically accepted) and on the other hand making use of regular plagiarism detection and rejection of submissions classified as plagiarized. We hope that this change of policy supports the motivating pedagogical concern: Students shall learn through problem solving on their own not through copying and—hopefully at best—only understanding the solutions of others.

Another policy change that we are planning is to introduce "spontaneous" tasks into the group exercises, i.e., within each group session of 90 minutes a slot of approx. 15 minutes will in the future be allocated for working on problems that are handed to the students within the session. This seems to be both necessary and feasible in the light of our experiences with the hybrid approach of combining e-learning and CAA with a traditional classroom based learning environment.

Acknowledgement

A number of colleagues and students have contributed to the design, implementation and deployment for successful every day usage of the eduComponents. We have to thank our former colleague M. Piotrowski for inspiring discussions and his contributions to the system, our students W. Fenske and S. Peilicke for their substantial implementations and our colleagues I. Blümel, M. Gnjatovic and M. Kunze for their valuable feedback from their experience in teaching with eduComponents.

References

1. Amelung, M., Piotrowski, M., Rösner, D.: EduComponents: Experiences in e-assessment in computer science education. In: ITiCSE 2006: Proceedings of the 11th annual conference on Innovation and technology in computer science education, pp. 88–92. ACM Press, New York (2006)
2. Rösner, D., Piotrowski, M., Amelung, M.: A Sustainable Learning Environment based on an Open Source Content Management System. In: Bühler, W. (ed.) Proceedings of the German e-Science Conference (GES 2007), Max-Planck-Gesellschaft (2007)
3. Amelung, M., Piotrowski, M., Rösner, D.: eduComponents: A Component-Based E-Learning Environment. In: ITiCSE 2007: Proceedings of the 12th annual SIGCSE conference on Innovation and technology in computer science education, pp. 352–352. ACM Press, New York (2007)
4. Amelung, M., Piotrowski, M., Rösner, D.: Webbasierte Dienste für das E-Assessment. In: Koschke, R., Herzog, O., Rödiger, K.H., Ronthaler, M. (eds.) Informatik 2007 - Informatik trifft Logistik. Beträge der 37. Jahrestagung der Gesellschaft für Informatik e.V (GI). Lecture Notes in Informatics, pp. 518–522. Bonn, GI-Verlag (2007)
5. Piotrowski, M., Rösner, D.: Integration von E-Assessment und Content-Management. In: Haake, J.M., Lucke, U., Tavangarian, D. (eds.) DeLFI2005: 3. Deutsche e-Learning Fachtagung Informatik der Gesellschaft für Informatik e.V. Lecture Notes in Informatics (LNI), vol. P-66, pp. 129–140. Bonn, GI-Verlag (2005)
6. Feustel, T.: Analyse von Texteingaben in einem CAA-Werkzeug zur elektronischen Einreichung und Auswertung von Aufgaben. Master's thesis, Fakultät für Informatik, Otto-von-Guericke-Universität, Magdeburg (2006)
7. Zeller, A.: Making students read and review code. In: ITiCSE 2000: Proceedings of the 5th annual SIGCSE/SIGCUE ITiCSE conference on Innovation and technology in computer science education, pp. 89–92. ACM Press, New York (2000)
8. Bloom, B.S., Engelhart, M.D., Furst, E.J., Hill, W.H.: Krathwohl: Taxonomy Of Educational Objectives: Handbook 1. In: The Cognitive Domain. Allyn & Bacon, Boston (1956)

Experiences of Hybrid Corporate Training Programmes at an Online Academic Institution

Kanishka Bedi

Universitas 21 Global, NSRCEL, Indian Institute of Management Bangalore,
Bannerghatta Road, Bangalore – 560076, Karnataka, India
kbedi@u21global.edu.sg

Abstract. During the past decade, many corporations world-wide have embraced hybrid training programmes to derive benefits of the conventional face-to-face (F2F) learning environment coupled with those of online learning environment for their employees. A majority of researches on hybrid learning focus upon blending of existing F2F programmes of brick 'n' mortar institutions with online component. This paper highlights the experiences of an online academic institution in blending its purely online courses with F2F component in order to better meet the training objectives of its corporate clients. It reports myriad of challenges faced during the creation and implementation of its initial hybrid corporate training programmes and how the lessons learned helped in blending its subsequent programmes for better learner and client satisfaction. It brings out the importance of redesigning/ modifying the blending proportion in future offerings of a programme through continual feedback of its corporate clients as well as the learners.

Keywords: Hybrid, Blended, Corporate, Training.

1 Introduction and Literature Review

The growing popularity of online education has inspired many conventional institutions world-wide to explore blending of their existing or new programmes with online pedagogy in order to cater to the needs of potential students, who are unable to attend campus-based full-time programmes. Blended learning is consistent with the values of traditional higher education institutions and has the proven potential to enhance both the effectiveness and efficiency of meaningful learning experiences [1]. The term "blended learning" or "hybrid learning" is relatively new and researchers have used different perspectives while defining it. Blended learning is defined as a combination of different training "media" (technologies, activities and types of events) to create an optimum training program for a specific audience [2]. For the purpose of a survey conducted on blended programmes in the USA, blended courses and programmes were demarcated as having 30% to 79% of the course content delivered online [3]. Irrespective of the blending proportion, it is a challenge for the designers designing a new blended programme to decide about the amount of blending to be performed between online and face-to-face teaching, keeping in view the overall objectives of

J. Fong, R. Kwan, and F.L. Wang (Eds.): ICHL 2008, LNCS 5169, pp. 271–282, 2008.
© Springer-Verlag Berlin Heidelberg 2008

the programme and the expectations of the students [4]. The amount of blending influences the operational issues related to the planning and execution of the programme.

Blended learning environment is increasingly getting popular in the executive education programmes of major corporations. The Shell Open University in collaboration with the University of Twente has successfully designed and implemented blended activity-based training programmes grounded in learner's actual workplace problems [5]. However, there are instances whereby corporations have struggled to adapt such blended programmes for their requirements. While illustrating the blended training approach adopted by Hyundai Motor Company, it is reported that despite efforts to align the curricula and content of the online and offline courses, overlaps and inconsistencies remained, partly due to different parties being responsible for conducting the offline and online courses [6]. Comparison of the blended approach to learning is natural vis-à-vis purely online and purely conventional face-to-face learning models. A study backed the hypothesis that the most efficient teaching model is a blended approach, which combines self-paced learning, live e-learning, and face-to-face classroom learning [7]. In another experiment, it was concluded that pre-service teachers in the experimental group subjected to a blended e-learning cooperative approach had higher achievement levels in their post-overall-course test 'comprehensive-score', and attitudes towards e-learning environments compared to those of the control group [8]. However, another study indicated no significant difference between the hybrid course and the traditional course in students' achievement, knowledge retention, satisfaction, and attitude [9].

Researchers have tried to explore various dimensions of blended approach to learning by using student surveys. An objective assessment instrument was developed and validated in order to capture the learner's views on blended learning and its implementation process [10]. According to a study, while students may believe that the hybrid courses have a negative impact on attendance, they do not self-report an actual impact [11]. In another study, a transformative education scale was used to show that teachers can be transformed through a blended and balanced programme which not only upgrades skills and knowledge, but also enables them to reflect on past and future practice [12]. Blended learning approach utilizes the collaborative power of online learning by encouraging peer-to-peer learning. The significance and power of "coaching" in a comprehensive blended learning strategy for improving the performance of learners has been emphasized upon [13]. "Power distance" is a term which signifies hierarchical difference as deemed legitimate by the members of a group or society [14], who feel that there are an elite few (higher up in the hierarchy) with more knowledge, skill and decision making ability [15]. In a study, it was concluded that in a hybrid learning environment, students with high power distance would prefer to seek feedback from fellow students rather than from the professor [16]. However, this study could not establish any significant positive relationship between power distance and participation on the electronic discussion board. In another study, it has been reported that students who perceived high levels of collaborative learning in the blended learning environment, also perceived high levels of social presence and were more satisfied with the course [17].

Faculty and technology with well developed pedagogy play a major role in the success of a blended programme. According to [18], blended learning adds value only when facilitated by educators with high interpersonal skills, and accompanied by reliable, easy-to-use technology. It has been reported that many students did not engage in the online resources of a blended programme possibly due to lack of awareness about the e-learning component, combined with inconsistent access to the computing facilities [19]. Thus, there is a clear need of training the students in online pedagogy and learning management system (LMS) before exposing them to online component in the blended programme. Many researchers have made useful recommendations for designing an effective blended learning programme. Guidelines have been provided for constructing successful combinations of elements in blended learning based upon criteria like stability and urgency, "touches" and cost, learning resources and experience [20]. Evaluation and revision of the blended programme based upon regular feedback from the students has been suggested by many researchers. It has been demonstrated how a holistic annual review framework can be helpful to blended learning educational designers to be sensitive to both their audience and the unintended and unanticipated consequences of their actions [21]. A study revealed that students have positive attitudes for hybrid learning [22]. In the same study, design, development, implementation, evaluation and revision are recommended as the five steps in the creation of a hybrid course. Some researchers argue that educationally useful research on blended learning needs to focus on the relationships between different modes of learning (for example, face-to-face and online) and especially on the nature of their integration. In particular, such research needs to generate usable evidence about the quality of the students' learning experiences and learning outcomes [23].

2   Universitas 21 Global (U21Global)

Established in 2001, U21Global is a premier online graduate school backed by 17 world renowned universities from around the world. U21Global has successfully enrolled over 4500 students from 60 countries since it opened its classes in August 2003. This paper highlights the experiences of this online academic institution in blending its purely online courses with F2F component in order to better meet the training objectives of its corporate clients.

2.1   Management Programme for Entrepreneurs and Family Businesses (MPEFB)

During early 2006, U21Global joined hands with N S Raghavan Center for Entrepreneurial Learning (NSRCEL) of the Indian Institute of Management Bangalore (IIMB) to create a hybrid programme entitled "Management Programme for Entrepreneurs and Family Businesses (MPEFB). The main objective of the programme was to provide an opportunity to the existing and aspiring entrepreneurs to undergo formal training in management, which they are rarely able to do due to their inability to be away from their business for long duration to attend a full-time campus-based programme. The genesis of the MPEFB can be traced back to the willingness of the two partner institutions to create a new learning paradigm for entrepreneurs by way of bringing out the best of both online as well as conventional face-to-face (F2F) learning. The big question faced by the instructional designers involved in the pro-gramme was to decide about the extent and proportion of blending. There are four paradigms of creating blended learning environments namely, the supplemental model, the replacement model, the emporium model and the buffet model [24]. In the supplemental model, the traditional F2F structure of the course is retained and is supplemented with out-of-class or within the class technology-based activities. How-ever, the supplemental model was adopted in MPEFB in a different manner, whereby the existing online content of selected courses in the U21Global MBA programme was supplemented with the F2F sessions by the IIMB faculty.

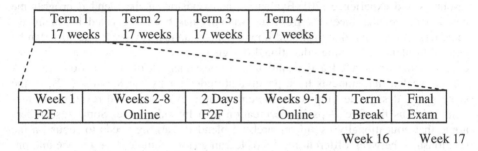

Fig. 1. Blending format in the first offering (batch 1) of MPEFB

Fig. 1 shows the blending format for the batch 1 of MPEFB. Each term (consti-tuted by two subjects) comprised of 17 weeks duration and the four terms resulted in 16 months duration of the programme. A high level of coordination was required for creating a joint programme like MPEFB involving two institutions with different inherent cultures and styles of functioning. The following challenges started erupting during the designing and implementation of the first batch of MPEFB:

- The participation from the IIMB faculty in the online faculty training programme (FTP) was only symbolic with many of them opting out of it, while others acting as mute spectators rather than active participants.
- During the customization of the online content (selection of modules, case studies, discussion topics), it was rather difficult to convince the IIMB faculty that micro-level changes within the modules would be very cumbersome and cost intensive.
- In some courses, there were contradictory views of the IIMB and U21Global fac-ulty counterparts with respect to the assessment components to be used.
- Apart from the first term, it became increasingly difficult to make the IIMB faculty aware of the merits of open book open web (OBOW) examination format and they preferred to use the "ready-made" cases from Harvard Business School Publishing (HBSP) and other sources for the examinations.
- The biggest challenge unfolded from the first term itself due to low faculty partici-pation/ presence in the online component of the programme. It became increasingly difficult to encourage the IIMB faculty members responsible for facilitating the online component to devote ample time with the LMS and guide the discussions on the discussion board.

- The above reasons had direct impact upon the engagement of students in the course, with about 15% of the students withdrawing from the programme over a period of time. Though, some students cited personal/ medical reasons at the time of withdrawing from the programme.
- In order to assess the situation, a survey instrument was designed to know about the expectations of the students from the course, their experiences and the problems faced by them during the first term. 34 students responded to the online survey conducted through *QuestBack* [25].

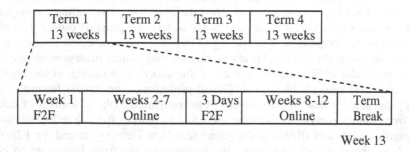

Term 1	Term 2	Term 3	Term 4
13 weeks	13 weeks	13 weeks	13 weeks

Week 1	Weeks 2-7	3 Days	Weeks 8-12	Term
F2F	Online	F2F	Online	Break

Week 13

Fig. 2. Modified format of blending in the second offering (batch 2) of MPEFB

The survey findings were useful in incorporating modifications in blending, *modus-operandi* and assessment system of the batch 2 of the programme. During the first offering of the programme, the directors found that it is operationally cumbersome to manage the 16 months duration programme due to overlaps with the subsequent offerings of the programme. In their opinion, one-year duration of the programme would be easier to manage as every year a new batch could be introduced after the culmination of the earlier batch. This decision also took into account the findings of the survey that the students preferred lesser duration for a "Certificate" programme in comparison to a "Degree/ Award" programme. The faculty capacity constraints did not warrant increasing the F2F component drastically. However, it was decided to increase the mid-term contact to three days. Also, while condensing the duration of the programme, the duration of the online component was reduced while slightly increasing the duration of F2F component (by one day). Thus, the F2F component increased in proportion substantially in relation to the online component (as desired by the students in the survey). As shown in fig. 2, each term in batch 2 comprises of 13 weeks duration compared to the 17 weeks duration in batch 1. Nevertheless, the content of the online component was kept unchanged while eliminating certain assessment components to ease-out the learning process on part of the students. Keeping in view the less than satisfactory participation of the IIMB faculty in the first offering of the programme, it was decided that from the second offering onwards, U21Global faculty would facilitate the online component of the programme while the IIMB faculty would conduct the F2F sessions.

2.2 Indian Oil Hybrid Programme in Project Management

Indian Oil Corporation Limited (IOCL) is currently India's largest company by sales with a turnover of US $51 billion, the highest-ever for an Indian company, and profits of US $1.73 billion for fiscal 2006. During the mid of 2006, U21Global created a hybrid programme on Project Management for IOCL. It's current (batch 3) blending format is shown in fig. 3. The two-day F2F at the beginning of the programme was meant to give the students a hands-on workshop in online pedagogy and the learning management system (LMS). This also provided the opportunity to the faculty to interact with the participants prior to the commencement of the online component of the programme. The mid-term two-day F2F had the objective of providing the opportunity to the participants to clarify any topics not understood properly during the online component of the programme. The last leg of F2F sessions is scheduled in Singapore to provide inputs to the participants about international project management practices through the faculty of National University of Singapore (NUS) along with evaluation of the team final projects by the U21Global professors. The typical feature of this hybrid programme is that the participants of the programme (the executives of IOCL) travel from various parts of India to the sprawling campus of the IndianOil Institute of Petroleum Management (iIPM) at Gurgaon (near New Delhi) to attend the F2F sessions. Also, the professor facilitating the sessions travels from Bangalore to New Delhi. Similarly, for the last part of F2F, all the participants and faculty travel to Singapore. Hence, substantial travel costs are associated with the F2F component of this programme. Over the past three offerings of the programme, the following changes in the blending format and modus operandi were brought about, keeping in view the feedback of the learners and the IOCL HR officials:

- In the first offering, the mid-term F2F was kept after the completion of the last online Segment 8. However, the participants felt that this F2F was very close to the last F2F held in Singapore. In batch 3, thus the mid-term F2F is being conducted after Segment 5.

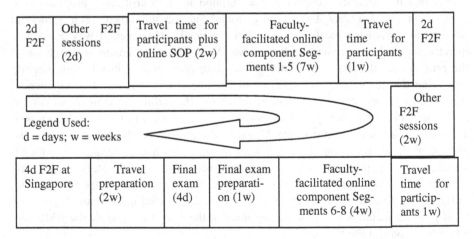

Fig. 3. The blending format in the IOCL Hybrid Programme in Project Management

- In the first batch, the mid-term F2F was conducted by a faculty other than the one facilitating the online component. However, feedback from the students revealed dissatisfaction and it was recommended to use the same faculty facilitating the online component for the mid-term F2F. This change in batches 2 and 3 has proved more effective as per the feedback of the participants.
- In order to offset the huge travel costs associated with the movement of the participants from different parts of India to iIPM, Gurgaon, from batch 2 onwards longer term breaks in the programme were introduced to conduct some additional F2F sessions (using experts apart from those of U21Global) there and to take care of the travel time before resumption of the online component.

2.3 Hero Honda – Tata Motors Programme in Operations Management

Incorporated in 1984, Hero Honda Motors Limited (HHML) is a joint venture between India's Hero Group and Honda Motor Company, Japan. It is currently the world's single largest two wheeler company and also one of the most successful joint ventures worldwide. Established in 1945, Tata Motors Limited (TML) is India's largest automobile company, with revenues of USD 7.2 billion in 2006-07. The company is the world's fifth largest medium and heavy commercial vehicle manufacturer, and the world's second largest medium and heavy bus manufacturer. During May 2007, both Hero Honda and Tata Motors enrolled their executives in a common online class of Operations Management at U21Global. Despite both the companies operating in the automotive sector, their products do not compete with each other. Ten executives of Hero Honda and twenty two executives of Tata Motors comprised the total thirty two students of the class. Hero Honda insisted upon blending the programme with three one-day F2F sessions at New Delhi with intervals of one month during the duration of the programme. On the contrary, Tata Motors preferred to have a purely online programme. Thus, in a unique arrangement, the faculty facilitating the course was assigned the responsibility of conducting the F2F sessions for Hero Honda executives (as per the blending format shown in fig. 4), while ensuring that Tata Motors participants are not made aware of such F2F sessions happening for the Hero Honda executives. The professor thus advised the Hero Honda executives not to share their F2F experiences with their Tata Motors colleagues in the online class. The F2F sessions for Hero Honda were used by the professor to provide supplementary inputs and to discuss latest case studies on the subject. It was felt by the professor that as a result, the performance of the Hero Honda executives during the online discussions also started improving. This was later substantiated by the fact at the end of the training programme, the average overall score of the Hero Honda executives was much higher at 89.56 compared to that of Tata Motors executives at 61.5. Noticeably, two participants of Tata Motors had withdrawn from the course while there was no withdrawal from the Hero Honda participants. The difference in grades and number of student withdrawals cannot be completely attributed to the blending of the programme for Hero Honda. Nevertheless, the findings are indicative of possible improvement in the satisfaction of the learners at Hero Honda due to blending of the programme. High acclaim from the Hero Honda HR department for the programme and approval of many more batches in future is another reason in favour of the hybrid nature of the programme.

Online component Segments 1-3 (4w)	1 day F2F at New Delhi	Online component Segments 4-5 (4w)	1 day F2F at New Delhi	Online component Segments 6-8 (4w)	1 day F2F at New Delhi	Final Exam (4d)

Fig. 4. The blending format in the Hero Honda Programme in Operations Management

2.4 Emirates NBD Hybrid "Certificate in Management" Programme

Emirates NBD is a leading banking group headquartered in Dubai (UAE). According to a study, blended learning is a viable means to teach interpersonal skills in a bank setting [26]. Interestingly, the findings of this study inspired U21Global to expose its corporate clients to online learning gradually through the hybrid learning approach. However, in the "Certificate of Management" hybrid programme developed for Emirates NBD, the proportion of the F2F component vis-à-vis online component has been further decreased compared to its earlier hybrid programmes by way of incorporation of real-time online "webinars" conducted through software like *Elluminate* and *Interwise*. As shown in fig. 5, the programme blends virtual classroom "webinars" and face-to-face sessions with online classes led by U21Global professors.

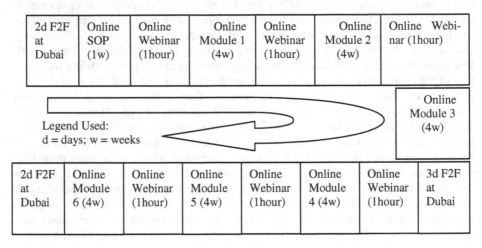

Fig. 5. The blending format in the Emirates NBD "Certificate in Management"

3 Comparing the Four Blending Models

All the four hybrid programmes discussed above involve a considerable amount of travel either on part of the students or faculty. A major challenge is finding the right mix in a blended learning environment that will leverage the advantages of asynchronous learning while maintaining quality interaction in the face-to-face classroom

[27][28][29]. The 'optimal mix' will be between 90% face-to-face and 10% computer-mediated instruction or vice-versa [30]. Some researchers are of the view that there is no standard approach to a blended environment because faculty design courses to fit their teaching styles and content [31]. Integration between the two environments is critical because students must see the relevancy of activities and rationale for a blended environment [29][31]. Table 1 compares the four hybrid training programmes at U21Global on various dimensions. Apart from the MPEFB, the demand for incorporation of F2F in purely online courses of U21Global had come from the side of the clients, who felt that their employees getting exposed to online pedagogy for the first time may not be "comfortable" with purely online content and delivery. This suggestion was well taken by the training designers at U21Global and was the primary reason in the genesis of these hybrid programmes. It can be seen that the proportion of F2F is the lowest in Emirates NBD programme amongst the four programmes. It is too early to predict the results of this latest experiment at U21Global, whereby the use of real-time online "webinars" would hopefully help in containing the faculty travel costs while retaining the flavor of the F2F interaction up to great extent.

Table 1. Comparing the four hybrid training programmes at U21Global

	MPEFB	IOCL	HHML–TML	Emirates NBD
Travel of faculty	No	Yes	Yes	Yes
Travel of students	Yes	Yes	No	No
Same faculty for online as well as F2F	No	Yes	Yes	Yes
Total duration of the programme	One year = 365 days	15 weeks = 105 days	14 weeks = 98 days	6 months = 180 days
Duration of the F2F	32 days	9 days	3 days	7 days
Proportion of blending (F2F viz. online)	8.77%	8.57%	3.06%	0.04%
Time intervals between consecutive F2F sessions	Approx. 1.5 months	Approx. two months	Approx. one month	Approx three months
Special Webinars	No	No	No	Yes
OBOW Exam	No	Yes	Yes	No
No. of students per batch	50	50	32	25
Number of batches	Two	Three	One	One
Time of Batch 1 launch	Dec., 2006	Aug., 2006	May, 2007	Feb., 2008
Learning Outcomes (Overall average score) in the most recent batch	85.90	75.55	First batch still in progress	First batch still in progress
Student Satisfaction in the most recent batch	4.53 on a scale of 5	4.69 on a scale of 5	First batch still in progress	First batch still in progress

4 Conclusion and Recommendations

Blended programmes are becoming more and more popular in major corporations world-wide due to synergy between the conventional F2F and online pedagogies. However, such programmes require high degree of synthesis and integration between such diverse modes of training delivery. If such a programme involves partner institutions, the challenge is even higher to coordinate the various aspects of design and implementation to fulfill the learning objectives and outcomes. This paper highlighted the experiences of an online academic institution in creating four hybrid training programmes for corporate clients and how the continual feedback from learners and clients resulted in modifying the blending format for better satisfaction of the stakeholders. The following recommendations will serve as lessons for other institutions planning to create hybrid corporate training programmes:

- Conventional institutions operating in face-to-face pedagogy must understand that online pedagogy may not be a cup of tea for each one of their faculty.
- It is a misconception that blended/ online component would reduce the effort/ involvement on part of faculty. Thus, faculty involved in blended programmes should perform their workload assessment before offering and committing their services for such programmes.
- An abysmal performance of the faculty in the online component of the blended programme may result in students getting wrong impressions about the utility of online education and thus, they may "demand" for more face-to-face component. It is suggested that in the blended learning context, continual moderation of student's postings by the instructor and student-to-student interaction, are likely to improve the student's perception about the online component of the learning environment as well as their grades [32].
- Despite providing proper training in online pedagogy, it would not be a good idea to use the faculty teaching online for the first time in every course of the programme. In-house professors already having experience in facilitating online classes for other programmes/ institutions should be involved at least in the initial few offerings of the programme. Otherwise, external faculty must be involved till the time in-house faculty is not full prepared to undertake the online facilitation.
- It is recommended that the designers of blended programmes should take care of the fundamental principles of adult learning viz. expectation of adults for personal relevance in what they learn, participation in setting their learning outcomes based on their real-world needs, self-direction of their learning resources and pathways and establishment of an active learning community [33]. It is thus imperative to take continual feedback of the students (particularly in executive development programmes) to fine-tune the blending proportion, assessment regime and *modus-operandi* of the programme to better understand and meet the expectations of the students in its future offerings.
- The institutions launching new hybrid programmes should be prepared to encounter teething troubles due to unique expectations of the various stakeholders involved in the programme (students, faculty, administrative staff etc.) and should accordingly prepare contingency plans. It may not be possible to always achieve the right blend in the first offering of the hybrid programme.
- Hybrid training programmes are a better means to expose the employees of corporations gradually to online pedagogy, some of whom may feel highly dismayed if abruptly exposed to the purely online mode of training delivery. The F2F sessions indeed act as cushions to make the learners more comfortable to this new paradigm of training.

- It is easier and more effective to use the same professor to facilitate F2F as well as online in hybrid training programmes, provided the professor is well-trained and passionate about both the pedagogies.

References

1. Garrison, D.R., Kanuka, H.: Blended Learning: Uncovering its Transformative Potential in Higher Education. Internet and Higher Education 7, 95–105 (2004)
2. Bersin, J.: The Blended Learning Book: Best Practices, Proven Methodologies and Lessons Learned. Pfeiffer, San Francisco (2004)
3. Allen, I.E., Seaman, J., Garrett, R.: Blending. In: The Extent & Promise of Blended Education in the United States. Sloan-C, USA (2007)
4. Graff, M.: Individual Differences in Sense of Classroom Community in a Blended Learning Environment. Journal of Education Media 28(2–3), 203–210 (2003)
5. Margaryan, A., Collis, B., Cook, A.: Activity-based Blended Learning. Human Resource Development International 7(2), 265–274 (2004)
6. Kim, D.M., Choi, C.: Developing future leaders at Hyundai Motor Company through Blended Learning. Industrial and Commercial Training 36(7), 286–290 (2004)
7. Alonso, F., Manrique, G.L.D., Viñes, J.M.: An Instructional Model for Web-based E-learning Education with a Blended Learning Process Approach. British Journal of Educational Technology 36(2), 217–235 (2005)
8. EL-Deghaidy, H., Nouby, A.: Effectiveness of a Blended E-learning Cooperative Approach in an Egyptian Teacher Education Programme. Computers & Education (2007), doi:10.1016/j.compedu.2007.10.001
9. Delialioglu, O., Yildirim, Z.: Design and Development of a Technology Enhanced Hybrid Instruction based on MOLTA Model: Its Effectiveness in Comparison to Traditional Instruction. Computers & Education (2007), doi:10.1016/j.compedu.2007.06.006
10. Akkoyunlu, B., Yılmaz-Soylu, M.: Development of a Scale on Learners' Views on Blended Learning and its Implementation Process. The Internet and Higher Education (2008), doi:10.1016/j.iheduc.2007.12.006
11. Yudko, E., Hirokawa, R., Chi, R.: Attitudes, Beliefs, and Attendance in a Hybrid Course. Computers & Education (2007), doi:10.1016/j.compedu.2006.11.005
12. Motteram, G.: Blended Education and the Transformation of Teachers: A Long-term Case Study in Postgraduate UK Higher Education. British Journal of Educational Technology 37(1), 17–30 (2006)
13. Stevens, G.H., Frazer, G.W.: Coaching: The Missing Ingredient in Blended Learning Strategy. Performance Improvement 44(8), 8–13 (2005)
14. Hofstede, G.: Culture's Consequences: Comparing Values, Behaviors, Institutions, and Organizations across Nations, 2nd edn. Sage, Thousand Oaks (2001)
15. Sagie, A., Koslowsky, M.: Participation and Empowerment in Organizations: Modeling, Effectiveness and Applications. Sage, Thousand Oaks (2000)
16. Hwang, A., Francesco, A.M.: Hybrid Learning Environment: Influences of Individualism, Collectivism and Power Distance. In: Academy of Management Best Conference Paper (2006)
17. So, H., Brush, T.A.: Student Perceptions of Collaborative Learning, Social Presence and Satisfaction in a Blended Learning Environment: Relationships and Critical Factors. Computers & Education (2007), doi:10.1016/j.compedu.2007.05.009

18. Derntl, M., Motschnig-Pitrik, R.: The Role of Structure, Patterns, and People in Blended Learning. Internet and Higher Education 8, 111–130 (2005)
19. Wakefield, A.B., Carlisle, C., Hall, A.G., Attree, M.J.: The Expectations and Experiences of Blended Learning Approaches to Patient Safety Education. Nurse Education in Practice 8, 54–61 (2008)
20. Rossett, A., Douglis, F., Frazee, R.V.: Strategies for Building Blended Learning. Learning Circuits, Alexandria, VA (2003), http://www.learningcircuits.org/2003/jul2003/rossett.htm
21. Stubbs, M., Martin, I., Endlar, L.: The "Structuration" of Blended Learning: Putting Holistic Design Principles into Practice. British Journal of Educational Technology 37(2), 163–175 (2006)
22. Olapiriyakul, K., Scher, J.M.: A Guide to Establishing Hybrid Learning Courses: Employing Information Technology to Create a New Learning Experience and a Case Study. Internet and Higher Education 9, 287–301 (2006)
23. Bliuc, A., Goodyear, P., Ellis, R.A.: Research Focus and Methodological Choices in Studies into Students' Experiences of Blended Learning in Higher Education. Internet and Higher Education 10, 231–244 (2007)
24. Twigg, C.A.: New Models for Online Learning: Improving Learning and Reducing Costs. Educause Review (September/ October), pp. 23–36 (2003), http://www.educause.edu/ir/library/pdf/erm0352.pdf
25. Bedi, K.: Utilizing First Term Experience in a Blended Programme for Improving Student Engagement: A Case Study. In: U21 Teaching and Learning Conference "Does Teaching & Learning Translate?", University of Glasgow (U.K.), February 21-22 (2008)
26. Callaway, K.L.: Learning Interpersonal Skills in Banking through Blended Learning. PhD Thesis, Capella University, ProQuest (2005)
27. Kerres, M., DeWitt, C.: A Didactical Framework for the Design of Blended Learning Arrangements. Journal of Educational Media 28(2/3), 101–113 (2003)
28. Martyn, M.: The Hybrid Online Model: Good Practice. Educause Quarterly 26(1), 18–23 (2003)
29. Reay, J.: Blended Learning: A Fusion for the Future. Knowledge Management Review 4(3) (2001)
30. Brown, D.G.: Hybrid Courses are Best. New Dimensions in Education Technology (2001), http://www.wfu.edu/%7Ebrown/Syllabus%20Articles/SylHybrid%20Courses.htm
31. Aycock, A., Garnham, C., Kaleta, R.: Lessons Learned from the Hybrid Course Project. Teaching with Technology Today 8(6), 1–6 (2002), http://www.uwsa.edu/ttt/articles/garnham2.htm
32. Ginns, P., Ellis, R.: Quality in Blended Learning: Exploring the Relationships between Online and Face-to-Face Teaching and Learning. Internet and Higher Education 10, 53–64 (2007)
33. Ausburn, L.J.: Course Design Elements Most Valued by Adult Learners in Blended Online Education Environments: An American Perspective. Educational Media International 41(4), 327–337 (2004)

Designing Programming Exercises with Computer Assisted Instruction[*]

Fu Lee Wang[1] and Tak-Lam Wong[2]

[1] Department of Computer Science, City University of Hong Kong,
Kowloon Tong, Hong Kong
flwang@cityu.edu.hk
[2] Department of Computer Science and Engineering,
The Chinese University of Hong Kong,
Shatin, Hong Kong
wongtl@cse.cuhk.edu.hk

Abstract. Teaching of computer programming has created significant difficulties to both teachers and students. Large class size is one of the major barriers to effective instruction. A well-designed pedagogy can make the instruction most effective. This paper will share our experiences of teaching programming courses with large class size. A set of programming exercises have been designed with help of computer assisted instruction. Evaluation has showed that the new pedagogy provide great flexibilities to both teaching and learning of computer programming. The students' academic results have been significantly improved in programming courses.

Keywords: Computer programming, large class size, stepwise learning, teaching and learning, computer assisted learning (CAI).

1 Introduction

Learning computer programming has been known to be difficult for many beginners (Boulay, 1989). A number of challenges have been identified for both teaching and learning programming (Sleeman, 1986). A programming course typically has a large class size. Large class size is one of the major barriers to effective instruction. It is difficult to closely monitor individual student's learning progress. The teachers do not have enough time to interact with all students in a class of hundreds of students within a few hours of lectures and tutorials each week. Teaching and learning computer programming has created significant difficulties to both teacher and students.

It has been showed that computer-assisted instruction (CAI) technology can be a more effective way of teaching introductory programming courses (Anderson & Skwarecki, 1986). This paper will share our experience in using CAI technology to teach computer programming with large class size.

---

[*] The work described in this paper was substantially supported by a grant from City University of Hong Kong (Project No.: 6000144).

J. Fong, R. Kwan, and F.L. Wang (Eds.): ICHL 2008, LNCS 5169, pp. 283–293, 2008.
© Springer-Verlag Berlin Heidelberg 2008

Students taking computer programming courses very often come with various backgrounds and ability levels. We have incorporated several teaching strategies in designing our teaching and learning activities for computer programming courses. We have designed programming exercises with different levels of difficulty to fulfil the need of students with various backgrounds and ability levels. We can ensure that each step is learned by stepwise learning (Schulman, 2001). The CAI technology allows us to have a close monitoring of students' learning progress. Moreover, we have designed programming activities in an incremental manner, so that the students gain the knowledge of large application development by implicit learning (Berry, 1997). This experience prepares the students ready to participation in a software development team.

The CAI technology provides great flexibilities for us to render the teaching and learning of computer programming more effectively. The students' academic results have been significantly improved. Students find the learning computer programming become interesting, and their programming skills are enhanced subsequently.

The rest of this paper is organized as follow. Section 2 gives an overview of computer-assisted instruction systems for computer programming. Section 3 describes the development of programming activities with multiple levels of difficulties. Section 4 presents incremental style of programming activities. Section 5 evaluates the new pedagogy. We conclude our work in Section 6.

2 Computer-Assisted Instruction for Computer Programming

Related research has showed that computer-assisted instruction (CAI) technology can be a more effective way of teaching introductory programming courses - for certain populations (Anderson & Skwarecki, 1986). Programming skill has to be acquired through lots of practice (Cheang, Kurnia, Lim & Oon, 2003). With the support of CAI, we are able to provide adequate practices to students.

Instant support to the students is a critical factor to the success of teaching and learning of computer programming. However, it introduces a huge pressure in the resources, and it may not be affordable by some universities. It has been showed that intelligent computer-assisted instruction technology can be a more effective way of teaching introductory computer programming courses (Anderson & Skwarecki, 1986). We have implemented a computer-assisted instruction system to support our teaching of computer programming courses. The detail functionalities, design and implementation can be found in (Choy, Nazir, Poon & Yu, 2005; Yu, Poon & Choy, 2006). Figure 1 shows the Programming Assignment aSsessment System (PASS). The PASS system is a web-based computer-assisted instruction system for computer programming (Choy, Nazir, Poon & Yu, 2005; Yu, Poon & Choy, 2006). The PASS system is a fully automated system to help students to study programming.

The PASS system allows the teachers to setup some programming problems. The teachers provide the input and the corresponding output to each test case. The students then submit their program for testing. The system automatically complies and executes the program submitted. By comparing the outputs generated by the students' program and the expected output provided by the teachers, the system will then provide feedbacks to the students. For example, if a student gets wrong in a certain

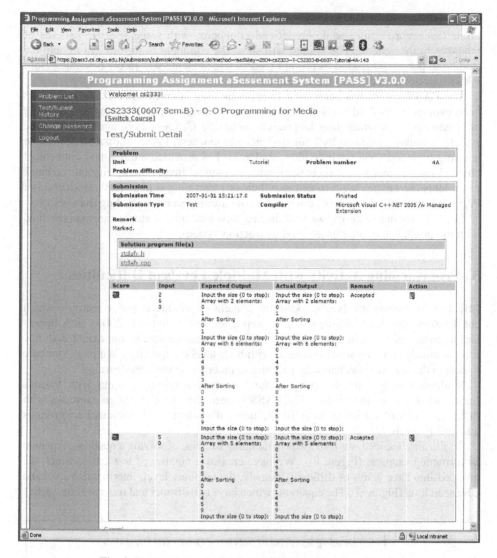

Fig. 1. Programming Assignment aSsessment System (PASS)

type of inputs, the system will show the attached annotation provided by the teachers to give some hints of possible mistakes to the student. The instant feedback provided by the system provides concrete assistances to students to revise their programs, and debugging will become more interesting.

A number of computer-assisted programming learning systems have been developed. The PASS system has a lot of advantages over the existing systems (Choy et. al., 2007). The program submitted will be tested automatically against a large number of test cases. The system will test whether the program is correct with respect to the selected test cases. When the submitted program is incorrect, PASS will indicate to the student exactly at which position the actual output differs from the correct output. Some teacher may store some predefined comments with some specific patterns of mistakes in the system. The system will show the comment to the student to help the student to debug. This kind of prompt feedback to students was rarely possible before PASS was developed (Choy et. al., 2005).

The PASS system has been used in programming courses since 2004, and it has been evolved to its third version. The system currently support teaching and learning of a number of programming languages, including C, C++, Java and Pascal. The system is highly evaluated by both students and teachers. PASS allows a tailor-made learning pace and style for individual student. It has provided a quick and convenient channel for students to test their work without manual involvement. Instant feedback to students encourages them to enhance their programming skills. The introduction of PASS has made the learning of computer programming more rewarding than before.

In the following sections, we will discuss how teaching strategies are incorporated with the intelligent computer-assisted instruction system.

3   Programming Activity with Multiple Levels of Difficulties

Effective instruction involves working the content to provide stepwise learning which checks along the way to assure that each step is learned (Schulman, 2001). It is important to ensure that students are well-trained in the fundamentals to the extent that they can eventually consider some problems with high-level complexity. We pay extra care to design the teaching and learning activities to incorporate stepwise learning.

Students taking computer programming courses very often come with various backgrounds and ability levels. The PASS system allows us to design exercises with different levels of difficulty to fulfil the need of students with various backgrounds and ability levels.

To illustrate the idea, we take the programming exercise of solving a quadratic equation as a running example (Figure 2). We have created a number of test cases, which are grouped into three levels of difficulty, namely, the beginner level, intermediate level and advanced level (Figure 3). The equations which have two distinct real roots are considered

---

A Programming Exercise of Solving a Quadratic Equation

Write a program to solve a quadratic equation. The general form of a quadratic equation is $ax^2 + bx + c = 0$, where a, b, c are real numbers. When $a \neq 0$, the solution of the equation is given by the quadratic formula $x = \dfrac{-b \pm \sqrt{b^2 - 4ac}}{2a}$.

In this exercise, the user need to input the value of a, b and c, then the program will output the answers accordingly. We assume that all the inputs are integers, and that the outputs are to be displayed in ascending order with 2 decimal point precision.

Fig. 2. Programming Exercise of "Quadratic Equation"

Test Cases of Quadratic Equation Programming Exercise

(a) Test Cases at the Beginner Level of Difficulty

Input	Expected Output
$a = 1, b = -5, c = 6$	$x = 3, 2$
$a = 2, b = -7, c = -15$	$x = 5, -1.5$
$a = 1, b = 6, c = 8$	$x = -2, -4$

(b) Test Cases at the Intermediate Level of Difficulty

Input	Expected Output
$a = 1, b = -2, c = 1$	$x = 1$
$a = 1, b = 2, c = 5$	$x = -1+2i, -1-2i$
$a = 2, b = 12, c = 18$	$x = -3$

(c) Test Cases at the Advanced Level of Difficulty

Input	Expected Output
$a = 0, b = 2, c = 4$	$x = -2$
$a = 0, b = 0, c = 0$	$x =$ any real numbers
$a = 0, b = 0, c = -4$	No solution

Fig. 3. Test cases of quadratic equation programming exercise at different levels of difficulty

relatively easier; and therefore we classify the corresponding test cases as at the beginner level (Figure 3a). The test cases which correspond to quadratic equations with one re-peated root or two complex roots are classified as at theintermediate level (Figure 3b). The exceptional cases (such as those corresponding to the cases when the equations be-come linear or identities) are classified as at the advanced level (Figure 3c).

The PASS system allows us to tell the students the level of difficulty of each exer-cise (Figure 4). For the same problem, students can attempt the exercises based on their capability. For example, the less talented students may design a simple program to solve the problem at the beginner level of difficulty (Figure 5a). If they submit their programs to attempt exercises at other levels of difficulty, they will fail in those test cases (Figure 5b). Instead, they must enhance their programs in order to solve the problem at the intermediate level of difficulty.

Unit	Prob. No.	Problem difficulty	Prob. Type
Quadratic Equation	Beginner Level	☆☆	Practice
Quadratic Equation	Intermediate Level	☆☆☆☆	Practice
Quadratic Equation	Advanced Level	☆☆☆☆☆ ☆☆	Practice

Fig. 4. Programming exercises at different levels of difficulty

No.	Input	Annotation	Expected Output	Actual Output	Result
0	1 -5 6		2.00, 3.00	2.00, 3.00	Accepted
1	2 -7 -15		-1.50, 5.00	-1.50, 5.00	Accepted
2	1 6 8		-4.00, -2.00	-4.00, -2.00	Accepted

(a) A Sample Run of Submission to an Exercise at the Beginner Level of Difficulty

No.	Input	Annotation	Expected Output	Actual Output	Result
0	1 -5 6		2.00, 3.00	2.00, 3.00	Accepted
1	2 -7 -15		-1.50, 5.00	-1.50, 5.00	Accepted
2	1 6 8		-4.00, -2.00	-4.00, -2.00	Accepted
3	1 -2 1		1.00	1.00, 1.00	Wrong Answer
4	1 2 5		-1.00-2.00i, -1.00+2.00i	Runtime error 207 at $00401115 $00401115 $0040123E	Wrong Answer
5	2 12 18		-3.00	-3.00, -3.00	Wrong Answer

(b) A Sample Run of Submission to an Exercise at the Intermediate Level of Difficulty

Fig. 5. Exercises at different levels of difficulty and sample runs of submissions in PASS

However, the talented students may work directly to solve the problem at the intermediate level of difficulty. They can even try to challenge the exceptional test cases by submitting their programs to solve the problem at the advanced level of difficulty. Eventually, they should come up with a single program which can solve the problem up to a certain level of difficulty. This approach allows the students to regulate their own learning pace. Additionally, we may require students to study the given test cases for each exercise to figure out how we select the test cases so as to learn how to test their programs on their own.

4 Incremental Style of Programming Activity

Traditional programming courses focus on the development of small applications. Without the support of related technology, students usually develop small applications by writing the code solely on their individual effort. The student may become an analyst programmer in the future and may be involved in some large scale projects.

Students often find it difficult to manage large software development jobs when they work in the industry. It is very important to provide students with experiences of software development in large scale applications while they are studying.

However, there are practical difficulties to require students to develop a large application. First of all, students' learning motivation drops very fast as the time they have to spend on study increases. If we require the students to code a large application, they are usually unable to see their results before the completion of the whole application. They will lose their interests in programming soon after they started. Lack of motivation is one of the major resistances to learning (Atherton, 1999). As we foresee the need, we consider large application development as an essential part of an advanced programming course. Some special arrangements have to be made to keep the students' learning motivation.

When we design a large application, we may divide the application into several modules. After the student has completed one module of the application, he/she can submit the modules to PASS. Some stubs or test drivers can be provided for testing their individual modules. It is important to reinforce the student's success upon his/her completion of one module. This approach also increases the student's confidence in learning. The intermediate results can keep students' learning motivation constantly high. The students will develop the application in a progressive manner. After the students have completed the entire application, they can submit it to PASS, which will test all the modules together as a single integrated application.

This approach highlights the modularity of computer programs. The students are exposed to programs that are built from modules so that they learn the concept of modularity of program by implicit learning (Berry, 1997). When developing an application, students will have to divide their solutions into modules as functions and classes.

Moreover, we require the students to archive all the files developed in their activities. When designing a programming activity, we intentionally require the students to make use of some modules developed in previous activities. For example, we may require students to develop a program to solve a quadratic inequality (Figure 6) based on the module developed earlier in the programming exercise of solving a quadratic equation (Figure 3).

Similarly, as before, we create exercises at different levels of difficulty (Figure 7). The least talented students can solve the inequality by using their simple programs that solve a quadratic equation, while the talented students can try some challenging test cases such as when the quadratic inequality has one solution or no solution. In this way, students will naturally acquire the concept of code reuse through their own experience of reusing the previously developed code, as concrete experience is important in the learning cycle (Kolb, 1984).

On the other hand, we sometimes ask students to exchange files and develop their applications based on modules written by other students. This gives students some experiences how to collaborate with other students. It prepares the students to work as a team member in a large project development team in the future. Moreover, the students need to ensure that their program depends fully on the program interface, so that their programs can work properly with the modules developed with other students.

A Programming Exercise of Solving a Quadratic Inequality

Write a program to solve a quadratic inequality based on the module you developed earlier in the programming exercise of solving a quadratic equation. In general, a quadratic inequality can be written in one of the following standard forms, where a, b, c are real numbers:

$$ax^2 + bx + c \geq 0$$
$$ax^2 + bx + c > 0$$
$$ax^2 + bx + c \leq 0$$
$$ax^2 + bx + c < 0$$

Suppose that the equation $ax^2 + bx + c = 0$ has two real roots x_1 and x_2, where $x_1 < x_2$. If $a > 0$, the solution sets of the inequalities are, respectively, as follows.

Inequality: $ax^2 + bx + c \geq 0$. Solution: $(-\infty, x_1] \cup [x_2, +\infty)$

Inequality: $ax^2 + bx + c > 0$. Solution: $(-\infty, x_1) \cup (x_2, +\infty)$

Inequality: $ax^2 + bx + c \leq 0$. Solution: $[x_1, x_2]$

Inequality: $ax^2 + bx + c < 0$. Solution: (x_1, x_2)

Fig. 6. A programming exercise based on a previously completed module

Unit	Prob. No.	Problem difficulty	Prob. Type
Quadratic Inequality	Beginner Level	☆☆☆	Practice
Quadratic Inequality	Intermediate Level	☆☆☆☆☆	Practice
Quadratic Inequality	Advanced Level	☆☆☆☆☆☆☆☆	Practice

Fig. 7. Programming exercises of "Quadratic Inequality"

5   Evaluation of the New Pedagogy

The new pedagogy is first developed for teaching computer programming courses in 2006. There are a number of differences between the new pedagogy with the old one. The most major change is the design of the programming exercises. The current programming activities are designed in incremental manner with multiple levels of difficulty. However, the exercises in the old design are disjoint from each other, and there is only one level in terms of difficulty.

The PASS system is currently used during tutorial class. The teacher assigns some programming exercises to the students. The student selects the difficult level of the exercises to attempt according to their capability. Moreover, some less talent students are unable to complete the tutorial exercises during tutorial session. These students can return home to continue their works. The system will be able to provide assistance to them even after school. As the system stores some patterns of common mistake, the system will give some pre-stored hints to the students if any of the patterns is identified.

The students taking programming courses are assessed by coursework and final examinations. The coursework is usually in the format of programming assignments, and the final examination is in the format of written examinations. We have compared the results of the students before and after the implementation of new pedagogy.

We have selected a typical programming course at the introductory level (Table 1). Because the class size of this course is very large, the statistical information of this course is worthy trusted. On the other hand, the materials of assessment are moderated by peer review to ensure the standard of assessment. No scaling of score has been conducted in this course. The score boundary for each grade has been fixed by the department. As a result, this graded distribution of students is a very important indicator to show the performances of teaching and learning.

Table 1. Statistics of a Computer Programming Course

		Year 2004	Year 2005	Year 2006
Total no. of students		277	253	251
Grade	Score Boundary	% of Students	% of Students	% of Students
A	69.5	7.94%	7.11%	26.00%
B	54.5	16.25%	17.79%	22.40%
C	39.5	35.38%	23.72%	23.60%
D	34.5	9.75%	12.65%	4.80%
F	below 34.5	30.69%	38.74%	23.20%

In years 2004 and 2005, only a small percentage of students got grade "A", while a large percentage of students failed the course in these two years (Table 1). After the new pedagogy was implemented in year 2006, the percentage of grade "A" students increased dramatically from 7~8% to 26% (Table 1). At the same time, the percentage of failure decreased significantly. As shown in the table, the students' performances in the programming course increase significantly. This is a strong evidence to show the success of the new pedagogy.

A focus group session has been held with students who enrolled in computer programming courses. A set of interview questions are designed by professionals in education development. The students are interviewed by an independent interviewer and none of the course lecturers were presented. All the students in the focus group believe that the new pedagogy can help them to learn programming courses more effectively. Few responses are extracted as examples:

Student 1:   The programming assignment with different levels is a fresh idea. I can control my learning pace.

Student 2:   *My fellow classmates teach me a lot. They know clearly of*
            my problem.
Student 3:   *Eventually, I can develop a computer game by myself.*

The preliminary results of interview show a positive feedback from the students. In order to get a more quantitative measurement for the course structure of programming courses, we have conducted a survey by questionnaires. The questionnaires are designed by professionals in education development in the similar way as (Harding, Kaczynski, & Wood, 2005). The students are asked to score each dimension of the course structure on the scale from 0 to 10, where a score of 10 represents the highest satisfaction, while 0 represents the least satisfaction. 50 students have participated in the survey. The results are summarized as Table 2.

Table 2. Evaluation of Course Design for a Computer Programming Course

Questions	Average Score
The PASS system is useful to my study of computer programming.	7.8
The PASS system helps me to have comprehensive testing of program.	8.2
I like the programming activity with different levels of difficulty.	8.1
I like the programming activity with incremental style.	7.3
The peer learning scheme is useful to my study.	7.8
The course design helps me to control my learning pace.	6.8
The course helps me to identify weakness.	7.5
The course encourages collaborations between students.	7.6
The course is effective in learning computer programming.	7.4

In Table 2, we can clearly see that the students are highly satisfied with the course structure. The students are happy with the flexibilities provided by the new pedagogy. They help the students to identify their weakness and control their own learning paces. Therefore, the students can learn computer programming effectively. Summing the above up, the new pedagogy is a good teaching and learning model for computer programming.

6 Conclusion

This paper has shared our experiences in design of teaching and learning activities for computer programming with large class size. By designing exercises at different levels of difficulty, we provide stepwise learning experiences to students, such that they can solve problems pertaining to their corresponding ability levels. Teachers can also define problems in various ways in PASS so as to make students familiar with modules programming and be prepared for large projects. The interviews have shown that new pedagogy is very effective in teaching and learning computer programming. The students' performances in the assessments have further confirmed our findings.

References

1. Anderson, J.R., Skwarecki, E.: The automated tutoring of introductory computer programming. Communications of the ACM 29(9), 842–849 (1986)
2. Atherton, J.S.: Resistance to learning: A discussion based on participants in in-service professional training programmes. Journal of Vocational Education and Training 51(1), 77–90 (1999)
3. Berry, D.C. (ed.): How Implicit is Implicit Learning. Oxford University Press, Oxford (1997)
4. du Boulay, B.: Some difficulties of learning to program. In: Soloway, E., Spohrer, J.C. (eds.) Studying the novice programmer. L. Erlbaum Associates, Hillsdale, N.J (1989)
5. Cheang, B., Kurnia, A., Lim, A., Oon, W.-C.: On automated grading of programming assignments in an academic institution. Computers & Education 41(2), 121–131 (2003)
6. Choy, M., Nazir, U., Poon, C.K., Yu, Y.T.: Experiences in using an automated system for improving students' learning of computer programming. In: Lau, R., Li, Q., Cheung, R., Liu, W. (eds.) ICWL 2005. LNCS, vol. 3583, pp. 267–272. Springer, Heidelberg (2005)
7. Choy, M., Lam, S., Poon, C.K., Wang, F.L., Yu, Y.T., Yuen, L.: Design and Implementation of an Automated System for Assessment of Computer Programming Assignment. In: Leung, H., Li, F., Lau, R., Li, Q. (eds.) ICWL 2007. LNCS, vol. 4823, pp. 584–596. Springer, Heidelberg (2008)
8. Harding, A., Kaczynski, D., Wood, L.N.: Evaluation of blended learning: analysis of qualitative data. In: Proceedings of the Symposium of Blended Learning in Science Teaching & Learning, 28th-30th September, pp. 56–62. The University of Sydney, Australia (2005)
9. Kolb, D.A.: Experiential Learning: Experience as the Source of Learning and Development. Prentice-Hall, New Jersey (1984)
10. Schulman, M.: Basic understandings for developing learning media for the classroom and beyond. Learning Technology Newsletter 3(1) (2001)
11. Sleeman, D.: The Challenges of teaching computer programming. Communication of the ACM 29(9), 840–841 (1986)
12. Yu, Y.T., Poon, C.K., Choy, M.: Experiences with PASS: Developing and using a programming assignment assessment system. In: Proceedings of the 6th International Conference on Quality Software (QSIC 2006), pp. 360–365. IEEE Computer Society Press, Los Alamitos (2006)

The Strategy and Practice of Blended Learning in Open and Distance Learning: Experiences from GDRTVU

Jun Le

Information Network Center, Guangdong Radio & TV University,
Xiatangxi Road 1, Guangzhou, 510091, P.R. of China
lejun@gdrtvu.edu.cn

Abstract. In this paper we introduce our experiences of blended learning for open and distance learning in our university in recent years. We form our basic philosophies to implementing blended learning and make one blended learning system with 10 subsystems, which is consisted of online learning environment, instruction design, interaction, space, time, curriculum, learning material, community of practice, instruction behaviour, and learning support service. We analyse their components and roles based on system theory, distance education theory, virtual learning community, instruction design, network flow measurement, and feedback information analysis method. We give some practical strategies, which include knowing and analysing our learners' characters, getting and analysing the feedback information, making compensated instruction dynamically, providing support services for different needs, integrating learning materials, forming virtual learning community, and introducing knowledge management. We also give a few cases.

Keywords: blended learning, distance learning, online learning environment, instruction design.

1 Introduction

Blended learning or hybrid learning has emerged in higher education for a few years, which combines online and face-to-face (F2F) instruction [1]. As a new delivery mechanism, it can bring effective learning, increase access and flexibility, and reduce cost [2][3]. But people today have to meet many complex challenges in the adaptive process in higher education [4][5].

For distance education institutes, some challenges come from the external socio-culture contexts and they add complexity of blended learning [6][7][8][9]. Few successful cases only give us finite solutions in special environments [10].

From the standpoints of pedagogy and effectiveness of technology application, the designers of blended learning should be seeking best practices for how to combine instructional strategies in F2F and e-learning environments that take advantages of the strengths of each environment and avoid their weaknesses in varied contexts [11]. Like many other design problems, people can make some different solutions based on different contexts.

J. Fong, R. Kwan, and F.L. Wang (Eds.): ICHL 2008, LNCS 5169, pp. 294–303, 2008.

In China, the Chinese RTVU system is a national organization system to provide open and higher distance education. The organizational structure has three levels that parallel the government administration structure. Central Radio & TV University is in the top and produces curriculums and learning materials, makes unified examinations. Guangdong Radio & TV University (GDRTVU) is in the middle level of the system and has 89 branch schools in Guangdong province. It implements instruction, makes supplementary materials, appoints and trains teachers, and provides support services. The branch schools recruit tutors and provide some learning support services in F2F.

Now the university is in the evolutionary process of blended learning. Here we introduce our experiences in practice from the point of view of GDRTVU.

2 Blended Learning System Analysis

Before 1999, the university used transmission ways of television, videotape, audiotape, correspondence and F2F for distance learning. Pedagogy is teacher-centered and class-based.

Since 1999, the university has been trying to make a new blended delivery way by information and communication technology (ICT). ICT application for open and distance learning (ODL) in the university is based on cost, access, effectiveness and service for teaching and learning.

2.1 Basic Philosophy for Blended Learning

Blended learning means different things to different institutes in practice. The university thinks that is a combination of multiple elements including mixed the learners' characters, delivery ways, learning theories, technologies and other educational resources.

The motive to implement blended learning for the university comes from different dimensions of learner, teacher, government, society, technology, and culture. These factors drive the university jointly to make use of blended learning.

Our trial goal is that develops a learner-centered blended learning mode for ODL step by step, which integrates the sociocultural factors, ICT, the university resources and the learner need.

2.2 System Component

Valiathan put blended learning into skill-driven model, attitude-driven model, and competency-driven model [12]. Graham [3] divided the interaction in the environment into four critical dimensions: space, time, fidelity, and Humanness.

From the view of general system theory, the process of implementing blended learning in one institute can be considered as a system. For ODL, we think that one blended learning system in distance higher education is a complex system, and it includes ten subsystems: online learning environment, instruction design (ID), interaction, space, time, curriculum, learning material, community of practice, instructional behavior, and learning support service.

2.3 Online Learning Environment

We use three network platforms to serve our information transmission. The first is the national TV network, which is consisted of the star TV and city cable TV system, it offers television programs and IP data transmission services. The second is Internet, the university and the branch schools separately connect Internet with 100M or 10M.The last one is the intranet based on the campus network and VPN, it connects the branch schools based on IP/SDH and IP/MPLS with 100M or 10M backbone. The university provides main application services with concentrated way. The learners can use these networks to access the university.

Our basic online learning environment (OLE) includes the university portal, learning management system (LMS), content management system (CMS), web-based videoconference system, web live broadcast system, e-mentoring system, digital library and some public application tools. The OLE can provide learning resources and virtual spaces. We not only need to build a usable OLE, but also need to overcome existent digital divide in our condition.

E-monitoring system is an important part of the OLE. It is a base for improving blended learning and provides feedback information of the system. It monitors the operation of the OLE, the resources using and the learning behavior [13].

2.4 Learning Support Service

Distance learners usually have many difficulties and especially need individual learning support services. The main services are information, resource, people, interaction, technological establishment, tutoring assistance, counseling, and personal development.

Blended learning also has particular need for strong learning support and provides learners with capacity to interact with systems and persons in the learning process. Effective learning settings must involve some forms of learner support.

In a word, we need to help distance learners to overcome obstacles in blended learning process.

2.5 Interaction

Interaction is important and necessary in ODL. It has three kinds: learner to learner; learner to teacher, tutor, and service worker; learner to learning content. The interaction between learner and teacher is the most welcome, but it needs to make much more great efforts to get the same effect in OLE than in F2F. The interaction between learners is a challenge problem.

Moore thought that the depth of talk, the flexibleness of self-paced learning and the structure intension of the course design affect the learning efficiency. The ID needs to blend online, offline, interaction based on technology-based and F2F into the system. In our instructional process we need to hold interaction.

2.6 Space and Time

The space and time in ODL are separated relatively. We usually can't finish an interview in F2F with all learners of registering the same course in classroom. Only some learners from the same location may be able to take F2F learning. We divide the virtual space into a few dimensions by communication way such as BBS, IM, and online read. In each space the learnering behaviors are time involved.

2.7 Community of Practice

We need to finish many tasks with a team way. Teachers, lecturers, tutors, instructional designers, technicians, support service workers, experts, and learners can be organized to form a community of practice for distance learning. This can promote learners' blended learning.

2.8 Behavior Analysis and Instruction Design

The active instruction behaviors in the space and time can show the state of the technology system, the time and period of the interaction, the using rate of the learning materials, and the participant rate of learners.

Based on the feedback information from the e-monitoring system, we can discover the information and knowledge of quality, instructional effectiveness, and learning behavior characters in the system. Then we can control and improve the blended learning system. Analysing the learning behaviors in the OLE is one of the important activities in blended learning.

The ID needs to make some learning media resources for self-directed learning, interaction activities based on problem and group collaboration learning, and curriculum learning guidance, etc.

3 The Practice and Strategy

Based on above our analysis and understanding to our blended learning system, we set up some action strategies and introduce a few practical cases of the course instructions for adult ODL here.

3.1 Knowing and Analysing the Learners' Characters

The characters of adult distance learners are much complex and there are many differences [14]. Before our ID based on learner-centered, we have to know our learners' characters and consider them how to affect blended learning.

A basic learner character system should include the information about the basic population, physiology, psychology, sociology, geography, ICT infrastructure, e-learning skill, learning behavior, learning favor, motive and wish, and the view on ODL and learning material.

We made an investigation form which has 47 questions based on above information classifications. Before our ID and making learning resource, we need to get some data.

Case 1: In 2005, we took a questionnaire investigation for the 5149 learners from 4 subjects, 3 registered years (2002, 2003, 2004), and 3 kinds of regions. The 689 samples were chose in 12% scale and returned 551 valid forms. We got some statistic data.

Almost all learners have their jobs and the main reasons of choosing ODL are that learning is part-time and self-paced. About the relations between the subject and the work, 20.9% are the same, 45.9% are correlative, 23% are adjacent, 9.1% are not correlative.

About Internet access, 32.3% can use Internet in home and 10.9% in work place.29.4% are less 2 hours-online time in one week, 30.9% are in 2-4 hours, and 23.6% are in 4-6 hours. Only 4.4% can get 2 hours one day. Network speed, stability, virus, and cost affect learning efficiency.

3.6% are short of the ability of using computer and Internet. 17.2% need improvement. 4.5% don't know online learning method.

About delivery mode, 3.8% agree total online learning, 18.5% agree that online learning is in the majority and F2F is assistant, 31.9% agree that online is assistant and F2F learning is in the majority, 21.6% agree that F2F learning is in the majority, online and based-resource learning are assistant. The reasons for F2F are tradition learning habit, the need of social intercourse and getting support service in time.

68.7% like to use different ways to talk with others, such as phone, email, MSN (QQ), mobile SM, BBS and F2F.

About learning materials, 31.4% like printing, 32.3% like multimedia, 4.5% like television program, 22% like integration of different media materials.

The data show the learners' characters and preferences are multiplex, most of them like to blended learning mode. If we want to hold our instructional philosophy and make use the advantages of blended learning, our ID system and the instructional processes have to satisfy their needs. The learners also drove us to adapt blended learning. The following cases show us how to adapt these new changes.

3.2 Getting and Analysing the Feedback Information of the OLE

We apply the tools of IP flow measurement, Sniffer, MRTG, and AWStats system to build a traffic-based monitoring system, and get some feedback information about the utilization of the web resources by IP flow function.

The online time, interactive time, media-based material use rate, people number and the involved learning contents are four kinds of critical data. Four mathematical functions are introduced that describes the learning behavior with above four variables and time variables. Dynamical system, statistics, and data cluster methods are applied for modeling [15].

These data can help us discover some information whether the materials are designed well, how many learners take part in interactive talk in BBS or hold self-paced online learning, and attention degrees on some topic in BBS, etc.

We define a real time traffic flow measurement function based on the IP flow. The function can be described online rate and attention degree on material or interaction.

Case 2: By the data clustering on the traffic flow data of visiting the LMS and the CMS from the March to the May in 2005, we find that learners' online time distribution. The learner numbers are the most in the time from 20 o'clock to 22 o'clock. The other online time are from 9 o'clock to 11 o'clock, from 15 o'clock to 17 o'clock. In these time tutors easily organize their online learning activity.

By the webpage clicking number and byte-based IP flow number, we also find that the most interested materials for the learners in the course, "Tax and Accountant", are multimedia coursewares.

3.3 Making Compensated Instruction Dynamically

Generally traditional ID models have "modifying teaching" module. The modifications rely on formative assess, like the famous Dick & Carey's model. Here we modify the blended learning system based on the dynamical feedback information from the system and make compensated instruction in the process.

The modification process of the ID system has 8 steps:

1. Evaluate requirement and make sure compensated teaching goal.
2. Analyze feedback information, learner's character and goal error.
3. Write instruction goal and content, construct online community.
4. Develop teaching and learning tactic.
5. Select media resource, design interaction.
6. Design formative assess.
7. Finish formative assess, collect feedback information.
8. Finish summarization assess.

Case 3: For the course, "Tax and Accountant", from the time of 10:47, March 3, 2006 to the time of 14:30, March 3, 2006, the feedback information in the BBS shows that learners' questions are different. Based on the web text analysis, we can get the following data table:

Table 1. The knowledge classiffication of the questions

Question & Number	Technology & Resource	Learning Method	Preparative Knowledge	Course Content	Profession Development
Total	4	2	2	9	4
Question Click	22.5	17	30	22	13.75
Reply Click	21.25	10.5	25.5	14.44	15.5

Based on the clicking numbers of learners and knowledge classifications, we chose corresponding pedagogical tactics for different groups: adding learning case materials, reinforcing self-paced learning material, guiding group to finish collaborative learning tasks, amending navigation, replying the problems individually by email and BBS, and holding few online lectures.

3.4 Providing Support Services for Different Needs

We not only provide some support services for different groups, but also pay attention to learners whose need are special and give individual support in time.

Case 4: One learner in the course "Tax and Accountant", his name was Alex200406, asked one question about the new change of The Chinese Value-Added Tax Regulation on 21:51:49, November 28, 2005. The question led enthusiastic talks during following two days in the community. 53 learners read the question, 33 learners answer the question. Follow on, he gave another correlative question, then 79 learners read it, 50 learners answer. In last, he gave anther correlative question and also got satisfaction answer. This time 35 learners read the question, 25 learners answered. This group inter-active behaviors showed that some learners were short of the knowledge.

For response to the group needs, we made two new learning cases in multimedia and gave two online lectures in webcast. In one week there are 182 learners to use these resources. In the end test of the term, 85% participants could apply the method to solve some practical problems.

Case 5: In the course, "Information Management Theory", 48 learners registered the course in Guangzhou, two of them had never been able to attend the F2F lecture or synchronous network talk, because of their works in nighttime. But our lectures were often arranged in daytime in the weekends and online talks were arranged in the nighttime for most learners. The teachers had to provide advices for each one by email or BBS. They passed the course in the end of the term.

3.5 Integrating Learning Materials

For one course, we usually arrange learning in F2F for about 30% contents and give live webcast in the same time. We also make them as digital resources in the CMS. The F2F teaching mode includes teacher-center lecture and learner-centered lecture, learning in practice, discussion, and seminars, etc.

For each course in blended learning, we generally make some learning materials based on digital media for self-directed learning. They maybe are problem-based, context-based, or case-based. Multimedia coursewares are often short and small for depth learning and self-directed learning.

Sometime we provide network-based self-test exercises and some open resources from Internet. Before that we often select adaptive materials and amend them to ac-cord with learners' needs.

Case 6: In the course, "Tax and Accountant", we provide 9 small multimedia coursewares for self-experiment, every one runtime does not exceed 5 minutes. The problems come from former many learners' wrong practices. 90% learners have read the materials. After that the later learners were able to solve the problems by using the materials.

3.6 Forming Virtual Learning Community

The basic framework for the virtual learning community in online setting is our good reference [16]. It is consisted of teachers, instruction designers, technicians, tutors and learners of learning the same course or subject. Sometime we maybe invite a few experts to attend our community activities.

Some tactics are effective for the vigor of the community:

1. Finding some protagonists.
2. Encouraging all learners to participate interaction by formative asses.
3. Making quick response to learners.
4. Talking between teacher and learner equally.
5. Designing value discussion topic from their work experiences.
6. Trying problem-based group collaborative learning.

Response to learners by interaction and designing the public topics by the teachers are the most important factors for the community. Here we also introduce a web2.0-based tool, called as the My Campus Space (MCS), to help to form some online learning communities from the course forum in BBS.

If it is possible, we arrange one tutor online to answer questions. Most of the questions can be solved during 24 hours. The community for the course, "Tax and Accountant", is the most welcome. The 80% learners had become the members of the community.

3.7 Introducing Knowledge Management

Knowledge management (KM) and distance education share some common elements such as knowledge sharing and knowledge creation. The distance education institutes can use the potential energy of KM to enhance learning and improve management efficiency.

Our basic KM goals are to share knowledge in the community, to improve support service, and to enrich the repository of the digital media resource for the course.

Some steps, programs, and strategies are applied to our work [17][18][19]. Data mining techniques and web-based text analysis methods are also applied to our knowledge discovery.

In the application process, we discover that some good questions are from the work experiences of some experienced learners, their social intercourse, the subjects of self-directed learning, and challenges in the professional development. The questions and their advices often attract some other learners' attentions. These can enrich the repository in the community.

Learning behavior can happen in the work and the social context. Our teachers and technicians need to help to transform the tacit knowledge to the explicit knowledge in the community by recording, collecting, dealing and presenting their individual information, problems and experiences. These tacit knowledges are especially useful to some learners which are short of similar experiences.

In fact, the problems in the case 6 are based on our discovery form accumulating information in the blended learning system. This is a typical KM application.

3.8 The Effect Analysis and Challenge

Although we are short of a systematic assessment method to the practice, we try to show some successful works. We take above cases and the course "Tax and Accountant" as example. The assessive method is based on the formative assessing and the term examination. If one can not pass because of lower examination score, we give one makeup in the same year. From the following table, we know that our instruction effects have been improving gradually since 2003.

Table 2. The pass rate of the learners from 2003-2006

Year	Total Registration Num.	Accepted Assessing Num.	Pass Num.	Pass Rate
2006	13545	1231	1168	91.18%
2005	966	918	826	89.98%
2004	542	510	399	78.24%
2003	591	567	362	63.84%

In one questionnaire investigation for 2813 graduates based on 5 subjects in 2005,the usable return forms have 546.We use 5 level satisfactional degree. The satisfactional rate for the instructional effect is 84.49%; The satisfactional rate for the instructional mode is 80.1%; The satisfactional rate for the instructional resource is 76.66%. The satisfactional rate for the skill of self-directed learning is only 6.6%,it is much lower.

From the investigation and our practice, the challenges are much more. Such factors as the learning resources, the tutors professional development, the skills of self-directed learning, and learning support service have been affecting the effect of blended learning.

4 Conclusion

Blended learning in ODL is a complex system with the integration of different medium, delivery methods, learning theories, instruction strategies, course knowledge, and support services. Distance higher institutes can apply blended learning to improve learning for open and distance learners and to enhance organization management efficiency. Since the factors are depended on the contexts, people maybe find some different solutions.

In order to implement blended learning for ODL, the teachers, support service workers and their institute have to meet many new challenges from the university, ICT application and socio-cultural contexts.

In here, our trials are not systematical and are short of assessment, but we have been able to improve ODL efficiency in some degree for our adult and distance learners. We will continue to research some problems further in the future.

References

1. Young, J.: Hybrid Teaching Seeks to End the Divide Between Traditional and Online Instruction. Chronicle of Higher Education 48(28), A33 (2002)
2. Lorenzetti, J.: Lessons Learned About Student Issues in Online Learning. Distance Education Report 9(6), 1–4 (2005)
3. Bonk, C.J., Graham, C.R.: Handbook of Blended Learning: Global Perspectives, Local Designs. Pfeiffer Publishing, San Francisco (2005)
4. Draffan, E.A., Rainger, P.: A Model for the Identification of Challenges to Blended Learning. ALT-J, Research in Learning Technology 14(1), 55–67 (2006)
5. Norman, V.: Perspectives on Blended Learning in Higher Education. International Journal on E-Learning 6(1), 81–94 (2007)
6. Moore, M.G., Kearsley, G.: Distance Education: A Systems View. Wadsworth Publishing Company, Belmont (1996)
7. Tony Bates, A.W.: Technology, E-Learning and Distance Education, 2nd edn. Routledge (2005)
8. Murphy, D., Carr, R., Taylor, J., Wong, T.M.: Distance Education and Technology: Issues and Practice. Open University of Hong Kong Press (2004)
9. Daniel, J.: Mega-University and Knowledge Media: Technology Strategies for Higher Education. Shanghai Higher Education Electrical Media Press (2003)

10. Kaur, A.: Blended Learning: Developing a Mix for Open University Malaysia. In: Bonk, C.J., Graham, C.R. (eds.) Handbook of Blended Learning: Global Perspectives, Local Designs, pp. 311–324. Pfeiffer Publishing, San Francisco (2005)
11. Martyn, M.: The Hybrid Online Model: Good Practice. Educause Quarterly 26(1), 18–23 (2003)
12. Valiathan, P.: Blended Learning Models (2002), http://www.learningcircuits.org/2002/aug2002/valiathan.html
13. Le, J.: Measurement and Analysis of Web-based Behavior Information in Distance Education. Distance Education in China 9, 65–68 (2006)
14. Qi, H., Le, J.: The Theory and Application of Feedback Information in Distance Instruction. Chinese Radio & Television University Press (2006)
15. Le, J., Qi, H.: Analysis and Application for Online Learning Feedback Information in Distance Education. Distance Education in China 9, 61–65 (2006)
16. McMurray, D.W.: The Psychological Dimension of Communities of Practice and their Relation to Online Learning. In: Proceedings of Third Pan-Commonwealth Forum on Open Learning, Dunedin, NZ, pp. 1903–1906 (July 2004)
17. Neil, B.: Knowledge Management Strategies for Distance Education. In: Proceeding of the Fourth Pan-Commonwealth Forum on Open Learning, Ocho Rios (2003)
18. Ranjit, P.: Knowledge Management and Online Education. In: Proceedings of the International Conference on Open and Online Learning 2003, University of Mauritius, Mauritius (2003)
19. Simon, W.: 12 Steps to a Successful KM Program. Knowledge Management Review 9(4) (September/October 2006)

Assessing the Effectiveness of Mobile Learning in Large Hybrid/Blended Classrooms

Minjuan Wang[1,2], Daniel Novak[1], and Ruimin Shen[2]

[1] Educational Technology, San Diego State University
[2] E-Learning Lab, Shanghai Jiao Tong University
mwang@mail.sdsu.edu, danielnovak@daniel-novak.com,
rmshen@sjtu.edu.cn

Abstract. This article describes a method we created to evaluate the impact of mobile learning on a large hybrid/blended computer science classroom of 562 students (about 90% being online). The impact of the mLearning system and learning activities is evaluated through pre- and post-surveys and from four aspects: 1) if student enjoyed the learning experience, 2) how students feel about interacting with fellow learners, 3) how students felt about their relationship to their instructors in the mobile blended learning environment, and 4) mobile blended classroom's effects on students' study habits. Cluster analysis is used to measure the validity of the surveys we used in this evaluation study. The cluster analysis confirms the validity of the survey results and also corroborates the statistical evidence of mLearning's positive influence on learning outcomes.

Keywords: Case study, interactivity in blended classrooms, mobile learning system, active learning, engaged learning, persuasive technology, mobile learning evaluation.

1 Introduction

Chinese classrooms, whether on school grounds or online, have long suffered from a lack of interactivity. Many online classes simply provide recorded instructor lectures to which students listen after downloading. This format only reinforces the negative effects of passive non-participatory learning. At Shanghai Jiaotong University (SJTU), researchers and developers actively seek technologic interventions that can greatly increase interactivity in the blended classes of their Online College. They developed a mobile learning system that can deliver live broadcasts of real-time classroom teaching to students with mobile devices.

The College's core philosophy concerning distance education is "learning anytime, anywhere." All lectures and activities that go on in a campus classroom are digitized simultaneously and broadcasted online, similar to online video programs and vodcasts (video podcast). Students can tune into live broadcasts or view archived videos of lectures online. However, the live broadcast system does not yet provide fully interactive venues. Distance students cannot ask questions or participate in any class

J. Fong, R. Kwan, and F.L. Wang (Eds.): ICHL 2008, LNCS 5169, pp. 304–315, 2008.

activities. The mLearning system recently implemented aims to promote active learning in large blended classrooms (more than 1000 students).

The use of mLearning in this college represents an attempt to encourage students' active participation in the learning process, and to engage them in constructivist learning through social and intellectual interactions. For the purposes of this paper, 'mLearning' refers to education and communication during class through mobile phones. Through adapting the current curriculum for interactive teaching and learning, researchers and developers in the E-Learning lab hope to set an example for pedagogic changes in China's system of higher education.

Successful trials indicate that the potential benefits of mobile learning will change the nature of the classroom, providing that instructional designers implement the devices effectively. For example, mobile learning currently enables researchers and students to bring the classroom into the field by enabling easy note-taking and audio/video recordings [1]. The ubiquity of mobile devices themselves further promises to accelerate the use of non-PC based digital learning, and to free students from the traditional classroom/field model.

The experiments reported in our study attempt to discover how much Chinese learners (who likely own cell phones and palm-top devices but rarely respond in the physical classroom) benefited from the mobile learning activities, to what degree students accept mobile learning as an instructional option, and how designers and instructors can better involve students in mobile learning activities.

1.1 Measuring Mobile Success

The penetration rates of internet-capable cell phones, personal digital assistants, and other handhelds and the data transmission rates of cellular networks increase with every passing quarter. As such, mobile learning (or, as some call it, mLearning) will play a greater role in classrooms in the coming decade. The question of how to measure the success and utility of this new technology will also appear, especially in today's results-oriented teaching culture.

Yet, how do we measure the quality and success of a program whose learners may never meet face to face? Anticipating this issue, John Traxler [2] identified nine qualities that any evaluation of a mLearning program must possess. Though these qualities do not provide proscriptive solutions to mLearning evaluation, they do offer some guidance. For example, Traxler asserts that evaluations must be consistent with the teaching and learning philosophy all the participants. He also notes that the evaluation must also be rigorous, efficient, appropriate to the specific learning technologies.. Another important factor is authenticity in terms of uncovering what learners really mean, really feel, really want from a learning environment.

However, Traxler [2] appears to mistrust system logs, participant observation, surveys, and questionnaire-based response, and ultimately mLearners as data sources on mLearning. In reference to those means of obtaining information, he notes:

"None of these elicitation techniques were particularly consistent with mobile learning technologies. And all accounts of such evaluations assumed that the evaluators were told the truth by subjects (that is, learners and teachers)..." (9).

In spite of this concern, researchers at SJTU decided to experiment with existing data about user experiences while participating in an mLearning project. The research team generated the questions for the questionnaire from 'common sense' concerns about the user's experience and from surveys used in past distance and e- learning surveys. This resulted in a focus on the end users' happiness and comfort in the virtual learning environment created by the mLearning classroom. The statistical consistency of the responses (indicated by a Cronbach Reliability Alpha of .95) indicates that either all learners lie equally, or that they have responded with some reasonable degree of 'truth.' From a positivist standpoint, this data proves statistically consistent and valid, and therefore provides a glimpse into the users' learning experience.

Using cluster analysis, a valid and oblique observational technique, researchers from San Diego State University collaborate with SJTU's E-Learning Lab to turn this data into a series of evaluative dimensions that measure student reception of the mLearning intervention. This responds to Traxler's concern about the inability of current techniques to describe mLearning phenomena. Cluster analyses often reveal obscured patterns of response that may not appear in more direct modes of statistical analysis. These evaluative dimensions, statistically valid but generated by mLearning data, will prove useful as researchers, administrators, and teachers gauge the usefulness and quality of their forays into the world of mobile learning.

Still, mLearning is slow in gaining traction in formal teaching and learning environments. The use of mobile learning in large blended classrooms is even less common. As such, researchers designed the surveys according to Traxler's principles of consistency, rigor, efficiency, appropriateness, and authenticity. Also, the survey questions conform to some of the recognized methods in evaluating online or distance learning [3] (Simonson, 1997). The survey collected both quantitative ratings and qualitative feedback, and thus balanced the traditional quantitative method [4] and more "modern" qualitative evaluation methods [3].

The survey questions are organized around the core issues that arise when evaluating distance learning: a) measures of activity, b) measures of efficiency, c) measures of outcomes, and d) measures of organization. In addition, the researchers also measured a few important constructs that don't fall into the aforementioned categories, such as student satisfaction, level of interaction (student-student, student-instructor), and sustainability of student participation in mLearning activities. Ample literature supports the idea that satisfaction is an important factor that affects learner choice of distance programs, as well as the high dropout rates associated with distance learning. Researchers also studied interaction because the mLearning systems at SJTU were designed to increase interaction in large classrooms.

2   M-Learning System and Its Implementation

2.1 System Function and Architecture

In a hybrid classroom at SJTU that is equipped with the mLearning system, instructors carry out multimedia instruction via a specialized station that supports handwriting on the computer screen, SMS messaging, and guided Internet use. Cameras and microphones that are connected to the computer capture live video of the classroom. A recording program, an integrated part of the mobile phone broadcasting sub-system, records all of these media components and relays them in customizable combinations to students.

During the class, the instructor station displays messages from campus and online students. It also reports their learning progress, their questions, and their feedback to the instruction. These messages are delivered as mobile phone text messages through a SMS (Short Message Service) protocol. To address these messages, the instructor can give oral explanations or reply through text-messages. In addition, this mobile learning system can also display the screen of any students' mobile device that are tuned into a live broadcast on a larger screen, allowing the instructor to supervise students' learning. The instructor can also take an instant poll on any aspect related to the instruction, including pace, clarity, content, and structure.

When the students connect their smart phones to the network, they can choose to view a live broadcast of the classroom. They can view it from the instructor's station (with the teacher's screen, audio, and a small video feed of the real-time classroom), from a 'virtual student' perspective (the video of the PowerPoint presentation and audio of the instructor), or from the 'front row' (close-up on the instructor's facial expressions and other body language). During the class, students can send short text messages to the instructor and participate in polls and other in-class activities. Thus, the instructors, students, and system administrators cooperate to create a blended classroom with real-time communications.

This model of mobile-supported hybrid learning can be used in many other classes. Students can use their mobile phones to send short text-messages to communicate with the instructor. The instructor can address these messages either by typing on the screen or giving an oral explanation that the entire class can see or hear.

2.2 Use of Mobile Learning in a Computer Science Class

This introductory computer science class teaches students a basic knowledge of computer science, Internet technologies, and the application of software in the business world. In this class, the instructor presented to both campus and online students at the same time. The computer system also archived videos of the course on the class's website for students to review at their convenience.

'Knowledge points,' or small, clearly defined units of knowledge or skills organize the class content. Knowledge points are an endemically Chinese mode of instructional design. While in some ways comparable to the American concept of instructional objectives, knowledge points do not necessarily require performance or demonstration of skills on the part of the learner. Rather, students listen to the knowledge points as delivered by the instructor, and are expected to remember them in detail at a later date.

In class, the instructor presented about the major knowledge points for that session. She then showed 10 multiple-choice questions on the computer screen. These questions allowed students to review the essential knowledge points that they should have learned from the instructor presentation. The instructor encouraged the students to answer these questions by sending text messages. She also presented real-world problems related to these knowledge points and encouraged students to discuss them through text messages.

3 Preliminary Survey

Researchers conducted a series of analyses to help determine how students respond to four major facets of the mobile learning system. Researchers explored these constructs (including satisfaction, interaction with content, social interaction, and effects on study habits) by using the raw data gathered from the survey. The survey's fifteen questions (translated into English from Chinese) appear in Table 1.

Table 1. Survey Questions (Translated from Chinese)

Question Number	Likert Scale (X-Y)	Question Text
1	1-4	Overall satisfaction with this class
2	1-5	The mLearning class was well organized
3	1-5	The course's activities were engaging
4	1-5	The activities strengthened my connections with my classmates.
5	1-5	The activities strengthened my connections with the instructor.
6	1-5	I had more opportunities to ask questions.
7	1-5	I had more opportunities to help my classmates.
8	1-5	I had more opportunities to practice what I learned.
9	1-5	Mobile learning helped me a great deal in studying the content of this class.
10	1-5	Mobile learning helped me grasp the course's main points.
11	1-5	Mobile learning changed my habit of studying alone
12	1-5	The modality of mLearn (words, audio, video) fits my learning style
13	1-5	I felt that my social skills have improved through the use of mobile learning.
14	1-5	I would like to recommend mobile learning to other students.
15	1-5	I would like to participate in future mLearn activities.

Researchers composed the survey to gather data relating to a number of practical questions. First, researchers wanted to determine if students enjoyed the mobile learning experience. If students did not enjoy participating in mobile learning activities, then developers may need to consider future design changes. Second, researchers hoped to gain insight into how students felt about interactions with fellow learners via the mobile classroom. This sought to address the concern that students may feel isolated or disconnected from one another. Third, researchers asked a number of questions concerning how students felt about their relationship to their professors in the mobile learning environment. In the Chinese classroom, students sometimes feel distanced or separated from their professors.

The Researchers wanted to know if the mobile environment affects student-instructor interactions. Fourth, researchers asked questions about the mobile classroom's effects on students' study habits and their ability to learn from the online system.

The survey yielded 245 unique responses from mobile learning students in this hybrid computer science course. This sample constitutes an adequate number of responses to represent a given university's population, and presents a rich source of data to mine. This data presents an opportunity to create a high quality metric system that can help future students, researchers, administrators, and faculty determine if mobile learning meets their needs.

4 Methods

Researchers determined that, by excluding demographic data, they could use the above survey to create a high-quality metric that could be used to generate future surveys and evaluations of mobile learning. A cluster analysis was conducted (based on the Pearson Correlation) to identify patterns amongst the scores. These similarities confirm that the constructs incorporated into the survey emerge in the results, and can therefore be measured in future surveys. The analysis that follows identifies some (though not necessarily all) of the important features of the mobile learning experience, and establishes ways to test them consistently. Ideally, future researchers will use the constructs identified in this paper to design surveys and evaluations that target mobile learning courses. These tests can also help future researchers determine if mobile learning performs as desired. Further, it represents a step towards the creation of a targeted and specific evaluation system for mLearning courses.

4.1 Cluster Analysis

Typically, researchers use cluster analysis to look for trends within large, unstructured surveys. This is an ideal strategy if one is looking for patterns amongst potentially linked ideas. The survey discussed in this paper is a Frankenstein's monster assembled from several different survey methodologies of varying ages and from varying media The questions and constructs were valid in their original contexts, but one cannot assume that they are valid when assembled into a different framework and applied to a different medium (mLearning). Therefore, a central concern of this study is confirmation that students responded to the *a priori* constructs that the researchers chose at the outset.

After this confirmation, the researchers hoped to identify new constructs by examining the clusters for patterns or missing features. This involved taking a close look at the patterns of response, and looking for larger patterns within the Finally, researchers hoped to identify ill-defined clusters or over-tested clusters, and thus refine the survey for future use. Table 2, generated by the statistical analysis software SPSS, clusters the questions into as few as 4 groups and as many as 9 using the Pearson Correlation method.

Table 2. Cluster Membership, using the Pearson Correlation

Case	9 Clusters	8 Clusters	7 **Clusters**	6 Clusters	5 Clusters	4 Clusters
Overall Course Satisfaction	1	1	**1**	1	1	1
mLearn was organized successfully.	2	2	**2**	2	2	2
The activities were engaging	3	3	**3**	3	3	3
The activities strengthend my connections with classmates	4	4	**4**	3	3	3
The activities strengthend my connections with the instructor.	5	5	**5**	4	4	3
I had more opportunities to ask questions.	5	5	**5**	4	4	3
I had more opportunities to help my classmates.	4	4	**4**	3	3	3
I had more opportunities to practice what I learned.	6	6	**6**	5	5	4
mLearn helped me a great deal in studying the content of this class.	7	7	**6**	5	5	4
mLearn helped me grasp the knowledge points.	7	7	**6**	5	5	4
mLearn changed my habit of studying alone	7	7	**6**	5	5	4
The modality of mLearn (words, audio, video) fits my learning style	8	8	**7**	6	5	4
I felt that my socialzing ability has improved.	9	8	**7**	6	5	4
I would like to recommend mLearn to other students.	8	8	**7**	6	5	4
I (very much) would like to participate in future mLearn activities.	8	8	**7**	6	5	4

After analyzing Table 2, researchers opted to use the seven-cluster breakdown. The four, five, and six cluster analysis created too few groups, and clustered several unrelated questions. The eight and nine cluster analysis created too many groups, and

Table 3. Questions Arranged by Cluster

Cluster – Cluster Title	Question Text (Translated from Chinese)	Likert Scale
Cluster 1 – Overall Satisfaction	Overall satisfaction with this class	1-4
Cluster 2 – Course Organization	The mLearning class was well organized	1-5
Cluster 3 – Course Activities	The course's activities were engaging	1-5
Cluster 4 – Student Interaction	The activities strengthened my connections with my classmates.	1-5
	I had more opportunities to help my classmates.	1-5
Cluster 5 – Instructor Interaction	The activities strengthened my connections with the instructor.	1-5
	I had more opportunities to ask questions.	1-5
Cluster 6 – Relationship to Content	I had more opportunities to practice what I learned.	1-5
	Mobile learning helped me a great deal in studying the content of this class.	1-5
	Mobile learning helped me grasp the course's main points.	1-5
	Mobile learning changed my habit of studying alone	1-5
Cluster 7 – Sustainability	The modality of mLearn (words, audio, video) fits my learning style	1-5
	I felt that my social skills have improved through the use of mobile learning.	1-5
	I would like to recommend mobile learning to other students.	1-5
	I would like to participate in future mLearn activities.	1-5

excluded thematically related questions from certain clusters. The seven-cluster method grouped most of the known constructs together, while revealing new and unexpected patterns in the questions. Table 3 shows the arrangement of questions by cluster.

5 Results

The above table lists the new and differentiated constructs that appeared within the original survey. Researchers noted certain important differences from their original research plan. For example, the questions in Cluster 1 (Overall Satisfaction) and Cluster 7 (Sustainability) were written with the belief that these questions measured related phenomena. The results of the cluster analysis indicate that a student's satisfaction and their willingness to participate in future mobile learning classes represent two different psychometric issues. Thus, survey researchers and school administrators must test for 'satisfaction' and 'sustainability' separately. Similarly, researchers wrote the survey believing that Clusters 2 (Course Organization) and 3 (Course Activities) represented the same construct. The cluster analysis shows that students consider these two survey questions representative of different phenomena.

Table 4, below, summarizes the evaluative dimensions and constructs that were revealed during this experiment, and their place in future research.

Table 4. Evaluative Dimensions and Explanations

Overall Satisfaction	A student's overall feeling of satisfaction after a course is as important in the mobile learning environment as in the classroom. If students do not feel satisfied, they will not continue taking mobile courses.
	Researchers and administrators should not ignore or discount the psychological importance of 'enjoyment' or 'satisfaction' in the classroom. These feelings enable learning.
Course Organization	Just as in a physical class, mobile learning students can lose focus if they feel that a course lacks direction. As such, surveys must ask whether students feel lost or confused by the course's direction.
	Both researchers and administrators stand to benefit from a close examination of students' feelings about course organization. Researchers can use this part of the survey to uncover substantive differences between the pedagogical organization of traditional and mobile classrooms. Administrators can use this portion to ensure that students are happy and are learning effectively.
Course Activities	The design of mLearning activities requires special attention to both the physical limitations of mobile devices (such as cellphones and personal digital assistants) and the psychological limitations and transactional distances of virtual communication.
	Designers and teachers must pay close attention to how their activities affect students. If one accepts that "the medium is the message," then one must design course activities that make full use of the affordances of the technology.
	As mobile learning courses develop, designers will need to work closely with administrators and research-hers to ask specific questions about learner preferences.

Table 4. (*continued*)

Student Interaction	The virtual world created by the mobile learning environment may isolate older learners while simultaneously engaging younger learners. Younger students (often called 'digital natives') feel comfortable in the virtual realities created by instant messaging, cellular telephone, and online games, while older learners (called 'digital immigrants') feel more comfortable in face-to-face environments. These questions can reveal how mixed-generation students feel about the content. Further, demographic information that researchers collect with the survey can reveal whether particular age groups feel alienated by (or comfortable in) the mobile learning environment.
Instructor Interaction	mLearning also carries the risk of distancing students from their instructors. Hybrid learning solutions (such as those employed in mobile learning experiments [5] at University of California San Diego (UCSD) show a distinct increase in learner-instructor interaction. In a series of experiments, researchers at UCSD found that students asked more questions when they could submit their questions via forums and mobile devices. This holds true in the mobile incarnation of the traditionally staid Chinese classroom. However, pure mobile courses may create a psychological distance derived from the lack of periodic, non-virtual interaction. Researchers must carefully study how mobile students interact with their online professors to ensure that students remain engaged and interested.
Relationship to Content	mLearning presents a number of new opportunities for instructional designers to change the relationship between students and course content. Students can access learning materials at any time and from any location. This may well lead to changes in how students study. The above survey included a question that addressed a problem that is prevalent in Chinese classrooms: studying alone. Research (e.g., [6]) shows that periods of group study increase efficiency in a variety of ways, yet Chinese students find themselves spending hours alone pouring over required texts. Mobile learning can increase group interaction if instructional designers and teachers tailor course activities to respond to this problem.

Table 4. (*continued*)

Relationship to Content	Future researchers should determine more specific responses to the problems posed and opportunities created by mobile learning. Asking questions from this dimension can provide valuable data about how students use this technology to interact with course content.
Sustainability	In this context, the phrase 'sustainability' refers to the long-term effects of mobile learning technologies. These include long-term student happiness, willingness to use mLearning tools, and the integration of mLearning solutions into courses. This is especially important as instructional designers look for ways to reduce the high attrition rates associated with eLearning and distance education programs. Administrators and researchers have a vested interest in this dimension. If students are unwilling to use mobile learning in the long run, then public and private sector institutions will not include the technology in their training plans. Non-adoption will further stunt development, and the cycle will continue. Therefore, researchers must study how students feel about the long-term use of mobile learning in their courses.

6 Conclusion and Future Recommendations

The seven dimensions uncovered by cluster analysis may well prove an excellent starting point for the study of mLearning's effects on learners. Future researchers will undoubtedly uncover other dimensions as the technology matures and gains wider acceptance. At this point, however, researchers have identified certain limitations to this study.

Culture and Language: Researchers conducted the original survey at a large Chinese university. The specifics of cultural attitudes towards learning dictate that some variation will occur from one culture to another. As mobile learning gains popularity in Europe, Africa, Australia, and the Americas, researchers may need to ask different questions to uncover how a specific learning group reacts to mLearning courses.

Repeated Testing: Future researchers must vet their surveys thoroughly before deploying them. Due to time constraints, researchers could not 'dry-run' the survey used to generate these dimensions on smaller focus groups.

Population: At present, few mLearning courses are available to students. Even at large-scale testing grounds, such as SJTU's Online College (17,000 students), only a small percentage of the students learn via mobile technologies. These students may differ from the larger student population in unexpected ways, including learning style preferences, social habits, physical environment, and educational goals. Researchers must work to isolate these variables if they wish to provide a more pure rubric for evaluating mobile learning.

Unaddressed Constructs: Though this study examined a variety of constructs and question styles, it is by no means complete. The context associated with the mLearning intervention may require more specific and tailored questions. Further, evolutions in the technological arena will also lead to the identification of unforeseen constructs in the future. The constructs identified here serve as a starting point for researchers who plan to design surveys for future studies, but by no means exclude other factors. This is an early link in the long chain of research and dialogue that will attend the evaluation of mobile learning programs.

Technological and instructional developments in the field of mobile learning are at a tipping point. Only careful observation, repeated testing, and systematic evaluation will ensure that the technology finds a place in the lifelong learning environment.

References

1. Milrad, M.: Mobile Learning: Challenges, perspectives and reality. In: The conference Communications in the 21st century The Mobile information Society (2002)
2. Traxler, J.: Defining, Discussing, and Evaluating Mobile Learning: The Moving Finger Writes and Having Writ.... International Review of Research in Open and Distance Learning 8(2), 1–12 (2007)
3. Simonson, M.R.: Evaluating Teaching and Learning at a Distance. New Directions for Teaching and Learning 7, 87–94 (1997)
4. Stufflebeam, D., Shinkfield, A.: A Systematic Evaluation. Kluwer-Nijhoff, Boston (1985)
5. Ratto, M., Shapiro, R.B., Truong, T.M., Griswold, W.G.: The ActiveClass Project: Experiments in Encouraging Classroom Participation. Computer Support for Collaborative Learning 2003. Kluwer, Dordrecht (2003)
6. Wang, M.J.: Designing Online Courses That Effectively Engage Learners From Diverse Cultural Backgrounds. British Journal of Educational Technology 38(2), 294–311 (2007)

A Hybrid Learning Course on Software Development— Requirements Validation of Tool Support[*]

Y.T. Yu[**], M.Y. Choy, E.Y.K. Chan, and Y.T. Lo

Department of Computer Science, City University of Hong Kong
{csytyu,csmchoy}@cityu.edu.hk, {chanyk,ytlo}@cs.cityu.edu.hk

Abstract. Learning of software development demands not only adequate supervision by the instructor, but also intensive interactions among students. In traditional classroom learning, the number of contact hours between the instructor and students is very limited. This severely restricts the amount of guidance and learning that students may receive in a course. In particular, the best practices in software development, such as design modelling, peer review, quality assurance and project management, all require ample practice that is hardly feasible in the traditional classroom learning setting. Supported by e-learning systems and tools, a large part of the interactions between instructors and students can now be done online. We propose a hybrid learning design of software development courses to take advantage of both the rich context available in classroom learning and the benefits of electronic communications. This paper presents the rationale for hybrid learning in such courses, and describes a pilot hybrid learning course on software development for preliminary evaluation and requirements validation of tool support.

Keywords: Course design, hybrid learning, requirements validation, software development, Web-based learning tool.

1 Introduction

Software development (SD) courses aim at educating students the theories, techniques, and best practices of the development of software systems. As such, project work is an integral component of SD courses [15]. Development of non-trivial software projects has to be done in teams. In doing the project work, members of a team have to collaborate closely, as effective communication is one of the critical success factors in software projects. Moreover, the instructor has to offer adequate supervision to project teams and monitor the progress of students. Thus, intensive communication among students and the instructor plays an important part in software project work.

The importance of communication is particularly prominent from the perspective of learning in SD courses. First, students have to learn from the instructor how to plan

---

[*] This work is supported in part by a grant (project number: CityU123206) from the Research Grants Council of the Hong Kong Special Administrative Region, China.
[**] Corresponding author.

J. Fong, R. Kwan, and F.L. Wang (Eds.): ICHL 2008, LNCS 5169, pp. 316–327, 2008.

a project and carry out the SD activities, which typically include requirements specification, design, implementation, testing and other quality assurance tasks. In this regard, ample guidance from the instructor is essential. Second, students have to learn from other members of the team through their collaboration in the project. During the project work, students invariably have to seek for supplementary learning materials which have to be shared among themselves. Third, modern SD best practices emphasise peer reviews and inspections, in which team members review the work of one another so as to remove any defects in the project deliverable as early as possible [2, 16]. Finally, members of a team can learn from the good work of other teams, provided there are opportunities for experience sharing and across-team reviews.

However, the number of face-to-face (F2F) contact hours between the instructor and students is usually very limited. This severely restricts the amount of guidance and learning that students may receive in a course. In particular, the best practices in software development, such as design modelling, quality assurance and project management, all require ample practice that is hardly feasible in a traditional classroom learning setting.

Web-based communications are more convenient, efficient, and flexible than F2F interactions as the former can be asynchronous and independent of the physical locations of the participants. Moreover, people can retrieve instant information from the Web and acquire new knowledge through it. Thus, the Web has opened up tremendous opportunities for improving the way that learning takes place.

Supported by e-learning systems, a large part of the interactions between instructors and students can now be done online. *Hybrid learning* [8, 12], also called *blended learning* [1, 6, 15], refers to the mode of education that requires the instructor and students to meet and interact not only in a traditional F2F classroom environment, but also online, typically through Web-based communication channels.

We have earlier proposed an outline of a hybrid learning design of SD courses [13], which takes advantage of both the rich context available in classroom learning and the benefits of communication by the electronic means. To facilitate the implementation of hybrid learning, we have built a Web-based course tool, known as TREASURE, to supplement an existing e-learning platform to provide the specific needs for learning of SD [14, 15]. For the purpose of preliminary evaluation and requirements validation of the tool support, we have recently completed a pilot run of a SD course based on the hybrid learning design and the use of TREASURE. This paper presents the rationale for hybrid learning in SD courses, and describes the learning activities in the pilot run.

The rest of this paper is organized as follows. Section 2 discusses the specific problems in conventional classroom learning in SD courses, and explains why it should be supplemented but not replaced by e-learning. Section 3 outlines the requirements, functionalities and design of TREASURE, which was custom-built for supporting hybrid learning in SD courses. Section 4 describes a pilot hybrid learning course on SD for preliminary evaluation and requirements validation of tool support. Section 5 briefly describes related work, and Section 6 concludes this paper with suggestions of further work.

2   Learning in Software Development Courses

2.1   Conventional Classroom Learning

The quality of software has become increasingly prominent since huge, complicated, and safety-critical software systems are now ubiquitous, affecting us in a myriad of ways in our daily life. To achieve high quality software, the SD process must be properly managed and well-disciplined. One common way of managing the SD process is to organise it into phases. A software process model is specified by the definition and sequencing of activities in these phases, together with the interactions among them. The most renowned software process model is the classical waterfall model, which is typically composed of a requirements definition phase, an analysis and design phase, a coding phase, a testing phase, and an operation phase. The waterfall model, which offers a structured approach to SD, provides distinct milestones and well-defined documentation in each phase of the process. It is perhaps for this reason that the waterfall model is commonly adopted in many SD courses [15], and also actually in most industrial SD projects [9, 10]. Here we present our ideas in terms of the waterfall model, but in fact the proposed course design can be implemented with the use of other process models, such as Boehm's spiral model and the agile processes [10].

In a typical SD course, the instructor has to form student groups, create software projects, allocate projects to different student groups, define the project phases, and prepare the document templates for students to record their intermediate and final work. When the work in each phase is completed, students should submit their intermediate deliverables to the instructor for assessment and feedback. The intermediate deliverables typically include requirement specifications, design models, test plans, progress logs and quality assurance reports [15, 16]. The performance of students should therefore be monitored and evaluated by assessing the quality of students' intermediate deliverables.

Learning of SD is communication and collaboration intensive. As each group works on the project, peer learning and review of intermediate work should be encouraged in order to maximise students' learning experiences. Thus, each group should share their work for comments by other groups. Fig. 1 depicts the flow of the tasks normally done by the instructor and students in a SD course [15].

Typically, tutorial sessions can be arranged so that students may discuss their work with other groups. However, such an arrangement has become increasingly difficult due to the limited F2F contact time, high student-to-instructor ratio and rigid class scheduling. Time and resource limitations often hinder the learning and teaching progress as well as the motivation of students in SD courses. Collaborative learning activities that are desirable beyond lectures and tutorials, such as in-depth group discussion, skills and experience sharing sessions, and technical information exchange, are also highly constrained when carried out in F2F settings. As such, students often receive little and/or delayed feedback from the instructor and fellow students. Moreover, this phenomenon is dissonant to the quality-centric notion that is advocated in SD courses and the industry's recommended best practices [2, 16].

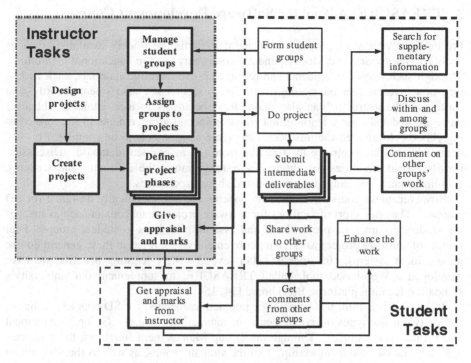

Fig. 1. Tasks to be done by instructors and students in a SD course [15]

2.2 E-Learning

More and more organizations begin to use e-learning as the major form of educational delivery, including universities, corporations, military institutions, and secondary schools [8]. On-demand availability of e-learning complements the routine structures of traditional classes by allowing students to participate and complete their coursework with flexible schedules in accordance with their daily family or work commitments, enabling more engaging learning materials to be accessible for a range of abilities and preferred learning styles, encouraging the development of an independent learning culture by making learning more inviting, and providing unique opportunities for active feedback from different participants. These benefits are particularly pertinent to our university in which the student population has a diverse background and different study modes, including the part-time evening mode [1, 16].

However, there are still values in the traditional classroom learning environment. In a typical SD course, the instructor has to offer guidance to students, encourage students to raise questions, provide comments and feedback, and act as the moderator to keep students on track. The classroom setting can promote social and cultural interactions among the instructor and students, facilitate mutual understanding through non-verbal communication mechanisms such as body language and eye-contact, and encourage peer-to-peer learning. As such, a hybrid mode of learning can be much more effective than pure F2F learning or e-learning alone [14].

3   TREASURE: A Tool for Software Development Courses

Presently, a variety of course management systems are widely available, such as WebCT, Blackboard, and Moodle, and are commonly used in educational institutions. Through such a system, students can retrieve course learning materials, such as lecture notes, recommended readings, quizzes, assignments, assessment records, and surveys. The instructor can also make announcements to alert students whenever there are updated course learning materials or special arrangements in the forthcoming classes. Moreover, the instructor can create assignments to be completed by students who can later retrieve their results from the assessment database. Discussion boards provide facilities for online discussions among the instructor and students, enabling them to exchange information and share experiences.

However, these course management systems are not specifically designed for SD courses. They fall short of facilities for software project management such as managing student groups on a project basis and assigning projects to student groups. Peer review of software project work is not conveniently supported in these general course management systems. In order to better leverage the e-learning benefits, we have developed a Web-based tool, called TREASURE, to supplement our university's standard e-learning platform, Blackboard [14, 15].

TREASURE is built to facilitate the interactions needed for SD courses. It has to satisfy two major types of requirements for interactions, namely, Group Management and Project Management. Through the Group Management functions, the instructor can keep track of the membership of all the student groups, as well as the assignment of projects to groups. The Project Management functions allow the instructor to define new projects and their phases, enable within-group discussions and information sharing, as well as peer inter-group reviews, and provide facilities for the instructor's appraisal and assessment of the intermediate or final products of the projects.

To make the best use of the existing e-learning system, we design TREASURE as a plug-in module to Blackboard. TREASURE utilizes many of the Blackboard system's built-in databases and facilities, including (1) the Student Groups database for group management, (2) the Grade Book database for assessment, (3) the Content Folder database for storing learning materials, and (4) Forum for students to hold online discussions.

We use Java Server Page (JSP) to implement the Web pages of TREASURE. Teachers and students access different pages according to their roles in Blackboard. To satisfy the Group Management requirements, we use the built-in Blackboard APIs to access the basic group management features provided by Blackboard. Our tool provides a single and easier-to-use interface for teachers to add, modify and delete student groups, and to enroll students to groups in a batch or manually one by one. A new Java class for managing an external database of all project information is created to satisfy the Project Management requirements. In this way, the contents of the Project database will not affect the integrity of Blackboard's internal system data.

Throughout the requirements validation and other stages of the development of TREASURE, all stakeholders [4] (including instructors and students) are invited to provide feedback to its intermediate versions to validate the requirements and functions. All these activities are instrumental in ensuring that TREASURE can be usefully incorporated into our proposed hybrid learning approach for SD courses [15].

4 A Pilot Hybrid Learning Course on Software Development

In this section, we describe a pilot postgraduate SD course for preliminary evaluation of the hybrid learning design. The course relies heavily on TREASURE to provide the e-learning facilities that support the hybrid learning implementation. We shall first outline the course and its project work, and then describe in detail the learning activities and the use of TREASURE in satisfying the requirements of these activities.

4.1 The Course and the Project

Software Quality Engineering is a course offered to part-time students in the MSc Computer Science programme. Most students are software practitioners with 1 to 5 years of working experience. One of the course objectives is to enable students to develop and apply a working knowledge of good management and engineering practices for the production of high quality software. The coursework component requires students to work in teams on a project for the development of part of a real software system, with emphasis on using the methods of software inspection, peer technical review and independent verification and validation (IV&V) as the means of effective software quality engineering.

The project requires students to collaborate with their teammates in analyzing and verifying the requirements, designing the architecture as well as implementing a prototype of the software system. The project is divided into phases. At each phase, the instructor needs to monitor the progress of the project groups, and provide supervision and feedback to students. In addition, students have to review and comment on other groups' work at some phases of the project for the purpose of IV&V. The project work includes individual work done by students at their own time, group work done via F2F meetings in tutorial classes, as well as work done via communications and interactions in TREASURE.

4.2 The Course Learning Activities

At the beginning of the course, students form project groups by themselves and notify the course instructor. The instructor then manages the project groups' details by using the group management functions provided by TREASURE (Fig. 2).

Before the project kicks off, the instructor has to design a project by defining the required phases and deliverables that students are required to submit. The instructor then assigns dedicated student groups to the projects and phases. In this pilot course, all student groups are required to do the same project. In other courses, different student groups may be assigned to do different projects.

Once the project commences, students apply the knowledge they acquire in their study to do the project and to produce the required deliverables for various phases. Fig. 3 shows a snapshot of the use of TREASURE, which provides a single entry point for students to manage their project in a convenient manner. Students may collect the required reading materials, submit deliverables, communicate with one another and receive appraisal from the instructor through this interface.

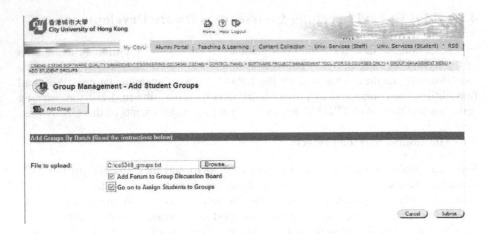

Fig. 2. Adding students to project groups

We now describe the course learning activities in detail. Initially, a requirements specification of part of a real software system, seeded with a number of defects by the instructor, is given to students. Students apply the various SQE techniques learned in class to complete the project based on the given requirements specification.

The project proceeds in 5 phases. In Phase 1 Requirements Inspection, students are required to study and analyze the requirements specification individually using the perspective-based reading (PBR) method [11]. They are required to submit the individual potential defect list and the project plan as the first part of the Inspection Report at the end of this phase via the submission link in TREASURE (Fig. 3). While the defect detection can be done individually, students in the same group have to collectively decide a project plan. Since all students have full-time job and it is very difficult to arrange F2F meetings within the short time duration of this phase, they have to communicate electronically in planning the project. The instructor may also participate in the electronic discussions to monitor students' progress or help those who have difficulties in their project planning.

In Phase 2 Requirements IV&V, students have to arrange two formal inspection meetings to review the requirements specification and to compile an agreed defect list and a revised requirements specification to be included in the second part of their Inspection Report. The first inspection meeting is held by the group members themselves. During the meeting, each group follows the Fagan's inspection process [5] as closely as practicable. The second meeting is held by a third party to perform IV&V. Both meetings are done in the classroom so that students can experience the F2F software quality assurance practice that takes place in real life.

In Phase 3, students work together to produce a detailed design document that includes system architecture and design modelled by data flow diagrams or UML diagrams, database tables, data structures as well as the algorithms of the system components. They have to surf the Web for supplementary learning resources. This kind of self-learning activities may apply to other project phases as well. To facilitate

Fig. 3. TREASURE allows students to manage their activities online

effective self-learning, we have compiled a set of useful Web resources for students' references. Fig. 4 shows the Web page of SD resources for the course.

After completing their work, students upload their draft intermediate deliverables to TREASURE for other groups to comment. In the mean time, the instructor may also comment on students' work drafts. Afterwards, each group can improve their work based on the comments they receive before formal submission for assessment.

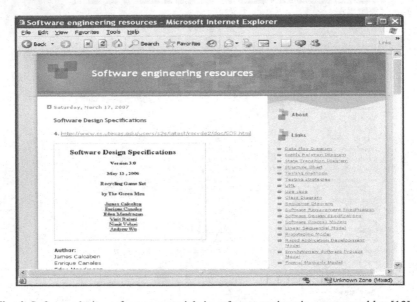

Fig. 4. Software design reference materials in software engineering resources blog [13]

Fig. 5 shows the interface of TREASURE through which students may view and comment on the work of other groups. In conventional classes, it may take a long time to complete this activity. To allow students to give F2F comments on the work of others, some precious tutorial class sessions may be needed. Similarly, it is also hard for the instructor to give appraisal promptly. Nor is it feasible for the instructor to give F2F comments to each student individually in class, as while talking to one student, other students would have to waste their time waiting for their turns in class. Without tool support, timely comments would be very difficult to implement.

At the completion of Phase 4 Prototype Development, students perform a F2F demonstration of their system prototype to other students and also review other students' draft prototype so as to provide comments for mutual improvement. The peer review of the system prototype is based on its conformance to the system requirements, consistency of the interface and usability of the system. The work in this phase is done F2F in tutorial classes. Similar to Fig. 5, there is another area in TREASURE for students to upload their comments in this phase.

In the final phase, students revise their draft system prototype according to the comments from the instructor and other students. Meanwhile, they have to submit an acceptance test plan together with a consolidated final report in which all relevant

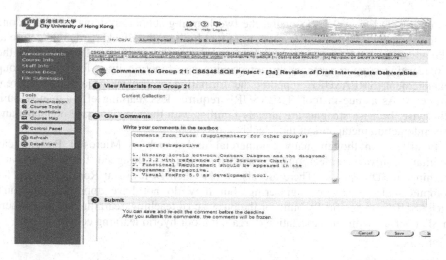

Fig. 5. View and comment on other groups' work

information about the prototype should be documented. Instructor can then mark the student submissions and give appraisals to each individual student via TREASURE.

5 Related Work

One work related to ours is the Web-based Collaboration Support Sub-system of an Education Support System developed in Tokyo Gakugei University [7]. The system allows instructors to act as inspectors to review and comment on the artifacts created by students. It also supports version and configuration management of the submitted artifacts. To monitor students' progress, the system keeps track of different states of the artifacts being inspected. A bulletin board is provided for discussion between individuals within group, among groups, and between groups and the instructor side.

Another related work is the ClassCompass system developed in the University of British Columbia as a distributed tool for group design mentoring [3]. It consists of several components: the ClassCompass Server, Instructor Client and Student Client. It provides a Web-based graphical editor for students to edit their UML diagrams. An automatic critique system generates expert advice when common design mistakes, such as association cycle and unnecessary realization, are found. Students can then revise their designs based on the generated advice. After submitting their own initial designs, students can critique on other groups' work, based on design principles that are pre-defined by the instructor. Instructors can act as experts to view the designs and manually provide feedback to students so that they may refine their design.

In short, the Web-based Collaboration Support Sub-system is designed to facilitate the inspection activities performed at the testing phase, and ClassCompass provides functionalities for mentoring the activities of students performed at the design phase. While each of these two learning support systems is specifically designed for a particular phase of the SD process, TREASURE realizes our hybrid learning approach at both the activity and course levels by assisting both the instructor and students in the entire SD life cycle. Secondly, the two learning support systems are standalone systems, whereas TREASURE is a plug-in tool built on the Blackboard architecture to take advantage of the functions of the existing e-learning platform. Thirdly, while the two learning support systems do not provide any functionalities for project group management, TREASURE supports the formation of project groups for different projects. As a plug-in tool, TREASURE requires less learning effort than if built otherwise, because students are already familiar with the user interface elements and user interaction metaphors of the Blackboard system.

Finally, even though many commercial tools, such as Microsoft Project, can facilitate software project management, they are not designed for teaching and learning in SD courses. There are also tools (such as Rational Rose) designed for computer-aided software engineering, but they do not have appraisal functions. TREASURE is specifically built for the purpose of teaching, learning and assessment in SD courses, with the expectation of realizing our hybrid learning course design.

6 Conclusion

In a conventional classroom, many factors hinder learning in a SD course, such as the limitation of time for interaction among participants, resource constraints such as high student-to-instructor ratio, and the diversity of students' backgrounds and study modes. A SD course requires students to do group project work to practise software engineering principles and proven techniques. Timely feedback and regular peer reviews are essential not only to ensure the quality of the product, but also to enhance students' learning experiences. The use of asynchronous communication can help improve students' skill of team work and time management. All these factors call for the adoption of a hybrid approach combining classroom learning and e-learning.

This paper has described the rationale of using a hybrid approach in SD courses and the learning activities in a pilot run of such a course, which utilizes our custom-built tool, TREASURE, to organize a non-trivial software project for students to learn the essentials of software quality engineering practices. Looking ahead, it would be desirable to integrate TREASURE with students' SD environment as far as possible. Most intermediate deliverables or products of a software project such as design models and software prototypes have to be assessed for evaluating students' progress. Further work may be done to automate more parts of the assessment processes by integrating our tool with other project assessment tools.

Acknowledgment. We thank Roy Au for his work in developing TREASURE, and Alfred Chan for helping out in the course. A preliminary version of this paper was earlier presented at the Symposium on Hybrid Learning 2007 [13].

References

1. Choy, M., Lam, S., Poon, C.K., Wang, F.L., Yu, Y.T., Yuen, L.: Towards Blended Learning of Computer Programming Supported by an Automated System. In: Workshop on Blended Learning 2007, pp. 9–18. Prentice-Hall, Englewood Cliffs (2007)

2. Ciolkowski, M., Laitenberger, O., Biffl, S.: Software Reviews: The State of the Practice. IEEE Software 20(6), 46–51 (2003)
3. Coelho, W., Murphy, G.: ClassCompass: A Software Design Mentoring System. ACM J. on Educational Resources in Computing 7(1) Article 2 (2007)
4. Damian, D.: Stakeholders in Global Requirements Engineering: Lessons Learned from Practice. IEEE Software 24(2), 21–27 (2007)
5. Fagan, M.E.: Design and Code Inspections to Reduce Errors in Program Development. IBM Systems Journal 15(3), 182–211 (1976)
6. Graham, C.R., Allen, S., Ure, D.: Benefits and Challenges of Blended Learning Environments. In: Khosrow-Pour, M. (ed.) Encyclopedia of Information Science and Technology, pp. 253–259. Idea Group, Hershey (2005)
7. Hazeyama, A., Nakako, A., Nakajima, S., Osada, K.: Group Learning Support System for Software Engineering Education – Web-based Collaboration Support between the Teacher Side and the Student Groups –. In: Zhong, N., Yao, Y., Ohsuga, S., Liu, J. (eds.) WI 2001. LNCS (LNAI), vol. 2198, pp. 568–573. Springer, Heidelberg (2001)
8. Koohang, A., Durante, A.: Learner's Perceptions toward the Web-based Distance Learning Activities/Assignments Portion of an Undergraduate Hybrid Instructional Model. J. Inform. Tech. Edu. 2 (2003)
9. Laplante, P.A., Neill, C.J.: The Demise of the Waterfall Model Is Imminent' and Other Urban Myths. ACM Queue 10(1) (2004)
10. Neill, C.J., Laplante, P.A.: Requirements Engineering: The State of the Practice. IEEE Software 20(6), 40–45 (2003)
11. Shull, F., Rus, I., Basili, V.: How Perspective-based Reading Can Improve Requirements Inspections. IEEE Computer 33(7), 73–79 (2000)
12. Young, J.R.: Hybrid Teaching Seeks to End the Divide between Traditional and Online Instruction. The Chronicle of Higher Education 48(28) (2002)
13. Yu, Y.T., Choy, M.Y., Chan, E.Y.K., Lo, Y.T.: Learning of Software Project Development: Towards a Hybrid Approach. In: Fong, J., Liu, L.C., Wang, F.L. (eds.) Hybrid Learning: Symposium on Hybrid Learning 2007, pp. 333–338 (2007)
14. Yu, Y.T., Choy, M.Y., Chan, E.Y.K., Lo, Y.T.: A Web-based Tool for Software Project Coursework: Requirements, Validation and Implementation. In: International Conference on ICT in Teaching and Learning, Hong Kong (2007)
15. Yu, Y.T., Choy, M.Y., Chan, E.Y.K., Lo, Y.T.: Requirements and Design of a Web-based Tool for Supporting Blended Learning of Software Project Development. In: Hirashima, T., Hoppe, U., Young, S.S.-C. (eds.) Supporting Learning Flow through Integrative Technologies — Proceedings of the 15th International Conference on Computers in Education (ICCE 2007), pp. 159–166. IOS Press, Amsterdam (2007)
16. Yu, Y.T., Poon, P.-L.: Designing Activities for Learning Software Quality Practices. In: 5th International Conference on Quality Software (QSIC 2005), pp. 333–338. IEEE Computer Society Press, Los Alamitos (2005)

Tools for Supporting Hybrid Learning Strategies in Open Source Software Environments

Francesco Di Cerbo[1], Paola Forcheri[2], Gabriella Dodero[1], and Giancarlo Succi[1]

[1] Center for Applied Software Engineering
Faculty of Computer Science
Free University of Bolzano-Bozen
Piazza Domenicani 1
39100 Bolzano-Bozen, Italy
{fdicerbo,gdodero,gsucci}@unibz.it
[2] Institute for Applied Mathematics and Information Technologies
Italian National Research Council
Department of Genoa, Italy
Via De Marini, 6
16149 Genoa, Italy
forcheri@ge.imati.cnr.it

Abstract. In this paper, we illustrate how a cooperative learning paradigm may benefit from cutting edge e-learning techniques. We use Web 2.0 resources (especially AJAX) to fulfill requirements for an interactive-constructivistic "learning space", extending an existing Free/Open Source Software Learning Management System, to create a cooperative and community-based learning space adherent to our proposal. The paper shows also how to use our toolset on two case studies.

Keywords: Open Source Software, virtual learning space, social communities.

1 Introduction

The development of the so-called "soft-skills" has become an indispensable complement to any discipline, be it technology oriented or in the humanities. With "soft skills", the European Community [1], identifies abilities in

- presentation of knowledge
- effective web search
- project work
- team work
- problem solving

These skills can be considered of paramount importance in any curricula, and as they can be effectively improved through the use of technologies, it is possible to refer to them as ICT-enhanced skills.

J. Fong, R. Kwan, and F.L. Wang (Eds.): ICHL 2008, LNCS 5169, pp. 328–337, 2008.

Methodologies have already been identified, which may be applied in order to achieve such results. Examples are "problem-based learning" [2], "troubleshooting" [3] or "case-based teaching" [4]. Several pilot experiences already support this claim (see for example [5] and [6]), even if an exhaustive experimentation involving e-learning specialists and students at various levels and disciplines is not yet completed.

As it is well known (see [7]) these methodologies, inspired to a constructivist basis ([8]), view learning as the result of student-centered activities, addressed by intentions and reflections, requiring to carry out authentic tasks and proposing concrete goals. Moreover, they integrate individual and collaborative work, thus including a socio-constructivist component ([9]).

Starting from the experiences collected in the European Project I*Teach ([10]), we started rethinking about the tools we used to effectively support our teaching experiences, and decided to initiate a new effort to put in practice the lessons we learned.

The work we present consists in the development of a technological infrastructure, suitable to support active learning methodologies. This development mostly concentrated on the possibility to pass from the learning environment concept (the status-quo of the market) to that of "dynamic learning space" (DLS, similar to [10]) which is the novelty of our approach. In such a DLS, people involved in learning are identified by their roles, attributes and behaviors, and meet each other to collaborate to the negotiation and construction of knowledge.

The concept of "dynamic learning space" is not originating in the virtual environment by itself. Indeed, in a real (not virtual) learning space, both teacher and his/her class participate to the creation of a shared knowledge; they build up meanings and concepts where every individual has its own role inside the process. Teachers have the supervision of the community, steering global effort towards learning targets, and every student may / must contribute to the global learning of the community.

In case of a virtual teaching, such as in hybrid and e-learning scenarios, a teacher should rely on a set of software tools, letting him involve his/her class, like during lessons in presence. We developed software to help teachers to coordinate such virtual communities, specifically at interaction level, in order to form a social network. Such a software has been called DIEL, Dynamic Interactive E-Learning system.

By DIEL, co-construction of learning materials and concepts is achieved through virtual experiences. Since it gives a precise and "automatic" track of activities conducted, without the distractive effect caused by recording them by hand, students and teachers may concentrate on the learning process. A detailed description of the pedagogical aspects taken into account in our design is available in [11].

The paper includes a description of the approach we followed, its implementation as well as two case studies to show the possibilities of DIEL.

2 The Approach

Our approach in the design of DIEL aimed at supporting learning activities using ICT technology. We targeted learning communities at academic level, but due to the easiness of use and the simple metaphors we chose, the tool may be used also for students of lower ages.

To implement DIEL, we decided to extend an existing Learning Management System (LMS), reusing a part of its tools and services, that are still useful in our vision. The Moodle open source LMS [12] was our starting point. Moodle is an open source environment which is broadly used around the world (with over 36,000 registered sites with 14 million users in 1.4 million courses, according to the Moodle website) and supports more than 70 national languages. Its adoption level leads us to choose Moodle as our target platform. The actual implementation at each installation may vary due to national options, and portal contents, visibility policy and interaction functionalities are implemented by such system as custom installation features, in order to better match actual needs of the users' community.

What really represents a discontinuity with all established solutions is a new metaphor, designed to highlight constructivistic approach in contents creation. Exploiting new technology capabilities (Java applets and AJAX, the engine of Web 2.0 paradigm, see [13]), DIEL creates a virtual environment where interactions are welcomed and eased, and where every community service contributes to the creation of a common knowledge as part of a structured learning process.

Each involved person, students as well as teachers, is free to operate and move in our virtual classroom: it is a place where to put opinions or contents, to meet the classmates, even to find amusement, without a fixed interaction stereotype. In such virtual environment, everyone is free to find his way to learn, in conjunction with the others and under teachers directions. Previous research in Human-Computer Interaction (for instance, the work of Gräther and Prinz [14]) on community and presence awareness, and especially the concept of social translucence [15] has been used as the basis for our metaphor. This concept allows each user of our community to be aware of what other users are doing in every moment.

Every user is associated to an avatar, which is free to move in a web page, where logical proximity of activities is naturally mapped into physical proximity of the avatars in the virtual space. In Figure 1, it is possible to see an example of an interaction between an avatar's client and a course material, for instance a book available to students. The avatar moves onto the picture representing the material, and a pop-up menu will appear, asking for possible actions to perform (in the example, the alternatives are: open, download, and cancel current action). Similar behaviors are associated to interactions between avatars and other elements (for instance, rooms, selected regions in virtual spaces connected through special passages rendered as doors), and also among avatars and avatars, such as the opening of a private chat session.

Other features that can be used in the virtual space include those which are usually supported by LMSs, like forums and wikis. We added to this basic set, a videoconferencing system based only on Java (applets and services) in a client/server architecture, and an AJAX [16] whiteboard, shared among the community. Both are browser independent and do not require additional software installation at client side.

DIEL is designed to be used as an additional set of feature to sum up to the original Moodle ones. In fact, DIEL supports group interactions even if conducted at unusualtimings, letting the users have a coordination point where to meet, after agreeing a specific appointment or even completely by chance. The latter possibility is permitted by the immediate feeling given by seeing the avatars online and the respective actions that are performed. DIEL can be also used to configure a part of a course created in Moodle; in fact, through the AJAX visualization, it is possible to create rooms as

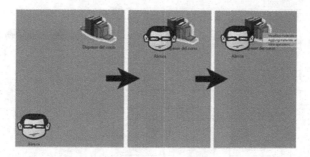

Fig. 1. Example of an interaction between an avatar and course material

wellas resources, besides the DIEL activities. This feature can be a help to speedup the Moodle learning curve for teachers that are not particularly skilled in the use of ICT.

3 Implementation

Our software consists on two main subsystems: one implements all the operations at client side, while the other is responsible for managing all the interactions between users and the system. We defined a set of system behaviors, called actions, regarding possible interactions between clients and server. Then, we also defined a set of widgets and utility objects to be used at client-side. Each object is associated to a number of actions that are needed to perform its own tasks. All these definitions have been formalized in XML documents, in order to be independent from any programming language (neither client- nor server-side, see example in Table 1). We refer to such definitions as "XML Interfaces".

Table 1. Example of a DIEL action using XML

```
<?xml ... ?>
<action name="move">
 <param name="avatar_name"/ value="Alexca">
 <param name="start_xy"/ value="10,15">
 <param name="end_xy"/ value="20,30">
  <url>...</url>
</action>
```

The development of objects both at client and at server side was based on such XML interfaces. Objects may exchange messages in XML format, if they can parse XML interfaces to produce XML requests accordingly. A representation of the two subsystems as well as XML interfaces is available in Fig. 1.

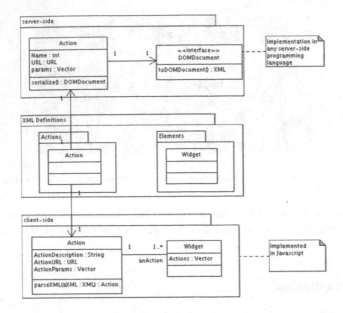

Fig. 2. Diagram of subsystems

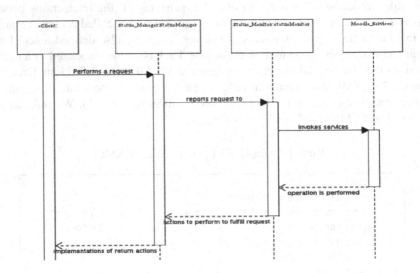

Fig. 3. Sequence diagram of interactions between Status Monitor and Status Manager

Two special entities are responsible for communication between client and server: Status Manager and Status Monitor. Both of them embed the concept of "status"; as DIEL is focused on live social interactions, we require that all the users share the same experience. As a consequence all users also have to share the very same status; we implemented this requirement keeping the status of the whole application at server-side, and exchanging periodic updates with clients. Once an action has been performed by one of the clients, all the others are notified within 1-2 seconds. This mechanism is based on the mentioned Status Monitor and Status Manager. A sequence diagram showing their interactions is available in Figure 3.

Status Monitor is an object managing all the client side tasks and operations. There are as many instances of Status Monitor as there are clients. In fact, it is responsible for creating the initial environment (avatars, rooms, widgets and so on), and to track any modification to its internal status (i.e., movement of the user's avatar, insertion of a new message in the real-time chat and so on). Once a modification happens, Status Monitor sends an update message to its server-side counterpart, Status Manager, receiving back (in the next update message) the actions to perform to show the actual status of the application to the user.

Status Manager sends to all Status Monitors an update message at predefined intervals; this message is created considering the past history of the Status Monitors since the last update message. The system has one and only Status Manager, as we need a central coordination point for the whole system.

4 Case Studies

We describe learning activities proposed within the project I*Teach [5], and their representation using DIEL. The aim of this section is to show concrete examples on what can be done with DIEL. The two cases show the flexibility of our metaphors, which allow different strategies with the same tool. The cases studies are held in a hybrid learning environment, including classroom face-to face lessons, group interactions and discussions, and online activities. The first one is more oriented to promote discussions and co-construction of contents, while the second shows how heterogeneous groups can find a support for their respective activities.

4.1 Case 1: Budget

Description: an activity focused on spreadsheet, supervised by the teacher, aimed at introducing spreadsheets concepts and tools. The activity is centered on the following problem: "A young family needs to know the flow of expenses in order to see if it is possible to limit them. Thus, it decides to build a household budget". Build such a budget and comment on it.
Active learning method(s): problem based learning
Learning objectives:

- introduce and analyze the budget concept
- Improve basic knowledge about worksheets and about (basic) functionalities of a specific spreadsheet program

Process:

- Task 1: Introduction of the budget problem as a decision problem
- Task 2: First planning of the budget
- Task 3: Analysis of some functionalities of a spreadsheet program and development of the budget

- Task 4: To develop the report on the work done
- Task 5: Comparison of the result with the expected outcomes

Case 1 using DIEL. DIEL virtual environment is partitioned into a set of rooms to be visited in sequence, as can be viewed in Fig. 4.

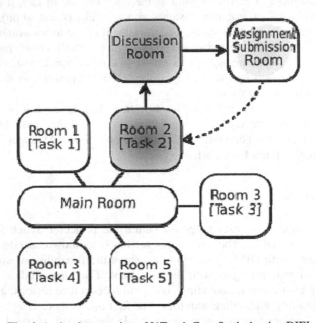

Fig. 4. An implementation of I*Teach Case Study 1 using DIEL

Initially, the teacher configures the system in order to enable the students to access the Main Room only. In that room, the teacher places a part of the learning material, as well as other resources that have to be available during all the duration of the course. Students gain access to the different rooms as the course develops, and the teacher decides when and what to show or to close, according to the progress of the course. Fig. 4 shows an example of the implementation of Task 2: such activity leads to the creation of an assignment, to be developed in groups, and usually a group discussion is required to clarify how to realize and structure the final budget. So, students, through their avatars, meet and exchange opinions, achieving a co-construction of shared knowledge, using audio/video services and/or a whiteboard, in a room (the discussion room) contiguous to the one of Task 2. When finished, they move and submit their work in another linked room (the assignment room), where they find a resource that is mapped on the existing assignment service exposed by Moodle. Finally, the teacher closes the discussion room, letting students to access Task 2 room, to fetch the didactic material eventually stored there. This way, DIEL rooms are a convenient metaphor to promote community interactions, through a more involving visualization and an integration of a set of useful community tools.

4.2   Case 2: Web Site Creation

Description: a group activity project to create a web site against the practice of doping into sport activities. Involved students have different backgrounds; in fact, some of them are studying biology, others computer science. Each student will develop those activities which are best suited for her/his study plan.

Active learning method(s): project based learning

Learning objectives:

- Analysis skills in understanding results coming from a web search
- Skills to produce a web text and a web biography
- Principles of web design

Process:

- Task 1: After dividing the class into heterogeneous groups, every group chooses a specific topic to explore (the risks to the health of doping, the importance of fair play and others)
- Task 2: The groups collect a bibliography on the argument, organize it and produce a wrap-up document
- Task 3: After a discussion of the material collected held at class level, every group updates its documents and transforms them into web pages, eventually adding images and videos
- Task 4: The last phase is the publication of the web pages created into a site for the whole project

Case 2 using DIEL. Case 2 can be implemented as a set of rooms, much in the same way as in the previous example. Fig. 5 shows a possible status of the virtual learning space after Task 1 is finished. The group has agreed with the teacher that Task 2 is

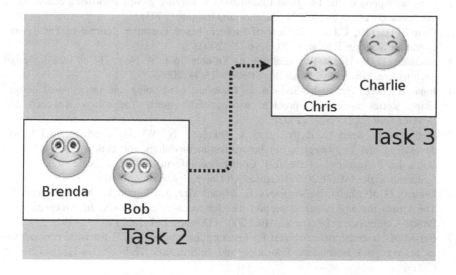

Fig. 5. A step in I*Teach Case Study 2 using DIEL

accomplished by two biologists, Bob and Brenda, who now are in Task 2 room. Two other group members, the computer scientists Chris and Charlie, in Task 3 room, are waiting for Task 2 to be completed. They will take over with web page implementation as soon as the biologists will "bring" them the collected files, images etc.

5 Conclusions

We have described the pedagogical approach, and implementation technologies that we have been employing in order to support social networking inside a new generation LMS, DIEL. Case studies support the claim that such new interaction models may encourage the teachers to use active learning methodologies in the virtual (as well as in the real) learning environment.

DIEL extends the well-known Moodle Free/Open Source software with a "dynamic learning space", providing a novel interaction model. At present, the system has been deployed on Moodle 1.8.3, and we are starting to extensively experience it with users (university teachers and students).

To evaluate our solution, we plan to collect both qualitative (through user assessment) and quantitative information. The latter come from automatic tools for collecting process metrics [17] already available and developed at the Free University of Bolzano-Bozen [18]. This will allow us to discover usability patterns inside users' experience, providing a base of evidence useful on two different scenarios: a technical one, to analyze introduced improvements and eventually refine them, and the pedagogical one, to bring quantitative confirmations for qualitative considerations.

References

1. Progress reports of the European Commission's working groups Improving education of teachers and trainers and ICT in education and training (2003)
2. Ward, J.D., Lee, C.L.: A Review of Problem-based Learning. Journal of Family and Consumer Sciences Education 20(1), 16–26 (2002)
3. Jonassen, D.H., Hung, W.: Learning to Troubleshoot: A New Theory-Based Design Architecture. Educational Psychology Review 18(1) (2006)
4. Jonassen, D.H., Hernandez-Serrano, J.: Case-based reasoning and instructional design: Using stories to support problem solving. Educational Technology Research and Development 50(2), 65–77 (2002)
5. Stefanova, E., Sendova, E., Nikolova, I., Nikolova, N.: When I*Teach means I*Learn: developing and implementing an innovative methodology for building ICT-enhanced skills. In: Proceedings of the IFIP Conference Informatics, Mathematics, and ICT: a 'golden triangle' IMICT 2007. Northeastern University, Boston (2007)
6. Dodero, G., Ratcheva, D., Stefanova, E., Miranowicz, M., Vertan, C., Musankoviene, V.: The virtual training center: a support tool for teachers community. In: Proceedings of Balkan Conference in Informatics (BCI 2007). Demetra Ltd (2007)
7. Barak, M.: Instructional principles for fostering learning with ICT: teachers' perspectives as learners and instructors. Education and Information Technologies 11(2), 121–135 (2006)
8. Bruner, J.: Toward a Theory of Instruction. Harvard University Press, Cambridge (1966)

9. Vygotsky, L.S.: Mind in Society. Harvard University Press, Cambridge (1978)
10. Pfister, H.-R., Schuckmann, C., Beck-Wilson, J., Wessner, M.: The metaphor of virtual rooms in the cooperative learning environment Clear. In: Streitz, N.A., Konomi, S., Burkhardt, H.-J. (eds.) CoBuild 1998. LNCS, vol. 1370, pp. 107–113. Springer, Heidelberg (1998)
11. Di Cerbo, F., Succi, G.: A proposal for interactive-constructivistic teaching methods supported by Web 2.0 technologies and environments. In: Wagner, R., Revell, N., Pernul, G. (eds.) DEXA 2007. LNCS, vol. 4653, pp. 648–652. Springer, Heidelberg (2007)
12. Dougiamas, M., Taylor, P.C.: Moodle: Using Learning Communities to Create an Open Source Course Management System. In: Proceedings of the EDMEDIA 2003 Conference (2003)
13. O'Reilly, T.: What Is Web 2.0 (December 12) (accessed, 2005),
    http://www.oreillynet.com/pub/a/oreilly/tim/news/2005/09/30/what-is-web-20.html
14. Gräther, W., Prinz, W.: Supporting cooperation awareness in common information spaces. In: Supporting the Social Side of Large ScaleSoftware Development, co-located with CSCW 2006 (2006),
    http://research.microsoft.com/hip/papers/ssslssdProceedings.pdf
15. Erickson, T., Kellogg, W.A.: Social translucence: An approach to designing systemsthat mesh with social processes. In: Trans. Computer-Human Interaction, vol. 1(7). ACM Press, New York (2002)
16. Murugesan, S.: Understanding Web 2.0. In: IT Professional, Piscataway, NJ, USA, vol. 9(4), pp. 34–41. IEEE Educational Activities Department, Los Alamitos (2007)
17. Humphrey, W.: Introduction to the Personal Software Process. Addison-Wesley, Reading (1997)
18. Scotto, M., Vernazza, T., Sillitti, A., Succi, G.: Managing Web-Based Information. In: Proceedings of ICEIS Conference, pp. 575–578 (2004)

L2Code: An Author Environment for Hybrid and Personalized Programming Learning

Ramon Zatarain-Cabada, M.L. Barrón-Estrada, J. Moisés Osorio-Velásquez,
L. Zepeda-Sánchez, and Carlos A. Reyes-García*

Instituto Tecnológico de Culiacán, Juan de Dios Bátiz s/n Col. Guadalupe, C.P. 88220
Culiacán, México
Tel.: +52 667 7131796
rzatarain@itculiacan.edu.mx
* Instituto Nacional de Astrofísica, Óptica y Electrónica (INAOE)
Luis Enrique Erro No. 1, Sta. Ma. Tonanzintla, Puebla, 72840, México
kargaxxi@inaoep.mx

Abstract. L2Code is an Intelligent Tutoring System used for teaching programming courses for different paradigms under a hybrid or blinded environment. It was designed and implemented to work with diverse types of modules oriented to certain ways of learning using principles of Multiple Intelligences. The author tool facilitates the creation of adaptive or personalized learning material to be used in multiple-paradigm programming language courses applying an artificial intelligence approach. The Tutoring System works with a predictive engine that uses a Naive Bayes classifier which operates in real time with the knowledge of the historical performance of the student. We show results of the tool.

1 Introduction

Teaching and Learning a programming language is in general considered a tough job, and programming courses usually have high abandon rates. Research has proven that for a beginner to become an expert programmer he might spend more than 10 years [1]. A great amount of educational research has been made to distinguish the characteristics of beginner programmers and to study the learning process and its associations to the different aspects of programming [2, 3]. Lately also differences between procedural and object-oriented education approaches have been studied, as Java and C++ have become common educational languages [4]. Some research show the difficulties of Object oriented programming by performing a web-based survey for both students and teachers [5].

Our proposal is an Intelligent Tutoring System (ITS) designed to accept diverse types of programming language paradigms oriented to different ways of teaching and learning like e-learning and classroom learning and by using the principles of Multiple Intelligences [6]. This system, named L2Code, can dynamically identify the learning characteristics of the student [7] and provide him personalized material according to his type of intelligence. The different programming modules can be conveniently produced by any instructor. It is only necessary to specify which resources refer to

J. Fong, R. Kwan, and F.L. Wang (Eds.): ICHL 2008, LNCS 5169, pp. 338–347, 2008.

which types of student intelligences, and which evaluation will be part of the different modules of the ITS. This is necessary in order to measure the student performance and to improve the prediction of the best learning resource. A predictive engine for L2Code works with a Naive Bayes classifier [8] which operates in real time with the knowledge of the historical performance of the student.

The organization of the paper is as follows: In Section 2, we present the architecture of L2Code describing each one of the module components. In Section 3, we discuss the implementation of several important algorithms used in the software. Test and results are shown in Section 4. Comparison to related work is given in section 5 and conclusions are shown in Section 6.

2 Architecture of L2Code

The general architecture of the system (Figure 1) includes a set of components that allow modularization, scalability, and maintainability of the system.

The server is the one in charge to provide the complete course that comes to be a package of different resources with its respective evaluations. The server is not more than an abstract entity, since can be distributed in internet by a Web site, or directly by the creator of the course.

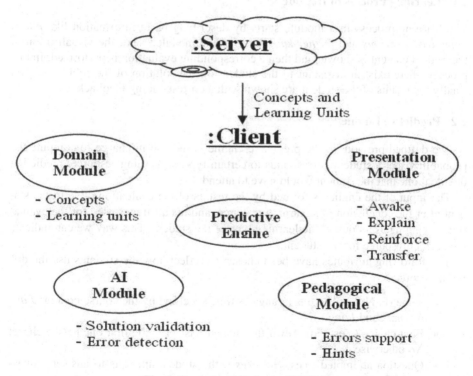

Fig. 1. General architecture of L2Code

The client contains the ITS. It has the following components:

- Domain Module. It is the one in charge to encapsulate the content of the course, such as concepts and learning units with their respective resources.
- Presentation Module. It is the one that works with certain unit of learning, like waking up the student, explaining some concepts, reinforcing the content or simply transferring new knowledge.
- Pedagogical Module. It is the one in charge of the tutor, making functions such as detecting errors in the answers of the student, and feed backing and guiding the student towards the correct solution.
- AI Module. Fundamental part in the operation of the pedagogical module, since it is the one that really detects the type of solution for the student, correct or incorrect, therefore the pedagogical module only worries about the feedback process.
- Predictive Engine. Its function is the one to calculate the probability that the student has taken the correct course, according to its type of intelligence measured in the degree of assimilation of the learning unit. With this calculation, the predictive engine is able to predict which would have to be the following resource that the student would have to take.

2.1 Learning Process in L2Code

The learning process in a module starts by describing basic information like *name*, *objectives*, *previous* and *further knowledge* of the module. Next, the visualization of theoretical content is shown, and then a corresponding evaluation is performed. In this process, there exist an assistant to the student on the solution of the problems. And finally the results of the student are shown with a corresponding feedback.

2.2 Predictive Engine

As we defined previously, the predictive engine is the one in charge to compute the probability that a student corresponds to certain type of learning resource, predicting the ideal one that the student would have to attend.

The input of the engine is formed by the results of the evaluation done to the student after the conclusion of a learning resource, and the attributes used for the evaluation, obtaining as an output the learning type of the student. This way we can indicate the correct resource for the student.

The following attributes have been chosen to reflect how the students use the different resources:

- Time (F, N, L). There is a range of time specified by the course creator: *Fast, Normal*, and *Long*.
- First choice (Yes, No). *Yes* if the student answer is the first one he/she chose; *No* otherwise.
- Question attempted (Yes, No). *Yes* if the student attempts to answer a question; *No* otherwise.

- Accuracy (0..1). Measures the approximation of the student answer with respect to the correct answer. This computation depends of the evaluation type defined by the course creator.
- After determining the probability of each question, the probability corresponding to the module (resource type) is calculated considering the following attributes:
- Repeat (Yes, No). *Yes* if the student had already seen this resource; *No* otherwise.
- Code value (0..1). This value is defined by the course creator and says what percentage must be assigned to code questions.
- Intelligence (VL, LM, VS, MR). It defines the type of student intelligence. According to Gardner theory [10] there are seven intelligences. We deal with four of them: *Verbal/Linguistic, Logical/Mathematical, Visual/Spatial,* and *Musical/Rhythmic.*

3 Implementation

The development of the system was made by following a cascade model with a modular development under the UML language [9, 10]. The system was implemented with Java™ [11]. L2Code makes use of two external packages that are: JDOM [12] for the XML reading and writing and SWT (Standard Widget Toolkit) [13] for the creation of native graphical interfaces.

3.1 Naive Bayes Classifier Algorithm

This algorithm (Figure 2) is in charge of the probabilistic computations for making prediction of the right student learning resource. During the interaction of the student with the learning module the attributes of this interaction are recorded and, when finishing it, the corresponding probability of the actual learning resource is updated.

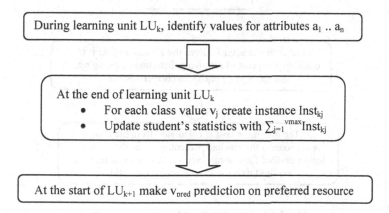

During learning unit LU_k, identify values for attributes $a_1 .. a_n$

At the end of learning unit LU_k
- For each class value v_j create instance $Inst_{kj}$
- Update student's statistics with $\sum_{j=1}^{vmax} Inst_{kj}$

At the start of LU_{k+1} make v_{pred} prediction on preferred resource

Fig. 2. Naïve Bayes classifier algorithm

3.2 Evaluation Algorithms

In the process of evaluation of the learning module we define four different evaluations:

- **Multiple Options.** It offers a series of possible answers, where only one answer is correct.
- **Keywords.** Here we evaluate the answer of the student based on the amount of correct keywords that the answer contains. The algorithm is explained in Figure 3.

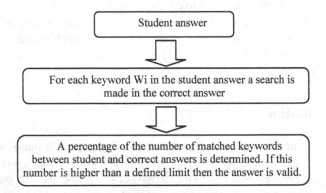

Fig. 3. Evaluation with keywords

- **Edit Distance.** It allows also free answers from the student, but the evaluation method is oriented to a minimum number of characters that must be eliminated, inserted or interchanged so the answer of the student is identical to the correct answer. This is explained in Figure 4.

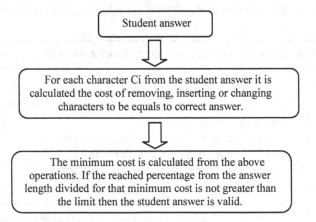

Fig. 4. Evaluation with edit distance algorithm

- **Practice Evaluation (Code Problem).** This type of evaluation (see Figure 5) was implemented to evaluate code and to provide hints to the student throughout its development and, at the end, a feedback of its answer is returned.

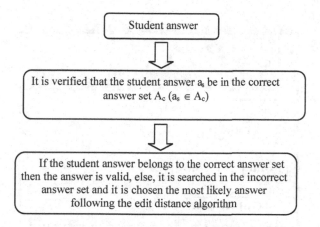

Fig. 5. Algorithm for practice evaluation (code problem)

4   Experimental Results

We will present an example for an object-oriented programming (OOP) course. This course is offered in the computer engineering program of our institution (Instituto Tecnológico de Culiacán). Figure 6 shows the interface of one of the topics. We can

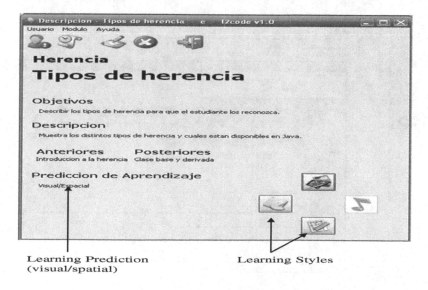

Fig. 6. Choosing the Learning Style

observe on the left bottom side of the figure, when the system makes a prediction of the learning style of the student (visual/spatial). We also observe at the right bottom side, the different learning styles the student can choose.

Topic content of multiple inheritances and topic assessment with results are shown in figures 7 and 8.

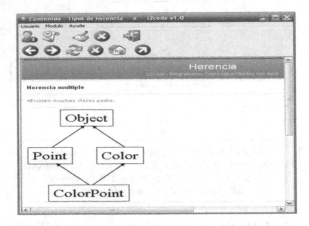

Fig. 7. Course Topic Content

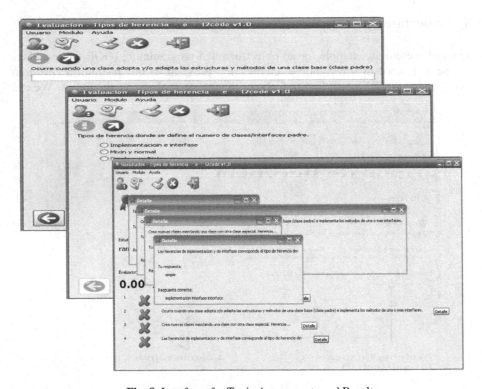

Fig. 8. Interfaces for Topic Assessments and Results

When the student has finished attending one learning module and has been evaluated, a probabilistic value is determined and used for the prediction of the type of intelligence. In order to be able of comparing the final calculation with the rest of the other learning resources and to determine the appropriate resource for the student, this probabilistic value is stored and merged with the rest of the calculations made to the learning resources of the same type. Table 1 shows a student interaction with L2Code. The interaction was in a module with Visual/Spatial intelligence type and the characteristics are shown in Table 2.

Table 1. Student interaction

Student answer	Response time
methods	10
Declaration and body	35
constructor	10
True	80
"()"	20
name body arguments	80
new	25
usr = new User()	100

Table 2. Module evaluation characteristics

Correct answer	Evaluation type	Normal time	Long time	Min. accuracy
method	Edit distance	15	60	80
Declaration body	Multiple options	10	60	100
constructor	Edit distance	15	60	80
False	Multiple options	10	30	100
{}	Multiple options	10	30	100
Return name	Keywords	15	60	75
new	Keywords	10	30	100
usr = new User();	Code problem	30	300	100

In Table 3 we show the results of the student interaction (probabilistic computations).

Table 3. Probabilistics results for student interaction

Accuracy	Probability
83	0.83
100	0.90
100	1.00
0	0
0	0
75	0.60
100	0.90
94	0.85

As this learning module had assigned a 20% to the practical evaluations (this is designed by the module creator), the probability that this resource has facilitated the learning to the student is of 0.65. This value later is added to the calculations done to other resources of the same type. Thus, at the beginning of another resource, the probabilities can determine that the student belongs to certain characteristics of learning.

In the last part, the results of the student evaluation are shown. It is necessary to indicate that the result is different from the one used for calculating the learning type.

5 Related Work

Research in this area has been oriented for teaching single programming languages and most of the time for introductory courses. ITEM/IP [14] is an ITS for teaching programming. ITEM/IP is only oriented to provide an introductory course to Turingal (a programming language). GREATERP [15] is another ITS based on Anderson's theory of learning and oriented for teaching the LISP programming language. A system named BITS [16] is also oriented for teaching only one programming language. One disadvantage of those systems is that they are oriented to just one programming language.

6 Conclusions

L2Code predicts the best learning resources and style for the students. The learning modules are a set of features that describe when the learning resource must be presented to the student. When starting any particular unit, the predictive engine calculates which resource the student must use for his learning process.

At present some empirical studies are taking place to analyze the reaction of students to the Object-Oriented Programming Course produced with L2Code. The course combines e-learning and classroom material. This study is examining instructional strategies due to the relationship between them and the learning performance.

Future work involves more implementation development of a user-friendly interface to create courses and further analysis in order to identify the relevance of different features. Also, we are working with other machine learning techniques.

References

1. Soloway, E., Spohrer, J.: Studying the Novice Programmer, p. 497. Lawrence Erlbaum Associates, Hillsdale (1988)
2. Barr, M., Holden, S., Phillips, D., Greening, T.: An exploration of novice programming errors in an object-oriented environment. SIGCSE Bulletin 31(4), 42–46 (1999)
3. Deek, F., Kimmel, H., McHugh, J.: Pedagogical changes in the delivery of the first-course in computer science: Problem solving. The Programming. Journal of Engineering Education 87, 313–320 (1998)
4. Wiedenbeck, S., Ramalingam, V., Sarasamma, S., Corritore, C.: A comparison of the comprehension of object-oriented and procedural programs by novice programmers. Interacting with Computers 11(3), 255–282 (1999)

5. McCracken, M., Almstrum, V., Diaz, D., Guzdial, M., Hagan, D., Kolikant, Y.B., Laxer, C., Thomas, L., Utting, I., Wilusz, T.: A multi-national, multi-institutional study of assessment of programming skills of first-year CS students. SIGCSE Bulletin 33(4), 125–180 (2001)
6. Gardner, H.: Frames of Mind: The theory of multiple intelligences. Basic Books, New York (1983)
7. Kelly, D., Tangney, B.: Predicting Learning Characteristics in a Multiple Intelligence Based Tutoring System. In: Lester, J.C., Vicari, R.M., Paraguaçu, F. (eds.) ITS 2004. LNCS, vol. 3220, pp. 678–688. Springer, Heidelberg (2004)
8. Lang, M.: Implementation of Naïve Bayesian Classifiers in Java, http://www.iit.edu/~ipro356f03/ipro/documents/naive-bayes.doc
9. Sommerville, I.: Software Engineering. Addison-Wesley, Reading (2001)
10. Martin, R.C.: UML for Java Programmers, http://books-support.softbank.co.jp/isbn/pdf/2513.pdf
11. Gosling, Joy, Steele, Bracha: The Java™ Language Specification
12. Hunter, J., McLaughlin, B.: JDOM™ Project, http://www.jdom.org
13. Eclipse Foundation: SWT (Standard Widget Toolkit), http://www.eclipse.org/swt
14. Brusilovsky, P.L.: Intelligent Tutor, Environment and Manual for Introductory Programming. Innovations in Education and Teaching International 29(1), 26–34 (1992)
15. Reiser, B., Anderson, J., Farrell, R.: Dynamic Student Modeling in an Intelligent Tutor for LISP Programming. In: IJCAI, pp. 8–14 (1985)
16. Butz, C.J., Hua, S., Maguire, R.B.: A Web-Based intelligent Tutoring System for Computer Programming. In: Proceedings of the 2004 IEEE/WIC/ACM International Conference on Web Intelligence, pp. 159–165 (2004)

VISOLE: An Example of Hybrid Learning

Jun Jie Shang[1], Morris Siu Yung Jong[2], Fong Lok Lee[2],
and Jimmy Ho Man Lee[2]

[1] Graduate Shcool of Education, Peking University,
Beijing, 100871, China
jjshang@gse.pku.edu.cn
[2] Centre for the Advancement of Information Technology in Education,
The Chinese University of Hong Kong, Hong Kong

Abstract. In this paper, we discussed the VISOLE learning mode, which is a hybrid learning that combined the game-based learning and the traditional learning. Briefly speaking, the VISOLE approach is composed of 3 phases in which students have to (Phase 1) preliminarily acquire some high-level knowledge in specific subject domains through teachers' scaffolding; (Phase 2) actively participate as game characters in a game-based virtual interactive environment to construct knowledge and skills through their near real-life game-play experiences; (Phase 3) reflect and generalize their game-based learning experiences through teachers' debriefing. During the design and develop process of the VISOLE, we paid close attention to the guiding function of teachers, and emphasized the subject position of students. Under the present research, we empirically found that most students were much more motivated during this learning process, and enhanced their knowledge, intellectual and non-intellectual skills. Therefore, VISOLE is a valuable learning mode worthy of promotion.

Keywords: Hybrid Learning, Blended Learning, Blending Learning, Educational Game, VISOLE.

1 Introduction

Since the 1990s, the applications of e_Learning in the field of education have been accelerated, which pushes forward reforms in education and generates many novel educational thoughts and ideas. People, however, begin to reflect the limitation and issues of e_Learning, and consider that the role of e_Learning should not be exaggerated and different problems should be solved by using different approaches [1]. By the reflection on e_Learning, the great importance has been attached to the Hybrid Learning (or Blended Learning, or Blending Learning) in the industry, for example, the e-Learning and the traditional face-to-face teaching mode are combined and enhance strong points and avoid weaknesses so as to achieve a better result in the learning.

Actually, hybrid learning is not to simply combine e-Learning and traditional teaching modes, but an in-depth integration according to their characteristics. Therefore,

J. Fong, R. Kwan, and F.L. Wang (Eds.): ICHL 2008, LNCS 5169, pp. 348–358, 2008.

people proposed varieties of combination modes from various angles, and put forward a great deal of designs and application principles for the hybrid learning (e.g., [2][3][4]).

In this paper, we will discuss the VISOLE learning mode, which is a hybrid learning that combines the game-based learning and the traditional learning.

2 Two Important Ideas of Hybrid Learning

Hybrid learning, in short, is a learning mode that combines the advantages of both the traditional learning and the e-Learning. The mode allows teachers to lead the learning process by guiding, illuminating and monitoring the students and the students, who actually learn in the process, to fully demonstrate their initiative, vigor and creativity [5].

According to the the definition and some scholoars' suggestions (e.g., [1][2][4][5]), two important ideads are very important to hybrid learning.

2.1 Highlight on the Combination of the Guiding Function of Teachers and the Subject Position of Students

Along with the rapid development of multimedia network technologies in 1990s, e-Learning has become very popular in many places all over the world. At the same time, constructivist learning theory has aroused attention around the globe and is becoming the basis of a revolution in traditional educational practice. According to some constructivism scholars, knowledge is not taught by teachers, but acquired by learners with the help of others (including teachers and fellow learners) based on necessary educational materials through meaning construction [6].

The constructivist theory vigorously promotes the change in education from traditional teacher-oriented mode to the student-oriented mode (e.g., [7]). Such change is of great significance in inspiring learning motives in students, fostering their self-learning abilities and cultivating creative talents. However, when too much emphasis is put on the subject position of students, the guidance provided by teachers may be ignored, e.g., in some classes teachers let students study totally by themselves without any guidance or help. This may result in unsatisfactory effect [5].

Hybrid learning aims at combining the advantages of e-Learning and traditional face-to-face learning, it shall elicit the initiative, enthusiasm and innovation of students, the ones who actually learn in the learning process, while having teachers take the lead in guiding, illuminating and monitoring the students in the learning process. In short, in the learning process the highlight should be put on the combination of the guiding function of teachers and the subject position of students [1].

2.2 Focus on Deep Hybrids

Though hybrid learning is commonly regarded as a quite effective learning mode, the fact is that we seldom see successful case of hybrid learning. The usual hybrid strategies are either too simple to achieve the expected effect or too complicated to implement.

According to some scholars' suggestions (e.g., [5][8]), hybrid learning is not the simple mixture of online learning and offline learning, but the hybrids on deeper layers. For example, classroom teaching is given while after-class discussion is held online. Such hybrid can achieve certain effect, yet it's still too narrow and the the hybrids in deeper layers are needed.

Moreover, according to Driscoll [2], hybrid learning should include four aspects. *1. To combine or mix modes of web-based technology (e.g., live virtual classroom, self-paced instruction, collaborative learning, streaming video, audio, and text) to accomplish an educational goal. 2. To combine various pedagogical approaches (e.g., constructivism, behaviorism, cognitivism) to produce an optimal learning outcome with or without instructional technology. 3. To combine any form of instructional technology (e.g., videotape, CD-ROM, web-based training, film) with face-to-face instructor-led training.4. To mix or combine instructional technology with actual job tasks in order to create a harmonious effect of learning and working.* Briefly speaking, in order to achive the leanring target, hybrid leanring should combine multiple learning modes, technologies, and learning theories.

In fact, Valdez [9] also states that *"Like chemistry, blended learning is about combining elements to create a desired reaction. However, both practices are not simply about the inclusion of elements but about how the elements are combined. The execution of the formula – by combining the right elements at the right time – creates the desired reaction."* This would imply us that the sequence of mixing the elements is as important as the elements itself in order to meet the desired outcome. Therefore, hybrid learning means the right person provides the right things to learn by using the right method through the right media.

3 A New Game-Based Learning Paradigm: VISOLE

In recent years, computer games have been the most pervasive entertainment in China and all over the word. In 2003, the sale of the video games was almost $16.9 billion across the world [10]. In China, the sale of the online games was almost RMB$6.5 billion in 2005 [11]. All the data showed that the computer games have been a maturing medium and industry, and games have been an important part of our culture as a whole (e.g., [12]).

Because computer games have been an important part of most students' leisure lives, some educators worry that the sex and violence in the games will influence them (e.g.,[13]). Nevertheless, many educators argue that games can be applied into education (e.g., [14]). They think the games can 'Make Learning Fun' (e.g., [15]) and can make 'Learning through Doing' (e.g., [16]), thus can enhance the student's Problem Solving, Collaborative and other skills (e.g., [17]).

During the last decades, lots of educational games have been developed and used in the classroom or outside the classroom, and many studies on the computer games in education have been done, such as CGE [18], MUVEE [19], and Game To Teach [20]. All the studies have shown that the games can arouse the students' intrinsic motivation, and improve the students' basic skills such as eye-hand coordination, problem solving skills, collaborative skills, and other skills (e.g., [21]). In addition, the games can facilitate the affective learning, active learning, situated learning, and collaborative learning (e.g. [22] [14]).

In order to explorer the educational potential of the educational games, Lee and Lee [23] has proposed a new Game-based Learning Paradigm--VISOLE (Virtual Interactive Student-Oriented Learning Environment), which aims to help students learn from near real-life experiences and social constructions of knowledge.

3.1 What's VISOLE?

VISOLE [23] is a learning mode that uses the virtual game environment to facilitate learning. The web-based game environment is a simulation of the real world where students participate as "citizens" and take part in shaping the development of the virtual world. It provides a platform for participants to apply the theoretical knowledge to solve problems in a near-real environment, as well as to develop high-level skills for communication and problem solving in addition to subject knowledge. VI-SOLE is usually divided into three stages [24]:

Stage 1: Scaffolding Learning

The first part of VISOLE is the scaffolding stage, where students are guided to learn different concepts in a series of formal lessons. In this stage, teachers act as facilitators to guide learners to construct the knowledge based on the reading materials provided and other authentic information on the Web.

Stage 2: Game-based Learning

In the second part, a virtual Game-based environment with near-real simulation is provided to students. In this stage, students are free to explore in the environment, to initiate changes, to solve problems arouse by players in the same environment, or any other activities that might happen in real environment. During this stage, students are expected to learn independently. However, teachers again act as facilitators in extracting scenarios and assist students in-group discussions and promote Reflection and Debriefing.

Stage 3: Debriefing and Reflection

In the last part, teachers play a more important role. They help students to reflect and debrief all the learning process and explain the representative scenarios and evaluate each group and each student.

Some educators (e.g., [25]) argue that simply using a simulation does not ensure that learners can generate the kinds of understandings that educators might desire. In order to solve the problem, some researchers (e.g, [26]) suggested that reflection and debriefing during or after the playing was the most effective approach.

In VISOLE, every group must submit a reflective journal every day after the playing. When the whole game is finished, every group must submit a group debriefing report and everyone must submit a personal debriefing report.

3.2 An Example of VISOLE – FARMTASIA

FARMTASIA [24] is the first series of educational resources that has been developed under the VISOLE framework, which involves the subject domains of geography, biology, natural environment and hazard, government, economics, production system and technology. In this one, the interdisciplinary context deployed in the VISOLE game is a farming system in which the students need to acquire knowledge and skills in cultivation, horticulture, pasturage and husbandry. In order for the teacher to easily review the students' activities in the farm and to more conveniently extract scenarios for conducting case studies in the class debriefing meetings, an innovative student game-play logging system and "replay" function [27] are implemented into the game system. Figure 1 shows the main screen shot of the game.

Fig. 1. Screen shots of FARMTASIA

3.3 Empirical Study of VISOLE

After finished the development of Farmtasia, we conducted an empirical study in Hong Kong [28], 254 high school students and about 28 teachers took part in the study. In this study, a mix of qualitative and quantitative methods was employed for data collection and analysis, including the knowledge pre- and post-tests, generic-skill test, perception survey, in-depth interviews as well as artifacts of students' reflective journals, reports and game-playing records. All of these intensively focused on investigating students' and teachers' perceptions, students' learning motivation, behaviors, effectiveness with respect to the VISOLE approach and researching the design strategies for situated educational games.

In the research, most of the findings were positive in general. For example, Students' perceptions on learning with VISOLE were collected through a self-developed questionnaire with 5-point likert scale. Table 1 shows the summary on students' general impression of system. As shown in table 1, the satisfaction percentage of all questions exceeded 50% and the satisfaction percentage of this learning activity achieved 72.8%. So the students were quite positive towards VISOLE.

Table 1. Students' General Impression on Learning with VISOLE

Questions	Strongly Agree(%)	Agree(%)	Neutral (%)	Disagree(%)	Strongly Disagree(%)
I am very satisfied with this learning activity.	15.5	57.3	23.5	2.3	1.4
I am very satisfied with this game.	12.7	49.8	23.0	8.0	6.6
I am very satisfied with the assistant materials and the support.	10.4	40.1	35.8	10.4	3.3
I am very satisfied with my achievement.	9.9	41.3	36.6	8.0	4.2

In addition, according to the result of pre-and post-tests for measuring students' advancement on the subject-specific knowledge and multi-disciplinary application, the average mark of the post-test was 13.7% higher than the average mark of the pre-test (p-value<0.001). Actually, the level of difficulty of the pre- and post-tests was the same. Each of them was composed of 25 multiple-choice questions, 15 true-or-false questions and 2 open-ended short questions.

On the other hand, it could tell from the qualitative evidence collected through, such as the observations and interviews that the participating teachers were quite positive towards the multi-disciplinary and constructivist learning paradigm of VISOLE. They also highlighted that it was a good motivational approach, especially for the students with less learning motive. A teacher made the following reflective argument –

> Every year I need to teach the topic of agriculture which is a part of the geography curriculum. My students hate this topic very much, they call "agriculture" as "uglyculture" ... they perceive it is the most boring topic in the curriculum. In fact, this is understandable as agriculture is so far away in their life, especially in Hong Kong ... I really want to adopt VISOLE and use FARMTASIA to help my teaching next year. I want to let my students know agriculture is not that boring and in fact can be very interesting and challenging. I would like them to learn constructively and authentically .....

Some teachers were amazed some passive-learning students became active learners in the VISOLE process –

> They actively questioned me some knowledge that seemed very vital for playing the game. I told them that they should look for the answer in the Knowledge Manual by themselves. They said they had done but nothing related could be found. Then I asked them to look it up from the Internet, they said they had done too .... This is the first time that they have been so active in participating in a learning activity ......

4 VISOLE and Hybrid Learning

In the foregoing paragraphs we discuss two important ideas in hybrid learning and give a brief introduction to our VISOLE research project. In this section we'll discuss in detail how the two important ideas work in VISOLE project.

4.1 Highlight on the Combination of the Guiding Function of Teachers and the Subject Position of Students

VISOLE is indeed a "student-oriented" learning mode. Students should arrange the study hours by themselves, play the games themselves, find and solve problems in the games by themselves, analyze the problems by themselves and write reflection reports. However, besides emphasising the subject position of students, we still put emphasis on the guiding function of teachers, and teachers are required to take the following actions in the games and out of the games [29]:

1. Guide and help students to learn related knowledge

In VISOLE, though students are expected to learn related knowledge spontaneously, teachers as intellectual constructor and helper still should guide and help students to learn. For example, in the scaffolding learning stage, teachers should guide students to learn the related knowledge from Knowledge Handbook, the Internet and libraries. Of course, the teachers do not teach the knowledge by explaining everything in detail as they usually do in traditional teaching process.

2. Encourage students in the learning process

Teachers should encourage students to learn in the whole learning process.

Activities of competition and cooperation, including resource competition, market competition, game championship, environmental protection, etc., are provided in the farm, and teachers should encourage the competitions and cooperation. It is also the teachers' responsibility to prevent unfair competition and maintain team-work spirit among students.

Communication is important to guarantee cooperation in the learning process. When a game is in progress, the students should be encouraged to communication with students in other teams, teachers and experts. Student discussions in online forums should also be encouraged.

3. Guide and help students to debrief and reflect

Many researchers regard it most effective to improve the learning effect by debriefing and reflecting the game experience during the games or after the games [25][26]. The role of teaches is very important in this aspect. During the games, they should check the student performances with the "Replay" function [27] of the system and give suggestions to typical scenarios, e.g., when a teacher sees a student planting wheat in December, the teacher should remind him / her to look up the game manual. During the learning process, teachers should lead students to debrief their performances and write reflective journals in their BLOGs; reflective journals on typical experiences should be picked out by the teachers for comment or explanation; after the games, the teachers should guide the students in writing debriefing reports to help them get firmer grasp of the knowledge they've learnt and be able to apply the knowledge they've learnt in virtual worlds to the realities.

Generally speaking, teachers are not getting less works in VISOLE, but more works and more complicated works.

4.2 Focus on Deep Hybrids

It has been stated already that hybrid learning is not the simple mixture of online learning and offline learning, but hybrids on deeper layers. In VISOLE, hybrids on deeper layers are shown in the follows aspects:

Firstly, the hybrid embodies at the combination of online leanring and offline learning. In "Scaffolding Learning" stage and "Debriefing and Reflection" stage, teachers shall organize students to learn related knowledge in class and arrange their debriefing and reflection in class, on the contrary, the "Game-based Learning" is done online and students may choose any time appropriate to them to log into the games.

Secondly, the hybrid includes multiple learning modes, technologies, and leanring theories. For example, a student may listen to his teacher in class to learn related knowledge, or learn such knowledge from an online Knowledge Handbook or Internet resources such as Wikipedia, he may also use library resources to learn the knowledge. As for cooperation in learning, students may discuss their experiences face-to-face in class, or in BBS of the official game website, or in their BLOGs. As for debriefing and reflection, teachers can guide students in their debriefing and reflection in class and students also need to write debriefing and reflective journals in their BLOG; after the games, students still need to write complete debriefing reports. In fact, the result of the empirical study of VISOLE [28] really showed that VISOLE can promote the active learning, situated learning, collaborative learning and problem-based learning.

Thirdly, maybe the most important, the hybrid embodies at the combination of "learning" and "practice", which focuses on applying what students learn to realities and how far they achieve in practice. This is just the very advantage of educational games. The games usually provide "almost real" virtual environments, in which players play the roles in the games, find problems, analyze problems and solve problems. In this process the players learn related knowledge as well as advanced skills including how to solve a problem, how to cooperate and how to cultivate innovation.

VISOLE also provides an "almost real" farm for students, the geographical, climate and economic models in VISOLE are built based on actual data, students need to decide, based on different situations, what and when to plant, when to harvest, what and how many animals to raise, etc. During the process, the students can apply what they've learnt in the scaffolding learning process to practice so as to check how far their study has achieved.

In fact, in an interview after the experiment [28], many students and teachers expressed that it is a learning mode which enables students to properly apply what they've learnt to the reality and helps students to have deeper understanding of the knowledge:

> *When a teacher teaches you something, you will probably forget it soon after the teacher finishes; now you have to use it to pass scenario after scenario, so you'll have an basic idea on what*

the thing can do, unlike in class, you will not feel confused (Student A).
    Such learning mode helps you to fully digest what you've learnt (Student B).

In a word, we tried to combine multiple learning modes, leanring theories, and technologies to achieve the learning targets.

5 Discussion and Conclusion

This paper discusses how the guiding function of teachers is emphasized and how hybrids deeper layers are implemented in VISOLE. From the experiment result [28], we can see VISOLE does help to motive students in learning process, encourages them to actively study things by themselves, to cooperate with each other and to do in depth researches. Such learning mode also helps them to make progress in dealing with knowledge, skills, emotions and values.

However, such hybrid of game-based learning and traditional learning does have problems of its own. For example, how to motive as many student as possible? How to converts their desire to recreate into study motive? How to improve learning efficiency in games? How to improve the advanced abilities of students more effectively? How to arrange the working hours of teachers? And so on.

In addition, the FARMTASIA we discussed above are used for elementary education, however, such learning mode also has a future in higher education. For example, Peking University has developed a complete course of "Decision Making Simulation" based on BUSIMU, a software application simulating company competition. This course creates a virtual environment for MBA students to practice their skills in company decision making. During the learning process, a team of 4 - 5 students forms a "company", in which a student may play the role of production manager, sales manager, etc. The students make decisions concerning production, marketing, human resources, and capital operation and development strategies based on the information provided by the software application on market environment, company condition and competitors, and they compete with other teams. The scores are given to the students based on the performance of their company after a number of simulations. Advanced educational management game, in which a student major in education management can run a virtual university, is also available.

To sum up, hybrid learning which combines game-based learning and traditional learning is a learning mode worth paying attention to, worth further researches and worth spreading.

References

1. Li, K.D., Zhao, J.H.: The application and principle of hybrid learning. E-education Research (7), 1–6 (2004)
2. Driscoll, M.: Blended learning: Let's get beyond the hype. Learning and Training Innovations (2002)
3. Singh, H.: Building Effective Blended Learning Programs. Educational Technology 43(6), 51–54 (2003)

4. Valiathan, P.: Blended Learning Models (2002),
    http://www.learningcircuits.org/2002/aug2002/valiathan.html
5. He, K.K.: A view of new trends in educational technology theories from the blending
    learning. E-education Research (3), 1–6 (2004)
6. He, K.K.: Constructivism: The theory basis to reform the traditional teaching. Chinese
    Teaching in Middle School (8), 58–60 (2002)
7. Levin, D., Ben-Jacob, T., Ben-Jacob, M.: The learning environment of the 21st century.
    AACE Journal, formerly Educational Technology Review 1(13), 8–12 (2000)
8. Four stages in hybrid learning,
    http://www.online-edu.org/
    viewthread.php?tid=5515&extra=page%3D1
9. Valdez, R.: Blended Learning: Maximizing the Impact of an Integrated Solution (a white
    paper), http://www.stratvision.net/Portal/uploads/blend.pdf
10. ELSPA.: Interactive Leisure Software: Global Market Assessment and Forecast to 2006.
    Report for ELSPA (The Entertainment and Leisure Software Publishers Association),
    http://www.elspa.com/serv/screendigestbrief.asp
11. iResearch. The 5th online game research report (2006), http://china.17173.com
12. Fromme, J.: Computer games as a part of children's culture. The international journal of
    computer game research 3(1) (2003)
13. Provenzo, Eugene, F.: Video kids : making sense of Nintendo. Harvard University Press,
    Cambridge, Mass (1991)
14. Prensky, M.: Digital Game-Based Learning. McGraw Hill, New York (2000)
15. Malone, T.W.: What Makes Things Fun to Learn? A Study of Intrinsically Motivating
    Computer Games. Xerox, Palo Alto (1980)
16. Thiagarajan, S.: The myths and realities of simulations in performance technology. Educa-
    tional Technology 38(5), 35–41 (1998)
17. Whitebread, D.: Developing children's problem-solving: the educational uses of adventure
    games. In: McFarlane, A. (ed.) Information Technology and Authentic Learning, pp. 13–
    37. Routledge, London (1997)
18. Becta. Computer Games in Education Project Report, 2001 (2001),
    http://www.becta.org.uk/research/
    research.cfm?section=1&id=2835
19. Dede, C., Ketelhut, D., Ruess, K.: Motivation, Usability, and Learning Outcomes in a Pro-
    totype Museum-based Muti-User Virtutal Environment. ICLS, Scattle, Washington (2002)
20. Squire, K.: Video games in education. International Journal of Intelligent Simulations and
    Gaming (2), 1 (2003)
21. Greenfield, P.M.: Mind and Media: The Effects of Television, Computers and Video
    Games. Harvard University Press, Cambridge, Mass (1984)
22. Bredemeier, M.E., Greenblatt, C.E.: The educational effectiveness of games: A synthesis
    of findings. Simulation & Gaming 12(3), 307–332 (1981)
23. Lee, J.H.M., Lee, F.L.: Virtual Interactive Student-Oriented Learning Environment (VI-
    SOLE): Extending the frontier of web-based learning. The scholarship of teaching and
    learning organized by University Grant Council, HKSAR (2001)
24. Jong, M.S.Y., Shang, J.J., Lee, F.L., Lee, J.H.M.: A new vision for empowering learning
    and teaching with IT: The VISOLE approach. In: Proceedings of the Hong Kong Interna-
    tional IT in Education Conference 2006: Capacity building for learning through IT, Hong
    Kong, February 6-8. HKSAR (2006)
25. Thiagarajan, S.: The myths and realities of simulations in performance technology. Educa-
    tional Technology 38(5), 35–41 (1998)

26. Jaques, D.: Debriefing debriefing. In: Ments, M.V., Hearnden, K. (eds.) Effective use of games & simulation: The proceedings of the 1984 conference of SAGSET, the Society for the Advancement of Games and Simulations in Education and Training at Loughborough University of Technology, pp. 57–65. SAGSET, Leicestershire (1985)

27. Shang, J.J., Jong, M.S.Y., Lee, F.L., Lee, J.H.M., Wong, M.K.H., Luk, E.T.H., Cheung, K.K.F.: Using the Record-Replay Function for Elaboration of Knowledge in Educational Games. In: Mizoguchi, R., Dillenbourg, P., Zhu, Z. (eds.) Learning by effective utilization of technologies: Facilitating intercultural, pp. 503–506. IOS Press, Netherlands (2006)

28. Jong, M.S.Y., Shang, J.J., Lee, F.L., Lee, J.H.M.: An Exploratory Study on VISOLE – A New Game-based Constructivist Online Learning Paradigm. In: America Educational Research Association Annual Meeting (AERA 2007), Chicago, April 9-13 (2007)

29. Jong, M.S.Y., Shang, J.J., Lee, F.L., Lee, J.H.M.: Two critical teacher facilitating tasks in VISOLE: Scaffolding and debriefing. In: Proceedings of 10th Annual Global Chinese Conference on Computers in Education, Beijing, China, June 2-5 (2006)

Designing an Automatic Debugging Assistant for Improving the Learning of Computer Programming[*]

Maria S.W. Lam, Eric Y.K. Chan, Victor C.S. Lee[**], and Y.T. Yu

Department of Computer Science, City University of Hong Kong
{marialam,csvlee,csytyu}@cityu.edu.hk, chanyk@cs.cityu.edu.hk

Abstract. Finding bugs in programs (debugging) is a core skill for practical programmers. However, debugging programs can be difficult to novice programmers. Even worse, repetitive failures may defeat students' enthusiasm for learning. The presence of a mentor giving hints and help face-to-face with students will surely make such a learning process much more effective and enjoyable. However, this requires lots of manpower and resources. To address this problem, we seek to capitalize on the potential advantages offered by hybrid learning. We are working towards a system for providing a certain level of automatic debugging assistance to students. Instructors can identify common errors in students' programs using the system and incorporate useful debug-guiding information into it so that students will be prompted with pertinent hints when common errors are detected in their programs.

Keywords: automatic debugging assistant, computer programming, PASS, test cases and annotations.

1 Introduction

Finding bugs in programs (debugging) is a core skill for practical programmers. However, debugging programs can be difficult to novice programmers. Even worse, repetitive failures may defeat students' enthusiasm for learning. The presence of a mentor giving hints and help face-to-face with students will make such a learning process much more effective and enjoyable. However, this requires lots of manpower and resources. To address this problem, we seek to capitalize on the potential advantages offered by hybrid learning (also called blended learning) [1], whereby students' learning experience through their face-to-face interaction with instructors and tutors is supplemented and enriched by the use of e-learning systems.

We are working towards an Automatic Debugging Assistant (ADA) which aims at providing a certain level of automatic debugging assistance to students. Instructors can identify common errors in students' programs using ADA and incorporate useful debug-guiding information into it so that students will be prompted with pertinent hints by ADA when common errors are detected in their programs.

---

[*] This work is partially supported by a Teaching Development Grant (project no. 6000145) from City University of Hong Kong.
[**] Corresponding author.

J. Fong, R. Kwan, and F.L. Wang (Eds.): ICHL 2008, LNCS 5169, pp. 359–370, 2008.

ADA is designed to be an extension of an existing Programming Assignment aSsessment System (PASS) developed at our university for improving the teaching and learning of computer programming [2]. Since 2004, PASS has been used in many computer programming courses to automate the programming assignment submission and grading process [3-5]. Through PASS, the instructor may upload the assignment and practice problems with some preset public test cases for students to obtain the problem specification and test their programs online. Students can submit their programs to PASS for assessment before the submission deadline specified by the instructor. Afterwards, upon the instructor's request, PASS can automatically produce the results of assessment of the students' programs [5]. Then students can read their grades, together with the feedback manually added by the tutor.

The sections that follow in this paper will explain the advantages and challenges of providing automatic debugging assistance for students. Then we discuss some relevant attributes of a test case, which is the core data entity of the automatic debugging assistant, and describe the design framework of the system. These are followed by a case study, some observations arising from it, and finally, some concluding remarks.

2 Problems in Manual Debugging

Solving problems by constructing correct computer programs is an iterative process. It is common to take more than a few iterations to debug and test programs before a correct version can be produced. However, debugging programs can be difficult, time-consuming, and prone to human errors. More bugs may be inadvertently introduced while revising the program if the original bugs cannot be correctly located and fixed during debugging.

There are many integrated development environments (IDEs) which provide facilities to computer programmers for software development. An IDE normally consists of a source code editor, a compiler and/or interpreter, build automation tools, and (usually) a debugger. They are designed to maximize programmer productivity by providing a user-friendly integrated environment with different components for users to edit, compile, build (create the executable program) and debug their programs. For debugging, the IDEs mainly help the programmers in removing the typing or syntax errors in the source code. However, the most difficult step in debugging is to find the logical software bugs which prevent the computer program from behaving as intended. Conventionally, the capability for detecting and fixing logical bugs depends heavily on the student's own experience, logical thinking ability and programming skills.

Practice is a major learning activity to gain experience and develop good programming skills. So, it is very important to arouse students' interest in doing more practice in a computer programming course. However, students nowadays will easily lose motivation and interest in program debugging, especially when they do not know if they are working in a right direction. An automatic debugging assistant, whose design is presented in the next section, will probably help motivate students to maintain the momentum of the search for a solution to their programming tasks.

3 Design of the Automatic Debugging Assistant

3.1 Attributes of a Test Case

A set of carefully designed test cases not only helps students partially verify the correctness of their programs, but also helps them identify possible semantic errors by comparing the program outputs with the expected ones. In addition, in case of wrong program outputs, meaningful annotation describing each test run can help students figure out the source of errors more efficiently. In a testing and debugging process, test case is a core data entity. We first discuss some relevant attributes of a test case.

Level of Difficulty. PASS allows the instructor to prescribe programming exercises and inform the students of the level of difficulty of each exercise. To extend this concept, the difficulty of developing a solution to the same programming exercise can vary substantially by prescribing different test cases that the student's program is required to pass. Thus, instructors can design and classify the test cases into different levels of difficulty so that students can construct their programs progressively and incrementally, and test their programs at each stage of development [4]. Moreover, students can easily learn that they are working in a right direction and get a sense of satisfaction when their programs can at least pass the test cases at a lower level of difficulty. This motivates them to put more effort to get their programs pass all the test cases at the higher levels of difficulty.

Visibility. Instructors can specify whether a test case is *open/public* or *hidden/private* [5]. For instance, in PASS, test cases for practice problems can be open for students (that is, all students know exactly what these test cases are) to check the correctness of their programs, while for assessment problems, like assignments or online quizzes, instructors can hide all or some of the test cases for the purpose of grading [2]. In another programming submission and testing system called Marmoset, Spacco et al. [6] further divide test cases into four visibility levels to serve different purposes, namely, *student tests* (those written by students), *public tests* (provided to students), *release tests* (selectively made available to students) and *secret tests* (not disclosed to students until after the submission deadline).

Inputs. Inputs are values to be fed into a student's program during execution. Depending on the problem specification, instructors may ask students to write programs which accept a single input, a specified number of inputs or an unlimited number of inputs until a specific value is entered or a specific key is hit. Also, whether any pre-processed input validation is required depends on the learning objectives of the problem. It is crucial to design a wide diversity of test inputs to cover most, if not all, possibilities to test the target program comprehensively. On the other hand, redundant test inputs that hint at the same bug may be eliminated to avoid a waste of debugging time. Nevertheless, it should be borne in mind that a program passing all the test cases can still be incorrect [2].

Expected Outputs. To check the correctness of students' programs, each test case is associated with a corresponding expected output. In this respect, PASS can be configured to display messages with varying amount of details. One option is to simply tell whether student's program output matches the expected output or not. Another option is to compare student's program output with the expected one and highlight their differences to provide more hints for students to figure out the possible source of errors [4].

Common Wrong Outputs with Annotations. Although there can be many different wrong outputs produced by different incorrect programs when they are executed with the same test case, some wrong outputs caused by typical program bugs usually appear more frequently than those caused by less common bugs. Our aim is to provide help to students who commit the common mistakes, as such help will have greater chances of benefiting more students.

In a recent study, Jadud [7] explored the behaviour of first-year university students who were learning to program in Java, and came up with a list of the most common errors they encountered related to the compilation of their programs. The list includes *unknown variable, missing or misplacement of semicolon, incorrect matching of brackets, unknown method,* and others. In another study, Morimoto et al. [8] developed a system, called TeCProg (which is a support system for Teaching Computer Programming), that analyzes the trend of past compilation errors to facilitate teachers to understand the common mistakes made by students in their programming work. In our work, we are more interested in detecting the logical errors made by students. To identify these errors, we examined a sample of incorrect programs submitted by students in their first programming course. Based on these sample programs, we prepared some annotations as debugging hints specifically for each of the bugs. Table 1 shows some typical program bugs that result in common wrong outputs and the corresponding debug-guiding annotations. Given the bug types, specific annotation for each test case can be entered manually by instructors or retrieved automatically from a repository. In the latter case, instructors can, if desired, further refine the retrieved annotations to provide more concrete hints to students to help them debug their programs.

General Annotation for Uncommon Wrong Outputs. It is impractical to capture all possible wrong outputs produced by incorrect programs when they are executed with a particular test case, as these programs can be written in myriads of ways. Besides the common wrong outputs, other wrong outputs or unexpected behaviour can be produced by an erroneous program, such as the lack of output, timeout, deadlock, or memory/resource leakage. These errors can only be identified by examining the program code line by line. In this case, the annotation may simply document the purpose of the test case as a hint for students to dig into the cause of bugs by themselves.

Table 1. Some typical program bugs

Type	Description	Annotation
Declaration	A declaration specifies the interpretation and attributes of a set of identifiers, which are used to define data types and initial values for variables, functions or constants in the source code. Many errors are caused by incorrect declaration statements. Example. Using an integer-type variable to store a real number may induce mathematical errors. Say, when the number 1.99 is stored as an integer, its value may be mistaken as 1.	Verify that the variables, functions and constants are correctly defined and initialized with appropriate data types and values.
Operator / Specifier Symbol	Many errors occur when the operators / specifier symbols are wrongly used.	Verify the use of operators / specifier symbols.
Boundary	Many errors occur when the input values are at the border of different parts of the input domain.	Verify or add codes to handle inputs at the border of different parts of the input domain.
Conditional Statement (if-then-else)	A conditional statement performs different computations or actions depending on whether its condition evaluates to true or false.	Verify the conditions in conditional statements.
Iteration	Errors commonly occur in loop constructs. In particular, failing to test the loop termination condition correctly may lead to an infinite loop or an incorrect number of iterations.	Verify the loop termination conditions.
Arithmetic Rounding	Rounding error is the difference between the calculated approximation of a number and its exact mathematical value. Example. To calculate (1/3 + 1/3) to 2 decimal places, if the value 1/3 is rounded to 0.33 before addition, the result will be 0.66. Otherwise, if rounding is done after addition, the result will be 0.67.	Verify the mathematical equations or calculations to avoid errors due to rounding.
Output Format	Incorrect formatting of the output, such as incorrect number of decimal places, wrong spelling of words, or occurrence of a redundant punctuation mark.	Verify that the format and wording of the program output conform exactly to the requirements stated in the program specification.
Exceptional / Abnormal	Some errors may occur when the program fails to handle gracefully the abnormal values, such as zero or negative values.	Verify or add exception value handling code, if applicable.

3.2 Design Framework of ADA

ADA is designed for use in the following way. Students submit their programs to PASS for testing. If a submission passes all the open test cases, PASS will prompt a successful execution message. Otherwise, ADA will provide the test case annotations together with a failure message. These annotations are either manually pre-set or derived from past submissions. Meanwhile, the current submissions, together with their wrong program outputs, will be recorded and subsequently become instances of past submissions for future annotation enhancement. In addition, submission statistics such as the number of attempts before successful execution will be recorded for analyzing the performance of students, the common mistakes committed by students, the level of difficulty of the problem or its associated test cases, and so on.

The design framework of ADA is shown in Fig. 1. It consists of six modules: *Test Case Editor / Upload, Result Processor, Submission Statistics Collector, Submission History Accumulator, Submission Post-processor* and *Annotation Repository*. The modules are briefly described as follows.

Test Case Editor / Upload Module. This module provides an interface for instructors to edit or upload test cases in a predefined format.

Result Processor Module. This module compares student's program outputs against expected outputs. For each correct program output, a successful execution message will be displayed. Otherwise, a failure message and an annotation for each wrong output will be provided. Depending on the preference of instructors, the expected outputs can be shown with the differences highlighted to provide more hints for students to revise their programs.

Submission Statistics Collector Module. Students are allowed to attempt and submit programs for testing any number of times before a given deadline. This module collects submission statistics such as the number of attempts before successful execution and the mean time between submissions. It also provides functions for instructors to organize and analyze the statistics for system performance evaluation.

Submission History Accumulator Module. All information in each submission, including the test cases, student programs and their outputs, will be recorded by this module for subsequent processing to identify typical bugs and derive respective annotations.

Submission Post-processor Module. This module analyzes the historical submission records and extracts useful knowledge or rules by artificial intelligence or data mining techniques to identify typical program bugs and derive respective specific annotations. It is a recursive process. The number of submission records will grow with time and more information can be used to refine the rules and enhance the quality of annotations or even track the trend of typical program bugs.

Annotation Repository Module. This module stores the typical program bugs and the associated specific annotations derived by the Submission Post-processor Module. This information can be accessed by the Result Processor Module to retrieve a particular specific annotation given a bug type.

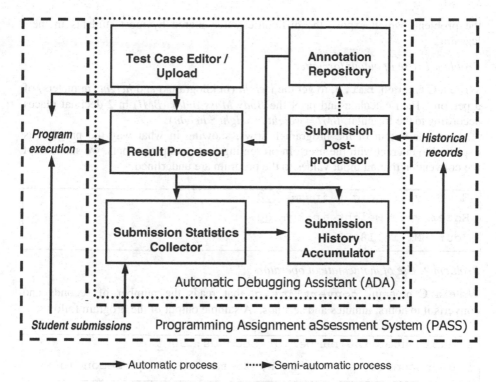

Automatic process   ⋯⋯▶Semi-automatic process

Fig. 1. Design Framework for Automatic Debugging Assistant

4 Case Study

To demonstrate the effectiveness of the output-specific annotation about helping students to find out the bugs of an incorrect program, a case study has been undertaken. In the rest of this section, the specification of the selected problems in a programming course are given first, followed by the creation of test cases and their annotations for the problems, and finally some observations and discussions.

4.1 Selected Programming Problems

We selected a foundation C programming course for the case study. Most students in this course are new to programming. In the course, students need to learn the basics of C programming, including data declaration, use of operators, as well as conditional statements and loops. During the learning process, they often feel frustrated to tackle the semantic errors in their programs, the issue which we are trying to address.

From the course's historical records in PASS, we selected the following three problems for detailed study, based on their complexity as well as their expected outputs' characteristics. Problems with too simple output(s), say, output values that are "Yes or No" or "True or False", are not selected. Problems with historically the highest attempt rate and failure rate from the remaining ones are selected. Thus, we selected firstly, the problems that contain various patterns of outputs, and secondly, the problems which expose the difficulties encountered by most students in their learning.

Problem 1: Use of output formatter

Write a C program, **bmi.c**, to get the *weight* (in kilograms) and *height* (in meters) of a person. Then calculate and print the *Body Mass Index* (*BMI*) in 2 decimal places according to the formula: *BMI = weight / (height * height)*.

   A sample output of the program follows, showing in what way the program is expected to interact with the user. In presenting these sample outputs, we shall adopt the convention that all input values to the program are underlined.

```
Enter your height in m: 1.8
Enter your weight in kg: 60
Your BMI is 18.52
```

Problem 2: Use of mathematical operators

Write a C program, **convertTime.c**, that reads the number of seconds and converts it to hours, minutes and seconds. A sample output of the program follows.

```
Please enter the number of seconds: 5000
5000 second(s) =  1 hour(s) 23 minute(s) 20 second(s)
```

Problem 3: Use of loop

Write a C program, **factor.c**, that reads a positive integer n and outputs all its factors k, where $1 < k \leq n - 1$. A sample output of the program follows.

```
12
2 3 4 6
```

   Below is another sample output of the program. Note that since the integer 7 has no factors other than 1 and itself, the program should produce no output.

```
7
```

4.2   Test Case and Annotation Creation

Because a variety of programming styles may be used by different students, it would be difficult to design test cases based on their program source code. Therefore, test cases for each problem are designed by considering the input and output domains.

Since input validation is not required in these problems, invalid inputs are omitted. Test cases and their corresponding annotations are created based on *Table 1*.

One class of typical test cases consists of exceptional cases to determine whether the programs can handle unusual values. For instance, if the input value of *weight* in Problem 1 is assigned to zero, the output *BMI* should be 0.00 (except when zero is assigned to the variable *height*). This test case can verify the correct substitution of the numerator and denominator. Stack overflow will occur if the program wrongly swapped the two variables. Similarly, if a program for Problem 3 did not treat zero as a special case before executing the while loop, the program may not terminate.

Another class of typical test cases consists of boundary test cases, where the input value(s) is (are) at the border of different parts of the input domain, such as an input of 60 or 3600 seconds, or inputs at the transition of seconds to minute or minutes to hour conversion in Problem 2. If the mathematical operators, such as division '/' and modulo '%' operators, have been wrongly used, the resulting number of seconds or minutes can become equal to or greater than 60, which is anomalous.

Normal test cases are used to determine whether the programs perform the normal computations correctly. Although a variety of outputs can result when the logic of the program is wrong, some specific errors will trigger certain definite wrong outputs. For instance, some students wrongly used an integer variable to store the input value of *weight* and a non-integer variable to store the input value of *height*, or vice versa.

There are two types of annotation which may provide assistance to students: *output-specific annotations* and *general annotations*. The creation of output-specific annotations is based on analyzing the wrong output corresponding to the test case. If the wrong output can be classified as a common wrong output, an appropriate message will serve as debug-guiding annotation to hint where the source code may get wrong. For instance, "check the correct position of the numerator and denominator" message is a specific annotation for the "stack overflow" exception output in Problem 1. For outputs that cannot be classified as common wrong outputs, stating the objective of the given test case will assist students to debug their programs. The general annotations are independent of the actual output produced by the student's program. For instance, one example of general annotation for Problem 3 can be "This input does not have any factor". The student may follow this reasoning to check why his/her code produces any output at all.

4.3 Observations

Fig. 2 to 5 show, respectively, some sample output messages for the chosen problems. The columns of each message include the serial number of the test case, the inputs, annotation, actual output and result. For simplicity, the expected output is omitted.

Fig. 2 shows the result of an erroneous program when 1.01 is input as the value for *height* and 62.99 as the value for *weight*, respectively, in Problem 1. Here, the program fails because the data type of the variable *weight* was wrongly declared as int (an integer variable), instead of float (a floating point variable) as stated in the annotation. Students can then check the code in the data declaration parts to debug their programs.

Fig. 3 shows an error case for Problem 2, in which the program fails to convert 60 minutes to 1 hour. Corresponding to such an output, ADA will produce a specific

368   M.S.W. Lam et al.

annotation "1 minute instead of 60 seconds and 1 hour instead of 60 minutes" to remind students to check the conversion formula.

Fig. 4 shows a "Time limit expired" error for Problem 3 caused by infinite loop when the input value is zero. The annotation "Check input 0 causes infinite loop" suggests the student to review the looping condition. With the hint of annotation, the student should be able to consider zero as one of the cases to terminate the while loop in his/her program.

Fig. 5 shows another programming error for Problem 3. The problem requires the program to output all factors of an integer except 1 and the integer itself. However, the input value itself is also printed in the output list. The specific annotation "No need to check equal to input in while loop condition" hints that the termination condition of the while loop is wrong.

No.	Input	Annotation	Actual Output	Result
1	1.01 62.99	The numerator should be declared as float instead of int	Enter your height in m: Enter your weight in kg: Your BMI is 60.78	Wrong Answer

Fig. 2. ADA prompts declaration error with annotation (Problem 1)

No.	Input	Annotation	Actual Output	Result
1	3600	1 minute instead of 60 seconds and 1 hour instead of 60 minutes	Please enter the number of seconds: 3600 seconds(s) = 0 hour(s) 60 minute(s) 0 second(s)	Wrong Answer

Fig. 3. ADA prompts boundary value error with annotation (Problem 2)

No.	Input	Annotation	Actual Output	Result
1	0	Check input 0 causes infinite loop		Time limit expired

Fig. 4. ADA prompts exceptional case error with annotation (Problem 3)

No.	Input	Annotation	Actual Output	Result
1	12	No need to check equal to input in while loop condition	2 3 4 6 12	Wrong Answer

Fig. 5. ADA prompts loop condition error with annotation (Problem 3)

4.4 Discussion

It is difficult to trace a semantic error in computer programs even for an experienced programmer. There is no debugger which is intelligent enough to tell the programmer why the program output is wrong. It would be hard to guess how to trace such an error as the program code listing grows longer and longer. ADA utilizes historical data to generate useful annotations for different kinds of common logical errors. It definitely is not intended to be fully automated. However, with the help of annotations as debugging hints, students can locate the bugs more effectively if such bugs have been committed by students in the past.

Our initial experience in the case study suggests that, with the assistance of test case annotations to serve as debug-guiding information, students can more precisely identify the location of bugs in their programs so that they do not need to rewrite the whole program again and again. Conversely, without the assistance of annotations, students may as well attempt to rewrite the programs and subsequently other new bugs may be introduced, making the problem even harder to solve. Worse still, students may eventually be fed up with frustration and abort their attempts.

5 Conclusion

This paper has described the design of ADA, an automatic debugging assistant that is an extension of PASS, a Web-based automatic programming assignment assessment system. Students can use PASS to test and verify their programming assignments online. The newly extended debugging assistant, ADA, aims to further relieve the workload of tutors in guiding students to find bugs in their program code. ADA is not intended to be intelligent enough to understand programs. Rather, it provides a platform for tutors to consolidate the causes of common programming errors and transform such information into helpful hints. This kind of automatic debugging assistance is expected to supplement our daily face-to-face teaching, hence realizing the potential benefits of hybrid learning in computer programming courses.

Enhanced by ADA, PASS will enable the instructor to return instant debug-guiding information to students. Initial responses from the users in our pilot case study are encouraging, and further work is underway to perform a systematic evaluation of the effectiveness of such a feedback mechanism and the debug-guiding information.

References

1. Graham, C.R., Allen, S., Ure, D.: Benefits and Challenges of Blended Learning Environments. In: Khosrow-Pour, M. (ed.) Encyclopedia of Information Science and Technology, pp. 253–259. Idea Group, Hershey (2005)
2. Yu, Y.T., Poon, C.K., Choy, M.: Experiences with PASS: Developing and Using a Programming Assignment aSsessment System. In: 6th International Conference on Quality Software (QSIC 2006), pp. 360–365. IEEE Computer Society Press, Los Alamitos (2006)
3. Chong, S.L., Choy, M.: Towards a Progressive Learning Environment for Programming Courses. In: Cheung, R., Lau, R., Li, Q. (eds.) New Horizon in Web-based Learning: Proceedings of the 3rd International Conference on Web-based Learning (ICWL 2004), pp. 200–205. World Scientific Publishing Co. Pte. Ltd, Singapore (2004)
4. Choy, M., Lam, S., Poon, C.K., Wang, F.L., Yu, Y.T., Yuen, L.: Towards Blended Learning of Computer Programming Supported by an Automated System. In: Workshop on Blended Learning 2007, pp. 9–18. Prentice Hall, Englewood Cliffs (2007)
5. Choy, M., Nazir, U., Poon, C.K., Yu, Y.T.: Experiences in Using an Automated System for Improving Students' Learning of Computer Programming. In: Lau, R.W.H., Li, Q., Cheung, R., Liu, W. (eds.) ICWL 2005. LNCS, vol. 3583, pp. 267–272. Springer, Heidelberg (2005)

6. Spacco, J., Hovemeyer, D., Pugh, W., Emad, F., Hollingsworth, J.K., Padua-Perez, N.: Experiences with Marmoset: Designing and Using an Advanced Submission and Testing System for Programming Courses. In: 11th Annual Conference on Innovation and Technology in Computer Science Education (ITiCSE 2006), pp. 13–17. ACM Press, New York (2006)
7. Jadud, M.C.: Methods and Tools for Exploring Novice Compilation Behaviour. In: 2nd International Computing Education Research Workshop (ICER 2006), pp. 73–84. ACM Press, New York (2006)
8. Morimoto, Y., Kurasawa, K., Yokoyama, S., Ueno, M., Miyadera, Y.: A Support System for Teaching Computer Programming based on the Analysis of Compilation Errors. In: 6th International Conference on Advanced Learning Technologies (ICALT 2006), pp. 103–105. IEEE Computer Society Press, Los Alamitos (2006)

Modeling and Simulation of Continuous Time-Invariant Systems in Simulation Based Learning Environments

Gang Chen[1], Yi Li[2], and Jinyang Shi[1]

[1] Educational Technology Department, School of Journalism and Communication
Yangzhou University, Yangzhou, 225002, China
chengangyz@gmail.com
[2] Educational Technology Department, School of Educational Science
Nanjing Normal University, Nanjing, 210097, China

Abstract. Simulation based learning environments are widely used in elementary and secondary science education. However, a large number of these learning environments are domain-dependent so that they are only useful in some special domains. In this paper, we put forward a new method of simulating continuous time-invariant systems by using frame based knowledge representation and interpretive structural modeling. This method is helpful to realize the separation of knowledge representation and simulation program, and promotes the reusability of a simulation based learning environment.

Keywords: simulation based learning environment, continuous time-invariant system, interpretive structural modeling, frame based knowledge representation.

1 Introduction

Science education has two primary goals: one is to teach learners about scientific knowledge about the natural world; and the other is to help them grasp scientific skills, methods and procedures [1]. Therefore, science learning is no longer seen as the more or less directed transfer of knowledge from an authority (e.g., a book or a teacher) to a learner, but as a process of knowledge construction in which learners play an active role [2]. In other words, learners should learn science by doing science just like scientists. This type of learning pattern is called "scientific inquiry learning".

To support this new learning pattern, many computer simulation based learning environments have come out, in which learners can learn science by discovering the knowledge behind the simulations of the natural world systems or building their own models according to their understanding of the natural world systems [3,4].

However, a large number of these simulation based learning environments are domain-dependent. That is, designers have embedded relative domain knowledge into the code of software in the phase of design, so that these learning environments are only useful in some special domains. For example, a learning environment for Newtonian's motion laws can not be used for gas state equation $P*V=n*r*T$.

J. Fong, R. Kwan, and F.L. Wang (Eds.): ICHL 2008, LNCS 5169, pp. 371–379, 2008.

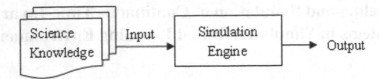

Fig. 1. Separating knowledge and simulation engine

In our opinion, domain-independence is a better idea. In other words, domain knowledge should be separated from the code of software, so that learning environments can model and simulate more natural world systems. Therefore, according to knowledge engineering methods, we have built a knowledge representation frame and simulation engine for natural world systems.

In this paper, we firstly analyze the characteristics of continuous time-invariant system to which the most of scientific knowledge in elementary and secondary education belongs; in section 3, we introduce the frame based knowledge representation of continuous time-invariant systems; in section 4, we discuss the key algorithms in the simulation engine.

2   Continuous Time-Invariant System

In elementary and secondary science education, learners often need to learn the relationships among several factors in the natural world. For example, when an iron block is under some liquid, the buoyancy has relationship with the density of the liquid and the volume of the block; if the latter two factors increase, the buoyancy will increase synchronously. The iron block and the liquid compose a system, which has the following characteristics:

(1) The factors of the system change continuously with respect to time;
(2) The equations describing the relationship of the factors don't change with respect to time.

All the systems that have the two characteristics are called continuous time-invariant system. The most of elementary and secondary science knowledge is about this type of system.

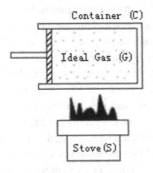

Fig. 2. Container-gas system

Table 1. Variables in the container-gas system

ID	Meaning	ID	Meaning
P_C	pressure of container	P_G	pressure of ideal gas
T_C	temperature of container	T_G	temperature of ideal gas
V_C	volume of container	V_G	volume of ideal gas
M_C	mass of container	n	the amount of ideal gas
SH_C	specific heat capacity of container	R	constant of ideal gas
PW_S	power of stove		

For the convenience of the following discussion, we give another detailed example of continuous time-invariant system. See figure 2. There is $20mol$ ideal gas in a closed container whose mass, volume, pressure, temperature, and specific heat capacity is $20kg$, $30m^3$, $120Pa$, $21.65K$, and $900J.kg^{-1}.K$ respectively. People can control the temperature of the container by burning the stove whose power is $100J$.

3 Knowledge Representation

3.1 Structure of Continuous Time-Invariant System

To describe the structure of continuous time-invariant systems, we depart a system into five parts: entities, variables, parameters, inputs and relations.

Entities are the most basic elements in a system, and can be seen as distinguishable objects in the natural world. Examples of entities in the container-gas system are the closed container, ideal gas, stove and so on. An entity is often denoted by a symbolic constant. We can use C to stand for the container, and use G to stand for the ideal gas.

A variable corresponds to a property of an entity, e.g. the volume, temperature and pressure of the ideal gas. Similar with an entity, a variable can also be represented by a symbolic constant. See table1. One can use T_C and T_G to stand for the temperature of container and ideal gas respectively. A variable is described by four attributes:

(1) the value, which is often numerical in continuous time-invariant system;

(2) the value range, which is the set of all possible values;

(3) the meaning, which the variable stands for, e.g. V_C stands for the volume of the container;

(4) the unit, e.g. the unit of V_C is m^3.

Parameters represent external factors, which influence a system and are not changed by factors inside a system. So, the difference between a parameters and a variable is that the former is a constant. Typical examples include the ideal gas constant whose value is $8.31\ Pa.m^3.mol^{-1}.K^{-1}$, the acceleration of gravity whose value is $9.8m.s^{-2}$ on the earth, and so on. Much like a variable, a parameter is also described by three attributes: value, meaning and unit.

An input corresponds to a simulation condition of a system, and is also called experimental framework by some researchers [5]. A continuous time-invariant system may have several different inputs, in which the system may have different behaviors. An input is usually defined as how some variables are controlled by a learner during a simulation. For example, in the container-gas system, the input is described as burning the stove whose power is 100J and keeping the volume constant. So, an input can be expressed by a function group, e.g.

$$\begin{cases} PW_{S(t)} = 100 \\ V_{C(t)} = 30 \end{cases} \tag{1}$$

(The symbol of t stands for the variable of time which counts from 0.)

Relations are math models of a system. They explain how variables are associated with each other, and can be used to predict how a system will change under a certain input. Relations are expressed in the form of a function group. In the container-gas system, the function group under the condition of heating the container and keeping volume constant is listed below:

$$\begin{cases} H_{(t)} = PW_S * t \\ T_{C(t)} = T_{C(0)} + \dfrac{H_{(t)}}{SH_C * M_C} \\ T_{G(t)} = T_{C(t)} \\ P_{G(t)} = \dfrac{n * R * T_{G(t)}}{V_{G(t)}} \\ P_{C(t)} = P_{G(t)} \\ V_{G(t)} = V_{C(t)} \end{cases} \tag{2}$$

($H_{(t)}$ stands for the quantity of heat abstracted by the container from time 0 to time t.)

What must be stressed is that every input corresponds to a special function group. For example, the function group (2) is not useful under the condition of changing the volume and keeping the temperature constant.

3.2 Frame Based Knowledge Representation

Frame based knowledge representation is a good approach to describe a system like the container-gas system. The fundamental idea of a frame is rather simple: a frame can be seen as a generic data structure about an object; and it is essentially a collection of slots and slot-values [6]. When a frame is being used, the slot-values can be altered to make the frame corresponding to the particular situation at hand.

According to the structure of a continuous time-invariant system, we build a frame to describe such systems. See table2 and table3.

Table 2. Frame structure of continuous time-invariant systems

System:
Entities:
Entity:
Name:
Variable:<Name, Value, Value Range, Unit, Meaning >
...
Entity:
...
Parameters:
Parameter: <Name, Value, Unit, Meaning >
...
Input:
Relations:

Table 3. Frame of container-gas system

System: container-gas system

Entities:

Entity:

  Name: *container*

  Variable:

  Name: P_C

  Value: *120*

  Range: $(0, +\infty)$

  Meaning: *pressure of the container*

  Unit: *Pa*

  Variable:

  Name: T_C

  ...

Entity:

  Name: *ideal gas*

  Variable:

  ...

Parameters:

Parameter:

  Name: *R*

  Value: *8.31*

  Unit: *Pa. $m^3.mol^{-1}.K^{-1}$*

  Meaning: *constant of ideal gas*

Input:

  $PW_{S(t)} = 100$;

  $V_{C(t)} = 30$;

Relations:

  $H_{(t)} = PW_S * t$;

  $T_{C(t)} = T_{C(0)} + H_{(t)}/(SH_C * M_C)$;

  $T_{G(t)} = T_{C(t)}$;

  $P_{G(t)} = n * R * T_{G(t)}/V_{G(t)}$;

  $P_{C(t)} = P_{G(t)}$;

  $V_{G(t)} = V_{C(t)}$;

4 Simulation Engine

4.1 Basic Simulation Procedure

We use a simulation engine to simulate different systems that are defined by frames. There is a simulation clock (SC) in the simulation engine. The basic simulation procedure is that the simulation engine calculates the functions in the relations part of the frame every other interval. See table4.

Table 4. Basic simulation procedure in simulation engine

Simulate ()	
{	
While (SC.CurrentTime <= SC.EndTime)	*// limit the time length of simulation*
{	
Calculate_Function_group();	*// calculate all the functions in relations*
If (any variable's value out of its value range) break;	*// make sure all variables do not beyond their value range*
SC.CurrentTime+=Time_Step;	*// add an interval to the current time of the simulation clock*
}	
}	

4.2 Deciding the Calculation Order of Functions

However, functions in a function group can be arranged in many different orders. It means the simulation engine needs to decide in which order these functions should be calculated. In fact, a function like $y=f(x_1, x_2, ...,x_n)$ implies there is a dependence relationship between y and $(x_1, x_2, ...,x_n)$. That is to say, one should calculate the value of $(x_1, x_2, ...,x_n)$ firstly, and then y. If there is another function $x_n=g(z_1,z_2,...z_n)$, the calculation order should be $(z_1,z_2,...z_n)$, $(x_1, x_2, ...,x_n)$, and then y. So, we can say a function group corresponds to a dependence digraph. What a simulation engine should do is to draw the dependence digraph and decide the calculation order according to it.

Interpretive structural modeling(ISM) method is helpful to solve this problem. ISM was proposed by David W. Malone in 1975 [7]. It is a method which can be applied to a system--such as a network or a society--to better understand both direct and indirect relationships among the system's components. The algorithm using ISM to decide the calculation order can be divided into five steps:

(1) Building a matrix for all variables in the left side of functions.
We assume all variables in the left side of functions compose a set $V= \{v_1, v_2,...,v_n\}$ (v_i is a variable). Build a matrix A *of size $n*n$*, and all elements of A is set to 0. The *ith* row and column correspond to the variable v_i. For example, to function group (2) ,
$V= \{H_{(t)}, T_{C(t)}, T_{G(t)}, P_{G(t)}, P_{C(t)}, V_{G(t)}\}$.
(2) Building an adjacent matrix according to dependence relationships in the function group.

In every function, we assume the variable on the left side is v_i. If there is a $v_j \square V$ and v_j appears in the right side of the function, then we set the element a_{ij} in matrix A to be 1, which means v_i depends on v_j. The new matrix A is called an adjacent matrix, whose operations are all Boolean.

	$H_{(t)}$	$T_{C(t)}$	$T_{G(t)}$	$P_{C(t)}$	$P_{G(t)}$	$V_{G(t)}$
$H_{(t)}$	1	0	0	0	0	0
$T_{C(t)}$	1	1	0	0	0	0
$T_{G(t)}$	0	1	1	0	0	0
$P_{C(t)}$	0	0	0	1	1	0
$P_{G(t)}$	0	0	1	0	1	1
$V_{G(t)}$	0	0	0	0	0	1

(a) adjacent matrix

	$H_{(t)}$	$T_{C(t)}$	$T_{G(t)}$	$P_{C(t)}$	$P_{G(t)}$	$V_{G(t)}$
$H_{(t)}$	1	0	0	0	0	0
$T_{C(t)}$	1	1	0	0	0	0
$T_{G(t)}$	1	1	1	0	0	0
$P_{C(t)}$	1	1	1	1	1	1
$P_{G(t)}$	1	1	1	0	1	1
$V_{G(t)}$	0	0	0	0	0	1

(b) reachability matrix

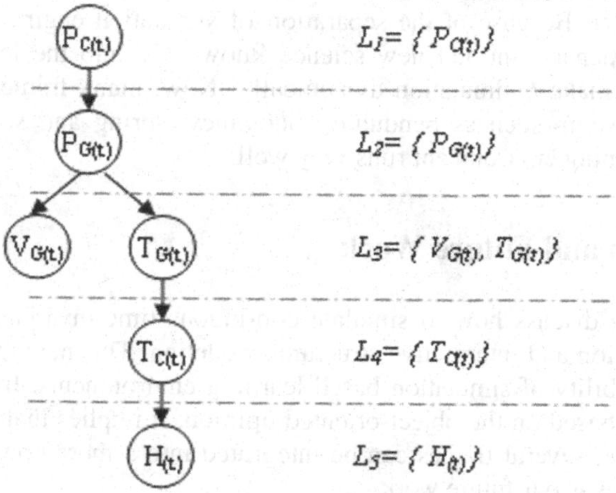

$L_1 = \{ P_{C(t)} \}$

$L_2 = \{ P_{G(t)} \}$

$L_3 = \{ V_{G(t)}, T_{G(t)} \}$

$L_4 = \{ T_{C(t)} \}$

$L_5 = \{ H_{(t)} \}$

(c) dependence relationship

Fig. 3. Using ISM to get calculation order of functions in container-gas system

(3) Building a reachability matrix.

Calculate $S=(A+I)^{n-1}$, where I is an identity matrix of size n. S is called a reachability matrix. If $s_{ij}=1$, then it means v_i depends on v_j directly or indirectly; otherwise, it means v_i doesn't depend on v_j.

(4) Getting the dependence digraph.

The reachability matrix S can be used to get the dependence digraph. To do this, we firstly define an antecedent set $A(v_i)$ for each variable $v_i \in V$, as all of those variables on which v_i depends. $A(v_i)$ is stated mathematically as: $A(v_i) = \{ v_j \in V \mid s_{ij} = 1 \}$.

Secondly, we define a reachability set $R(v_i)$ for each variable $v_i \in V$, as all of those variables which depend on v_i. Stated mathematically: $R(v_i) = \{ v_j \in V \mid s_{ji} = 1 \}$.

Then, we define $(L_1, L_2,..., L_k)$ as levels of the dependence relationship among all variables from top to bottom, and

$$L_k = \{ v_i \in (V - L_0 - L_1 - ... - L_{k-1}) \mid R_{k-1}(v_i) = R_{k-1}(v_i) \cap A_{k-1}(v_i) \}.$$

Where L_0 is defined as an empty set ϕ for convenience of calculation, $R_{k-1}(v_i)$ and $A_{k-1}(v_i)$ stand for the reachability set and antecedent set of v_i in the set of $(V - L_0 - L_1 - ... - L_{k-1})$ respectively.

(5) Deciding the calculation order of functions.

Therefore, the calculation order of functions is that variables in L_k should be calculated firstly, then L_{k-1}, L_{k-2}… until L_1. To every variable in the same L_j, there is no special order.

5 Implementation

We have developed a simulation based learning environment for elementary and secondary science education based on the method introduced in this paper. Technically, the frame structure is defined as a XML schema, and simulation engine is programmed using C#. Because of the separation of simulation engine and knowledge representation, teachers can add new science knowledge into the learning environment which will make a simulation dynamically. Now, many frames of continuous time-invariant system--such as pendulum, buoyancy, spring and so on--have been built, and the learning environment runs very well.

6 Conclusion and Future Work

In this paper, we discuss how to simulate continuous time-invariant systems using frame representation and interpretive structural modeling. This new method is helpful to improve reusability of simulation based learning environments. In fact, the frame representation is based on the object-oriented opinion. It implies that a frame is reusable. For example, several frames can be integrated into a more complex frame. So, the reuse of frames is our future work.

Acknowledgement

This work was supported by the project "Thinking with Graphs" funded by social science research foundation of Yangzhou University.

References

1. Li, J., Klahr, D.: The Psychology of Scientific Thinking: Implications for Science Teaching and Learning. In: Rhoton, J., Shane, P. (eds.) Teaching Science in the 21st Century. National Science Teachers Association and National Science Education Leadership Association. NSTA Press (2006)
2. van Joolingen, W.R., de Jong, T.: Design and implementation of simulation-based discovery environments: the SMISLE solution. Journal of Artificial Intelligence and Education 7, 253–277 (1996)
3. De Jong, T., van Joolingen, W.R.: Scientific discovery learning with computer simulations of conceptual domains. Review of Educational Research 68, 179–201 (1998)
4. Forbus, K., Carney, K., Sherin, B., Ureel, L.: Qualitative modeling for middle-school students. In: Proceedings of the 18th International Qualitative Reasoning Workshop, Evanston, Illinois, USA (August 2004)

5. Wang, W.: Modeling and simulation. Science publishing house, Beijing (2001)
6. Lassila, O., McGuiness, D.: The Role of Frame-Based Representation on the Semantic Web. Linkoping Electronic Articles in Computer and Information Science 6 (2001)
7. Malone, D.W.: An introduction to the application of interpretive structural modeling. Proceedings of IEEE 63, 397–404 (1975)

Imagistic Digital Library for Hybrid Medical Learning

Liana Stanescu[1], Dan Burdescu[1], Anca Ion[1], Andrei Panus[2], and Ligia Florea[2]

[1] University of Craiova, Faculty of Automation, computers and Electronics, Craiova, Romania
{stanescu_liana, burdescu_dumitru, soimu_anca}@software.ucv.ro
[2] University of Medicine and Pharmacy, Craiova, Romania
{apanus,florealigia}@hotmail.com

Abstract. The paper presents an e-learning platform (TESYS) that enhances the possibilities of the traditional medical teaching. It allows students to use modern tools for information access and continuously testing their knowledge. Although medical learning cannot replace direct transfer of knowledge performed during hospital practice hours, when the teacher presents to students different medical cases with all complementary information (medical investigations, diagnosis, applied treatment, disease evolution), the e-learning solution can offer significant advantages It can be said that the hybrid learning is the best solution for the medical teaching. An element of originality brought by the TESYS platform is a medical imagistic database that can be updated by the specialists with images acquired from different patients in the diagnosis and treatment process. A series of alphanumerical information: diagnosis, treatment and patient evolution can be added for each image. The second element of originality is the content-based visual query that uses characteristics that were automatically extracted from medical images (color, texture, regions). It can be used both in the training process and e-testing process. Using content-based visual query with other access methods (text-based, hierarchical methods) on a teaching image database allows students to see images and associated information from database in a simple and direct manner. This method stimulates learning, by comparing similar cases along with their particularities, or by comparing cases that are visually similar, but with different diagnoses.

Keywords: hybrid medical learning, imagistic medical database, content-based visual query, color feature, texture feature, color region.

1 Introduction

The hybrid or blended learning describes the learning method in which some traditional face-to-face "seat time" has been replaced by online learning activities. The purpose is to take advantages of both face-to-face and online learning [11], [12].

Although medical learning cannot replace direct transfer of knowledge performed during hospital practice hours, when the teacher presents to students different medical cases with all complementary information (medical investigations, diagnosis, applied treatment, disease evolution), the e-learning solution can offer significant advantages which were highlighted in medical literature: increased accessibility to information,

J. Fong, R. Kwan, and F.L. Wang (Eds.): ICHL 2008, LNCS 5169, pp. 380–391, 2008.

better updating solutions, personalized training, better distribution, standardization of content, better efficiency in achieving knowledge and aptitudes [4], [5], [7], [8], [9].

Due to all these advantages medical e-learning has become more and more important and more frequently used in the last decade [1], [2], [3], [6], [7]. The technological development and the Internet contributed to the development of e-learning resources. Repositories and digital libraries for access to e-learning materials were established (MedEdPortal, Association of American Medical Colleges, End of Life/Palliative Resource Center, The Health Education Assets Library, Multimedia Educational Resource for Learning and Online Teaching, International Virtual Medical School) [10].

The accomplished studies, including those focusing on medical domain, indicated that the students substantially appreciate the e-learning method, due to the facilities offered (easy access to materials, navigation, interactivity, friendly interfaces), but they don't consider it as a replacement of the traditional learning which has other advantages [8].

The introduction of the multimedia components (text, images, sound, video, graphics, animation) for the improvement of the learning content led to the necessity of the concept which precedes even the Internet, i.e. the multimedia learning. Both teachers and students consider that the multimedia learning improves the process of teaching and learning [10].

There is an increasing need to assess aspects of professional behavior and competence within the health system. The right evaluation of the students in the medical area represents an important problem and should be done in a complex manner, guaranteeing that the students will become competent and professional doctors. That is why the testing should be more complex than multiple-choice tests of knowledge and multi-station tests of "presupposed" clinical skills using simulated patients.

The paper presents an e-learning platform (TESYS) that enhances the traditional medical learning methods, allowing students to access modern methods to transmit information and test their knowledge.

Besides traditional functions, an element of originality brought by the TESYS platform in the hybrid medical teaching is a color digital images library, structured as a database updated by the specialists with images acquired in the diagnosis and treatment process, from different patients. Each image can include a series of alphanumerical information: diagnosis, treatment and patient evolution. It means that along with the electronic teaching documentation for the classic teaching methods, there will be a database with medical images.

In the medical learning process, the courses in traditional or electronic format, are accompanied in many cases by a series of images. For example, at a gastroenterology course, for the presentation of the ulcer diagnosis, the teacher presents to the students images that are relevant for this diagnosis, highlighting the changes in color, texture or shape of the sick tissue, in comparison to a health one.

In general, the presented images number is minimal. Accordingly, the existence of a database with medical images (of order of hundreds) that could be collected by the teacher in the process of patients' diagnosis and investigation raises considerable the variety of communicated knowledge.

This digital library with images can be used both in the learning and testing process. It uses a modern query method, namely content-based visual query. Medical learning is the most important direction for using content-based visual query, besides diagnostic aid and medical research, as presented in the specialty literature [15].

The students can use the medical imagistic database in the training process. They can query the database in two different ways:

- Traditionally, by the text-based method; for example, the diagnostic is written and all the images associated to it are searched in the database.

- Content-based query; in this case keywords or other texts are not used. The query uses the characteristics extracted from images (for example color or texture). This type of query is implemented taking into account the whole image, or only parts of it (regions). In the first case the name of the query is content-based image query. It will find in the database all the images that are significantly similar to the query image. In the second case, the name of the query is content-based region query. It needs to be selected one or several regions used as query regions and it searches in the database all the images that contain the selected regions. In this case it is necessary to have an automated region extraction algorithm for images, using certain characteristics (for example color) [13], [17].

To use the imagistic collection and content-based visual query in the testing process, the TESYS platform offers a solution that can replace or complete a usual mode for knowledge testing: the teacher presents to the student the image of a patient and he/she has to study it, establish a diagnosis and make observations. More than this, the electronic solution challenges the student to recognize similar images that are included in the same diagnosis class, or visually similar images, but of different diagnosis. Such complex testing allows the teacher to evaluate student's knowledge more efficiently and deeply so that he can take the right decisions. The role of proficient testing methods is very important in the medical domain, where establishing a wrong diagnosis based on the imagistic investigations can have serious consequences on a patient.

Using content-based visual query with other access methods to medical imagistic database allows students to see images and associated information in a simple and direct manner. They only have to select a query image and find similar ones. This method stimulates learning, by comparing similar cases or by comparing cases that are visually similar, but with different diagnoses [15].

2   Medical e-Learning Platform Description

The main goal of the application is to give students the possibility to download course materials, take tests or sustain final examinations and communicate with all parties involved. To accomplish this, four different roles were defined for the platform: sysadmin, secretary, professor and student.

2.1   Roles

The main task of sysadmin users is to manage secretaries. A sysadmin user may add or delete secretaries, or change their password. He may also view the actions performed by all other users of the platform. All actions performed by users are logged. This way the sysadmin may check the activity that takes place on the application. The logging facility has some benefits: an audit may be performed for the application with the logs as witness; security breaches may also be discovered.

A sysadmin user may block an IP so that no user will be able to access the application from that IP. Finally, the overall activity of users represents valuable data. This data may be off-line analyzed using machine learning or even data mining techniques so that important conclusions may be obtained regarding the quality of service for the application. The quality of service may have two indicators: the learning proficiency of students and the capability of the application to classify students according to their accumulated knowledge.

A statistics page is also available. It displays the number of users that entered the application, the total number of students, and the number of students with and without activity, as well as other information that gives an overall view on the activity on the application.

Secretary users manage sections, professors, disciplines and students. On any of these a secretary may perform actions like add, delete or update. These actions will finally set up the application so that professors and students may use it. In conclusion, the secretary manages a list of sections, a list of professors and a list of students. Each discipline is assigned to a section and has as attributes a name, a short name, the year and the semester of study when and the list of professors teaching the discipline which may be of maximum three. A student may be enrolled to one or more sections.

The secretaries have also the task to set up the structure of study years for all sections. They have the possibility of searching students using different criteria like name, section, year of study or residence. The secretaries have a large set of available reports regarding the student's status. Among them there is a list of students who took all the exams, a list of students who requested grants for taking an exam one more time and many other reports specific to secretary work.

The main task of a professor is to manage the assigned disciplines while the discipline is made up of chapters. The professor sets up chapters by specifying the name and the course documentation. Only students enrolled in a section in which a discipline is studied may download the course's document and take tests or examinations. Besides setting up the course's document for each chapter, the professor manages test and exam questions. For each chapter the professor has to define two pools of questions, one used for testing and one used for exams. He specifies the number of questions that will be randomly extracted to create a test or an exam. Let us suppose that for a chapter the professor created 50 test questions and 60 exam questions and he has set to 5 the number of test questions and to 10 the number of exam questions that are to be randomly withdrawn. It means that, when a student takes a test from this chapter, 5 questions from the pool of test questions are randomly withdrawn. When the student takes the final examination at the discipline from which the chapter is part, 15 questions are randomly withdrawn: 5 from the pool of test questions and 10 from the pool of exam questions. This way of generating tests and exams is intended to be flexible enough for professor.

All tests and exams are taken under time constraints. For each chapter the professor sets up a number of seconds necessary to answer questions of that chapter. When a test or exam is taken all the seconds are summed up thus obtaining a maximal interval of time in which the student has to finish the test. The elapsed and remaining time are managed by the server and presented to the student after each answered question.

The professor has also flexibility for creating and editing questions. A question may contain pictures, and thus equations, formulas or other graphics may be imbedded in it. For each question the professor sets up the visible answers and the correct answers. There are two implemented formulas that may be used for calculating grades. For each discipline the professor chooses and sets any of the formulas such that it will be used for all tests and exams taken at that discipline.

Professors have also the possibility of searching students using different criteria and a large set of available reports that help them in working with students.

The application offers students the possibility to download course materials, take tests and exams and communicate with other parties involved, as professors and secretaries. Students may download only course materials for the disciplines that belong to sections where they are enrolled. They can take tests and exams with constraints that were set up by the secretary through the year structure function.

Students have access to personal data and can modify them as needed. A feedback form is also available. It is composed of questions that check aspects regarding the usability, efficiency and productivity of the application with respect to the student's needs.

All users must authenticate through username and password. If the username and password are valid the role of the user is determined and the appropriate interface is presented. The platform assigns a set of actions that the user may perform. Each time a user initiates an action the system checks if that action is allowed. This approach ensures security at user's level and makes sure that a student may not perform actions that are assigned to professor, secretary or sysadmin users.

A record of sustained tests is kept for all students. In fact, the taken test or exams are saved in full for later use. That is why a student or a professor may view a previously taken test or exam if needed. For each question is presented what the student checked, which was the correct answer, which was the maximum score that could be obtained from that question and how many points did the student obtain. At the end it is presented the final formula used to compute the grade and the grade itself.

Besides these core functions for the on-line testing some other are implemented or currently under development. A message board is available for professors, secretaries and students to ensure peer-to-peer communication. This facility is implemented within the platform such that no other service (e.g. email server) may be necessary.

2.2 Imagistic Digital Library

Further on, this paper presents the way in which a medical imagistic library is managed for educational purposes. This implies the insertion of images and the launch into execution of some pre-processing algorithms for extracting information related to color and texture, as well as the significant color regions. Thus the images are prepared for the next stage, which is that of content-based query by color and texture.

Database Structure and Management. The system offers professors the possibility to insert new images in the database, together with their relevant information, namely: path and name of the image file, the diagnosis, as well as supplementary information that include specialists' observation regarding the disease and the way in which it is illustrated by image, treatment and evolution.

For realizing the content-based visual query, all the images loaded in the database are automatically processed, in three steps:

o   the extraction of color feature
o   the extraction of texture feature
o   the extraction of significant color and texture regions

The extraction of color feature. The images are pre-processed, namely they are transformed from the RGB color space to HSV color space and quantized to 166 colors, being thus prepared for a future query. The HSV color space is preferred, for its properties (compactness, completeness, naturalness and uniformity) which allow it to be proper for usage in the content-based visual retrieval [13], [17].

For the quantization of the HSV color space, the solution with 166 colors was chosen. Because the hue represents the most important color feature, it needs the finest quantization. In the circle that represents the colors, the primary colors red, green and blue are separated by 120 degrees. A circular quantization with 20 degree step separates sufficiently the colors. The saturation and the value are each quantized to three levels. The quantization produces 18 hues, 3 saturations, 3 values and 4 greys, that means 166 distinct colors in the HSV color space. The color information from the image is represented by means of the color histogram and by the binary color set. The color information is stored in the database as a vector with 166 values and it is used furthermore in the content-based image query and content-based region query [13].

The dissimilitude between the query and target image is computed using the histogram intersection [13], [17]:

$$d_{q,t} = 1 - \frac{\sum_{m=0}^{M-1} \min(\ h_q[m\ ],\ h_t[m\ ])}{\min(\ |h_q|, |h_t|)} \tag{1}$$

The extraction of texture feature. Together with color, texture is a powerful characteristic of an image, which is present in nature and in medical images also. Thus a disease can be indicated by changes in the color and texture of a tissue [15].

There are many techniques used for texture extraction, but there is not any certain method that can be considered the most appropriate, this depending on the application and the type of images taken into account. The effectuated studies on medical images indicated that among the most representative methods of texture detection are the Gabor representations, reason for which it was chosen for extracting the colour texture feature from medical images in the database [15].

In the case of Gabor filters, starting from the representation of the HSV colour space, the colour in complex can be represented [14], [16]:

$$b(x, \ y) = S(x, \ y) \cdot e^{iH(x, \ y)} \tag{2}$$

The computation of the Gabor characteristics for the image represented in the HS-complex space is similar to the one for the monochromatic Gabor characteristics, because the combination of colour channels is done before filtering [14], [16]:

$$C_{f,\varphi} = (\sum_{x,y}\ (FFT^{-1}\{P(u,\ v) \cdot M_{f,\varphi}(u,\ v)\}))^2 \tag{3}$$

The Gabor characteristics vector is created using the value $C_{f,\varphi}$ computed for 3 scales and 4 orientations [16], [18]:

$$f = (C_{0,0}, C_{0,1}, ..., C_{2,3})$$ (4)

So the texture feature is represented for each image as a 12-dimension vector stored in the database.

The dissimilitude between the texture characteristics of the query image Q and the target image T is defined by the metric [14], [16]:

$$D^2(Q,T) = \sum_f \sum_\varphi d_{f\varphi}(Q,T), \text{ where } d_{f\varphi} = (f^Q - f^T)^2$$ (5)

Extracting the color regions. For detecting color regions, it was chosen the color set back-projection algorithm, introduced initially by Swain and Ballard and then developed in the research projects at Columbia University, in the content-based visual retrieval domain [13]. This technique provides the automatic extraction of regions and the representation of their color content. The extraction system for color regions has four steps [13]:

1. the image transformation, quantization and filtering (the transformation from the RGB color space to HSV color space and the quantization of the HSV color space at 166 colors)
2. back-projection of binary color sets
3. the labeling of regions
4. the extraction of the region features

The color regions detected by applying this algorithm on each medical image are stored in the database with the following characteristics: the color set, the area (the number of pixels) and the minimum-bounding rectangle that bounds the region. All this information is used later in the e-testing process that uses content-based region query.

Medical Imagistic Database Query for Learning Purpose. The medical imagistic database can be visualized by browsing the images and their attached information, or can be simply queried by text. For example, the student introduces a diagnosis and the images included in the specified diagnosis will be returned from database.

A more modern solution is that of an imagistic database query based on content. This supposes that there are not keywords or other textual information, but only an image is chosen from database, and the system will return a number of images similar with the query image taking into consideration the following characteristics: color, texture or shape automatically extracted. This process is called content-based image query [13], [17].

The retrieval can be done also by taking into consideration the significant color regions automatically detected from color medical images. A relevant region that indicates the existence of a disease is selected, and the system will retrieve a number of relevant images, meaning images that contain a similar region with the query one.

The student can analyze a lot of images from the same diagnosis, he can see the changes in color, texture or shape of the seek tissue reflected in the image. The content-based visual query offers to the student a variety of options, raises his curiosity, because the student can select any image from the database and the query response can be different because the database is permanently updated.

Content Based Image Query Based on Color and Texture Features. It requires the selection of an image as a query image and the retrieval of all those images from database which best resemble it, taking into consideration the color and texture features, each in equal parts. Also, for every image detailed information is displayed.

Content-based visual query is a searching method based on similarity and not on the equality. It will return images visually similar with the query image, with the same diagnosis, or different diagnosis. For computing the dissimilitude between a query and a target image from database, the color characteristic (represented by a 166 values vector) and the texture characteristic (represented by a 12 values vector), in equal weights were considered. The color dissimilitude is calculated using the equation 1, and the texture vectors dissimilitude using the equation 5. The overall distance between the query and target image is the average of these two values. The images are displayed to the student in the ascending order of the computed dissimilitude.

Content-Based Region Query. It is necessary to select an image and to display the color regions detected with the color set back-projection algorithm. Next, the user must tick one or more color regions for content-based region query. The result is a set of images from the database that contain the query region(s), based on ascending order of the computed distance. Taking into account that the color information of each region is stored as a color binary set, the color similitude between two regions is computed with the quadratic distance between color sets [13]:

$$d_{q,t} = \sum_{m_0=0}^{M-1}\sum_{m_1=0}^{M-1}\left((s_q[m_0]-s_t[m_0])a_{m0,m1}\,(s_q[m_1]-s_t[m_1])\right) \tag{6}$$

The window in figure 1 displays the images containing the regions on which the database query was made.

e-Testing Solutions based on the Medical Imagistic Database. The medical imagistic collection and content-based visual query can be used in e-testing also. The original e-testing solution proposed in the TESYS platform, can be done in two different ways:

o   using content-based image retrieval
o   using content-based region retrieval

In the first case, the testing process is the following: an image from the database that represents the query image is displayed. The student is asked to establish the diagnosis and to give details that will be added in text type controls. The "Content-based Image Query" option should be activated next. The content-based image query system will return a number of images from database that can be relevant or non-relevant for the query. For each image retrieved by the system, the student has to

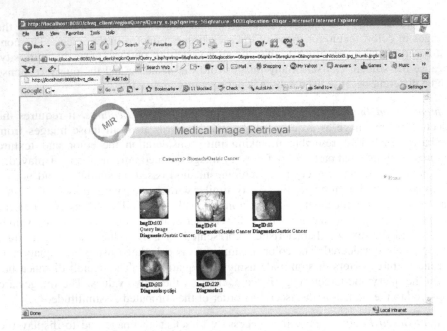

Fig. 1. The results of the content-based region query

establish if this is relevant or non-relevant for the query image, meaning the image is or not included in the same diagnosis. The number of similar images retrieved automatically by the system can be established by the teacher before the testing (for example between 5 or 10 similar images). Also, the teacher has the possibility to establish the number of images on which the testing is done and to what diagnosis they belong.

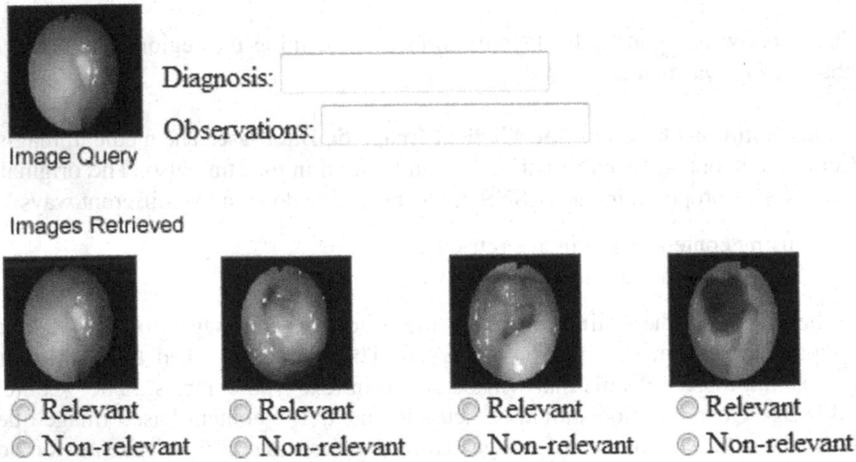

Image Query

Diagnosis:

Observations:

Images Retrieved

Relevant
Non-relevant

Relevant
Non-relevant

Relevant
Non-relevant

Relevant
Non-relevant

Fig. 2. An example of e-testing using the content-based image query on medical imagistic database

The utilization of this testing system for medical hybrid learning shows that such testing environment is recommended to contain 3 query images and for each of them to be retrieved 5 similar images. This modality keeps students interested and offers the teacher a good idea about their capacity to accumulate knowledge necessary to establish a correct diagnosis for certain patology.

At the end of the test, the student will be automatically marked. He will receive the corresponding mark for each relevant image retrieved (the relevance is automatically established based on diagnosis) and also the correct diagnosis from the database and other information introduced by teacher will be displayed. Also, the student can visualize the correct solution of the test. This way, he can observe his errors and understand why images similar by color and texture are included in different diagnosis.

The electronic testing that uses the content-based region query comes to complete the first modality of testing. This is considered more complex, because a fine granularity approach to image retrieval is adopted. The student's testing takes into consideration the relevant color/texture regions automatically detected from medical images. The student has to select the option 'Regions Detection' and the relevant regions will be detected automatically by the system. In general, in an image there are many normal regions (healthy tissue) and a single relevant region for the diagnosis, which presents changes in color and texture in comparison to the normal one; the student has to recognize the abnormal region in the image. After that, the student has to mark the corresponding region and select the option "Content-based region query", which will retrieve a number of images from database (5 up to 10), that contain regions similar to the query region. The student has to establish which images from the images automatically retrieved by the system are relevant for the query region. Also, in this case, the student is automatically marked, getting the points for each relevant region recognized, relevance established based on the image diagnosis from the database and can visualize the correct results.

3 Conclusion

The paper presents in detail the functions of an original platform for medical e-learning that completes the traditional way of performing this activity. The implemented platform creates an environment in which students can take tests or exams at different disciplines.

As an original element, the implemented system offers students a multimedia medical database that apart from the traditional information also contains medical images. Within the learning process, the image database can be consulted in a modern way, image or region-based manner.

The paper also presents an e-testing modality of students from medical domain that uses the same database and the two modern query methods.

The medical imagistic collection and content-based visual retrieval used in the training and e-testing processes help to increase the students' ability to find the correct diagnosis and to choose between very similar images as color and texture, but that are included in different diagnosis, reducing the probability for the future physician to establish a wrong diagnosis, which may have serious consequences on patient's health.

For each kind of pathology, the teacher can determine the student's level of knowledge and also, at general level, the student's capacity to establish a correct diagnosis based on the imagistic investigations, frequently used nowadays.

The solution of teaching and e-testing using content-based visual query in a database with medical images is used in parallel with traditional techniques at the University of Medicine and Pharmacy. During the year 2007, 60 students used the e-training module based on imagistic database and content-based visual query in study of the gastroenterology discipline. Each of them accessed the database for approximately 9 times, spending in average 200 minutes.

The 60 students participated also at the electronic testing, using the imagistic database and content-based visual query at the same discipline. It was recorded an improvement of the correct established diagnosis number based on medical images. In 2006, when this multimedia component was not used, the average number of images correctly analyzed and diagnosed was 5 from 10, and in 2007, using the multimedia database, was obtained an average of 7. This improvement, in such relative short time (one year) clearly indicates that this modality can bring important benefits in raising the student education. Of course, this development can be influenced by other factors (the intellectual capacity of the students, for example), so the system efficiency must be observed for a longer period of time.

The students found it attractive, innovative, and with big advantages in testing the level of achieved knowledge.

References

1. Ozuah, P.O.: Undergraduate medical education: thoughts on future challenges. BMC Med. Educ. 2, 8–10 (2002)
2. Nair, B.R., Finucane, P.M.: Reforming medical education to enhance the management of chronic disease. Med. J. Aust. 179, 257–259 (2003)
3. Leung, W.C.: Competency based medical training: review. BMJ 325, 693–696 (2002)
4. Rosenberg, M.: E-Learning: Strategies for Delivering Knowledge in the Digital Age. McGraw-Hill, New York (2001)
5. Wentling, T., Waight, C., Gallaher, J., La Fleur, J., Wang, C., Kanfer, A.: E-Learning: A Review of Literature,
   http://learning.ncsa.uiuc.edu/papers/elearnlit.pdf
6. Moberg, T.F., Whitcomb, M.E.: Educational technology to facilitate medical students' learning: background. Acad. Med. 74, 1146–1150 (1999)
7. Ward, J.P., Gordon, J., Field, M.J., Lehmann, H.P.: Communication and information technology in medical education. Lancet 357, 792–796 (2001)
8. Gibbons, A., Fairwether, P.: Computer-based instruction. In: Tobias, S., Fletcher, J. (eds.) training& Retraining: A Handbok for Business, Industry, Government and the Military. McMillan Reference USA, New York (2000)
9. Clark, D.: Psychological myths in e-learning. Med. Teach. 24, 598–604 (2002)
10. Ruiz, J., Mintzer, M.J., Leipzig, R.M.: The Impact of E-Learning in Medical Education. Academic Medicine 81(3) (2006)
11. Reynard, R.: Hybrid learning: Challenges for teachers. The Journal (2007)
12. Reynard, R.: Hybrid learning: Maximizing Student Engagement,
    http://campustechnology.com/articles/48204_1/

13. Smith, J.R.: Integrated Spatial and Feature Image Systems: Retrieval, Compression and Analysis. Ph.D. thesis, Graduate School of Arts and Sciences, Columbia University (1997)
14. Palm, C., Keysers, D., Lehmann, T., Spitzer, K.: Gabor Filtering of Complex Hue/Saturation Images For Color Texture Classification. In: Proc. JCIS 2000, pp. 45–49 (2000)
15. Muller, H., Michoux, N., Bandon, D., Geissbuhler, A.: A Review of Content-based Image Retrieval Systems in Medical Application – Clinical Benefits and Future Directions. Int. J. Med. Inform. 73(1), 1–23 (2004)
16. Zhang, D., Wong, A., Infrawan, M., Lu, G.: Content-Based Image Retrieval Using Gabor Texture Features. In: Proc. IEEE Pacific-Rim Conference on Multimedia, pp. 392–395 (2000)
17. Del Bimbo, A.: Visual Information Retrieval. Morgan Kaufmann Publishers, San Francisco (2001)

Web Design Requirements for Improved Web Accessibility for the Blind

Rehema Baguma and Jude T. Lubega

Faculty of Computing and Information Technology, Makarere University,
P.O. Box 7062, Kampala, Uganda
{rbaguma,jlubega}@cit.mak.ac.ug

Abstract. Considerable research has been done on how to make e-learning systems accessible. But Learners in electronic and hybrid learning environments utilize many Web based systems beyond what the instructor and institution provides and can control such as search engines, news portals and research databases. This paper presents Web design requirements that can improve the accessibility of such websites for PWDs particularly the blind. The requirements were derived from both theoretical and quantitative data gathered from both literature and a case study. It was observed that graphical user interfaces, non-linear navigation, forms, tables, images, lack of key board support, non-standard document formats and acronyms and abbreviations hinder Web accessibility for the blind. Therefore in order to improve Web accessibility for the blind, the following requirements were suggested; a text only version of the website or a combination of design considerations namely: text alternatives for visual elements, meaningful content structure in the source code, skip navigation link(s), orientation during navigation, ensure (tables, frames and forms) are accessible if any is used, test the website with keyboard only access, use or convert documents into standard formats and expand abbreviations and acronyms the first time they appear on a page. Meeting the given requirements in the Web development process improves Web accessibility for all blind Web users including those engaged in hybrid learning.

Keywords: Web Accessibility, Requirements, Blind, Hybrid Learning, E-learning.

1 Introduction

With the Web, People with Disabilities (PWDs) can undertake a number of tasks that would otherwise be difficult or impossible. Learners with visual, audio, cognitive, learning and physical disabilities can take all or most of the courses in the comfort of their homes. They can access course content online, interact with the instructor, participate in online discussions with classmates, research on the subject, buy books/software and read news including that related to class modules. However this is only possible when designers of such systems consider their special access needs. Considerable research has been done on how to make e-learning systems accessible [1], [2],

J. Fong, R. Kwan, and F.L. Wang (Eds.): ICHL 2008, LNCS 5169, pp. 392–403, 2008.

[3], [4]. This has resulted into systems like VisiCAST [5], SMILE [6] and the EVI-DENT [7] which are trying to address the need for accessible learning materials for PWDs. But learners utilize many other Web systems during their learning experience beyond what the instructor and institution provide and can control. They use search engines and research databases for additional study material, buy books/software online, access news portals for articles on class modules and may need to interact with classmates and other learner groups on social networking sites like Facebook [8]. Besides educational needs, the Web offers opportunities for all PWDs to do more things themselves without external support. They can shop, read news and pay their bills online among other things.

This paper provides Web design requirements that can improve accessibility of websites such as search engines, e-commerce sites, news and general portals for PWDs particularly the blind. The requirements are based on both theoretical and quantitative data gathered from literature and a case study involving blind and sighted Web users on sample websites. Meeting the given requirements in the Web development process improves Web accessibility for blind Web users such as those engaged in hybrid learning. Other than PWDs, accessible websites offer other benefits to other users and owners namely: better page download speed, easier to use for all, easier maintenance and upgrade and better visibility for search engine indexing [10]. The remainder of the paper has methods, results, discussion of the results, Web accessibility requirements for the blind, conclusion and future work.

2 Methods

The objective of this work was to establish the Web accessibility requirements of blind Web users. This was achieved by reviewing the major guidelines, policies and published literature on Web accessibility for PWDs particularly the blind and a case study involving blind and sighted Web users. The case study was used to verify if the requirements given in the guidelines and literature were correct, complete or otherwise. The case study involved blind and sighted Web users who performed tasks on five sample websites covering common Web applications: search engines, news portals, e-commerce and a tourism portal. Each website had one or more of the features reported in literature to hamper accessibility for the blind. Features not found in the sample websites or that could not be sufficiently assessed using the sample websites were tested by the researchers using Job Accessibility with Speech (JAWS) 8.0 screen reader. A website designed to be accessible to PWDs was included in the sample to compare its usability with others. Only participants with intermediate web usage skills and above were involved in order to minimize expertise related other than visual disability related problems with the tasks. The tasks and associated questions made participants interact with the website features reported to affect Web accessibility such as graphical user interfaces (GUIs), forms and tables.

Participants were required to open sample websites, perform specified tasks, give feedback about the results and any problems encountered. The questionnaire was e-mailed to 10 participants on 1st July 2007 to be returned by 30th July 2007. Five of the participants were university students and the rest were working class. We fell short of our target sample of 20 blind Web users because blind people that could use the Web in Uganda were found limited. During the time of the assessment, we checked the sample websites in the morning and afternoon to ensure the features referred to in the tasks were available and functioning as required. Five sighted Web users were also assessed on the sample websites using the same tasks and questions to compare the experience of the two groups. The next section presents results of the review of the major guidelines, policies and research efforts followed by the results from the case study.

3 Review of Guidelines, and Policies and Other Literature

The guidelines reviewed included Web Content Accessibility Guidelines (WCAG) 1.0 and its successor WCAG 2.0 draft, Americans with Disabilities Act (ADA) 1990, Section 508 of the US Rehabilitation Act, Australian Disability Discrimination Act (ADDA) and National Institute on Aging (NIA) Guidelines. The review revealed that only WCAG 2.0 draft mentions which guidelines benefit the blind. But it is still a draft under review hence not stable. WCAG 1.0 contains all key points for Web Accessibility [10], [11] and most of the other guidelines are comparable to it. But WCAG 1.0's guidelines are general and not specific to different types of disabilities. NIA only covers low vision. The academic literature revealed that some sites only try to comply with the guidelines without understanding the needs underlying Web accessibility [12]. This results into supposedly compliant websites that are neither accessible nor usable to PWDs. Suggestions on WHAT could make Web applications accessible based on user experience could supplement existing guidelines. Other important findings from the literature were that: there is low accessibility despite the increasing number of PWDs [13], [14], [12], [15], [16], [11] the focus of many Web developers is often limited to meeting standards and regulations at the expense of the human interaction aspects [17], [10] but also there are significant efforts towards enhancing Web accessibility for PWDs such as those in [11], [19], [20].

Also from the literature, a number of Web application features that hamper Web accessibility for the blind were reported namely: graphical user interfaces (GUIs) [13], [11], [20]; non-linear navigation approach for the Web environment [10], [18], [12]; visual elements [22], [13], [11]; tables [23], [13], [21], [11]; forms [13], [24], [17]; frames [24]; lack of keyboard support [23], [24], [11]; lack of orientation [10], [22], [10]; non-standard document formats [23], [13], [11]; and abbreviations and acronyms [24]. In order to verify whether these features are indeed a problem and if there were any other problems, we carried out a case study on actual blind and sighted Web users. The next section presents the results obtained.

4 Results

4.1 Web Accessibility Experience of Blind Web Users on the Sample Websites

The sample websites covered common Web applications used by my many groups including hybrid learning students: search engine, news portal, e-commerce and a general portal. Each of the websites had one or more of the features reported to hamper accessibility for the blind. Participants were required to use a screen reader to open the website, perform the given task that was related to the feature of interest and answer given questions. The questions covered: if the user was able to perform the task, how long it took to access a given information item, what happened in cases where the task could not be successfully executed and any problems faced while performing the task.

The features tested on each websites were as follows:

- A simple form on **Google** (www.google.com) used for its search functionality. The task was to search and read about the theme of the 2007 Common Wealth Heads of Government Meeting (CHOGM 2007) which was due to take place in Kampala, Uganda from 23rd to 25th November 2007 and preparations were in high gear involving almost every citizen.
- A detailed form on **Amazon** (www.amazon.com) used for ordering goods. The task was to search for any book of interest, order for one up to submission of shipping address.
- Tables (layout) and images on New Vision (www.newvision.co.ug). The task was to open the national link on the home page and read the first story.
- Flash on **About Uganda** (www.aboutuganda.com). The task was to open the home page, listen to its contents.
- Images on the designed to be accessible **British Broadcasting Corporation (BBC)** (www.bbc.co.uk). The task was to open the News link on the home page and read the first story. The interest was to find out if images on this website were accessible to the blind in comparison to the images on the New Vision.

The questionnaire was administered to 10 blind Web users in Kampala, the capital city of Uganda out of which 8 responded (80%).

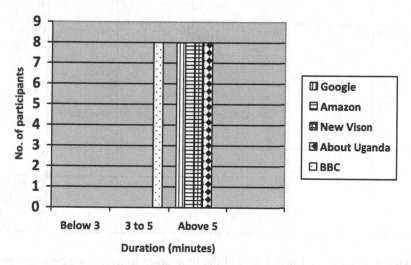

Fig. 1. Time taken by the Blind to access a given Information Item on Sample Websites

Table 1. Quantitative Results about the Experience of Blind Web users

Question	Google		Amazon		New Vision		About Uganda		BBC	
	Yes	No	Yes	No	Yes	No	Yes	No	Yes	No
Found Required information item	8	0	7	1	8	0	8	0	8	0
Could use info item obtained to perform given task	0	8	0	7	8	0	8	0	8	0
Understood content in text form	NA	NA	NA	NA	8	0	NA	NA	8	0
Understood content in image form	NA	NA	NA	NA	0	8	NA	NA	8	0

Table 2. Summary of the Qualitative Results about the Web Accessibility Experience of Blind Web users

What happened?	Couldn't get info Item Required	Couldn't use info obtained to perform given Task	Couldn't Understand Text	Couldn't Understand Images	Any other Problems
Google	Nil	Could get to list of links but screen reader could not read results (8)	NA	Nil	Nil
Amazon	Failed to open homepage(1)	Couldn't get info on how to proceed after getting search results(7)	Nil	NA	Not able to order book of interest due to lack of relevant cues (8)
New Vision	Nil	Nil	Nil	-Screen reader kept silent on certain sections (5) -Got vague messages 'out of field'(3)	Difficulty tracing headlines (4)
About Uganda	Nil	Nil	Nil	Nil	Nil
BBC	Nil	Nil	Nil	Nil	Difficulty determining which story came first (6)

Figure 1 and Tables 1 and 2 present the time taken to access a given information item on each website and a summary of the quantitative and qualitative results respectively. 'NA' in Table 1 means that a particular question did not apply to that website and 'Nil' in Table 2 means that there was no problem for that task.

4.2 Web Accessibility Experience of Sighted Web Users on Sample Websites

The sample websites were also tested on 5 sighted users on similar tasks to compare the experience of the two groups. All the 5 (100%) responded.

They all took less than three minutes to access a given information item on all the websites, performed the tasks successfully and understood the content in text as well as image form. However, two of them faced problems with the task on the Amazon website. A first time online shopper did not find guidance on how to shop, the second participant was sensitive about submitting a functioning e-mail address. Other complaints on Amazon were: too much clutter, difficulty finding the shopping cart and the need to scroll to read content. Other than Amazon, participants also complained of many flash images on 'About Uganda' that made page loading slow. The next section discusses the results obtained from both groups.

5 Discussion of Results

5.1 Time Taken to Access Required Information Items

All the blind users took above 5 minutes to access a given information item on all websites except BBC where they took 3 to 5 minutes. The sighted took less than three minutes on all the websites. Four of the five websites had graphical intensive user Interfaces (UI), a feature that affects accessibility for PWDs [13]. Only BBC had a text intensive interface and a text only version. The results confirmed the fact that Graphical User Interfaces (GUI) affect Web accessibility for the blind. Less GUI interfaces improve access speed for the blind as evidenced on the BBC. Moreover this does not affect access speed for the sighted as evidenced by the same duration taken by sighted users on both BBC and the other websites.

5.2 Execution of the Tasks on Each Website

- **Forms on Google and Amazon:** The search function was successful for both the blind and sighted on both websites but all the blind were not able to use the obtained results to perform the required tasks. The sighted had no problem using the results on Google probably because they use the mouse rather than the keyboard but two were not successful with the task on Amazon, a problem they related to the poor usability of the website. The problem on Google was not the form based search function but the format of the results which could not be navigated with a keyboard and opened by the screen reader. Web designers should ensure that results from search forms are accessible for such functions to be useful to PWDs. Interestingly, Amazon had a link to an accessible version of the website on the home page but all the blind participants never realized so. Thus Web designers need to test such links with relevant assistive technologies to be sure they are accessible as required.
- **Tables on New Vision:** All the blind users were able to get the news link of interest that was presented with other website items in a table based layout. But they found it difficult to trace the headlines. The sighted users had no problem with the

task. Therefore using tables for layout makes accessibility of web pages difficult for the blind.

- **Images on New Vision and BBC:** The blind did not recognize images on New Vision but did so, on the BBC where the screen reader read out alternative textual descriptions and the users understood what the images were about. The sighted users had no problem on both websites. Therefore images on general audience websites also pose accessibility problems to the blind.

- **Flash on About Uganda:** All the blind and sighted participants were able to understand the content of interest that was primarily presented in flash. This was made possible because the content in flash had alternative text describing the flash images. All web pages with flash should emulate this practice. However one sighted user complained that the flash images made the site slow. Such users especially those with slow internet links can benefit from designs with out flash just like the blind where flash can be avoided.

- **Orientation during navigation:** Orientation is the user's understanding of their current location, and their own movements and their grasp of their current navigation context [11]. Sighted users had better orientation on all the sample websites given the less time taken to identify the required information item. On Amazon, all the blind and one sighted participant failed to get cues on how to order hence addressing this problem benefits both groups. On New vision, the blind had problems tracing the headlines. Interestingly, two blind participants also found it difficult to determine which news story came first on BBC. One of them said, "I only had to guess which story came first". This is a revelation that even websites designed to be accessible can still have some problems for PWDs hence further research to identify such issues and possible solutions is desirable.

- **Frames:** All the websites surveyed did not use frames. We failed to get one with frames to include in the sample.

- **Lack of keyboard support:** All the sample websites supported use of the keyboard for input tasks and navigation. This was tested using JAWS 8.0 screen reader and navigating the websites with the keyboard. In addition, no participant reported a keyboard related problem.

- **Non-standard document formats e.g. PDF:** This was not tested on the participants but New Vision had images of scanned text documents. Such documents pose the same problems as images without alternative text. This was verified and confirmed by the researchers using JAWS 8.0 screen reader.

- **Acronyms and abbreviations:** Using JAWS 8.0 screen reader, we tested an MS word document with acronyms and abbreviations. The screen reader read the acronyms and abbreviations as one word, which makes the user unable to decipher them. Hence acronyms and abbreviations that are not expanded cannot be understood by users of assistive technologies such as screen readers.

5.3 Other Issues from the Assessment Other Than the Features Tested in the Case Study

- Pop ups disorient blind users when they pop up in a page.
- Images without alternative text is the biggest problem for the blind.

- On websites with many images, the blind use sighted guides which interferes with their privacy.
- Lack of information on the page download progress frustrates the blind especially on slow links
- Designers in Uganda are ignorant about the diversity of their clientele
- There is limited effort by internet cafes in Uganda to install screen readers.

In the next section, we present suggestions on WHAT needs to be done in order to address the difficulties faced by blind Web users.

6 Web Accessibility Requirements for the Blind

This section discusses Web design considerations that can address the difficulties faced by blind Web users on websites such as those covered in the case study.

6.1 Provide a Text Only Version of Entire Website

Assistive technologies used by the blind such as screen readers have plain interfaces that sequentially verbalize Web content in the order it is structured in the source code [12], [21]. This makes it difficult for the blind to identify and use information items on graphical intensive websites compared to sighted users as was evidenced on the 4 out of the 5 websites. It took all the blind users more than 5 minutes to access a given information item on the graphical intensive websites and 3 to 5 minutes on the text intensive BBC. The sighted took less than 3 minutes on all the websites to perform the same tasks. Therefore a text only version of the entire website can improve the access speed for blind users.

6.2 Apply a Combination of Web Design Considerations

Other than a text only version, Web accessibility for the blind can be improved with out having two website versions by applying a combination of Web design considerations as follows:

- **Provide Text Alternative for every Visual Element:** Web content conveyed using visual elements with out alternative text excludes persons who are blind from accessing such information because screen readers cannot interpret such content [14], [12] and as was established on the New Vision website. Web designers should provide a text alternative for every visual element and avoid elements that cannot be presented in this form [24], [12]. Screen readers can adapt text into audio formats for the blind users to access. The common method of achieving this is to use the 'alt' attribute of the 'IMG' tag which allows for a short textual description of information contained in an image. For complex images such as charts and graphs, the 'D-link' attribute to link to a file or page with a detailed description of the image is recommended and preferred over the 'Longdesc' attribute. The latter is not widely supported by screen readers [18]. Images that do not convey important information should have null 'alt' text. Designers should ensure that the alternative content conveys the same function or purpose as the image, for it to be useful to the blind [24], [12]. Alternative text can also be useful to people without disabilities e.g. those using handheld devices with small screens and limited graphics capabilities and increases usability for all users [18].

- **Structure Content Meaningfully in the Source Code:** This is possible through use of markup such as HTML's structural tags like heading (<H1>, <H2>...), Paragraph <P> to describe the document structure [12]. Markup embeds information structure and relationships among page elements into content of a document thereby adding a layer of meaning to the website document structure. This enhances the capacity of screen readers and voice browsers to read and interpret Web documents to blind users. They can easily find, skip or go back to content items given the logical presentation [21]. Markup can also provide additional functionality to the user such as document overview using heading tags. However, mark up should be used for the intended function for it to yield accessible applications.
- **Provide Skip Navigation Links:** Traditionally, Web pages are written in Hypertext Markup Language (HTML) whose documents are presented in a non-linear form. But screen readers present information sequentially using a text-to-speech (TTS) engine. Hence the blind have to go through all the clutter such as adverts and repeated navigation on each page. From the case study, a content item that took less than 3 minutes to locate by sighted users, took more than 5 minutes to reach using the screen reader. Even on BBC, it took blind users more time than the sighted (3 to 5 minutes and less than 3 minutes for the sighted). Skip navigation links [18] enable users of screen readers to skip repeated or peripheral content and go straight to the main content. This saves time and improves usability for the blind. More over the link(s) can be made invisible by using an invisible image link so as not to affect the visual layout [13].
- **Provide for Orientation during Navigation:** To improve orientation for the blind, Web designers should mark up different sections of Web pages with predefined semantics such as main, heading, navigation and adverts [21]. This makes it possible for them to navigate to different sections of the website including the ability to skip certain sections. In addition, some screen readers like Home Page Reader (HPR) support heading navigation mode with the 'ALT' + 1 command and using the arrow keys to move from current, previous and next headings [18]. Other suggestions include: put main content after the title followed by navigation for table layouts; provide clear 'alt' text on each area of the client side image map; provide redundant text links for all hot spots of server-side image maps. Asakawa [12] proposes fragmentation e.g. the XML fragmentation recommendation (XFrag) for the benefit of both blind and users of small screen devices.
- **Create Accessible Tables:** Tables on the Web are used for layout and data presentation. The former is however discouraged in favor of cascading style sheets (CSS). For those that still insist on using tables for layout, Thatcher et al., [17] advises that they should put content after the title instead of left navigation and put navigation in the right column after main content. Alternatively since tables are read a row at a time, if main content can be the only content in row two and navigation menu in row three, then content can be read first. On the other hand, data tables can be either simple or complex. A table is simple if the column headers for any given data cell is in the same column as the cell and the row headers for any given data cell is in the same row as the cell [17], [24]. To create accessible simple tables, designers should identify table headers in the first row and first column or use the table

header <TH> element or scope attribute. Complex data tables are tables with two or more logical levels of row or column headers. They can be made accessible by associating heading information with the data cell using the 'id' attribute of the <TH> element [18].

- **Create Accessible Frames or Provide Alternative Content:** To design accessible frames, frame elements should have meaningful titles and name attributes and all frame pages must have meaningful titles. Some assistive technologies such as Lynx and JAWS depend on the name attribute of the frames. Others such as Window-Eyes and Home Page Reader use the title element on the actual frame pages [17]. Frame title and name attributes should explain the role of the frame in the frame set, e.g. navigation or title. Alternatively, designers can provide alternative content with out frames [21], [23].

- **Create accessible forms:** To make form based content accessible to blind Web users, Web designers should explicitly and programmatically associate form labels with their controls e.g. place text information for text entry fields and combo boxes to the left (or above) the control and put the prompt for a checkbox or radio button to the right of the object. When the prompt is programmatically connected to the <input> element, all the screen readers make the correct announcement [17]. The alternative approaches are to place titles in the <input> elements that identify the purpose of the control, to use the <label> element to associate the correct text prompts with each form control with the 'for' attribute and to use the <FIELD-SET> and <LEGEND> tags to structure complex forms so that they are clearer and simpler to understand. For forms used for search functionality, designers should ensure that results from the search are accessible e.g. with the keyboard and screen reader.

- **Test the application with Keyboard only Access:** The blind Web users rely on keyboards as their primary input device. To be sure that all parts of a Web application are usable with the keyboard, designers should test the application with keyboard only access.

- **Use or convert documents into available standard formats:** Web designers should use or convert documents into available standard formats such as those recommended by W3C [23].

- **Expand Abbreviations and Acronyms:** Designers should expand abbreviations and acronyms the first time they appear on a page. This will enable users of screen readers to get their full meaning hence making them understandable to them [23].

7 Conclusion and Future Work

We have presented Web design requirements that can improve Web accessibility for PWDs particularly the blind like blind hybrid Learners. The requirements are derived from both theoretical and quantitative data gathered from both literature and a case study. It was observed that graphical user interfaces, non-linear navigation, forms, tables, images, lack of key board support, non-standard document formats, acronyms and abbreviations hinder Web accessibility for the blind. In order to address the challenges faced, we suggest a text only version of the website or a combination of Web design considerations namely: text alternatives for visual elements, structure content meaningfully in the source code, skip navigation link(s), orientation during navigation, accessible (tables, frames and forms), test the website with keyboard only access, use or convert documents into standard formats and expand abbreviations and acronyms the first time they appear on a page. Meeting the given requirements in the Web development process improves Web accessibility for all blind Web users including those engaged in hybrid learning. In future, we plan to carry out the same case study in another country to compare results and infer a wider perspective.

References

1. Coombs, N.: Reflections on the State of Accessibility in E-learning in the Sciences (2008)
2. Mirabella, Kimani, Catarci: A no-frills approach for accessible Web based learning material. In: W4A 2004, New York, USA (2004)
3. Kelly, et al.: One World One Web but Great Diversity. In: W4A 2008, Beijing, Japan (2008)
4. Karampiperis, Sampson: Designing Learning Systems to Provide Accessible Services. In: W4A 2005, Chiba, Japan (2005)
5. ViSiCAST Project, Virtual Signing: Capture, Animation, Storage and Transmission, http://www.niwi.knaw.nl/en/oi/nod/onderzoek/OND1277077/toon
6. SMILE Project, A Sign Language and Multimedia-based Interactive Language Course for the Deaf for the Training of European Written Languages, http://www.arcsmed.at/projects/smile
7. VIDENT Project, European Versatility in Deaf Education using Multimedia Technology, http://www.niwi.knaw.nl/en/oi/nod/onderzoek/OND1276
8. http://www.facebook.com/ (accessed May 15, 2008)
9. Lazar, et al.: Improving Web accessibility: A study of Webmaster perceptions. Computers in Human Behavior, 269–288 (2005)
10. Harper, et al.: Web Mobility Guidelines for Visually Impaired Surfers. J. of Research & Practice in Information Technology 33(1) (2001)
11. Horton, S.: Designing Beneath the Surface of the Web. In: W4A 2006, Edinburgh, UK (2006)
12. Asakawa, C.: What's the Web Like If You Can't See It? In: W4A 2006, New York, USA (2005)
13. Chiang, et al.: Computer and World Wide Web Accessibility by Visually Disabled Patients: Problems and Solutions. Survey of Ophthalmology 50(4) (2005)
14. Shi, Y.: The accessibility of Queensland Visitor Information Center's websites. Tourism Management (2005)
15. Becker, S.A.: E-government Visual Accessibility for Older Adult Users. Social Science Computer Review 22(1), 11–23 (2004)
16. Abanumy, et al.: E-government website Accessibility: In-Depth Evaluation of Saudi Arabia and Oman. The Electronic Journal of e-Government 3(3) (2005)
17. Thatcher, et al.: Constructing Accessible Web Sites, Web professional to Web professional, an Apress imprint (2002)
18. Takagi, et al.: Accessibility Designer: Visualizing Usability for the Blind. In: ASSETS 2004, pp.18–20 (2004)
19. Borodin, Y.: The HearSay NonVisual Web Browser. In: W4A 2007, Banff, Canada (2007)

20. Leventhal: Structure Benefits All. In: W4A 2006, Edinburgh, UK (2006)
21. Huang, C.J.: Usability of E-Government Web Sites for PWDs. In: HICSS 2003 (2003)
22. Patil, S.R.: Accessible Image File Formats-The Need and the Way. In: W4A 2007, Banff, Canada (2007)
23. Chisholm, et al. (ed.): WCAG 1.0 (Retrieved February 13, 2007), http://www.w3.org/TR/WAI-WEBCONTENT/
24. Brewer, J. (ed.): How PWDs Use the Web (Ret. on April 20, 2005) (2007), http://www.w3.org/WAI/EO/Drafts/PWD-Use-Web/Overview.html

Towards a Better Blended Learning: Experiences of Adult Learners in Hong Kong

Po Wan Ruby Lee[1] and F.T. Chan[2]

[1] Faculty of Education, Monash University, Clayton, Australia
[2] HKU SPACE, The University of Hong Kong, Hong Kong, China
ruby.lee@education.monash.edu.au, ft.chan@hkuspace.hku.hk

Abstract. The rapid development of information and communication technology brings along many impacts to education and training. Though delivery of courses solely based on e-learning on its own is not totally satisfactory to students and course providers, distance learning and face-to-face courses benefit from the use of e-learning as a support in the teaching and learning process. Surveys of Hong Kong part-time students clearly indicated that they preferred a blended learning mode that retains some form of face-to-face teaching and utilizes e-learning at the same time. However, effective blended learning is not simply using technology as an additional communication means or organizing extra learning activities. Web-based technology should be used as communication and collaborative tools. Pedagogy has to be adjusted to incorporate e-learning as an integral part of the teaching and learning process. Through the proper design of course, better integration of assessment, learning activities and use of technology for facilitating interactions via online community, meaningful blended learning experience can be resulted.

Keywords: blended learning, hybrid learning, adult learners, distance learning, higher education.

1 Introduction

The advancement in information and communication technology (ICT) brings a lot of hope to education institutes, especially those providing distance education. A wide range of e-learning tools, such as computer-mediated education software, online forum, blog and wikis, have been developed. Some institutes make use of technologies to enhance their delivery of distance education courses. Some go for new ventures in offering courses solely using the electronic platform. However, these purely e-learning courses are largely not successful in delivering learning experience to the satisfaction of the students and in achieving cost effectiveness to the satisfaction of the institutes. The potential benefits of e-learning nevertheless flourish when use together with existing models of course delivery. A comprehensive discussion on the development of blended learning and utilizing e-learning to enhance teaching and learning effectiveness can be found in Macdonald [1] and Naidu [2]. This article reports the experiences and research findings of the authors in the past eight years.

J. Fong, R. Kwan, and F.L. Wang (Eds.): ICHL 2008, LNCS 5169, pp. 404–414, 2008.

In the following sections, the development of e-learning activities introduced into distance education courses experienced by the authors is reviewed; the trend of students' preferences on delivery modes is analyzed based on surveys conducted in various years; and the good practices of blended learning approaches are described. Thereafter, implications and experiences for designing hybrid learning courses for adult learners are discussed, followed by the conclusion section.

2 Stages of Blended Learning

Since 1990, the School of Professional and Continuing Education, The University of Hong Kong (HKU SPACE) collaborated with Charles Sturt University (CSU) in Australia their first joint course using a distance education delivery mode. Students were largely working adults and studied part-time. For each subject, the adult learners were given a set of distance learning package that consisted of a Subject Outline, a Study Guide, and a collection of required Readings. The Subject Outline stated the objectives and overview of the subject, information of the Subject Coordinator, the proposed self-learning schedule, the assessment items, the marking criteria, and the list of reference materials. About 8 sessions of face-to-face teaching/tutorial sessions of 2 to 3 hours each, depending on the subject, were organized by HKU SPACE using a local teacher to support the students. These sessions were scheduled after office hours or during the weekends to match the availability of the students.

Students could communicate with CSU Subject Coordinator through email. At that time, email was far less popular than today. Most students had not used email before they joined the course. They needed to use a modem to dial in to a computer server operated by the University Computer Centre. Many did not have computers at home and few had modems. Before 2000, less than 50% of the households in Hong Kong had one or more PCs at home. Out of these households with PC, about 73% had access to the Internet [3]. The local Course Coordinator acted as the communication bridge between students in Hong Kong and the CSU Subject Coordinator in Australia.

Since 1994, CSU started to supplement the printed learning package with a computer disk. Hyperlinks and computer animations of flowcharts and computer programs were added to increase the interactions between students and the learning materials. Students generally felt that printed materials had the advantage of physical portability. They could bring along the printed materials and read them during traveling or waiting at some places. Electronic materials simply mirroring the printed version were not welcomed. Additional features such as hyperlinks to relevant resources, computer animations, and multimedia presentations were needed to justify the development and production of electronic materials [4].

Starting from 1999, a more comprehensive online support services were offered in the form of a Subject Web Page. In addition to CSU, Monash University (Monash) in Australia also jointly offered degree programs with HKU SPACE since 2002 using a web-enhanced distance education delivery mode, supplemented by face-to-face teaching conducted by local teachers in Hong Kong. For each subject, the set of distance learning materials were put online. In addition, Forum was set up to enhance communication between the overseas university subject teacher and students from different places. The Forum also facilitated discussions among the students themselves.

Students from different places used the Forum as a platform to share their learning experiences. However, in 2002 connection to the Internet in Hong Kong was largely through modems. Students needed to occupy a phone line at home and suffered from annoying unexpected disconnections.

Recently more Hong Kong people had access to Internet at home. In 2003 the percentage of households that had PCs at home increased to 67.5% (more than 30% increase in three years) and out of these households 88.8% had access to the Internet. Effectively, the percentage of households that had access to Internet at home increased from 36.5% to 60%. An increase of 64% of households in Hong Kong had Internet access at home in the three years from 2000 to 2003. The survey in 2006 revealed that 71.7% of households had PCs at home and 93.6% of them had access to Internet. The percentage of households that had both PCs and Internet access rose to 67%. The latest survey in 2007 revealed that 74.2% of households had PCs at home and 94.5% of them had access to Internet [5]. There is an increase of 93% of households in Hong Kong had Internet access at home in the seven years from 2000 to 2007. The advancement in information and communication technologies supported the development of blended learning. Yet, to the students, there were learning elements of face-to-face sessions that could not be totally replaced by online learning.

3   Student Surveys on Preferred Learning Modes

In order to understand learners' preferences of various learning modes, surveys of students studied in the blended learning programs described above were conducted from 2000 to 2005.

3.1   Student Survey 2000

The first questionnaire survey was carried out in 2000 [6, 7] with two groups of students. One group of 24 students studied a graduate diploma in library program and the other group of 21 students studied a Master of Information Technology program. Both courses utilized a blended learning mode that some subjects were taught face-to-face and some subjects were based on distance learning but with some supporting face-to-face tutorials. These students studied part-time while working full-time. They were asked to select the teaching mode they preferred most from the following options, assuming they were given a choice:

- face-to-face teaching for all the subjects (FtF);
- some face-to-face taught subjects and some distance learning subjects with supporting tutorials (BL1);
- distance learning with face-to-face tutorials (BL2);
- pure distance learning mode (DL).

The survey findings revealed that almost all students rejected the pure distance learning mode. Yet, not too many of them preferred a purely face-to-face teaching mode, probably due to the fact that they were working full-time. The majority wanted to have the benefits of both worlds, having face-to-face sessions and distance learning

Table 1. The Most Preferred Teaching Mode – Students' Perspective in 2000

Learning Mode	IT Students n=21	Library Students n=24	Combined n=45
FtF	9%	21%	16%
BL1	**67%**	**50%**	**58%**
BL2	24%	25%	24%
DL	0%	4%	2%

at the same time. A summary of the findings is given in Table 1. IT students did not necessarily favored distance learning supported by technology when compared with the library students.

3.2 Student Surveys 2002-2003

Similar surveys on the learning experiences of part-time postgraduate students taking distance learning courses with blended learning were conducted in 2002 and 2003. In February 2002, a survey on the distance learning experience of the two Master's IT degree programs jointly offered by HKU SPACE and Australian Universities was conducted. 58 successfully completed questionnaires were received for the February 2002 survey [8]. During December 2002 and January 2003, students from a diploma course, an undergraduate program and five postgraduate programs that were jointly operated by HKU SPACE and universities from Australia and the United Kingdom were invited to participate in the 2002-2003 survey. In this survey, the full-time face-to-face study was refined to include both part-time and full-time study [9]. In early 2003, 130 returns were received. The results of all the surveys, which conducted between 2000 and 2003, on the most preferred learning mode are summarized in Table 2.

Table 2. The Most Preferred Teaching Mode – Students' Perspective in 2000 - 2003

Learning Mode	2000 n=45	Feb 2002 n=58	2002-03 n=130
FtF (part-time)	16%	11%	15%
FtF (full-time)	N/A	N/A	16%
BL1	**58%**	**54%**	**52%**
BL2	24%	35%	15%
DL	2%	0%	2%

3.3 Student Survey 2005

The latest survey was conducted in late 2005 with an extended scale [10]. More programs and recent graduates as well as active students from four undergraduate programs and four postgraduate programs were included. 274 successfully completed questionnaires were received out of 1,357 distributions. The response rate was about 20%. As e-learning was much more developed and became so pervasive, the

Table 3. The Most Preferred Teaching Mode – Students' Perspective in 2005

Learning Mode	2005 n=274
FtF supplemented with e-Learning	42%
BL1	22%
BL2	27%
Total online learning with some FtF support	6%
Total online learning with no FtF	3%

preferred teaching modes were redefined and the survey results on the most preferred learning modes are shown in Table 3.

The demographic details of the 2005 survey respondents were similar to the survey respondents of 2002 and 2003. Most of the 2005 survey respondents were male (76%). Majority of them (83.8%) were aged between 21 and 40 (32% age 20–30, 51.7% age 31–40, 15% age 41-50, 1.5% age above 50). 43.2% of them obtained a Bachelor degree and 35.9% had a Master Degree. Regarding the working experience, 21.2% of the respondents worked for five years or less, 32.6% worked for six to ten years, and 46.2% worked for more than ten years. Most of them (81.3%) had broadband access to Internet both at home and at office. The respondents in general were experienced online and distance learners. Among the respondents, 9.9% had experienced in complete online learning, 52% had experienced in web-enhanced distance learning and 16.8% experienced face-to-face teaching supplemented by online support. Only 21.2% of the 2005 survey respondents (as compared to 39% of the 2002-2003 survey respondents) did not have any e-Learning experience. In brief, most of the 2005 survey respondents were male aged between 21 and 40 who had a Bachelor degree or higher degree. These working adults had high accessibility to Internet, and were experienced in various online learning modes. There was no significant correlation found between the preference of learning mode and the demographic factors of the 2005 survey respondents (including age, working experience and previous online learning experience).

The findings of the 2005 survey about the preferred learning mode are similar to the previous survey results of 2000, 2002, and 2003. Blended learning modes were highly preferred by Hong Kong's adult learners. The results of the 2000-2005 surveys indicated that blended learning modes with more face-to-face elements were more welcomed by the respondents. Web-enhanced distance learning with no face-to-face element was not preferred by student respondents from 2000 to 2005 as only 2% to 3% of them preferred such learning mode. The results of these surveys confirmed the predominant acceptance of the mixed delivery modes over pure distance learning and online learning. This further indicated that Hong Kong adult learners perceived face-to-face sessions as highly valuable.

3.4 Adoption of Blended Learning Strategies

The findings of these surveys lead the authors to think what blended learning strategies can better integrate e-learning tools with face-to-face sessions to achieve higher teaching and learning effectiveness, especially for the part-time adult learners. The main features of the blended learning strategy that we have been adopting so far are as follows:

- Distance learning package available online and in printed form;
- Face-to-face sessions at regular intervals throughout the semester;
- Deploying asynchronous online environment (email, forum, subject webpage) for communication, discussion and access to resources.

The number of face-to-face sessions ranges from 6 to 10 for a semester-long subject. Each session lasts for 2 to 3 hours. The actual arrangement depends on the nature of the subject and the level of the program. For example, more sessions are organized for a bachelor degree program than a postgraduate program. Longer hours per session are organized for a subject involving practical components. During the face-to-face sessions, the local teacher can choose to do one or more of the following activities:

- teach the more challenging topics of the subject;
- discuss questions raised by students;
- discuss the assessment items.

These face-to-face sessions also serve as checkpoints to keep students' paces of learning progress and allow for peer-sharing and mutual support.

The key questions are how to integrate face-to-face sessions and e-learning to achieve the greatest synergy. For the good practice in blended learning, Macdonald [1] stated that "if there is currently a recipe for a blended strategy, it is a broth of pedagogy, heavily peppered with pragmatism". In the next section, we describe the practices of a blended learning approach of an education program and compare it with the approach advocated by Albon and Trinidad [11].

4   Good Practices of Blended Learning Approaches

4.1   Integration of Online Learning and Face-to-Face Teaching

In 2005-2006, the delivery approach of a postgraduate subject in an Education Diploma program for part-time adult learners in Hong Kong was examined. The subject was taken by a group of twenty students. In the subject, an e-learning platform was used to support the following functions online:

- Announcement – releasing of announcements related to the subject or program;
- Resources – presentation slides, handouts, and other reference materials;
- Forum – discussion forum for students to post views and questions as well as responses to other students' submitted views and questions.

For this postgraduate subject, students were divided into three groups. Students received a set of pre-class reading materials for the next weekly class meeting. Each group was assigned to work on an activity as stated in the materials. Every member of the group was required to post his/her views or proposed solutions in the Forum before the next class. On top of their own postings, students were encouraged to post responses or follow up questions to items posted by their classmates, either of the same group or the other two groups. Each activity provided a scenario for the students to analyze, they were then asked to prepare their responses to some questions. Typical questions, for example, read something like:

> *What do you think about these views? Which one do you like more?*
> *How do these teachers see motivation differently? Or can you integrate these different approaches to motivate the class to learn?*

During the class meetings, members of each group would get together to discuss their postings and any follow up postings. They formulated some concluding findings and presented these findings to the whole class. A summary report of the findings was then posted to the Forum. As part of the assessment, the timely submission of the postings in the Forum and the presentations in class meetings contributed up to 20% of the final score. In addition, each student was required to compile the set of their own postings in the Forum together with their responses to other students' postings as part of the final assignment for submission to the teacher at the end of the teaching term.

The number of postings of each lesson for this subject ranged from 30 to 50. The average number of postings per lesson was 36.8. The average number of postings per lesson per student was 1.84. These figures were regarded as indicators of active engagement by the students. Students learnt more effectively in this subject in several ways due to the design of the blended learning. In each class meeting, students were required to follow up on what they had prepared by studying the reading materials and the postings on the Forum. Without such pre-class learning, they would not be able to work on the in-class activity effectively. By design student learning was built upon the integration of the face-to-face session and the use of the online forum outside class. The grouping of students helped not only achieving collaborative learning but also exerting positive group pressure for each group member to submit online forum posting on time. Otherwise, other members could not read and prepare for the in-class discussion.

The weekly postings not only counted as part of the final score but also formed an essential part of the final assignment submission. The importance of using the online forum was appropriately reflected in its weighting in the assessment. This example illustrated how the use of internet-based technology was integrated into the learning process and continuous assessment, as well as how adult learners were motivated to participate in online forum discussion.

4.2 Mediated Learner Approach (MLA)

A similar model can be found in the Mediated Learner Approach (MLA) developed by Albon and Trinidad [11]. They believed technology could be used to act as vehicles for driving the model in which communication and collaboration among the learner, peers and the lecturers could be facilitated. Mediated learning occurred through the building of a learning community. In addition to the technology component, another key component was assessment which was learner-focused and performance-based. In the MLA, learning was driven by assessment which was "part of the learning process", and learning was about "developing competency in applying knowledge" [11, p. 53], not just simply knowing the content.

It was believed that assessment tasks were essential and drove the learning as they "emphasise planning, writing, and revising ideas mediated through the learning community, and encourage deep meaningful learning" [11, p.56]. It was through the embracement of the multiple views of learners and the learning community that meaningful and deep learning could be achieved in this MLA approach.

The MLA approach was illustrated in a first year unit offered in an Australian University about 'Teaching, Learning and Assessment' to show how "the assessment drives the learning, and the technology drives the model, creating a simultaneous and harmonious building of a learning community" [11, p.56]. Students were grouped into groups of four to develop a website, and all groups were encouraged to act as communities of learners. The assessment components consisted of the tasks of developing a website which included Journal of Andragogy, chapter summary, quiz, teacher interview, video, journal articles, internet articles/sites, links to other unit topics, and critique of peer websites. Technology, such as the bulletin board, e-mail, online journals and databases, was used to facilitate the communication and collaboration so that mediated learning among the learners, peers, and lecturers was possible in the MLA approach. Positive feedbacks were received from the students to embrace the MLA. This MLA approach demonstrated how the integration of technology, assessment, and pedagogy such as the social constructivist theory which combining with mediation could create a powerful teaching and learning approach.

The postgraduate subject case and the MLA approach show that several key elements are needed for good blended learning, which include:

1) Proper design and integration of the online and in-class activities;
2) Integrate usage of technology throughout the whole learning process;
3) Proper design and integration of assessment into the learning process and activities.

5 Discussion

After reviewing the survey results during 2000 to 2005 and the good practices of blended learning approaches, some implications on the design of hybrid learning courses for adult learners are identified. To support more meaningful learning for adult learners, several aspects need to be considered in order to set up a blended learning program, including (1) Course design and learning activities; (2) Role of web-based technology; and (3) Use of assessment.

(1) Course design and learning activities

- All online learning activities, for examples, use of newsgroup discussion and constructive wikis, should be designed to closely link with face-to-face class activities (such as presentation or in-class discussion) and become an integral part of the overall assessment.
- The requirements for individual learning and collaboration among peers, as well as the purposes of the online activities and class activities should be stated and communicated clearly.

- The value of participation in the online learning community and the importance of process of knowledge construction should be elaborated clearly to the students.

The clarification of requirements and purposes as well as motivating learners comply with the characteristics advocated by Knowles about learning environments involving adult learners as learners need to know and be informed of why something is important to learn [12].

(2) **Role of Web-based technology**

- Web-based technology should be used as communication tools and collaborative tools to facilitate interactions among the human actors (for examples the student, peer learners and the teachers) throughout the whole learning process for co-construction of knowledge. As mentioned in Albon and Trinidad [11, p. 50], interactive technologies should act as "important instruments in learning as today's students are learning with technology, as opposed to learning about technology".
- Simple use of technology coupled with good integration of assessment can yield better learning outcomes.

(3) **Use of assessment to motivate active participation**

- Proper integration of activities and assessment throughout the learning process is essential. As adult learners are always constrained by life commitments such as career and family responsibilities, if posting on newsgroup forum is entirely voluntary and not counted as formal assessment items contributing to scores of the final grades, only very limited online participation will occur. Whereas, if the learning activities are blended neatly with assessment components and the learners are clearly informed about the goals and objectives of the activities, adult learners will perceive the value of the activities and be motivated to participate. The priority of these activities will then be raised.
- Besides of using individual assessment educators are encouraged to consider more use of group works to encourage the adult learners to work and learn collaboratively. Not only can the learners learn from each other when they build up a community, they can also exert positive group pressure and provide mutual social support in keeping their learning spirits.

We believe that more meaningful blended learning experiences can be resulted through proper course design, which emphasizes on student-centered learning, and proper integration of learning activities, assessment and web-based technology.

6   Conclusion

Learning at a distance from the campus was not a new thing. With the development of ICT, e-learning has firmly established its importance in education and training courses, no matter these courses are conducted in conventional face-to-face mode or through distance learning. In our studies, we find that throughout the last decade most students in Hong Kong studying part-time postgraduate and undergraduate IT programs indicated their preferences in retaining some form of face-to-face teaching while at the same time utilizing the advantages of e-learning. A pure form of delivery mode, whether it is face-to-face teaching or distance learning, is not appealing to the adult learners in Hong Kong.

Cheng [13] commented that regarding students in Asian culture, it was uncertain whether they preferred to study at home and communicate electronically with their teachers.

> *"Students in Asian culture are also not used to expressing themselves and exchanging views. They are more used to listening, keeping analyses in their minds, and express themselves only when it is very necessary. As such it remains to be seen whether the extension of the physical classroom to the cyberspace would further discourage or encourage interaction among students."* [13, p.204]

Through the 2000-2005 surveys and the review of good practices of blended learning approaches, it is concluded that Hong Kong students take a pragmatic approach towards e-learning. They can be active learners in the cyberspace if a proper pedagogy is adopted. To make blended learning more effective, it is more than simply introducing the technology component in the teaching and learning process. The right teaching approach and assessment strategies have to be employed. For example, it is evidenced that participation in online forum discussion becomes more active and fruitful when such activity is designed as an integral part of class teaching and contributing to the assessment.

As mentioned by Macdonald [1, p.54], different parts of a blended strategy were inter-related and there was much to learn about the ways to integrate e-learning with face-to-face support. And as suggested by Albon and Trinidad [11, p.51], educators in any disciplines should "ask themselves a fundamental question: how does learning occur? The answer informs the learning process and strategy selection irrespective of whether the environments are paper-based, face-to-face, online, or a mixture of delivery modes". With the high accessibility rate to Internet at home nowadays, it is time for Hong Kong teachers to explore how they can deploy online tools together with their class teaching as well as encourage learning and interactions in the online environments. It is through the proper design of course, better integration of assessment, learning activities and use of technology for facilitating interactions via online community that meaningful blended learning experience can be resulted.

References

1. Macdonald, J.: Blended Learning and Online Tutoring: A Good Practice Guide, Aldershot, Hants, England, Gower (2006)
2. Naidu, S. (ed.): Learning and Teaching with Technology: Principles and Practices. Kogan Page, London (2003)
3. Census and Statistical Department, HKSAR Government website (March 2007), http://www.censtatd.gov.hk/hong_kong_statistics/statistics_by_subject/
4. Messing, J., Chan, F.T.: Hands Across the Ocean: Using Information Technology in a Distance Education Course. In: Castro, F., Lai, R., Wong Sr., M. (eds.) Proceedings of the Fifth Hong Kong Web Symposium, pp. 227–241 (1999)

5. Census and Statistical Department. Usage of Personal Computers and Internet Services by the Hong Kong Residents from 2000 to 2007. Hong Kong Monthly Digest of Statistics, Hong Kong (2008) (February 2008),
   `http://www.censtatd.gov.hk/products_and_services/products/publications/statistical_report/feature_articles/science/index_t.jsp`
6. Chan, F.T., Messing, J.: A Joint Venture in Distance Education Program between Hong Kong and Australia. In: IVETA Conference 2000 (2000)
7. Chan, F.T., Mills, J.: Collaboration for Success in Open and Distance Education: A Case Study of Australia and Hong Kong. In: Distance Education, an open question? Conference 2000 (2000)
8. Lee, P.W.R., Chan, F.T.: Mixed Mode of Delivery - An Effective Collaboration Model. In: ASAIHL 2002 Lifelong Learning Conference, Proceedings of ASAIHL 2002: Lifelong Learning, June 17-19, pp. 155–163. Nanyang Technological University, Singapore (2002)
9. Lee, P.W.R., Dooley, L., Chan, F.T.: Enhancing Adult Learning via E-Learning: the Perspectives of Students and Teachers in Hong Kong. In: VIEWDET 2003 Vienna International Conference on eLearning, eMedicine, eSupport, November 26 – 28. Vienna University of Technology, Austria (2003)
10. Lee, P.W.R., Dooley, L.S., Chan, F.T.: Effective E-Learning: Perspective of Adult Learners in Hong Kong. In: HKITEC 2006: Hong Kong International IT in Education Conference – Capacity Building for Learning through IT, Proceedings of HKITEC 2006, Hong Kong, February 6–8. EMB, pp. 66–75 (2006)
11. Albon, R., Trinidad, S.: Building learning communities through technology. In: Appleton, K., Macpherson, C., Yeppoon, D.O. (eds.) International Lifelong Learning Conference: refereed papers from the 2nd International Lifelong Learning conference, Central Queensland, Australia, June 16-19, pp. 50–56. Central Queensland University Press, Rockhampton, Qld (2002)
12. Knowles, M.S., Holton, E.F., Swanson, R.A.: The Adult Learner: The Definitive Classic in Adult Education and Human Resource Development, 6th edn. Elsevier, Amsterdam (2005)
13. Cheng, Kai-Ming: Institutional collaboration in higher education: challenges of the information era. In: Ronnie Carr (edn. 1999), The Asian Distance Learner, pp. 196–206. Open University of Hong Kong Press, Hong Kong (1999)

Internet Usage Status among Chinese College Students

Yan Li

Department of Education, Zhejiang University
Tian Mu Shan Rd. # 148, 310028
Hangzhou, Zhejiang Province, P.R. China
yanli@zju.edu.cn

Abstract. The study was carried out to determine Internet usage status among Chinese college students and how personal differences impact students' online activities. Quantitative research was employed and the findings were descriptive in nature. Results showed that the majority (80%) of participating Zhejiang University (ZJU) students (N=596) currently owned PCs. Averagely, they spent 3.11 hrs per day using computer, within which 2.51 hrs with online activities. ZJU students participated in nine of the fifteen listed online activities frequently. Half of them used study-related websites and browsed online programs frequently. Only 39% used major related websites frequently. Most students did not use English websites or use Internet to communicate with teachers frequently. Few students knew how to make web page. Gender and other five factors had different impact on students' different online activities.

Keywords: Internet usage, computer, college students.

1 Introduction

Internet has been adopted rapidly worldwide as an innovative tool for information record and diffusion. At present, there are about 970 million Internet users in the world, accounting for 15.2% of world population. According to the 17th "Statistical Survey on the Internet Development in China" issued by China Internet Network Information Center (CNNIC), up to Dec. 31st, 2005, China had 111 million Internet users, accounting for 8.5% of Chinese population. Out of hem, 85% had an educational background of college level or higher (CNNIC, 2006). Studies showed that 80% of Chinese college students have looked online activities as an important part of their daily life (Liu, 2005; Sun, Hua, & Xiao, 2002; Xu, 2005; Yu, 2005).

Computer and Internet has dramatically changed the learning styles and daily habit of current college students, especially in information searching, communication, and resources sharing (Hannan, 2005; Lee & Tsai, 2004; Liu, 2005). Literature found that Chinese college students focused online activities mainly in four areas: 1) online chatting; 2) game playing and other entertainments; 3) sending and receiving emails; and 4) browsing news and searching information related to personal hobbies (Tian, 2005; Zhang & Jia, 2002; Yu, 2005).

J. Fong, R. Kwan, and F.L. Wang (Eds.): ICHL 2008, LNCS 5169, pp. 415–427, 2008.
© Springer-Verlag Berlin Heidelberg 2008

Studies found that computer and Internet has become important tools for students' communication and entertainment; however, it has not yet become a useful tool for their study (Zhang & Jia, 2002). Three reasons might explain this phenomenon: 1) online resources currently available for Chinese college students were not abundant in quantity or good in quality; 2) students were not familiar with information searching tools or searching methods (Wu, 2004; Xu, 2005; Zhang & Jia, 2002); and 3) incompetent English language ability limited students from visiting foreign websites, especially those English websites related to their study or majors (Zhang & Jia, 2002).

Based on the literature, the researcher found that it would be meaningful to make a systematic study about the detailed online activities of Chinese college students and how personal factors impact their online behaviors. That is the purpose of the study.

2 Methods

The study used random sampling method to collect data. And the author selected Zhejiang University (ZJU) as a representative university of Chinese higher education. ZJU, which was founded in 1897, currently has 22 colleges and it is now one of the largest and comprehensive universities in China. The target population of this study was 42,000 enrolled full-time ZJU students. The sample number was derived by using the table of "Determining Sample Size for Research Activities" (Krejcie & Morgan, 1970). Between October 20th, 2005 and January 20th, 2006, 650 students were randomly chosen from across the ZJU's five campuses.

The research instrument was a two-part questionnaire, which was designed based on the review of literature. The first part was to determine students' status of Internet usage by asking their agreements about participating in fifteen online activities. Participants could respond to a series of statements on a five-point Likert-type scale. The second part was to gather data about students' differences, including major, gender, and etc. To test its reliability, the survey instrument was tested among 20 sophomores who were from the Department of Education, ZJU in September, 2005. A repeated test was done six weeks later. The results showed good reliability (r=0.80).

The researcher finally got 633 surveys back and among these responses, 37 were uncompleted, resulting in a usable response rate of 91.7% (N=596). The collected data were analyzed using the Statistical Package for Social Sciences (SPSS, 11.0). Descriptive statistics were used to describe each variable.

3 Findings

In the study, participants (*N* = 596) from 22 different colleges were randomly selected and the number of students from each college ranged from 18-35. Among them, 327 were male and 269 were female. Participants were distributed evenly according to their grades (18% freshmen, 19.6% sophomore, 21.6% junior, 19.8% senior, and 21% graduates).   80% of participants had PCs. Half of students bought PCs within 1-2 years and the other half owned PCs more than two years. On an average, ZJU students spent 3.11 hrs per day in using computer. About 44% of students used computer no more than 2 hrs everyday; 45.5% used computer within 2-6 hrs everyday; and 10.5% used computer more than 6 hrs everyday (Table 1). As for the Internet usage, ZJU students averagely spent 2.51 hrs online everyday. Three fourths of them used Internet less than 3 hrs; 20% between 3-6 hrs; and 5% used Internet more than 6 hrs everyday. As to the purposes of Internet usage, "study" was indicated by 41.2% of students as their first purpose, and "communication" and "entertainment" were indicated as the second and third purpose of internet usage by 42.5% and 38.4% of students, respectively. Other activities, such as browsing news, online shopping, etc. were indicated by 40.7% of students as the fourth purpose of using Internet (Table 2).

Table 1. Distribution of participating ZJU students by computer and Internet usage (N=596)

Owing computer's time			Using computer's time per day			Using Internet's time per day		
Year	f	%	hour	f	%	hour	f	%
0<t≦1	152	32.1	0<t≦1	118	20.8	0<t≦1	195	34.4
1<t≦2	86	18.1	1<t≦2	131	23.1	1<t≦2	135	23.8
2<t≦3	101	21.3	2<t≦3	89	15.7	2<t≦3	92	16.2
3<t≦5	76	16.0	3<t≦4	90	15.8	3<t≦4	72	12.7
t>5	59	12.4	4<t≦6	80	14.1	4<t≦6	44	7.8
			>6	60	10.6	>6	29	5.1
Total	474	100	Total	568	100	Total	567	100

Table 2. Distribution of participating ZJU students by their priorities of using Internet (N=596)

	Study			Communication			Entertainment			Others	
No.	f	%	No.	f	%	No.	f	%	No.	f	%
1	**196**	**41.2**	1	138	29.3	1	141	30.7	1	27	29.7
2	137	28.8	2	**200**	**42.5**	2	123	26.8	2	10	11
3	132	27.7	3	126	26.8	3	**176**	**38.3**	3	17	18.7
4	11	2.3	4	7	1.5	4	19	4.1	4	**37**	**40.7**
sum	476	100	sum	471	100	sum	459	100	sum	91	100

Table 3. Distribution of participating ZJU students by their Internet usage status (N=596)

	n	M	SD	D	N	A	SA
I use LAN frequently.	595	4.39	2	19	43	211	320
I use Chinese websites frequently.	594	4.39	1	5	34	275	279
I use online text resources frequently.	594	3.98	4	24	105	305	156
I use non-major related website frequently.	592	3.95	4	26	113	300	149
I use entertainment and daily life related websites frequently.	592	3.94	6	26	109	310	141
I use online audio resources frequently.	592	3.87	8	44	117	268	155
I often use Internet to communicate with students.	589	3.85	12	49	107	268	153
I use online visual resources frequently.	592	3.82	7	34	148	274	129
I use WAN frequently.	592	3.71	10	71	150	213	148
I use study related websites frequently.	591	3.42	14	72	222	219	64
I watch online programs frequently.	585	3.3	32	106	182	187	78
I use major related websites frequently.	591	3.21	26	126	208	160	71
I use English websites frequently.	593	2.83	72	178	180	106	57
I often use Internet to communicate with teachers.	595	2.76	60	176	231	102	26
I know how to make web page.	594	2.56	111	205	139	114	25

Note: M value: 1=Strongly Disagree(SD); 2=Disagree(D); 3=Neutral(N); 4=Agree(A); 5=Strongly Agree(SA)

The majority of ZJU students (ranging from 61% to 93.3%) agreed or strongly agreed with statements about nine online activities (M>3.50)(Table 3). However, only half of participating ZJU students indicated that they used study related websites frequently or watched online programs frequently. As to "I use major related websites frequently", 39% agreed or strongly agreed, 35% kept neutral, and 26% disagreed or strongly disagreed. Most students did not used English websites or used Internet to communicate with teachers frequently. Few of them knew how to make web page.

Six personal differences (gender, grade, computer PC or not, owning computer's time, using computer's time per day, and using Internet's time per day) had different impact on the fifteen online activities of ZJU students (Table 4). Gender had no significant impact on students' most online activities except these two: 1) using online text resources frequently, t (592)=2.24, $p<0.05$; and 2) knowing how to make web page, t (592)=2.61, $p<0.05$. Female students used online text resources more frequently than did male students. And Male students knew more about how to make web page than did female counterparts.

Table 4. Distribution of participating ZJU students Internet usage by six factors (N = 596)

Online Activities	Gender		Grade		Owning PC or not		Owning computer's time		Using computer's time per day		Using Internet's time per day	
	t	p	F	P	t	p	F	P	F	p	F	P
I use LAN frequently.	0.22	0.83	14.18*	0.00	8.01*	0.00	1.94	0.10	12.80*	0.00	6.43*	0.00
I use WAN frequently.	0.77	0.44	8.72*	0.00	1.87	0.06	8.67*	0.00	1.69	0.14	2.61*	0.02
I use Chinese websites frequently.	1.99	0.05	3.28*	0.01	4.33*	0.00	0.81	0.52	1.92	0.09	1.97	0.08
I use English websites frequently.	0.71	0.48	21.13*	0.00	3.00*	0.00	5.45*	0.00	9.29*	0.00	6.35*	0.00
I use major related websites frequently.	0.87	0.39	19.21*	0.00	0.55	0.58	1.87	0.11	2.73*	0.02	1.24	0.29
I use non-major related websites frequently.	0.26	0.80	1.45	0.22	1.94	0.05	2.47*	0.04	1.81	0.11	1.32	0.25
I use study related websites frequently.	1.69	0.09	3.40*	0.01	1.85	0.07	1.02	0.40	0.69	0.63	0.84	0.53
I use entertainment and daily life related websites frequently.	1.41	0.16	2.75*	0.03	3.75*	0.00	0.50	0.74	3.25*	0.01	3.68*	0.00
I use online text resources frequently.	2.24*	0.03	4.60*	0.00	5.01*	0.00	1.69	0.15	7.18*	0.00	5.24*	0.00
I use online visual resources frequently.	0.24	0.81	3.03*	0.02	5.85*	0.00	1.32	0.26	2.84*	0.02	2.98*	0.01
I use online audio resources frequently.	0.03	0.97	2.78*	0.03	5.14*	0.00	2.82*	0.03	3.30*	0.01	4.17*	0.00
I often use Internet to communicate with teachers.	1.57	0.12	4.20*	0.00	0.90	0.37	0.87	0.48	2.46*	0.03	1.68	0.14
I often use Internet to communicate with students.	0.04	0.97	0.66	0.62	1.33	0.18	1.59	0.18	1.07	0.38	1.72	0.13
I watch online programs frequently.	0.09	0.93	2.43*	0.047	2.08*	0.04	0.86	0.49	1.38	0.23	1.86	0.10
I know how to make web page.	2.61*	0.01	6.48*	0.00	2.32*	0.02	5.30*	0.00	1.72	0.13	2.29	0.045

Grade had significant impact on most online activities of ZJU students ($p<0.05$): 1) I use LAN frequently, F (4, 595)=14.18; 2) I use WAN frequently, F (4, 592)=8.72; 3) I use Chinese websites frequently, F (4, 594)=3.28; 4) I use English websites frequently, F (4, 593)=21.13; 5) I use major related websites frequently, F (4, 591)=19.21; 6) I use study related websites frequently, F (4, 591)=3.40; 7) I use entertainment and daily life related websites frequently, F (4, 592)=2.75; 8) I use online text resources frequently, F (4, 594)=4.60; 9) I use online visual resources frequently, F (4, 592)=3.03; 10) I use online audio resources frequently, F (4, 592)=2.78; 11) I use Internet to communicate with teachers frequently, F (4, 595)=4.20; 12) I watch online programs frequently, F (4, 585)=2.43; and 13) I know how to make web page, F (4, 594)=6.48 (Table 5). Generally speaking, students from higher grades participated in the above thirteen online activities more frequently than did students from

Table 5. Grade had significant impact on students' thirteen online activities (N=596)

	Graduate	Senior	Junior	Sophomore	Freshman	Average
I use LAN frequently.	4.53	4.60	4.43	4.43	3.92	4.39
I use WAN frequently.	4.02	3.96	3.63	3.46	3.44	3.71
I use Chinese websites frequently.	4.40	4.56	4.34	4.38	4.26	4.39
I use English websites frequently.	3.46	2.99	2.83	2.50	2.27	2.83
I use major related websites frequently.	3.86	3.11	3.21	2.90	2.89	3.21
I use study related websites frequently.	3.68	3.36	3.39	3.36	3.28	3.42
I use entertainment and daily life related websites frequently.	4.04	3.97	4.02	3.88	3.73	3.94
I use online text resources frequently.	4.05	4.09	4.09	3.96	3.70	3.98
I use online visual resources frequently.	3.66	3.98	3.88	3.87	3.67	3.82
I use online audio resources frequently.	3.74	3.97	3.98	3.97	3.69	3.88
I often use Internet to communicate with teachers.	2.95	2.64	2.91	2.74	2.50	2.76
I watch online programs frequently.	3.48	3.41	3.20	3.29	3.08	3.30
I know how to make web page.	2.38	2.98	2.54	2.33	2.56	2.56

Note: M value: 1=Strongly Disagree; 2=Disagree; 3=Neutral; 4=Agree; 5=Strongly Agree

lower grades. However, graduate used online visual or audio resources less frequently than did undergraduate. Graduate also showed less confidence in making web page than did undergraduate.

Owning PC or not had significant impact on the following online activities of ZJU students ($p<0.05$): 1) I use LAN frequently, t (591)=8.01; 2) I use Chinese websites frequently, t (590)=4.33; 3) I use English websites frequently, t (589)=3.00; 4) I use entertainment and daily life related websites frequently, t (588)=3.75; 5) I use online text resources frequently, t (590)=5.01; 6) I use online visual resources frequently, t (588)=5.85; 7) I use online audio resources frequently, t (588)=5.14; 8) I watch online programs frequently, t (591)=2.08; and 9) I know how to make web page, t (590)=2.32 (Table 6). Students having PCs attended these activities more frequently than did those without PCs.

One third of their online activities (five items) were significantly affected by the time students owned PCs ($p<0.05$). These activities includes: 1) using WAN frequently, F (4, 470)=8.67; 2) using English websites frequently, F (4, 471)=5.45; 3)

Table 6. Owning PC or not had significant impact on students' nine online activities (N=596)

	Owning	Not Owning
I use LAN frequently.	4.51	3.90
I use Chinese websites frequently.	4.45	4.16
I use English websites frequently.	2.90	2.55
I use entertainment and daily life related websites frequently.	4.00	3.69
I use online text resources frequently.	4.07	3.66
I use online visual resources frequently.	3.92	3.41
I use online audio resources frequently.	3.97	3.49
I watch online programs frequently.	3.34	3.11
I know how to make web page.	2.61	2.35

Note: M value: 1=Strongly Disagree; 2=Disagree; 3=Neutral; 4=Agree; 5=Strongly Agree.

using non-major related websites frequently, F (4, 471)=2.47; 4) using online audio resources frequently, F (4, 471)=2.82; and 5) knowing how to make web page, F (4, 472)=5.30 (Table 7). Generally speaking, the longer students owned computer, the more frequently they would participate in these five online activities. However, students who owned computer for less than one year showed higher frequencies in using non-major related websites than the average. Also, students who owned computer for 1-2 years indicated the highest agreement with "I use online audio resources frequently."

Table 7. Owning computer's time had significant impact on students' five online activities (N=596)

	$t>5$ yrs	$3<t\leqq 5$ yrs	$2<t\leqq 3$ yrs	$1<t\leqq 2$ yrs	$t\leqq 1$ yr	Average
I use Wan frequently.	4.22	3.97	3.87	3.64	3.43	3.75
I use English Website frequently.	3.08	3.09	3.17	2.74	2.59	2.88
I use non-major related websites frequently.	4.22	4.04	3.98	3.79	4.01	4.00
I use audio resources frequently.	4.07	4.01	3.94	4.22	3.84	3.99
I know how to make web page.	2.92	2.75	2.81	2.65	2.28	2.62

Note: M value: 1=Strongly Disagree; 2=Disagree; 3=Neutral; 4=Agree; 5=Strongly Agree.

As showed in Table 8, half of the students' online activities were significantly affected by the time they spent in using computer everyday ($p<0.05$). These activities includes: 1) I use LAN frequently, F (5, 567)=12.80; 2) I use English websites frequently, F (5, 565)=9.29; 3) I use major related websites frequently, F (5, 563)=2.73; 4) I use entertainment and daily life related websites frequently, F (5, 564)=3.25; 5) I use online text resources frequently, F (5, 567)=7.18; 6) I use online visual resources frequently, F (5, 564)=2.84; 7) I use online audio resources frequently, F (5, 564)=3.30; and 8) I often use Internet to communicate with teachers, F (5, 567)=2.46. Generally speaking, the longer the time students spent in using computer everyday, the more frequently they participated in these eight online activities. Students who used computer for 1-2hrs per day participated in the following five activities more frequently than the average level: using LAN, using entertainment and daily life related websites, using online visual resources, using online audio resources, and using Internet to communicate with teachers.

As indicated in Table 9, almost half of ZJU students' online activities were significantly affected by the time they spent in using Internet everyday ($p<0.05$). These activities includes: 1) using LAN frequently, F (5, 566)=6.43; 2) using WAN frequently, F (5, 563)=2.61; 3) using English websites frequently, F (5, 564)=6.35; 4) using entertainment and daily life related websites frequently, F (5, 563)=3.68; 5) using online text resources frequently, F (5, 566)=5.24; 6) using online visual

Table 8. Using computer's time per day had significant impact on students' eight online activities (N=596)

	t>6hrs	4<t≦6hrs	3<t≦4hrs	2<t≦3hrs	1<t≦2hrs	t≦1hr	Average
I use LAN frequently.	4.55	4.53	4.67	4.55	4.46	3.97	4.42
I use English website frequently.	3.42	3.11	2.91	2.93	2.65	2.38	2.83
I use major related websites frequently.	3.52	3.33	3.31	3.19	3.15	2.97	3.21
I use entertainment and daily life related websites frequently.	4.05	4.03	4.08	3.95	3.97	3.68	3.94
I use online text resources frequently.	4.18	4.01	4.28	3.94	3.98	3.66	3.98
I use online visual resources frequently.	3.83	3.94	4.06	3.76	3.85	3.63	3.81
I use online audio resources frequently.	3.88	4.08	4.00	3.85	3.92	3.60	3.87
I often use Internet to communicate with teachers.	2.78	2.84	2.97	2.73	2.84	2.52	2.77

Note: M value: 1=Strongly Disagree; 2=Disagree; 3=Neutral; 4=Agree; 5=Strongly Agree.

Table 9. Using Internet's time per day had significant impact on students' seven online activities (N=596)

	t>6hrs	4<t≦6hrs	3<t≦4hrs	2<t≦3hrs	1<t≦2hrs	t≦1hr	Average
I use LAN frequently.	4.41	4.57	4.64	4.61	4.49	4.21	4.43
I use WAN frequently.	4.14	3.64	3.94	3.78	3.69	3.58	3.72
I use English website frequently.	3.45	2.91	3.17	2.91	2.95	2.53	2.85
I use entertainment and daily life related website frequently.	4.03	3.95	4.11	4.02	4.08	3.76	3.95
I use online text resources frequently.	4.31	3.86	4.21	4.07	4.08	3.79	3.99
I use online visual resources frequently.	4.14	3.70	3.97	3.95	3.90	3.68	3.84
I use online audio resources frequently.	4.07	3.84	4.08	3.91	4.04	3.65	3.88

Note: M value: 1=Strongly Disagree; 2=Disagree; 3=Neutral; 4=Agree; 5=Strongly Agree.

resources frequently, $F (5, 563)=2.98$; and 7) using online audio resources frequently, $F (5, 563)=4.17$. Comparing with students who used Internet for more than one hour per day, students who used Internet for less than one hour showed lower agreements with these seven online activities. Students who had online activities for 3-4 hrs or more than 6 hrs per day participated in the following five activities most frequently: using WAN, using English websites, using online text, visual and audio resources.

4 Conclusions and Recommendations

The majority of ZJU students owned PCs and half of them bought PCs within 1-2 years. Averagely, ZJU students spent 3.11 hrs in using computers and 2.51 hrs online everyday. About 44% of students used computers for no more than 2 hrs per day, 45.5% between 2-6 hrs, and 10.5% for more than 6 hrs. Three fourths of students used Internet for less than 3 hrs per day, 20% between 3-6 hrs, and 5% for more than 6 hrs.

ZJU students participated in the following nine activities frequently (ordered by their frequencies): using LAN, using Chinese websites, using online text resources, using non-major related websites, using entertainment and daily life related websites, using online audio resources, using Internet to communicate with students, using online visual resources, and using WAN. Half of them used study related websites and watched online programs frequently. Four tenths of students used major related websites frequently. And the majority of ZJU students did not think that they: 1) used English websites frequently; 2) used Internet to communicate with teachers frequently, or 3) knew how to make web page. Six personal differences had different impact on students' different online activities. Conclusions and suggestions are made as below:

4.1 Computer and Internet Have Become an Important Part of the Daily Life of Chinese College Students

Having PCs and doing various kind of online activities are very popular among college students in China. College student used LAN most frequently and campus network has become very important source of information for them. The majority of college students mainly browse Chinese websites and they prefer to multi-media materials, from text to audio and video. Comparing with using study or major related websites, college students showed higher frequencies in using entertainment and daily life or other non-major related websites. At the same time, comparing with using Internet to communicate with teachers, college students showed higher frequencies in using Internet to communicate with their peers. The study also found that small proportion of students (about one fifth) knew how to make web page.

Most of college students used computer and Internet in a relatively rational way and they would spend certain amount of time everyday in using computer and/or doing online activities. However, it is obvious that a small group of students spent too much time everyday in using computer and Internet. New technology, as we know, is a double-edged sword and it would bring both opportunities and challenges for college students. In 2002, ZJU dismissed 120 students who failed to pass certain amount of courses due to problem of Internet Addiction (IA). Therefore, educators and researchers should be sensitive about the emerging passive problems that computer and Internet might bring to students.

Based on these findings, the researcher recommends that further qualitative studies are needed to investigate the following questions: (1) whether those students who spent too much time on online activities had tendency of IA; (2) comparing with using Internet to communicate with peers, why students showed lower frequencies to communicate with teachers through Internet.

4.2 The Usage Status of Study and Major Related Websites by Chinese College Students Is Not So Satisfactory

Results of the study found that only 40-50% of students used study and major related websites frequently and fewer students (27.5%) indicated that they used English websites frequently. There are two possible explanations for such phenomenon. One might be limited useful resources related to major studies, as mentioned in literature. Although Chinese universities have been putting lots of efforts in constructing online resources in recent years, there are still many challengeable problems facing the practitioners, such as how to make the online content more attractive and more user-friendly, how to integrate online resources effectively into curriculum design in different principles, and etc. Solutions to these problems would have direct impact on the quality of digitalization of Chinese universities. As faculty members are key factors in constructing study and major- related websites, more faculty training programs related to educational technology and constructing online resources would also be very helpful. Decision-makers of universities should propel the construction of e-universities through providing sufficient incentives to faculty, staff and students.

Secondly, some students might be unfamiliar with searching methods and skills, especially those skills related to international websites that are in English. Although more and more educators realized the importance of information searching ability in era of information exploration, it is still noticeable that lots of college students feel unconfident in major study because of limited ability of information searching.

As to English education, it is actually heavily emphasized by the whole higher education system in China. Students must pass the national College English Test (CET) Band 4 before getting the bachelor degree and pass the CET Band 6 before getting the Master's degree. Students know the importance of English. However, current English education is limited largely in class and is mainly aimed at exam.

Thus, the researcher recommends that it might be a good idea for Chinese faculty, especially those who are familiar with international resources on the web, to develop and/or to improve college students' Internet searching ability, together with their major study and language ability, by teaching them skills about searching international websites related to their majors, like online journals or online information about specific professional associations. In this way, students could learn language more practically as well as learn major knowledge more efficiently.

4.3 Internet Has Contributed to More Convenient Student-Student Communication; However, It Hasn't Revealed Its Potential Power in Student-Teacher Communication

Communication is the foundation of education. Better communication means better teaching and learning experiences. With the emergence of Web-based educational circumstances and the availability of state-of-art communication technologies, these tools are expected to change the manners of traditional educational communication by providing quicker and more diverse ways of communication. The study found that college students' online communication with their peers is very active. However, the status of student-teacher online communication was not so satisfactory. Since e-learning become more and more popular on campus, universities and faculty should be encouraged to be more involved in online communication with students.

To improve student-teacher online communication, some basic questions are worthy of our rethinking. These questions include what is the new role for teachers in information era; what's needed to be done during the process of transition from traditional education to IT-based education; how to make teacher-student interaction more effectively with the help of new multimedia communication tools (such as email, instant messages, personal web page, blog, and etc). Answers to these questions would contribute to a better relationship between students and teachers in the new era.

4.4 Gender Has Little Impact on Most of College Students' Online Activities

The study found that gender had no significant impact on most of ZJU students' online activities. Male students and female students have similar online experiences. However, female students were reported to use online text resources more frequently while male students felt more confidence with making web page. Such differences might be explained by different learning style and different strongpoint aroused by gender. It seems that female students more like text materials than do male students. While male students are more able in activities that need hands-on ability, such as webpage making, than do their female counterparts.

4.5 Grade Has Significant Impact on Most of College Students' Online Activities

The study found that, except two items (using non-major related websites or using Internet to communicate with students), grade had significant impact on most of college students' online activities. Generally speaking, students from higher grades tended to participate in the following online activities more frequently than did students from lower grades: using LAN and WAN, using Chinese and English websites, using major and study related websites, using entertainment and daily life related websites, using online text, audio and visual resources, watching online programs, using Internet to communicate with teachers, and knowing how to make web page. Experiences with computer and Internet would correspondingly increase students' learning experience. And it seems that college life would contribute to students' better knowledge and skills of using resources on the web.

The study also found that, as to the frequencies related to using online visual or audio resources, graduate students and freshmen showed lower agreement than did sophomore, junior or senior students. For freshmen, the tense brought by brand-new learning and life style in college as well as relatively limited knowledge and skills related to online resources might contribute to their lower frequencies in using visual or audio resources. For graduate, pressure from research work and concerns of time might be the explanations. As to knowing how to make web page, although most of students showed negative answers, senior students' agreements are obviously above other groups of students. It might be because senior students would like to learn more practical skills for better opportunities in job marketing.

Based on these findings, the researcher proposes two suggestions. (1) More communications among college students from different grades might improve computer and Internet- related knowledge and skills of lower-grade undergraduate. (2) When curriculum planners arrange courses for students or when faculty teach specific course, it is recommended to provide students with more information about how to utilize online resources. Such activities as inviting experienced students to sharing experiences of using computer and Internet in class, holding contests related to multimedia design or course design at the college or university level, providing seminars about history & future of lifelong learning or IT-based education reform, and etc, would improve college students' experiences with information technology.

4.6 Owning Computer Could Partly Contribute to College Students' Better Online Experiences: But It Is Not a Prerequisite for Students' Better Learning Experiences

The study found that students owning PCs participated in nine of the listed 15 items of online activities more frequently than did students without PCs. These online activities include using LAN, using Chinese and English websites, using entertainment and daily life related websites, using online text, visual and audio resources, watching online programs, and knowing how to make web page. However, owning computer or not had no significant impact on the following activities: using WAN, using major or study related websites, using non-major related websites, using Internet to communication with teachers or students. Therefore, owning PCs would partly contribute to students' better online experiences. But it is not a prerequisite for students' better learning experiences or better online communication with others.

The study also found that the length of owning computer's time had significant impact on one third of college students' online activities. Generally speaking, the longer students owned their PCs, the more frequently they would do these five online activities: using WAN, using English websites, using non-major related websites, using online audio resources, and knowing how to make web page. New owners who owned computers less than one year had higher agreement about "I use non-major related websites frequently" than the average level. Students owing computer for 1-2 years used online audio resources more frequently than did others.

The findings indicate that universities are important places where the majority of students experienced from having no PCs to owning PCs, from being unfamiliar with Internet to being skillful with it, and from participating in online activities blindly to using online resources more rationally. Thus, to enhance students' knowledge and skills of computer and Internet, universities' computer center and every department should provide sufficient opportunities for all of students to access computer and Internet, even though the proportion of the students who had no PCs is small. Proper guidance is also useful for students' better online learning experiences. Guidance could be related to how to search for major and study related resources and how to improve communication with teachers and peers through computer and Internet. .

4.7 The Length of Time Students Spent in Using Computer or Internet Per Day Have Significant Impact on Many of College Students' Online Activities

The study found that the length of time students spent with computer and Internet had significant impact on such online activities as using LAN, using English websites, using entertainment and daily life related websites, and using online text, visual or audio resources. Generally speaking, the longer time students spent in using computer and Internet, the more frequently they would do these activities. However, when students spent 3-4 hours in using computer or Internet per day, they would have the highest frequencies in doing those activities. And students who use computer or Internet less than one hour had obviously lower frequencies in doing the online activities mentioned above than did other students. The length of time students spent in using computer or Internet showed no significant impact on the following activities: using Chinese websites, using study-related websites, using Internet to communicate with students, watching online programs, or knowing how to make homepage.

Therefore, to utilize online resources more sufficiently, college students are recommended to spend more than one hour per day in using computer and Internet. Although the appropriate length of time for better use of online resources would vary from person to person, the study showed that 3-4 hours per day are suitable length for students' sufficient utilization of online resources. (2) Faculty should give appropriate guidance for students about skills related to computer-assisted or web-based learning.

5 Limits of the Study

Due to the limited time and other constraints, the study hasn't explored problems such as how major impact students' Internet usage status, or how helpful Internet would be in facilitating students' major study. The researcher hopes that more studies would be done in near future to answers the two questions and other concerns mentioned above.

References

1. China Internet Network Information Center: The 17th China Internet development statistic report, http://tech.sina.com.cn/focus/cnnic17/index.shtml
2. Caplan, S.: Problematic Internet use and psychosocial well-being: Development of a theory-based cognitive-behavioral measurement instrument. Computers in Human Behavior 18, 552–575 (2002)
3. Hannan, A.: Innovating in higher education: contexts for change in learning technology. British Journal of Educational Technology 36(6), 975–985 (2005)
4. Krejcie, R.V., Morgan, D.W.: Determining sample size for research activities. Educational and Psychological Measurement 30, 607–610 (1970)
5. Lee, C.-I., Tsai, F.-Y.: Internet project-based learning environment: the effects of thinking styles on learning transfer. Journal of Computer Assisted Learning 20(1), 31–39 (2004)
6. Lindner, J.R., Murphy, T.H., Briers, G.: Handling nonresponse in social science research. Journal of Agricultural Education 42(4), 43–53 (2001)
7. Liu, B.: The impact of BBS as a campus Internet culture on students' learning. Modern Distance Education Study (in Chinese) (2), 24–27 (2005)
8. Liu, Y.: Thoughts on college students' online activities. E-education Research (in Chinese) (6), 61–64 (2003)
9. Morahan-Martin, J., Schumacher, P.: Incidence and correlates of pathological Internet use among college students. Computers in Human Behavior 16, 13–29 (2000)
10. Nie, N.H., Erbring, L.: Internet and society: A Preliminary Report. IT & Society 1(1), 275–283 (2002)
11. Nie, N.H., Hillygus, D.S.: Where does Internet time come from?: A reconnaissance. IT & Society 1(2), 1–20 (2002)
12. Sun, S., Hua, H., Xiao, Z.: A survey of the college students surfing on Internet. Journal of Nanjing University of Science and Technology (in Chinese) 15(6), 80–83 (2002)

13. Tian, P.: On the negative influence of and solutions to college students' addiction to the Internet. Journal of Nanjing University of Aeronautics & Astronautics (Social Sciences) (in Chinese) 7(3), 75–78 (2005)
14. Wu, H.: Study on university students' utilization of network information resources. Science/Technology Information Development & Economy (in Chinese) 14(4), 47–48 (2004)
15. Xu, H.: A survey report on students' online learning behavior. E-Education Research (in Chinese) (6), 61–63, 73 (2005)
16. Young, K.S.: Internet addiction: The emergence of a new clinical disorder. In: 104th annual meeting of the American Psychological Association (1996)
17. Yu, X.: Investigation about the use of Internet among college students. Higher Education Exploration (in Chinese) (3), 82–86 (2005)
18. Zhang, J., Jia, H.: Survey analysis about college students Internet usage. Chinese Journal of Medical Library and Information Science (in Chinese) 11(4), 51–53 (2002)

Relationships between the Learning Strategies, Mental Models of Learning and Learning Orientations of Post-secondary Students in Hong Kong

Dennis C.S. Law[1] and Jan H.F. Meyer[2]

[1] Caritas Bianchi College of Careers, Hong Kong
dennislaw@cbcc.edu.hk
[2] University of Durham, UK
j.h.f.meyer@durham.ac.uk

Abstract. The present study is based on analyses of data resulting from an administration of a Chinese translation of the Inventory of Learning Styles (ILS) to a large sample of post-secondary students in Hong Kong. The ILS is a research instrument developed by Vermunt to capture variation in contrasting forms of learning strategies, mental models of learning, and learning orientations. In what are believed to be the first analyses of ILS data obtained in a Chinese response-context, empirical support is found for the theoretical model that underpins the ILS. Findings also confirm the posited central explanatory role of regulation strategies. In particular, students' processing strategies are found to be most directly influenced by their regulation strategies, while the influence of students' mental models of learning and students' learning orientations on their processing strategies is mostly indirect, via students' regulation strategies.

Keywords: Student Learning, Inventory of Learning Styles, Regulation Strategies.

1 Introduction

With the rapid expansion of the post-secondary education sector of Hong Kong in its educational reform [1], the question of how students engage in learning, and with what likely consequences, is an important consideration for various stakeholders. One well established methodology for addressing this question lies in the development of appropriate research instruments for capturing variation in students' educational experiences [2], and particularly their experiences of learning insofar as these can inform endeavours aimed at enhancing the quality of both learning and teaching. The Inventory of Learning Styles (ILS) is one such research instrument developed to capture variation in students' processing and regulation strategies, mental models and orientations of learning, and has been widely used and validated in a number of studies in western higher education contexts. In extending the student learning research literature involving the ILS, the present study utilizes a Chinese translation of it in a new and previously unreported response context; that of post-secondary education in Hong

J. Fong, R. Kwan, and F.L. Wang (Eds.): ICHL 2008, LNCS 5169, pp. 428–438, 2008.

Kong involving six institutions. Reported here are the initial analyses of the relationships between the conceptually discrete learning constructs operationalized by the ILS, and the proposal of a more general theoretical model to capture and interpret these relationships.

2 Context of the Present Study

Students participating in the present study came from six institutions of Caritas Adult and Higher Education Service (CAHES)[1], an organization which operates under the auspices of Caritas – Hong Kong. At the time of undertaking the study these students were enrolled in various kinds of post-secondary Certificate, Diploma, Associate Degree and Higher Diploma programmes. Over a three month period (March – May, 2005), and with the assistance of teachers from the participating institutions, access to *convenient samples* was made possible the aim being to involve the entire student population. Precise enrolment data for the programmes involved was not collected but the total student enrolment (size of the population) was estimated to be 2515 based on the number of copies of the research instrument (see Section 3) requested by the individual institutions for use in the study. Valid responses were obtained from 1572 students, representing a response rate of 62.5%.

3 Research Instrument

The research instrument employed in the present study is a Chinese translation of the 100-item version of the Inventory of Learning Styles (ILS). The ILS was originally designed by Vermunt [3] for research in the Dutch higher education sector, and it is based on an integrative theory and conceptualization of student learning that encompasses students' processing strategies, regulation strategies, learning orientations and mental models of learning. Details on the development of the ILS can be found in [4] and [5], and [6] provides an excellent review studies based on its application.

Among the four ILS components, *processing strategies* refer to the thinking activities that students use to process the content of learning. These activities lead directly to learning outcomes in terms of, for example, knowledge and understanding. In terms of Vermunt's theorization three main processing strategies are operationalised in five scales: (a) a deep processing strategy which combines the learning activities of *Relating and Structuring* and *Critical Processing,* (b) a stepwise processing strategy which reflects the learning activities of *Memorizing and Rehearsing* and *Analyzing*; and, (c) a *Concrete Processing* strategy with concretizing and applying as its major learning activities.

Regulation strategies refer to students' activities for regulating and controlling the processing strategies and they therefore indirectly lead to learning outcomes. Vermunt distinguishes contrasting aspects of regulation in terms of internal versus external control, with three main strategies or experiences being consistently observed and operationalized by five scales: (a) a *Self-regulation* strategy (comprising two scales) in

---

[1] Caritas Adult and Higher Education Service (CAHES) is renamed as Caritas Community and Higher Education Service (CCHES) with effect from 1 September 2007.

which students perform most regulative activities for their learning, (b) an *External Regulation* strategy (comprising two scales) in which students let their learning activities be regulated by teachers, textbooks and other external means and, (c) *Lack of Regulation* in which students face difficulties resulting from both their inability in self-regulation and their experience of insufficient external regulation. It should be noted that students' application of regulation strategies in their learning is in fact an active area of research, see [7] for some examples.

Learning orientations refer to the whole domain of students' personal goals, intentions, motives, expectations, attitudes, concerns and doubts with regard to their studies. Instead of developing theories on each and every aspects of this whole domain, Vermunt identified major sources of variation among students in this domain and incorporated them into the ILS as five scales; namely *Personally Interested, Certificate-oriented, Self-test-oriented, Vocational-oriented,* and *Ambivalent.*

Mental models of learning refer to a coherent system of knowledge and beliefs about learning and related phenomena, such as the nature of knowledge and the roles that should be assumed by teachers, classmates and the students themselves in learning. In the ILS, five scales are employed to capture the variation among students in this regard, namely *Construction of Knowledge, Intake of Knowledge, Use of Knowledge, Stimulating Education,* and *Cooperative Learning.*

In its adaptation for the present study, the ILS was translated into Chinese and then back translated into English for verification purposes. It was also construct validated for application in the previously unexplored context of the post-secondary education of Hong Kong, mainly through considerations of exhibited values of *Cronbach's coefficient alpha* (for assessing the internal consistency of the discrete scales, see [8] for brief introduction), and *exploratory factor analysis* (for assessing the construct validity of the scales in relation to empirical structure, see [9] for brief introduction). Space limitations prevent disclosure of these detailed analyses and it is simply mentioned here in summary that the alpha values associated with the 20 ILS scales ranged between 0.50 and 0.79, with 12 of them greater than 0.70[2]. These results are comparable to those in three other studies; namely, the original study of the ILS in a Dutch response context as reported in [5], a study by Ajisuksmo and Vermunt [10] in which the ILS was adapted for use in an Indonesian response context, and a cross-checking study of the ILS in a British response context as reported in [11]. In terms of construct validity, the variation in the learning patterns of students found in the present study resembles more closely the findings of [10] rather than those of [5]. This observation is not surprising given that the response context of the former study (Indonesia) arguably resembles more closely that of the present study.

Unlike earlier inventories used in many previous studies of student learning (such as the Study Process Questionnaire (SPQ) and the Approaches to Studying Inventory (ASI), see Chapters 5 and 6 of [12] that focus on students' processing strategies and learning motivations, the ILS is a second generation instrument. It is based on more recent conceptualizations about student learning, and seeks to locate these within a wider range of exploratory constructs (especially students' regulation strategies). With the development of the ILS, Vermunt proposed his model of 'regulation of constructive

---

[2] Many researchers consider an alpha value of at least 0.7 as desirable or adequate, see [8] for more details.

learning processes', and hypothesized the central role of regulation strategies in this model (see Figure 1). The main purpose of the present study is to test Vermunt's hypothesis and to investigate whether his model is applicable in its empirical manifestation to the post-secondary Hong Kong response context.

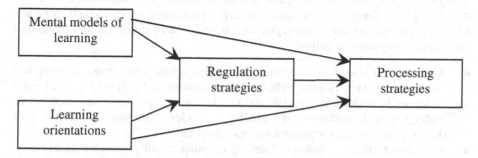

Fig. 1. The Model of Regulation of Constructive Learning Processes Adapted from Vermunt [5]

4 General Theoretical Model for Analysis

The approach taken here to explore the relationships between the ILS components is based on a more general theoretical model (see Figure 2) proposed by Richardson [13] to investigate the relationships between students' demographic background, perceptions, study behaviour, and outcome measures, and the model proposed by Richardson [14] to investigate the relationships between students' demographic background, motives and attitudes, study behaviour, and outcome measures. The functional relationships depicted in these models arise from the sophisticated application of multiple regression analyses in which the relationships between the constructs being modelled can be determined as being possibly direct, indirect or spurious effects according to the analyses of statistical significance and magnitude of the standardized regression coefficients.

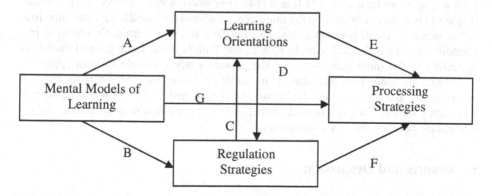

Fig. 2. A General Theoretical Model of Relationships between the Components Measured by the ILS

For example, the relationship between students' learning orientations and processing strategies may contain a direct effect (Path E) and an indirect effect (Path D → F). The relationship may also be a spurious effect with students' mental models of learning being a common cause for the variations in learning orientations and processing strategies (directly through Path A and Path G, or indirectly through Path B → C and Path B → F). However, the regression of students' processing strategies on their mental models, learning orientations and regulation strategies can identify the contribution of these three components as follows:

- A *direct effect* of students' learning orientations on processing strategies is implied by standardized regression coefficients that are statistically significant even when variations in both mental models and regulation strategies are controlled. These findings provide evidence that variations in students' learning orientations give rise to variations in their processing strategies (Path E).
- An *indirect effect* of students' learning orientations on processing strategies is supported by standardized regression coefficients that are significant when only variations in mental models are controlled but that are attenuated, eliminated or even reversed when variations in both mental models and regulation strategies are controlled. These findings provide evident that variations in students' learning orientations give rise to variations in their regulation strategies (Path D) and that variations in their regulation strategies in turn give rise to variations in processing strategies (Path F).
- A *spurious effect* is implied by standardized regression coefficients that are significant when variations in mental models and regulation strategies are not controlled, but are attenuated, eliminated or even reversed when only variations in mental models are controlled. These findings provide evidence that variations in students' mental models are simply the common cause of variations in their learning orientations (Path A and/or Path B → C) and variations in their processing strategies (Path G and/or Path B → F).

More details on analysis of possible causal relationships among the components of such a model can be found in [13] and [14]. It is worth noting that Vermunt's model (Figure 1) is in fact embedded in the more general model (Figure 2), with the same four boxes denoting the ILS components, and the five links in Vermunt's model corresponding to Path B, Path D, Path E, Path F, and Path G in the more general model. In appealing to the more general model the present study was able to both apply the techniques developed by Richardson in analyzing the relationships among the ILS components, and also explore the status of Paths A and C which do not appear in Vermunt's model. The present study is believed to be the first to thus analyze the relationships between the ILS components.

5 Results and Discussion

Due to space limitations, only the results for analyzing the possible relationships between students' learning orientations and their processing strategies, and the possible relationships between students' regulation strategies and their processing strategies are reported in this section. The results are meant to be examples to show how analyses are conducted using the general theoretical model in Section 4 to delineate the possible direct, indirect and spurious effects among the various student learning constructs, and to provide evidence on the fact that students' processing strategies of learning are mostly influenced by their regulation strategies, both directly and indirectly.

5.1 Relationships between Students' Learning Orientations and Students' Processing Strategies

Table 1 shows the standardized regression coefficients relating students' learning orientations to their processing strategies[3]. The findings indicate that *Certificated-oriented* students tend less to adopt *Relating and Structuring* in their learning, as indicated by the negative direct effect being significant even when variations in students' mental models and students' regulation strategies are controlled. The positive effect of *Personally Interested* or *Self-test-oriented* is mainly an indirect one mediated by students' regulation strategies, as the coefficient becomes insignificant when variations in regulation strategies are controlled.

For Critical Processing, the significant direct effects indicate that Vocation-oriented students tend less, and that Ambivalent students tend more, to adopt this processing strategy in their learning. The positive effects of Personally Interested or Self-test-oriented and the negative effect of Certificate-oriented are mainly indirect ones mediated by students' regulation strategies, as the respective coefficients become insignificant when controlling for variations in regulation strategies.

Students' learning orientations have no direct effect on *Memorizing and Rehearsing*. The positive effect of *Self-test-oriented* is mainly an indirect one mediated by students' regulation strategies, as the coefficient becomes insignificant when variations in regulation strategies are controlled. The positive relationship of *Vocation-oriented* and *Memorizing and Rehearsing* is a spurious effect with students' mental models being the common cause, as it becomes insignificant when only variations in mental models are controlled. A combined consideration of the relevant analysis results among all the learning constructs involved (not reported here due to space limitations) indicate that this effect is caused by *Construction of Knowledge*, with the effect on *Vocation-oriented* being direct (via Path A of Figure 2), and the effect on *Memorizing and Rehearsing* being indirectly mediated by regulation strategies (via Path B → F).

Students' learning orientations also have no direct effect on *Analyzing*. The findings indicate that when *Certificate-oriented* students tend less, and *Self-test-oriented* students tend more, to adopt this processing strategy in their learning, the main underlining cause is the indirect effects mediated by students' regulation strategies. The positive relationship of *Personally Interested* and *Analyzing* is a spurious effect with students' mental models being the common cause, as it becomes insignificant when only variations in mental models are controlled. A combined consideration of the relevant analysis results among all the learning constructs involved (not reported here

---

[3] Following Richardson, a significance level of 0.01 is adopted in this study to reduce the likelihood of Type I errors.

Table 1. Standardized regression coefficients relating students' learning orientations to their processing strategies

Relating and Structuring			
Predictor Variable	Direct, Indirect and Spurious Effects[a]	Direct and Indirect Effects[b]	Direct Effects Only[c]
Personally Interested	+0.155***	+0.106***	+0.007
Certificate-oriented	-0.193***	-0.166***	-0.072**
Self-test-oriented	+0.210***	+0.167***	+0.029
Vocation-oriented	-0.025	-0.044	+0.023
Ambivalent	+0.021	+0.022	+0.026
Critical Processing			
Predictor Variable	Direct, Indirect and Spurious Effects[a]	Direct and Indirect Effects[b]	Direct Effects Only[c]
Personally Interested	+0.172***	+0.126***	+0.027
Certificate-oriented	-0.156***	-0.128***	-0.036
Self-test-oriented	+0.181***	+0.139***	+0.005
Vocation-oriented	-0.112**	-0.141***	-0.071**
Ambivalent	+0.070**	+0.072**	+0.085***
Memorizing and Rehearsing			
Predictor Variable	Direct, Indirect and Spurious Effects[a]	Direct and Indirect Effects[b]	Direct Effects Only[c]
Personally Interested	+0.056	+0.025	-0.036
Certificate-oriented	-0.020	-0.028	+0.026
Self-test-oriented	+0.174***	+0.137***	+0.028
Vocation-oriented	+0.092**	+0.060	+0.050
Ambivalent	-0.001	-0.015	-0.020
Analyzing			
Predictor Variable	Direct, Indirect and Spurious Effects[a]	Direct and Indirect Effects[b]	Direct Effects Only[c]
Personally Interested	+0.122***	+0.077*	-0.010
Certificate-oriented	-0.108**	-0.093**	-0.018
Self-test-oriented	+0.225***	+0.181***	+0.038
Vocation-oriented	-0.021	-0.049	-0.031
Ambivalent	-0.014	-0.018	+0.016
Concrete Processing			
Predictor Variable	Direct, Indirect and Spurious Effects[a]	Direct and Indirect Effects[b]	Direct Effects Only[c]
Personally Interested	+0.159***	+0.082**	+0.014
Certificate-oriented	-0.159***	-0.139***	-0.073**
Self-test-oriented	+0.157***	+0.092	-0.021
Vocation-oriented	+0.145***	+0.042	+0.061
Ambivalent	-0.020	-0.020	-0.029

[a] Not controlling for variations in students' mental models of learning and regulation strategies.

[b] Controlling for variations in students' mental models of learning, but including any indirect effect mediated by students' regulation strategies.

[c] Controlling for variations in students' mental models of learning and regulation strategies
*$p<0.05$, **$p<0.01$, ***$p<0.001$ (two-tailed test).

due to space limitations) indicate that this effect is caused again by *Construction of Knowledge*, with the effect on *Personally Interested* being direct (i.e. via Path A of Figure 2), and the effect on *Analyzing* being indirectly mediated by regulation strategies (via Path B → F).

Certificate-oriented students tend less to adopt *Concrete Processing* in their learning, and this negative effect comprises mainly a direct component, and to a lesser extent an indirect component mediated by students' regulation strategies. The effect of *Personally Interested* on *Concrete Processing* is largely an indirect one mediated by students' regulation strategies. Both the relationship of *Self-test-oriented* and *Concrete Processing* and the relationship of *Vocation-oriented* and *Concrete Processing* are spurious effects, with students' mental models being the common cause. A combined consideration of the relevant analysis results among all the learning constructs involved (not reported here due to space limitations) indicate that in both cases, the association is caused by the direct effects of *Construction of Knowledge* and *Use of Knowledge* on the constructs concerned (via Path A and Path G of Figure 2).

Overall, the above findings suggest some direct effects of students' learning orientations on their processing strategies, which are mainly manifested in the negative influence of *Certificate-oriented* on *Relating and Structuring* and *Concrete Processing*, the negative influence of *Vocation-oriented* on *Critical Processing*, and the positive influence of *Ambivalent* on *Critical Processing*. Again, it is worth noting that the magnitude of many of the standardized regression coefficients in Table 1 is substantially reduced when variations in students' regulation strategies are controlled (and consequentially some of these coefficients become statistically insignificant), indicating the significant roles of students' regulation strategies in the indirect effects of students' mental models on their processing strategies.

In a number of the cases reported above, spurious effects have been identified, with the mental model *Construction of Knowledge* being the common cause of variations in the respective learning orientations and processing strategies of students. These findings suggest a minor omission in the theoretical model proposed in [13] and [14] namely that spurious effects from the common cause may not only be exercised via the direct routes (Paths A and G), but also via the indirect routes (Path B → C and Path B → F).

5.2 Relationships between Students' Regulation Strategies and Students' Processing Strategies

Table 2 shows the standardized regression coefficients relating students' regulation strategies to their processing strategies. For *Relating and Structuring*, the effects of the two self-regulation strategies are basically direct, as indicated by the fact that the respective coefficients remain significant with magnitudes changed only slightly when variations in students' mental models and students' learning orientations are controlled. The effect of *Lack of Regulation* is also direct, but in view of the low magnitude of the coefficient concerned it is less important than those of the self-regulation strategies.

For *Critical Processing*, it was also found that the effects of the two self-regulation strategies are basically direct, as indicated by the fact that the respective coefficients remain significant with magnitudes changed only slightly when variations in students'

Table 2. Standardized regression coefficients relating students' regulation strategies to their processing strategies

Relating and Structuring		
Predictor Variable	Direct, Indirect and Spurious Effects[a]	Direct and Indirect Effects[b]	Direct Effects Only[c]
Self-reg.: L. Proc. & Results	**+0.512*****	**+0.505*****	**+0.499*****
Self-reg.: L. Content	**+0.287*****	**+0.274*****	**+0.268*****
External Reg.: L. Processes	+0.025	+0.031	+0.035
External Reg.: L. Results	+0.002	+0.017	+0.019
Lack of Regulation	**+0.058****	**+0.067*****	**+0.062****
Critical Processing		
Predictor Variable	Direct, Indirect and Spurious Effects[a]	Direct and Indirect Effects[b]	Direct Effects Only[c]
Self-reg.: L. Proc. & Results	**+0.472*****	**+0.471*****	**+0.463*****
Self-reg.: L. Content	**+0.319*****	**+0.308*****	**+0.296*****
External Reg.: L. Processes	-0.063*	-0.056*	-0.038
External Reg.: L. Results	+0.044	+0.054*	**+0.071****
Lack of Regulation	+0.042*	+0.048*	+0.020
Memorizing and Rehearsing		
Predictor Variable	Direct, Indirect and Spurious Effects[a]	Direct and Indirect Effects[b]	Direct Effects Only[c]
Self-reg.: L. Proc. & Results	**+0.247*****	**+0.247*****	**+0.253*****
Self-reg.: L. Content	**+0.137*****	**+0.139*****	**+0.148*****
External Reg.: L. Processes	**+0.228*****	**+0.222*****	**+0.213*****
External Reg.: L. Results	**+0.178*****	**+0.175*****	**+0.163*****
Lack of Regulation	**+0.094*****	**+0.092*****	**+0.099*****
Analyzing		
Predictor Variable	Direct, Indirect and Spurious Effects[a]	Direct and Indirect Effects[b]	Direct Effects Only[c]
Self-reg.: L. Proc. & Results	**+0.387*****	**+0.385*****	**+0.379*****
Self-reg.: L. Content	**+0.248*****	**+0.237*****	**+0.234*****
External Reg.: L. Processes	**+0.195*****	**+0.202*****	**+0.207*****
External Reg.: L. Results	**+0.142*****	**+0.154*****	**+0.158*****
Lack of Regulation	-0.017	-0.009	-0.014
Concrete Processing		
Predictor Variable	Direct, Indirect and Spurious Effects[a]	Direct and Indirect Effects[b]	Direct Effects Only[c]
Self-reg.: L. Proc. & Results	**+0.381*****	**+0.328*****	**+0.326*****
Self-reg.: L. Content	**+0.176*****	**+0.182*****	**+0.179*****
External Reg.: L. Processes	+0.010	+0.012	+0.008
External Reg.: L. Results	**+0.218*****	**+0.211*****	**+0.208*****
Lack of Regulation	**+0.077*****	**+0.083*****	**+0.097*****

[a] Not controlling for variations in students' mental models of learning and learning orientations.
[b] Controlling for variations in students' mental models of learning, but including any indirect effect mediated by students' learning orientations.
[c] Controlling for variations in students' mental models of learning and learning orientations
$*p<0.05$, $**p<0.01$, $***p<0.001$ (two-tailed test).

mental models and students' learning orientations are controlled. After the said control of variations a direct effect of *External Regulation on Learning Results* is found, but it is less important than those of the self-regulation strategies, as indicated by the low magnitude of the coefficient concerned.

Relationships with *Memorizing and Rehearsing* are found in all the regulation strategies. Relationships with *Analyzing* are found in all the regulation strategies except *Lack of Regulation*; and relationships with *Concrete Processing* are found in all the regulation strategies except *External Regulation of Learning Processes*. Each of these relationships comprises a basically direct effect, as the respective coefficients remain significant with their magnitudes changed only slightly when variations in students' mental models and students' learning orientations are controlled.

Overall, and as expected, the above findings suggest significant direct effects of students' regulation strategies on their processing strategies. When the magnitudes of the standardized regression coefficients are taken into account, the direct effects are mainly manifested in the positive influence of self-regulation strategies on *Relating and Structuring*, *Critical Processing* and *Concrete Processing*, and the positive influence of all regulation strategies except *Lack of Regulation* on *Memorizing and Rehearsing* and *Analyzing*.

6 Conclusion

The analytical approaches used here are relatively novel and the direct application of Richardson's model and analytical methodology for analyzing the ILS data has been fully justified. Valuable insights have emerged. In particular, and apart from the possibility for the existence of Path A and Path C, the dynamics of Vermunt's model have, in effect, been empirically reconstituted in the Hong Kong post-secondary education response context. Findings also confirm his hypothesis for the central role of regulation strategies; namely that students' processing strategies are most directly determined by their regulation strategies, and that the influence of students' mental models of learning and students' learning orientations on their processing strategies is mostly indirect (via their regulation strategies). Through the real-life examples of *Construction of Knowledge* being the common cause of variations in students' learning orientations and processing strategies (cf. Section 5.5), a minor omission in the models proposed in [13] and [14], namely the possibility of indirect spurious effects has furthermore been identified.

It is also acknowledged that, notwithstanding the novelty of the analytical approach, the inherent problem of causal ambiguity arising from correlational assumptions cannot be completely avoided. As student learning is a complex phenomenon involving many constructs [15], the possibility of the model as depicted in Figure 2 being an insufficient representation of the real world, and thus its associated analyses leading to incorrect causal inference needs to be acknowledged.

The results of the present study are believed to be the first analyses of ILS data obtained in the Chinese response context of the post-secondary education in Hong Kong. These results indicate that the ILS is able to capture the variation in students' learning strategies, mental models of learning and learning orientations in this new response context, and can thus form the basis for the development of an instrument to obtain students' feedback on their learning patterns in the next stage of the research. The quality of student learning is of paramount concern in the educational reform of Hong Kong, especially for the post-secondary education sector in which a substantial expansion in student participation has occurred. The present study demonstrates that Chinese translation of the ILS can be employed by institutions in the sector as part of a diagnostic system for addressing the possible problems of students in their learning, or as a formal means to collect data as part of an evidence-based process to improve the quality of teaching and student learning.

References

1. EMB (Education and Manpower Bureau): Review of the Post-secondary Education Sector, March 2006, Hong Kong Special Administrative Region Government (2006)
2. Richardson, J.T.E.: Instruments for Obtaining Student Feedback - A Review of the Literature. Assessment & Evaluation in Higher Education 30(4), 387–415 (2005)
3. Vermunt, J.D.: Inventory of Learning Styles in Higher Education. ICLON-Graduate School of Education. Leiden University, The Netherlands (1994)
4. Vermunt, J.D.: Metacognitive, Cognitive and Affective Aspects of Learning Styles and Strategies: A Phenomenographic Analysis. Higher Education 31, 25–50 (1996)
5. Vermunt, J.D.: The Regulation of Constructive Learning Processes. British Journal of Education Psychology 68, 149–171 (1998)
6. Vermunt, J.D., Vermetten, Y.J.: Patterns in Student Learning - Relationships between Learning Strategies, Conceptions of Learning, and Learning Orientations. Educational Psychology Review 16(4), 359–384 (2004)
7. Boekaerts, M.: Self-Regulated Learning: A New Concept Embraced by Researchers, Policy Makers, Educators, Teachers, and Students. Learning and Instruction 7(2), 161–186 (1997)
8. Cortina, J.M.: What Is Coefficient Alpha? An Examination of Theory and Applications. Journal of Applied Psychology 78(1), 98–104 (1993)
9. Hayton, J.C., Allen, D.G., Scarpello, V.: Factor Rentention Decisions in Exploratory Factor Analysis - a Tutorial on Parallel Analysis. Organizational Research Methods 7(2), 191–205 (2004)
10. Ajisuksmo, C.R.P., Vermunt, J.D.: Learning Styles and Self-Regulation of Learning at University - An Indonesian Study. Asia Pacific Journal of Education 19(2), 45–59 (1999)
11. Boyle, E.A., Duffy, T., Dunleavy, K.: Learning Styles and Academic Outcome - The Validity and Utility of Vermunt's Inventory of Learning Styles in a British Higher Education Setting. British Journal of Educational Psychology 73, 267–290 (2003)
12. Richardson, J.T.E.: Researching Student Learning - Approaches to Studying in Campus-Based and Distance Education. SRHE and Open University Press, Buckingham (2000)
13. Richardson, J.T.E.: Investigating the Relationships between Variations in Students' Perceptions of Their Academic Environment and Variations in Study Behaviour in Distance Learning. British Journal of Educational Psychology 76, 867–893 (2006)
14. Richardson, J.T.E.: Motives, Attitudes and Approaches to Studying in Distance Learning. Higher Education 54, 385–416 (2007)
15. Meyer, J.H.F.: Variation in Student Learning - An Empirical Nested Model. Centre for Learning, Teaching and Research in Higher Education. University of Durham (2001-2004)

Japanese Students' Attitudes towards Hybrid Learning

Yoko Hirata and Yoshihiro Hirata

Faculty of Engineering, Hokkai-Gakuen University
Sapporo, Japan
{hira, hirata}@eli.hokkai-s-u.ac.jp

Abstract. This paper summarizes the research work conducted for a survey of a group of Japanese University students' attitudes towards a hybrid language learning course. It determines how two different ways of teaching, traditional in-class structured and online unstructured lessons, significantly affected their perceptions about their learning English in a foreign language (EFL) course. As an introduction to the reader, a brief background of implementation of hybrid learning into the classroom is provided, followed by the description of hybrid approaches in Japanese educational settings. Then the objectives and the results of the present study are explained. The findings suggest that some instructional factors, such as flexibility, goal focused approach as well as closely connected relationships between in-class and online instructions, are indispensable for students to acquire a set of skills and strategies for successful language learners in hybrid learning environments.

Keywords: Japanese, language learning, online instructions.

1 Introduction

As computers have become widely used in the language classroom, interest in mixed-mode learning or hybrid learning has significantly increased throughout the world [1] [2]. The courses based on hybrid learning are defined as "classes in which instruction takes place in a traditional classroom setting augmented by computer-based or online activities which can replace classroom seat time"[3]. Numerous studies have indicated that using the combination of traditional and online instructions is regarded as a panacea for the students' development of language skills and is more effective than before [4, 5]. This approach has also been recognized as a perfect solution to support individualized learning as well as to help students' lifelong learning even outside the classroom [6]. One of the problems of this growing trend is that not much time has been spent to examine how to combine both online-based and classroom-based approaches for an effective structure of hybrid learning. A mix of these approaches does not "fit easily into the organizational structure of higher education administration"[7]. In addition, focus has often been placed on a variety of applications of online activities and computer programs rather than on different students' perceptions of this innovative language learning environment. More emphasis should be placed on the exploration of specific key factors which affect students' attitudes towards various approaches implemented in the hybrid learning modes.

J. Fong, R. Kwan, and F.L. Wang (Eds.): ICHL 2008, LNCS 5169, pp. 439–449, 2008.
© Springer-Verlag Berlin Heidelberg 2008

2 Hybrid Learning in Japan

E-learning courses in Japanese tertiary institutions have recently begun to play an increasingly important role in the teaching and learning of foreign languages. 69.3 percent of the national universities surveyed in Japan have offered e-learning classes [8]. Computer-based educational platforms, such as Blackboard and WebCT, have also been introduced into many language courses as an integral part of their curriculum designs [4, 6]. With the development of these e-learning technologies, hybrid learning courses have been implemented either as a mainstream methodology or as a supportive or supplementary role to the traditional courses [6, 9]. Although this technology in the language classroom is a rather new development in Japan, there are two major problems with regard to the effective implementation of hybrid learning.

The first major concern to be considered is how the instructor should deal with students' culture-specific styles of language learning. In the Japanese traditional educational contexts, the teacher-centered classroom structures are still highly valued. As in many other Asian countries, students are accustomed to a lecture type class where they are passive recipients of knowledge offered by the instructor [10]. This learning culture and individual students' commitment directly affect their learning process and their motivation to learn a language in a new environment. This is because e-learning, in general, requires more responsibility on the part of the student. In order to promote students' self-directed learning strategies and to stimulate their interest to the learning process, the development of pedagogical approaches that are sensitive specifically to Japanese cultural traditions is indispensable.

Another challenge to be considered in hybrid learning is a lack of understanding of an effective combination of traditional classroom instructions and online learning. Using online learning as supplement classroom instruction or extra follow-up practices is based on the assumption that, by simply giving individuals access to technology, it is expected to enhance student autonomy and support individualized learning [6]. However, how to blend two different modes of instructions, which will successfully improve the quality of the learning experience, has not been fully examined. It is important for the instructor to evaluate students' perceptions and attitudes when integrating new online teaching approaches into the conventional face-to-face component in a language course.

3 Listening and Language Awareness Activities

It is generally recognized that listening comprehension plays an important role in facilitating successful language learning [11, 12]. For students studying English, however, learning 'listening' has long been regarded as one of the most problematic areas which requires appropriate use of a variety of different approaches, skills and strategies [13]. In Japanese educational settings, how to effectively develop students' listening skills has long been the subject of much concern and debate. It has been well accepted that Japanese students find listening to English extremely difficult. This is partly due to a fact that Japanese students do not have much opportunity to be exposed to vast amounts of authentic English information in everyday contexts. In order to overcome this inherent problem, a variety of online listening activities have recently been developed in tertiary institutions. These activities are resources which can be used in and out of the class. Although these technology-enhanced listening lessons and practices are valuable resources which are readily available online, they commonly include drill exercises and gap filling comprehension tests. They are simply opportunities for students to practice listening to English and, therefore, are often regarded as passive activities [14]. As research has indicated, merely exposing students to these kinds of listening exercises is not adequate instruction for improving listening comprehension [15].

Recent studies on a more active approach to developing listening skills have pointed to the key role in identifying and grouping lexical and syntactic forms in the spoken discourse. This is based on the notion that spoken texts are determined by the context which includes word combination and structural patterns [16]. Having students access language data and discover the lexical patterns, that are associated with a specific word or phrase, is one of the effective approaches for developing their language learning skills [17-19]. This approach, called 'data-driven learning' (DDL), as defined by Johns [20], allows students to pay closer attention to the target word in rich contexts and to make reasonable conclusions about the structural rules of the target word. However, relatively little research has been conducted to determine how this teaching approach encourages Japanese students to increase their language awareness and helps them to engage in a more active process of learning a language.

4 Program Design and Development

Realizing the importance of developing a computer system which helps Japanese students understand phrases and sentence patterns effectively and efficiently in language data, the authors designed and developed a computer program, called *Lex*, which performs the simple function of searching and extracting all the occurrences of a certain key word or phrases in language data. *Lex* is a user-friendly program for retrieving and displaying collocational and lexical patterns, which are associated with the key word, from any kind of text data. The search results can be displayed in Key Word In Context (KWIC) mode in a plain text document. Key words are displayed with approximately six words on either side. This program, with a simplified easy-to-use interface, has been designed specifically for students without any lexical experience. *Lex* was installed in an Apache web server with Tomcat on a Linux computer. With this program, students can independently consult various collocational and lexical patterns which are associated with the key word. This program is accessible on campus or at home. Its access is restricted to registered students. Figures 1 and 2 demonstrate two different interfaces of *Lex*. Figure 2 shows that the words *make* and

Fig. 1. Interface design of *Lex*

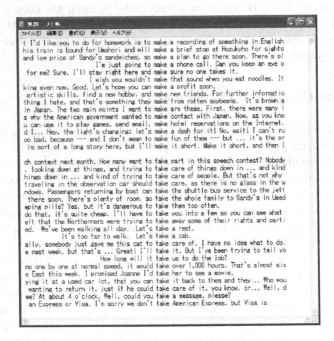

Fig. 2. Search results by *Lex*

take occur in the language data. As seen from these examples, it is possible for students to formulate basic rules about the way *make* and *take* work. For example, *make a friend, make contact with, make a reservation, take a rest, take care of.*

5 The Study

5.1 Purpose

The primary aim of this study is to determine how students who are used to passive and deductive learning approaches perceive hybrid learning in a language course. This course was designed to assist students to improve English listening by emphasizing the development of lexical skills. The following issues were specifically focused on.

1. What is the impact of the hybrid learning environment on students?
2. How do students perceive the difference between the traditional face-to-face learning and the web-based independent learning?

How this new technology can enhance students' language learning will be determined based on previous studies of the effectiveness of using hybrid learning systems in the language classroom.

5.2 Students

The respondents consisted of thirty five first year undergraduate students studying engineering at a Japanese national university. They were used to traditional teacher-directed step-by-step instructions in a large lecture-type classroom. They were also familiar with passive and sequential learning approaches which can often be seen in most engineering education [21]. Many students had limited computer competency with no previous experience of independent learning. 51% of the students had almost no experience in listening to English in their daily lives. All of the students had learned English for at least six years in secondary school in which listening was not a skill that was given much attention. Therefore, most of the students were properly motivated to improve their listening ability. Their level of English ranged from high-beginners to intermediate.

5.3 Course Design

A hybrid learning course was designed in order to encourage students to improve their English listening and lexical skills. This course was compulsory. Although the course comprised of both conventional teacher-directed instructions and online self-paced independent studies, these two different educational approaches were closely related with regard to the content and the materials the students used. Therefore, the entire course was a continuous process rather than a discrete event. The class was scheduled for one and a half hours each week over a 14-week course in a computer assisted language learning (CALL) classroom. The course which was divided into two phases is outlined as follows.

	First Phase	Second Phase
Objectives	Using a textbook, the students engaged in listening comprehension practices in the traditional teacher-directed classroom.	Based on textbook data, the students independently consulted various lexical patterns by using *Lex*. They were encouraged to understand patterns of usage and work out the rules for themselves.
Details	The first seven-week phase consisted of the traditional classroom teaching mode, in which the students were provided with listening comprehension lessons, with a variety of spoken texts and recordings with transcripts. These lessons were designed to help students comprehend main ideas, details, inferences, and language functions.	The second seven-week phase is the web-based independent component of this course. The aim was to increase the students' awareness of important language features and their functions in the discourse community. This component was also designed to focus on the understanding of a variety of lexical phrases which would be useful for enhancing students' interpretation of discourse.

Before the project started, there was a period of guidance which was offered by the instructor for the purpose of making students understand the basic concepts and techniques for the works. In addition, sample activities were given to the students about how to understand various language forms from the data. The students were instructed to organize their finds by focusing on various language features such as the use of adjectives, verbs and prepositions, and to examine collocations and other lexical combinations. After that, the students compared their own work with other students and discussed the use of words and expressions in the classroom.

5.4 Student Responses

After the course had been completed, data was collected from a 14-item questionnaire which was distributed to the students. The purpose was to gauge their opinions and attitudes towards their hybrid learning including the advantages and disadvantages of the course. The students were required to answer the questions anonymously. The rating scale used in the questionnaire was a 10-point Likert Scale with 1 representing "strongly disagree" and 10 representing "strongly agree". In order for students to fully understand the questionnaires, the questions were written in Japanese. For the purpose of attaining a mean response for each question, the responses were totaled and averaged. Standard deviation was then obtained for the purpose of examining statistically significant differences between students' responses. The data is presented in this paper as mean ±SD. The questionnaire was also analyzed by using Spearman's correlation to determine correlations between responses and significant factors underlying their responses. Correlation is significant at the .01 level (2-tailed). For the purpose of determining whether the type of course and the way of teaching significantly affected students' attitudes toward their hybrid learning, the students were required to answer open-ended questions and report how they felt about the course.

6 Findings

The results revealed the students' different values and attitudes to the hybrid learning approach. With regards to the effectiveness of the online independent learning mode, the overwhelming majority of students preferred the flexible online component to the conventional language courses. The Average (±SD) of this response was 9.00 (±1.18). In addition to the fact that many respondents highly valued the online component of the course itself, they felt that the close combination between in-class instructions and online lessons offered by the course was effective. The online activities encouraged students to assess what they had learned in the previous teacher-directed component of the course. There was a moderate correlation between those who valued the online component and those who valued the close combination between in-class instructions and online lessons ($r = .717$, $p < .01$). In addition, many students found the online component helpful in understanding lexical phrases and improving their listening skills. The analytical process of consulting various lexical patterns by *Lex* helped to enhance and clarify the understanding of various useful expressions and key phrases. The Average (±SD) of this response was 7.66 (±2.08). The correlation of .449 was significant between those who valued the analytical process and those who valued the close combination between in-class and online components. There was no correlation between those who required plenty of online training and those who did not value the effectiveness of the hybrid learning.

Table 1. Correlation between factors for effectiveness of the hybrid course

	High appreciation of the hybrid approach	Close combination between in-class and online	Future need for the hybrid approach
High appreciation of the hybrid approach	1.00	-----	-----
Close combination between in-class and online	.717**	1.00	-----
Future need for the hybrid approach	.741**	.780**	1.00

*Notes: Correlation Matrix (N=35), **p < .01.*

In addition, there was a moderate correlation between those who appreciated the effectiveness of the hybrid methodologies and those who required similar approaches in their future studies ($r = .741$, $p < .01$). Many students stated their willingness to use the web as a source of linguistic data for their language learning. The Average (±SD) of this response was 6.94 (±1.71). Those who highly rated the close combination between in-class and online components had a moderate correlation with those who

Table 2. Correlation between factors for effectiveness of the hybrid approach

	Close combination between in-class and online	Improving lexical skills	The use of the web
Close combination between in-class and online	1.00	-----	-----
Improving lexical skills	.449**	1.00	-----
The use of the web	.660**	.369**	1.00

Notes: *Correlation Matrix (N=35), **p < .01.*

Table 3. Correlation between factors for effectiveness of the hybrid course

	Improving listening skills	Goal focused approach	Effectiveness of independent component
Improving listening skills	1.00	-----	-----
Goal focused approach	.743**	1.00	-----
Effectiveness of independent component	.498**	.423**	1.00

Notes: *Correlation Matrix (N=35), **p < .01.*

valued the use of the web as a student learning resource ($r = .660$, $p < .01$). As for the amount of language data the students were exposed to the majorities of students stated that they were appropriate. The Average (±SD) of this response was 7.17 (±1.83).

There was a moderate correlation between those who realized the effectiveness of the course in improving their listening skills and those who valued the goal focused approach offered by the course ($r = .743$, $p < .01$). The correlation of .498 was significant between those who found the effectiveness of the course in improving their listening skills and those who valued the goal focused approach.

As for the negative aspect of the online component, 28.5% of the students stated that they frequently visited Websites which were not relevant to the class. However, there was no correlation between those who were frequent visitors of irrelevant Websites and those who did not value the effectiveness of this hybrid learning.

6.1 Student Comments

The students expressed distinct opinions about the course they had taken. In their comments, students suggested that the experience of hybrid learning was beneficial to the students in the following two ways. Firstly, when asked about the advantages of the course, the majority of students reported that they highly valued its independent, self-paced component during the online lessons. The flexible delivery of the materials, such as digital audio data, *Lex*, and accessing from remote sites, also brought enormous benefits for their language study. This finding is in accordance with the results of the students' questionnaire explained above. The comments made by the students also suggest that they highly valued the flexibility in analyzing the language data and deciding what worked and what did not work for improving their language skills on their own. These students liked taking an active role in directing their own study at their own pace more than following sequential step by step instructions. Ten students stated that they were fully satisfied with an educational environment which they could actively engage with and control by themselves. These students didn't seem to have any problems with shifting from lecture-type instructions to student-centered instructions.

Secondly, the students' constructive comments have shown that another advantage of this course is the fact that it encouraged students to engage in critical thinking and reflect on what they had learned through their previous language learning experiences in the face-to-face instructions. In combination with traditional classroom-based education, the students stated that the web-based analytical activities helped them raise their awareness of various meanings and usages of the words and expressions they had previously listened in the classroom. Sixteen students stated that discovering the results from the data was highly motivating and rewarding. None of the students had difficulties in identifying regularities in the language data. This integration of reflective and experiential learning process aided them in considering not only what and how they had learned a language but also how they would be able to solve their own language problems in their future studies. These comments also support the results of the questionnaire described in the previous section.

With regards to what they didn't like about the course, three students stated that the analysis of the language data by using *Lex* was time-consuming and laborious. Some students reported that they did not know what to do in front of their computers once they had completed their own activities. Other students reported that they also did not know what to do in front of their computers because the activities offered were too difficult for them to deal with. In addition, some participants indicated that there was a problem with the different levels of involvement in the activities throughout the course. Without the instructor, some students seemed to be at a loss what to do during the online independent lessons.

7 Discussion and Conclusions

Although the sample size is too small to allow any generalization, at least in the statistical sense, the data collected in this study offered valuable information which instructors should take into account when implementing hybrid learning approaches in language courses in Japan.

First of all, the results of this study suggest that the hybrid approach can foster the development of students' critical and reflective thinking, under the condition that flexibility as well as the successful combination of both in-class instructions and online lessons are provided. This is consistent with earlier studies [1, 22]. As the findings suggest, as would-be engineers who were inclined to enjoy researching data, the students acknowledged the value of examining patterns and occurrences of particular words or phrases on their own with the aid of *Lex*. It is also important to note that many students were observed to be actively involved in the analytical process even if the instructor was not directly involved in the instructional process during the online lessons. There is an indication that different modes of instructions were fully appreciated by many students as long as the course accommodated the students' learning needs and preferences. In order to make a hybrid course effective and productive, both the classroom lead by the instructor and independent learning should be goal-oriented and well-organized. It is also important for the instructor to encourage students to be more aware of their learning process and help them consciously examine their own contribution to this process.

Secondly, the instructor should acknowledge the fact that there are always some students who feel more secure when being spoon-fed instructions. The results suggest that there were some students who were reluctant to take charge of their own learning during the unsupervised lessons. This finding is in accordance with the fact that the students who were involved in independent learning still showed a strong preference for teacher-directed learning environments [23]. Based on the data given by this study, it was concluded that the Japanese students perceived their language learning in different ways and different approaches provided them with different impacts. These results are in accordance with the findings of Jung and Suzuki [24] who claim the importance of online education which deals with the diversity of language learners.

Although more research is necessary and many different factors should be explored, it is hoped that the findings of the present study will create new research questions. For example, what are the major characteristics of the students who can maximize their computer-based independent learning effectively? What should the instructor do to accommodate multiple teaching methods when dealing with a more diverse student population in the classroom? Answering these questions will enormously contribute to the future development of successful hybrid language courses.

Acknowledgement

The authors would like to express their sincere thanks to Mr. Hideki Ooyane for his dedication and tremendous help in developing WWW version of *Lex*.

References

1. Lindsay, E.B.: The best of both worlds: Teaching a hybrid course. Academic Exchange Quarterly 8(4), 16–20 (2004)
2. Papadima-Sophocleous, S.: A hybrid of a CBT- and a CAT-based new English placement test online (NEPTON). CALICO Journal 25(2), 276–304 (2008)
3. Scida, E.E., Saury, R.E.: Hybrid courses and their impact on student and classroom performance: a case study at the University of Virginia. CALICO Journal 23(3), 517–531 (2006)

4. Hinkelman, D.: Blended Learning: Issues Driving an End to Laboratory-based CALL. JALT Hokkaido Journal 9, 17–31 (2005)
5. Oblender, T.E.: A hybrid course model: one solution to the high online drop-out rate. Learning and Leading with Technology 29(6), 42–46 (2002)
6. Gitsaki, C.: Course Design to Promote Student Autonomy and Lifelong Learning Skills: A Japanese Example? In: Anderson, H., Hobbs, M., Jones- Parry, J., Logan, S., Lotovale, S. (eds.) Supporting independent learning in the 21st century. Proceedings of the second conference of the Independent Learning Association, pp. 9–12. Independent Learning Association Oceania, Auckland (2005)
7. Ross, B., Gage, K.: Insight from WebCT and our customers in higher education. In: Bonk, C.J., Graham, C.R. (eds.) The Handbook of Blended Learning, pp. 155–168. Pfeiffer, San Francisco (2006)
8. Ozkul, A.E., Aoki, K.: E-Learning in Japan: Steam Locomotive on Shinkansen. In: 22nd ICDE World Conference on Distance Education: Promoting Quality in On-line, Flexible and Distance Education (2006),
   http://aide.nime.ac.jp/research/ICDE2006_Ozkul&Aok_
9. Redfield, M., Campbell, P.D.: Comparing CALL approaches: self-access versus hybrid classes. The JALT CALL Journal 1(3), 50–61 (2005)
10. Kennedy, J.: Perspectives on cultural and individual determinants of teaching style. RELC Journal 22(2), 61–78 (1991)
11. Rost, M.: Teaching and Researching: Listening. Pearson Education, Harlow (2002)
12. Vandergrift, L.: Facilitating Second Language Listening Comprehension: Acquiring Successful Strategies. ELT Journal 53, 168–176 (1999)
13. Wilson, M.: Discovery listening --- improving perceptual processing. ELT Journal 57(4), 335–343 (2003)
14. Field, J.: Skills and strategies: towards a new methodology for listening. ELT Journal 52(2), 110–118 (1998)
15. Hisaoka, T.: On the use of shadowing for improving listening ability: theory and practice. Gakusyuin Kotoka Kiyou 2, 13–30 (2004)
16. Hunston, S.: Corpora in Applied Linguistics. Cambridge University Press, Cambridge (2002)
17. Chambers, A.: Integrating corpus consultation in language studies. Language Learning and Technology 9(2), 111–125 (2005)
18. Gaskell, D., Cobb, T.: Can learners use concordance feedback for writing errors? System 32(3), 301–319 (2004)
19. Vannestål, M.E., Lindquist, H.: Learning English grammar with a corpus: experimenting with concordancing in a university grammar course. ReCALL 19(3), 329–350 (2007)
20. Johns, T.: Should you be persuaded - two samples of data-driven learning materials. In: Johns, T., King, P. (eds.) Classroom Concordancing. Birmingham University English Language Research Journal 4, Birmingham, pp. 1–13 (1991)
21. Felder, R.M., Linda, K., Silverman, L.K.: Learning and teaching styles in engineering education. Engr. Education 78(7), 674–681 (1988)
22. Graham, C.R.: Blended learning systems: definition, current trends, and future directions. In: Bonk, C.J., Graham, C.R. (eds.) The Handbook of Blended Learning, pp. 3–21. Pfeiffer, San Francisco (2006)
23. Felix, U.: Integrating multimedia into the curriculum: A case study. On-CALL 11(1), 1–13 (1997)
24. Jung, I., Suzuki, K.: Blended learning in Japan and its application in liberal arts education. In: Bonk, C.J., Graham, C.R. (eds.) The Handbook of Blended Learning, pp. 267–280. Pfeiffer, San Francisco (2006)

Blended Learning:
A Case Study for Japanese Language Studies

Kenneth K.C. Lee[1] and Melody P.M. Chong[2]

[1] Department of Computer Science, City University of Hong Kong
[2] Department of Chinese, Translation and Linguistics, City University of Hong Kong
{kenkclee, ctchong}@cityu.edu.hk

Abstract. This article examines the link between e-learning and instructor-led teaching in a local university in Hong Kong. It employs a case study to examine the relation in a sample of undergraduate students studying Japanese language. More specifically, the study aims to pose a challenge to the existing and dominant instructor-led teaching method. The paper also provides implications for the design of course structure and content that will improve students' performance and motivation while enhancing the effectiveness of teaching and learning as a whole.

Keywords: blended learning, language studies, Japanese language, e-learning.

1 Introduction

In recent years, e-learning has assumed greater importance in educational sectors as it has been recognized as contributing to overall quality, effectiveness, convenience and cost of learning experiences [1]. In view of growing significance of blended learning in language studies, it is absolutely essential to develop efficient blended learning practices capable of providing excellent quality of teaching. Today, we can understand better how learning experiences could be improved by the "blended" combinations of both traditional and technology-based learning methods [1] and how it can have significant effects on students' learning processes in terms of motivation, performance, and effectiveness.

In this paper, some insights are provided relating the application of blended learning in language studies. In particular, Japanese language study is discussed. This paper first explores the distinctive features of Japanese language. Then it intends to justify blended learning by analyzing the respective merits of instructor-led and e-learning paradigms. We also demonstrate how the blended approach could match perfectly to the demanding nature of Japanese studies using a case study research method in a sample of undergraduate students studying Japanese language in a local University in Hong Kong. We hope that the propositions of our recipe of blended learning could bring incites and insights to educational practitioners in similar academic disciplines.

J. Fong, R. Kwan, and F.L. Wang (Eds.): ICHL 2008, LNCS 5169, pp. 450–462, 2008.

2   Blended Learning and Its Development in Language Studies

Since Sir Tim Berners Lee invented World Wide Web in 1989, there have been revolutionary changes in our way of life. The Internet shows its influences in the areas from business, mass media to entertainment. Education, as one of the major elements in governmental expenditure, is no exception. E-Learning and later Blended learning is widely adopted in Hong Kong and most developed countries in hope of increasing productivity. E-learning is characterized by online resources and Virtual Learning Environments (VLE) such as WebCT/Blackboard [2] which supports self-motivated and self-paced learning. Meanwhile blended learning further complements e-learning by providing activities such as instructor-lead classes, role-play and discussion group alongside with e-resources. It is well believed that blended learning is a better learning paradigm than e-learning and the fact is supported by a recent study conducted by Thomson and NETg [3]. The study showed that the speed and accuracy performed by the "blended" student group was considerably superior to that of the pure e-learning group by 30-40%. With the uprising urge of "enhanced productivity" and "cost effectiveness", blended learning has become an ideal and only solution to educational practitioners and business training experts.

E-learning and Blended learning is inherently superior to its traditional counterpart in many ways. In logistic point of view, the use of hyperlinks and e-documents nowadays not only reduces the time and cost, but also allows rapid information dispersion at any time and anywhere. In pedagogic point of view, e-learning and blended learning helps memory reinforcement since it encourages self-paced learning and self assessment during non-contact hours. In the long run, blended learning helps on class progress since it reduces the asynchronies and variance of progress among students. (At times, the progress of class is *"dictated by the slowest learners in the group"* [4].) However, e-learning is no silver bullet. Online resources and VLE do show their short sides from time to time. One major problem is that students are generally inexperienced and hence personal guidelines and study models are needed in order to keep them from wandering around the sea of online resources without target. Another issue is that e-solution generally lacks personal interaction which is important in disciplines such as second language acquisition [5]. To conclude, we need tailor-made blended learning schemes for different subjects and careful stock picking of pedagogic activities is indispensable.

Among all those academic and vocational subjects, language studies are probably the most challenging areas. The reason lies in the fact that language is not a single skill but *a collection* of literary and communicational skills which requires high degree of proficiency. It is a long and painstaking process that it takes years to train up the language ability of a student to a level which enables direct communication with native speakers. Language study is also distinctive in a way that the learning of high level concepts or syntaxes heavily depends on how well a student can grasp the fundamental ones. For example, to learn the passive voice in English, students have to master the past participles. This implies that foundation building is particularly important during the course of study. In this research, we attempted to investigate different learning dimensions to figure out a combination of pedagogic approach and teaching media for effective language learning.

3 Methodology

The present research employed a case study research approach. Case study approach is that the researcher systematically gathers in-depth information on a single entity such as an individual, a group, an organization or a community using a variety of data gathering methods. Particularly, picking the right cases for study and understanding and correctly translating the dynamics to one's own situation are critical for successful problem solving [6]. Cases to study may range from *dancehall musicians to student physician*, and a case may be *a single child, a classroom or clinic or a charity* [7]. A case study approach is considered the most appropriate methodology to answer the **what, how** and **why** research questions. As Yin [8] indicates, exploratory case study is good in dealing with proposition development and tracing links between concepts or incidence. This research method allows the researchers to study the central phenomenon in depth. The case study was conducted between September 2007 and February 2008. The case being studied was an intermediate Japanese language course. The case included forty-two undergraduate students aged around twenty years old.

4 A Case Study for Japanese Language Study

In this study, we use the well-known Japanese Language Proficiency Test (JLPT) [9] as a benchmark to generate the ideas. In particular, we try to sketch the full picture by referring to four vital dimensions in language studies: writing-vocabulary, listening skills, reading-grammar and oral skills. Each sub-session first highlights the problems faced in traditional classrooms with refer to the distinctive linguistic features of Japanese language. We then demonstrate how the *quality of learning and teaching* could be improved after blended learning came into picture.

4.1 Study of Japanese Vocabulary

In most instructor-led classes, instructors teach students about 180 new vocabularies in one semester. For decades, compilation of personal wordlist is the only means for students to master a huge amount of vocabularies. But yet, compilation of word list is not a no-brainer and considerable planning is needed. Let alone the tremendous time and effort required, study of Japanese vocabulary is especially difficult due to problems rooted from the linguistic features. The same kanji may contain two or more different pronunciations. For example, the word 'day' (日) could be pronounced as *hi/bi* (ひ/び), *nichi* (にち) or *jitsu* (じつ). Even in daily conversations, in which Kanji writing is not necessary, the situation is no better. Japanese is flooded with huge amount of homophones (sound-alike words). According to Mochizuki [10], Japanese homophones are three times more numerous than those found in Chinese. Given a pronunciation, one could easily find three or more words which pronounce exactly the same (Fig. 1). For extreme case such as こうしょう, a single pronunciation could even carries 43 different meanings. As the mental database of vocabularies grows, memory tends to "interfere with each other". [11]

Pronounciation	Possible meanings and corresponding Kanji (Chinese character)		
Koto	Capital (古都)	Affair (事)	Piano (琴)
Kōtō	Oral (口頭)	Nice baseball pitching (好投)	High level (高等)
Kōdo	Height (高度)	Brightness (光度)	Hardness (硬度)
kōdō	Action (行動)	Lecture Hall (講堂)	Highway (公道)

Fig. 1. Homophones in Japanese

From the learner's point of view, there is a need of automatic instrument which helps vocabulary management and self-assessment. From the educator's point of view, there is a need to encourage students to actively learn new vocabularies so that they could accumulate thousands of vocabularies before the JLPT exam. With respect to the vocabulary dimension, it is expected that the e-technology will create synergy by speeding up the wordlist compilation and classification process for students' self-learning. The "huge information volume" and "high searching speed" properties of e-resources match perfectly to the demanding wordlist compilation task. Students can store the words in an electronic form instead of hand-written text on small paper cards. It allows students update the personalized wordlists and review them at anytime and anywhere. Students could also share or exchange wordlists in VLE platforms, forums, blogs or even personal wiki solutions [12] with their fellows.

In this case study, Blackboard [2] system was set up for an intermediate Japanese language course. Like other web-assisted courses, lecture handouts are released online. Yet instead of using Internet as merely a data-release medium, we intend to treat it as a learning platform. Several discussion groups are being set up to encourage students exchanging ideas (Fig. 2). Students are encouraged to ask any questions either in Japanese, English or Chinese relating Japanese language or culture. We believe that this can help stimulate students' motivation in learning the language, especially for those students who have learnt the language for one or two years. Hyperlinks to interesting resources are also posted in VLE in order to stimulate students' interest. For instance, students are encouraged to visit YouTube[13] (Fig. 3) to view *selected* music clips with Japanese subtitles and lyrics. Despite the fact that grammars

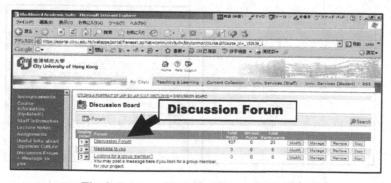

Fig. 2. Japanese discussion forum on Blackboard

Fig. 3. Music Clip in YouTube [13] together with Japanese lyrics

in songs are not perfect, it is hoped that students could build up a habit in learning vocabularies and Japanese culture from real-life resources.

To build up comprehensive and ordered vocabulary list, students are encouraged to make use of existing online systems such as the excellent Yahoo! Dictionary Service [14]. Online dictionaries (Fig. 4) are inherently superior to the paperback ones in terms of a large word counts and related resources. Apart from that, online dictionaries are usually equipped with value-added features. As shown in Figure 4, the Yahoo! Dictionary not only provides related synonym and antonym, but also displays entries

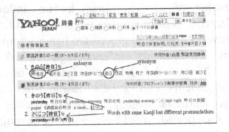

Fig. 4. Yahoo Online Dictionaries [14]

Fig. 5. Yahoo! Translation [17] (left) and Babel Fish Translation [18] (right)

with the *same Kanji but different pronunciations*. (Yahoo! Dictionary shows two entries for "yesterday": *kinō (きのう)* and *sakujitsu (さくじつ)*). This feature is invaluable to students who intend to take JLPT. Apart from the Yahoo! Dictionary, the Goo dictionary [15], which displays Wikipedia [16] entries related to queries, is also a good choice. At the same time, the Yahoo! Translation [17] or the Babel Fish [18] (Fig. 5) also helps students to translate texts, or even websites from Chinese or English to Japanese. Despite most translation sites are only capable for short sentence translation; students can still use these free web-sites to assist their self-learning.

4.2 Study of Japanese Listening Skill

In traditional in-class training, most instructors find difficulties in improving the listening skills of their students. Given that the contact-hours are limited, most of the times have been spent on vocabulary and grammatical explanations. Nowadays, standard teaching aids used are those companion tapes or CDs included in textbook. Each chapter accounts for about 5-7 minutes of recording, including the recitation of main text/article, sound-only roleplay and listening questions. Considering that time needed for students to write down the answers and for instructors to reveal the correct answer together with vocabulary and grammatical explanations, one could easily draw a conclusion that instructors are simply not able to afford playing the tape many times within the standard 50-minute listening lab session in classroom. Needless to say, playing real-life recordings such as news broadcast or radio program in class is simply out of the question. The outcome of all those is that the listening abililty among students in class could be highly asynchronus, which in turn, affects the progress of class. It is especially problematic that a considerable number of Japanese courses are taught in Japanese itself by native teachers.

In our opinion, switching from tape to digital media is inevitable. Of course, the media itself is inherently superior, in the sense that it supports random access and bookmarking. However, the real significance come from the fact that electronic recordings make information dispersal easy and it promotes self-learning.

Recorded Japanese passages and dialogs in mp3 format are available to students via Blackboard (Fig. 6). Students in need could listen to the recordings as many times as they want after the scheduled listening lab session. This helps alleviating the

Fig. 6. Japanese recording (mp3) on Blackboard

pressure of limited time. Apart from mechanical examples included with textbook, students where also given chances to be exposed to interesting real-life materials. For instance, short animation clips from the famous films "My Neighbor Totoro" (となりの トトロ) and "Spirited Away" (千と千尋の神隠し) [19] were shown to students by using the YouTube video (Fig. 7). Those films are targeted to juvenile audience in Japan and hence the language used, as well as the speed is appropriate to intermediate level students. Students were given the Japanese transcript of the films beforehand and they could try to follow during animation playback. This serves a trio advantage: First of all, students could practice their listening skill, with dialog *(and dialect)* by native speakers. Also, students were exposed to the "everyday language" used among local Japanese people. More importantly, it stimulates students' interest and encourages them to be active learners.

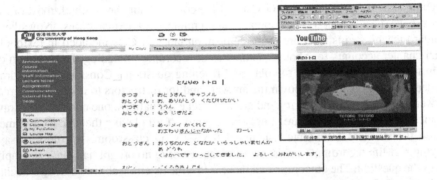

Fig. 7. Animation "Totoro" from YouTube with the corresponding transcript

4.3 Study of Japanese Grammar

Despite the fact that Japanese vocabularies are affected by Chinese language, Japanese grammar itself did not significantly change [20]. Some scholars [21] urge that, in particular, the Japanese particle system is a major hurdle for second-language learners in college-level Japanese courses, due to its complexity and its absence from the learners' first language. The picture is further complicated by the fact that a single particle is usually overloaded with multiple usages. For example, the particle と could be used to represent accompaniment *(similar to "and" in English)* or conditional events *(similar to "if" in English)*. As a result, Japanese teachers usually found themselves spending most of the times in teaching grammatical concepts to students.

The use of a blend of e-technology and traditional tutoring is prooved useful in levelling the learning curve and improving students' writing and grammar skills. Nagata's [21] experimental study suggests that the computer's metalinguistic feedback program can lead learners to develop general grammatical competence in the use of particles. In addition, we try to help stuents learning grammar by posting managed articles and summaries on the Blackboard environment. Apart from listing articles in a time-oriented manner *(from week 1 onward)*, we also try to summarize the knowledge taught in different semesters to formulate grammar-oriented summaries.

Fig. 8. Linguistic summaries which consolidate grammatical rules learnt from different levels (left). List of usages and examples for particle か (right).

As shown in Fig. 8, learning materials related to Japanese grammar (i.e. exercises and explanatory notes for outside benchmark language tests or summary of particular patterns) have been uploaded to the Blackboard. This feature helps students to manage their memory better and is particularly useful for students who intend to attend the JLPT, since examinees are always asked to fill in the blanks by selecting a correct particle from a list of multiple choice questions.

To promote self-learning and self-assessment, selected exercises, such as the questions from past JLPT papers are posted on Blackboard (Fig. 9). Evenever students have queries regarding Japanese grammar, students could freely raise their questions on the Q&A forum in Blackboard (Fig. 10). With online forum, students' questions could be answered within a short time without being delayed until the next lecture. Also, it is observed that forum answers not only help the student who questioned, but usually also benefit the whole class as well, since questions among peers are usually similar or overlapped. By uploading the revision exercises and linguistic summaries, instructors can save time from performing mechanical routine jobs. They can concentrate to spend more time for areas which require face-to-face instruction and interaction with students, such as oral training.

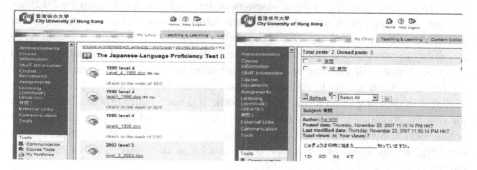

Fig. 9. Exercises and JLPT past papers for self-assessment

Fig. 10. Online Question & Answer forum in Blackboard

4.4 Study of Japanese Oral Skill

Like most languages, the accent and intonation of spoken Japanese may be the most difficult parts to learn. In Japanese language, there are many words with same pronunciations. However, a change in the accent would change the meaning of the word. For instance, *ame* can be 'candy' (*ame*) or 'rain' (*ame*). Unlike English which has stress accent, Japanese has pitch accent which means that after an accented syllable, the pitch falls. Another distinct feature of Japanese language is the honorific expressions. Japan is well-known as a hierarchical society. Japanese has an extensive system to express politeness and formality. The position of a person is determined by a variety of factors including job, age, experience, or even psychological state [22]. This makes Japanese expressions difficult for the overseas learners [23].

Type	Person with whom to speak	Expressions
Casual	Friends, Siblings, Juniors	食べなさい、食べて、食べてください
Honorific	Seniors, Teachers, Guests	召し上がってください、お召し上がりください

Fig. 11. Differences between casual and honorific expressions **Source:** *A Manual for Using Honorifics* [24]

Figure 11 shows two sets of possible expressions used to invite someone to eat. The first row shows the 'casual' daily expressions used among friends and the second row shows the honorific expressions. It can be seen that the sentence structures and the words used are quite different. It is believed that the best way to enhance oral ability may be to maintain face-to-face interactions between tutors and learners. As Yamazaki [25] suggests, ideal speech translating systems are far from mature and considerable future work is needed on resolving various acoustic and linguistic phenomena such as colloquial idioms, occasional omission of words and inversion of word order. Nevertheless, in reality, it is infeasible to have intensive training between teachers and students. Hence, net resources, offline assessment and feedback mechanism via VLE are suggested to supplement normal face-to-face tutorial sessions. In here we focus our discussion to three related aspects: 1) the ability to pronounce a single vocabulary, 2) the ability to pronounce a complete sentence with correct tone and intonation, and 3) the presentation skill and interaction among peers. In each lesson, some 15-20 new vocabularies from textbook are taught. Since pronunciation audio clips are always available in the companion resource of textbook, it is not a major problem. Meanwhile for new vocabularies students *learnt outside class*, the use of electronic dictionary or online Text-to-Speech (TTS) systems is suggested. For instance, the NeoSpeech system (Fig. 12) available online supports pronunciation of vocabularies or even short phases.

Students can use the system to input simple vocabularies such as the mentioned vocabularies 'candy' (*ame*) or 'rain' (*ame*) to practice the pronunciation. Further, according to our rudimentary experiments, it was found that the system is rather

Fig. 12. Pentax NeoSpeech [26] – Online Japanese Text-to-Speech (TTS) system

intelligent because it can handle complex Japanese pronunciation rules well. For instance, the system can distinguish the pronunciations even the vocabularies are written the same but with different meanings. An example is illustrated in Figure 13. In Japanese language, the meaning of the vocabulary "十分" could be "ten minutes" or "adequate." Pronunciation differs depending on the meaning. It was found that the NeoSpeech system can distinguish the pronunciation perfectly.

Meaning	Pronunciation
今、十時十分です。 Now is ten minutes past ten.	→ じゅっぷん／じっぷん (*Juppun or Jippun*)
日本語はまだ十分ではありません。 My Japanese is still not very good.	→ じゅうぶん (*Jubun*)

Fig. 13. Test of NeoSpeech – pronunciation of the same word in different sentence structure

Students were also encouraged to use the provided link (i.e. the NeoSpeech) or software (i.e. mp3 recording) to enhance the quality of their reading and oral assignments. Students could make good use of this advanced systems so as to improve their pronunciation and intonation. For learning the pronunciations of single vocabularies, online text-to-speech systems provide variable degree of usefulness. However, to train up the ability to pronounce sentences or documents, we suggest the use of offline assessment and feedback mechanism to complement face-to-face oral sessions, since we also found the software is incapable of presenting the sentences or dialogues together with appropriate emotional expression. Apart from mere pronunciation, the presentation skills and interaction during conversation are also considered important. As suggested by Chaudron [8], the interaction in the classroom between peers is one of the most significant factors for successful learning of the second language acquisition (SLA). From time to time, students' performance during class is recorded with camcorder and some outstanding ones will be uploaded to Blackboard. Not only could it help the instructors to understand the students better, but it also allow students learning from each other, by observing the good practices as well as the weak points which require refinement.

5 Conclusion

In our previous research, we discussed and proposed how facilitators can enhance the teaching activities effectively by four dimensions of Japanese language learning. Suggested activities are highlighted in Figure 14 [27]. In the present research, we

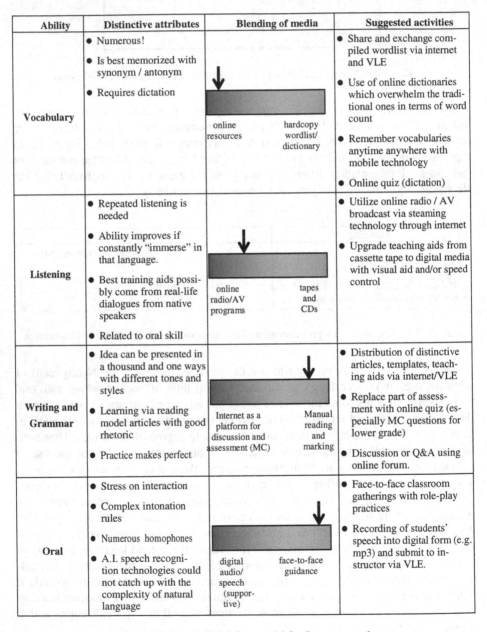

Ability	Distinctive attributes	Blending of media	Suggested activities
Vocabulary	• Numerous! • Is best memorized with synonym / antonym • Requires dictation	online resources → hardcopy wordlist/ dictionary	• Share and exchange compiled wordlist via internet and VLE • Use of online dictionaries which overwhelm the traditional ones in terms of word count • Remember vocabularies anytime anywhere with mobile technology • Online quiz (dictation)
Listening	• Repeated listening is needed • Ability improves if constantly "immerse" in that language. • Best training aids possibly come from real-life dialogues from native speakers • Related to oral skill	online radio/AV programs → tapes and CDs	• Utilize online radio / AV broadcast via steaming technology through internet • Upgrade teaching aids from cassette tape to digital media with visual aid and/or speed control
Writing and Grammar	• Idea can be presented in a thousand and one ways with different tones and styles • Learning via reading model articles with good rhetoric • Practice makes perfect	Internet as a platform for discussion and assessment (MC) → Manual reading and marking	• Distribution of distinctive articles, templates, teaching aids via internet/VLE • Replace part of assessment with online quiz (especially MC questions for lower grade) • Discussion or Q&A using online forum.
Oral	• Stress on interaction • Complex intonation rules • Numerous homophones • A.I. speech recognition technologies could not catch up with the complexity of natural language	digital audio/ speech (supportive) → face-to-face guidance	• Face-to-face classroom gatherings with role-play practices • Recording of students' speech into digital form (e.g. mp3) and submit to instructor via VLE.

Fig. 14. Suggested blending model for Japanese study

continue to explore how educators and learners can be benefited from blended learning with proposed activities in relation to vocabulary, listening, grammar and oral skills. As Singh and Reed (2001) point out [1], *"Blended learning focuses on optimizing achievement of learning objectives by applying the "right" learning technologies to match the "right" personal learning style to transfer the "right" skills to the "right" person at the "right" time."* In addition, effectiveness of blended learning also depends on whether an instructor or facilitator can match the appropriate delivery media to existing teaching activities and to catch up with the e-learning paradigm.

In this paper, students are suggested using online dictionaries and pop-culture materials to assist vocabulary learning. The informative online resources not only save time for knowledge management and retrieval but also free students from schedule and geographical restrictions. E-resources also benefit listening training which allows students to access real life programmes and broadcasts from Japan. For grammatical training, we suggest the use of VLE and online forums with assistances from e-helpers or e-mentors. Instructors may also encourage students to ask questions on the VLE so as to save time from in-class activities while enhancing students self-learning ability. Finally, with respect to oral skill training, the system NeoSpeech is introduced to improve pronunciation particularly for vocabulary and short sentence.

This case study demonstrated that instructors can use different levels of "blend" in different learning areas to improve students' motivation and performance, and thus also enhance the effectiveness of teaching and learning as a whole. However, like other revolutionary institutional policies, 'human' is the ultimate factor which governs *make or break*. Despite the availability of robust *hardware* (technology), we also need appropriate *software* (instructors) to make things happen. Instructors must be well trained, both technically and mentally, and accommodate themselves to the new-generation instructional media.

References

[1] Singh, H., Reed, C.: A White Paper: Achieving Success with Blended Learning. Centra Software, 1 (2001)
[2] Blackboard – Educate. Innovate. Anywhere,
    http://www.blackboard.com/us/index.Bb
[3] Thomson Job Impact Study - The Next Generation of Corporate Learning,
    http://www.netg.com/NewsAndEvents/PressReleases/top
[4] Masterworks International - Distance Learning,
    http://www.masterworksinternational.com/faq.asp
[5] Chaudron, C.: Second Language Classrooms: Research on Teaching and Learning. Cambridge University Press, Cambridge (2004)
[6] Cavana, R.Y., Delahaye, B.L., Sekaran, U.: Applied Business Research: Qualitative and Quantitative Methods, p. 112. John Wiley & Sons, Australia (2003)
[7] Silverman, D.: Doing Qualitative Research, p. 126. Sage, London (2005)
[8] Yin, R.K.: Case Study Research, Design and Methods, p. 6. Sage, Thousand Oaks (2003)
[9] The Japanese Language Proficiency Test (JLPT), Japan Educational Exchanges and Services, http://www.jees.or.jp/jlpt/en/index.htm

[10] Mochizuki, Y.: Homophones in Japanese and Chinese. In: The 2nd volume of A Contrastive Study of the Japanese and Chinese Languages. U. of Foreign Languages, Osaka (1977)

[11] Body & Brain Magazine,
http://www.bodynbrain.com/01_magazine/news_view.asp?SeqNO=36

[12] List of wiki software,
http://en.wikipedia.org/wiki/List_of_wiki_software

[13] Youtube – Broadcast Yourself, http://www.youtube.com

[14] Yahoo! Japan – Dictionary, http://dic.yahoo.co.jp/

[15] Goo Online Dictionary, http://dictionary.goo.ne.jp/

[16] Wikipedia – The Free Encyclopedia, http://www.wikipedia.org/

[17] Yahoo Translation – Text Translation, http://honyaku.yahoo.co.jp/

[18] Alta Vista – Babel Fish Translation, http://babelfish.altavista.com/

[19] Studio Ghibli, http://www.ghibli.jp/

[20] The Japanese Language,
http://www.wsu.edu/~dee/ANCJAPAN/LANGUAGE.HTM

[21] Nagata, N.: The Effectiveness of Computer-Assisted Metalinguistic Instruction: A Case Study in Japanese. Foreign Language Annals 30(2), 187–200 (1997)

[22] Wikipedia – Japanese Language - Politeness,
http://en.wikipedia.org/wiki/Japanese_language#Politeness

[23] Ogata, H., Yano, Y.: How ubiquitous computing can support language learning. In: Proceedings of KEST 2003, Honjo, Akita, Japan, pp. 1–6 (2003)

[24] Asada, H.: A Manual for Using Honorifics. Japan: Nagumodo (南雲堂) [In Japanese] (2002)

[25] Yamazaki, Y.: Research activities on spontaneous speech translation. Denshi Tokyo 33, 109–114 (1995)

[26] Pentax NeoSpeech, http://www.neospeech.com/

[27] Lee, K.K.C., Chong, M.P.M.: An Observational Study on Blended Learning for Japanese Language Studies in a Local University in Hong Kong. In: Workshop on blended learning 2007, Edinburgh, pp. 88–100 (2007)

Distance Education Network for Strengthening the Education Movement in Nigeria

Ezeja Ogili

Department of Staff Development and Distance Education
School of Distance Learning and Continuing Education
Institute of Management and Technology, Enugu – Nigeria
ezejaogili@yahoo.com

Abstract. Nigeria is the largest race in African continent with a population of 140,000,000 people. It also contributes to the high rate of illiterates among the nine populous countries of the world. Existence has always meant for man, a succession of challenges. Moreover, the preservation and utilization of natural resources can only be assured through heavy investments in knowledge and ability aimed at all inhabitants of our country Nigeria. Education represents the conscious, deliberate and well equipped aspect of that steady progression which is the law of all human beings. Challenges are still with us and have not loss nothing in each particular life or given community they arise in different combination and obey a different order of priorities.

1 Overview

The advent of this era requires a higher-order thinking skills to effectively utilize the technological tools of the emerging century. Distance Education has emerged as an intrinsic part of many national education system with the power conferred on it as a genuine effort of the society to exploit all this abilities of the time, all the contributions of the past, and all the hopes of the future. The rational for Distance Education (DE) practice in Nigeria include its cost effectives, time effectives, individualization of the instructional attractiveness and compressing of the world into a global village. Distance Education network is the response to a growing needs of the society that need to expand education rapidly and cheaply, it is an academic discipline in its own right with a liberal practice of taking care of the socially, and geographically isolated of the society. Therefore, it is necessary to take education seriously and actively to its promotion development which calls for serious attention.

2 Introduction and Background

Today according to Green Street (1989), it is unrealistic to face future with relatively rigid and less adoptive set of educational programme and structures. We are faced with a situation in which education have become increasingly significant and crucial (Omolewa, 1980). On a worldwide scale, attitudes and polices on education in general

J. Fong, R. Kwan, and F.L. Wang (Eds.): ICHL 2008, LNCS 5169, pp. 463–471, 2008.
© Springer-Verlag Berlin Heidelberg 2008

are fast changing, while there has been particular interest in Distance Education. It is therefore necessary to take education seriously and actively to its promotion development (Ogili, 1998[a & b]). We should not only look at our strategies as practitioners but also redefine our concepts that would create genuine functional education especially in Nigeria. Wangoola (1989) reiterates that a network can be describes as reiterates a process by which individual, groups and institutions are put in contact in a manner which enable them to learn from each other, strength their own work, supplement each other, take joint action and mobilize and deploy latent resources and energize for social advancement. Thus a network is defined as the totality of all the units connected by a certain type of relationship which enhance the sharing of experiences, knowledge, and skills in a particular field of activity designed to raise this quality of life (Ogili, 2004).

It is clear that no group or profession can survive at whatever level, unless there is ample opportunities for individual initiatives and the entire such conduct that civilized moves it forward and develops it in a wholesome way.

Today the world is undergoing tremendous changes in arts, science and technology. There are also dramatic, social, economic, political and ecological changes across the globe. The extent to which people perceive and actually are sensitized to these change depends on a number of variables which include exposure, experience and direct interaction with one's environment (Ogili 1995&1996). The term Distance Education (DE) grew out of a need for a concept broader than correspondence study that could encompass new communications technology for the delivery of Education at a distance. It is an over-arching concept that appears not to have serious rivals for international usage. Ogili (2006) defines distance education as the various forms of study at all levels which are not under the continuous levels which are not under the continuous immediate supervision of facilitators present with their learners in lectures rooms or on the same premises, but which, nevertheless, benefit from planning, guidance, and tuition of a tutorial organization." This definition has remained unchanged for a period of nearly ten years (Holmberg 1986). It is interesting to note that planning, guidance and tuition are a function of an organization as compared to a teacher.

In another context, Moore (1973) states that DE may be defined as the family of instructional methods in which the teaching behaivours are executed apart from the learning behaivours including those that are n a continuous situation would be performed in the learner's presence, so that communication between the facilitator and the leaner must be facilitated by print, electronic, mechanical or other devices. In contrast to Holmberg's definition that focused on the "tutorial organization" Moore has emphasized the importance of communication between a facilitator and learner and the family of instructional methods appropriate to Distance Education.

A may be seen, several characteristics of DE have emerged, as have a number of issues. Keegan (1986) analysed a number of definitions and produced a descriptive definition consisting of seven elements of DE as follows:

1. The quasi-permanent separation of teacher and learner throughout the length of the learning process; this distinguishes it from conventional face-to-face education.
2. The influence of an educational organization both in the planning and preparation of learning materials and in the provision of it from private study and teach – yourself programmes.

3. The use of technical media; print, audio, or computer, to unite facilitator and learner and carry the content of the course.
4. The provision of two-way communication so that the learner may benefit from or even initiate dialogue; this distinguishes it from other uses of technology in education.
5. The quasi-permanent absence of the learning group throughout the length of the learning process so that people are usually taught as individuals and not in groups, with the possibility of occasional meetings for both didactic and socialization purpose.
6. The presence of more industrialized features than in conventional oral education.
7. The privatization of institutional learning.

In order to reduce internal inconsistencies in the preceding classification, Ogili (2007) provided three criteria on which to judge the process of DE.

1. DE implies that the majority of educational communication between (among) facilitator and learner(s) occurs noncontiguous.
2. DE must involve two-way communication between (among) facilitator and learners(s) for: the purpose of facilitating and supporting the educational process.
3. DE uses technology to mediate the necessary two-way communication.

Ogili (2004) believes that perceived control occupies a central position in communication theory which may be especially relevant in educational settings. This is because our society has, for good reason, been referred to as the information age. Today, over half of the labour force in the world work in the information sector. However, he further said that the information age emerged as a result of a crisis of control in the last century but the advances in the way information is created, processed, and communicated has spawned a control revolution and the information age.

Ogili (2006) agreed that the developments in educational technology have seen a gradual shift from an all-encompassing reliance on mass media...as alternative systems for the delivery of instructions to a concern for the individual, personal media...for instance in the home, at work, and in that classroom. It is further believed that the information revolution based upon microelectronics is a revolution of greater significance; it is nothing than an "intelligence revolution" making possible the intelligent application of information to perform tasks of ever increasing complexity.

Garrison (1989) and Ogili (1996:b) summed up the importance of information technology with the following assumptions.

a)   That the human species and the things that its members undertake generate vast quantities of data and information that is of interest or value to someone somewhere.
b)   That in order to exist and survive in a complex competitive world members of the human species need to have access to and capable of processing significant quantities of information (Barker, 1985). As a result of existing and emerging communication technology, distance education is experiencing a shift of emphasis from packaging content economically to facilitating dialogue and support for the educational transaction (Ogili, 2004).

3 The Relevance of Network in Distance Education

According to Tandon (1989), the relevance of Network includes that newer idea; visions and perspectives can be elaborated and sharpened. Hence, a Network is the most efficient and flexible mode of sharing information, experiences and ideas across like-minded persons, groups and organizations spread geographically and working on diverse issues. In conditions of grassroots efforts towards education, the organization of the poor and social change inevitably invite retaliation from those with vested interest in status quo. This retaliation takes three forms over repression, negation and cooption. This has proved more relevant and effective as the principles and ideas of participatory research seem to be congruent with the practice of Networking. Participatory researchers share common visions, dreams and struggles. Even though they operate from different geographical locations, entry points, focus etc, they have essentially a common approach to different geographical, social, economic and political context in their work.

Characteristic of a Network

1. It is an informal and flexible mechanism based on the initiative and interest of individuals and groups. No centralized planning and implementation is done in a Network.
2. It recognizes the value of experiences of its ordinary members and eschews the concept of expertise.
3. Members are encouraged and supported to take over the activities, direction and resources of a Network.
4. It entails shared responsibility among the members for sustaining, strengthening and managing the Network. New members are invited and existing member are encouraged by all the existing active members.
5. It has the capacity to mobilize its membership and their resources for collaboration around common issues at a rapid space.
6. It requires some animators, convenors, or co-ordinators to act as modes for energizing and sustaining information, ideas, and resources among members of the Network.

In a network, interaction is encouraged. As intelligence and ability give us power in the first place, knowledge which is scattered among members is tapped for the benefit of the group. In a network therefore, there is shared knowledge, shared experience, and collaboration of the greater benefit of all expressed by the term synergy or synchronized energy (Ingalis 1973). Synergy is manifested in shared values and expectations in a network which brings likeminded people together to achieve common objectives.

4 Operational Justification of Distance Education Network

Ogili (1995) pointed out that the operational justification of DE network is because the society is changing very fast in the present age. Hence, education is actually faced with the challenge of fulfilling the needs of a changing society which include, knowledge explosion, expansion of educational institutions, increase in learners enrolment, shortage of professional facilitators, non-committed political will, poverty of many families etc has therefore arisen. Also Ogili (2004) stressed that the justification for using DE network in Nigeria is the power conferred on the programme as the genuine effort of man take up into himself all the abilities of the time, all the conditions and contributions of the past, and all the hopes of the future. Hence, DE network creates viable chances to those who could not go to the formal school because of financial, social, geographical and medical reason. It is more succinctly clear that the attributes of network include: to save costs, save time in bringing education to the individual and to the door step of all. Secondly, is an investment in human resources development as it seeks to equip at least an individual in his own way with skills, and a capability of import and share their skills. This is because we in Nigeria, have lived with the belief and practice of being our brothers keepers, which we now extend to DE delivery. Ensuring that at the end, we shall not just be improving on the well-being of our families, but shall be building self-reliance nation (Ahmed, 1992).

Ogili and Eluka (1997) affirms that with the emergency of DE network in Nigeria, the desire of removing culture of silence, ignorance assistentialism, dehumanization, disparity and disabilities also emerged. The operational justification of DE network is the capacity to create the required change in skills, values, attitude, knowledge, etc that are relevant to the development of people and the nation. Thus, Ogili (1997) describes DE as a part of our struggle for securing a national goal of securing social justice, equity, liberty and removal of illiteracy and poverty in Nigeria in this millennium.

Ogili (1995) and (1996 [a&b]) asserts that DE network is best in meeting the vision and growing needs of the society which is impossible to meet by conventional schools. These include:

- Ensuring that learners learn in scattered communities covering sparsely populated, large geographical areas such as found in Nigeria. Hence making it possible for a few facilitator to reach large number of learners.
- Creating possible opportunities for learners to learn while they continue to earn. Learners do to need to be removed from their productive activity while they earn.
- DE does not require new schools to be built; it can only rely on the spare-time use of existing buildings and equipment. While all ranks can receive learning concurrently without apathy.
- Liberation of both the socially and geographically isolated learners from the culture of illiteracy and relapsing into illiteracy. Also, there is no age limit to learn thereby promoting lifelong education.
- It is cost effective. Teaching is economical, once the facilitating materials have been produced and the system is established, additional learners can be enrolled with only marginal costs. The more learners they are, the less the cost per learner.
- DE brings into learning circle expert knowledge, rare experiences and stimulating personalities. Hence professionalism is respected.
- It is most effective in national campaigns. Today health, child development, nutrition and political issues are initiated through DE network. Hence, the cost effectiveness of DE in absorbing very large numbers of learners with many following each course has made it attractive for a country with vision that need to expand education rapidly and cheaply.

5 Some Major Problems of Distance Education Network in Nigeria

Most African countries especially Nigeria are facing many obstacles in the running of the DE system. Some of these problems include:

- Inadequate trained distance educators: even the few experts available require constant retraining to keep abreast of the fast rate of technological changes;
- Dependence on consultants outside Nigeria as a result of shortage of experts needed;
- Lack of finance and culture of preventive maintenance in our societies;
- Lack of effective cooperation among the DE institutions because of non-formation of a clearing house for cross fertilization of ideas and information at a given time for exchange of experts;
- Geographical remoteness which result to learners lack of access to institutions and other resources when needed most.
- Scarcity of light for reading after day light hours,
- Radio receivers and cassette players are often expensive in Nigeria in relation to not only average wage and salaries earners (Ogili, 2006).
- Postal services are unreliable and irregular in some area in Nigeria which is a major drawbacks in DE network system. This make learners travel long distance to centres of distribution with economic implications etc (Holmberg, 1989).
- Non availability of educational media where needed;
- Lack of information about what DE is;
- Long periods of training which are necessary before entering any profession do not seem to have take off seriously in DE,
- Lack of intellectual techniques in the field of DE, the current practitioners from making popular acclaimed achievement in the solution of Nigeria's educational problems.
- Existence of personal jealousness, and rivalness, conflict of personality, favoritism, cliques, and faction, prejudices. And idiosyncrasies resulting from the political relations between persons; difficulties in communications, and imperfections in organizational structure (Ogili, 1996 and 1997).
- Gender disparity in developing nations on education issues,
- Bad leadership, corruption, political instability and poor economic management of our nation,
- The economic crisis which has led to mass unemployment thereby creating fear of future and helplessness among the nations (Okeem, 1990).

6 Recommendations

Distance education has drawn widespread and growing interest in this decade as a result of the emergence of sophisticated communication technology (Ogili and Nzeneri, 2004).

They further affirmed that formal and institutionally based conventional educational programme are often luxuries we cannot afford. As such DE Network has become the new imperative of our time and therefore, in other to bring about effective telmatic learner, there is need for the followings:

- Setting up a very strong professional association of distance educations with vigour;
- Engaging in regular publications of its activities and achievements through the Nigeria Distance Education Journals and other academic/professional journals;
- Organizing regular conference, seminars, workshops; courses for its members and other interested or reference group.
- Recruitment and retention of professionally trained distance education personnel (academic/technical) to man the study centres and other areas.
- Seek support service of the related agencies in terms of human and material resources;
- Provision of logistics for developing distance education programme practice;
- Regular evaluation of practices to allow for extensive and intensive understanding of negative or positive achievements for adjustment and/or modification.
- Organization of support services such as broadcast, learner fora, study groups, study centres, equipment, course, set kits on a serious basis so that each learner undertake to one suitable to him based on his circumstance (Ogili 1995[d]).
- Provision of grants-financial to distance educators in Nigeria to enable them attend both long-term and short term course;
- The Nigeria Association of Distance Educator (NADE) should be formed and strive to come of age by establishing a permanent secretariat with a paid secretary to co-ordinate the activities on a day-to-day basis.
- Federal, state and local governments should set aside at least 10 percent of their budget for the provision of electronic, mechanic and other materials. This will be supported with adequate security and maintenance culture.
- Establishment of National satellite Education programmes.
- To establish a network of co-operation between different systems of DE institutions;
- Creation of data base concerning the different types of DE materials, video equipment, audio equipment, printed materials and computer facilities.

7 Conclusion

The prosperity of a country depends not on the abundance of its revenue or on the strength of its fortifications and beauty of public building, but on the number of cultivated citizens, its men of character and enlightenment. The justification of Distance Education Network for strengthening education movement in Nigeria is the development of DE into an acceptable academic discipline with some underline criteria: in the growth in theoretical and conceptual depth, the growth in the degree of relevance to real and important problems: interrelationship between its fundamental ideas and professionalisation of distance educators beyond training programmes. Hence the rationale of Distance Education Network to Nigeria. Network is for strengthening education movement in its capabilities of bringing reasonable expectations, experience, and insights into useful order.

Finally, education movement that is actual and functional needs certain conditions such as open-door policy, foresight, accessibility and information while all these factors must operate in optional combination synergically in order to achieve the desired educational objectives.

References

1. Afigbo, A.E.: Nigeria and Open University. New Africa, Owerri (1983)
2. Ahmed, A.I.: Mass Literacy Policy and Delivery in Nigeria. NMEC, Abuja (1992)
3. Barker, P.: Information Technology, Education and Training. British Journal of Education Technology 16(2), 102–115 (1985)
4. Bates, A.W.: The Role of Technology, Distance Education. Croom helm, London (1984)
5. Garrson, D.R.: Understanding Distance Education: a framework for future. Routlage, London (1989)
6. Greenstreet, M.: The Concept of Network in Adult Education. Journal of AALAE 5(4), 22–26 (1989)
7. Holmberg, B.: Theory and practice of Distance Education. Routlage, New York (1989)
8. Ingles, H.T.: Cutting-edge developments in educational technology: prospects for the immediate future. In: Brown, J.W., Brown, S.N. (eds.) Educational media yearbook. Libraies Unlimited, Colorado (1984)
9. Keegan, D.: The Foundations of Distance Education. Croom Helm, London (1986)
10. Moore, M.G.: Towards a theory of Independent earning and teaching. Journal of Higher Education 44, 666–679 (1973)
11. Ogili, E.E.: Distance Education: A liberal vision in Nigeria. Journal of Education and Psychology in Developing Africa 2(1), 38–40 (1995a)
12. Ogili, E.E.: Teacher Education and Distance Education in Nigeria: An imperative for national development. In: Conference organized by NCCE, September 25th – 29th, Kaduna (1995b)
13. Ogili, E.E.: Evaluation of distance Education programmes in Nigeria. Ph.D. Thesis Seminar presented to department of Adult Education, University of Nigeria Nsukka March (unpublished, 1996a)
14. Ogili, E.E.: Factors Militating Against the Development of Distance Education in Nigeria. Journal of Nigeria Research in Social Sciences and Education 1(1), 4–10 (1996b)
15. Ogili, E.E.: Distance education VISION AND Gerontology for a better tomorrow. Journal of Research in science and Technology Education (JORSTED) (2), 204–212 (1996c)
16. Ogili, E.E.: Information Technology Application in Distance Education and Training: A Strategy for professionalism in Adult Education. Journal of CITADEL 1(3), 451–460 (1977a)
17. Ogili, E.E.: Stress and Crisis in distance Education in Nigeria. Stress Crisis in science and Technology Education in Nigeria (ed.). A publication of Dept. science and Technical Education, ESUT, Enugu, pp. 47–57 (1977b)
18. Ogili, E.E.: Challenges of Open and Distance Education in Achieving Education for All in Nigeria Malaysian. Journal of Distance Education 6(2), 67–74 (2004)
19. Ogili, E.E.: Strategies for Effective Communication in Educational Instructions in Nigeria madysiaan on line. Journal of Instructional Technology (MOJIT) 2(1) (2005) (7th paper), http://pppjj.usm.my/mojit
20. Ogili, E.E.: Distance Education Approaches. ADELS foundation Publishers, Enugu (2006)

21. Ogili, E.E.: Introduction to Distance Education Technology. ADELS foundation Publishers, Enugu (2007)
22. Ogili, E.E., Eluka, M.A.: Distance Education programmes and Operational justification in Nigeria Towards vision 2010. Educational Technology Conference, pp. 22–25. IMO STATE University, Owerri (1997)
23. Ogili, E.E., Nzeneri, S.I.: Quintessential crises in Distance Education practices on Achieving Education for all in Nigeria. In: 21st ICDE World Conference on Open learning and Distance Education, Hong Kong, February 18-21, p. 336 (2004)
24. Okeem, E.O.: Education in Africa; Search for Realistic Alternative. IFFA, United Kingdom (1990)
25. Race, Philip: How to win An open Learner. London CET (1988)

Author Index

Lecture Notes in Computer Science

Sublibrary 1: Theoretical Computer Science and General Issues

For information about Vols. 1– 4855
please contact your bookseller or Springer

Vol. 5008: A. Gasteratos, M. Vincze, J.K. Tsotsos (Eds.), Computer Vision Systems. XV, 560 pages. 2008.

Vol. 5004: R. Eigenmann, B.R. de Supinski (Eds.), OpenMP in a New Era of Parallelism. X, 191 pages. 2008.

Vol. 5000: O. Grumberg, H. Veith (Eds.), 25 Years of Model Checking. VII, 231 pages. 2008.

Vol. 4996: H. Kleine Büning, X. Zhao (Eds.), Theory and Applications of Satisfiability Testing – SAT 2008. X, 305 pages. 2008.

Vol. 4988: R. Berghammer, B. Möller, G. Struth (Eds.), Relations and Kleene Algebra in Computer Science. X, 397 pages. 2008.

Vol. 4985: M. Ishikawa, K. Doya, H. Miyamoto, T. Yamakawa (Eds.), Neural Information Processing, Part II. XXX, 1091 pages. 2008.

Vol. 4984: M. Ishikawa, K. Doya, H. Miyamoto, T. Yamakawa (Eds.), Neural Information Processing, Part I. XXX, 1147 pages. 2008.

Vol. 4981: M. Egerstedt, B. Mishra (Eds.), Hybrid Systems: Computation and Control. XV, 680 pages. 2008.

Vol. 4978: M. Agrawal, D.-Z. Du, Z. Duan, A. Li (Eds.), Theory and Applications of Models of Computation. XII, 598 pages. 2008.

Vol. 4975: F. Chen, B. Jüttler (Eds.), Advances in Geometric Modeling and Processing. XV, 606 pages. 2008.

Vol. 4974: M. Giacobini, A. Brabazon, S. Cagnoni, G.A. Di Caro, R. Drechsler, A. Ekárt, A.I. Esparcia-Alcázar, M. Farooq, A. Fink, J. McCormack, M. O'Neill, J. Romero, F. Rothlauf, G. Squillero, A.Ş. Uyar, S. Yang (Eds.), Applications of Evolutionary Computing. XXV, 701 pages. 2008.

Vol. 4973: E. Marchiori, J.H. Moore (Eds.), Evolutionary Computation, Machine Learning and Data Mining in Bioinformatics. X, 213 pages. 2008.

Vol. 4972: J. van Hemert, C. Cotta (Eds.), Evolutionary Computation in Combinatorial Optimization. XII, 289 pages. 2008.

Vol. 4971: M. O'Neill, L. Vanneschi, S. Gustafson, A.I. Esparcia Alcázar, I. De Falco, A. Della Cioppa, E. Tarantino (Eds.), Genetic Programming. XI, 375 pages. 2008.

Vol. 4967: R. Wyrzykowski, J. Dongarra, K. Karczewski, J. Wasniewski (Eds.), Parallel Processing and Applied Mathematics. XXIII, 1414 pages. 2008.

Vol. 4963: C.R. Ramakrishnan, J. Rehof (Eds.), Tools and Algorithms for the Construction and Analysis of Systems. XVI, 518 pages. 2008.

Vol. 4962: R. Amadio (Ed.), Foundations of Software Science and Computational Structures. XV, 505 pages. 2008.

Vol. 4961: J.L. Fiadeiro, P. Inverardi (Eds.), Fundamental Approaches to Software Engineering. XIII, 430 pages. 2008.

Vol. 4960: S. Drossopoulou (Ed.), Programming Languages and Systems. XIII, 399 pages. 2008.

Vol. 4959: L. Hendren (Ed.), Compiler Construction. XII, 307 pages. 2008.

Vol. 4957: E.S. Laber, C. Bornstein, L.T. Nogueira, L. Faria (Eds.), LATIN 2008: Theoretical Informatics. XVII, 794 pages. 2008.

Vol. 4943: R. Woods, K. Compton, C. Bouganis, P.C. Diniz (Eds.), Reconfigurable Computing: Architectures, Tools and Applications. XIV, 344 pages. 2008.

Vol. 4942: E. Frachtenberg, U. Schwiegelshohn (Eds.), Job Scheduling Strategies for Parallel Processing. VII, 189 pages. 2008.

Vol. 4941: M. Miculan, I. Scagnetto, F. Honsell (Eds.), Types for Proofs and Programs. VII, 203 pages. 2008.

Vol. 4935: B. Chapman, W. Zheng, G.R. Gao, M. Sato, E. Ayguadé, D. Wang (Eds.), A Practical Programming Model for the Multi-Core Era. VI, 208 pages. 2008.

Vol. 4934: U. Brinkschulte, T. Ungerer, C. Hochberger, R.G. Spallek (Eds.), Architecture of Computing Systems – ARCS 2008. XI, 287 pages. 2008.

Vol. 4927: C. Kaklamanis, M. Skutella (Eds.), Approximation and Online Algorithms. X, 289 pages. 2008.

Vol. 4926: N. Monmarché, E.-G. Talbi, P. Collet, M. Schoenauer, E. Lutton (Eds.), Artificial Evolution. XIII, 327 pages. 2008.

Vol. 4921: S.-i. Nakano, M.. S. Rahman (Eds.), WALCOM: Algorithms and Computation. XII, 241 pages. 2008.

Vol. 4919: A. Gelbukh (Ed.), Computational Linguistics and Intelligent Text Processing. XVIII, 666 pages. 2008.

Vol. 4917: P. Stenström, M. Dubois, M. Katevenis, R. Gupta, T. Ungerer (Eds.), High Performance Embedded Architectures and Compilers. XIII, 400 pages. 2008.

Vol. 4915: A. King (Ed.), Logic-Based Program Synthesis and Transformation. X, 219 pages. 2008.

Vol. 4912: G. Barthe, C. Fournet (Eds.), Trustworthy Global Computing. XI, 401 pages. 2008.

Vol. 4910: V. Geffert, J. Karhumäki, A. Bertoni, B. Preneel, P. Návrat, M. Bieliková (Eds.), SOFSEM 2008: Theory and Practice of Computer Science. XV, 792 pages. 2008.

Vol. 4905: F. Logozzo, D.A. Peled, L.D. Zuck (Eds.), Verification, Model Checking, and Abstract Interpretation. X, 325 pages. 2008.

Vol. 4904: S. Rao, M. Chatterjee, P. Jayanti, C.S.R. Murthy, S.K. Saha (Eds.), Distributed Computing and Networking. XVIII, 588 pages. 2007.

Vol. 4878: E. Tovar, P. Tsigas, H. Fouchal (Eds.), Principles of Distributed Systems. XIII, 457 pages. 2007.

Vol. 4875: S.-H. Hong, T. Nishizeki, W. Quan (Eds.), Graph Drawing. XIII, 402 pages. 2008.

Vol. 4873: S. Aluru, M. Parashar, R. Badrinath, V.K. Prasanna (Eds.), High Performance Computing – HiPC 2007. XXIV, 663 pages. 2007.

Vol. 4863: A. Bonato, F.R.K. Chung (Eds.), Algorithms and Models for the Web-Graph. X, 217 pages. 2007.

Vol. 4860: G. Eleftherakis, P. Kefalas, G. Păun, G. Rozenberg, A. Salomaa (Eds.), Membrane Computing. IX, 453 pages. 2007.

Printed in the United States
By Bookmasters